Windows® 2000 Server

Architecture and Planning

2nd Edition

Morten Strunge Nielsen, MCSE

President and CEO
Keith Weiskamp

Publisher
Steve Sayre

Acquisitions Editor
Charlotte Carpentier

Product Marketing Manager
Tracy Rooney

Project Editor
Greg Balas

Technical Reviewer
Martin O'Reilly

Production Coordinator
Carla J. Schuder

Cover Designer
Jody Winkler

Layout Designer
April E. Nielsen

CD-ROM Developer
Chris Nusbaum

Windows® 2000 Server Architecture and Planning, 2nd Edition
© 2001 The Coriolis Group. All rights reserved.

Limits of Liability and Disclaimer of Warranty
The author and publisher of this book have used their best efforts in preparing the book and the programs contained in it. These efforts include the development, research, and testing of the theories and programs to determine their effectiveness. The author and publisher make no warranty of any kind, expressed or implied, with regard to these programs or the documentation contained in this book.

The author and publisher shall not be liable in the event of incidental or consequential damages in connection with, or arising out of, the furnishing, performance, or use of the programs, associated instructions, and/or claims of productivity gains.

Trademarks
Trademarked names appear throughout this book. Rather than list the names and entities that own the trademarks or insert a trademark symbol with each mention of the trademarked name, the publisher states that it is using the names for editorial purposes only and to the benefit of the trademark owner, with no intention of infringing upon that trademark.

The Coriolis Group, LLC
14455 North Hayden Road
Suite 220
Scottsdale, Arizona 85260

(480) 483-0192
FAX (480) 483-0193
www.coriolis.com

Library of Congress Cataloging-in-Publication Data
Nielsen, Morten Strunge.
    Windows 2000 server architecture and planning / Morten Strunge Nielsen.--2nd ed.
      p. cm.
    ISBN 1-57610-607-1
    1. Microsoft Windows 2000 server.   2. Operating systems (Computers) I. Title.

QA76.76.O63 N537 2001
005.7'13769--dc21   00-043142

Printed in the United States of America
10 9 8 7 6 5 4 3 2 1

The Coriolis Group, LLC • 14455 North Hayden Road, Suite 220 • Scottsdale, Arizona 85260

Dear Reader:

Coriolis Technology Press was founded to create a very elite group of books: the ones you keep closest to your machine. Sure, everyone would like to have the Library of Congress at arm's reach, but in the real world, you have to choose the books you rely on every day *very* carefully.

To win a place for our books on that coveted shelf beside your PC, we guarantee several important qualities in every book we publish. These qualities are:

- *Technical accuracy*—It's no good if it doesn't work. Every Coriolis Technology Press book is reviewed by technical experts in the topic field, and is sent through several editing and proofreading passes in order to create the piece of work you now hold in your hands.

- *Innovative editorial design*—We've put years of research and refinement into the ways we present information in our books. Our books' editorial approach is uniquely designed to reflect the way people learn new technologies and search for solutions to technology problems.

- *Practical focus*—We put only pertinent information into our books and avoid any fluff. Every fact included between these two covers must serve the mission of the book as a whole.

- *Accessibility*—The information in a book is worthless unless you can find it quickly when you need it. We put a lot of effort into our indexes, and heavily cross-reference our chapters, to make it easy for you to move right to the information you need.

Here at The Coriolis Group we have been publishing and packaging books, technical journals, and training materials since 1989. We're programmers and authors ourselves, and we take an ongoing active role in defining what we publish and how we publish it. We have put a lot of thought into our books; please write to us at **ctp@coriolis.com** and let us know what you think. We hope that you're happy with the book in your hands, and that in the future, when you reach for software development and networking information, you'll turn to one of our books first.

Keith Weiskamp
President and CEO

Jeff Duntemann
VP and Editorial Director

Look for these related books from The Coriolis Group:

Windows 2000 Active Directory Black Book
By Adam Wood

Windows 2000 Registry Little Black Book
By Nathan Wallace

Windows 2000 Security Little Black Book
By Ian McLean

Windows 2000 System Administration Black Book
By Stu Sjourwerman, Barry Shilmover, and James Michael Stewart

Windows 2000 Systems Programming Black Book
By Al Williams

Windows 2000 TCP/IP Black Book
By Ian McLean

Windows 2000 Professional Advanced Configuration and Implementation
By Morten Strunge Nielsen

Also recently published by Coriolis Technology Press:

SQL Server 2000 Black Book
By Patrick Dalton and Paul Whitehead

XML Black Book, 2nd Edition
By Natanya Pitts

For Magnus, our beloved son. Wish you were still here.

❧

About the Author

Morten Strunge Nielsen is a Microsoft Certified Systems Engineer (MCSE), who holds a Master of Science in Electronic Engineering. From 1993 to 1996, he was chief technologist at the Danish State University Hospital. During this tenure, he designed and implemented a NetWare 4.x based LAN with Windows 95 clients. This LAN catered to the needs of the approximately 8,000 employees at the hospital. He also held strategic responsibility for the Unix-based servers, which were implemented at the hospital during the same period.

While at Aston IT Group A/S (formerly NETLOG Technology A/S), a Microsoft Certified Solution Provider (MCSP) Partner specializing in systems integration, Mr. Nielsen designed and oversaw the implementation of several Windows-based environments. Among these, was a 2,500+ PC environment, based entirely on Microsoft products, a Nortel Networks ATM backbone, and Europe's first fully-fledged Windows 2000 installation developed from Dell-based equipment (which went live in February 2000).

Since 1998, Mr. Nielsen has spearheaded Aston IT Group's initiative to become one of the foremost systems integrators in Windows 2000. This initiative has resulted in Aston IT Group being appointed as a Windows 2000 Rapid Deployment Program (RDP) Partner.

Mr. Nielsen is also a highly appreciated keynote speaker at seminars and conferences on technical issues. His Windows 2000-related speaking engagements included the prestigious Microsoft Tech-Ed 2000 Conference. He has also contributed more than 1,000 articles as a freelance writer for a variety of leading computer magazines in Denmark, and has published nine books (the latest being *Windows 2000 Professional: Advanced Configuration and Implementation*, also published by The Coriolis Group). Some of these titles have been translated, or are being translated, into German, Russian, Japanese, Chinese, Italian, Spanish, Hungarian, and Swedish.

Mr. Nielsen lives in Glostrup, Denmark, with his wife, and his two children.

Acknowledgments

Before you start reading, I just want to acknowledge the magic from the hardworking folks at The Coriolis Group. They really deserve thanks because I've been hell to work with. I've repeatedly broken the deadlines, due to immense pressures at my daytime work, where I've been incredibly busy doing Active Directory designs, and getting these designs implemented in the real world.

So, I really want to extend a big thank you to the people at The Coriolis Group: Charlotte Carpentier, my Acquisitions Editor, for not giving up on me, and an even bigger thanks to my very capable Project Editor, Greg Balas, who must have had a hell of a time rescheduling everything so many times. As incredible as it may sound, Greg actually managed to be a nice guy all the way through this ordeal.

Likewise, I feel that Stephanie Wall, Ann Waggoner Aken, and Tom Lamoureux, who were instrumental in the making of the first edition, deserve to be mentioned in this edition. After all, if it weren't for them—and especially, their angel-like patience—there would be no second edition.

Thanks also to Carla Schuder, my Production Coordinator, April Nielsen for designing the layout, Jody Winkler for designing the cover, and Tracy Rooney for her marketing efforts. In addition, I would like to thank Martin O'Reilly for tech reviewing, Paulette Miley for copyediting, Dorothy Bungert for typesetting, Andrea Stonerook for proofreading, and David Astra for indexing the book.

Also, I want to extend a thank you to my Danish publisher, IDG Denmark Books, and Carl Rosschou, in particular, for helping me reach an even larger audience than before.

And then there's my life companion, Helena Strunge Nielsen, who's much better than me at making the kids stay quiet (even though it doesn't work that often, when you think about it). She has also been great at starting me up during the times when I was paralyzed from being behind schedule on virtually everything. And of course, my

Acknowledgments

daughter, Camilla, who, despite her early age, is an avid user of the mouse, the keyboard, and the on/off button on my various PCs, and is very proficient at showing off these skills at the worst of times. I sure don't hope that her younger brother, Thorbjørn, will turn out the same.

Last, but not least, I want to extend a thank you to my current employer, Aston IT Group, and some of the good folks found at the Microsoft team for keeping me ahead of the pack. A special thanks go to my colleagues Panagiotis Mitkas and Peter Per Rhovan, for feedback and suggestions on a couple of important matters during the development of the second edition.

—*Morten Strunge Nielsen*

Contents at a Glance

Table of Contents

Introduction

Not Just Any Revolution

You don't have to be an avid Web surfer of the Microsoft Web pages, or a technophile to have heard about Windows 2000 Server. And no, the declarations by Microsoft and a large proportion of the IT press that Windows 2000 is a revolutionary improvement on the Windows NT technology aren't just shallow promotional talk.

Windows 2000 Server *will* be a revolutionary experience for you if you fully exploit its Active Directory features. And, as evidenced by history, revolutions should not be taken lightly if you want to keep your head—or, in today's pacifist environment, your job.

Why Active Directory Is so Important

If you're used to working with Windows NT Server-style domains, directory services will indeed turn your world upside down—and will most certainly cost you an obscene amount of time to put everything back into place.

But all your efforts should pay off quite handsomely, because you will have prepared your organization for the directory services future. In fact, the future has been headed in the direction of directory services ever since X.500, NDS, and Exchange Server. I still feel that everybody was right to call Novell's NDS a breakthrough for computing when it was released back in 1993. There was just one precious thing missing from Novell's directory services: the unequivocal backing from a fair percentage of their customers, as well as Independent Software Vendors (ISVs) and hardware manufacturers.

The whole point of a directory service is to ease the management and integration of all kinds of corporate applications and platforms. Unfortunately, Novell never managed to persuade the major application developers and operating system providers to build the necessary NDS hooks into their products, which is what makes the whole directory services notion shine.

This is exactly why I feel confident that Active Directory—and Windows 2000 Server—will become a much bigger success than you can currently see from the sales figures. Microsoft is firmly in control of the client platforms, and it has already hooked up with so many different application developers and suppliers of different hardware components, that a very broad support of Active Directory will develop inside the next few years. And just as support from third-parties proved to be one of the reasons for Novell's relative fiasco with NDS, it will likely prove to be the basis of the success of Windows 2000.

So, please do not be narrow-minded when you look at the concept of directory services, which I will introduce in Chapter 3. Actually, easier user management is only the tip of the iceberg when it comes to the wide-ranging benefits of directory services. I am quite certain that we all will be amazed by the power and potential of directory services, when a significant percentage of the current NT Server 4 installations have migrated to Windows 2000 Server.

Knowledge Counts, but Experience Is Everything

Right now, chances are fairly good that you will prove almost as lacking in knowledge and experience with regard to Active Directory, as I was when I set out to implement my first large directory services-based network. I had been reading a lot about Novell's NDS and directory services in general, but nothing had actually prepared me for the real thing.

You are pretty much left in the same situation as I once was, no matter how experienced you may be with Windows NT Server, because your NT experience simply doesn't apply to Active Directory. Your current NT know-how will primarily help you ease the transition when part of your environment is still running on NT 4. In fact, in moving from a current NT environment to Active Directory, the only useful knowledge is that which you've acquired in your experience with Exchange (or Novell's NDS or Banyan's StreetTalk). However, the skill set used with Exchange Server 5.5 is still a far cry from what you will need for Active Directory.

So, please, take some advice from a man who has been there before. You need to understand Active Directory and get all the experience you can before venturing into the world of directory services. Second, you should not underestimate the time and complexity of doing it—which is exactly why Windows 2000 Server has been off to a relatively slow start (sales-wise), and why you should get started today, in order to get finished not too many years from now.

I can't advise strongly enough to plan for Active Directory today. When you get into the planning phase, it might be necessary to carry out some fairly radical adjustments or changes within the IT organization. It's advisable to address—and tackle—these issues from the outset, because it won't get any easier later on. By ensuring that all decisions starting today take the Active Directory fundamentals into account, you might be able to avoid some of the worst migration woes, and reap all the directory services rewards for your company.

Implementation Time Estimates

Based on my previous directory services experiences, and some working with Active Directory, I estimate that it will take a medium-sized organization (that is, one with 1,000 to 5,000 clients) between four and nine months to get trained, plan for, test, and start migrating to Active Directory. A large organization will have to spend at least nine months, and most probably around 12 to 18 months, to complete the same task. It can, of course, be done faster if the organization is very easy to model, and if the necessary corporate knowledge, as well as technical know-how are at hand. But, judging from my experiences with large IT infrastructure projects, it's more probable that the migration project will drift toward the long end of the time range because of internal skirmishes, limited resources in the IT department, a lack of Active Directory know-how, or some other reasons.

Getting the Most Out of this Book

Anyone who has a working knowledge of Windows NT will be able to profit from the information delivered in this book. But do not be mistaken. This book is written with computer professionals in mind. IT strategists, IT planners, IT designers, and current administrators with a working knowledge of Windows NT—or a wish to achieve this knowledge—are the ones who will get the most from the book.

This book can also help maximize your returns if you are planning to become a Microsoft Certified Systems Engineer (MCSE), because it covers the full curriculum for the Microsoft Certified Professional exams "Designing a Microsoft Windows 2000 Directory Services Infrastructure" (70-219), and "Upgrading from Microsoft Windows NT 4.0 to Microsoft Windows 2000" (70-222).

Note
The courses for passing MCP exams 70-219 and 70-222 are Designing a Microsoft Windows 2000 Directory Services Infrastructure (MOC 1561), and Designing a Microsoft Windows 2000 Upgrade Strategy (MOC 2010), respectively.

However, you should understand that the overriding focus of this book is to provide you with all the theoretical and real-life experiences needed to get safely through the planning and designing of Active Directory. Thus, it's quite likely that you'll be able to pass the two above-mentioned tests just from studying this book carefully. But you might want to supplement this book with the applicable Exam Crams in order to be on the safe side, because Microsoft does tend to refine their MCP exams over time—and the Exam Crams will allow you to check out the exact curriculum, and pit yourself against a fair number of the probable questions.

Also, this book actually goes well beyond the curriculum for the two exams, which together represent five course days—it's really only the base information provided here that will prove of relevance to passing the exams, as all the tiny details seem to be too practical to be covered by a curriculum. So chances are that you will be able to pass the two tests without understanding every little detail covered in this book.

But I would like to stress that you will do well to heed all of the advice provided throughout this book, because it's based on my experience with putting Active Directory solutions into life, and as such should prove to be very useful when you need to put your own Active Directory knowledge to work afterwards. As any MCP will know: It's one thing to pass the exams, but it's quite another thing to accomplish a successful design and implementation of a complex infrastructure solution.

Understanding the Book

The aim of this book is to give you a thorough understanding of Microsoft Windows 2000 Server from a design and planning perspective. The implication of this is that virtually everything I will explore in deeper detail is seen from the perspective of Active Directory.

This book is divided into five parts:

- *Part I, "Overview"*—Chapters 1 and 2 give a rundown on all the major capabilities and features of Windows 2000 (all editions from Professional to Datacenter Server), and some marketplace background relevant to Windows 2000.

- *Part II, "Planning"*—Chapters 3 through 13 initiate a very thorough discussion of all the major new Active Directory features of Windows 2000 Server that are of interest to a reader who needs to understand the finer points of Windows 2000 Server architecture. You should also take a look at Appendix B that provides you with a couple of Active Directory design cases.

- *Part III, "Advanced Planning Topics"*—Chapters 14 through 16 include a discussion of the advanced planning tasks that will be of interest to enterprise planners and security specialists, among others.

- *Part IV, "Testing"*—Chapters 17 through 20 provide an introduction to installing Windows 2000 Server and implementing Active Directory for testing purposes. And believe me: You will definitely want to take a look at Chapter 20, which includes a lot of advice on how to optimize your design for just about any situation.

- *Part V, "Fitting into a Current Infrastructure"*—Chapters 21 through 23 (including Appendix B) frame an advanced discussion on how to plan for Windows 2000 Server today, integrating with Windows 2000 Server, and doing full or partial migration to Windows 2000. This part is rounded off with an appendix, which describes the Windows 2000 Server migration project basics.

Guiding You through the Book

As I pointed out already, the book starts out with two chapters that supply you with a broader view of the marketplace in which Windows 2000 is introduced. The first chapter focuses on the market situation—today and in the years to come—which will prove to be of great consequence to Windows 2000 Server and all IT professionals. The next chapter provides a full-fledged introduction to all the features and capabilities of Windows 2000 Server.

After that, you have reached the "introduction" to the very heart of the book. That is, while Chapter 6 through 12 really constitute the heart of the book, which will provide you with all necessary knowledge about the finer details of Active Directory, Chapters 3 through 5 will prove invaluable for getting an overview of all the Active Directory constituents, and thus getting more in-depth with the planning of the major properties of the directory. Chapter 3 gives an introduction to directory services in general; Chapters 4 and 5 will start you off by introducing the key features and building blocks of Active Directory.

Tip

You should be able to skip Chapters 3 through 5 if you already have been introduced to Active Directory on several occasions, because these chapters are only there to provide you with an overview before you head into each of the areas. Also, you might want to note that Chapters 4 and 5 will prove fairly tough reading: They represent an Active Directory crash-course, so please don't get turned off by reading those two chapters. Everything will get so much better (and easier to understand) after them.

With Chapter 6, you get some of the "real" planning know-how intertwined with the presentation of Active Directory. Chapter 6 is about analyzing the organizational and physical settings for Active Directory, which will be the lifeblood of any successful implementation of directory services.

Chapter 7 delves into DDNS and DHCP (and WINS), which are crucial prerequisites of a working Active Directory. The fact that I have yet to meet a person with a PC-only background, that really is very hardcore in the DNS area, has caused this chapter to grow rather large.

Chapter 8 is about the planning of the domain structure (including OUs and delegation of administration); Chapter 9 puts the planning of user accounts and groups into play. And Chapter 10 delves deep into the intricacies of the new Delegation of Administration and Group Policies features. Chapter 11 focuses on planning directories that have more than one domain (that is, directories that include several domains or domain trees). Chapter 12 looks at the planning of the physical infrastructure, which will ensure that Active Directory does not run amok on the network. And then the whole Active Directory "base" planning section is sealed off with Chapter 13, which provides a very brief review of the most important lessons and best practices from the different parts of the planning phase.

Chapter 14 goes on to tackle the many new security features and challenges, including a discussion on Active Directory security, Kerberos, IPSEC, EFS, and Certificate Services.

Chapter 15 provides you with the lowdown on how to get Exchange Server 5.5 integrated into your Active Directory—and how to move from this point to Exchange 2000 Server.

Chapter 16 gives insight into the subject of Active Directory-aware applications. Although much more can—and will—be said on this important subject, this chapter should put you in a great position to delve further into this topic with your enterprise's own mission-critical applications.

Now you've come to the testing phase. Chapter 17 gives the necessary information for installing Windows 2000 Server and implementing a single Active Directory domain with OUs (Organizational Units) and the most common objects. And in Chapter 18 you get a crash course on the most useful "advanced" Active Directory topics, such as creating sites, implementing Group Policies and administrative delegation, and much more.

In Chapter 19 you learn how to plan for, prepare, and ultimately modify the directory schema. Chapter 20 teaches you how to assess the database size and replication load generated in your Active Directory environment, as well as how to optimize Active Directory for just about any LAN or WAN scenario.

The last three chapters (21 through 23) focus on how to fit Active Directory into your current infrastructure. Chapter 21 details how you can implement new platform solutions today with your sights set on Windows 2000 Server and Active Directory. Chapter 22 provides you with detailed insight into how to migrate your current NT Server platforms to Active Directory.

Chapter 23 lays out your possibilities for short-term or long-term coexistence with regard to today's most prevalent legacy server platforms and client platforms, with special emphasis on DNS and other networking issues.

Finally, Appendix A supplies you with the outline of a project plan for pre-planning, design, prototyping, building, testing, and implementing for Windows 2000 Server/Active Directory, and Appendix B presents you with a small handful of educative Active Directory design cases from the real world—which hopefully will work to give you a bit of inspiration for your own designs. Appendix C provides a quick glimpse into the next release of Windows 2000 Server, the Whistler version.

I Already Have the Book: What's New?

The fact that this is a second edition means that I've fixed a number of small errors and omissions from the original book. And I've also had the privilege of updating things that did change from the beta version of Windows 2000 to the finalized version of Windows 2000 (including Service Pack 1).

But that's not all: This book also includes a host of new material—much of it based on my practical experiences with Active Directory—that has mostly been integrated into the existing chapters. And it's not just window dressing: This new material has made the book more than one-third larger than the original.

In order to make it easier on all of you who have purchased the first edition, here is a rundown on the major changes and additions found in the second edition of *Windows 2000 Server Architecture and Planning*:

♦ *Chapter 7*—Includes a lot more practical advice for getting the DNS structure in place (including information on how to handle Active Directory-integrated DDNS, as well as WINS).

♦ *Chapter 9 and 10*—Expand on the former Chapter 9, including more information on the Windows 2000 security fundamentals, as well as more planning and practical advice on Group Policies.

♦ *Chapter 12*—Includes more information on the rather crucial File Replication Service (FRS), adds a section on Distributed File System (DFS), and provides a much more in-depth treatment of Active Directory replication, with a keen eye to the minor details that tend to grow quite crucial in practice.

♦ *Chapter 14*—A new chapter that presents you with an in-depth treatment of all the advanced security options (such as Kerberos, PKI, EFS, and IPSEC) introduced with Windows 2000 Server.

♦ *Chapter 15*—A new chapter that gives you the information needed for how to integrate with Exchange Server 5.5, and the consequences of migrating to Exchange 2000 Server.

♦ *Chapter 16*—A new chapter that provides a treatment of the possibilities brought forward by implementing Active Directory-aware applications. This includes a treatment of Microsoft Metadirectory Services (MMS), which seems destined to become an integral part of Windows 2000 in the next couple of years.

♦ *Chapter 20*—Features a new and very unique section focused on improving your understanding of Windows 2000's network behavior, which provides a lot of suggestions for improving upon the default settings.

♦ *Chapter 22*—Includes a lot of new information on how to migrate from Windows NT Server to Windows 2000 Server. This includes an in-depth treatment of the crucial Active Directory Migration Tool (ADMT), available for free from Microsoft.

♦ *Chapter 23*—Includes new information on migration and coexistence with non-Microsoft environments, especially Unix and Novell.

♦ *Appendix B*—A new appendix that provides you with some very interesting examples of Active Directory designs for companies of very different sizes.

♦ *Appendix C*—A short preview of what type of changes you should expect to Active Directory, when moving forward to the next release of Windows 2000 Server (this being the Whistler version).

With the rather large improvements in depth, as well as breadth of treatment, I feel fully confident that this book does represent the "bible" to design and planning for Windows 2000 Server—and as such, most of you probably won't be able to find any other books that will get close to the completeness and quality of this one. But, well, enough about that. Let's all get started on the actual book.

The Very Last Words

In case you should come across any errors or shortcomings in this book, please let me know. I can be reached at **morten@strunge.com**. My new Web presence can be found at **www.strunge.com**.

To all of you sitting out there, I hope you will enjoy reading this book just as much as I've (mostly) enjoyed writing it.

Morten Strunge Nielsen
December 3rd, 2000

Part I

Overview

Chapter 1
Overview of the Market

R egardless of your personal feelings about Microsoft, nobody
can deny that the Windows platform rules the PC client. In
fact, the Windows platform has led the field for quite some time.
In 1995, more than 60 million Windows 3.1x-based PCs were in
use globally, and by late 1997, Microsoft announced that it had
sold more than 100 million copies of Windows 95.

The conventional wisdom about Microsoft's dominance in the
desktop operating system (OS) marketplace is dramatically un-
derscored by studies from virtually any business analyst. For
example, Dataquest anticipated that Microsoft's 93.5 percent projected 1998 market share of all OS shipments worldwide would
increase to 95 percent by 1999. And they were right!

Windows 2000 Professional not only represents the latest and greatest Windows platform from Microsoft for business use, it also
represents the platform on which Microsoft intends to build all future Windows versions, and thus should prove very important with
regard to whether or not Microsoft will be able to keep its current
stronghold on desktop operating systems in the new decade.

The desktop OS isn't the only market segment that is virtually owned
by Microsoft—its Office suite also dominates the market for PC
desktop software. Depending on who you ask, Microsoft's Office
suite has a comfortable worldwide market share of 80 to 90 percent
in this segment. Additionally, in recent years Microsoft has enjoyed
a booming demand for its Internet Explorer Web browser. Windows dominates the desktop so thoroughly that it is beginning to
resemble a monopoly, which is part of the reason for Microsoft's
recent legal troubles with the U.S. Department of Justice.

Currently, Microsoft is making serious inroads into the server market, too, with its server OSs and BackOffice applications (most notably Exchange Server). Windows 2000 Server and its variants represent Microsoft's new crop of server OSs, and judging from the market's reception to Windows 2000 Server, Microsoft seems poised to continue to make inroads into this important market.

Microsoft Is Everywhere

In June 1997, Microsoft announced that it had sold more than 77 million copies of Windows 95, and this staggering figure was increasing at a rapid rate. This meant that Microsoft had sold an average of four million copies of Windows 95 per month since its launch, which equals more than one copy sold per second. These incredible numbers confirmed what everyone had already suspected—Windows' reign over client-side desktop computing couldn't be challenged.

The impressive sales figures didn't noticeably slow down during the latter half of 1997—Microsoft announced in late 1997 that it had sold more than 100 million copies of Windows 95! And although sales decreased slightly in 1998 and 1999, compared with the "dream figures" quoted later in this chapter, the sales of Windows 98 (released June 25, 1998) really haven't been that bad.

Sales of Microsoft Office are yet another key indicator of Microsoft's desktop domination. Office has been a dramatic success over the last four to five years. On July 23, 1997, Paul Maritz, Microsoft's Group Vice President of Platforms and Applications, stated that Microsoft had shipped nearly 25 million copies of Office in its fiscal year that ended in June 1997 (that figure covered both new and upgrade copies). At the end of 1997, Microsoft estimated that the number of users currently working with Microsoft Office was more than 60 million.

Aside from Microsoft's own assertions about the Office suite, virtually everybody acknowledges that, in volume, Microsoft Office is easily the most important nonfreeware application on the PC platform. Office has become a major phenomenon in the PC industry in its own right; of any single application that PC users depend on, Office is at the top of the list.

Only one application (including freeware) is more successful than Office on desktop clients: the Web browser. The success of Web browsers is exactly why Microsoft has been heavily targeting the Web browser market with its Internet Explorer product, which has also become hugely successful in the last few years.

Lately, Windows 95/98's big brother, Windows NT Workstation 4, has also been growing in popularity. By May 1997, more than three million copies of NT Workstation had been sold, and the growth rate was approximately 400,000 NT Workstations sold per month. That figure continued to increase sharply until, by the middle of November 1997, Microsoft announced that it had sold more than 11 million copies of NT Workstation.

By June 17, 1998, sales of Windows NT Workstation had surpassed the 15 million mark, an increase of 4 million licenses sold in approximately six months, which means that the market is moving (albeit rather slowly) in the direction that Microsoft wants it to—toward Windows 2000 Professional (see the sidebar in the next section, "Microsoft Stakes Its Future on the NT Kernel," for an explanation of the new name).

The preliminary sales figures for Windows 2000 also seem quite encouraging. Actually, at the end of April 2000, Microsoft was able to announce that it had licensed more than one-and-a-half million copies of Windows 2000 (meaning Windows 2000 Professional, Windows 2000 Server, and Windows 2000 Advanced Server) in the first two months since launch.

This number of licenses represents four times the rate of Windows NT 4 adoption. This sure does sound promising, especially when one considers the fact that the one-and-a-half million copies don't include licenses acquired through enterprise agreements from Microsoft's largest customers around the world.

NT vs. Windows 9x

The big question is whether Windows NT's growth will continue to build into the future as it transitions into Windows 2000. The short-term picture is confusing to the client, because of the early success of Windows 98. Even though Microsoft has clearly been pushing Windows NT Workstation 4—and now Windows 2000 Professional—for a while over Windows 95 and Windows 98, Windows 98 has turned out to be the smash hit that Microsoft intends Windows 2000 Professional to be.

Although the Windows 98 launch wasn't anywhere close to the marketing extravaganza that was put on for Windows 95, it has already carved out a rather important place in software history. And this might also end up being the case of Windows 98's heir—Windows Millennium Edition, which is getting even less marketing attention at Microsoft than its predecessor.

Note

You should take note of the fact that Windows Millennium Edition (also known as Windows Me) is specifically targeted at home users and consumers, not businesses. Actually, Microsoft has lifted from the Millennium Edition several of the businesslike features found in Windows 98, and all of its new features are geared toward the home user. In addition to sporting the basic Windows 2000 user interface, Millennium Edition is promised to include numerous stability and performance improvements, new multimedia capabilities, and the hardware and software support that consumers expect. However, because Windows Millennium Edition has been positioned as the end of the line for Windows 9x, it will most likely be a minor upgrade.

The overnight success of Windows 98 happened despite the fact that Microsoft was unusually straightforward regarding its plans for Windows 98: *extinction*. Actually, initially Microsoft was intent on having Windows 98 be the last hurrah for the current architecture. But because of pains with scaling the Windows 2000/NT kernel down to the current typical configuration of

Microsoft Stakes Its Future on the NT Kernel

Microsoft's early promotion (1997) of NT Workstation 4 over Windows 98 as the choice for business users was foreshadowing Microsoft's plans to base the next generation of Windows on the NT kernel rather than on Windows 3.x/95/98. Consider the following statement from Jim Allchin, Senior Vice President of the Personal and Business Systems Group at Microsoft (appearing in a November 1997 Microsoft press release):

Customers are asking for the easiest path to move to Windows NT; in purchasing new business PCs, customers should deploy Windows NT Workstation 4, our recommended business operating system. Customers are finding that a combination of powerful yet aggressively priced new hardware platforms, the rapid movement of applications to a 32-bit environment, and their desire to lower their total cost of ownership make Windows NT Workstation the best operating system choice for business.

Microsoft confirmed its plans at the end of October 1998, when it announced that some major name changes would occur for the next versions of its NT product family. Windows NT Workstation 5 was renamed *Windows 2000 Professional*; Windows NT Server 5 was called *Windows 2000 Server*; Windows NT Server Enterprise Edition was called *Windows 2000 Advanced Server*; and a new high-end server OS product (*Windows 2000 Datacenter Server*) was announced. Acknowledging the confusion that might occur initially, Microsoft states in its announcement, "To help make the change clear for customers who are accustomed to the previous name, all Windows 2000 products will be accompanied by the tagline, 'Built on NT Technology.'"

It is important to note that this rather drastic name change most probably serves two purposes: taking out a trademark on the Windows 2000 term (which can't be done with NT because Microsoft has allowed the use of this name in many products and services for too long) and positioning the next generation of NT as the future Microsoft OS. Microsoft has acknowledged that it is busily planning for a low-end version of the NT kernel, which is to supplant Windows Me. This low-end version will most probably be named something along the lines of Windows 2000 Standard.

I guess you've got it by now. The name change is a ploy for strengthening the name recognition of all Microsoft OSs in order to establish a brand name that is comparable to Coca-Cola or Pepsi in worldwide recognition. Until then, the world will be a confusing place to be, because virtually everyone inside the computing sector has grown used to the NT.

a home PC and the kernel's limited backwards-compatibility, Microsoft has put together yet another version of the old Windows 9x OS line, going by the name of Windows Millennium Edition (Me).

However, Microsoft promises that Windows Me *will* be the end of the line for the old 16-bit Windows code base. The next version of Microsoft's consumer OS—probably to be called Windows 2000 Home Edition, Standard, or something along those lines and thus representing a "downscaled" version of Windows 2000 Professional—is destined to be based on the Windows NT kernel. This is Microsoft's attempt to accelerate revenue by putting some excitement in the NT marketplace. It is sending a clear message to corporations that NT kernel-based products are the wave of the future, not Windows 9x/Me.

Windows NT Server Is on the Move

In 1993, Windows NT was introduced to the market after five years of development. The Windows NT OS was, and is, designed for use at servers and workstations. During the following years, Windows NT Server developed a reasonable market stronghold, but it never came close to the ultimate goal of replacing mainframes, Unix servers, and PC servers.

But Windows NT Server has been slowly gaining ground in the last few years, as has been the case for Windows NT Workstation. Actually, Windows NT Server has become the most prevalent choice for new server deployment inside the last few years. However, it still is no match for the "big guys" and faces some tough competition in the PC server market from Novell on one side and Linux on the other.

Currently, most analysts subscribe to the notion that two trends are occurring in the server market: One trend is "volume" deployment of PC-based server OSs for departmental use, and the other trend is "value" deployment of Unix (and maybe the old mainframe-like OS environments, such as MVS [IBM's mainframe OS], OS/400, and VMS [DEC's mainframe OS]) onto larger hardware, for centralized management.

According to the IDC report titled *Server Operating Environments: 1998 Worldwide Markets and Trends*, some of the key trends in the server OS market include the following:

♦ Large organizations will continue to use—into the next century—mixed-vendor environments for server operating environments, because of the wide variety of tasks that need to be performed in these organizations.

♦ Windows NT Server had the fastest sales growth of new worldwide software licenses in 1997, with a 73 percent increase, compared to Unix, which grew at only 17 percent.

♦ More than half the new NT Server licenses in 1997 were for file/print server use; only 10 percent of new Unix server licenses were used for this function during the same period.

♦ Novell NetWare shipments, which outpaced Unix, declined nearly 7 percent in 1997; IBM OS/2 declined 36 percent.

IDC's figures also indicate that Windows NT Server has consistently achieved the highest unit sales in the server OS market in 1997, 1998, and 1999. If this trend continues (and most analysts agree that it will), Windows NT/2000 Server soon will also be able to claim the largest installed base. See Figure 1.1 for the number of new server OS shipments from 1995 to 1999 for Windows NT Server, NetWare, and Unix.

Although much of the growth of Windows NT Server has been occurring in the small and midrange markets, it is also making a dent in the large systems environments. In May 1998, data from Computer Intelligence showed a 200 percent increase in the number of Fortune 1000 companies that had deployed Windows NT Server in the past 12 months. As of March 1998, more than 86 percent of these organizations had deployed Windows NT Server; Unix deployments remained at 61 percent.

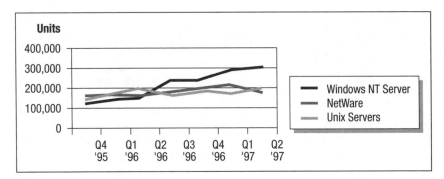

Figure 1.1
According to IDC's figures for new server OS shipments from the end of 1995 through mid-1997, sales of Windows NT Server have been gaining momentum.

The reason for Microsoft's focus on this segment is simple: Fortune 1000 companies lead the industry in innovation and continually push technology to its limits, according to Jim Allchin, Microsoft's Senior Vice President, Personal and Business Systems Group. And although Microsoft's ambitions seem to be satisfied by the significant gains Windows NT/2000 Server has been making inside the PC server market, there still is much to be desired for large systems solutions.

Windows 2000 Server for the High End

Microsoft has been very intent on making their server OSs capable of handling even the largest applications for several years now, which translates into directing much effort toward enhancing reliability, scalability, and availability, as well as interoperability and porting of strategic Unix and mainframe applications. The early results of that focus became apparent in the form of an improved emphasis on the stability of the Windows NT Server 4 platform. Correspondingly, many of the features and capabilities that have been added to Windows 2000 Server are highly responsive to mission-critical solutions—for example, Windows 2000 Server includes a tangible reduction in the number of situations in which rebooting from the server is necessary after a system reconfiguration.

While everybody expects Microsoft to fare much better in the high-end market with the release of Windows 2000 Server, it was actually already beginning to do well in the high-end market before the advent of Windows 2000, largely because of its focus on a select number of strategic application vendors and an addition to the Windows NT Server 4 product line: Windows NT Server 4 Enterprise Edition (which is on par with Windows 2000 Advanced Server).

Microsoft's business strategy for Windows 2000 Advanced Server (and its big brother, Windows 2000 Datacenter Server) is quite simple: to supply greater scalability and manageability than found in their "kid brother," Windows 2000 Server. Windows 2000 Advanced Server and Windows 2000 Datacenter Server are designed for use in high-availability settings or very large server solutions, respectively.

Linux: A Word on the Only Real Threat to Windows 2000

At the moment, the fragmented Unix community and the stagnant NetWare society don't seem to provide any real threat to the momentum of Windows 2000. Recently, however, one possible threat has surfaced. This threat is Linux, which is a public domain implementation of Unix that is available as a client and a server.

Linux is the brainchild of Linus Torvalds, who created it while he was an undergraduate student at the University of Helsinki. In addition to an Intel 80386-based kernel, Linus wrote keyboard and screen drivers to attach to PC hardware and provided this code free for all on an FTP site in the summer of 1991. Today, Linux is widely perceived to represent a best-of-breed Unix that performs very well on the Intel platform, can be trusted in mission-critical applications, and has a long-term credibility that exceeds many other Unix variants. Also, most of the primary applications that people require are already available free for Unix. Linux was believed to be running on some seven million PCs in mid-1998 and is showing an impressive annual growth rate of 20 percent.

Although the Linux threat isn't imminent, it does seem to be the cause of some wrinkles at Microsoft HQ. Microsoft's thoughts on Linux were brought to the computer media in the form of two internal Microsoft memos (dubbed Halloween I and Halloween II) in November 1998. These two memos and a lot of complementary materials can be found at **www.opensource.org**.

Besides the fear of lost revenues and the eventual risk of facing a "real" challenge to the Microsoft game plan with regard to developers (some of the main Microsoft adversaries have already announced support for Linux), as well as customer mindshare, Microsoft also fears the revolution that Linux might represent to the current business model for software. The basic idea behind Linux is open source; that is, it provides the means for all programmers to read, redistribute, and modify the source of Linux. This in turn gives everyone the power of improving it, adapting it, and fixing bugs at speeds that seem astonishing compared to the pace of conventional software development.

However, many previous attempts of this kind have sooner or later fallen victim to the laws of gravity, or the lowest common denominator principle. Such has become the case with the Internet, in which all new standards seem to be evolving at a snail's pace because of the inherent inefficiency of getting a large number of people and organizations to agree on each and every tiny detail. If you take a look at the Internet's standards, you will find that hardly anything has changed in recent years.

So, the key question is whether or not Linux can stay free of these ills and start working its way into the corporate heartland (which traditionally has demanded services and support, which in turn slows progress and requires a unity unheard of in the Linux community). Because Linux is such a different entity, only time will tell.

However, the Windows 2000 Server product family still requires a lot of improvement in its performance of mission-critical jobs. The existing Unix and mainframe solutions simply perform better for the majority of real-life tasks. Furthermore, Windows 2000 Server hasn't been sufficiently tested for fault tolerance. In mission-critical terms, the system must be operational in a matter of seconds after an error occurs, regardless of what type of error it is. Moreover, the administrative tools still aren't fully on par with what the other enterprise-oriented OS platforms offer.

The key factor isn't the capability to perform one billion transactions—it is the capability to deliver *reliable* transactions. But defining precisely what is required for Windows 2000 Server to succeed in the high-end market is quite complicated. For example, Unix still hasn't been accepted as a way to handle the heaviest tasks, even though the most common Unix platforms can handle at least 16 processors with almost linear scalability for most tasks. Thus, Unix has an architecture that has the capability of handling at least the capacity of the current mainframes, which are several times more expensive than Unix. So far, Unix is widely accepted only for certain data-crunching tasks (notably data warehousing), whereas batch processing still belongs to the mainframe domain.

In Pursuit of New Business Opportunities

In addition to keeping its current market share in the market segments in which it dominates or has a strong presence, Microsoft is constantly looking for new business opportunities. One such business opportunity is actually part of an old plan: Microsoft's 1990 "Information at Your Fingertips" strategy.

The philosophy behind "Information at Your Fingertips" is to create a world in which all information is only a mouse-click away from the user. Nevertheless, the essence of the strategy is essentially the same as Bill Gates' "Windows Everywhere" vision from 1987, insofar as Microsoft not only wants to be present in all major segments of the computer market, but also wants to be number one—from the smallest mobile computers, portable PCs, and stationary PCs, up to workstations and megaservers.

In other words, "Information at Your Fingertips" is really Microsoft's strategy of gaining close to a 100-percent market share of every OS niche. This strategy is tripartite: PCs today, servers tomorrow, and in the future, everything that requires an OS, including PDAs (Personal Digital Assistants), office equipment, consumer electronics, TV-top boxes, and video servers.

Personal Digital Assistants

For some time now, Microsoft has been trying to remedy its remaining Achilles' heel regarding the full implementation of "Information at Your Fingertips": the small, cheap units for communication, entertainment, and mobile data processing. Microsoft has previously carried out some remarkably unsuccessful attacks in this area with, among others, Windows for Pen Computing (for PDAs and pen computers) and Microsoft Bob (a GUI for computer beginners).

Inside the consumer handheld computer market segment, Microsoft bets on a new OS entry that goes by the name of *Windows CE*. Windows CE is an entirely new, 32-bit, processor-independent multitasking and multithreading OS, built with the sole purpose of gaining access to the consumer market. However, two important common denominators exist between Windows CE and the other Windows products: Windows CE is equipped with the well-known Windows user interface, and it operates with part of the Win32 API (it isn't supported by the entire Windows API, but is compatible with Windows).

Unlike the rest of the Windows product line, Windows CE isn't available as a software package, simply because it is supposed to be an OS for consumer units. Windows CE will only be sold directly to those who are developing and manufacturing these hardware units.

Until now, Windows CE has been quite unsuccessful compared with its closest competitors. And that's probably some of the reason why Microsoft is putting such big expectations on the third iteration of Windows CE (version 3), which was released in April 2000. However, you will most probably be seeing the Windows CE-based devices being marketed as Pocket PCs.

Thin Clients

Lately, Microsoft has also concentrated some effort on the concept of *thin clients*, clients that have very little program code. Such clients were unheard of at the inception of "Information at Your Fingertips." Microsoft's thin client product was introduced as another variant of Windows NT Server 4, which is named Windows NT Server 4, Terminal Server Edition. The reason for the separate packaging of Windows NT Server 4 was that the Terminal Server functionality demanded a change of several services at the very heart of Windows NT (that is, at the kernel level). However, these changes have been implemented in Windows 2000 Server, so that the Terminal Server functionality is handled as just another service.

Terminal Services adds Windows-based terminal support to Windows 2000 Server and adds a "super-thin client" to the Windows family product line. In other words, Terminal Services enables the familiar Windows graphical user interface (GUI) to be presented to users of new Windows-based terminals (based on Windows CE), legacy desktops (including Windows 3.x; for Macintosh and Unix, you will have to supplement Terminal Server with third-party extensions like Citrix MetaFrame), and the newer 32-bit Windows desktops. The concept is simply to execute the Windows program code at the server, transmit the display data to the client, and transmit the movements of the keyboard and mouse back to the server. This is the same principle that was used for the old visual display terminals (VDTs).

The Windows terminal concept is quite attractive, because a vast number of corporate PCs are relatively outdated. Converting all of those old computers to Windows terminals enables corporations to use them for a few more years, usually by assigning them to users whose computing needs are less demanding. The Terminal Service concept might also be a good idea for a company that wants to use a certain application that requires a newer version of an OS than is currently deployed on the desktop.

Integrating Television

Microsoft is also busy investigating the opportunities for integrating digital TV with PCs, integrating the Web with TV, and many other initiatives that center on providing full coverage for the expected convergence of different technologies in the coming years. Microsoft has purchased several companies operating inside this area, including some cable operators.

Although Microsoft might venture into many new markets during the coming years, it will no doubt keep a strong focus on desktop clients, operating systems, its Office suite, and its servers—the foundation for both "Information at Your Fingertips" and Microsoft's healthy earnings—unless it is forced away from that because of the anti-trust case running!

Understanding the New Microsoft Mantra: Digital Nervous Systems

These days Microsoft isn't referring to "Information at Your Fingertips" as much as it used to. This is perhaps because that strategy is already very well implemented, or perhaps because the typical Microsoft customer increasingly is buying technology for strategic purposes rather than simply buying whatever is the latest release.

Rather, Microsoft is pushing a new concept, called the "Digital Nervous System," which is essentially a vision of how technology can enhance business in the future. A Digital Nervous System relies on solutions that make information flow rapidly and accurately through a corporation, enabling the best ideas to be gathered from employees at all levels of an organization, to create a new kind of corporate intelligence. A Digital Nervous System will help accomplish the following:

♦ Motivate everyone to act more quickly and make more informed decisions.

♦ Close the gap between your company and its customers.

♦ Prepare your company to react to unexpected events.

♦ Enable people to focus on business, not technology.

Or, as Bill Gates is quoted as saying: "Virtually everything in business today is an undifferentiated commodity except how a company manages its information. How you manage information determines whether you win or lose." Microsoft also provides a technology-bound definition of a Digital Nervous System, which is built on a commitment to the following six principles:

♦ A PC computing architecture

♦ All information in digital form

♦ Universal email

♦ Ubiquitous connectivity

♦ Common end-user productivity tools

♦ Integrated business-specific applications

But one still has to recognize the fact that a Digital Nervous System is more than what is mentioned above. It's how the elements work together; how they're integrated.

As Figure 1.2 demonstrates, a Digital Nervous System places heavy requirements on every part of the corporate computing infrastructure—from the desktops and desktop productivity tools, through the networking layer, up to the servers and application services offered. These heavy demands almost certainly translate into a need for a lot of new technology, and Windows 2000 Server, which includes a multitude of new infrastructure technologies, appears to be especially well suited to fill these requirements.

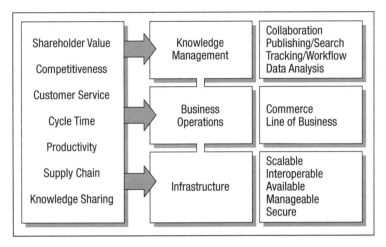

Figure 1.2
Reading from left to right, the corporate requirements become more detailed regarding how they can be handled inside the Digital Nervous System framework.

The vision of Digital Nervous Systems (see Figure 1.3) also aligns with Microsoft's plan to strike strategic partnerships in select vertical markets (financial services, education, real estate, distribution, engineering, health care, hospitals, government, the law, media, manufacturing, retail, and utilities) and select horizontal markets (Enterprise Resource Planning [ERP], customer management, document management, e-commerce, and tools).

On a more purely technological note, the incredibly vital Windows Distributed interNet Applications Architecture (Windows DNA) is also built in full compliance with the Digital Nervous System vision—and vice versa. In the newest release of Windows DNA—Windows DNA2000—Windows 2000 Server is featured as the foundation of Windows DNA.

It's All Leading to Windows 2000 Server

Windows 2000 Server fulfills the requirements of the Digital Nervous System vision. And although Microsoft claims that the Windows DNA framework is designed around open protocols and built on the standards approved by the World Wide Web Consortium (W3C) and the Internet Engineering Task Force (IETF), you can only get the "whole package" using Windows 2000 Server.

For example, the Windows DNA approach differs markedly from the common, Unix-based, layered middleware approach, in which application services reside above the OS and use different sets of services for security, maintenance, and other functions.

Windows DNA's true purpose is to integrate capabilities directly into the OS, such as a high-performance Web server, a scalable object request broker, a distributed transaction manager, a messaging-oriented server, and other application servers. Not surprisingly, all of

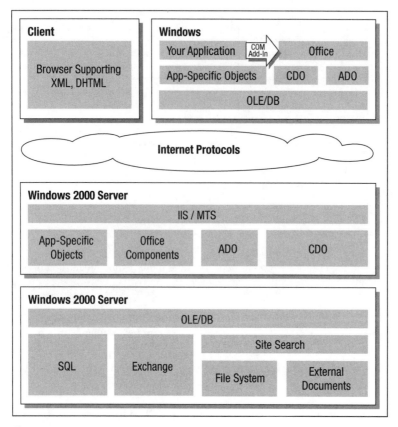

Figure 1.3
The core of the Digital Nervous System that Microsoft presents is built on top of Microsoft Office and BackOffice technologies.

these application services—including distributed security functions, scalable X.500, LDAP directory services, and built-in networking support for TCP/IP and other protocols—are designed to work with a common infrastructure: Windows 2000 Server.

The same compatibility issues apply to the two new extensions to Component Object Model (COM)—COM+ and DCOM. COM+ is an enhancement of COM (which is the foundation of such things as OLE) that integrates additional services, including transactions, data binding, events, garbage collection, and security functions. *Distributed* COM (DCOM) is an object bus that allows components in distributed applications to communicate with other components and to access distributed Windows platform services, regardless of whether the objects are running locally or on a remote machine. COM+ and DCOM won't be fully implemented until the advent of Windows 2000 Server. Likewise, the integration of business applications—which is part of the Digital Nervous System vision—isn't possible without Windows 2000 Server's Active Directory.

In addition to its compliance with the Digital Nervous System strategy, Windows 2000 Server provides a perfect match to the goals of the "Information at Your Fingertips" strategy. Windows 2000 Server includes a lot of new capabilities and features that are relevant to conquering the high-end server market—and some very persuasive integration gains on the desktop side, if the customer chooses to deploy Windows 2000 Professional.

Windows 2000 Server is also destined to help increase the market standing of Microsoft's BackOffice applications, for the following reasons:

♦ Windows 2000 Server demonstrates that Microsoft is committed to the future of the Internet.

♦ Windows 2000 Server's Active Directory will deliver large improvements in the integration between BackOffice applications and the OS, between two or more BackOffice applications, and between BackOffice and third-party applications.

Finally, Windows 2000 Server is integral in accomplishing Microsoft's ambitious target of providing market-leading team collaboration via Exchange 2000 Server, Outlook 2000, and Office 2000. These three products are destined to form Microsoft's future messaging and collaboration platform, but the "glue" needed for reaping the full rewards of an intense collaborative environment resides within Windows 2000 Server.

This chapter could easily go on and on discussing how crucial an ingredient Windows 2000 Server is to all of Microsoft's strategies and products, but you probably have figured that out by now.

Chapter 2
Windows 2000 in Brief

Windows 2000 isn't just another upgrade. It is quite simply Microsoft's biggest and most important new operating system since Windows 95 and the first release of Windows NT. Even though Bill Gates said it a rather long time ago, I still think he put it best in his remarks at the Professional Developer's Conference in September 1997 (prior to NT's name change to Windows 2000).

It's fair to say Microsoft has bet its future on Windows NT Version 5. We'll be driving the business market to use that product as rapidly as possible, and then we'll do a variation using the same technology that will drive into the consumer market. And so, some time in not too many years, new personal computers will come with the refinement of Windows NT Version 5 in the same way they come with Windows 95 today.

Since that time, Bill Gates and many other Microsoft employees have delved much deeper into why Windows 2000 is such an important product for Microsoft and its customers. But usually it can more or less be summed up to the following statement uttered by Bill Gates at one time: "It's the biggest release of NT that we've ever done. There are more new lines of code in this than even in any of the releases we've done. And it's the directory, it's the security, it's the IntelliMirror breakthrough for cost of ownership, and it's the platform for building the rich distributed applications."

This chapter goes into much more detail about the new capabilities and functionality that Microsoft offers with Windows 2000.

Windows 2000 Is an Enormous New Release

In terms of the sheer number of program lines, Windows 2000 represents a 150-percent increase over NT 4. And aside from requiring more available hard disk space, Windows 2000 also taxes CPUs and demands more memory than the previous version. For example, Microsoft has upped the minimum requirements for Windows 2000 Server to a 133MHz Pentium CPU, 1GB of free hard disk space, and 128MB RAM (256MB recommended). The minimum requirements for running Windows 2000 Professional are a 133MHz Pentium CPU, 650MB of free hard disk space, and 32MB RAM (64MB recommended).

Please note that these requirements cover only the base OS. You have to add processor muscle, hard disk space, and RAM to cover your applications. In other words, many current systems that handle Windows NT 4 reasonably well will no longer be feasible for running Windows 2000.

What do you have to gain from Windows 2000 then? In short, quite a lot, regardless of which parts of the OS you are most interested in. Windows 2000 is a very broad product release. For example, Windows 2000 sports a much-improved application architecture, a full-fledged directory service architecture, a new security architecture, and a lot of things to reduce cost of ownership.

Microsoft's overall goal for Windows 2000 Server is to:

♦ Deliver great servers for the following:

  ♦ File/Print/Web services

  ♦ Application services

  ♦ Infrastructure services

  ♦ Communications services

♦ Deliver great workstations for the following:

  ♦ Corporate desktops

  ♦ Mobile/laptop systems

♦ Deliver the best reliability ever

One of the many signs of improved reliability is a dramatic reduction in the number of reconfiguration scenarios that require a reboot. Windows NT 4 demands a reboot in 50 to 80 reconfiguration examples (depending upon how you count them), whereas Windows 2000 cuts that number to 7 to 20!

Windows 2000 Server for File, Print, and Web Services

When Windows 2000 Server is used for file services, its greatest features are the following:

♦ Ease in locating and accessing the following info:

  ♦ Volumes published in Active Directory

- Content indexing via Indexing Service
- Distributed File System (DFS)

- Improved storage management
  - Disk quotas
  - Hierarchical Storage Management (HSM)
  - Dynamic volume management
- Improved performance
  - 20-percent faster file access
  - Distributed replicas

For print services, the highlights of Windows 2000 Server include the following:

- Easier printing
  - Printers published in Active Directory
  - Improved user interface and administration
- Broad device/protocol support
  - Internet Printing Protocol (IPP)
  - New Postscript subsystem
  - More than 2,500 printer drivers
- Improved performance
  - Faster printing
  - More efficient queue management
  - Network printing driver improvements

For Web services, Windows 2000 Server offers the following:

- Robust Web service delivery
  - Higher performance
  - CPU throttling
  - Server scriptlets
- Improved manageability
  - Command-line scripting
  - Management wizards
- Support for the latest standards
  - Distributed Authoring and Versioning (WebDAV)
  - Digest authentication
  - HTTP compression

As an application server, Windows 2000 Server includes the following:

♦ Higher performance and scalability

 ♦ Improved memory support (available only in Windows 2000 Advanced Server and Windows 2000 Datacenter Server)

 ♦ Better symmetrical multiprocessing (SMP) scaling

 ♦ Support for Intelligent I/O Architecture (I2O)

♦ Greater availability

 ♦ Fewer planned/unplanned reboots

 ♦ Improved Cluster Service (available only in Windows 2000 Advanced Server and Windows 2000 Datacenter Server)

 ♦ Auto-restart of failed services

♦ Reach to new desktops

 ♦ Terminal Services

Windows 2000 Server for Application, Infrastructure, and Communications Services

With Windows 2000 Server, Microsoft also focuses on catering to the needs of three "new" types of servers:

♦ Infrastructure

♦ Custom line-of-business

♦ Communications

Windows 2000 Server as an infrastructure server has the following features:

♦ Physically decentralized and logically centralized

 ♦ Active Directory

 ♦ IntelliMirror server support

 ♦ Policy-based management

 ♦ Remote/scriptable administration

♦ Advanced security services

 ♦ Kerberos

 ♦ Public key infrastructure

 ♦ Security Configuration Editor

 ♦ Smart Card support

The custom line-of-business server delivers the following:

- Distributed application services
    - Component/Transaction Services (formerly known as Microsoft Transaction Server)
    - Message Queuing Services (formerly known as Microsoft Message Queue Server)
    - Streaming Media Services
- Service level control
    - Job object
    - Advanced cluster management tools (available only in Windows 2000 Advanced Server and Windows 2000 Datacenter Server)

The main capabilities of the communications server include the following:

- Policy-based networking
    - Directory-enabled networking
    - Quality of service
- Network security
    - Encryption of IP packets (IPSEC)
    - Integrated packet filtering
    - Improved Virtual Private Networking
- Rich connectivity
    - Integrated routing
    - Dynamic DNS
    - ATM and gigabit Ethernet
    - Telephony services (primarily handled via Telephony Application Programming Interface [TAPI])

Windows 2000 Professional

The highlights of Windows 2000 Professional on the corporate desktop include the following:

- Flexibility
    - Internet Explorer 5, DirectX 7
    - Automatic network setup
    - Exploitation of advanced hardware
    - Improved language support

- Robustness
    - Fewer reboots
    - Windows Installer service
- Leveraging of existing assets
    - Broad application compatibility
    - Broad hardware compatibility
    - Automatic private IP addressing (APIPA) in case of DHCP failures and the like

Windows 2000 Professional adds the following features to the mobile environment:

- Advanced hardware support
    - Plug and Play
    - PC Card
    - Power management
    - Hot docking functionality
- Mobile user support
    - Easier Remote Access Services (RAS)
    - Encrypting File System (EFS)

Windows 2000 Professional and Windows 2000 Server form the perfect partnership, offering a package that includes these features:

- Managed enterprise desktops
    - IntelliMirror client support
    - Policy-aware workstations
    - Machine deployment/replacement
    - Centralized application management
- Roaming user support
    - Offline folder access
    - Distributed File System (DFS) location transparency

Don't despair if you feel overwhelmed by the number of acronyms and names in the preceding pages. More details are presented next.

Understanding Windows 2000

Summarizing the key features of Windows 2000 is somewhat complicated by the fact that it includes five different products:

- Windows 2000 Professional
- Windows 2000 Server

- ◆ Windows 2000 Advanced Server
- ◆ Windows 2000 Datacenter Server
- ◆ Windows 2000 Small Business Server

To help you understand the main variants of Windows 2000, this section sums up the major new features and functionality of Windows 2000 Professional, followed by Windows 2000 Server, and then Windows 2000 Advanced Server, and Windows 2000 Datacenter Server. The Small Business Server variant of Windows 2000 Server is not covered, because it isn't closely related to the subject of this book (you should be able to find explanations of this product on Microsoft's Web site).

Table 2.1 lists and explains the most important features and functionality of Windows 2000 Professional.

Table 2.1   The major features of Windows 2000 Professional.

Feature	Description
Active Directory support	With Windows 2000, logon and searching for network resources is easier and more flexible than ever. With Active Directory integration, Windows 2000 publishes all shared network resources in the directory, thus providing users with an easy way to locate resources quickly (from the Search menu) and in effect improving the capabilities across the network.
Microsoft MMC	A new framework for the operating tools that ensures a uniform GUI for all system tools used in the Windows 2000 Professional environment, which include the built-in tools and the management tools for third-party applications.
Internet Explorer 5	The latest version of Microsoft's popular Web browser, offering superior integration with the Windows platform.
Windows Scripting Host (WSH)	Enables you to automate GUI or command-line actions via a script. WSH includes support for Visual Basic and Java scripts and sports a language-independent architecture that enables you to build script interpreters for other programming languages.
FAT32 support	FAT32 is an improved version of the FAT file system already used by Windows 98 and the OEM Service Release (OSR) versions of Windows 95.
NTFS 5	The new version of NTFS is faster and has many new capabilities, such as per-user disk quotas; EFS, which offers on-the-fly file encryption; the capability to add disk space to an NTFS volume without rebooting the system (dynamic volumes); and Distributed Link Tracking, which often will be able to resolve lost shortcuts and OLE links to NTFS files that have undergone a name or path change.
Universal Disk Format (UDF)	A new file system that handles DVD drives and CDs.
Defragmenting utility	The built-in Windows 2000 tools include a tool for defragmenting the disk, regardless of whether it is FAT-, FAT32-, or NTFS-formatted.
Removable Storage Manager (RSM)	RSM presents a common interface to robotic changers and media libraries, which enable multiple applications to share local libraries and tape or disk drives and to control removable media within the system.

(continued)

Table 2.1   The major features of Windows 2000 Professional *(continued)*.

Feature	Description
New backup utility	The built-in backup tool has a new user interface that is media-centric rather than tape-centric because of the introduction of RSM, which Backup uses. The tool provides support for most of the common storage media.
Windows Installer technology	A new technology for improved software installation, which enables you to remove each part of the installed software without wreaking havoc on other applications. It also includes support for lockdown (allows application installations to be completed even if users logged on to the network don't have the privileges to install applications) and "just-in-time" installation of applications.
Internet Printing Protocol (IPP)	Enables users to print directly to a URL over the intranet or Internet, view printer status by using a browser, and install printer drivers from a URL.
Plug and Play	New native support of Plug and Play, allowing for much-improved support for portable computers.
ACPI Power Management	Improved Power Management standard that is much better at saving power and handling the peripherals correctly when users go into one of the power save modes that are available.
Universal Serial Bus (USB) support	Enables you to connect many devices to the same port (unlike the old style serial/COM ports). USB requires very little user knowledge, which could make it very popular with end users.
IEEE 1394 support	This new standard for high-performance communications can deliver up to 100, 200 and 400Mbps sustained bandwidth.
WDM driver architecture	The new driver architecture for 32-bit Windows, mainly for use with new types of peripherals. WDM drivers can be used by Windows 98 and vice versa.
Smart Card support	Microsoft envisions a lot of potential uses for Smart Cards, which is why Windows 2000 Professional fully supports Smart Cards (including the ability to use Smart Cards for login).
Fibre Channel support	Fibre Channel supports transmission speeds of up to 4Gbps (to be exact, there's support for transmission rates of 133, 266 and 531 Mbps and 1.06, 2.12 and 4.25 Gbps in each direction). This technology is used mainly for server storage as of now.
64-bit processor support	Gives users the capability to better exploit the performance advantages offered with PCs based on the future Intel 64-bit processors. This new technology will likely be used for high-performance servers.
Intelligent Input/Output Architecture	Enables you to eliminate some of the processing of I/O (I2O) support tasks from the central processor (CPU), which can then be carried out by separate support logic instead, resulting in lower CPU utilization and improved I/O performance.
Accelerated Graphics Port (AGP) support	New standard for 3D graphics that provides improved performance on "plain-vanilla" PCs.
Multimedia Extensions (MMX) support	Just like Windows 98, Windows 2000 Professional supports the special Intel MMX instructions. MMX is a Pentium superstructure that improves performance with multimedia tasks via numerous special instructions. Intel's MMX and Pentium II processors, AMD's K6, and Cyrix's 6x86MX all are furnished with the extra MMX instruction set.

(continued)

Table 2.1 The major features of Windows 2000 Professional *(continued)*.

Feature	Description
Quality of Service (QoS)	Enables applications to request and, if possible, obtain the necessary service quality from the network. Includes support for the QoS standards, Resource Reservation Protocol (RSVP), Differentiated Quality of Service (Diff-serve), and 802.1p (an IEEE standard for providing QoS in 802-based networks).
Telephony Application Programming Interface (TAPI)	Unifies IP and traditional telephony, which enables developers to create a new generation of powerful computer telephony applications.
Network Driver Interface Specification (NDIS)	The newest edition of the Windows network architecture, which now features support of multicasts and bandwidth reservation, among other things.
TCP/IP enhancements	The TCP/IP protocol stack delivered with Windows 2000 Professional has been updated to include support for several important performance-enhancing functionalities, such as TCP scalable window sizes (RFC 1323 support), Selective acknowledgements (SACK), and improved round-trip time (RTT) estimation. Additionally, there's support for many other things, such as Internet Group Management Protocol (IGMP) v2, which allows multiple clients to share a common multicast session.
Asynchronous Transfer Mode (ATM)	Gives applications the advantage of all of the capabilities of ATM straight from the OS, which might very well be just what it takes to have ATM come in from the cold in regard to servers.
More simultaneous monitors used	The capability to connect as many as four monitors to the system and still have them regarded as just one monitor by the OS (and thus by applications).
DirectX 7	The latest version of Microsoft's collection of APIs, which is especially developed to meet the high sound and sensation demands of entertainment software.
Task Scheduler	New scheduling tool that puts a more user-friendly GUI on top of the current AT service. This interface is the same as the one found in Windows 95/98.
Personal Fax for Windows	New version of the well-known fax tools.
Disk duplication (SysPrep)	The setup tools include a mechanism that enables you to duplicate fully installed systems on identical hardware.

Because of the wide-ranging code sharing between Windows 2000 Professional and Windows 2000 Server, all the functionalities listed in Table 2.1 are also included in Windows 2000 Server. In addition, Windows 2000 Server includes the key features and functionalities listed in Table 2.2.

Please note that Windows 2000 Server supports up to four processor (meaning four-way SMP), just as was the case with Windows NT Server 4. However, according to Microsoft, the SMP implementation in Windows 2000 Server offers a much more linear scaling when processors are added, than was the case in Windows NT Server 4.

Table 2.2 The major features of Windows 2000 Server.

Feature	Description
Active Directory	Directory service that enables you to consolidate information on all available network objects and services into one and the same place.
Dynamic DNS (DDNS)	Replaces the present WINS service for name resolution. DHCP and DDNS are closely integrated. Additionally, the Windows 2000 implementation of DDNS has an option for integrating DDNS and Active Directory, which eliminates the requirement to maintain a separate DNS replication topology.
Distributed File System (DFS)	Enables you to establish a virtual file system directory tree that is split between several servers (even non-Windows 2000 servers), and to introduce fault tolerance by duplicating the same part of the file structure onto several servers.
QoS Admission Control	Gives QoS-prepared applications access to reserve network bandwidth and to prioritize network traffic even on a shared segment. With QoS Admission Control, you can control the amount of bandwidth that applications and users can reserve, based on policies configured in Active Directory—thus preventing overstretching of the network.
IP security (IPSEC)	An IETF proposed standard for encrypting IP traffic. IPSEC is controlled through Windows 2000 Server's system policy management tools and thus enables you to enforce encryption between systems, transparent to the end user.
Group Policy Objects (GPOs)	Allows the administrator to enforce a set of rules (for such things as policies, login/logoff scripts, folder redirection, and application deployment) for users and computers as they are applied to a particular site, domain, or organizational unit (OU) in Active Directory. The Software Installation functionalities will enable you to specify a set of applications that will always be available to a user (or group) that is using Windows 2000 Professional. If a required application is unavailable when needed, it is automatically installed on the desktop.
Remote Storage Service (RSS)	RSS provides Hierarchical Storage Management (HSM) functionality to Windows 2000. RSS monitors the amount of space available on your local hard disk and springs into action when the free space on your primary hard disk dips below a predefined level.
Internet Information Server (IIS)	Version 5 of Microsoft's immensely successful Web server. Some of the added functionality in IIS 5 includes process accounting (information about how each Web site uses CPU resources on the server), CPU throttling (limiting the amount of CPU processing time that a Web application or site can use over a predefined period of time), multiple user domains (supports hosting multiple Web sites on a single server, while offering unique name spaces for each site), and support for new standards, such as WebDAV and HTTP compression.
Transaction Services	Gives access to administer the various COM/COM+ components via the traditional transaction-processing techniques for improved load balancing, security, and reliability. Transaction Services is an integral part of Microsoft Component Services. (Also available in an earlier version for Windows NT Server 4 as part of the Option Pack.)
Message Queuing Services	A message and queuing system that is Microsoft's shot at ensuring reliable delivery of messages and data in a distributed environment. (Also available in an earlier version for Windows NT Server 4 as part of the Option Pack.)

(continued)

Table 2.2   The major features of Windows 2000 Server (*continued*).

Feature	Description
Indexing Service	Enables you to index all text and properties of various types of text files, including HTML and Microsoft Word files. (Also available for Windows NT Server 4 as part of the Option Pack.)
Certificate Services	Enables you to implement a fully-fledged Public Key Infrastructure (PKI) based on all the prevalent standards, which can be utilized for such things as authentication and digital signatures.
Routing and Remote Access Service (RRAS)	An extension to RAS that enables you to use the server as a router on IP- and IPX-based networks. The new version of RRAS includes Network Address Translation (NAT) and Layer 2 Tunneling Protocol (L2TP), among other things. (An earlier version of RRAS is available for Windows NT Server 4 via Microsoft's Web site.)
Windows Internet Name Service (WINS)	Provides name-to-address resolution for NetBIOS client requests. Even though WINS isn't used in a native Active Directory setup, Windows 2000 Server includes a new version of WINS that eliminates the most common WINS headaches, with capabilities such as persistent connections, manual tombstoning, dynamic record deletion, and tools to check the consistency between various WINS servers.
Job object	An extension to the process model called a job. A job object's basic function is to allow groups of processes to be managed and manipulated as a unit. A job object gives you access to control the attributes associated with a group of processes. Setting a maximum on CPU utilization to a specific process or group of processes is just one of the very useful ways of tapping the potential of the job object.
Windows Management Interface	Supports the Desktop Management Task Force (DMTF) Web-Based Enterprise Management (WBEM) standard, which simplifies the instrumentation of drivers and applications. Also includes a management application called Real World Interface from Computer Associates for viewing WBEM data.

Microsoft Windows 2000 Advanced Server is a variant of Windows 2000 Server, which is designed for organizations that require an improved level of scalability, reliability, and availability. Windows 2000 Advanced Server contains all the features and functionality of the standard version of Windows 2000 Server plus the key features set forth in Table 2.3.

For the highest attainable level of scalability, you will find yet another variant of Windows 2000, called Windows 2000 Datacenter Server. Windows 2000 Datacenter Server contains all the features and functionality of Windows 2000 Advanced Server plus the following features:

♦ 32-way SMP

♦ four-node clustering

♦ memory sizes up to 64GB (the 64GB support is provided by Enterprise Memory Architecture [EMA] on Intel PAE-compliant systems)

♦ WinSock Direct (which enables applications that use WinSock to perform faster and with less overhead when communicating across a system area network [SAN], out of the box)

Table 2.3   The major features of Windows 2000 Advanced Server.

Feature	Description
Intel Physical Address Extensions (PAE) support	Servers that have support for PAE will be able to use as much as four times more physical memory (16GB of RAM) than possible with Windows 2000 Server. A large physical memory can dramatically improve performance in various applications, when exploited by the products.
Cluster Service (previously known as Cluster Server)	Microsoft's clustering solution, which also is an integral part of Windows NT Server, Enterprise Edition 4. Just as its predecessor, Cluster Service only contains support for high-availability facilities (bringing an offline system online in case of disaster on the primary system) with two nodes. However, Windows 2000 Advanced Server contains a newer version of Cluster Service, which has support for rolling upgrades (sequential upgrades of the OS on each node, thus eliminating the downtime of cluster services) of both OS releases (versions, service packs, and hot fixes) and layered products. Additionally, more OS services (for example, DHCP, WINS, and DFS) are now cluster-aware than was the case with Windows NT Server 4.
Network Load Balancing Service (formerly Valence Research Convoy Cluster)	Complements Cluster Service by providing clustering of TCP/IP services between as many as 32 nodes. Network Load Balancing Service operates in a fully transparent manner to both your server applications and TCP/IP clients, meaning that clients can access the cluster as if it were a single computer, by using one IP address. Under normal operations, Network Load Balancing Service automatically balances the networking traffic between the clustered computers, scaling the performance of one server to the level that you require. When a computer fails or goes offline, Network Load Balancing Service automatically reconfigures the cluster to direct the client connections to the remaining available computers. Please note that Network Load Balancing Service is of real value only for use in stateless client applications, such as Web browsing, because it does not have any support for synchronizing of the server states.
Enhanced SMP scalability	Supports up to eight-way Symmetrical MultiProcessing (SMP) out of the box. Please note that this is the same as what was available in Windows NT Server 4 Enterprise Edition. Microsoft has promised that improvements in the implementation of the SMP code provide for better "linearity" of scaling between the eight processors than users are accustomed to from Windows NT Server 4.
High-performance sorting	Optimizes commercial sorting performance on large data sets. This sort typically is used to prepare data for loading in data warehouse and data mart applications and to prepare large, sort-sensitive print and batch operations.

The First Revolution: Active Directory

The biggest news in Windows 2000 Server is Active Directory (see Figure 2.1), Microsoft's bid for a scalable, hierarchical directory service capable of competing with Novell NDS and other such directory services.

Note

The introduction of Active Directory may seem contradictory to seasoned observers of NT Server/Windows 2000 Server, because—since the launch of NT Server 3.51— Microsoft has insisted that NT Server offers a directory service. Microsoft's arguments are that NT Server requires a single login and that all users within the domain are replicated, so if a user's computer is moved to a different physical location, that user still can be authenticated and still can access their network resources (for example, a satellite office on the company network). When NT Server 4 was launched, Microsoft started to refer to its solution as a "directory service." However, these two facilities alone are far from sufficient to create a "real" directory service (see Chapter 3 for more discussion of this topic).

A genuine directory service has the following properties:

♦ Storage of information on the environment in a distributed form

♦ Support for searching "white pages" (search on the basis of a certain attribute, such as a name or telephone number) and "yellow pages" (search on the basis of fairly precise classifications, such as "all color printers or 1200 dpi printers on the second floor")

♦ Option of having the login to the directory cover new applications and services

♦ Option of totally removing dependence on physical locations

All the properties mentioned in the preceding list have only been available within the non-Microsoft products, such as Novell NDS. But now Microsoft is also there with Active Directory.

Like its competitors, Active Directory is very similar to the X.500 directory service model, which defines the *directory schema* (how information is stored in the directory). Active Directory uses a scaled-down version of the X.500 schema, which consists of object classes and attributes. And, like the other directory service providers, Microsoft envisions a future in which the directory will be extended with all sorts of new objects to cover

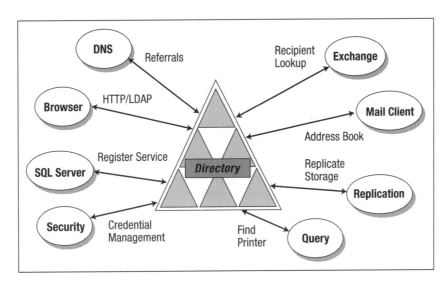

Figure 2.1
Active Directory delivers an extensible and hierarchical namespace for use with all types of infrastructure information.

special-purpose corporate demands and information structures that are vital to the operation of the installed applications.

To add new objects and data to Active Directory, you should use either the *Active Directory Services Interface (ADSI)* or the *Lightweight Directory Access Protocol (LDAP)* C API. Active Directory also provides support of MAPI, but this is just a solution that is provided for backward-compatibility, and thus should not be utilized by anything but legacy solutions.

Because Active Directory uses the DDNS protocol to localize examples of the directory and LDAP 3 for directory queries, it effectively makes TCP/IP the standard protocol for Windows 2000 Server and relegates NetBIOS and WINS to a legacy solution. However, to ensure backward-compatibility, Windows 2000 Server is still able to handle WINS and other "older" network protocols, such as NetBEUI.

Windows 2000 Server is based on multimaster replication, to ensure high availability of the directory and to ease the distribution of administrative rights throughout the company. *Multi-master replication* means that each domain controller (DC) contains a master replica of the directory and that all changes are automatically spread to all DC servers. Multi-master replication eliminates the current division into *Primary Domain Controller (PDC)* and *Backup Domain Controller (BDC)* that is used by NT Server 4's single-master replication scheme. To ensure backward-compatibility, an Active Directory DC can still act as a PDC, when running in mixed mode (see Figure 2.2).

One of the distinct technical drawbacks of Active Directory—compared with NT Server 4's domain-based solution—is that the new structures increase the complexity of trusts in the environment. This is why Windows 2000 Server includes support for transitive trusts, which are defined by default between Active Directory domains.

A *transitive trust* means that, by defining a single trust connection between two domains, all the domains trusted by the two domains are trusted by the other domains. Transitive trusts are a great relief for administrators, who previously had to define their own bi-directional trust relationships between each and every domain pair that needed to trust each other. In instances with a lot of domains, that could easily become an administrative nightmare.

The Second Revolution: Microsoft Management Console

In addition to Active Directory, Windows 2000 Server builds on another technology—*Microsoft Management Console (MMC)*—that delivers large administrative advantages compared to its predecessors. MMC is an administrative tools framework for the Windows 2000 Server environment, designed to centralize and unify the user interface for the tools used to configure or monitor computers and applications—whether they are responsible for a single workstation or an entire network of computers. The whole point of MMC is to deliver a similar "look and feel" to all administrative tools (and tools for viewing network functions) through the following features:

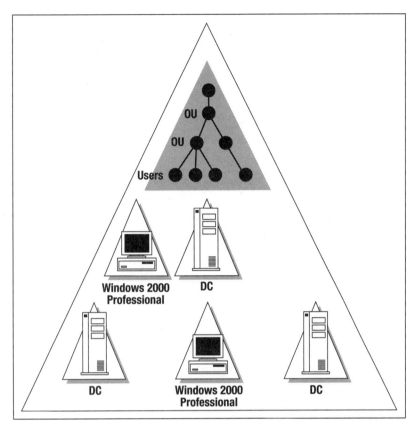

Figure 2.2
Domains and DCs will still be among the most vital building blocks in the Active Directory age. But you should be aware that the domains and DCs in Windows 2000 Server are very different from the domains and DCs used in NT Server 4.

♦ A graphical console hosts the programs (known as *snap-ins*) that give access to administer the individual parts of the Windows 2000 environment.

♦ The various snap-ins are loaded into the console and then organized in a tree structure.

♦ The various windows in the console can offer different views of the same structures, thus enabling you to complete different tasks as easily as possible.

♦ Web pages can be incorporated into the console.

In other words, MMC is nothing by itself; it just provides a standardized way of presenting the administrative tools of Windows 2000 and third-party applications. MMC is merely a set of APIs, a GUI shell (the console), and a set of guidelines for building administration tools. MMC is a *tool host*—it provides no management functionality of its own. The individual components (snap-ins) provide all the functionality.

Besides the GUI standardization, MMC also enables you to mix and match different tools inside a single console, instead of having to switch between different windows. This means that an MMC tool can include more than a single application—a tool can include one or more snap-ins, and, in turn, each snap-in can contain additional extension snap-ins.

The modular structure of MMC enables you to reduce significantly the costs associated with systems management, by grouping snap-ins into custom tools that provide only the view and set of options that you want. Thus, you can place all parts of a particular administrative job or routine in a single console, regardless of which server applications or parts of Windows 2000 need administration.

Additionally, you can save each custom tool as an MMC-saved console (MSC) file and supply it to whoever is delegated to perform the administrative tasks associated with that console. This functionality enables you to create a custom-built set of tools for end users and administrators to ease their work.

In short, MMC makes it much easier for you to handle task delegation, to group tools and processes logically, and to organize your tools and tasks for the jobs at hand (see Figure 2.3).

Some of the most important MMC snap-ins provided with Windows 2000 Server are explained in Table 2.4.

You might as well start getting used to MMC today, because Microsoft intends to supply MMC snap-ins for all their applications and services. Also, Microsoft most probably will make MMC snap-ins a requirement for the next release of the BackOffice logo (actually, Microsoft intended to make it a requirement for the new Windows 2000 logo; however, it was dropped because of delays in their support documentation for application developers).

Table 2.4 Windows 2000 Server snap-ins used with MMC.

Snap-in	Description
Active Directory Users and Computers	Enables you to manage users, groups, OUs, and all other directory objects (including computers that are part of the domain). This tool is the heart of all Active Directory administration.
Services	Enables you to stop, start, pause, and resume services on local and remote computers. (Replaces the Services Control Panel application of the previous NT versions.)
Shared Folders	Enables you to create shares and manage the sessions and connections on local or remote computers. (Replaces functionality previously found in the Server Control Panel application.)
Security Configuration and Analysis	Provides a one-stop security configuration and analysis tool for Windows 2000. It enables you to configure various security-sensitive Registry settings, access controls on files and Registry keys, and security of system services. Additionally, it enables you to define security configurations as a template and then apply the template to selected computers, using a Group Policy Object (GPO), in one operation.

(continued)

Table 2.4   Windows 2000 Server snap-ins used with MMC *(continued).*

Snap-in	Description
Computer Management	The administrator's computer-configuration tool. It provides access to the base Windows 2000 Server tools (to view events, create shares, manage devices, and so on) and dynamically discovers which server services and applications are available. It is designed to work with one computer, and all of its features can be used remotely, enabling you to troubleshoot and configure a computer from any other computer on the same network. Computer Management comprises a range of different snap-ins, including Shared Folders, Device Manager, Disk Management, and Services.
Disk Management	A graphical tool for managing disks (replaces the NT 4 Disk Administrator) that supports partitions, logical drives, and the new dynamic volumes. It contains short-cut menus and wizards to simplify creating volumes and initializing and upgrading disks.
Group Policy	Responsible for managing the settings of Group Policy Objects (GPOs), which can be applied to a specific site, domain, or OU. The GPO can be used for application deployment, policy options for computers and users, scripts, and folder redirection.
Device Manager	Enables you to configure devices and resources on your computer (change device properties, unplug or eject devices, and resolve hardware conflicts).

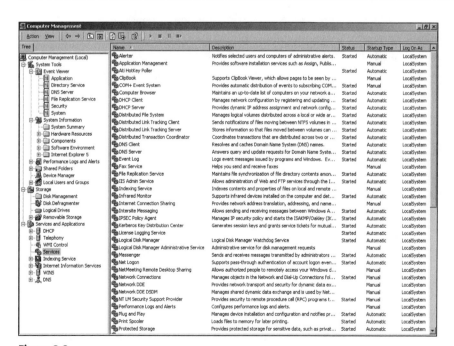

Figure 2.3
The standard configuration of the Computer Management Administrative Tools, which is just one of the many predefined MMC consoles that are delivered as part of Windows 2000.

The Third Revolution: IntelliMirror and Other Technologies to Ease the Desktop Burden

IntelliMirror is another very thrilling addition to Windows 2000 Server. The capabilities of IntelliMirror include the following:

♦ *Reduce Total Cost of Ownership (TCO)*—Supports centralized, policy-based administration of your PC infrastructure, utilizing technologies such as Active Directory and Group Policies.

♦ *Comprehensive software management*—Helps manage each step in the software life cycle, from installation over upgrades and repairs to removal.

♦ *Support for roaming and mobile users*—Enables users who roam the network to have their documents, settings, and applications automatically follow them wherever they go. Enables mobile users to have their files and folders brought up to date automatically, whenever they're on-line.

♦ *Easy replacement of PCs*—Enables a PC to connect automatically to a server and install Windows 2000 Professional via Remote OS Installation Services, thus enabling easy replacement of PCs that have failed or need to be replaced.

IntelliMirror is not a single new technology, but a group of new technologies that can be used separately or together to preserve the users' state, data, and preferences. The goal of IntelliMirror management technologies is to ensure that the PC is always available and protected, regardless of place, time, or problems that desktop machines may have in communicating with the server.

Please note that IntelliMirror is a set of technologies that depends on both the server and the client, which is why the IntelliMirror feature set is available only when you use Windows 2000 Server in combination with Windows 2000 Professional.

Microsoft has no immediate plans to bring the IntelliMirror services to other client OSs, such as Windows 98, which probably is related to Microsoft's strategy to use IntelliMirror as one of the most important arguments for establishing Windows 2000 Professional as the preferred desktop environment for corporate PCs. Thus, you still have to invest in another robust application distribution platform (such as Microsoft Systems Management Server) if you need application deployment functionality for Windows 95/98, Windows 3.x, or other OS platforms.

Selective Mirroring of Files and Folders

One of the technologies central to IntelliMirror is its ability to mirror each user's personalized workspace—that is, files and folders—and use client-side storage for local access to data. This technology enables you to deliver offline access to files (and folders) when the network version of the file is unavailable or when you don't want to load the server with file requests. In other words, this technology enables you to provide all network users with access to a familiar desktop environment, regardless of whether they are online or offline or they log on from a new or existing client.

And although each user enjoys the performance of local data access, management functions can still be performed centrally with minimal or no user participation. So, without a sacrifice in performance, administrators and users gain the security and convenience of "anywhere, anytime" access to the personalized workspace, automatic system updates and data protection, and fast, complete recoveries from downtime.

Offline files and folders are sometimes referred to as *server-side mirroring*, or *client-side caching*, so don't be confused if those terms are used. Regardless of the wording, this technology is great for users, because they don't need to learn new file names (the cached copy of a file on the client's hard drive uses the same file name and directory path as when the client is connected to the network), and the synchronization of data that occurs when connecting to the network is totally transparent to the user, except when a replication collision is encountered—that is, when a file has been changed at the server, as well as at the client, since the last synchronization.

Windows Installer

Windows Installer technology, another key IntelliMirror technology, is a new transaction-based application installer that is responsible for application management. Windows Installer technology comprises the following:

♦ A standard package format and a built-in installation service that handles installation, repair, removal, and dependency tracking of certain components. A standard package (also called an *MSI package*) actually specifies a relational database that contains all the information necessary to describe how to install an application. This permits granular control over the application, its features, updates, and broken or missing files. It also provides Windows Installer with information on every change (such as file and Registry changes) that a particular application makes, which enables it to remove all pieces of the application, if needed, and dramatically reduces the potential for DLL conflicts (also known as "DLL Hell").

♦ Increased resilience, through its capability to repair or reinstall applications, perform rollback on installation transactions, and establish redundant install points.

♦ Just-in-time (JIT) installations, enabling future applications to be designed to install components on demand and as they are needed. (Microsoft has promised to utilize this JIT functionality in future Windows 2000 Service Packs and in Office 2000.) Windows Installer technology also includes functions for locating and forcing the installation of components.

♦ Support for *lockdown*, which enables you to install deployed applications completely, even if users logged on to the network don't have the privileges to install applications (Windows Installer technology is implemented on Windows 2000 Server as a service: *Application Management Service*).

An important complement to Windows Installer is Software Installation MMC snap-in, which enables you to control when a user or computer can have an application published, deployed, or assigned—and whether it should be upgraded or removed.

Together, Windows Installer technology and the Software Installation MMC snap-in give you the power to implement effective software management and to delegate power to the user, when appropriate. These tools can help you reduce TCO by reducing the costs associated with lost productivity when users tinker with their systems.

Other Tools for Desktop Administration

On top of all the preceding IntelliMirror technologies, you will find heaps of other worthy tools and services that help ease the life of the desktop administrator. For example, Windows 2000—as well as Windows 98—offer built-in support of scripts via Windows Scripting Host (WSH).

WSH is a language-independent scripting host for 32-bit Windows platforms that includes both VBScript (Visual Basic Scripting Edition) and JavaScript (JScript) engines. WSH enables you to execute scripts directly on the Windows desktop or command console, making it a much-needed improvement to the previous state of affairs, where one only had MS-DOS style batch files (and the KiXtart Resource Kit utility).

Also, Windows 2000 is, by far, the most world-ready Windows product that Microsoft has released so far. Windows 2000 is "multilingual" regarding APIs, tables of characters, keyboard layout, and so forth, which makes developing applications that cover many different languages much easier (Windows 2000 supports 64 languages). If third-party application developers start taking advantage of the extensive language-awareness functionality built into Windows 2000, companies that cover several language areas or that are situated in small language areas will benefit greatly.

Windows 2000 Server introduces *Group Policies*, which enable an organization to reduce administration by standardizing user and computer configurations. Group Policies are an advanced successor to NT 4's System Policies. For example, Group Policies offer greater granular control, because they can be applied at the site (a collection of computers with a local affinity), domain (a group of computers that shares the same security boundary), or OU (a container that holds objects and delegates administrative rights for domains and sites). Group Policies can also be hierarchically inherited or filtered with security groups. Table 2.5 includes the areas covered by Group Policies.

Table 2.5 Coverage of Group Policies.

Area Covered	Description
Administrative templates	Includes all Registry-based policies. Administrators can use administrative templates to customize the Registry settings that provide the personalization of system services, desktop settings, and application settings.
Folder redirection	Allows folders that are used by the user to be redirected to folders on the server. Thus, users can establish a roaming profile, enabling them to move from computer to computer and still have access to the same folders.
Logon/logoff and startup/shutdown scripts	Determines which scripts are run during the user logon or logoff process and computer startup or shutdown process, respectively. The benefit of these scripts is that you can customize each desktop according to specific needs, based on domain, OU, site, and/or group memberships.
Software installation	Specifies which applications are to be deployed, assigned, and published to desktop systems, based on the container's (site, domain, or OU) policy settings.
Security settings	Controls how access to certain files, folders, Registry keys, and system services is configured and managed for any object or group of objects in the directory. Also known as security templates.

The Fourth Revolution: Real Security

The security infrastructure in Windows 2000 Server is another revolutionary feature. Windows NT Server 4 leaves a lot to be desired in the area of security, whereas Windows 2000 Server proves that Microsoft is finally putting a lot of emphasis on server security. The security infrastructure in Windows 2000 Server includes the key technologies set forth in Table 2.6.

Windows 2000 Server's primary authentication mechanism is Kerberos (with public key certificates as an option), but it retains backward-compatibility with the old LAN Manager authentication methodology (also known as NTLM).

Table 2.6 The security infrastructure of Windows 2000 Server.

Technology	Description
Security Configuration and Analysis	Convenes all security-specific settings in one place. It is a "define once, apply many times" technology, which means that it enables you to define security configurations as a template and then apply the template to selected computers simultaneously using a Group Policy.
Kerberos authentication	Replaces the weak NTLM as the primary security protocol for access to resources within or across Windows 2000 domains. Kerberos currently is the best available standardized security protocol for distributed systems. Windows 2000 Server has full support for the Kerberos Version 5 protocol.
Public Key Certificate Services	Enables you to integrate X.509-based public keys with Active Directory for authentication and issue public key certificates to the organization's own users without depending on commercial Certificate Authority services.

(continued)

Table 2.6   The security infrastructure of Windows 2000 Server *(continued)*.

Technology	Description
Smart Card infrastructure	Provides tamper-resistant storage for protecting private keys, account numbers, passwords, and other forms of personal information. Smart Cards are a key component of the public key infrastructure. Also, Microsoft views Smart Cards as a big enhancement to the current software-only solutions to client authentication, single sign-on, secure storage, system administration, and the like.
IP Security Protocol (IPSEC)	Provides an IETF standard for encrypting TCP/IP traffic, enabling you to establish end-to-end secure communications between systems that are fully transparent to end users. IPSEC supports network-level authentication, data integrity, and encryption.
Encrypting File System (EFS)	NTFS encryption provides protection for sensitive data and can be enabled on a per-file or per-directory basis. Uses public-key-based encryption technology and runs as an integrated system service, which makes it easy to manage, difficult to attack, and transparent to the end user.
Delegation of administration	Allows you to delegate administrative privileges to others in just about any way you may need—be it for a subset of operations or objects. The very fine-grained delegation of administration features brought forward by Active Directory allows you to match the privileges given to each person exactly to their job responsibilities.

The Fifth Revolution: Preparing for the Distributed Future

Windows 2000 actually represents the final piece in Microsoft's much talked about *Cairo* jigsaw puzzle. Cairo is the code name for the distributed services that Microsoft has promised Windows-based customers and servers since the early 1990s.

Note

Occasionally, you may hear "Cairo" and "Windows 2000 Server" used interchangeably, which is a misnomer, because Cairo simply is the code name that Microsoft has been using for years to refer to its distributed services functionality that has finally seen the light of day as part of Windows 2000 Server.

These much-hyped distributed services comprise the following:

♦ COM+ or Distributed COM (DCOM, previously known as Network OLE or distributed OLE)

♦ Distributed File System (DFS)

♦ Transaction Services (previously known as Transaction Server)

♦ Message Queuing Services (formerly known as Message Queue Server)

♦ Active Directory, the "glue" that holds together all of these technologies

These technologies are a prerequisite for *Windows DNA* (refer also to Chapter 1), Microsoft's framework for building a new generation of n-tier computing solutions.

Distributed Component Object Model (DCOM)

DCOM actually arrived with Windows NT 4 in 1996. However, really harnessing the potential of DCOM hasn't been possible until the advent of Active Directory, which is why DCOM has been relatively obscure until recently.

DCOM enables software developers to spread component-based applications anywhere on the network. DCOM is Microsoft's extension of the COM object model (used for OLE/ActiveX). It is designed to make the network transparent to the application developer, which makes it an attractive tool to build object-oriented programs that can be placed on multiple PCs for reasons of scalability and/or reliability.

Basically, DCOM enables you to use objects across the network as if they were present on the local system, without requiring any changes to the object's program code. Thus, DCOM enables all existing "well mannered" ActiveX applications (OLE applications) to function flawlessly over the network.

However, DCOM is close to being unusable in real life without Active Directory, because of several fundamental problems. Without Active Directory, DCOM has to be operated via point-to-point communication against one particular machine that has been designated the OLE server holding the specific COM/COM+ components—which is quite complicated in terms of administration, scalability, and fault tolerance. Active Directory enables you to place the DCOM program components everywhere on the network, thus creating the necessary degree of scalability, fault tolerance, and administrative ease.

Besides the fact that Active Directory now covers the very important "missing link" of a DCOM infrastructure, Microsoft is promoting DCOM to the extent that it has gone into several licensing agreements for spreading DCOM to non-Windows platforms. DCOM is currently available for the most popular Unix and mainframe platforms—and Microsoft and its partners promise that more porting announcements will be heading your way in the future.

Distributed File System

DFS brings the distributed school of thought to the world of volumes and files. DFS has been available for some time for NT 4 as an add-on, but that is an earlier version of DFS which lacks much of the fault tolerance functionality that is part of Windows 2000 Server's DFS. With the new version of DFS, separate network-connected volumes can be combined into what looks and behaves as a single, logical network volume or share. Furthermore, you can increase fault tolerance by duplicating all or part of the given volume across two or more servers.

DFS is organized as a logical tree structure that is independent of physical restrictions. The DFS tree topology is automatically stored in Active Directory, which makes it possible to establish the necessary level of fault tolerance in the DFS solution.

Transaction Services and Message Queuing Services

Both of these services were first made available with the Microsoft Windows NT 4 Option Pack. Transaction Services is a transaction processing system that is designed for COM. It is component-based middleware for assembling simple building blocks that can reliably and efficiently execute complex transactions across widespread distributed networks.

Message Queuing Services is geared to handle "data on the move," thus enabling standard message methods for online and batch messages. Actually, Message Queuing's primary purpose is to shield applications from the complexity of the network and enable the served application to continue its other tasks, without wasting more time and resources by handling the message. The Message Queuing Services constitute a "shoot and forget" mechanism. You simply have to be able to identify to which queue you want to send the message. As long as the served application doesn't require an immediate confirmation of the message, it can continue processing data, knowing that sooner or later the message will reach its destination.

As with the other distributed technologies, Active Directory is integral to Transaction Services and Message Queuing Services. For example, Message Queuing Services uses Active Directory to store information about message queues, which enables applications to locate message queues easily across the network.

Getting the Right Perspective

Windows 2000 Server builds on the strengths of Windows NT Server 4; without sacrificing the backward-compatibility, it provides a platform that is faster, more reliable, and easier to manage.

Actually, you will soon discover that NT Server 4 and Windows 2000 Server are very similar, if you narrow the focus to the core OS (the *kernel*). A large part of the OS code in Windows NT Server 4 with the latest ServicePack (recent ServicePacks actually include a few features that were first built and tested for Windows 2000 Server) is identical to the code in Windows 2000 Server. And, just as with NT 4, quite a lot of code sharing occurs among the five different variations of Windows 2000 Server.

In other words, you have to go outside the kernel to identify the differences between NT Server 4 and Windows 2000 Server that make Windows 2000 Server a revolutionary experience. Its real dynamite lies in its comprehensive set of distributed infrastructure services and the major improvements to security, manageability, enterprise-scale performance, and availability. All of these things basically are benefits of the new Active Directory—or vice versa.

And so, Active Directory no doubt will be the foundation that any future Windows 2000-based enterprise is built upon, which is why the rest of this book focuses almost exclusively on the Active Directory infrastructure and its consequences for planning and implementing new Windows 2000–based solutions.

Part II
Planning

Chapter 3
Introducing Directory Services

Active Directory is clearly the jewel in Windows 2000's crown. Not only is Active Directory the most revolutionary and promising single new feature of Windows 2000, but it is also something that many Microsoft customers should be clamoring for—a genuine directory service.

Today, a growing number of companies are starting to view an enterprise-wide directory, such as Active Directory, as a key building block of their future integrated system architectures. The reason is that directory services carry the potential to unify scattered and proprietary systems, give users easier access to computing resources, and lay the groundwork for interconnected applications that support all corporate processes. For example, the current drive to bring together business partners and suppliers in an integrated supply chain more or less requires a unified directory that is able to track users, system resources, and data traversing companies' interconnected networks.

Often, the need to manage better the growing complexity of the IT environment is key to the decision of adopting a directory service. Also, the directory services segment is starting to feel the positive influence of a rising pool of directory services skills, a heightened awareness on issues such as total cost of ownership (TCO) and integration, several standards initiatives, and the resolution of early technical problems. Furthermore, a growing number of applications are able to tap the potential of a directory service, from network administration tools to Web-based data-management programs.

If this is getting your attention, you aren't alone. Gartner Group, Inc., estimates that by 2001, *metadirectories* (the integration of existing directories found in databases, email systems, and other applications) and *directory synchronization* (the process of ensuring that all the data in these various directories is up to date and in agreement) will be used by 70 percent of large enterprises.

This chapter provides an overview of directory services and is intended to establish a common ground for readers who have different backgrounds. As such, this chapter doesn't focus too much on the nitty-gritty of Active Directory, but instead focuses on the overall concepts of directory services and the unique properties and features that constitute a thoroughbred directory service.

What Comprises a Directory Service?

Generally speaking, a directory can be defined as a specialized repository that contains lists of various kinds of objects. A telephone book is an example of a directory that consists of phone numbers, names, titles, and addresses.

A computer directory (such as Windows 2000 Server's user database) usually contains lists of systems users, access rights, computers, printers, groups, and so forth. Besides functioning as a storage container for several types of data, the (computer) directory also functions as a kind of network white pages, giving users a simple way to locate applications, print services, and the computing resources available.

A directory service is a superset of a directory. A directory service goes beyond the function of a directory by combining the basic information source of a directory with a flexible service for enabling other parties to find information in the directory.

Whereas a directory has approximately the same interpretation, whether it is used inside or outside of the computing segment, a directory service has a distinct "add-on" definition when used in connection with computing. In computing, a directory service also includes the options to add, delete, arrange, and manage directory objects and attributes. In other words, a directory service is a type of modular storage container that can be uniquely customized for a specific use.

Unfortunately, providing a precise, all-encompassing definition of a directory service is an impossible task, because people using the term today have wildly diverging views about what actually constitutes a directory service. The following are two different definitions of a directory service, the second being a bit more technical than the first:

♦ A customizable information store that enables users to find information and network resources from a single point—even though they are located in a distributed environment—that provides a single point for administrators to define, arrange, and manage objects and their attributes, so that they are available to users and applications.

- A (usually distributed) database that has an extensible schema describing its data, and protocols to access and manipulate that data.

From the standpoint of users and administrators, the following list is a very useful description of what elements a good directory service includes:

- A storage container that can take on a *distributed form* (the information generally is distributed between several physical containers, but still looks like one).

- A storage container in which new information objects can be added, as required—and vice versa.

- A searchable information storage that can provide users and administrators, as well as applications, with the answers they need.

- A structure that conceptually eliminates the dependency on physical locations.

- The Utopia of computing that can cover all needs on the network information infrastructure for both users and administrators.

Essentially, the concept of a directory service is to provide a flexible and distributed database that can service the infrastructural information needs for all parties present on the network.

In the context of current enterprise directories, the directory service holds the promise to eliminate the need for multiple directories—at present, you'll find that directories exist in many applications, ranging from network operating systems and asset management systems to email and Relational Database Management System (RDBMS) applications.

The proliferation of businesses using several disparate and often proprietary directories translates directly into a rather high TCO in the form of management complexity, lost end-user productivity, and application complexity. And that high TCO is one of the key reasons why many large companies have designated the need to obtain a single directory that integrates these diverse systems as a top priority.

Most importantly, a directory service is a tool for integrating applications and business units that traditionally have worked as standalone systems. The business value of a unified directory is quite compelling: the elimination of redundant information and the automation of business processes across an entire enterprise.

Why Directory Services?

If you still need some convincing regarding the significance of directory services, consider all the applications (such as Exchange Server, SQL Server, Microsoft Transaction Server, and others) that solve the same problem of representing user information and other properties. Imagine the immense negative implications of user and administrator productivity at a prototypical company with 500 users, knowing that the 500 users actually equate to more than

1,000 user accounts that need to be maintained on various servers and services. These accounts consist of 500 users who share file and printer services, 500 email users, and a varying number of users of database systems, remote access services, production systems, and other specialized systems.

Undoubtedly, network administrators in such companies dream of a simpler way of handling users and their data. After all, who wouldn't want to escape all the duplicate work of handling workers, services, and data? Unfortunately, in the real world, a directory that has the same users connected to several servers and an environment filled with fragmented or duplicate data is the rule rather than the exception.

Actually, you don't have to look further than the prevalent network operating systems of today and yesterday. You will find a large number of these one- or two-dimensional name services still in operation throughout corporations. For example, as shown in Figure 3.1, Novell NetWare 2.x and 3.x bindery are both good examples of one-dimensional name services. In these instances, a user account must be set up for every server that the user has access to. Windows NT Server introduced a two-dimensional name service, as shown in Figure 3.2. A two-dimensional name service is an extension of a typical one-dimensional name directory, which makes it conceptually possible for users to be defined only once. However, this method is ripe with limitations regarding real-life administration, information storage, usage, and application scope.

The consequences of having several incompatible directories running in the enterprise include the following:

♦ Users must use multiple user accounts and passwords to log in to different systems, and they must know the exact locations of information on the network.

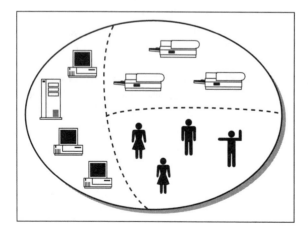

Figure 3.1
The Novell NetWare 2.x and 3.x bindery.

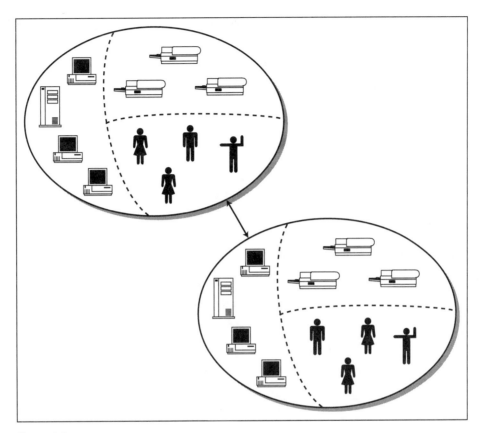

Figure 3.2
A typical one-dimensional name directory extended into two dimensions.

♦ Administrators must understand how to manage each directory within the network and must cope with the fact that many duplicate steps are required when a procedure, such as adding a new employee to a company, involves several different directories.

♦ Application developers must write different logic for every directory their applications need to access.

So, even though the storage requirements for infrastructure information are basically the same among server applications, practically every available server application provides a different solution to the problem. This results in a linear increase in operating expenses for every server application that is added, because the number of users administered is more or less directly proportional to the number of server applications implemented. Additionally, the expense resulting from users being confused by the many different usernames and passwords tends to increase exponentially with the number of directories.

A directory service solves virtually every problem encountered by all parties by providing the following benefits within a single schema:

♦ A common place to store information

♦ A single logon for users

♦ A single point of administration

♦ A common naming scheme

The best choice in both practical and theoretical terms (as shown in Figure 3.3) is a genuine, three-dimensional directory service, which enables users to log on to the network just once and lets the directory service take care of the rest. The same applies to the network administrator regarding his or her administrative chores and to the application developer, regarding his options for reuse of system functionality.

Some of the obvious applications for a directory service include the following:

♦ Find addresses, mail servers, Web servers, and files.

♦ Store information about people, such as names, phone numbers, passwords, and so forth.

♦ Store information of and about applications.

♦ Store public key certificates for users.

♦ Provide a single login to all applications (including email and secure Web access).

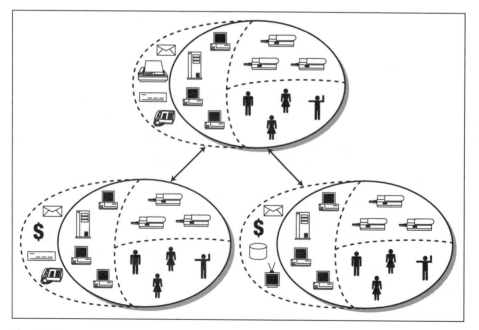

Figure 3.3
A three-dimensional directory service.

◆ Store profile and configuration information (for example, Web links and personal customizations of the desktop).

◆ Store identifying information on application components.

◆ Provide a class store.

Furthermore, directory services can be used for many future applications, such as for devices that become networked—copy machines, fax machines, PBXs, security systems, heating and air conditioning systems, and so on—that need to be accessible from anywhere in a totally connected global network.

Many people define a directory service as being a kind of sophisticated phone book for networks, but it's far more than that. To understand the full capability of directory services, consider what is required to access and manage network resources in a fully distributed global network. You may want to take a look at Figure 3.4 to get an idea of the more earthly capabilities involved in doing that, which coincidently represents Microsoft's initial vision of what its directory service should be used for.

A primary feature of directory services is that the database schema is *extensible* (which enables it to accommodate both new informational objects and extensions to existing objects), and provides answers to queries about the contents of the directory in a variety of ways. Stated in another way, a directory service is "just" a database that is optimized to handle core network information objects.

As a short-term goal, most companies want to incorporate a directory service to reduce administrative costs by aggregating information into a single place. As a long-term goal, a

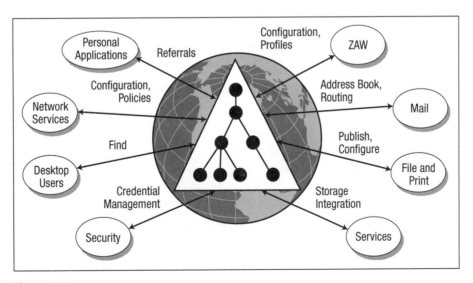

Figure 3.4
Microsoft's vision of its directory service.

directory service is adopted for its potential of enabling the company to standardize many of its business and technical processes, instead of operating in a fragmented, disparate environment.

An increasing number of organizations is beginning to realize that directory services have a very important long-term mission: If a company starts the unification process now via a directory service, it'll be in a better position to leverage the directory service for future applications, such as e-commerce tasks, in which enterprise-wide security and issuance of digital certificates will prove crucial.

X.500 Is Common Ground

The various attempts by software companies to create a directory service have one common denominator: X.500.

The X.500 specification is a set of protocols that has been approved as a formal standard by the International Telecommunications Union (ITU) and the International Organization for Standardization (ISO). The aim of X.500 is to provide standards that enable the creation of a truly interoperable, distributed, worldwide directory service.

The X.500 standard dates back to 1988 and was followed by a 1993 edition (which includes replication and access control) that is interoperable with its predecessor.

X.500 can be used to support messaging systems (X.400 and others), but it isn't restricted to email usage. X.500 provides a hierarchical structure that fits the world's classification system (countries, states, cities, streets, and so on), the goal from the outset being to build a distributed, global directory. The rewards of the early, careful consideration that went into the design of X.500 are being realized today.

The following are the key features of the X.500 model:

♦ *Decentralized maintenance*—Each site running X.500 is responsible only for its local part of the directory, so updates and maintenance can be done instantly.

♦ *Powerful searching capabilities*—X.500 provides powerful searching facilities that allow users to construct complex queries.

♦ *Single global namespace*—Much like Domain Name System (DNS), X.500 provides a single, homogeneous namespace to users. However, the X.500 namespace is more flexible and expandable than DNS, which means X.500 is capable of supporting an enormously large potential namespace.

♦ *Structured information framework*—X.500 defines the information framework used in the directory, thus allowing for local extensions.

♦ *Standards-based directory services*—Because X.500 can be used to build a standards-based directory, applications that require directory information (email, automated resource locators, special-purpose directory tools, and so forth) can access all available information in a uniform manner, regardless of where they are based or currently running.

The X.500 directory as a whole is quite complex and rather difficult to understand. To help you understand what the information looks like and how it is distributed and managed, various models are described in the 1988 version of the X.500 standard. Each model presents a simplified view of just one aspect of the directory information.

One of these models gives a view of the directory information as a typical user sees it. This model, the *Directory Information Model*, doesn't recognize that the directory is distributed. From its perspective, a large amount of information is held in the directory, and users can access all of it, provided that they have the appropriate access rights.

To enable the correct information to be accessed, users need a way to identify the items that they want to access. Consequently, chunks of information are given globally unambiguous names. This model is sufficiently general to allow any sort of information to be held in the directory.

This model constitutes a hierarchical, object-oriented structure that resembles a tree turned upside down, with a root at the top and branches that hang down (see Figure 3.5). This structure guarantees that any object in the tree is always unique, provided that its location (traversing the tree from the top) and locally unique name (all branches originating at a particular object have separate names) are known.

The objects in the tree that have branches are generally denoted *container objects* (or *nonleaf nodes*), and the rest of the objects are called *noncontainer objects* (*leaf nodes*). Each piece of information that describes some aspect of an object is called an *attribute*, which consists of an attribute type (for example, username) and one or more attribute values (for example, "Viggo Mortensen").

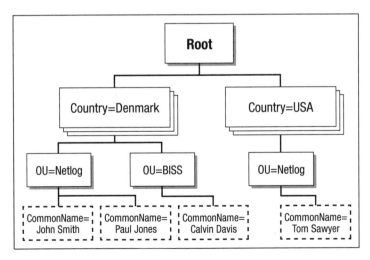

Figure 3.5
The structure of an X.500 directory—and other hierarchical directory services—from the perspective of users.

However, for implementations of X.500 to be widely accessible, a subset of this information must be internationally standardized, so that implementations worldwide can understand it. As stated earlier, X.500 was well planned from the beginning. Consequently, the X.500 standard defines a subset of the types of user information that can be held in the directory, to aid the international use of X.500.

Most directories contain a varying number of different container objects. The X.500 standard includes the following standard container objects:

◆ O (Organization)

◆ OU (Organizational Unit)

◆ Country

◆ Locality

Correspondingly, among the noncontainer objects you find users, groups, aliases, servers, volumes, computers, print servers, print queues, and printers.

One of the main reasons for having a distinction between the objects that have branches and those that do not is that objects need to inherit the attributes of the objects that are placed above them in the tree, which enables the directory service to be extended in a safe and uniform manner. Unfortunately, as has been the case several times before in the history of setting standards in international organizations—such as the OSI (Open Systems Interconnection) network protocol standard that was supposed to occupy the place that now belongs to TCP/IP—X.500 turned out to be a paper tiger.

In its attempt to create a directory service that truly meets all the demands that can sensibly be made of it, the ITU ended up with a specification so complex and compressed that most vendors' X.500 products didn't comply fully with the standard. To complicate matters, X.500's complexity resulted in its various implementations being mutually incompatible and delivering incredibly poor performance. Also, many of the parts that constitute the X.500 standard were intertwined with the OSI protocol, which didn't help its progress.

Luckily, both designers and buyers have been quick to realize that the overall goals and features of the X.500 directory are extremely sensible, and thus they have adopted the X.500 structure outright. All the currently popular directory services are modeled on the basic features of X.500—in other words, the differences are not in the base architecture, but in the protocols that are used and the implementation details. The directory service designers have looked closely at the X.500 model and then "stolen" freely the parts of the specification that are relevant to their directory solutions.

Know Thy LDAP!

The influence of X.500 on today's directory services extends even further with one other key technology: *Directory Access Protocol (DAP)*. DAP is used by clients to gain access to a

X.500 directory. DAP is a full OSI protocol that contains extensive functionality, much of which is not used by most applications.

The much-discussed *Lightweight Directory Access Protocol (LDAP)* is modeled on DAP. Actually, LDAP is just a simplified version of DAP. When LDAP was first introduced, it required the use of X.500 servers; specifically, their directory information storage features and capability to pass unfilled service requests to other directory servers. Refinements and sample implementations have made LDAP relatively more independent (allowing its use for LAN and application-level directory systems) as well as a directory data store in its own right.

Four primary differences exist between X.500 DAP and LDAP:

♦ LDAP supports the much simpler and more common Internet TCP/IP protocol instead of OSI.

♦ LDAP simplifies the X.500 model by eliminating the list and read operations, emulating them in the search operation, and retaining only the most commonly used features.

♦ LDAP uses a simpler encoding scheme.

♦ LDAP chases referrals, so that clients don't have to. X.500 generally just informs the user that it can't satisfy the user's request and refers the user to another server that may have the information. LDAP follows up on the referrals.

The simplifications included in LDAP make coding queries easier in LDAP than in DAP—and, most importantly, LDAP queries are processed much faster than DAP queries and require less horsepower from the clients' machines. However, these advantages come at a price: LDAP is clearly less comprehensive than its predecessor.

Nonetheless, the price is worth paying in return for establishing a single standard on directory queries, which LDAP seems destined to provide. LDAP has much potential as the future gateway standard for directory services, because most of the heavyweights (notably Netscape, Sun, Microsoft, Cisco, and IBM) now view LDAP support as a checkmark item. As early as April 1996, 40 companies (including Microsoft, Netscape, and Novell) separately announced support for LDAP in their directory service products, with the goal that they may interoperate with each other's products and integrate with the Internet.

LDAP consists of the following components:

♦ A *data model*—Defines the syntax of the data in the directory. The data model is centered on the same building blocks as found in X.500 (objects that are composed of attributes, where each attribute has a type and one or multiple distinct values). Which attributes are required and which are optional in an object is controlled by a special **objectClass** attribute in every object.

♦ An *organizational model*—Defines how data is organized in the directory; the structure is a tree (the same hierarchical model as X.500).

♦ A *security model*—Defines how information in the directory is accessed in a secure manner. The authentication model of LDAP version 2 is based on clear-text or Kerberos password authentication, whereas LDAP version 3 defines an extensible model based on *Simple Authentication and Security Layer (SASL)*, which implements a layered architecture to use different security providers. In addition to SASL, LDAP version 3 supports secure connections by using the *Secure Sockets Layer (SSL)* protocol.

♦ A *functional model*—Defines the operations for querying and modifying the directory. It includes operations to add an entry to the directory, delete an entry from the directory, modify an existing entry, change the name of an existing entry, and query for an entry in some part of the directory, based on a criterion specified by a query filter.

♦ A *topological model*—Defines how the directory service integrates with other directory services, to form a global directory service on the Internet/intranet. This model gives LDAP referral capabilities that enable it to implement a global directory structure of independent LDAP servers that appear to the client as a single LDAP server.

LDAP support is broadly available in most popular applications, such as Web browsers and email programs. OS vendors, such as Sun Microsystems, Microsoft, and Novell, are all busy implementing LDAP across the board in their products. Likewise, networking equipment vendors Cisco Systems and Nortel Networks are adding LDAP support to their networking products. And application server vendors, such as Netscape and Net Dynamics, and new Web applications, such as Oblix IntraPower, use LDAP to integrate multiple applications and computing environments into a coherent whole.

However, before you dismiss all of your reservations about LDAP, you need to recognize that the current LDAP technology has its limits:

♦ The LDAP standard is still evolving and currently, in its third release, provides the lowest common denominator for directory integration.

♦ LDAP lacks a uniform and convincing way to replicate data across LDAP servers (a serious gap that standard makers are scrambling to fill). Replication is a major concern for large enterprises that deal with data distributed across many servers and clients and, possibly, multiple directories. Even after the replication hitch is solved and directory services are more widely deployed than today, you may still discover a need for richer functionality than LDAP provides (remember that the *L* in LDAP stands for *Lightweight*).

But why focus on the eventual shortcomings of tomorrow? LDAP is here today and is the only sensible choice currently available!

Today's Directory Services

Today, only two directory services from the traditional network operating system (NOS) suppliers have succeeded in the market:

♦ Banyan Systems (now ePrescence) StreetTalk directory service, which has been included in the Vines NOS for more than 11 years. However, StreetTalk and Vines are currently being phased out, and ePrescence recommends migrating to Active Directory. All support for StreetTalk and Vines ended May 1, 2000.

♦ Novell Directory Services (NDS) (also called NetWare Directory Services, because it is an integral part of the NetWare 4 NOS) entered the market more than seven years ago.

Both of these directory services are proprietary systems, built on the X.500 foundation (outlined earlier in this chapter). Unfortunately, until today, none of the established directory service solutions has been able to meet the inherent potential of a directory service. This doesn't imply that companies who have introduced these solutions into their network environments haven't gained from doing so, because they clearly have. Instead, it means that directory services have a lot of untapped potential.

A number of surveys demonstrate a reduction in operating costs for companies that have implemented directory services, compared with companies that use name services. This reduction in operating costs has shown to be closely tied with the size, complexity, and division of labor in an organization. Generally, small organizations that have a simple organizational structure and one central IT department gain little (or nothing) by implementing a directory service, whereas large organizations that have a complicated organizational structure and a decentralized IT department gain quite a lot by investing in a directory service.

Until now, the directory services solutions have been utilized almost exclusively for traditional network services (such as file, print, mail, and remote access services) and tend to be limited to these purposes. This isn't because of narrow-mindedness or lack of vision on the part of directory service providers, but instead is a result of all too few third-party applications being "directory-services aware." Also, most midsize and large companies still operate several OS platforms for their servers and, as a rule, can't agree on one single directory service solution.

The following are two important steps that you should take when choosing directory services:

♦ Examine closely the level of support offered by each directory service for the server and client platforms, as well as the networking equipment that currently is in use—and whether that equipment will continue to be used in the near future.

♦ Compare the statement of direction (or, even better, the current products) regarding directory services support that are available from your current provider(s) of client and server applications. Likewise, because the number of corporate directory service applications has been steadily rising in the last 10 years, you should take into account the software community's general sentiments on which directory services to bet on.

With this advice in mind, take a look at the following sections, which provide a quick overview of each of the remaining two directory service contenders: NDS and Active Directory.

NDS

Despite a relatively poor beginning, figures indicate that Novell Directory Services is doing quite well. According to Novell, NDS counts more than 70 million users. However, I surmise this is a marketing phrase, which represents a consolidation of all licenses sold for all NDS versions (in spite of the fact that many Novell users have upgraded several times and so are counted several times). But, the figures notwithstanding, there's no doubt that NDS is the only real competition to Microsoft's Active Directory directory service.

Because of its age, NDS is a rock-stable and feature-rich directory service. And NDS has much more to show in regard to multiplatformness than any Microsoft products will ever show. Beside the native NetWare OS, Novell has ported NDS to Windows NT Server (NDS for NT), and has entered into agreements with Hewlett-Packard (HP), Sun, and SCO to build NDS support into their Unix OSs. In July 1997, Novell experienced a major breakthrough, through its agreement with IBM to port NDS for the IBM mainframes and AIX systems. This was quite a surprising step—albeit a positive one—for Novell, because IBM had previously aimed at a directory service solution based on a distributed computing environment (DCE). IBM seems to be indicating that it is considering changing over completely to NDS, although it argues that the NDS porting is just a "supplement" to its own DCE solution. This explanation deserves credit, because DCE has been of limited success, and IBM doesn't have any great marketing impetus to support NDS at this time, because too few companies have implemented NDS thus far. However, this explanation also enables IBM to wait and see in which direction the market is headed, before it throws its full support behind NDS.

Currently, NDS is ported (or soon will be ported) to the following operating systems by various third parties: SCO UnixWare; Hewlett-Packard HP-UX; Caldera OpenLinux; Sun Solaris; Fujitsu DS/90; and IBM's AIX, OS/400, and MVS OSs. However, thus far, NDS can be implemented only on networks where some NetWare/IntraNetWare 4.x servers are present.

With the latest edition of NDS (version 8, which was released in May 1999), Novell has changed its ways by becoming truly multiplatform—that is, removing the need for having one or multiple NetWare servers running at the LAN. NDS 8 is solely available for NetWare.

The support of other platforms is handled with the so-called NDS eDirectory product. NDS eDirectory is a fully platform-independent LDAP directory built for e-business, which can run without NetWare. Currently, NDS eDirectory is available for Linux, Sun Solaris 7, Microsoft Windows NT Server 4, and Microsoft Windows 2000 Server.

If you want the full feature-set known from the earlier versions of NDS (including version 8), you will need to add NDS Corporate Edition to your NDS eDirectory platform. NDS Corporate Edition is a network resource management tool built on top of NDS eDirectory to enable companies to integrate resources (user accounts, printers, routers, NT domains, etc.) across the network and simplify network management.

On the application side, integration to NDS is found only in Novell's own server applications and in relatively few other third-party server applications. And only very few of the fairly well-known business applications—including Attachmate, PC Docs, and Oracle—from third-party providers are truly NDS-prepared (in the form that actually takes advantage of the directory service). To be fair, there are many directory integration tools (backup, antivirus, and all sorts of other infrastructure-focused tools) to be found for NDS.

Tip

In case you should be interested, you can find some exhaustive lists of NetWare solutions (which you shouldn't mistake for directory services-aware applications) inside the different application categories at ***http://developer.novell.com/solutions/ platformpage/netware.htm***.

Clearly, the level of integration offered from business applications isn't impressive enough to sway potential NDS buyers. So, Novell is currently quite aggressive in their bet for improving the level of support for NDS at the most important server applications. Until now, Novell's focus on software developers only has seemed to pay off in regard to e-business applications.

Additionally, most analysts predict that Novell's chances of a runaway success with server applications are slim, because Microsoft's Active Directory already has won the favor of many software developers.

Active Directory

Although Microsoft is a newcomer to the directory service market, it has already garnered an incredible amount of attention—and even excitement—among customers and third-party suppliers.

Microsoft only delivers Active Directory with the Windows 2000 Server variants, and you only will find full support for Active Directory at the Windows 2000 Professional client (Active Directory clients that have limited functionality are also available for Windows 95/ 98 and Windows NT Workstation 4). However, regarding platform coverage of Active Directory, Cisco is allowed to port Active Directory to Unix and to implement it on its large and extensive line of network components (through the Unix-like IOS OS). However, Cisco hasn't announced how much emphasis it is putting on the Unix rights, except a statement of direction that mentions possible ports to the Sun Solaris and HP's HP-UX Unix variants.

But the Cisco-Microsoft partnership on Active Directory might very well turn out to be one of the keys to the success of Active Directory inside the infrastructure segment. Cisco's move has prompted all of Cisco's competitors in the networking segment to consider support for Active Directory.

Also, Microsoft has developed its own directory services API, Active Directory Services Interface (ADSI). The idea of ADSI is to enable software developers to write their applications to a single API, regardless of the directory service to which they primarily want to provide integration, because ADSI supports all the popular directory services (such as Exchange Server, Lotus Notes, and Novell NDS).

ADSI undoubtedly is Microsoft's Trojan horse, which it intends to use to lure application developers further away from writing to the native APIs used by their competitors. And the response by the competition hasn't taken long: Novell and Sun have defined a competing, Java-based API called *Java Naming and Directory Interface (JNDI)*.

However, Microsoft has made a smart move that none of its competitors have been able to match thus far: Active Directory provides a native support for LDAP! Microsoft is thus aiming at the evident alternative to openness: standardization. In Microsoft's opinion, directory services must be implemented through harsh standardization combined with the use of the LDAP standard to handle other platforms, particularly the Internet.

As stated earlier, Active Directory shows all the early signs of becoming the most supported directory services environment with respect to applications. Microsoft can already boast an impressive list of more than 250 application developers—including producers of practically all the popular server applications—who intend to support Active Directory. However, the application developers don't supply any information on the extent of Active Directory integration that is planned for in their products, nor do they predict any delivery schedules.

But perhaps application developers won't have much of a choice anyway. Sooner or later, Microsoft likely will make an extensive integration of Active Directory compulsory to achieve the prestigious BackOffice logo.

Warning

The current BackOffice logo for Windows 2000 Server only puts up some very basic demands for Active Directory integration. So it's fair to expect that we'll have to wait several years for the "real" Active Directory integration to surface at the third-party server applications, unless they start doing it themselves because of customer demands or for staying competitive with Microsoft's own server applications, which already sport quite a fair level of integration with Active Directory (please note that this only goes for the versions of Microsoft's server applications that were released in the year 2000).

Even though Active Directory has been a latecomer compared with its competitors from Novell, analysts generally agree that Microsoft isn't too late—and the move by Banyan/ePrescence to embrace Active Directory offers convincing proof of that. The majority of analysts even suggest that Active Directory stands a real chance of becoming the leader in the directory services market, because relatively few corporations have managed to implement truly integrated directory service solutions until now.

Directory Services Are Coming Your Way

Basically, directory services are repositories for information about network-based entities, such as applications, files, printers, and people. Directory services are important because they provide a consistent way to name, describe, locate, access, manage, and secure information about these resources.

A directory service possesses the potential to span all the components that are available in your network infrastructure, including network equipment, operating systems, server applications, and client applications. That is why the advantage of harnessing a single directory service is obvious: It makes your life less complex and provides the foundation for new, innovative solutions.

Some of the hallmarks of an apt directory service solution are the following:

♦ Single sign-on to all systems and applications.

♦ Single point of administration of all systems and applications.

♦ Pervasive security for authentication, as well as authorization for the networking infrastructure as a whole via rules-based administration.

♦ A high level of fault tolerance and accessibility through distribution and replication.

♦ Easy access to extensive customization of the network infrastructure, enabling administrators to design a good fit for the organization, instead of vice versa.

♦ Good scalability for handling any size and type of network infrastructure and providing for future growth.

Apart from being a necessary prerequisite for cutting the day-to-day operating expenses for the corporate network infrastructure, the directory service also represents "the missing link" for client/server and true distributed data processing, because the directory service will enable users to find and access applications, regardless of where the applications might be placed. Thus, directory services will enable administrators to move data and services everywhere on the network at their discretion, without bothering the users—actually, without the mainstream users ever noticing it.

Despite general agreement that directory services provide the only way to cope with the ever-increasing administrative workload for company networks, few companies have implemented them. The reasons vary, but most analysts point out that realizing the advantages of directory services, before they are implemented, is quite difficult. A shift from today's name services to a global directory service is also such a large-scale change that most IT departments instinctively withdraw from it.

But directory services are here to stay—they are destined to be part of everyday life for network administrators in a matter of years, because all popular server and network OS choices now include a directory service.

On the other hand, today's directory services are still a long way from the ultimate goal of being able to administer all resources and data on any existing computer platform. However, just as imagining a globally unified telephone directory is difficult—which, all things considered, ought to be a more practicable task than gathering data from all computer systems in a directory service—the technology of directory services is still in its formative stages.

The tremendous speed with which the Internet is expanding will make it absolutely necessary to establish an electronic equivalent of an international telephone directory very soon. In step with the Internet's turning into an electronic counterpart of an old-fashioned marketplace, in which everyone sells their output (including working capacity), it is becoming increasingly urgent to set up a single, albeit very flexible, storage place in which any information can be located.

It's still much too early to predict which directory service(s) will turn out the winners, but the jockeying for position between the various directory services probably isn't going to focus as much on technological qualities and standards as on something very simple: how many platforms and applications a particular directory service can call on for support, because broad applicability is the only way in which directory services can reach their full potential.

Amazingly, despite its disadvantage of being released much later than the competition, Active Directory is already well on its way to gaining the strongest support from the application developer community and providers of networking components (led by Cisco, which is Microsoft's Active Directory partner).

Because of the many diverse approaches to directory services, some common denominator likely will be needed among the various directory services—unless one directory service is declared a clear winner very soon. Because most corporations are unlikely to change their server platforms any time soon (as it's an intensely painful exercise), LDAP could very well wind up on top.

Chapter 4

Understanding Active Directory

A s Chapter 3 discussed, information about people, applications, and resources is scattered throughout the network infrastructure in the majority of enterprises. Almost all current operating systems and applications (ranging from email to Enterprise Resource Planning [ERP] systems) provide their own repositories—or *directories*—to store information about users and resources. And as most companies continually increase the number of applications and platforms that they use and support, the number of different repositories increases as well.

This rapid increase in repositories forces companies to manage information in many different places—even though those places contain duplicated and related information. To minimize costs and increase their ability to respond to changes, companies need an enterprise-class directory service that provides a common place to store, access, and manage corporate information—and that doesn't sacrifice application and operating system functionality. Active Directory is Microsoft's bid for one such enterprise-class directory service.

This chapter provides a review of all the key Active Directory terminology and how it relates to the Windows 2000 Server core components. As the key terms are defined and the inner workings are singled out, your understanding of Active Directory should grow rapidly. Over the course of the upcoming chapters, your understanding of Active Directory will be transformed into knowledge that you can utilize to design and plan for your own Active Directory implementation.

Understanding the key Active Directory concepts and terminology presented in this chapter is essential for the planning of a Windows 2000 Server environment and a prerequisite for successfully completing the rest of the book. However, don't despair if you are a bit overwhelmed by this chapter's *tour de force* into Active Directory terminology. The new Active Directory concept presents a lot of information to learn (and relearn), regardless of your current level of NT 4/Windows 2000 Server experience. For that reason, the next chapter also reinforces the definitions of the key Active Directory concepts.

Enter Active Directory

Two of the most critical corporate assets in today's economy are people and information systems. Unfortunately, from a technical point of view, in the typical Windows NT 4-based network, these resources have no knowledge of each other—whatsoever.

For example, every time a new application is installed or a new employee is hired, administrators typically must create multiple directory entries to match new users with the proper resources. Simple events such as a new hire can turn into a laborious exercise, requiring enrollment in email systems, ERP systems, intranet systems, remote access systems, and others. Similarly, if an employee leaves the company, that user must be removed immediately from all of these systems.

Promotions, too, can quickly turn into nightmares for the administrators, because they can't simply drag-and-drop users from one Windows NT domain to another Windows NT domain. Instead, they must delete the person being promoted from one domain and completely re-create that person in another domain. (And moving entire groups between domains is far more difficult.)

Data from Forrester Research helps put the scale of this task into perspective: On average, a Fortune 1000 company has more than 180 separate directories at its network. Thus, in today's fast-paced world of mergers, acquisitions, divestitures, and reorganizations, ensuring that employees have proper access to company resources can be a full-time job for an army of IT workers. Furthermore, the technical fallouts of NT 4 don't result only in cost and replication of effort—they touch upon the very flexibility and security that safeguard vital corporate information.

Unifying corporate directories does far more than just ease management woes, improve flexibility, and eliminate many inherent security risks. An industrial-strength directory service can serve as a central repository to store information that impacts every part of the performance and functionality of the corporate network. And this centralized directory plays an essential role in supporting such tasks as creating and enforcing policies to prioritize traffic, manage bandwidth, and control access to corporate information.

Essentially, a directory service has the potential to become the heart of the enterprise. And, as the last chapter should have made clear, the Windows NT 4 domain system doesn't provide the functionality needed to fulfill this role. Windows NT 4 domains are plagued by numerous and well-known shortcomings: limited object types, flat namespaces, Byzantine trust relationships, difficult APIs, and much more.

Fortunately, Microsoft now offers Active Directory to remedy the weaknesses of the NT 4 domain. The Active Directory directory service is included with Windows 2000 Server. Active Directory represents a revolution compared to the directory included in Windows NT Server 4. Active Directory includes many of the same traits of Windows NT Server 4—a single network logon, a single point of administration and replication, and full integration with the Windows 2000 OS. However, Active Directory includes much more than NT Server 4:

♦ Active Directory is built from the ground up, using Internet-standard technologies, with an emphasis on security, distribution, partitioning, and replication.

♦ Active Directory is designed to work well in installations of any size, from a single server with a few hundred objects to thousands of servers and millions of objects.

♦ Active Directory is designed to be a consolidation point, so that organizations can isolate, migrate, centrally manage, and reduce the number of directories that they maintain. This ought to make Active Directory an ideal long-term foundation for corporate information sharing and common management of network resources, including applications, network OSs, and directory-enabled devices.

Basic Directory Services Definitions

Before venturing into the key terms that are specific to Active Directory, you should understand some of the basic definitions that are universal to Active Directory and almost all current directory services. Many of the terms and concepts may seem very abstract at first, so staying on track all the way through this section may take some effort—but it will prove to be a worthwhile investment later on.

Objects and Attributes

An *object* is a distinct, named set of attributes that represents something concrete, such as a user, a printer, or an application. The *attributes* (also referred to as *properties*) hold data that describes the subject identified by the directory object. Attributes of a user might include the user's given name, surname, and email address, such as the example shown in Figure 4.1.

Container

A *container* is an object that can contain other objects. In the same way that a file folder is a container for documents, a directory container is a container for directory objects.

Figure 4.1
A sample user object and its attributes.

Tree

Tree is used throughout this book to describe a hierarchy of objects. A tree shows how objects are connected, by displaying the path from one object to another. Visualizing the structure of a file directory helps most people understand the abstraction (and fundamental properties) of a tree structure.

In a tree, the end points are called *leaf nodes*. Inside the realm of directory services, leaf nodes often are referred to as *noncontainer objects*, because they can't contain other objects. Nodes in the tree (points at which the tree branches) are known as *nonleaf nodes*—or simply *containers*. A *contiguous subtree* (shown inside the dotted circle in Figure 4.2) is any unbroken path in the tree, including all members of any container in that path.

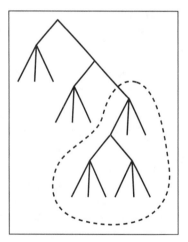

Figure 4.2
A tree in which a contiguous subtree is shown inside the dotted circle.

Namespace

Active Directory is actually a *namespace* (much like any other directory service), which is any definable space or context in which a specified name can be resolved. The following are examples of namespaces:

♦ A telephone directory forms a namespace in which the names of telephone subscribers can be resolved to telephone numbers.

♦ The Windows 2000 Server file system forms a namespace in which the name of a file can be resolved to the actual file.

Active Directory forms a namespace in which the name of an object in the directory can be resolved to the specific object. The namespace also defines the scope of replication.

Naming Contexts and Partitions

Active Directory consists of one or more naming contexts (also known as *partitions*). A *naming context* is any contiguous subtree of the directory, and it's the unit of replication (meaning that each naming context is replicated separately, and replications that cover less than the whole naming context aren't allowed).

Each Active Directory server always holds at least three naming contexts (see also Figure 4.3):

♦ The schema naming context

♦ The configuration naming context

♦ One or more user naming contexts (also known as the *domain partition*)

Schema Naming Context

Basically, the schema naming context defines which objects can be created in the directory and which attributes can be assigned to those objects. To be more precise, the schema partition comprises the set of all object classes and attributes that can be stored in Active Directory. The more specific details of the Active Directory schema are the following:

♦ Each *class* consists of a list of attributes that the class—that is, the instances of that class (the objects)—must or may contain. For example, a value for the First Name attribute is required for a user account object, whereas a value for the Address attribute is optional.

♦ Each attribute is defined utilizing a syntax that allows you to control what kind of data each attribute can hold and optional range limits.

♦ The schema is *extensible*, which means that new classes and attributes can be added at your discretion.

It is worth noticing that the Active Directory schema naming context is implemented as a set of object class instances, stored in the directory database. Many of the competing directories

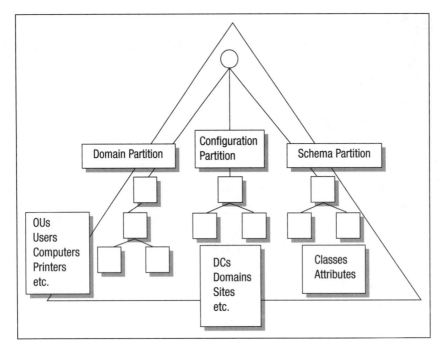

Figure 4.3
The Active Directory directory actually is partitioned into three distinct parts.

have a schema, which is stored as a text file to be read at startup. Storing the schema in the directory database has many advantages. For example, applications can read the schema to discover which objects and properties are available, and the Active Directory schema can be updated dynamically.

Configuration Naming Context

The configuration naming context contains all the globally relevant Active Directory setup information. And so, objects that have a global scope should always be published in the configuration naming context because this partition is being replicated to every Domain Controller (DC) in the whole forest.

By default, the configuration naming context includes information on the replication topology, the site setup, specifications on how to display the various Active Directory objects in the user interface (optionally this will even allow you to specify how to display objects in several different user interfaces), and the configuration of a range of services and cross-references between the different user naming contexts. It's expected that the future Active Directory-integrated applications and services will store a fair percentage of their data in the configuration partition.

User Naming Contexts

The user naming contexts (also known as domain partitions) are subtrees that contain the actual objects in the directory (please remember that the range of possible types of objects is specified in the schema naming context). Each Active Directory domain constitutes one user naming context. Therefore, you'll always have at least one user naming context (that is, one for the first domain defined when creating the directory) in each Active Directory forest.

Name

Active Directory is based on the concept of representing every single object in the directory with its own name. Names are structured in a hierarchical manner, so that you can build paths that relate back to the original name.

The following are the two fundamentally different kinds of name addressing:

♦ *Distinguished name (DN)*—Every object in Active Directory has a DN that identifies (or *distinguishes*) the domain that holds the object and the complete path through the container hierarchy by which the object is reached. The following is a typical DN that identifies the "Viggo Mortensen" user object in the **Netlog.com** domain (see Figure 4.4):

/O=Internet/DC=COM/DC=Netlog/CN=Users/CN=Viggo Mortensen

♦ *Relative distinguished name (RDN)*—The part of the object's DN that is an attribute of the object itself. In the preceding example, the RDN of the "Viggo Mortensen" user object is CN=Viggo Mortensen. The RDN of the parent object is CN=Users.

Name Resolution

Name resolution is the process of translating a name into some object or information that the name represents. Active Directory uses the *Dynamic Domain Name System (DDNS)* to resolve names.

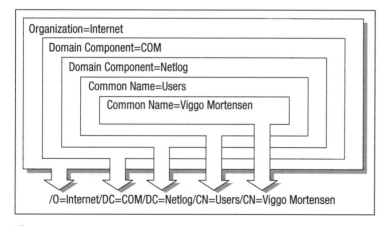

Figure 4.4
A graphical representation of a distinguished name. Understanding the DN is key to determining the relative distinguished name.

Domains: Logical Partitioning of the Directory

The domain is the core unit of logical structure in Active Directory (as it was in Windows NT Server 4 and earlier versions). However, an Active Directory domain is much different from its Windows NT Server namesake.

In Active Directory, the domain represents a logical grouping of objects, as well as a boundary for replication and security. The following are the major features and benefits of Active Directory domains:

♦ Each domain provides object-grouping functionality (that is, it allows you to impose a hierarchy on the objects stored in that domain using containers), to reflect the company's organization.

♦ Each domain stores information only about the objects located in that domain. By splitting up, or *partitioning*, the directory information in this way, Active Directory can be scaled to accommodate virtually as many objects as should ever be needed in any kind of company.

♦ Each domain is also a security boundary. Security policies and settings (such as users, administrative rights, and access control lists) do not cross from one domain to another. The administrator of a domain has absolute rights to set policies only within that domain.

♦ A domain can span more than one physical location. The use of domains actually is a purely logical way of partitioning the directory—domains don't have any bearing on the physical side of things, such as the actual placing of servers and clients.

The Active Directory can have one or more domains. The domains are joined together in one or multiple trees, each of which will be part of a forest. In other words, a forest consists of one or multiple trees, each of which consist of one or multiple domains.

> **Note**
> *Even though "domains" are still the fundamental building blocks for Active Directory, don't confuse Active Directory domains in Windows 2000 Server with NT Server domains. Active Directory domains are totally different from the domains used in Windows NT Server.*

Trees

A *domain tree* (or simply *tree*) constitutes several hierarchically organized domains that share a common schema and configuration, forming a contiguous namespace. The domains in a tree are linked together by trust relationships. Stated another way, when multiple domains are connected by trust relationships and share a common schema, configuration, and Global Catalog, they form a domain tree.

The minimal domain tree is a single Windows 2000 Server domain. Trees can be viewed in one of two ways:

♦ By the namespace of the domain tree

♦ By the trust relationships between domains

Viewing the Namespace

In the namespace view, all domains within a single domain tree share a hierarchical naming structure. The first domain in a tree is called the *root* of the tree. Additional domains in the same tree are called *child domains*. Domains immediately above other domains in the same tree are called *parent domains*. The domain name of a child domain is the RDN of that child domain added to the beginning of the name of the parent domain. For example, hq.acme.com is a child domain of the acme.com parent domain.

Often, drawing a picture of the domain tree based on its hierarchical namespace can help you thoroughly understand the domain tree. For example, as shown in Figure 4.5, you can use the drawing as a straightforward way to determine an object's DN, by following the path up the domain tree's namespace.

Viewing Trust Relationships

All domains in a tree are automatically joined together through two-way, transitive trust relationships. Active Directory establishes trust relationships between domains via the Kerberos security protocol. Kerberos trust relationships are two-way and transitive—that is, if domain A trusts domain B, and domain B trusts domain C, then domain A also trusts domain C. The properties of transitive trusts used by Active Directory effectively minimize the number of trusts necessary between domains compared with nontransitive trusts (which is used by Windows NT Server 4 and earlier releases), almost regardless of the particular application.

In Active Directory, a domain that joins a domain tree immediately has trust relationships established with every domain in the tree—no administrative intervention is required—

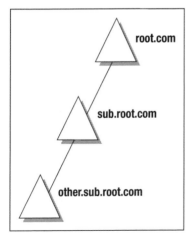

Figure 4.5
Viewing a domain tree as a hierarchical namespace almost always will prove of benefit for understanding the specific domain model.

because Active Directory automatically creates a transitive trust to the parent domain. With the necessary trust relationships being established from the outset in the tree, all the objects in all the domains will be available to users and computers from any domain in the tree. Thus, no trust relationships need to be defined for users to be able to perform a single login in which they're authenticated and granted access throughout the entire network (depending upon the user's privileges, of course).

Just as drawing a picture of the hierarchical namespace helps you grasp the intricacies of the domain tree, drawing a picture of a domain tree based on its individual domains and their mutual trusts will help you understand the domain's trust relationships (see Figure 4.6).

The Forest

A *forest* is a set of one or more domain trees that does *not* form a contiguous namespace—that is, the individual domains in a forest don't share a common root, unless the forest consists of only one domain tree. For example, the domains **hq.com** and **sales.com** have no obvious relationship to each other. This is an example of *disjointed naming*, in which the two domains can't be part of the same domain tree, but have to be joined in a forest.

Combining trees in a forest provides you with the flexibility of both contiguous and disjointed naming conventions. This can be useful, for example, in companies with independent divisions that must each maintain their own DNS names.

All trees in a forest must share a common schema, configuration, and Global Catalog and must trust the other trees of the forest via transitive hierarchical trust relationships—just as is the case for a domain tree. Thus, the only marked difference between a tree and a forest is

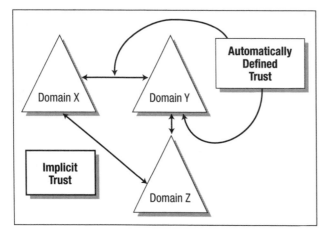

Figure 4.6
Drawing a domain tree based on its trust relationships helps to clarify the full implications of your domain model.

The Trusts Have Become Transitive

Trusts are also needed in an Active Directory environment in order to allow for secure communications among the domains in a tree and among the domain trees in a forest. However, the trust relationships are now automatically defined between the domains comprising the forest, unlike the trusts available in the previous versions of Windows NT Server.

You should take note of the heavy changes brought about by the transitive, two-way nature of the Windows 2000 Server trusts—before somebody with harmful intentions does!

---

that each tree in a forest has its own unique namespace, instead of having a contiguous namespace (which is also why a forest is sometimes referred to as a *noncontiguous* or *disjoint namespace*).

A forest exists as a set of cross-referenced objects and trust relationships known to its member trees. The domain trees in a forest form a hierarchy for the purpose of trust; the tree name at the root of the trust tree (that is, the first domain tree created in the forest) is used to refer to that particular forest (see Figure 4.7).

In other words, to make the resources in a domain or domain tree available to the other network users, you simply join a domain to an existing tree or create a new domain tree that is part of the pre-existing forest. When a domain joins a tree, a trust is created between the joining domain and the parent domain. When two trees are associated in a forest, the trust is created between the root domains of each tree. The underlying trust relationships are transparent, and no further management of the trust relationships is necessary. Because domain trees linked together in a forest are linked by transitive, two-way Kerberos trusts, users have access to resources in any domain in the entire forest.

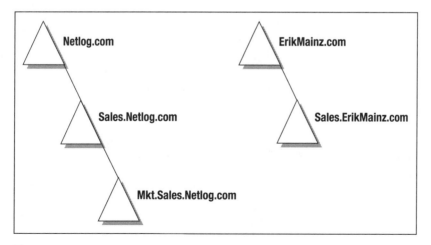

Figure 4.7
When combined, these two separate domain trees form a *forest*, because the DNS names of the two domain trees don't have any common parts.

Note, however, that the chief advantage of the domain tree (that is, a contiguous namespace) over the forest is that an LDAP search from the root of the namespace effectively searches the entire hierarchy, whereas with a forest, you can search only the Global Catalog and the local domain tree. This difference is the primary reason that you should always strive to establish domain trees rather than a forest. So you should look to the forest as a way to deliver the necessary flexibility for making Active Directory viable in real-life applications, only when no other alternatives are available. Or, to state it more directly: A forest should be considered only when it simply isn't possible to get the work done using a domain tree.

Organizational Units: Logical Partitioning of Domains

Organizational Units (OUs) are just one among many types of directory objects that can be created inside a domain. However, an OU probably is the most important kind of domain directory object, because it allows you to create yet another level of partitioning of the logical namespace.

OUs are container objects that can be used to organize objects within a domain into logical administrative groups. These logical containers can carry many interesting objects, such as user accounts, groups, computers, printers, and even other OUs.

The combination of domains and OUs provides you with a powerful, flexible way to organize your directory for the most effective administration (that is, you've got the option to impose two levels of hierarchy to your logical structure). When you create OUs within domains, you can organize your logical structure on as many levels as you want, while still having the benefits of creating and managing a small number of domains.

Even more importantly, OUs provide an administrative model that can be scaled to the smallest size necessary. And with the new delegation features of Active Directory, users and groups can perform very detailed administrative work, such as resetting passwords and maintaining special rights in particular containers, based on OU membership. For example, a user can be granted administrative rights for only a subtree of OUs, a single OU, or even a subset of the objects found in a single OU.

Global Catalog: Another Key Feature of Active Directory

Active Directory can consist of many domain partitions (or user naming contexts), and so you'll need to know most of the DN of an object to be able to locate a replica of the partition that holds a specific object (after which you're able to perform an LDAP search to retrieve the object in case the full DN isn't known).

Many times, however, the user or application doesn't know the DN of the target object, or even which partition contains the object. And that's where the *Global Catalog (GC)* comes into play, because it enables users and applications to find objects in Active Directory without performing a costly (and rather slow) forestwide search, even if the user or application knows only one or a few attributes of the target object. Using the GC allows fast queries of all objects in the entire forest.

The reason the Global Catalog is a good alternative to exhaustive searches is that it simply holds a subset of the attributes for all objects found in all of the Active Directory domains that are part of the forest.

The point of the GC is to provide a service and a store that:

♦ Contains a replica of every domain object in the particular Active Directory forest.

♦ Contains a subset of the object attributes, which is defined by Microsoft. Administrators are allowed to add attributes to be included in the GC in order to meet their organization's needs for making the most frequently searched for properties available to its users.

♦ Is built automatically by Active Directory's replication system.

Typically, each physical site should have at least one GC server available locally in order to allow for local access to look up information about any object in the forest (and thus avoid wasting precious bandwidth for that). A search of the Global Catalog can be initiated in one of several ways:

♦ By a subtree or one-level LDAP search rooted at the null DN (the root of the namespace)

♦ By a direct reference to the GC port at a GC replica

♦ By an explicit reference to the GC ADSI provider (GC://)

Domain Controllers and Sites: The Directory's Physical Parts

Until now, all the terms and concepts discussed have been purely logical—that is, they are not bound in any way by physical limitations and thus don't take important physical limitations into account.

Active Directory is adapted to the physical side of life through two important features:

♦ Domain Controllers (DCs)

♦ Sites

Domain Controllers

As mentioned earlier, the domain structure and the physical structure are independent concepts. A single domain can span geographical sites, and a single site can include users and computers that belong to multiple domains.

Additionally, Active Directory breaks away from the need to distinguish between Primary Domain Controllers (PDCs) and Backup Domain Controllers (BDCs). Unlike the single master model used by Windows NT 3.51 and NT 4, with its PDCs and BDCs, all Active Directory DCs are peers, and each DC contains a writable copy of the domain's directory. Any DC can change its copy of the directory, and the changes in the directory on one DC will be passed on to the remaining DCs in the domain.

Thus, all the DCs that are members of a particular Active Directory domain are able to receive changes directly and replicate those changes throughout the domain. And so, Active Directory also does away with the annoying single point of failure found in the single master replication model.

Note

In a single master replication model, all domain members (being the BDCs) are relying on a single DC (being the PDC) for updates. Thus, if the PDC is down, nobody will be able to impose any changes (including password changes) to the domain nor be able to update the BDCs with the changes that were implemented since the last replication round.

Additionally, the peer controller architecture enables you to promote any standalone or member server to the role of an Active Directory DC—or vice versa. Thus, any computer running Windows 2000 Server can potentially become a DC, which also makes moving DCs between domains a very straightforward operation.

A DC can either join an existing domain or be the first DC in a new domain. A DC that joins an existing domain is called a *replica DC*, because it receives a copy of the domain's directory and participates in the directory replication. When a DC becomes the first DC in a new domain, the act of promoting the server to a DC actually creates the domain. A domain cannot exist until it has at least one DC.

Sites

To make sure that replication among the DCs for a particular domain can be fit to the physical bounds (that is, the bandwidth between the geographical sites), Active Directory includes a site concept.

A *site* is by definition a location in a network that contains Active Directory servers and consists of one or multiple well-connected TCP/IP subnets. Typically, a site has the same physical boundaries as a local area network (LAN)—but it doesn't necessarily have to be like that.

When a user logs on, the Active Directory client will try to find the needed Active Directory logon services on servers in the same site as the user. This is accomplished easily, because

---

Domain Controllers: Starting All Over Again!

When Windows 2000 Server is first installed, it is installed as either a standalone server or a member server:

♦ A *standalone server* is a computer that is running Windows 2000 Server and that *isn't* a member of a Windows 2000 Server domain. If you install a server as a member of a workgroup, that server is a standalone server.

♦ A *member server* is a computer that is running Windows 2000 Server and that *is* a member of a domain, but not an Active Directory DC. Member servers don't receive copies of the directory. They typically are dedicated to application services or resource services, such as a file and print server or a fax server.

Windows 2000 Server uses the Active Directory Installation Wizard (formerly Domain Controller Promotion Wizard, DCPROMO) to promote a standalone or member server to a DC role or to demote a DC to a standalone or member server. Also, please note that Windows 2000 Server no longer distinguishes between PDCs and BDCs. In Active Directory networks, all DCs are peers and contain writable copies of the directory.

---

the user's workstation already knows what TCP/IP subnet it is on, and subnets translate directly to Active Directory sites. The client will only start looking elsewhere if the needed services aren't available in the site.

Correspondingly, defining a site also allows administrators to quickly and easily configure Active Directory's access and replication topology to take the properties of the physical network properly into account.

Tip

How does a workstation discover its site? A workstation discovers its site by presenting its subnet (that is, by applying its subnet mask to its IP address) to the first Active Directory server contacted. The first server contacted uses the presented subnet to locate the Site Object for the site in which the workstation is located. If the current server isn't in that site, the server notifies the workstation of a better server to use.

Key Active Directory Features

Some of the other features that are integral to a full understanding of Active Directory's functionality are: DNS integration, Kerberos security, the wire protocols used to access the directory information, and replication. Each and all of these functions are crucial for bringing and keeping the Active Directory in operation. That is, not all of them have to be taken into consideration when doing the actual designing of the Active Directory structures, but they have to be properly understood by Windows 2000 Server administrators to keep the Active Directory up and running.

DNS Integration

Active Directory is tightly integrated with the Domain Name System (DNS). DNS is the distributed namespace used on the Internet to resolve computer and service names to TCP/IP addresses. Most enterprises that have intranets already use DNS as their name resolution service—and now they have to expand this use to cover Active Directory.

Windows 2000 Server domain names are DNS domain names. For example, **astonitgroup.com** is a valid DNS domain name, and thus can also be the name of a Windows 2000 Server domain. When an Active Directory DC is installed, it publishes itself via *Dynamic DNS (DDNS)*, a recent extension to the DNS standard that defines a protocol for dynamically updating a DNS server with new or changed values. Prior to DDNS, administrators had to configure manually the records stored by DNS servers.

Active Directory servers publish their addresses in a form that enables a client to find them even if the client knows only the domain name. Active Directory servers are published via Service Resource Records (SRV RRs) in DNS. The SRV RR is a DNS record that is used to map the name of a service to the address of a server that offers that service. The name of a SRV RR takes the following form: *<service>.<protocol>.<domain>*.

Because Active Directory DCs use the Lightweight Directory Access Protocol (LDAP) service over the TCP protocol, the names published by Active Directory are in the following form: *_ldap._tcp.<domain>*.

The SRV RR also allows the administrator to indicate the priority and weight for each server, enabling clients to choose the best server for their needs.

> ### Tip
> *How does a workstation find a directory server? A workstation finds a directory server by querying DNS. Directory servers for a particular domain publish SRV Resource Records in DNS with names in the form: **_ldap._tcp.<domain>**. Thus, a workstation logging in to **acme.com** will query DNS for SRV RRs for **_ldap._tcp. acme.com**. A server will be selected from the list and then contacted. The contacted server uses the subnet information presented by the workstation to locate a DC that is in the same site as the workstation.*

Kerberos Security

In Active Directory, authentication is performed using the Kerberos version 5 protocol. This protocol is fully integrated with the Windows 2000 Server security architecture for authentication and access control. Just as you know from Windows NT, the initial domain logon is provided by the WinLogon single sign-on architecture. And so, the only difference is that the initial authentication now is performed using Kerberos rather than NT LAN Manager (NTLM) protocol.

The Kerberos version 5 protocol is a "shared-secret" authentication protocol, in which the user and the authentication service both know the user's password or the one-way encrypted password. The Kerberos protocol defines the interactions between a client and a network authentication service, known as a *Key Distribution Center (KDC)*. Active Directory implements a KDC as the authentication service on each DC. The KDC use the Active Directory as an account database. The Active Directory allows only three different account types (also known as security principals): users, groups, and computers.

Accessing Active Directory

Access to Active Directory is accomplished via *wire protocols*, which define the formats of messages and interactions between the client and server. Supported protocols include the following:

♦ *Lightweight Directory Access Protocol (LDAP)*—The Active Directory core protocol. LDAP versions 2 and 3 are supported.

♦ *Messaging API-Remote Procedure Call (MAPI-RPC)*—Active Directory supports the remote procedure call Mail API (MAPI) interface for backward-compatibility.

Various APIs give developers access to these protocols. Supported APIs include the following:

♦ *Active Directory Services Interface (ADSI)*—Provides a simple, powerful, object-oriented, language-independent interface to Active Directory developed by Microsoft. Developers can use many different programming languages, including Java, Visual Basic, C, C++, and others. ADSI can also be used from scripts (including VBScript), which will no doubt make it popular with administrators. ADSI was developed by Microsoft with the express intent of abstracting the many details of LDAP communications.

♦ *LDAP C API*—The LDAP C API, defined in RFC 1823, is the standard low-level interface to LDAP stores like Active Directory. The LDAP C API can only be accessed from the C and C++ programming languages.

♦ *Messaging API*—Active Directory supports MAPI for backward-compatibility. New applications should use ADSI or the LDAP C API.

Replication

Active Directory builds on *multi-master replication*, which means that all replicas of a particular partition (that is, the DCs) are writable, enabling updates to be applied to any replica of that partition. The Active Directory replication system propagates the changes from one replica to all other replicas. Replication is automatic and transparent to the users and administrators.

Some directory services use timestamps to detect and propagate changes. In these systems, the clocks on all directory servers must always be synchronized. Historically, time synchronization within a network has proven to be a difficult undertaking. Even with good network time synchronization, the time at any particular directory server can be incorrectly set, which in turn can lead to lost updates.

To avoid synchronization problems, the Active Directory replication system doesn't depend exclusively on time for update propagation. Instead, it uses an *Update Sequence Number (USN)*, a 64-bit number maintained by each Active Directory DC server. When the DC writes any property to Active Directory, the USN is advanced and stored with the property that was written. This operation is performed *atomically*—which means that the incrementing and storage of the USN and the writing of the property succeed or fail as a single unit of work.

Each DC also maintains a table of USNs that are received from replication partners. The highest USN received from each partner is stored in this table. When a DC is notified by a particular partner that replication is required, those two DCs quickly will be able to establish which changes are needed—being all USNs greater than the last USN value received. This is a very simple approach that doesn't depend on the accuracy of timestamps.

Because the USN stored in the table is updated atomically for each update received, recovery after a failure also is quite simple. To restart replication, a server simply asks its partners for all changes with USNs greater than the last valid entry in the table. Because the table is updated atomically as the changes are applied, an interrupted replication cycle always picks up exactly where it left off, with no loss or duplication of updates.

In a multi-master replication system, such as Active Directory, the same property may be updated at two or more different replicas. When a property changes in a second (or third, or fourth, and so on) replica before a change from the first replica is fully propagated, a *replication collision* occurs. Collisions are detected through the use of Property Version Numbers. Unlike USNs, which are server-specific values, a Property Version Number is specific to the property of an Active Directory object. When a property is first written to an Active Directory object, the version number is initialized.

An *originating write*—a write to a property at the system initiating the change—advances the version number. Property writes caused by replication are *not* originating writes, and thus don't advance the version number. For example, when a user updates his or her password, an originating write occurs and the password version number is advanced. Replication writes of the changed password at other servers don't advance the version number.

A collision is detected when a change is received via replication in which the property version number received is equal to the locally stored Property Version Number, and the received and stored values are different. When this occurs, the receiving system applies the update that has the later timestamp. This is the only situation in which time is used in Active Directory replication.

When the received version number is lower than the locally stored version number, the update is presumed stale and thus discarded. When the received version number is higher than the locally stored version number, the update is accepted.

The Active Directory replication system allows *loops* in the replication topology, enabling an administrator to configure a replication topology with multiple paths among the servers, which enhances performance and availability.

What Happens to WINS?

The Windows Internet Naming Service (WINS) functionality is unchanged for Windows 2000 Server. Actually, Windows 2000 Server includes a new and much-improved version of WINS. However, Windows 2000 clients (and Windows 95/98 clients with the Active Directory upgrade installed) no longer need to use NetBIOS on top of the TCP/IP stack—they use DDNS to resolve network names, instead.

WINS is still required for down-level (that is, legacy) clients to find servers, and vice versa. So, when no more down-level clients and servers are in the forest, all the WINS servers can be turned off.

Active Directory's replication system performs *propagation dampening* to prevent changes from propagating endlessly and to eliminate redundant transmission of changes to replicas that are already up-to-date. *Up-to-date vectors*—lists of server-USN pairs held by each DC server—are used to dampen propagation. The up-to-date vector at each server indicates the highest USN of originating writes received from the server in the server-USN pair. An up-to-date vector for a server in a particular site lists all the other servers (where an originating write has occurred) in that site.

When a replication cycle begins, the requesting server sends its up-to-date vector to the sending server. The sending server uses the up-to-date vector to filter changes sent to the requesting server. If the highest USN for a specific originating writer is greater than or equal to the originating writer USN for a particular update, the sending server does not need to send the change; the requesting server is already up-to-date with respect to the originating writer.

How Active Directory Fits within the Windows 2000 Server Architecture

The core architecture of the Windows 2000 Server operating system is very similar to its predecessor, Windows NT Server 4 (see Figure 4.8). For example, Windows 2000 Server is built on the same *modular* architecture as found in Windows NT Server, which means that it is composed of several separate and distinct components, each of which is responsible for its own functions.

This modularity is also the reason that Active Directory hasn't forced any major changes on the OS kernel. Active Directory is simply part of the Security subsystem component (which is run in User Mode). This means that Active Directory is a full participant in the Windows 2000 Server security infrastructure, because all objects in Active Directory are protected through Access Control Lists (ACLs); any attempt to access an object or attribute in Active Directory is validated against the ACL.

The Security Subsystem consists of several components (the Windows 2000 Server Resource Kit provides a complete review of the Security Subsystem), one of which is the *Local Security Authority* (LSASS.EXE). LSASS.EXE is a protected subsystem that maintains the security for the local computer, ensuring that users have the proper system access permissions.

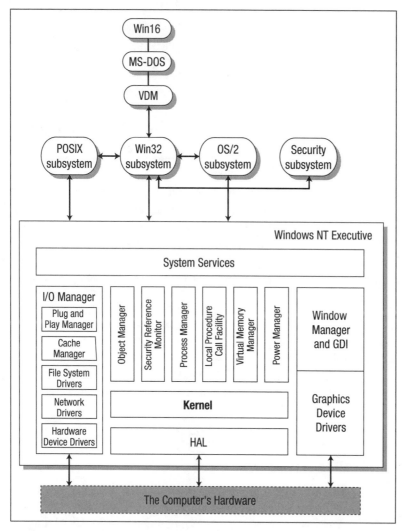

Figure 4.8
The Windows 2000 Server architecture looks much akin to that used in Windows NT Server 4. However, there are a couple of changes to be found.

Active Directory is located in the Directory Service Module inside LSASS.EXE, as shown in Figure 4.9. Specifically, the LSASS.EXE subsystem of Windows 2000 Server includes the components listed in Table 4.1.

Of these components, the Directory Service Module (NTDSA.DLL) is the most vital to the Active Directory functionality. The Directory Service Module consists of three components and several interface agents (see Figure 4.10) that work together to provide directory services that are compatible with legacy systems (such as Windows NT 4) and other systems (including something as mundane as Outlook clients).

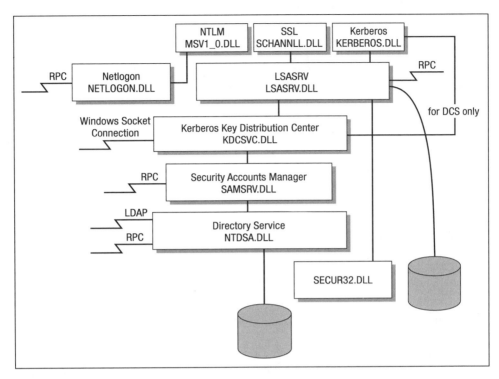

Figure 4.9
Active Directory is located in the Local Security Authority (LSASS.EXE) component inside the
Security Subsystem.

Table 4.1 The components of LSASS.EXE.

Component	Description
Netlogon.DLL	A command-line utility that maintains the computer's secure channel to a DC. In Windows 2000 Server, Netlogon uses DNS to locate the DCs.
MSV1_0.DLL	The NTLM authentication protocol that is used by previous versions of Windows NT.
KERBEROS.DLL	The Kerberos authentication protocol, the default authentication protocol of Active Directory.
KDCSVC.DLL	The Kerberos Key Distribution Center (KDC) service, which is responsible for granting tickets to clients.
SCHANNEL.DLL	The SSL authentication protocol, which can be used as a supplement—or substitute—to Kerberos.
LSASRV.DLL	Enforces security policies.
SAMSRV.DLL	The Security Accounts Manager (SAM), which stores local security accounts, enforces local policies, and supports the legacy Windows NT APIs.
NTDSA.DLL	The Directory Service Module. This module handles the replication of the user naming context and LDAP accesses to the directory and manages the naming contexts.
SECUR32.DLL	The multiauthentication provider that holds together all the components.

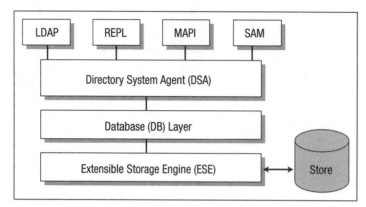

Figure 4.10
Directory Service Module (NTDSA.DLL) is a central part of Active Directory.

Table 4.2 describes the three components of the Directory Service Module, which act as layers (from the top down).

Table 4.3 lists and describes the four interface agents that access the Directory Services Module.

Table 4.2 The components of the Directory Service Module (NTDSA.DLL).

Component	Description
Directory System Agent (DSA)	Provides access to the store. This is done by creating a hierarchical tree-like namespace from a flat namespace (the NTFS file, which constitutes the Active Directory database), which in turn enables others to view users and resources in a more logical manner. The DSA also includes support for replication, enforces the directory schema, updates rules and security, and contains Active Directory policy information, such as partitioning and referrals.
Database Layer (DB layer)	An internal abstraction layer that provides access to database storage and search functionality. All database access is routed through the DB layer.
Extensible Storage Engine (ESE)	An improved version of the Jet database engine that is used in Microsoft Exchange Server. ESE stores all Active Directory objects. The database currently has a limit of 16TB, which means that every domain theoretically can hold at least ten million objects. Also worth mentioning is that ESE reserves storage only for the space that actually is used (for example, if an object can have 50 attributes, but a new instance of that object is created with only 4 attributes, space is consumed only for the 4 attributes actually used).

Table 4.3 The interface agents that access the Directory Service Module.

Interface Agent	Description
LDAP	Used to communicate with LDAP and ADSI clients.
REPL	Governs the intersite and intrasite replication that can use different transports (RPC and SMTP).
MAPI	Mail API, used to communicate with Outlook clients.
SAM	Security Account Manager, used for legacy communication with NT 4 BDCs and thus employing NT 4 NET APIs.

Active Directory, in Summary

Table 4.4 contains the most important terms and features of Active Directory, for your review.

Table 4.4   The primary features of Active Directory.

Feature	Description
Domains	The fundamental logical building block for the partitioning of Active Directory. Partitioning is a important concept to directory services, because it allows the designer to implement multiple directory databases rather than one massive store. Because each domain's directory needs to store only the information about the objects located in that domain, the partitioning allows Active Directory to scale to virtually any size.
Domain tree	The prevalent way of structuring multiple domains. The structuring is done in such a way that the domains form a hierarchy.
Forest	A way of connecting several domain trees. A forest enables administrators to join two domain trees that have no common root (for example, in a merger of two separate companies with separate DNS roots).
OU (Organizational Unit)	Allows the administrator to partition the domain without the costs (more DCs) imposed by creating new domains. The intended use of OUs is to build a hierarchy that models the real properties (departments, teams, and so forth) of a particular organization.
Directory schema	Defines which objects can be created in the directory and which attributes can be assigned to those objects. The directory schema of Active Directory is fully extensible, allowing administrators or applications to add to the directory new object types or attributes that service the specific needs of the network users or the applications in use.
Global Catalog	A service that allows users and administrators to query for and find any object available in the Active Directory forest very quickly. The Global Catalog (GC) can be thought of as Active Directory's indexing engine that allows for fast and easy querying. You should note that the GC service only returns a list of the resources that are allowed to the person who posed the query, as a matter of security.
Replication	Active Directory is based on multi-master replication, which means that directory changes can be written to any DC in the domain. The DC then replicates the changes to its replication partners. Multi-master replication provides the scalability and fault tolerance needed to handle such a crucial network service as Active Directory.
DNS integration	Active Directory uses DNS as its domain naming and location service. DNS is the most widely used directory service in the world, because DNS is the locator service used on the Internet and in most private intranets. Because Active Directory uses DNS as its location service, Windows 2000 Server domain names are also DNS names.

Chapter 5
The Key Concepts of Active Directory

If Active Directory represents your first "real-life" encounter with directory services, your head probably still is reeling from the many new and very abstract concepts introduced in the last few chapters. The goal of this chapter is to eliminate most (if not all) of the confusion that you may have. However, you'll also learn quite a few new feats along the way to that—so, to all you directory services buffs who fear this chapter is going to be a mere repetition of the key Active Directory terms: I can assure you this won't be the case.

Chapter 4 presented the key concepts in a scholarly and pedagogical way, with rather detailed definitions (and, hopefully, easy-to-understand explanations) of each important term. But the designing and planning for Active Directory also require a deep and all-encompassing understanding of all key concepts. And that's why the aim of this chapter is to provide an alternative explanation that is structured in such a way that relationships and interdependencies between the various Active Directory concepts become clearer.

In effect, this chapter strives to present a rare insight into the Active Directory concepts and terminology as a whole, to give you a lasting understanding—and appreciation—of each of the key Active Directory terms before the book delves deep into the intricacies of each Active Directory concept.

Domains and Organizational Units

The domain contains objects, such as users, computers, printers, and files—just as you may be used to from NT 4. However, the

Windows 2000 domain also introduces several new objects, one of which is called an *Organizational Unit (OU)*. Understanding the concept of OUs is quite important, because it offers a structuring mechanism for the rest of the objects that can be stored inside the domain.

Domains

As in Microsoft's Windows NT 3.x/4.0 architecture, the core unit in Windows 2000 Server's Active Directory is the domain. In Active Directory, a *domain* is simply a partition of the namespace that forms a security boundary.

More practically speaking, the effect of being a partition in the namespace is that you are one fairly independent part of a larger namespace. In an Active Directory domain, the independence comes from two sources:

♦ You have a *scope of complete administration*, which means that you can hold full administrative privileges only if you are part of the domain.

♦ The system policies—especially security policies—that can be defined are limited to the domain boundaries. In other words, a domain forms a *physical security boundary*, thus containing full administrative control within each domain.

Another easy-to-remember consequence of being a partition in the namespace (from which you can deduce many of the more minute details about what constitutes a domain) is that all *domain controllers (DCs)* in the same domain hold the entire directory database—that is, the user naming context—for the domain and thus have identical directories, because object replication always happens on the domain level. DCs *never* replicate their domain objects to DCs in different domains.

Organizational Units

The other key term in Windows 2000 Server's Active Directory is the *organizational unit*. The OU is a *domain container object*—an object that can host other objects, including itself.

OUs reside in the domain and act as *facilitators* (see Figure 5.1); for example, they enable you to delegate administrative rights almost effortlessly. OUs make it possible to improve the overall structuring of network objects, and enforce differentiated rules on the network objects, based on their location in the OU hierarchy.

You may want to split some part of your logical namespace into multiple OUs, if any of the following conditions apply:

♦ You want to reflect within a domain the details of your company's structure and organization.

♦ You want to delegate administrative control over smaller groups of users, groups, and resources.

♦ Your company's organizational structure is likely to change later.

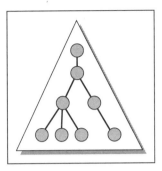

Figure 5.1
A domain with OUs is usually shown with the domain represented as a triangular shape, encompassing a number of OUs represented by circles. The OUs form a hierarchical tree structure inside the domain.

Stated another way, OUs enable administrators to structure network objects in a way that is logical and straightforward to administrators and users alike. (For example, you might want to structure the directory objects in an OU hierarchy that mimics the organizational diagram.) OUs also provide a simple way for administrators to assign to specific users and groups the permissions to create and change attributes on the objects stored in one or more OUs, and to assign differentiated rules or policies to network objects—based on their position in the OU hierarchy. OUs also provide *inheritance of access rights*, enabling you to restrict to members of an OU the access to resources that are specific to their particular organization.

Using the analogy of file systems, you can compare a domain to a volume and an OU to a directory:

♦ A *volume* includes the information about the file system type, number of disks, and other relevant information that covers all the files and directories stored on the volume, whereas the *domain* includes all core information regarding both the domain's network objects and the domain itself.

♦ The *directory* (or *folder*) in a file system is a container that holds files or other directories, whereas a *Windows 2000 OU* is a container that holds other objects or other OUs for the sake of imposing a structure.

Trees and Forests

Trees and forests also are essential to grasping the essence of Active Directory domains, because they encompass the ability to link separate domains to each other.

Trees

Usually, a tree structure is used to link multiple domains within Active Directory. A *domain tree* is a hierarchical structure of domains that form a contiguous namespace and share a common schema, configuration, and Global Catalog, with Kerberos trust among all members of the tree.

In other words, when linking as a tree, users in the linked domains can access resources in other domains via the transitive trust relationships that exist hierarchically among all the domains in the tree. However, administrative rights are not inherently transitive. Thus, an additional layer of complexity (and security) is added by limiting the scope of administrative rights to each domain.

The domain tree forms the foundation of Active Directory, because the minimal tree is a single, standalone Windows 2000 Server domain (thus everything is managed as a domain tree from the Active Directory's point of view). From this foundation, larger domain trees are constructed simply by joining additional standalone domains as children, to form a larger, contiguous namespace.

Every domain tree has a name, which is *always* the DNS name of the domain at the root of the tree, per the definition of being a contiguous namespace. The DNS names of the children of a tree root reflect this naming scheme; for example, if **astonitgroup.com** is the root of the domain tree, the child domains of **astonitgroup.com** are always children of **astonitgroup.com** in the DNS namespace—such as **child1.astonitgroup.com**, **child2.astonitgroup.com**, and so forth, as seen in Figure 5.2.

Forests

A forest is the only available alternative to a tree when you need to link domains. A *forest* is a set of one or more domain trees that do *not* form a contiguous namespace (see Figure 5.3). All trees in a forest share a common schema, configuration, and Global Catalog, and all trees in a forest trust each other via Kerberos trust relationships—just like the domain tree.

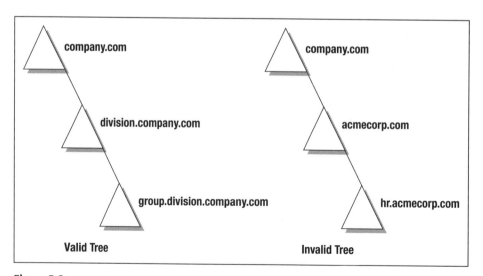

Figure 5.2
A domain tree always forms a contiguous namespace—the children must *always* reflect the name of the immediate parent, and so on up the tree.

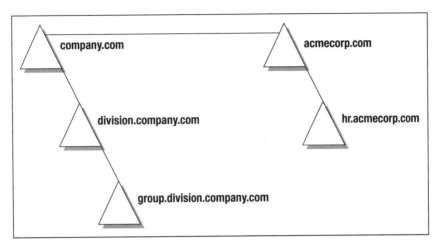

Figure 5.3
The whole point of a forest is to provide a way to link domain trees that don't share any commonality in their names.

Thus, the only real difference between trees and forests is that a forest doesn't grow out of a common root, because a forest exists as a set of cross-referenced objects and Kerberos trust relationships that are known to the member trees. Essentially, a forest provides you with the option to construct Active Directory domain hierarchies from separate, distinct, disjointed namespaces, if needed.

Comparing Trees and Forests

The following compares the important lessons regarding forests and trees.

A domain tree is one or more domains with:

♦ A common schema, configuration, and Global Catalog

♦ Transitive trust

♦ A *contiguous* namespace

A forest is one or more domain trees with:

♦ A common schema, configuration, and Global Catalog

♦ Transitive trust

♦ A *noncontiguous* namespace

The major difference between a forest and a domain tree, then, is the removal of the requirement in a forest that the member domains always form a tree. A forest joins together different domain trees arbitrarily, which, for example, makes the trust hierarchy in a forest less than intuitive because the forest is formed (by default) in the order that the trees are joined to the forest; that is, the "top" is the root domain of the first tree, and subsequent trees trust the "top" domain. However, this trust hierarchy is exposed only to the administrator, for management purposes, because users don't know or care what the trust tree looks like.

The same nonintuitiveness resulting from the arbitrary order in which domain trees are joined to a forest has an even worse impact on search behavior, because LDAP search operations are propagated only if the child is contiguous with the parent (that is, they are part of the same domain tree). So an LDAP search is effectively restricted to the domain tree in which the search was initiated, which is why a search from the root of the namespace always will search the Global Catalog instead of the domain tree. None of these search properties is by any means intuitive or understandable to the user.

Consequently, the nonintuitive nature of the trust hierarchy and the search behavior, among other things, point to the same conclusion: A domain tree should always be chosen over a forest. Use a forest only when the use of a domain tree isn't possible.

Putting the Vital Pieces Together

The first thing you need to remember when thinking about trees, forests, domains, and OUs is that these terms are purely logical—they aren't restrained by any physical limitations.

However, this doesn't mean that these logical terms can't be modeled on physical properties (such as the cities in which a particular company is based, or something similar). Actually, as later chapters of this book explain, some combination of the virtual world (such as organizational properties) and real world (such as physical properties) often represents the best way to fit the Active Directory architecture to the needs of an enterprise.

By now, you should recognize that an Active Directory tree consists of a hierarchy of domains. A domain can implement a tree of OUs within itself, which creates two levels of hierarchies inside the Active Directory structure—the hierarchy of the domains and the hierarchy of OUs within the domains. The OU hierarchy inside a domain is an independent structure of other domains—each domain can implement its own OU hierarchy. Understanding that both hierarchies are purely logical in nature is of paramount importance; that is, the hierarchies shown in Figure 5.4 have no bearing to the "real" or physical world of servers, network segments, and such things.

The domain tree is key to the scalability of Active Directory. A single domain can start very small and, in theory, grow to contain some 15 million objects. When a more complex organizational structure is required, or a large number of objects must be stored, multiple Active Directory domains can easily be joined to form a tree. With Active Directory, a domain tree theoretically could contain hundreds of millions of objects.

Also, unlike some other directory services that consist of a single tree structure and require a complex "top-down" partitioning process, Active Directory provides a simple and intuitive "bottom-up" method for building a large tree. In Active Directory, a single domain is a complete partition of the directory, and these domains can then be subdivided into OUs for administrative purposes.

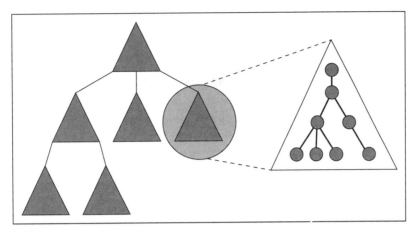

Figure 5.4
Active Directory gives access to two levels of hierarchy, the domain hierarchy (domain tree) and
the container hierarchy within a domain (OUs).

A Real Shocker: Groups Are Still There

Judging from the many new terms that introduce a level of hierarchy, and thus inheritance, you
could easily make the mistake of believing that every part of Windows 2000 has been turned into a
native part of the Active Directory's hierarchical structures.

Not so! For several reasons (primarily backward-compatibility), Microsoft has carried the group
concept into Windows 2000 Server, even though this totally offends the concept of directory services: Groups aren't aware of the directory hierarchy and still require unique names (depending on
the scope of the group). And you don't have any chance to escape the group concept, because
Active Directory can't use the OU as a security principal—it has to use groups, user accounts, or
computers, just as is the case with Windows NT.

However, despite the many bad things that rightfully can be said about groups with regard to administration, a few ever-so-small positive aspects exist: Groups enable you to create complex, distributed
groups that span several different OUs, which often will be needed to support *ad hoc* or multidisciplinary
corporate groups. Also, in an effort to lessen some of the pains of using groups, Microsoft has introduced a new kind of group, the Universal Group, to supplement the Domain Local Group and Global
Group. As its name suggests, a Universal Group can span multiple domains.

The two-tiered hierarchical structure of Active Directory also allows a great deal of flexibility in administering domain trees. For example, an entire domain tree can be owned and
administered by a central IT team. The IT team can create the same OUs in all domains—
such as an "IT" OU, in which local IT user accounts reside, or a "technical support" OU, to
hold support employees. Additional OUs can be formed to meet users' needs in a particular
domain. For example, in the headquarters domain, a "human resources" and a "finance"
OU can be created. For a regional office domain, an OU for the "office sales team" can be
created. Administrative rights for these particular OUs can be delegated to specific users or

groups, so that these users can administer their own areas without involving central IT. And because these users have administrative rights only on their own OUs, they can never interfere with central IT's global rights and responsibilities.

You can see an (albeit very simplistic) example of how to transform an organization diagram to an Active Directory structure in Figures 5.5 through 5.8. Reviewing these examples should give you a better grasp of the difference between domains, trees, forests, and OUs.

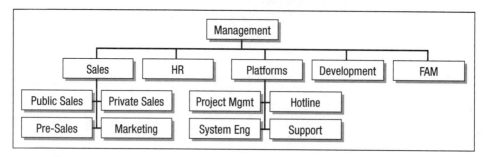

Figure 5.5
Still puzzled about domains, trees, forests, and OUs? This is a real-life example that shows a simplified organizational diagram of a company.

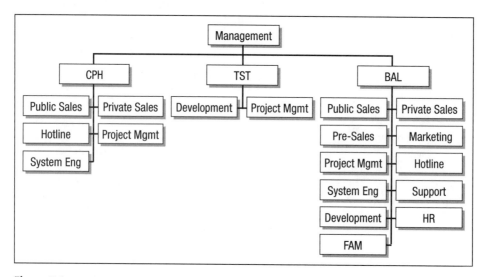

Figure 5.6
An expansion of the organizational diagram shown in Figure 5.5, which takes into account geographical conditions.

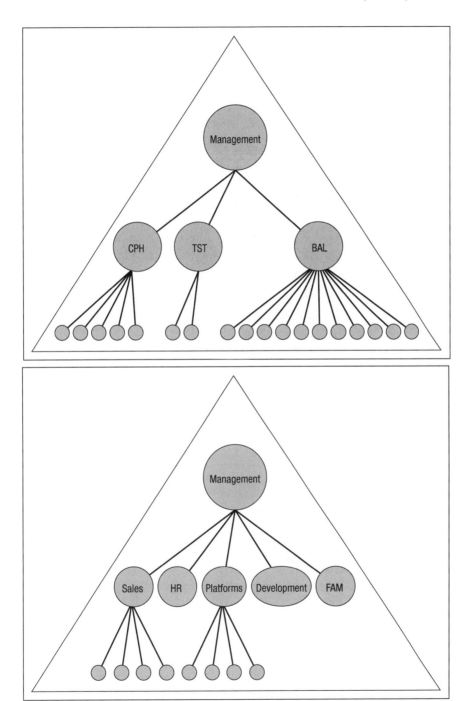

Figure 5.7
Two viable candidates for modeling the corporate structure in Active Directory. Which one you choose (if either) to use depends on a wide range of issues.

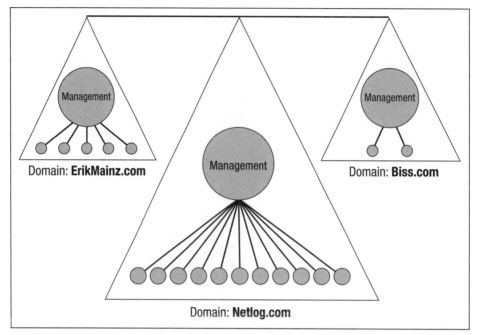

Figure 5.8
The company presented is the result of the merger of three separate companies (Netlog, Biss, and Erik Mainz). Thus, this represents a viable candidate for integrating three separate namespaces into a common directory by way of a forest.

DNS and LDAP

Active Directory uses DNS as its locator service. In Active Directory, Active Directory domain names are DNS names (see Figure 5.9). Also, users will find that Active Directory uses the same simple naming conventions that are used on the Internet. For example, **astonitgroup.com** can be both a DNS domain (an area of addressing) and an Active Directory domain. And **ViggoMortensen@astonitgroup.com** can be an Internet email address, as well as a user name in the **astonitgroup.com** domain.

DNS has historically been somewhat difficult to manage because it requires manual maintenance of text files containing the name-to-address mappings for every computer and service in an organization. In response, Active Directory is built to support several new DNS extensions that eliminate this problem.

Dynamic DNS

Dynamic DNS is one of the new DNS extensions that Active Directory supports. Dynamic DNS enables clients and servers to register directly with the DNS server and update the DNS table on-the-fly. This, in turn, frees administrators from the time-consuming (and error-prone) process of manually updating DNS entries. However, it also requires a DNS server that follows the RFC 2136 specification for Dynamic DNS.

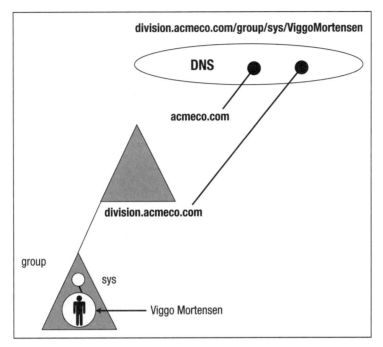

Figure 5.9
Active Directory domains can be located on the Internet (and intranet) in the same way that any resource is located on the Internet, because Active Directory now supports the DNS integration.

You can use Windows 2000 Server without Dynamic DNS support, but the network administrator's workload will increase significantly, because of the work involved in manually updating DNS information.

The DNS server must support the service locator record type (SRV record) defined in RFC 2052. SRV records are a generalization of the MX record concept, in which several different servers can advertise a similar service. Active Directory utilizes the SRV record for pointing to the services offered, such as the domain controllers (DCs). For example, a typical SRV record for the domain **sales.astonitgroup.com** would be:

_ldap._tcp.sales.astonitgroup.com 0 IN SRV 0 0 389 server01.sales.astonitgroup.com.

Lightweight Directory Access Protocol (LDAP)

To communicate with the directory, native Active Directory clients use LDAP. LDAP requires object names in the directory to be formed according to RFC 1779, which defines the X.500 naming style as the standard for naming objects in a directory.

Active Directory implements a DNS-based naming style that is founded on the LDAP proposals. In LDAP proposal naming hierarchy, the single components of the DNS domain names are expanded to domain component (DC) entries that should *not* be mistaken for

---

The Choice of DNS Servers

The DNS integration present in the Active Directory invokes the need for having DNS servers in the infrastructure. Although you don't have to use Windows 2000 Server's built-in DNS Server, doing so provides several significant advantages. First, Windows 2000 Server's DNS Server supports Dynamic DNS, which is highly recommended because it enables Active Directory servers to register automatically the necessary records in DNS. Second, Windows 2000 Server's DNS Server can store the DNS zones for which it has the authority in Active Directory. In that case, DNS data is being replicated among Microsoft DNS servers by Active Directory replication—not by a separate DNS replication topology using DNS Zone transfers.

And, while touching upon the interoperability matter, be keenly aware that most of the RFCs central to Active Directory's DNS functionality—and the much-vaunted administrative ease of Active Directory in regard to DNS—still aren't ratified by the Internet Engineering Task Force (IETF). Additionally, Windows 2000 Server's DNS Server is a native implementation created by Microsoft's own programmers, not a port of the public domain BIND implementation, which just about anyone else seems to be using these days.

---

the Active Directory DC concept. For example, for an Active Directory domain that carries the DNS name **sales.astonitgroup.com**, the DNS-style LDAP name is:

DC=sales,DC=astonitgroup,DC=com,O=Internet.

See Figure 5.10 for another example of this.

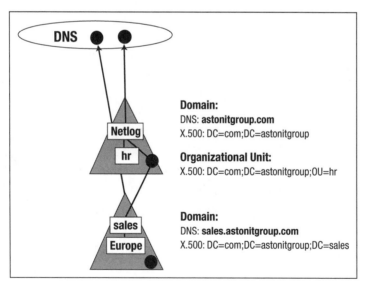

Figure 5.10
A simple domain tree structure in DNS, as well as X.500/LDAP, lingo.

LDAP and ADSI

LDAP has emerged as an industry-accepted technology for exchanging information between different, incompatible directories. LDAP promotes interoperability by offering four components:

♦ A standardized networking protocol for accessing a directory

♦ An information model (or *schema*) defining the form and characteristics of the information stored in a directory

♦ A namespace outlining how the information is referenced and organized

♦ An emerging model defining how these objects can be distributed

Currently in its third generation, LDAP enables software developers to write applications that are based on open standards, ensuring compatibility among most directories. Although LDAP goes a long way toward providing a unified architecture for directories, it still has some kinks that must be ironed out. For that and other reasons, Microsoft's *Active Directory Services Interface (ADSI)* deserves some attention. ADSI provides a fairly clean and simple interface to the directory structure, compared to the rather cryptic C-based LDAP API.

In an LDAP directory, the namespace can be organized in either a contiguous or a disjointed namespace. In a *contiguous namespace*, the name of a child domain always contains the name of the parent domain as part of its name. For example, if an Active Directory domain with the LDAP name DC=sales,DC=coriolis,DC=com is a child of DC=coriolis,DC=com, a contiguous namespace was used. The name of the parent domain can always be constructed by removing the first part of the child domain's name.

In a *disjointed namespace*, the names of the parent and child domains are not directly related to each other. Examples are the Active Directory domains DC=examcram,DC=com and DC=coriolis,DC=com, which clearly aren't related because the child domain does not carry the name of the parent domain as part of its own name (the com domain is owned by the Internet domain authorities).

The use of a contiguous or a disjointed namespace affects LDAP search operations in the Active Directory. In a contiguous namespace, a DC always creates referrals to the child domains. Using a disjointed namespace, however, terminates the search operation—referrals are never created.

The use of both contiguous and disjointed namespaces within the Active Directory has led to much confusion about how search operations really work. For that reason, the domain structuring model was refined for Active Directory to introduce the concept of the domain tree and the forest.

The Global Catalog

The Global Catalog (GC) is yet another concept introduced with Active Directory. The *Global Catalog* holds all objects from all domains in the Active Directory forest, as well as a subset of each of the object's properties. These attributes are contained in an abbreviated catalog. This technique, known as *partial replication* (see Figure 5.11), allows many common queries to be resolved from the GC without requiring a computationally intensive search in the domains that are part of the forest.

The GC is really just a partial index of select attributes in the forest, combined with a search engine. Designed for high search performance, the GC enables users to find an object easily—regardless of where it is in the forest—by searching based on the attributes that have been replicated to the GC.

Internally, the GC implements the same hierarchy as the domain tree does. LDAP queries, however, usually return results in a flat record set or list. This allows the GC to be used as a repository that functions like a global address book (that can be compared to the Microsoft Exchange Global Address book; actually, Exchange 2000 Server does use the GC for storing the Global Address book).

To find a resource in the forest, a user queries the Global Catalog for that resource, based on one or more known attributes of the target resource. The GC returns the location of the specified resource. One of the object attributes included in the GC is the object's Access Control List (ACL). This reduces the obvious security risk posed by the GC. If a user does not have rights to access an object, the user's query will fail. Thus, the GC does not provide a single point of risk exposure from a security perspective.

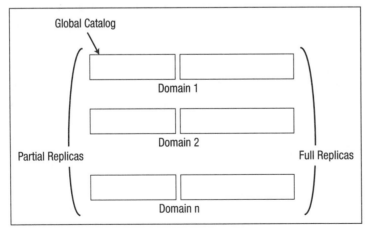

Figure 5.11
The Global Catalog structure provides access to full and partial replication.

Definition: The Naming Context

Active Directory consists of one or more naming contexts, or partitions. A naming context is any contiguous subtree of the directory and the unit of replication.

In Active Directory, a DC always holds at least three naming contexts:

- *Configuration Naming Context*—Contains the physical data for sites, services, and partitions in the forest, such as a list of which domains are trusted by each domain.
- *Domain Naming Context*—Contains the actual objects in the domain, such as user accounts, printers, and OUs. Also known as the domain partition.
- *Schema Naming Context*—Contains the schema defining the objects that can be created inside the Active Directory forest.

Tip

Including at least one GC in each site is a good idea. By doing so, clients always have a local repository for performing forest-wide search operations. Also, because the GC is accessed by the clients when they log on, a fair amount of WAN bandwidth will be saved in this respect.

The Physical Side of Things: Sites and DCs

A *site* is an area of the network where connectivity among machines is assumed to be good. Active Directory defines a site as one or more TCP/IP subnets, based on the assumption that computers with the same subnet address are connected to the same network segment, typically a LAN or other high-bandwidth environment. Unfortunately, the site concepts used in Windows 2000 Server and the different Microsoft server applications don't match. But Microsoft has promised that all their server-based applications eventually will evolve to the Windows 2000 site concept (thus, you have more than one reason to learn the ropes on sites).

It's very important to understand that a site is *not* a logical term and thus isn't part of the domain namespace (that is, the user naming context). Site structure is stored elsewhere in the directory (to be more precise, in the configuration naming context).

Stated in another way, site structure is totally independent of the Active Directory domain structure. *Site* is a term invented purely for the sake of fitting Active Directory to the physical limitations and possibilities of the LAN/WAN environment (see Figure 5.12).

When you define your network's site structure, you are in fact optimizing the behavior of Windows 2000 Server for your network's physical structure. Network traffic within a site generally should prove to be much higher than traffic between sites.

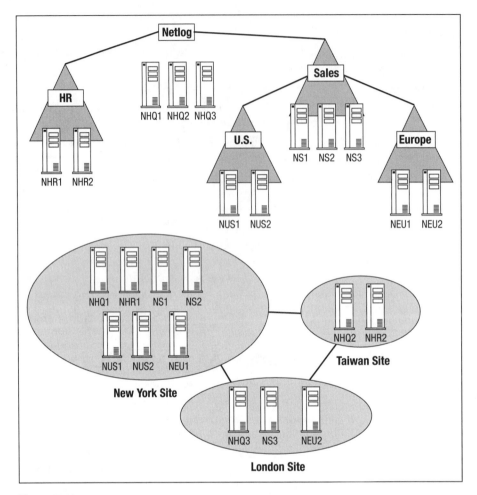

Figure 5.12
Sites are completely distinct from the logical Active Directory terms and concepts.

How you set up your network's site structure affects Active Directory in two main ways:

♦ *Workstation logon*—Sites help clients find DCs that are close to them.

♦ *Directory replication*—Sites can help keep to a minimum the replication traffic traversing slow or costly WAN networks.

The native Active Directory clients use site information to locate an Active Directory DC server, nearby to the user. When a client connects to the network, it receives a TCP/IP address from a DHCP server, which also identifies the subnet to which the workstation is attached. Clients that have statically configured IP addresses also carry statically configured subnet information.

The DC locator attempts to locate an Active Directory DC server located in the same site as the user, based on the subnet information known to the client. When a client logs on and no DC is available in the same site, the client will need to find another DC. However, that other DC could be across a slow link, because the workstation has no way to determine which other DC is closest, except the site identifier and the DC's response time.

Replication within a site (*intra-site* replication) and between sites (*inter-site* replication) follows different topologies. The Active Directory replication system automatically generates a ring topology for replication among Active Directory DCs and GCs in a particular site. Unlike Microsoft Exchange Server 4 and 5, Active Directory enables you to manipulate the replication topology within a site. For example, you could opt to change the bi-directional ring (default replication topology) for another architecture, such as a star layout.

However, the directory service always makes sure that the topology isn't broken and that no DC is excluded from the replication process. The *Knowledge Consistency Checker (KCC)*— a process that runs on all DCs—checks this. If the replication topology is broken, it will automatically be remedied by the KCC. Also, Active Directory dictates the schedule for intra-site replication.

When it comes to inter-site replication, the administrator will need to decide on the *path* (which servers are able to do replication, and in which order they try to replicate), the *schedule* (when replication is allowed to occur) and *frequency* (how often to check for replication updates) for the replications. Replication will only occur at the scheduled times. If replication can't occur when it's supposed to (as defined by the frequency setting), Active Directory will keep on trying to perform the replication until it eventually succeeds.

Intra-site directory replication is always performed via the *remote procedure call (RPC) protocol*, a TCP/IP-based programming interface that allows one program to use the services of another program in a remote machine. Inter-site replication can be selectively configured to use RPC or SMTP. (Note also that the replication protocols that are available for inter-site replication use compression to attain minimum bandwidth utilization.)

Even though Active Directory works to minimize and optimize replication by replicating only revised attributes—rather than whole objects, which is the case with Windows NT Server and Exchange Server 4/5—a site should only encompass an area in which bandwidth is:

♦ Available

♦ Plentiful

♦ Cheap

Typically, for a network connection to be considered fast, it must be at least 512Kbps. However, an available bandwidth of 128Kbps or higher might prove sufficient in many cases (the precise number depends on the actual load realized on the wire caused by Active Directory replications, server application traffic, client traffic, etc. See Figure 5.13).

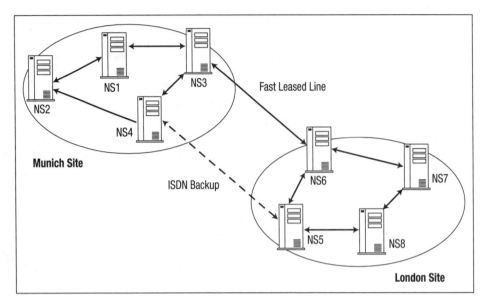

Figure 5.13
The site concept is simply a question of providing the necessary means to properly handle the LAN/high-speed connections and WAN/low-speed connections.

When you plan your sites, you also need to consider the placement of DCs, as well as GCs. Sites can be used to determine which DC is local to the client and thus most suitable for logons, whereas the decision on GC server placement is a bit more muddy. When you consider sites and DCs, you should keep in mind the following:

♦ A DC must be able to respond to requests in a timely manner.

♦ For best logon performance (and the least WAN load), you generally need at least one DC in each site that contains users or computers that belong to that domain.

When considering sites and the Global Catalog servers, you should focus on the following:

♦ The best logon and query performance comes from placing a DC (on a small site) with a GC server, enabling the server to do local logon and local resolving of queries about all the objects in the entire forest.

♦ However, adding a GC server increases the amount of data to be replicated, so you don't want every DC to be a GC server. Also, keep in mind that a GC server must have the storage capacity to hold all objects from all other domains in the Active Directory forest (today and in the future; so remember to add room for growth).

In essence, the placement of GC servers is a balancing act between query and logon performance and replication load, which is why you might find that placing a GC in each major site provides the best trade-off (where a "major site" could be a regional IT hub or simply locations on your WAN where a large collection of users and resources intersect).

Domain Controllers: It's a Whole New Ball Game

In Active Directory-based networks, you no longer have to distinguish between primary domain controllers (PDCs) and backup domain controllers (BDCs). Unlike the single-master model used by Windows NT 3.51 and 4, in Active Directory networks, all DCs are peers and each contains a writable copy of the domain's directory. Any DC can change its copy of the directory, and any changes in the directory on one DC are then passed on to the remaining DCs in the domain.

Additionally, the peer controller architecture enables you to promote any standalone or member server to the role of DC—or vice versa. Thus, any computer running Windows 2000 Server can potentially become a DC. Also, moving DCs between domains becomes quite simple. You just demote it, move it, and finally promote it.

Each DC is part of a specific site. However, the DCs for a particular domain can be placed in multiple sites, and a site may contain DCs for several domains. A domain can't exist without at least one DC—just as was the case with Windows NT Server. And so, the biggest departures from Windows NT Server really lie in the introduction of the multi-master replication and the site concept, which gives the network administrator a lot more control over LAN/WAN performance and, thus, the tools necessary to keep tight control over the situation at hand.

A Word on Replication

Active Directory is based on multi-master replication, which enables administrators to use and treat all DCs as peers, so that objects can be created or manipulated on any DC—and changes then can be propagated to the remaining DCs.

The introduction of multi-master replication replaces the master-slave approach used by Windows NT Server, in which updates can be performed in only one place: on the master copy of the directory (the PDC), which then is replicated to the slave copies (the BDCs). The master-slave approach is adequate for a directory with few copies and an environment in which all the changes can be applied centrally, but this approach really doesn't scale well beyond medium-sized organizations, nor does it address the needs of organizations that have a global presence.

Although the multi-master approach is conceptually simpler, it requires a stable and well-thought-out mechanism for transferring data among DCs, which must include a way to reconcile contradictory information sets among the different DCs. Luckily, the mechanism introduced in Active Directory meets this requirement.

For example, replication in Active Directory is not based primarily on time, but instead on *Update Sequence Numbers (USNs)*, which are 64-bit numbers maintained by each DC server. Each DC holds a table that contains entries for its own USN and the USNs of its replication partners. When the server writes any property to Active Directory, the USN is advanced and stored with the property written. This operation is performed *atomically*—that is the incrementing of the USN and the write of the property to the Active Directory will succeed or fail as a single unit of work.

FSMOs: A Small Limitation on the Peer Principle

The principle that Active Directory no longer features a single DC that processes all changes—and that changes can be made simultaneously at all the various sites and DCs within a domain—has one small caveat. Some actions actually still are based on the master-slave principle. For example, actions that have consequences for the entire domain tree, such as the addition or deletion of a domain or changes in the domain object schema, still use a lockout mechanism to ensure that changes are propagated prior to the beginning of the next domain-wide change.

Active Directory's lockout mechanism builds on the so-called *Flexible Single-Master Operation (FSMO)* roles, which need to be assigned to either a single DC within the forest or a single DC within each domain. Only one DC can serve as the FSMO for a given FSMO role at any point in time. At different times, different DCs can assume this role. In the event of a failure of a DC that is currently holding an FSMO role, another DC can be promoted to take on this role.

During replication, the DC compares the last known USN of its replication partner (saved in the table) with the current USN that the replication partner provides (see Figure 5.14). If changes have occurred recently (that is, if the replication partner provides a higher USN), the data store requests all changes from the replication partner (known as *pull replication*). After receiving the data, the directory store sets the USN to the same value as that of the replication partner (see Figure 5.15).

If properties on the same object are changed on different DCs, the DCs reconcile the data in the following order:

1. *By version number*—All properties carry a version number that is used to determine which property should be declared the correct one. Active Directory always uses the higher version, which isn't always the correct solution. However, the use of an unequivocal algorithm ensures that reconciliation can be performed locally, without negotiating with the replication partner, and that the outcome always results in the same data being used on all DCs.

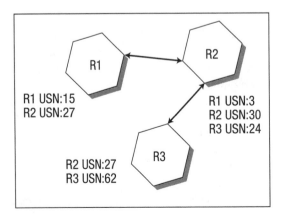

Figure 5.14
A simple example of the USN replication methodology, just before the replication starts.

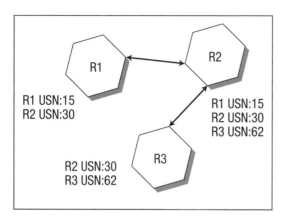

Figure 5.15
The situation after replication has been carried out between the DCs shown in Figure 5.14.

2. *By timestamp*—If the version numbers on the changed property are the same, the DC uses a timestamp to reconcile the property data. The timestamp is always created in addition to the property and the version number. The attribute that has the latest timestamp is used. DCs have to assume that time information is accurate because they don't negotiate the time as an integral part of the Active Directory replications, but a time synchronization scheme is automatically set up between all Active Directory DCs, as well as the members of the Active Directory domain (servers as well as clients). Just as is the case with using the highest version number, using the timestamp isn't always the correct solution. However, the use of this algorithm ensures that the DCs continue to serve the clients, rather than performing lengthy and potentially troublesome negotiations on which property value to choose.

3. *By buffer size*—If both the version number and the timestamp are the same, the DC performs a binary memory copy operation and compares the buffer size. The higher buffer size wins. If the two buffers are equal, the attributes are the same from a binary perspective and thus one can be discarded.

Note that all reconciliation operations are logged in a separate Active Directory container, and thus administrators have the option of recovering any values rejected by the directory.

Tip

Each Windows 2000 Server machine can hold only one domain. Consequently, you must provide at least one server that acts as a DC for every single domain in your enterprise. For example, with Active Directory, a network that has 10 domains needs at least 10 servers: one for each domain. In "real-life," however, Active Directory needs at least 20 servers (one for each domain and a backup for each domain), because nobody wants to risk total standstill of a domain, which would be the effect of a serious DC breakdown.

Name Types and Naming Conventions in Active Directory

The Active Directory terms are inherently logical. That is, "Active Directory" itself is just a name. This unique name represents all objects within Active Directory. Likewise, every object inside a directory is also known by a unique name. The use of unique names is the *central* idea that constitutes the entire (albeit very simple) idea of directory services.

Namespace is the technical term that describes the unique name of each Active Directory partition. Several different name types exist for directory objects:

♦ *Distinguished name (DN)*—At the outset, every object has exactly one name—its distinguished name. The DN uniquely identifies the object and contains sufficient information for a client to retrieve the object from the network. This is done by identifying the container that holds the object, as well as the complete path through the container hierarchy (for example, CN=Viggo Mortensen, OU=hr, OU=sales, DC=astonitgroup, DC=com). DNs are guaranteed to be unique for every object in the directory because Active Directory doesn't permit two objects that have exactly the same name to exist under the same parent (just as it's the case in a file system). Because DNs are too complex to remember and are subject to change, using other means to retrieve objects will prove of immense value in practice.

♦ *Relative distinguished name (RDN)*—The relative distinguished name is the part of the name that is an attribute of the object itself. In the example in the preceding bullet, the RDN of the hr object is Viggo Mortensen.

♦ *User Principal Name (UPN)*—The UPN is available for all security principals (that is, users and groups) and is a "friendly" name, because it is shorter than the DN and easier to remember. The UPN is composed of a shorthand name for the object and a DNS name (by default it will be the name of the container in which the object resides). Referring again to the preceding example, the object might have a UPN of **ViggoM@astonitgroup.com**. The UPN must be unique for every object because it is used for logon and authentication purposes.

♦ *Globally Unique Identifier (GUID)*—The GUID is a 128-bit number that is unique by definition. When they are created in Active Directory, all directory objects are assigned a GUID via an algorithm that ensures uniqueness in the generation of GUIDs. The GUID is never changed, even if the object is moved or renamed (which forces a change to the DN and possibly the UPN and RDN). In other words, applications can store the GUID of an object and be assured of retrieving that object, regardless of the object's current DN.

The UPN highlights one of the serious shortcomings of Active Directory: Although UPNs help users, because UPNs are much easier to remember (and, incidentally, also can double as their Internet email address), the requirement of global uniqueness for every UPN puts a heavy workload on administrators.

First of all, each user needs a unique UPN that is meaningful to that particular user. Second, and worst of all, the UPN also is used for groups, but without the possibility of associating each group object with a UPN suffix (the part after the @ sign). Effectively, this means that groups don't translate into the hierarchy of Active Directory—instead, they implement a flat namespace similar to the one known from the Windows NT Server domain model.

To use the previously listed name types in practice, you also need a naming convention to adhere to. Active Directory includes support for several of the common name formats for directories, defined as formal, as well as *de facto* standards. This extended support for diverse name formats enables users and applications to use the format with which they are most familiar when they access Active Directory.

So, don't be perplexed by the diverse name formats presented in the following list. Rather, simply choose the name format that you feel most comfortable with and take note of the other possibilities:

♦ *RFC822 Names*—RFC822 names are in the form **somename@somedomain**, and are familiar to most users as Internet email addresses (for example, **UserName@ MyCompany.com**). As previously mentioned, Active Directory provides the UPN in RFC822 form.

♦ *HTTP URL Names*—Active Directory supports access from Web browsers via the HTTP protocol and Microsoft Internet Information Server (IIS). HTTP URLs are familiar to most users who have Web browsers, and take the form **http://somedomain/path-to-page**. Active Directory supports access to its contents via HTTP URLs (but it's only a subset of the Active Directory objects, which actually can be of use inside a Web browser), in which *somedomain* refers to a server running Active Directory services, and *path-to-page* represents the path through the Active Directory hierarchy to the object in which you are interested. For example: **http://SomeServer.MyCompany.com/BIN/Division/Product/Ssys/UserName**.

♦ *LDAP URLs and X.500 Names*—Active Directory supports access via LDAP from any LDAP-enabled client. LDAP names are less intuitive than Internet names, but the complexity of LDAP naming is usually hidden within an application. LDAP names use the X.500 *attributed naming* convention. An example LDAP (RFC 1779) name could be CN=UserName, OU=Sys, OU=Product, OU=Division, O=MyCompany, C=US. Also, you can use LDAP URL names that point to the server holding Active Directory services and the attributed name of the object. For example: **LDAP://SomeServer. MyCompany.Com/CN=UserName,OU=Sys,OU=Product, OU=Division, O=MyCompany,C=US**.

♦ *Universal Naming Convention (UNC) Names*—Active Directory supports the UNC used in earlier Windows NT Server-based networks to refer to shared volumes, printers, and files. A user can refer to a shared file published in Active Directory by a UNC name, such as **\\MyCompany.com\division.product.Sys. SomeVolume\XLSheets\status.xls**.

The Logical Structure Elements of Active Directory

The core definitions also include terms that describe the logical structure elements of Active Directory. The following three elements are essential to understanding the logical structure of Active Directory:

♦ *Object class*—Defines the policies pertaining to a certain type of object, such as users, computers, domains, and OUs. The individual characteristics that together constitute the object class are called object attributes.

♦ *Object*—A concrete item that shares a common set of attributes and can be organized by classes. Examples of objects are users, computers, printers, and applications.

♦ *Object attribute*—Attributes (also referred to as *properties*) are categories of information that define the characteristics for a certain entity. That is, all objects of the same object class have the same attributes—it's the values of the attributes that make the object instance unique. For example, First Name is an attribute used in the User Account object, and the First Name attribute contains a string value, such as Viggo.

The schema in Active Directory defines which objects and properties can be created in the directory. When Active Directory is installed on the first DC of a forest, the directory service creates a default schema. This schema includes all objects and properties that are required for the Active Directory to get up and running, and is replicated to all DCs that join the forest later on.

Active Directory enables you to extend the schema to create new properties and classes for all the information that you may want to add. New classes can be derived from existing classes and can inherit all properties from the previous classes. New attributes can be created, and these attributes can be added to classes. Each of those attributes are either "must" attributes or "may" attributes—that is, they are either required or optional:

♦ *Required attributes* (those with "must") need to be filled out in order for Active Directory to create a new object. The attributes comprising the object class can be changed in the schema at a later date, but they can never be deleted. For example, a user object must contain a common name (cn), a SamAccountName used for backward-compatibility, and a password.

♦ *Optional attributes* (those with "may") can be added or changed at any time. These properties are not required to be filled out for being able to create an object, but they can be used for holding additional information that might prove highly useful for system administration or for other users. For example, a user object can contain a phone number, an office number, and information about the person's manager.

Definition: Containers

A *container* is a directory object that is capable of holding other objects (sometimes including other containers of the same type). Domains and OUs are both examples of containers.

The Active Directory Data Store

The data store for Active Directory is the *Extensible Storage Engine (ESE)*. ESE is an improved version of the Jet database that was used in Microsoft Exchange 4/5, as well as in Access and WINS.

The improved storage engine enables you to create a database up to 16 terabytes in size. That gives the database the (theoretical) potential of storing in excess of 15 million objects.

Note that ESE reserves storage only for those properties that actually have a value. For a user object, the default schema predefines approximately 50 properties. If you create a user, and you set only four properties—such as first name, last name, common name, and password—the database uses space for these four attributes only. If you add more values later, the database dynamically allocates storage for the data. Also, ESE can store multivalue properties. This feature allows the storage of multiple values for a single property—for example, because of the multivalue attribute, the database can store a virtually unlimited number of phone numbers for a single user without the need for defining multiple phone number attributes.

The extensibility of Active Directory is a key feature because it makes the directory a great place to store information on behalf of other applications—thereby enabling you to attain a previously unheard-of level of integration throughout the corporate network.

One example of such a mutually beneficial integration could be a human resources (HR) application. The directory already includes a great deal of information about users—such as their first and last names, office numbers, phone numbers, and perhaps home addresses and job titles. Although all of this information is useful to a human resources application, it is not enough, so additional information has to be added—such as the employees' salaries, social security numbers, tax withholding information, and health insurance information. And this isn't just a theoretical example, because the security granularity of Windows 2000 enables you to grant read and write access to these added properties only to members of the HR department. So although the individual user might be offered read access to his or her HR data, other administrators can be prevented from gaining access to these attributes altogether.

Active Directory Security Features

Active Directory is part of the Windows 2000 Trusted Computing Base and is a full participant in the Windows 2000 security infrastructure. The following are the prominent ideas behind the security:

- Object protection
- Delegation
- Inheritance
- Trust relationships

Object Protection

Access Control Lists (ACLs) protect all objects in Active Directory. ACLs determine who can see the object and what actions each user can perform on the object. The existence of an object is never revealed to a user who is not allowed to see it. Any attempt to access an object or attribute in Active Directory is validated against the ACL by the Windows 2000 Server access-validation routines.

An ACL is a list of *Access Control Entries (ACEs)* stored with the object that it protects. In Windows 2000 Server, an ACL is stored as a binary value as a part of the *Security Descriptor*. Each ACE contains a *Security Identifier (SID)*, which identifies the principal (user or group) to whom the ACE applies and shows information on what type of access the ACE grants or denies.

ACLs on directory objects contain ACEs that apply to the object as a whole and ACEs that apply to the individual attributes and/or actions that can be performed on the object. This allows an administrator to control not only which users can see an object, but also which properties of an object particular users can see and what they're allowed to do with the object. For example, all users might be granted read access to the email and telephone number attributes for all other users, but security properties of users might be denied to all but members of a special security administrators group. Also, individual users might be granted write access to personal attributes, such as the telephone number and mailing address on their own user objects.

Delegation

Delegation is one of Active Directory's most important security features, because it enables a higher administrative authority to grant specific administrative rights for containers and specific object classes inside the containers to individuals and groups. This feature goes a long way toward eliminating the need for creating a lot of "Domain Administrators" who have sweeping authority over large segments of the user population, which was close to being a given when using Windows NT Server.

ACEs can grant specific administrative rights on the objects in a container to a user or group. Additionally, rights can be granted for specific operations on specific object classes via ACEs in the container's ACL. Thus, the user or group can be allowed to perform some specific operations, but might not be able to create any other object classes nor affect users in any other containers (unless, of course, ACEs grant the user or group that access on these other containers, too).

Inheritance

Inheritance enables a specific ACE to propagate from the container in which it was applied to all children of the container. Inheritance can be combined with delegation to grant administrative rights to a whole subtree of the directory in a single operation.

Trust Relationships

As previously mentioned, a transitive trust relationship exists among the domains in an Active Directory forest. When a domain is joined to an Active Directory domain tree, a Kerberos trust relationship is automatically established between the joined-from domain and its immediate parent domain in the tree.

The transitiveness of Kerberos trust relationships eliminates the need to maintain and manage explicitly the two-way trusts between all the domains on a corporate network, which every Windows NT Server administrator is familiar with as the $N*(N-1)$ problem. In this simple multiplication problem, N represents the number of NT Server domains, and the product of the problem represents the number of trust relationships required for creating a complete trust relationship. Thus, 15 domains equals 210 (that is, the result of 15 times 14) trust relationships. This is so complex because trusts in NT Server are nontransitive; that is, if domain B trusts domain A, and domain C trusts domain B, domain C still won't have access to domain A, because these two domains don't trust each other.

The following are the two trust mechanisms available in Active Directory:

◆ *Transitive Kerberos trust relationships*—Allow users to gain access to resources anywhere within the Active Directory forest (subject to access control), by just setting up single explicit trusts (which happens automatically, when the domain is created) to another domain participating in the forest.

◆ *Explicit one-way trust relationships*—Allow either domains that are members of another Active Directory forest or domains that don't support Active Directory authentication to have access to a given Active Directory domain. The one-way trust relationship limits the scope of the authenticated access to the member domain that is explicitly trusted (exactly as is the case with the old-style Windows NT Server trust relationships). Thus, the explicit one-way trust relationships provide a mechanism for limiting the network resources that are visible and available to outside parties to just a single domain.

Moving On

Windows 2000 Server introduces Active Directory, an extensible, scalable directory service. Active Directory gives network administrators, developers, and end users access to a directory service that provides:

◆ *Flexible querying*—Users and administrators can use the GC to rapidly find any object in the forest quickly, using any attribute of that object. For example, an administrator is able to find users by their first name, last name, email name, office location, or other attributes of their user account.

◆ *Single point of administration*—Active Directory supports a single point of administration for all published resources, which can include files, peripheral devices, host connections, databases, Web access, users, other arbitrary objects, services, and so forth.

♦ *Flexible administration*—An ACL (or permissions) is used to protect every object in the directory. An object's ACL lists what specific actions users can perform on the object. The administrator can grant access specifically for each individual attribute of an object. For example, all users can be granted access to see the names and office telephone numbers of all users on the network, but be restricted from access to all other user attributes, such as home phone numbers, home addresses, and other personal information.

♦ *Delegation of authority*—Active Directory security supports both inheritance and delegation of authority. Inheritance makes the specific permission set of a directory object available to all of its child objects. Administrators can use delegation of authority to grant specific administrative rights for containers and subtrees to other individuals and groups. With delegation of authority, instead of granting administrators sweeping authority over large parts of the network, much more stringent administrative rights can be granted for each part of the network.

♦ *Security of information*—Windows 2000 Server supports a variety of network security protocols. This provides stronger, more effective security mechanisms, interoperability with outside entities such as the Internet, and compatibility for existing clients. The default protocol for network authentication in Active Directory is the Kerberos 5 protocol, a mature security standard for distributed environments.

♦ *Replication of information*—The directory is replicated, or copied, to each server running as a DC inside each domain. And so, if the domain contains multiple DCs, the directory is replicated to multiple servers. Each DC in the domain stores and maintains a complete copy of the domain's directory. Replication of this directory provides the level of fault tolerance, load balancing, and high availability requested by administrators.

♦ *Partitioning of information*—With Active Directory, instead of using one massive store, the directory of each domain stores information only about the objects located in that domain. By enabling the use of multiple domains and multiple trees, Active Directory can provide a perfect fit and the necessary scaling to any size of application—from the smallest of companies to the largest. Both small and large companies will reap several administrative benefits from being able to implement fewer domains than was the case with Windows NT Server. Meanwhile, large companies now are able to scale up Active Directory to just about any size wanted, simply by configuring multiple domains.

♦ *Extensibility of the directory*—Active Directory has an extensible schema, which means that administrators can add new object types to the directory and add new attributes to existing object types. For example, the administrator can add a purchase authority attribute to the user's object class, and then store each user's purchase authority limit as part of the user's account.

♦ *Integration with DNS*—DNS is a set of protocols and services used throughout the Internet and other TCP/IP networks to provide name registration and name-to-address resolution services. Active Directory uses DNS as its location mechanism.

♦ *Interoperation with other directories*—Active Directory supports several protocols for accessing the directory, such as versions 2 and 3 of LDAP, and MAPI. LDAP, the native protocol of Active Directory, is an industry-standard directory service protocol that enables Active Directory to share information with any other directory service that supports LDAP (meaning virtually any other directory). By supporting LDAP, Active Directory can expand its services across multiple namespaces, and possesses the potential of dealing with information and resources located on the Internet, on other operating systems, and in other directories. Active Directory support of MAPI provides backward-compatibility with Microsoft Outlook clients.

♦ *Full backward-compatibility*—Active Directory supports and interoperates with the earlier versions of Windows NT. Servers running different versions of Windows NT can interoperate within an Active Directory domain because the Active Directory DCs will appear to earlier-version clients and servers as Windows NT Server PDCs and BDCs.

By now, you should be able to couple most of the features in the preceding list to one or several Active Directory concepts. And, if this chapter and the last chapter have fulfilled their purpose, you are beginning to appreciate and gain insight into the fundamental workings of Active Directory.

Really, if everything has gone as expected, you are ready for the nitty-gritty of architecting and planning for Active Directory, which is the central subject of the rest of the book. If you still are unsure about the basics of Active Directory, I urge you to read through Chapters 4 and 5 again.

Before venturing into the next chapter, you must realize that not just anybody is able to design an efficient and sensible directory. To solve the challenges of architecting and planning, you need to have an in-depth understanding of every major part of Active Directory and your organization, and possess some experience in Active Directory modeling for the "real world."

Although mapping an organization's structure into an Active Directory namespace often appears relatively simple to casual observers, you must be keenly aware that many possible mappings exist—and that often, only one mapping provides the right match for a specific organization. And although realizing the correct Active Directory design is vital, it is far from being all that is involved in implementing a Windows 2000 Server infrastructure (for an in-depth discussion of the work processes and steps involved, you might want to take a look at Appendix A).

And beware: Even the smallest mistakes can prove fatal. For example, the wrong domain tree design can entail a dramatic reduction in the stability and productivity of the network environment—just as if the network design itself proves wrong. Regarding the design, pay special attention to such things as whether the domain tree(s) is built using the organizational structure or the world geography as its point of departure, how the replication and conditions of replication are configured, and many other similar details.

Architecting a medium-sized Active Directory solution is on par with designing a building from the ground up (with almost no predefined elements). Everybody knows that designing a building takes a lot of skill and innovation. Today, not too many people recognize that the same is true for creating a blueprint for a successful directory service implementation. I sure do hope that most people will realize this, before too many projects go terribly wrong.

Chapter 6

Identifying the Directory for Your Organizational Setting

The first step in planning for your organization's implementation of Windows 2000 Server is to examine your organization's business structure and operations in detail. You need to take this course of action to establish the environment in which Active Directory will operate.

This chapter provides an introduction to the most essential concepts for identifying corporate structures. It isn't intended as an organizational primer (you need to look elsewhere for that information, or recruit someone with organizational expertise into your Active Directory working group). Additionally, this chapter helps you to review your current network infrastructure, to ensure that it has the attributes that are necessary to implement Active Directory, including the physical network infrastructure properties that you need to have available in order to be able to bring your Active Directory design to life.

The overall goal of this chapter is to supply you with the information that you need to identify the pertinent details about your company's organizational structure and conduct, as well as its technology and infrastructure requirements. Such analyses, along with a plan for your company's future technological needs, are prerequisites for a successful Active Directory design. For your convenience, the end of this chapter presents a checklist that specifies the information that you absolutely must obtain to plan properly for your Active Directory implementation.

A Word Regarding the Planning Team

Experience shows that the implementation of a directory service has a rather heavy impact on the entire organization. Therefore, the need to form a central working group whose sole responsibility is to plan for the implementation of Active Directory can't be emphasized enough. Specifically, you want to avoid having multiple separate groups planning different Active Directory implementations.

Apart from people from the IT department, the Active Directory working group really should include some members from upper management—or, at the very least, should report to a group that has a high level of authority within the organization. Because your Active Directory design might very well turn out to be a representation of the entire organization, the Active Directory working group ideally also will include people from the different business and technology areas of the company—or, at the very least, be reviewed by several businesspeople who are thoroughly briefed on the long-ranging organizational effects of implementing Active Directory.

From the outset of your planning for Active Directory's implementation, remember that a successful design requires that you analyze each layer of the organization and its requirements. Thus, when the Active Directory working group is formed, it should begin its work by addressing the following planning activities:

♦ Obtain approval and authority from upper management to analyze and document the needs of the entire organization. Optimally, the working group should include one or several persons from upper management, because this furnishes the group with the necessary organizational leverage to obtain the information needed.

♦ Identify and document all details on how the organization conducts business.

♦ Identify and document all details on the organizational structure.

♦ Identify and document all details on how the current IT infrastructure is being managed (including the current administration of users, information, resources, and security). Please be aware that this might very well vary by location or even by the "personal preferences" of particular administrators.

♦ Identify and document all people in the organization whose current responsibilities include administration of systems and operations.

♦ Identify and document the enterprise network infrastructure map. The layout of the enterprise network infrastructure can impact rather heavily on many Active Directory implementation decisions.

♦ Finally, the working group should try to anticipate major events that may later cause profound changes to the business, because such events, in the worst-case scenario, could render the whole Active Directory architecture obsolete overnight.

Armed with this information, chances are very good indeed that you'll be able to plan adequately for the Active Directory implementation. For a more detailed discussion of the work process and the steps involved in executing an implementation project on Windows 2000 Server, see Appendix A.

Before you organize the Active Directory working group, you need to be keenly aware that, as an IT person developing an organizational hierarchy, you may be venturing into a potential hotspot of corporate politics, and thus should proceed with extreme caution.

The obvious reason that you should proceed cautiously is that when you implement a directory service, people might suddenly find themselves confronted with their position in the organizational hierarchy. Naturally, this will foster more focus on where each department and individual is placed in this hierarchy. Also, regardless of how political or nonpolitical your organization's behavior is in the pre-directory service era, no company seems to be immune to a dose of organizational perspective coming from its IT systems. In fact, organizations that don't have much focus on the corporate hierarchy before implementing a directory service often suffer the most post-implementation political implications.

Consequently, getting the proper organizational sign-offs on your planned Active Directory working group from the start is essential. If you don't heed this all-important advice, sooner or later you will hit an organizational stumbling block that will require you to go to the very top of the organization for resolution. And hopefully, you will hit that snag before Active Directory is put into production rather than later.

Identifying Organizational Characteristics

At its best, Active Directory includes a wide range of very important organizational objects, yet is able to represent those objects as a unified, well-structured organization. Thus, the need for Active Directory's implementation to reflect the way that the organization actually conducts business is of paramount importance. For example, if an organization has many offices all over the world, but virtually all major business decisions are made centrally (or in very few places), Active Directory should reflect this centralized power structure, because that is how the company actually conducts its business.

To prepare your company's plan for implementing Active Directory, you need to obtain information about the organization in the following areas:

♦ The organizational structure

♦ The geographical structure

♦ The potential for major reorganizations or other events that will have an impact on Active Directory

♦ The security requirements and preferences (for example, how users, information, and resources are handled and who handles this work)

♦ The enterprise network infrastructure (such as bandwidth, Internet access, and so forth)

Before you begin your work exploring the above-mentioned areas, you need to identify and document all details on how the organization conducts its business (as outlined in the prior section). That is, you should try to uncover the underlying properties of your organization (and each of its business units) and its position in the marketplace, such as the organization's purpose, mission, and strategy, as well as its size, technology, and changes in environmental circumstances. This information, in turn, will help you to establish the very specific blend of business, application, information, and technology needs that exist in the organization—and ultimately help you to pinpoint some critical business activities that may need more support, as well as areas that are still based on obsolete business processes or goals.

When you uncover how your organization conducts business, be aware that users and customers may have similar needs and preferences—although this might not necessarily be the case. You should use a variety of methods to identify how the organization conducts business, including the following:

♦ Identify key decision makers and develop business scenarios with them. Also, strive to understand potential strategy changes that are underway.

♦ Identify the core competencies and major improvements that are deemed necessary.

♦ Review the organization's annual report and other documents for insights into the corporate standing and the immediate corporate needs.

♦ After having exhausted the alternative options, conduct internal (and possibly external) surveys of issues that aren't covered adequately.

After you gather an overview of how the organization executes its business, you should review whether the current IT infrastructure goals align with the overall goals and needs of the organization. Some of the questions that you should answer are the following:

♦ Have you assessed how your business requirements and IT capabilities match up today?

♦ Do you have a vision statement of your business and IT goals (including one-year, three-year, and five-year plans for business needs and the IT functionality and services needed to meet those needs)?

♦ Do you have a roadmap that helps guide you through the steps needed to reach your IT and business goals?

♦ Is all the vital corporate raw data turned into useful information?

♦ Do the information systems meet the needs of users in different departments?

♦ Is IT used for competitive breakthroughs (in other words, have you evaluated the possibilities offered by business process reengineering, supply chain integration, knowledge management, and so on)?

♦ Is IT helping the company to connect to its customers or suppliers?

♦ Does a plan exist for updating obsolete systems?

♦ Is the company capitalizing on advances in the IT field?

The timeframe for an IT planner is much shorter than in virtually all other fields, because organizational IT needs and opportunities change rapidly, as do the tools that can help address IT needs.

One of the hallmarks of a skilled enterprise IT architect is a conceptual framework that helps the IT department manage the demands brought about by the growth of the organization. This framework includes the logical and physical development of the corporate network and the management of the network's growth, so that when an organization adds offices, divisions, or new markets, its network is able to integrate the new users and business entities logically.

Optimally, the IT infrastructure plan that you create and manage does much more than support the business—it should also help the organization exploit new strategic opportunities for growth. However, you need to make sure that it's the business needs that are the driver for all of the substantial improvements implemented to the corporate use of information technology, and not the other way around.

Finally, be aware that companies often make serious mistakes during the planning process by trying to leap too far forward at one time, which is why you should make sure that IT plans are implemented gradually, by integrating future goals with current fundamental business needs.

Microsoft recently studied several large companies that consistently do an excellent job of using IT to deliver substantial value to their organizations. According to Microsoft, its survey revealed that cutting-edge technology isn't the primary factor in the success of these companies. Rather, success is based on managing IT functions just like any other strategic business functions and processes. The study revealed six key characteristics that can help make your IT infrastructure more successful:

♦ *Make IT a business-driven line function, not a technology-driven staff function.* According to the IT managers who were surveyed, many organizations do a poor job of linking IT to business strategies and the day-to-day work processes that support them.

♦ *Base IT funding decisions on the same ROI (return on investment), cost-benefit, and strategic considerations as any other corporate expenditure.* IT spending decisions should be reached in the same way that manufacturing evaluates an investment in a new business location or a major new machine for the factory floor. Decisions must be based on rigorous cost-benefit analyses and mature insights into the organization's strategic direction and priorities.

♦ *Strive for simplicity and flexibility throughout the technology environment.* The best companies enforce solid architectural IT standards and make exceptions to those standards only after rigorous scrutiny. They believe strongly in reducing the number of technologies and platforms that they deploy, and design their implementations for maximum flexibility and ease of implementation.

♦ *Demand near-term business results from development efforts.* Nobody working today has to deal with faster turnover in technologies than IT professionals. That is why you should favor incremental project rollouts and, wherever possible, packaged software over custom software. And when custom development is necessary, focus on the 20 percent of the functionality that typically deliver 80 percent of the value.

♦ *Strive for constant year-to-year operational productivity improvements.* You should measure performance against internal and external benchmarks and standards and strive for constant improvements. While new investments should be treated like capital decisions, operations should be evaluated against aggressive cost and service targets.

♦ *Build a business-smart IT organization and an IT-smart business organization.* The IT and business organizations have to be well integrated. That is, they must speak the same language, communicate, and understand each other's capabilities and needs.

Wherever possible, you should check that these six ingredients of success are incorporated as short- and long-term goals of the enterprise.

After you've acquired an intimate understanding of the corporate culture and business goals, you should be ready to move forward with the more palpable parts of the information gathering for the Active Directory design. However, before you venture into identifying the organizational structure, you should understand very clearly that the information gathering described in this section usually doesn't impose any direct consequences on the design of Active Directory. But, still, it is a very significant activity, because the information collected provides the participants in the working group with a consensus on the corporate goals, which the Active Directory implementation also has to honor. And, more often than not, this information proves invaluable for ensuring that the right decisions are made (now and in the future) when laying down the architecture of Active Directory and adding new functionality.

You might want to note that the real value of that information often won't be apparent to the participants in the working group, because these decisions often seem obvious or intuitive—which simply means that someone has done a good job identifying the corporate "heartland" at the outset.

Identifying the Organizational Model

The first thing that you do to identify the organizational structure is to discover which basic organizational concept (which Microsoft often refers to as the *Administrative Model*) your company builds upon.

In essence, the three types of organizational models to choose from are the following:

♦ The centralized organizational model

♦ The decentralized organizational model

♦ A combination of the centralized and decentralized organizational models

The Centralized Organizational Model

Many companies (especially the smaller ones) are built on a *centralized model* (shown in Figure 6.1), in which a single entity controls the core administrative and operational areas within the organization. In other words, an organization in which most decision-making authority is held by a central upper-level management team. Typically, these companies have strong IT departments that define the network infrastructure and implement that model down to the smallest details—including operations and planning matters.

The Decentralized Organizational Model

Other organizations, especially large enterprises, may be structured in a very decentralized way (similar to the structure shown in Figure 6.2). In the *decentralized organization*, multiple business units or departments perform their own core administrative and operational activities,

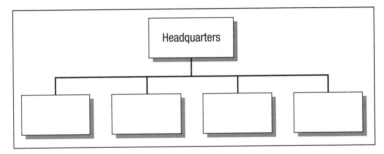

Figure 6.1
The structure of an organization using a centralized model.

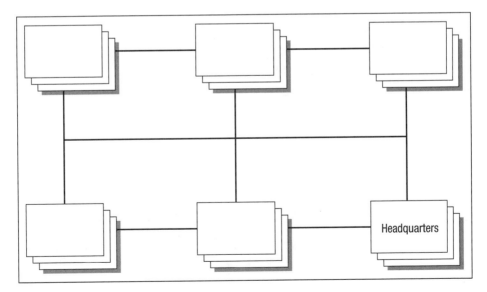

Figure 6.2
An example of an organization that is built on a decentralized model.

and the corporate headquarters simply can be treated as another business unit or department. In other words, under a decentralized model, an organization delegates a great deal of decision-making authority to levels of management at points below the top.

A company may use a decentralized organizational model if the company actually comprises several different businesses, each of which is very focused upon its own conditions, which have no bearing on the other constituent businesses. Or, a company may choose a decentralized model simply as a matter of organizational likes and dislikes, geographical necessity, or managerial preference.

When a decentralized approach to managing the organization is used, often no single point in the corporation exists from which the network infrastructure can be controlled or managed. Therefore, the network infrastructure (including operations and planning) usually is more or less split up on the units or divisions and treated as a part of them.

The Combination Model

The third model (represented in Figure 6.3) reflects the fact that some organizations use a combination of the centralized and decentralized organizational models. The number of different possibilities for combining centralization and decentralization is nearly infinite.

Usually, the model that a company uses is simply a result of practical reality; for example, the need for centralization of certain corporate functions, such as upper management, auditing, and IT, leads to a centralized model. Of course, the choice may also simply be a matter of organizational likes and dislikes.

Identifying the Organizational Structures

After you determine your company's organizational model, you are ready to move a step closer to "real life" by focusing on the organizational structures—the way the corporate infrastructure appears one or two steps down from the top level.

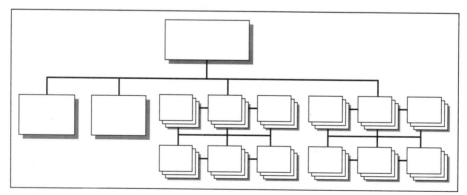

Figure 6.3
An example of an organization that is partly centralized and partly decentralized.

The following are the building blocks of an organizational structure:

♦ *Specialization*—Identifying the specific jobs that need to be performed and designating the people who will perform them.

♦ *Departmentalization*—Grouping jobs into logical units (this can be supplemented by the *profit center* concept, in which each separate company unit is responsible for its own costs and profits). The departmentalization most often is one of the following types:

♦ *Customer departmentalization*—Based on the types of customers likely to buy a particular product.

♦ *Product departmentalization*—Based on the specific products created.

♦ *Process departmentalization*—Based on the production processes used to create certain goods or services.

♦ *Geographic departmentalization*—Based on the areas served by a business.

♦ *Functional departmentalization*—Based on the organization's groups, functions, or activities.

♦ *Process organization*—Based on the units or teams responsible for all the various processes involved in getting products to consumers.

The most prevalent organizational structures found are the following:

♦ *Functional organization*—Authority is determined by the relationships between group functions and activities. An example is the line-staff organization (see Figure 6.4 later in this chapter).

♦ *Divisional organization*—Corporate divisions (a division is a department that resembles a separate business because it's more or less producing and marketing its own products in isolation; the divisional organization is dubbed a conglomerate if the divisions making up the organization are unrelated) operate as relatively autonomous businesses under the corporate umbrella. An example is a product organization.

♦ *Matrix organization*—Work is being done by forming teams, and team members report to two or more managers. Matrix organizations are often implemented in organizations, where a need exists for tightened cross-functional cooperation and/or tearing down the existing power lines that might be stifling the company.

Many different organizational structures exist in addition to these three, so you have to be open-minded when trying to determine the corporate structure. For example, international organizational structures often include some novel approaches, developed in response to the need to manufacture, purchase, and sell on a global scale.

The line-staff and product organizations are inherently hierarchical in their structure, whereas the matrix organization is quite anarchic (meaning diametrically opposite to the two other structures), because it is based on a matrix in which every person and project can be mapped to functional units. So, whereas the hierarchical constructions are very static in their concepts, much of the idea of the matrix construction lies in its inherently dynamic characteristics.

Hierarchical Structures

The traditional hierarchical structure has the properties shown in Table 6.1. Often, traditional, hierarchically structured companies strive to remove or reduce some of the worst cons of this inherently static organizational structure. The means with which they attempt to remove the cons are generally referred to as *integration mechanisms*, which include the following:

♦ Rules and procedures

♦ Planning processes

♦ Referring problems "up the hierarchy"

♦ Strong horizontal communication among functional managers

♦ "Project leaders" or liaison departments within functional units

♦ Task forces

One of the hierarchical structures typically found is the *line-staff* organization (represented in Figure 6.4). The line-staff organizational structure is characterized by the following:

♦ Senior managers are at the top of the organizational hierarchy.

♦ Project managers are employed to "blur" the harsh hierarchical boundaries.

♦ Department managers have responsibility but limited authority.

♦ The authority given to project managers often results in a "web" of relationships and concomitant conflicts.

Dissatisfaction in the line-staff organization most often stems from one or several of the following traits:

♦ Inability to cope with problems of shared authority.

♦ Reluctance to relinquish authority.

♦ Limited scope of project management authority.

Another popular hierarchical structure is the *product* organization (an example of which is shown in Figure 6.5). The product organization is characterized by the following:

♦ Everything is ordered by product membership. Instead of project managers, product managers often are employed.

Table 6.1   The pros and cons of the traditional hierarchical structure.

Pros	Cons
Better control	No project-oriented emphasis
Low communications bandwidth	Coordination is complex
Continuity within functional areas	There is no customer focal point
Potentially quick response	Responsibility can be diffuse
	Motivation and innovation can be inhibited

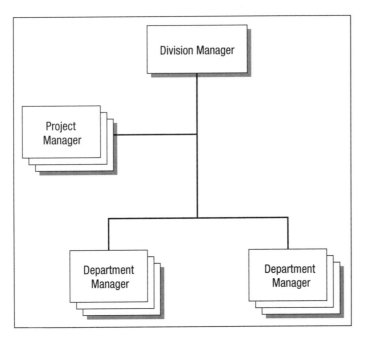

Figure 6.4
A representative line-staff organization.

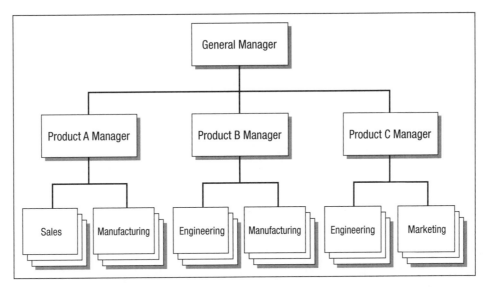

Figure 6.5
The typical hierarchy of a product organization.

- Line authority is employed over projects.
- Redundant resources exist across the product boundaries.
- A potential for problems exists in sharing facilities and equipment.
- Less skill development and career opportunity are fostered within each functional unit.

Matrix Structures

The whole idea of the *matrix* organization is to tear down the many layers of decision-making—which in the worst case turn out to work as decision inhibitors—that are part of any large hierarchical organization. This is done by removing the hierarchy and implementing a matrix, which gives way to two axes of authority (see Figure 6.6).

Matrix organizations have proven to be particularly appealing to firms that want to speed up the decision-making process. However, some major shortcomings also exist:

- The matrix organization may not allow long-term working relationships to develop.
- Inherent problems exist in using multiple managers for one employee. Conflict-management skills for managers in the "two-boss" situation are absolutely essential.
- Employees are easily confused regarding manager evaluation and accountability.

The matrix organization often uses the x-axis for project responsibility and the y-axis for functional responsibility (or, more broadly, one is usually functional and the other aligned to markets), as shown in Figure 6.6. The matrix organization is characterized by the following:

- Project managers have maximum project control.
- Projects can have distinct policies.
- Project managers have authority to commit resources.
- Rapid response is possible.
- Dual reporting is part of the scheme, which can lead to excessive supervisory overhead.
- Priorities are inherently dynamic, but there is a risk of decision strangulation (too many parties), or some people may confuse matrix with group decision making.
- Long-range plans may suffer if a determination isn't made regarding which of the two axes really controls the power in the organization. Generally, one axis controls the direction and policy decisions, while the other axis controls resources.
- Lessons learned may not be propagated, due to organizational islands or anarchy.
- A severe risk of conflicts and confusion of authority arises from the inherent power struggle between the horizontal and vertical responsibilities.

Because of the many positives and negatives that have to be considered in this very different organizational structure, the matrix organization largely has been superseded by refinements such as the *network* organization—or, more recently, the *learning* organization.

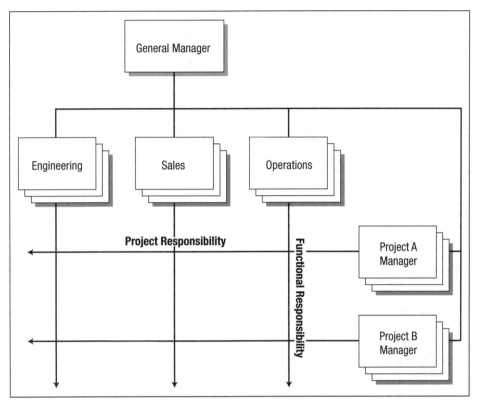

Figure 6.6
A matrix organization should be viewed as the opposite of hierarchical organizations.

When you examine the organizational structure, you should also strive to map the essential organizational *authority* to the units and persons that are part of the structure. Authority, or the right to decide, generally can be subcategorized into these three forms:

♦ *Responsibility*—The obligation to meet a goal.

♦ *Accountability*—The state in which authority and responsibility are coextensive.

♦ *Power*—The ability to influence others.

Although this mapping of organizational authority isn't strictly necessary prior to your implementation of Active Directory, uncovering beforehand the more or less officially sanctioned power lines in existence often will work to ease some of the implementation pains.

Organizational Chart

After you've identified your company's basic organizational model, you should try to synthesize this model into a comprehensive organizational chart that depicts the company's structure and shows where all employees fit into its operations. This chart should cover all the divisions, business units, locations, departments, and formal groups that constitute the company. (Don't include ad hoc or temporary, cross-boundary groups, although you should document them in some way, because you will need this information later on in the Active Directory design process).

Also, you should identify who manages the following IT-specific properties:

- Name resolution issues
- Network standards, policies, and issues
- General problem resolution for users and administrators
- Capacity planning
- Security issues
- User administration

Identifying the Geographic Structure

After you've resolved the many intricacies of the corporate organizational model and structure, you still need to carry out the relatively straightforward task of identifying all geographic locations in which the company has offices and users.

Ideally, these geographic locations should be identified (similar to Figure 6.7) by their specific physical location (for example, country, state or province, and city), size (such as number

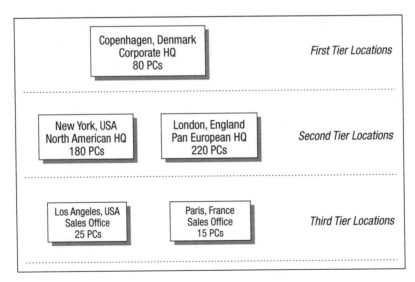

Figure 6.7
An example of a geographical mapping of a company.

of users and PCs), and functions. For example, you could choose to distinguish between the following location types:

♦ Main sites

♦ Secondary sites (such as the headquarters for each country or function)

♦ Local offices

♦ Remote sites

♦ Subsidiaries

Of course, you may find that another way of dividing the locations makes more sense to your situation.

Besides identifying all the preceding details regarding geographic location, you will often find that the implementation phase will be easier if you have determined the following details for each location:

♦ Number of buildings

♦ Number of floors in each building

♦ Square footage of each floor in each building

♦ Business functions performed on each floor or at each location

♦ Number of PCs on each floor

♦ Location of servers and other central infrastructure components

Projecting Organizational Changes

As long as an organization continues to grow, merge, reorganize, downsize, go after new markets, and otherwise change, its directory service will have to change in order to adapt to the changing environment of the enterprise.

Consequently, the Active Directory working group must also try to anticipate events that may affect the corporation. Factoring in things such as growth and reorganization translates into addressing the following variables:

♦ The corporate short- and long-term growth projections:

  ♦ Whether differentiated growth projections for specific parts of the company are needed.

  ♦ Correspondingly, whether specific departments, business units, or locations within the corporate boundaries are likely to shrink in the future.

♦ The potential for reorganizations (the best indicator often is the corporate history):

  ♦ When reorganizations occur, are departments simply renamed or are personnel reorganized into completely different departments?

  ♦ When reorganizations occur, do they usually cause profound changes in the organizational model or structure employed?

- The chance of merging with or acquiring other companies:
  - If mergers and acquisitions are expected, how is the integration typically performed—is the other company being completely dismantled or simply made another autonomous corporate unit?
- The chances of increased integration and partnerships with suppliers, customers, and other parties, requiring tighter integration between the IT systems across the usual corporate boundaries.

Ultimately, as long as new technologies are constantly being introduced, the ideal IT solution from five years ago may not be appropriate today. Likewise, the solution that you identify today will have to be updated to meet your organization's needs some years down the road.

However, because a corporate IT solution can't simply be replaced every so often, the success of your network infrastructure depends on the working group forming a mature, high-level vision of what your organization will look like in three, five, or even 10 years. This vision should address high-level questions such as the following:

- How will the roles of management and employees change?
- How will the core businesses, processes, and systems evolve?

Even if the changes are relatively modest, they can have a dramatic impact on your IT infrastructure. By anticipating those changes and planning for them, you ensure that your network will indeed meet future needs.

Hopefully, such a vision—or something resembling it—will be readily available to the working group (or be formed along the way), so that it can be incorporated into the planning of the Active Directory implementation.

Identifying Security Requirements

Ultimately, you need to delve into the corporate IT security policies and requirements, to get a complete picture of corporate shortcomings and needs. Security is receiving an ever-more prominent place on the IT agenda, because client/server systems and intranets are distributing data ever more widely, making information more available and more useful to employees than ever before. Correspondingly, the points of vulnerability and potential sources of attack are on the rise.

So, how can you protect your valuable information when it's so widely distributed? The key, according to IT managers and security analysts, is to get the right people and tools in place to implement and revise the corporate security policies. Furthermore, the need to take an all-or-nothing approach to security is very important for it to be efficient. This entails constant scrutiny of the entire security infrastructure (including oversight of firewalls, encryption techniques, network access control, virus protection, and disaster recovery) and adoption of standards and guidelines for just about every component in the IT infrastructure. Fortunately, with Active Directory, somewhat less vigilance should prove adequate.

The following are the central tasks and considerations when determining your organization's security requirements:

◆ Identify the user and network security policies that already are in place.

◆ Pinpoint who currently performs administrative tasks, such as creating user accounts, file shares, and groups, as well as resetting passwords, and so on. This should include documenting which rights these people and groups need.

◆ Establish what kinds of relationships exist between locations, business units, departments, vendors, customers, and joint venture partners. This encompasses finding out the following:

   ◆ The policy concerning rights to access, view, and change data and resources.

   ◆ Whether users already are grouped together for security-management purposes.

   ◆ Whether application access is restricted, and if so, how.

   ◆ What information is available to the entire company, and what information is available only to a select number of people (whether this might be based on membership of certain business units, groups, or something else).

Your work could benefit from your having evaluated the current security and encryption standards and reviewed the many innovations (such as public key certificates and support for Smart Card logon) that are delivered with Windows 2000 Server in advance to the security assessment. You should check out Chapters 9 and 14 for a detailed description of the security functionality brought forward by Windows 2000 Server/Active Directory.

Analyzing the Enterprise Network Infrastructure

When you are designing your future network and determining the best way to implement Active Directory, knowing the fundamental properties and current use of the enterprise network is vital. This obviously doesn't apply if you plan to remove all network and workstation hardware over a weekend and replace it with new, state-of-the-art equipment, all proven to interoperate. But that is an unlikely scenario. Even though this type of "clean-cut" philosophy is by far the most desirable for most situations, the majority of companies (out of financial, technical, or organizational necessity) phase out legacy hardware and software over a period of time, lasting anywhere from a few months to a year or more.

This section focuses on how to get the major properties of your existing network structure properly documented (including the speed of network links, the load on the network links, profile of the user community, interoperability concerns, and connectivity to internal and external networks). You need this information in order to be able to determine whether enough capacity is available to implement Active Directory and how it should be mapped to your network infrastructure.

Tracking a Key Network Property: Bandwidth

You need to have extensive knowledge of the speeds of the links between locations and the current bandwidth utilization of each individual link, because the corporate network infrastructure will represent either an enabler or a restraint to Active Directory. You should start this task by documenting the network's physical structure, because a large drawing (like the one shown in Figure 6.8) showing all the hardware in your network will be invaluable in order to get a good understanding of the network infrastructure. Also, the drawing can prove very helpful later, when implementing Active Directory. Often, the implementation requires you to determine at which nodes the network can and can't be expanded, the best network traffic routing, and the optimum placement of servers and other network services.

When you have the drawing ready, you should start documenting the network traffic flows, including the speed and utilization of every network link (see Figure 6.9). Ideally, this bandwidth utilization should include a network analysis to determine your average overhead (or background) network traffic as well as the peak conditions.

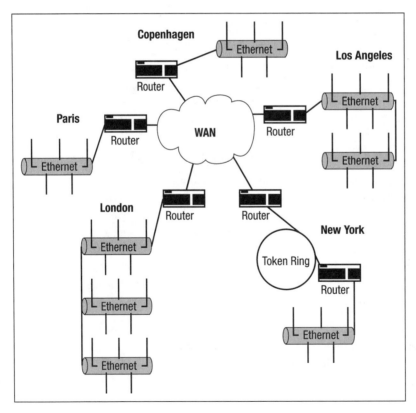

Figure 6.8
An example of the physical structure of the network (LAN as well as WAN).

After your drawing includes the answers to all of the following questions, you have the information that will prove absolutely necessary in order to create a suitable Active Directory design:

♦ What is the speed of each link between each location and within each location (such as between buildings and network segments)?

♦ Which networking technology is utilized for each link?

♦ What is the available bandwidth on each of these links during ordinary conditions—that is, what is the average bandwidth during business hours (the baseline) and at peak hours?

♦ How much growth in network traffic and the speed of links do you anticipate?

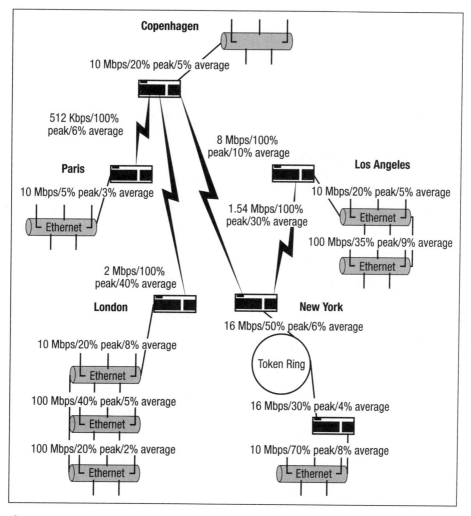

Figure 6.9
An example of how network traffic flows can be documented.

And remember, the current link speed and—even more importantly—the current bandwidth utilization on all links can (and should) be determined rather precisely. This can be done by using a network analyzer of some sort.

Identifying the User-Specific Properties

When you analyze the individual physical locations in your network infrastructure, you also have to review the user properties or characteristics. The questions that you should address at this stage include the following:

♦ How many users are at each corporate location?

♦ How large an increase or decrease in the user community should be projected? Should any individual adjustments be made in regard to specific locations?

♦ How big a change should be projected in user functions and requirements?

♦ How many users are utilizing remote access?

♦ What is the "intuitive" organization of the user's function (division, business unit, department, product line, or something else) from the user's point of view?

♦ Do any of the users participate in a joint venture with other organizations? If so, how many users does it involve?

♦ Are any of the users multilingual? If so, which languages, how many users, and how are they distributed?

♦ If possible, you should try to project how much strain each different group of users will put on the infrastructure. Often, this is done by attaching an informal rating (such as light users, medium users, and power users) to each of the users or groups of users.

Tracking a Key Network Property: Internet

Windows 2000 Server and Active Directory are built for TCP/IP networking. That is, Microsoft anticipates that you'll be using IP, DHCP, and DDNS—actually this is a requirement for being able to run Active Directory. Proper knowledge of current DNS usage and configuration will usually prove to be absolutely essential for the successful Active Directory design. This is quite opposite to IP and DHCP, where the issues usually don't arise until the implementation stages.

A detailed study of DNS is crucial because it indicates how the organization is known—internally as well as externally—and every Active Directory domain is registered as a DNS name (see Figure 6.10). Apart from staying clear of DNS name clashes, the company has to choose whether to use one or two namespaces—that is, whether the internal and external namespaces should be the same or not.

You will find a much more thorough discussion on the DNS naming subjects in the next chapter, but before moving on to that you might as well document the answers to the following questions, because they represent the business side of your DNS choices:

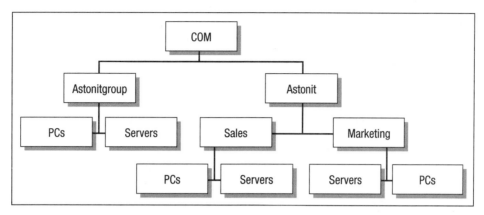

Figure 6.10
An example of how to document the corporate DNS namespace.

♦ Does the company have access to the Internet? If not, does it plan to do so in the future?

♦ Does the company currently have a presence on the Internet? If not, does it plan to do so?

♦ If your company does have an Internet presence, will it be using the same DNS names for internal and external purposes, or will another name be needed for internal purposes?

♦ Is DNS currently used on your corporate network? If so, how are the DNS naming and replication structures, and which DNS servers are employed?

Determining the Interoperability Needs

Larger enterprises commonly have several different operating system platforms and many different application software products running. To determine the interoperability issues that may arise, you need to identify the hardware and software components currently in use, including the following:

♦ Determine the operating systems currently in use.

♦ Do an inventory of the software in use.

♦ Determine the future prospects of each OS platform. Whether you need to migrate one platform or many, you need to plan how to do it. Your upgrade strategy should include what the upgrade or migration path should be, and what preparatory upgrades are needed, among other things.

♦ Determine the future prospects for each software package. Besides doing a study of the migration challenges on each software package, you should be specifically aware of the following:

  ♦ If you want to migrate mail-based directories, you often want to migrate the information contained in the existing directory (and maybe even the email boxes).

  ♦ The need for interoperability with other providers (i.e., LDAP or X.500 services).

♦ Other DNS servers in use that will have to interoperate with Windows 2000 Server's DNS or host the Active Directory namespace.

♦ A need for interoperability with security services on other platforms and from other vendors.

What You Need and Why

Table 6.2 presents a checklist that specifies the information that you absolutely must obtain to plan properly for Active Directory.

Table 6.2   Preparing a plan for the implementation of Active Directory.

Task	Reason
Obtain approval and authority from upper management to analyze and document the needs of the entire organization.	Getting the necessary organizational buy-in on the Active Directory hierarchy, which helps avoid what can otherwise quickly turn out to be a stage for internal power struggles.
Identify how the organization conducts business.	Uncovering the underlying properties of your organization and its position in the marketplace will help you to identify the very specific blend of business, application, information, and technology needs that exist in the organization, thus establishing the settings that the Active Directory has to fit into.
Identify the organizational structure.	Establishing the organizational model and organizational structure is important for choosing between a domain tree and a forest, designing the Active Directory domain tree(s), and designing the Active Directory OUs.
Identify how the organization is technically structured, including the current administration of users, information, resources, and security.	Locating all people in the organization who currently have administration of systems and operations as part of their responsibilities will help you to design the Active Directory OUs, and thus the overall concept of administrative delegation.
Identify the geographical structure.	Geographic location information is important for determining the design of sites, the placement of DCs and GCs, and the partition requirements for replication.
Identify the potential for major reorganizations or similar events.	Forecasting major events that may cause profound changes to the business in the future helps reduce the chances that Active Directory's architecture could be rendered obsolete overnight.
Identify security requirements and preferences.	Security requirements will have an influence on the design of each domain and the domain tree structure. Also, the security requirements can have a rather large influence on some of the key design decisions, such as the number of domains implemented.
Identify the speed and bandwidth utilization in the enterprise network infrastructure.	Network infrastructure information is needed to configure replication, configure sites, and analyze which of the network infrastructure upgrades may be needed to secure adequate performance.

(continued)

Table 6.2   Preparing a plan for the implementation of Active Directory *(continued)*.

Task	Reason
Profile the user community.	User information is important for the proper design of the domain structure.
Identify Internet presence and usage.	Internet needs are important for designing a DNS naming scheme that reflects current and future requirements.
Identify interoperability needs.	Interoperability is important in regard to the implementation concept that you choose.

Moving On

By now, you should realize that Windows 2000 Server is a very powerful and flexible network operating system. But that power and flexibility impose some large responsibilities on you—namely that you have to plan carefully to use the many features in support of your business and IT infrastructure goals.

That is exactly the reason why you are under obligation to examine the organization's business structure and operations in detail before you venture into the nitty-gritty of designing and planning for Windows 2000 Server and Active Directory.

Most of today's companies are built on the centralized organizational model. Luckily, this kind of organizational model provides the most straightforward fit to Active Directory. However, other organizations, especially large enterprises, tend to be somewhat decentralized. These companies have multiple businesses, each of which is very focused, and they need decentralized approaches to managing their business relationships and networks. In such forest operations, more thought often needs to go into the design of Active Directory, if you are to be successful.

The coming chapters discuss how to turn the insight that you've got for your particular organizational structure and network infrastructure into a fully fledged Active Directory design. During the course of the next six chapters, you will learn how to make an informed decision between one or multiple domains, domain trees, and forests, and how to model the OUs, DCs, sites, and much more.

When designing for Active Directory, you should almost always start with the domains. The following are the top three priorities for that:

♦ Being able to accommodate organizational changes without expensive domain changes.

♦ Being able to evolve the domain design in sync with the changes in the organizational needs.

♦ Implementing domain names that won't need to change. Often, you will find the easiest answer is to organize geographically, because geographical names tend to change very rarely in the developed countries.

Because the single domain is the simplest domain structure to create and administer, this structure should always be your first consideration. This is especially so because you're allowed to implement OUs within a single domain to better reflect your organization, and thus usually will be able to achieve the same goals as would be possible by implementing additional domains.

Note

Active Directory's OU object works to reduce the number of domains needed to create your company's management hierarchy compared to the situation in Windows NT Server.

But before you get into the intricacies of domain modeling, you have to endure a detailed introduction to the Domain Name System (DNS), which is the subject of the next chapter. The fact that DNS is the cornerstone of the Internet and, also, a prerequisite for Active Directory, means that it pretty much holds the key to choosing the proper naming standards on your network as well as ensuring a good operations record.

Chapter 7
Determining the DNS Structure

After you've collected the corporate information outlined in Chapter 6, you are ready to delve into the core design tasks. The first part of the design phase is primarily a question of names; that is, establishing what your DNS naming scheme of the Active Directory domains should look like. In addition to choosing the proper names and perhaps laying out naming conventions, the naming process includes the decision of whether the names should be the same on both the Internet and the corporate intranet, how to establish redundancy for resilience and load balancing of the name resolution, how the naming replication structure should be set up, and how to address several different interoperability concerns. Making all of these decisions requires that you understand the intricacies of the Domain Name System (DNS) standard, which Active Directory uses as its location service.

As you work through this chapter, you will recognize that choosing the proper names probably is the least of your troubles in the naming process. If you have a PC-only background, understanding DNS likely will be your biggest challenge in determining the naming standards. Judging from experience, most of you have exactly that background, which is why this chapter starts with a large segment on DNS fundamentals. If you are already familiar with DNS, you can breeze through the segment that serves as a DNS primer.

Note
The DNS primer includes information on Dynamic DNS (DDNS) and the other new standards used by Active Directory, so I would advise against skipping the DNS section altogether—no matter how experienced with DNS you might already be.

However, I urge you to evaluate your DNS skills closely before you choose to skip the DNS primer, because DNS is a very fine art that isn't well understood, even by most resolute Unix users. Actually, one of the main reasons that DNS is quite hard to master is the same reason that Active Directory poses a challenge: DNS is a hierarchical namespace. But don't let that intimidate you. Although DNS is a hard trade to master, it is by no means impossible.

> ### Note
> *You might want to note that this chapter also features a discussion on the base properties of WINS, because my real-life experience has shown it to be impossible to avoid having some kind of NetBIOS name resolution functionality present in the network infrastructure. So, chances are that you'll have to implement this terrible invention unless you want to try your luck with distributing LMHOSTS files to your hosts.*

An Example of DNS in the Active Directory Setting

Microsoft has chosen to harness DNS for the Active Directory location service. In Active Directory, Windows 2000 Server domain names are DNS names. And so, it follows that the same simple naming conventions, which are used on the Internet also apply to Active Directory. For example, if **astonitgroup.com** is the name of an Active Directory domain, it will also be the name of a DNS domain (which is the default setting; however, the domain name and DNS name don't have to be the same). Correspondingly, **JamesSmith@astonitgroup.com** can be both an Internet email address and a username in the **astonitgroup.com** domain.

DNS is the tool that enables you to resolve Active Directory domains and domain host computers into their TCP/IP addresses, which constitute the "native" language of the underlying network infrastructure and hence are needed to establish a network connection to Active Directory. So, although you could save a lot of complexity by using TCP/IP addresses from the outset, doing so probably won't get you anywhere in terms of usability. Common network users typically won't comprehend—and even more important, won't be able to remember—the proper TCP/IP address for their needed services, whereas they are much more likely to remember a name, depending on the complexity and familiarity of your naming scheme.

The most important single application for DNS (see Figure 7.1) is the resolution of an Active Directory domain name and the subsequent identification of a directory server that serves the particular Active Directory domain. An example is when an Active Directory-compliant client needs to log on to Active Directory over the network (the NetLogon process), which occurs as follows:

1. The networking part of the NetLogon process starts off by querying DNS for the SRV records (which indicate the domain controllers [DCs] that serve the requested directory) for the particular Active Directory domain, which is in the same site as the client. If the client wants to log in to the **astonitgroup.com** domain in the London site, the query

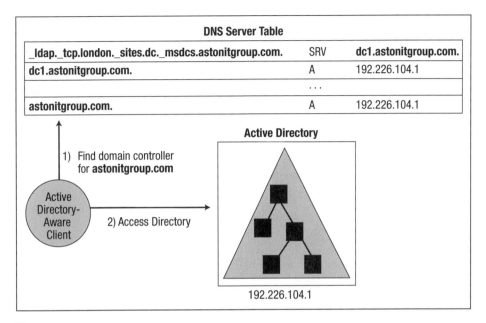

DNS Server Table		
_ldap._tcp.london._sites.dc._msdcs.astonitgroup.com.	SRV	dc1.astonitgroup.com.
dc1.astonitgroup.com.	A	192.226.104.1
	...	
astonitgroup.com.	A	192.226.104.1

1) Find domain controller for **astonitgroup.com**

Active Directory-Aware Client

2) Access Directory

Active Directory

192.226.104.1

Figure 7.1
DNS lookup is used as part of many different processes, such as NetLogon.

requests the SRV records for **_ldap._tcp.london._sites.dc._msdcs.astonitgroup.com**, which is held in the DNS Server.

2. Upon receiving the server list of DCs serving the **astonitgroup.com** domain in the London site, the client selects a server from the list and tries to make contact with it—getting the IP address from the DNS A (Address) record for the target server.

3. The contacted DC will then use the subnet information presented by the client to determine the DC closest to the workstation (this is defined via the Active Directory site concept). If the current DC is not in that site, the server will notify the client of a better DC to use.

From then on, it will pretty much be business as usual (that is, pretty much the same as with NetLogon in Windows NT Workstation 4) to complete the authentication of the client for the domain. However, there are differences to be found. For example, the client will be logging on using Kerberos rather than NTLM, the client will synchronize its clock with the server's, and the Active Directory is queried for GPOs using LDAP. (Chapter 20 includes a more complete discussion on the various steps of the login process).

As you can see, the functionality needed by the NetLogon process (and many other processes that likewise need to access a DC that serves a particular Active Directory domain) depends on the registration with DNS—by the Windows 2000 Server domain controllers (DCs)—of one or more SRV records, along with the usual A-type record and PTR-type record (see the section "The Standard Resource Record Format" for more information on these records).

This registration is done automatically if the particular DNS Server supports the new Dynamic DNS standard. Otherwise, the DNS Server administrator needs to add the records and keep them updated manually. And, to make matters worse, the same goes for all the Active Directory-aware clients on the network. Each client has to be present in the DNS table as an A-type record and a PTR-type record (that is, forward and reverse lookups), specifying a mapping of the client DNS name to an IP address, and vice versa. This alone should present you with a very persuasive argument for not employing anything but DNS Servers that support DDNS in an Active Directory setting. You might also want to note that any on-the-fly changes in the IP addresses of the network resources listed in the DNS table will be updated automatically, if you have implemented the Microsoft DHCP Server and employ DDNS Servers.

From WINS to DDNS

Even though a network looks completely different today than it did 10 years ago, Microsoft's approach to networking has changed surprisingly little from the introduction of its first network operating system (LAN Manager) in 1987 until the advent of Windows 2000 Server.

At the time when LAN Manager was launched, NetBIOS and NetBEUI were the name of the game. And while NetBEUI met increasing opposition during the 1990s, culminating with the change to TCP/IP as the default setting in Windows NT 4, NetBIOS has continued to hold its ground—until now.

With Windows 2000 Server, Microsoft has turned NetBIOS into a legacy solution in favor of a pure TCP/IP solution that is based on the familiar DHCP and DNS standards—and thus eliminated the need for Microsoft's proprietary *Windows Internet Name Service (WINS)* in the process, because WINS is a name service designed for machines that communicate using NetBIOS on top of TCP/IP. Thus, if you already have experience with NT Server 4, your WINS skills will be outdated as soon as you update to Active Directory (ironically, Windows 2000 Server includes a new and much-improved version of the WINS service that can be used for backward-compatibility purposes). But that isn't necessarily bad news for you, because WINS has several disadvantages that make the time you spend learning DNS worthwhile:

♦ WINS is a Microsoft proprietary technology, whereas DNS is not.

♦ WINS has earned a solid reputation of being rather flaky inside large environments and is neither easy to administer nor troubleshoot, largely because NetBIOS was originally designed for implementing user-friendly names on a small LAN.

♦ WINS replication facilities are so weak that they don't contain any genuine security facilities (for example, to guard against unauthorized WINS Servers).

♦ With the advent of the Internet, most people have introduced the DNS name service on their LANs anyway.

Field experiences have shown that NetBIOS isn't all that dead after all. The reason is as simple as it's annoying: Microsoft evidently forgot to remove Windows 2000's reliance on NetBIOS in a few places. So, you should keep that WINS architecture in place in order to avoid any unfortunate surprises.

DNS was designed from the outset for high performance and a stable operation on large networks. For example, the hierarchical namespace of DNS provides the best possible starting point for searches and assures that names are globally unique, even though they have only been inspected locally. The hierarchical namespace also gives you a much more varied universe of names from which to choose than does WINS, which restricts you to 15 characters in a totally flat namespace—regardless of the number of hosts.

DNS includes features that allow implementation of much greater fault tolerance than is possible with WINS. Furthermore, DNS contains a greater variety of more advanced and flexible setup options, enabling you to adapt its administration, operation, and security far more precisely to your organization's needs.

Overall, DNS has only four disadvantages—and a long range of weighty advantages, especially for use in large networking environments—compared to WINS/NetBIOS:

♦ DNS names can be a bit more difficult to understand for an ordinary user, because they consist of several parts and the use of separators (periods). However, the explosive growth of the Internet has largely diminished this problem, because Internet users are exposed regularly to DNS names.

♦ DNS doesn't include standardized capabilities for registering network services beyond mail servers in the name table. However, this shortcoming is addressed by a proposed extension to DNS (documented in RFC 2052) that specifies a new resource record (RR) type.

♦ DNS doesn't contain capabilities for passing off updates from the primary to the secondary DNS Servers, in case of changes in the name table. DNS only allows for defining the secondary servers doing a pull of information stored on the primary server with certain intervals. However, this shortcoming is removed by a proposed extension, **DNS NOTIFY** (documented in RFC 1996).

♦ DNS is limited to *static* names, which means that the names on all network resources (servers and the like) must be input manually by the administrator. This concept is feasible only for situations in which few changes happen once in a while. This shortcoming also is addressed by a proposed extension, Dynamic DNS (documented in RFC 2136 and 2137).

Introducing the Domain Name System

The DNS naming system usually can be found in use on any "pure" TCP/IP network (for example, those networks where Unix systems are employed). DNS names basically work the same way as NetBIOS names. Just like NetBIOS names, DNS names are used to identify the accessible resources on the network in a more user-friendly way than IP addresses (which always are in the x1.x2.x3.x4 format, wherein x1 through x4 are integers between 0 and 255 that define the address, such as 10.1.4.1). Requesting access to a server via a name rather than a numerical network address is much easier, because users typically don't comprehend nor have any familiarity with a network address. You probably are already familiar with DNS names because they are used on the Web—for example, **www.microsoft.com** and **www.coriolis.com**.

DNS is a well-known and widely accepted Internet standard for naming and registering resources, which can also be used on private TCP/IP-based networks. DNS names are constructed in a slightly different way from NetBIOS names, because the world of NetBIOS is as flat as a pancake, whereas DNS is a hierarchical namespace. DNS computer names consist of several parts (or *hierarchies*), each of which is separated by a period.

For example, in the naming of computers, NetBIOS names are limited to the actual computer name (or even an abbreviation of that name, because NetBIOS names are limited to a maximum of 15 characters), whereas DNS names consist of two parts: a computer name (called a *host name*) and a *domain name*. When the two parts of the DNS name are combined, they form a *fully qualified domain name (FQDN)*. An example of an FQDN is **ntbeta.microsoft.com**, where the computer name is **ntbeta** and the domain name is **microsoft.com**.

As mentioned, the Web (among others) is based on DNS names. This means, for example, that when the URL **http://www.astonitgroup.com** is typed in the Web browser, the browser treats the URL as a DNS name request. The request searches for a computer named **www**, located in the **astonitgroup.com** domain. When the DNS Server on which this computer is registered is found, the server sends back an IP address to the browser, which then can use it to contact Aston IT Group's Web server (this is what the "http:" protocol specification tells it).

Why DNS?

DNS was designed in 1984 to solve escalating problems with the old name-to-address mapping system used on the Internet. The old system consisted of a single file, known as the host table, maintained by the Stanford Research Institute's Network Information Center (SRI-NIC). As new host names trickled in, SRI-NIC added them to the table. Systems administrators would grab the newest version and update their domain name servers. But, as the Internet grew, the host table became unwieldy and clearly wasn't the most practical or effective way to update and distribute the information.

With DNS, no single organization is responsible for keeping the domain namespace up-to-date. DNS is a distributed database, which means that it exists on many different name servers around the world, with no one server storing all the information. Because of this, DNS has the capacity for almost unlimited growth.

Understanding DNS

Viewed in a slightly more abstract way, DNS forms a distributed database system that provides a hierarchical namespace for identifying computers on the Internet—in exactly the same way as is the case with Active Directory, which also is built on the hierarchy premise. That is also why DNS constitutes such a good match to Active Directory.

DNS was designed to solve the problems that arose when the number of computers on the Internet grew drastically in the beginning of the 1980s. The fundamental specifications for DNS were defined in RFCs 1034 and 1035, which were accepted as Internet Engineering Task Force (IETF) standards in 1987 and remain in force today. Naturally, the DNS specification has been updated several times since 1987, which has resulted in some new RFCs. If you want to study DNS in depth, your minimum reading requirements should be the RFCs shown in Table 7.1.

Note

Several RFCs in Table 7.1 are not part of the official DNS standard, but instead include invaluable advice on DNS. The tips on common errors and strategies for troubleshooting, for example, often provide educational and enlightened insights that surpass the more abstract description of the actual DNS standard.

The conceptual namespace on which DNS is based is a hierarchical and logical tree structure, which is called *domain namespace*—which colloquially has become DNS.

The top level in domain namespace represents the most general groupings, and these domain names are standardized. Currently, 7 top-level generic domains and approximately 200 top-level geographical domains exist. The top level in domain namespace is currently administered by the *Internet Authorized Numbers Authority (IANA)*, which is responsible for

Table 7.1   RFCs relevant to DNS.

RFC Number	Title
1034	Domain Names—Concepts and Facilities
1035	Domain Names—Implementation and Specification
1101	DNS Encoding of Network Names and Other Types
1464	Using the Domain Name System to Store Arbitrary String Attributes
1536	Common DNS Implementation Errors and Suggested Fixes
1591	Domain Name System Structure and Delegation
1664	Using the Internet DNS to Distribute Mail Addresses Mapping Tables
1706	DNS NSAP Resource Records
1712	DNS Encoding of Geographical Location
1713	Tools for DNS Debugging
1794	DNS Support for Load Balancing
1912	Common DNS Operational and Configuration Errors

the delegation of administrative responsibility for parts of domain namespace and registration of domain names. For example, IANA has delegated responsibility for the four most important generic top-level domains to the Internet Network Information Center (InterNIC, at **www.internic.net**).

Domain names are administered through the use of a distributed database system, in which the name information is kept on name servers that are spread across the Internet. Every name server has database files (known as *zone files*) that contain the registered information for a chosen region within the domain tree hierarchy.

As mentioned, the names in the DNS database form a logical tree structure called domain namespace. Figure 7.2 demonstrates the top level in the Internet domain namespace hierarchy for the U.S. (while it's actually the generic domain namespace, it nonetheless is the primary delivery vehicle for U.S.-bound entities sporting an Internet presence). Table 7.2 shows the type of organization represented by each domain extension (even though the original intent with the **.com**, **.net**, and **.org** top domains isn't being enforced anymore). Table 7.3 shows the domains for the rest of the world.

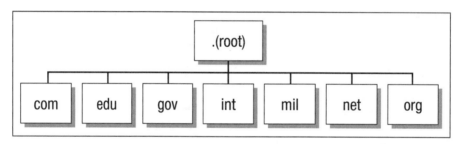

Figure 7.2
Because DNS is a hierarchical namespace, the top generic domains in the Internet DNS hierarchy should be represented in this manner.

Table 7.2   The top-level Internet domain in the so-called generic DNS hierarchy.

Top Domain	Type of Organization
.com	Commercial
.edu	Educational
.gov	U.S. Government
.int	International
.mil	U.S. Military
.net	Networking
.org	Nonprofit

Table 7.3   The top domains outside the generic domains contain an abbreviation for each country.

Country Code	Country
ac	Ascension Island
ad	Andorra
ae	United Arab Emirates
af	Afghanistan
ag	Antigua, Barbuda
ai	Anguilla
al	Albania
am	Armenia
an	Netherlands Antilles
ao	Angola
aq	Antarctica
ar	Argentina
as	American Samoa
at	Austria
au	Australia
aw	Aruba
az	Azerbaijan
ba	Bosnia, Herzegovina
bb	Barbados
bd	Bangladesh
be	Belgium
bf	Burkina Faso
bg	Bulgaria
bh	Bahrain
bi	Burundi
bj	Benin
bm	Bermuda
bn	Brunei Darussalam
bo	Bolivia
br	Brazil
bs	Bahamas
bt	Bhutan
bv	Bouvet Island
bw	Botswana
by	Belarus
bz	Belize
ca	Canada
cc	Cocos (Keeling) Island
cd	Congo, Democratic People's Republic
cf	Central African Republic
cg	Congo, Republic of

(continued)

Table 7.3   The top domains outside the generic domains contain an abbreviation for each country *(continued)*.

Country Code	Country
ch	Switzerland
ci	Ivory Coast/Cote D'Ivoire
ck	Cook Islands
cl	Chile
cm	Cameroon
cn	China
co	Colombia
cr	Costa Rica
cs	Czech Republic
cu	Cuba
cv	Cape Verde
cx	Christmas Island
cy	Cyprus
de	Germany
dj	Djibouti
dk	Denmark
dm	Dominica
do	Dominican Republic
dz	Algeria
ec	Ecuador
ee	Estonia
eg	Egypt
eh	Western Sahara
er	Eritrea
es	Spain
et	Ethiopia
fi	Finland
fj	Fiji
fk	Falkland Island (Malvinas)
fm	Micronesia, Federal States of
fo	Faroe Islands
fr	France
ga	Gabon
gd	Grenada
ge	Georgia
gf	French Guiana
gg	Guernsey
gh	Ghana
gi	Gibraltar

(continued)

Table 7.3 **The top domains outside the generic domains contain an abbreviation for each country** *(continued)*.

Country Code	Country
gl	Greenland
gm	Gambia
gn	Guinea
gp	Guadeloupe
gq	Equatorial Guinea
gr	Greece
gs	South Georgia and Sandwich Islands
gt	Guatemala
gu	Guam
gw	Guinea-Bissau
gy	Guyana
hk	Hong Kong
hm	Heard and McDonald Islands
hn	Honduras
hr	Croatia/Hrvatska
ht	Haiti
hu	Hungary
id	Indonesia
ie	Ireland
il	Israel
im	Isle of Man
in	India
io	British Indian Ocean Territory
iq	Iraq
ir	Iran
is	Iceland
it	Italy
je	Jersey
jm	Jamaica
jo	Jordan
jp	Japan
ke	Kenya
kg	Kyrgyzstan
kh	Cambodia
ki	Kiribati
km	Comoros
kn	Saint Kitts and Nevis
kp	Korea, Democratic People's Republic
kr	Korea, Republic of
kw	Kuwait

(continued)

Table 7.3 **The top domains outside the generic domains contain an abbreviation for each country** *(continued).*

Country Code	Country
ky	Cayman Islands
kz	Kazakhstan
la	Lao, People's Democratic Republic
lb	Lebanon
lc	Saint Lucia
li	Liechtenstein
lk	Sri Lanka
lr	Liberia
ls	Lesotho
lt	Lithuania
lu	Luxembourg
lv	Latvia
ly	Libyan Arab Jamahiriya
ma	Morocco
mc	Monaco
md	Moldova, Republic of
mg	Madagascar
mh	Marshall Islands
mk	Macedonia, former Yugoslavia Republic
ml	Mali
mm	Myanmar
mn	Mongolia
mo	Macau
mp	Northern Mariana Island
mq	Martinique
mr	Mauritania
ms	Montserrat
mt	Malta
mu	Mauritius
mv	Maldives
mw	Malawi
mx	Mexico
my	Malaysia
mz	Mozambique
na	Namibia
nc	New Caledonia
ne	Niger
nf	Norfolk Island
ng	Nigeria
ni	Nicaragua
nl	Netherlands

(continued)

Table 7.3 The top domains outside the generic domains contain an abbreviation for each country *(continued).*

Country Code	Country
no	Norway
np	Nepal
nr	Nauru
nu	Niue
nz	New Zealand
om	Oman
pa	Panama
pe	Peru
pf	French Polynesia
pg	Papua New Guinea
ph	Philippines
pk	Pakistan
pl	Poland
pm	St. Pierre and Miquelon
pn	Pitcairn Island
pr	Puerto Rico
pt	Portugal
pw	Palau
py	Paraguay
qa	Qatar
re	Reunion Island
ro	Romania
ru	Russian Federation
rw	Rwanda
sa	Saudi Arabia
sb	Solomon Islands
sc	Seychelles
sd	Sudan
se	Sweden
sg	Singapore
sh	St. Helena
si	Slovenia
sj	Svalbard and Jan Mayen Islands
sk	Slovakia
sl	Sierra Leone
sm	San Marino
sn	Senegal
so	Somalia
sr	Suriname
st	Sao Tome and Principe
sv	El Salvador

(continued)

Table 7.3   The top domains outside the generic domains contain an abbreviation for each country *(continued).*

Country Code	Country
sy	Syrian Arab Republic
sz	Swaziland
tc	Turks and Caicos Islands
td	Chad
tf	French Southern Territories
tg	Togo
th	Thailand
tj	Tajikistan
tk	Tokelau
tm	Turkmenistan
tn	Tunisia
to	Tonga
tp	East Timor
tr	Turkey
tt	Trinidad and Tobago
tv	Tuvalu
tw	Taiwan
tz	Tanzania
ua	Ukraine
ug	Uganda
uk	United Kingdom
um	US Minor Outlying Island
us	United States
uy	Uruguay
uz	Uzbekistan
va	Vatican City State
vc	St.Vincent and the Grenadines
ve	Venezuela
vg	Virgin Islands (British)
vi	Virgin Islands (US)
vn	Vietnam
vu	Vanuatu
wf	Wallis and Futuna Islands
ws	Samoa
ye	Yemen
yt	Mayotte
yu	Yugoslavia
za	South Africa
zm	Zambia
zr	Zaire
zw	Zimbabwe

Domain namespace forms the entire tree structure—from the top level in the domain to the lowest level, where the hosts are located. A domain that contains another domain is called a *parent* domain, and as you know from X.500 and Active Directory, each domain has one, and only one, parent. At the top of the DNS tree is the *root* domain, which has no parent. A domain that is contained within another domain is a *child* domain—which is more commonly referred to as a *subdomain*.

The conventions for presenting the tree structure as a DNS name are quite simple: The domain names are written from the child domain up through the tree hierarchy of the parent domains, and each level in the domain (and the computer name) is separated by a period. In principle, every domain name can be seen as a combination of one or more domain components. The following are the four domain components that are ordinarily worked with:

♦ *Top-level domain (also known as the root domain)*—Always indicated farthest to the right in the DNS name. The top level typically consists of a name code of two or three characters that identify either a country or a type of organization (refer to Tables 7.2 and 7.3). For each top-level domain, IANA formally appoints one responsible party, called a *registrar*, who is responsible for the delegation of the subdomains of each top-level domain.

♦ *Second-level domain*—Consists of a unique name of varying length that has been formally registered by the registrar for an individual or an organization connected to the Internet.

♦ *Subdomain name*—A registered domain can be divided further into a random number of underlying domains by adding subdomains.

♦ *Host name*—Placed farthest to the left in the domain name, a host name identifies a specific computer on the network.

Note

To understand the meaning of a domain name, read it from right to left. You should note that the ordering from specific to general in domain namespace is the opposite of the elements in an IP address, in which the first (leftmost) number represents the most general division.

The hierarchical structure—and the possibility to subdivide the domains to match the needs of a specific job—is the founding concept of DNS domains (see Figure 7.3). It's the hierarchical structure, which guarantees that the Internet will never run out of domain names, even if the growth doesn't stop until everybody in the world has registered their very own domain. The hierarchical structure also enables network administration to be divided in a manner that is logical, as well as easy to understand—each organization on the Internet can be allocated the authority for a large or small part of domain namespace, meaning that the organization's administrator is responsible for the administration, subdivision, and naming in that domain namespace partition.

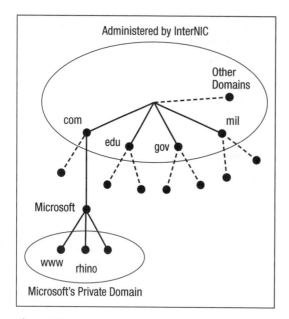

Figure 7.3
DNS is based on a hierarchical tree structure, which is shown here from Microsoft's point of view.

Every time InterNIC (or another delegation authority) accepts a new second-level domain, the particular organization is allocated authority to administer the contents of its own resources within that domain, in the form of subdomains, zones, and computer names. A DNS name can consist of as many as 255 characters. Each level in domain namespace can consist of as many as 63 characters and must be unique relative to the overlying level, to ensure that all DNS names in the world are unique—a necessary prerequisite for the execution of correct name resolutions. According to the RFC, for a domain name to be compatible across the Internet, it may consist only of the English alphabet, decimal numbers, and hyphens. No distinction is made between lowercase and uppercase letters in DNS names (in other words, they are case-insensitive).

DNS Servers

The practical handling of domain namespace happens through the name servers, also known as *DNS Servers*. DNS is based on a client/server model, in which the name servers contain information about a subset of the DNS database (the *zone*) and make this information accessible to clients (called *resolvers*). According to the DNS model, a client requests information about a DNS name from a name server, which can, if necessary, ask other name servers for the information if it doesn't have the information at its own disposal.

Besides handling requests, a name server usually has responsibility for one or more zones. A zone is the smallest administrative unit for a name server, and it can cover a large or small part of domain namespace. A zone can consist of a single domain or a domain that has underlying domains (that is, second-level domains or subdomains). A zone is rooted by a specific domain node, which is called the *root* domain of the zone. Each zone assumes the form of a file. A zone file consists of resource records (RRs), which are standardized divisions of the zone's configuration information. Among the RRs is the pool of DNS names and their corresponding IP addresses, which is where the name resolution has its starting point.

It is crucial to understand the difference between a domain and a zone. A *domain* refers to a single node and all the nodes placed under it in the domain tree. A zone, however, covers only those RRs that are delegated to a specific name server. Each zone is anchored at a specific domain node—referred to as the zone's *root domain* (see Figure 7.4). A zone, as such, may coincide with a domain, but can also include only part of a domain (the rest of which could be delegated to other name servers). So, multiple zones may exist within a domain and vice versa. To put it in another way, a zone is a point of delegation in the DNS tree. It contains all names from a certain point downward, except for those that are delegated to other zones.

Whereas the concept of a domain is what makes DNS a very simple and effective device, zones make DNS effective to administer and use. By delegating zones to different name servers spread across the entire network, the speed of name resolution can be improved, while simultaneously placing the administration tools exactly where events occur. Zone delegation sometimes also results in a more effective replication of the domain information.

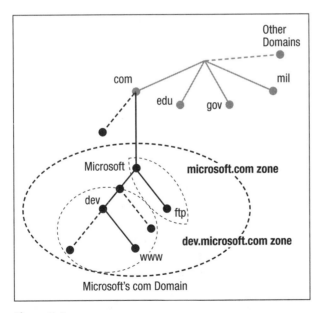

Figure 7.4
Each zone is rooted in a specific node in the domain (the root domain). In return, a domain always consists of all the subdomains and computer names that are placed below the root of the domain.

If you want a specific DNS Server to answer requests within a certain part of domain namespace, that DNS Server must be configured to have authority within that zone. This authority is configured with a special RR called the *Start of Authority (SOA)*, which is typically placed at the start of the zone file. A SOA record's presence in a server's zone file indicates that the server is the best source of information about that specific part of domain namespace. Consequently, DNS administrators distinguish between two kinds of name servers:

♦ A *primary server*—Contains the "original" copy of the data files for a particular zone (identified by the SOA RR), including RRs for all underlying domains and computer names. The server gets its zone data from its own local file. Changes for the zone are carried out on this server.

♦ A *secondary server*—Receives data for its zone(s) from another name server. The process of receiving this replicated zone information (meaning the actual zone database file) is carried out periodically from another authoritative name server—the *zone transfer*. When defining a zone on a name server as secondary, you must designate a name server from which to obtain the zone information. The source of zone information for a secondary server is referred to as a *master server* (which can be either a primary or secondary server). When a secondary server is initialized, it will contact the master server and initiate a zone transfer with that server.

Note

You might also be confronted with yet another set of terms in regard to name servers. Here, the primary name server is known as the primary master server and the secondary servers are referred to as slaves. In some cases, the slaves are segmented into masters and slaves, with the masters being secondary name servers from which one or multiple secondaries are pulling zone information.

It is important to understand that these name servers represent a separate concept from the DNS Server as a whole. Because the information for each zone is recorded in a separate file, the names "primary server" and "secondary server" are relative to each zone. Thus, a specific DNS Server can function both as a primary server for one or multiple zones and as a secondary server for other zones.

But remember that one—and only one—primary server must be present for each zone. For compliance with the RFCs, at least one secondary server is needed for each primary server zone that is established, because a secondary server is needed for securing the operational stability of the zone (that is, to avoid a zone's going missing because of a crash at a server). Additional secondary name servers may be advantageous, depending on fault-tolerance requirements, the need for name resolution from distant locations, and the need to reduce the load on the primary server. Actually, if you're used to Windows NT Server, you might benefit from thinking of the name server characteristics as being the same as they were with domain controllers (one PDC and multiple BDCs for each domain).

The Definition of a DNS Server

A DNS Server is simply a computer running DNS software that services queries placed on a specific TCP port. DNS Server software can be found by a variety of names, depending on the operating system. The built-in Windows 2000 Server service is simply referred to as DNS Server Service, while Unix users usually depend on Berkeley Internet Name Daemon (BIND), which implements an Internet name server for Berkeley Software Distribution (BSD)-derived versions of the Unix OSs. BIND consists of a server (or daemon) called "named" and a resolver library.

DNS software generally consists of two elements: the actual name server (in Windows 2000 Server: The DNS Server Service) and a resolver (in Windows 2000: The DNS Client Service). Whereas the name server only is needed at a computer that is being used as a DNS Server, the resolver is needed on all computers that use DNS—so you might want to think of the resolver as being the DNS client. The name server responds to resolver requests by supplying name-to-address conversions. When it doesn't know the answer, it asks another name server for the information. A listing of the available resolver methods appears under "Registration and Resolution of DNS Names," later in the chapter.

When the DNS Server is initialized, it (per definition) needs the name of a boot file that contains the names of the database files that contain the DNS information. The first record in the boot file contains setup directives, which often include directory information and point to the directory in which the DNS zone files reside. Each of the remaining records in the boot file contains a field that describes the base properties of a DNS database file. One of the fields might read like this:

primary **foo.com foo.com.zone**

To be precise, each field specifies the type of DNS information (how the name server is acting for the zone specified), the zone specified in the file, and its file name. In the example shown above, the fields specify that it's a primary zone for the **foo.com** domain, which is stored in the **foo.com.zone** file.

The final record in the boot file always should define where the DNS cache information for the root domain (**"."**) can be found—the so-called root hints. This isn't a "real" cache, but rather a set of fixed pointers to the higher-level DNS databases (usually the IP addresses of the top-level name servers, if the DNS Server is part of the Internet namespace) that will be used by the name server for forwarding any name queries that it can't resolve on its own and doesn't have any clue as to which name server to forward it to. The correct way to treat the root hints table file is to download a new copy periodically from the InterNIC at **ftp://rs.internic.net/domain/named.cache**. However, several DNS Servers treat the content of this file as being fixed forever—thus, essentially hard-coded into the DNS Server. You should be keenly aware of the contents of the root hints table file, especially if you are using the DNS Server in a setting that isn't part of the Internet (as you might find the DNS Server to be unable to resolve some DNS queries because they go "into the blue" as they're forwarded to these top-level name servers that can't be reached).

For the sake of completeness, you also should know about another "type" of name server, which actually is just a specialized instance of the name server's setup. But because you might run into this term when communicating with battle-hardened DNS admins, you have to be familiar with it:

♦ *Slave server*—Always forwards queries that it can't satisfy from its cache to a fixed list of forwarding servers, instead of interacting with the name servers for the root and other domains. One or more forwarding servers may be sent the queries, and each one of them will be tried in turn until the list is exhausted. A slave-and-forwarder configuration is typically used when you don't want all the servers at a particular site to interact with the rest of the Internet servers. No prohibition exists against declaring a server to be a slave, even though it also has primary and/or secondary zones; the effect is still that anything in the local server's cache or zones is answered, and anything else is forwarded by using the forwarder's list.

Additionally, many DNS administrators refer to yet another type of name server that can serve no zones and only answer queries via the cache. However, this concept does induce a fair level of confusion, because—contrary to the other terms mentioned in this section—it is referring to the DNS Server as a whole, not just a zone:

♦ *Caching-only server*—A server that is able to work only on information received from other name servers, which is stored in its cache until the records expire (the expiration of each record is based on a Time-To-Live field that is specified by the server that initially fulfilled the name resolution request). By definition, a caching-only server isn't authoritative for any zone. That is, a caching-only server isn't associated with any specific DNS zone (namely, it isn't used as a primary server nor secondary server for any zone) and doesn't contain any active database files. When first activated, a caching-only server doesn't have any knowledge whatsoever of the DNS domain structure. But every time the server makes a request to a DNS Server on behalf of a client, it will register the information in its name cache, which consequently can grow quite comprehensive over time because it will have all the results of names previously resolved.

Note

In Microsoft's DNS Server, a subdomain is added to an existing zone by choosing the New Domain...option on the short cut menu. You define a new zone inside an existing domain by choosing New Delegation...on the short cut menu. For defining an entirely new domain (and zone), you'll have to choose the New Zone... entry, which is only available outside of the existing zones (that is, on the Forward Lookup Zones and Reverse Lookup Zones folder entries).

The Standard Resource Record Format

As mentioned in the last section, each zone file consists of a number of resource records. The generalized format of each RR is as follows:

{name} {TTL} *addr-class   Record Type   Record Specific data*

The first field in any DNS RR is always a domain name, which is optional. If it is missing, then the name/address from the previous record is implied. Note that all absolute names should end with a trailing dot. Absolute addresses (FQDNs) are relative to the root.

The second field is an optional Time-To-Live (TTL) field. This specifies the length of time that the information in this field should be considered valid. By leaving this field blank, the default Time-To-Live is specified by the Start Of Authority (SOA) RR.

The TTL value is very important. High values lead to lower network traffic and faster response times, whereas lower values tend to generate lots of requests, but allow faster propagation of changes. Only changes and deletions from the zone are affected by the TTLs. Additions propagate according to the Refresh value in the SOA. Internet sites typically use default TTLs for their zones that vary from around half a day to seven days.

The third field indicates the address type. In today's DNS databases, it's usually the string "IN", which indicates an Internet address. This field is present for historical purposes (when more types of addresses existed than the one used by TCP/IP) and backward-compatibility with older systems.

The fourth field states the type of the RR. This field is followed by optional parameters that are dependent on the type of the RR. The most common RRs are the following:

♦ *Start of Authority (SOA) records*—Indicate the authoritative name server for a given zone and a few additional administrative items like the following items in this list:

  ♦ *Serial number*—An incremental counter that tracks changes to the database, which in turn makes the server able to keep track of when a zone transfer is needed.

  ♦ *Refresh interval*—Specifies how often secondary name servers should poll for updates. The default value is 15 minutes.

  ♦ *Retry interval*—Specifies how long a secondary name server should wait before trying to reconnect to the primary name server when the previous connection failed. The default value is 10 minutes.

  ♦ *Expire time*—Specifies how long a secondary server should continue to respond to name resolution queries after having failed to connect to the primary name server. The default value is 24 hours.

  ♦ *Minimum TTL value*—Determines the minimum time that any RR registered in the zone will have to stay valid (in other words, how long you can safely include it in a cache). The default value is 1 hour. You're allowed to assign different TTL values to the individual RRs.

♦ *Address (A) records*—Supply the IP address for a specific host name. Known as **host** in Microsoft's DNS Server.

♦ *Canonical Name (CNAME) records*—Specify the alias or nicknames for the official host names. Nicknames are useful when a well-known host changes its name. In that case, having a CNAME record is usually a good idea, so that people and applications still using the old name will be sent off to the right network location. Multiple A records are also allowed for a particular address, thus providing alias (or alternate) host names. However, it is usually easier (and less prone to human error) to supply one A record for an address and to use CNAME records to define alias host names for that address. Known as **alias** in Microsoft's DNS Server.

♦ *Pointer (PTR) records*—Associate a host name with a specific IP address, which is called *reverse name lookups* (obtaining the host name from an IP address). PTR RRs can't be registered in the "normal" database files—that is, the ones that hold A RRs, MX RRs, etc. Rather, they can only be stored in the so-called reverse database file, which is a specialized type of domain database file that is designed exclusively for the needs of doing reverse name lookups. The name of a reverse lookup domain is the reverse-dotted-decimal notation of the domain's IP address segment, followed by **in-addr.arpa.dns**, an indication of the use of IP addresses within the ARPA address assignment domain. The name of a PTR RR is the reverse-dotted-decimal notation of the IP address, followed by **in-addr.arpa**. The **in-addr.arpa** nomenclature is a holdover from when more than one type of address was in use and more than one addressing authority existed.

♦ *Mail Exchanger (MX) records*—Define the SMTP mail system(s) that are configured for a particular domain name. The number preceding the address is known as the preference value. When a remote user sends mail to **some_user@some_domain.com**, the remote mail system looks up the MX record in the zone that pertains to **some_domain.com**, and then the remote mailer attempts to establish an SMTP connection with the mail system that has the lowest preference value. If the system isn't available, the remote mailer will try to connect to the next mail system (if applicable)

Reverse Lookups

DNS includes one of the worst examples of when standards work goes haywire: the reverse lookup record. Reverse lookups are needed to obtain the host name from an IP address. The fact that the administrator has to do the registering of IP addresses to DNS names manually makes perfect sense, because the IP addresses need to be registered in the zone that "owns" the IP subnet in question, which need not coincide with the zone that "owns" the domain.

However, this doesn't explain the very clumsy syntax of the reverse lookup record (PTR RR). The syntax of rearranging the IP address (including turning around the decimal notation of the domain's IP address) and adding **in-addr.arpa** is quite awful. Allegedly, the reason the reverse lookup record looks so stupid is that the designers of DNS forgot to address the need to obtain the host name from the IP address. Consequently, the PTR RR was implemented as a last-minute resolution for avoiding the only other possible method: to conduct a thorough search of all domains in the DNS namespace, which would be too exhaustive, if not impossible, to perform in any practical way. And for some strange reason, no one has thought to revise the syntax of the PTR RR until now. So, instead of imposing a small syntactic change on a fairly simple standard before the Internet grew into its current enormous size, DNS administrators worldwide have had to live with this major annoyance for the last 15 years and counting.

---

that covers the same domain and has the second-smallest preference value. The remote mailer will keep trying the different mail systems specified until it either is able to deliver its mail, or the list of MX records is exhausted).

♦ *Name Server (NS) records*—Define the name server(s) responsible for a domain name, creating a delegation point in the domain namespace and a zone. The name field specifies the name of the zone that is serviced by the name server(s) specified in the record-specific data. A zone needs to be serviced by at least one name server (and it should always be serviced by at least two name servers in order to avoid a single point of failure). The full set of authoritative name servers (that is, the primary name server and all the secondary name servers) for the zone usually will be listed in the NS records of the parent zone. The full set of servers must by definition always be listed in the zone file itself, usually under the "@" name, which is a magic cookie that means the particular "top level" or "root" of the zone. To put it in another way, you are allowed to list servers in the zone's top-level "@" NS records that aren't in the parent's NS delegation, but you can't list servers in the parent's delegation that aren't present in the zone's @.

Some examples of RRs (all of which can't be part of one and the same zone) are listed in Table 7.4.

You might want to note that, although the case is preserved in names and data fields when loaded into the DNS Server, all comparisons and lookups in the DNS Server database are case-insensitive. So, it won't make any difference whatsoever if you write **ASTONITGROUP.COM**, **astonitgroup.com**, or **AstonITGroup.com**.

Registration and Resolution of DNS Names

A client will always request the closest DNS Server (which is either defined in the network property settings or indirectly in the settings for the applicable DHCP scope) to do the actual resolution of a DNS name to an IP address. Regarding the actual resolution of DNS

Table 7.4   Examples of RRs. To avoid any confusion on this important topic, I would like to stress that the RRs listed can't be part of a single zone.

astonitgroup.com	IN	SOA	dns.astonitgroup.com. dnsowner.astonitgroup.com. (1998010500; serial # (date format)
			10800; refresh (3 hours)
			3600; retry (1 hour)
			604800; expire (1 week)
			86400); TTL (1 day)
astonitgroup.com.	IN	NS	dns.astonitgroup.com.
astonitgroup.com.	IN	MX	20 mail.astonitgroup.com.
dns.astonitgroup.com.	IN	A	10.1.200.1
www.astonitgroup.com.	IN	CNAME	dns.astonitgroup.com.
200.1.10.in-addr.arpa.	IN	PTR	dns.astonitgroup.com.

names, you should take care to understand that a DNS Server can, in fact, also function as a client in relation to another DNS Server. This isn't that rare an occurrence. If the DNS Server doesn't have the information necessary to handle the request, it will act as a client to one or several other DNS Servers by using one of the following three types of name resolution to produce an answer:

♦ Recursion

♦ Iteration

♦ Caching

Recursion

A *recursive request* means that the client expects an answer to the question and isn't satisfied with a reference to another DNS Server. So, through recursion, the DNS client (usually a DNS Server) will take over the responsibility for the name resolution process and be obligated to continue the recursive transfer of the request to other servers, until a positive or negative answer to the request is established definitively.

A positive answer occurs when the client finds the information needed. In this situation, the information will be sent back to the computer that initiated the request. A negative answer occurs when a server with authority indicates that the name or the requested data type doesn't exist. A server "with authority" is a name server that is configured to be either a primary or secondary zone server for the domain in question.

Recursive name resolution puts all the work of the name resolution on the client, which is why the administrator specifically must allow that facility on many DNS Servers. However, Microsoft's DNS Server permits recursive name resolution from the outset.

Iteration

In the strictest sense of the word, *iteration* can be called nonrecursive name resolution, because the DNS Server contacted by the initiator of the request will answer the request based on its best knowledge about the requested information. For example, the DNS Server's answer to the client may consist of references to those DNS Servers most likely to have the answer, after which the client can make direct contact to those DNS Servers as part of the completion of the name resolution process. However, with iteration, the DNS Server may also choose to assist in carrying out the name resolution, besides simply returning the "best answer" to the client—but this assistance isn't obligatory.

Caching

While the local DNS Server processes requests, it finds a lot of information about domain namespace. To increase the DNS performance and ease the pressure on other DNS Servers, the local DNS Server will keep this information handy in a local cache. Caching can be particularly advantageous if the DNS Server is located on a LAN segment that is linked to the rest of the world through a slow connection. Caching-only servers also are an option. A caching-only server is a DNS Server whose only task is to carry out requests, embed the answers in the cache, and return the results. Such servers have no authority over any domains and contain only the information that they have intercepted while processing requests from other computers.

In each case of a request for name resolution, the local DNS Server will check its own zone information (the static DNS entries), as well as its cache (the dynamic entries learned from previous requests), to find an answer. Even if no exact match exists for the requested address, the local DNS Server may be able to find some information about, or a reference to, a usable DNS Server—and thus reduce the number of DNS Servers involved in finding the answer to a name resolution request.

In a worst-case situation for the resolution of a DNS name, the local DNS Server starts out from the very top of the DNS tree, using one of the Internet root servers specified in the root hints table, and works its way down through the tree until the requested data is found. However, this situation is quite uncommon, because the DNS Server learns a lot over time as it handles such requests, and this information is readily available in the DNS Server's cache.

Conversely, certain limits apply to what a cache can solve by itself. When the information is embedded in the cache, a TTL value is also attached to each RR, to ensure that the data is renewed at regular intervals—and that out-of-date information won't stay in the cache forever. However, on Microsoft's DNS Servers, a few cache entries—the root hints table— are loaded from the beginning and, by default, never will become outdated. These entries are references to DNS Servers for the roots on the Internet (the .com domain, .org domain, and so forth), which should never change.

Getting Used to DDNS and the Other New DNS Features

Since DNS was promoted to the standard for name resolution on the TCP/IP protocol via IETF, numerous refinements to DNS have been suggested—and a dozen refinements currently are in the pipeline for standardization.

As mentioned earlier, with the advent of Active Directory and Windows 2000 Server, Microsoft has chosen to place all bets on DNS. However, this creates a need for a DNS standard with functionality equaling the dynamic registration functionality available in WINS. This need has prompted Microsoft to include some of the DNS refinements, even though some of them were quite far from being ratified as Internet official protocol standards at the time of the inclusion.

For the DNS Server that comes with Windows 2000 Server, Microsoft has chosen to use a fair number of RFCs that weren't ratified as Internet official protocol standards at the time. All the RFCs that weren't ratified as Internet official protocol standards when Windows 2000 Server was being designed are listed in Table 7.5.

Table 7.5   RFCs not ratified as Internet official protocol standards, when Windows 2000 Server was designed.

RFC Number and Abbreviation	Title
1995 (DNS-IZT)	Incremental Zone Transfers in DNS
1996 (DNS-NOTIFY)	Mechanism for Prompt DNS Notification of Zone Changes
2052 (DNS-SRV)	DNS RR for Specifying the Location of Services (DNS SRV)
2136 (DNS-UPDATE)	Dynamic Updates in the Domain Name System (DNS UPDATE)

As of mid-June 2000, all the RFCs listed in Table 7.5, except RFC 2052, are at the proposed standard level.

RFC 2052 is an experimental-level RFC. When the Internet community found that Microsoft had adopted this very RFC in Windows 2000, the DNS working group at IETF was persuaded by Microsoft to take yet another look at the standard. With some lobbying on the part of Microsoft, the DNS working group eventually sponsored the development of RFC 2782, "A DNS RR for specifying the location of services (DNS SRV)", which obsoletes RFC 2052. RFC 2782 is currently at the proposed standard level.

What's in an Internet Official Protocol Standard?

The Internet Architecture Board maintains the list of documents that define standards for the Internet protocol suite (the latest version of these documents can be found at **ftp://ftp.isi.edu/in-notes/std/std1.txt**) and the state of the IETF RFCs (an evolving series of official documentation of reports, proposals for protocols, and protocol standards used by the Internet community at large).

Protocols that are being considered as Internet standards go through a series of states, or maturity levels—proposed standard, draft standard, and, finally, standard—involving increasing amounts of scrutiny and testing. The advancement of a protocol to the level of proposed standard is a very important step for any RFC, because it marks the protocol as a potential candidate for standardization (by putting the protocol "on the standards track"). Likewise, the advancement to the level of draft standard is another major step, because it demonstrates that, unless major objections are raised or flaws are discovered, the protocol is likely to become a standard—sooner or later.

Like all standardization, IETF RFCs are progressing at a moderate pace. To allow time for the Internet community to consider and react to standardization proposals, a minimum delay of six months occurs before a proposed standard can be advanced to a draft standard, and a minimum of four months then occurs before a draft standard can be promoted to a standard. Also, in practice, no proposed standard can be promoted to draft standard without at least two independent implementations, and the promotion from draft standard to standard generally requires operational experience and demonstrated interoperability of two or more implementations.

Several other intermediate states of maturity, other than the three standard levels, are in existence. One of them is the experimental state, which denotes any useful document that demonstrates the important results of early protocol research and development work. Note that experimental RFCs are not even to the point of being considered for standardization.

In other words, the prospects are pretty good for the functionality that Microsoft added to their DNS Server, including that which was initially specified in RFC 2052. So, before anyone starts Microsoft bashing, they should at least give Microsoft credit for trying to adhere to the most widely recognized (and freely available) specifications in existence.

Note

You should note that Microsoft's DNS Server currently doesn't support any of the looming RFC standards—Domain Name System Security Extensions (RFC 2535) and Secure Domain Name System Dynamic Update (RFC 2137)—for adding security to your DNS registrations. Because it looks very much as if both standards will indeed be supported by virtually anyone except Microsoft, this might very well turn out to be a major drawback to the Microsoft DNS Server in multiplatform environments.

Bluffer's Guide to DDNS

DNS-NOTIFY and **DDNS-** work to remove the last two large disadvantages of DNS compared to NetBIOS: the restriction to static names and the lack of an on-demand replication mechanism. **DNS-UPDATE**, which is commonly referred to as Dynamic DNS or simply DDNS, specifies a method to make *dynamic updates* (appending or deleting one or more entries in the name table of the name server) of the data on the primary name server. These updates are distributed in the usual manner to the secondary name servers, when they ask to be brought up to date.

In other words, Dynamic DNS mends one of the major drawbacks of DNS: the ability to support only static changes to a zone database, thus requiring the DNS administrator to do all adds, removes, or modifications of the RRs by hand. DDNS enables hosts (servers as well as clients) to register their computer name and IP address information at the time that the hosts are initialized on the network. The dynamic data may be new or changed computer-name-to-IP-address data or service identification.

Note

The NetLogon service at the DCs uses DDNS to maintain all the DNS entries used to access Active Directory services. Clients register DNS address records when they boot either directly or via the DHCP Server.

The primary DDNS-compliant name server may, incidentally, be configured to accept updates that are initiated by certain other servers (which can include secondary zone servers, DCs, and other servers that perform network registration for clients, such as WINS and DHCP Servers). You may also set up several different conditions that must be met for a dynamic update to be carried out. Apart from these improvements, DDNS works in the same way as DNS.

Unfortunately, DDNS doesn't address another major shortcoming of DNS that becomes much more crucial with the introduction of DDNS: The primary server for each zone is a potential single point of failure when performing update operations. The dynamic updates are allowed to occur only on the primary name server for the given zone, which means that if the server is down, no updates can be made of the DNS database.

Although the DDNS standard does nothing to address this rather terrifying single-point-of-failure, it does seem to leave some of the implementation up to interpretation, which might allow for some indigenous improvements inside this vital area. Who knows, it might actually be possible to introduce a fair level of fault tolerance into a DDNS implementation that will work to avoid having the network clients left to their own devices because the primary DNS Server is down for a short time. But then again, this is not the case at the present time, so you shouldn't set your hopes too high on this account.

Note

The single-point-of-failure problem when performing update operations can be eliminated if you choose to base the DNS zone infrastructure on Windows 2000 Server's built-in DDNS Server and use Active Directory's database as its data store rather than the usual zone file—this functionality is dubbed Active Directory-integrated DNS by Microsoft. In this case, all the DDNS Servers that also function as DCs are able to act as the primary DNS Server. You can read more on Active Directory-integrated DNS in the section "Getting a Handle on Active Directory-Integrated DDNS."

Besides, DDNS still has to prove its worth in the many unpredictable situations that are experienced in the real world before it can be considered an improvement to DNS that's here for good.

Tip

You should note that the Dynamic DNS protocol described in RFC 2136 doesn't describe the security measures used on the DNS RRs. So, in the absence of any security technology (such as the one described in RFC 2137) in use, the DDNS protocol will actually allow anyone who can reach an authoritative name server to alter the contents of any zones on that server.

This represents a rather serious increase in vulnerability compared to DNS (where only the administrator was able to change the RRs), which is why it's strongly recommended that Dynamic DNS not be implemented without the proper security technologies and security measures in place.

Bluffer's Guide to **DNS-NOTIFY**

DNS-NOTIFY is a push mechanism that enables the primary server to notify secondary zone servers when changes have taken place in the zone file. While this does work to reduce unneeded network traffic, it also helps improve the data consistency across all authoritative zone servers, because the zone servers are notified at the moment a change occurs, instead of having to wait for the next scheduled replication.

The **DNS-NOTIFY** process typically works like this:

1. The local zone file on the primary name server is updated. When the updated zone file is written to disk, the serial number field in the SOA record is incremented to indicate that a new version of the zone file has been written to disk.

2. The primary server sends a notify message to other name servers that are part of a *notify set* (this being a list of secondary servers specified at the primary name server using the NS RR).

3. All secondary name servers that receive the notify message respond by initiating an SOA-type query back to the notifying server (usually the primary server) to determine whether the notifying server's zone file is a later version than the currently stored copy of the zone file.

4. If a notified server determines that the serial number used in the SOA record of the notifying server's zone file is higher (more recent) than the serial number used in the SOA record for its current zone copy, a zone transfer is initiated. Otherwise, no update occurs and the notified server logs the attempted notify-update transaction as an error.

Bluffer's Guide to Incremental Zone Transfers

DNS-IZT, incremental zone transfers, is the ideal complement of **DNS-UPDATE**, because it describes a method for achieving more efficient propagation of zone file updates between the primary name server and the secondary name servers within a zone.

According to the current DNS standards, any request for an update of zone data requires a full transfer of the entire zone database (a so-called AXFR-type request). With the incremental zone transfer (**DNS-IZT**) available, a more effective replication of zone files can be provided, because the data transfer can be limited to the data that has changed.

Incremental zone transfers use the following process to manage updates and replication of zone data when a secondary zone server asks for an update:

1. The primary name server maintains a copy of the most recent version of the zone file, along with a recent version history. This history observes all record changes that occurred in the most recent version updates of the zone file.

2. When an incremental zone transfer request is forwarded by a secondary server to a primary name server, the primary server does a query check to compare the secondary server's current zone version number (that is, the serial number value in the SOA record) with its own current version number.

3. If the primary server has a newer version of the file, it forwards to the secondary server only those record changes that have occurred between the two different versions of the zone file. If the primary and secondary name server both share the same version number, no new or revised zone data is transferred. Otherwise, if incremental zone transfers are not supported by the primary server, a full zone transfer (AXFR) can be initiated as an alternative method for updating the zone.

Bluffer's Guide to SRV RRs

Microsoft's DNS Server also contains support of **DNS-SRV**, which specifies a new RR type (the service record, or SRV RR). The service record can be used to specify those TCP/IP network services that are accessible within the particular zone. This, in turn, enables a client to send a request asking which servers offer a certain service or protocol within the local DNS zone and to receive the names of any available server. (For example, if a **DNS-SRV**-compliant Web browser wants to find the Web services available in the **www.asdf.com** DNS domain, it can just do a lookup of **_http._tcp.www.asdf.com**, which then returns the registered Web services available inside that domain.)

The SRV RR represents a major improvement over current methods, whereby you must either know the exact address of a service to contact it or broadcast a question. Besides easing the lives of the client users quite a bit, **DNS-SRV** also has several good things in store for the administrators: The SRV allows administrators to offer the same service or protocol on several servers, to move services with little fuss, and to designate some hosts as primary servers for a service and others as backups.

Note

The new RFC 2782, which supersedes RFC 2052, has changed the SRV definition quite dramatically by inserting underscores in front of the Service and Proto segments. This has been done to avoid collisions with DNS labels that occur in "nature." However, this is a very problematic solution, as the underscore, strictly speaking, isn't supported by the current DNS character set. Hopefully, you won't experience any problems on this account, but the potential is surely there. So, you should tread cautiously if you're employing DNS Servers other than the one built in to Windows 2000.

In Active Directory, clients harness **DNS-SRV** (among other things) to locate DCs that provide logon to a given Active Directory domain. A typical SRV record for the Active Directory domain **marketing.astonitgroup.com** would be:

_ldap._tcp.marketing.astonitgroup.com 0 **IN SRV** 0 0 389 **dcs.marketing. astonitgroup.com**

In addition, Active Directory introduces a number of other DNS entries for identifying various services offered by the DC (including the GC service). For example, a typical SRV record for an Active Directory domain controller that is writable would be:

_ldap._tcp.writable.marketing.astonitgroup.com 0 **IN SRV** 0 0 389 **dcs.marketing. astonitgroup.com**

And a DC that is located in the site CPH would be identified by the following RR:

_ldap._tcp.cph.sites.marketing.astonitgroup.com 0 **IN SRV** 0 0 389 **dcs.marketing. astonitgroup.com**

Chapter 17 provides a detailed description of all the SRV RRs registered by Active Directory.

How to Read the SRV RR

SRV records are a generalization of the MX record concept, in which several different servers can advertise a similar service. Active Directory employs the SRV record for pointing to several kinds of network services. RFC 2782 specifies the SRV RR to have the following format (whose DNS type code is 33), with its individual segments explained in the list that follows:

_Service._Proto.Name   TTL Class SRV Priority Weight Port Target

- *Service*—The symbolic name of the requested service, as defined in IANA's Assigned Numbers table or locally. The Service is case-insensitive.

- *Proto*—TCP and UDP are currently the most useful values for this field, though any name defined by Assigned Numbers or locally may be used (the same as for Service). Proto is case-insensitive.

- *Name*—The domain name that this RR refers to.

- *TTL*—The standard DNS Time-To-Live parameter.

- *Class*—The standard DNS class "IN".

- *Priority*—Defines the priority of this target host and is used in the same way as with the better-known MX record. A client must attempt to contact the target host with the lowest number that it can reach; target hosts with the same priority should be tried in pseudo-random order. The allowed range for the priority value is 0 to 65,535.

- *Weight*—A load-balancing mechanism. When you select a target host among those that have the same priority, the chance of trying this one first should be proportional to its weight. The allowed range of this value is 1 to 65,535. Domain administrators are urged to use Weight 0 when no load balancing exists, to make the RR easier to read for humans.

- *Port*—Defines the port used by the service on the target host. The allowed range is 0 to 65,535. The port number will usually be specified in Assigned Numbers, but the official port number doesn't have to be used.

- *Target*—The DNS name of the target host. One or more A records must be available in the applicable zone specifying the IP address for this name.

Getting a Handle on Active Directory-Integrated DDNS

Microsoft's DNS Server introduces a new proprietary feature called *Active Directory-integrated DNS zones*, which offers several interesting capabilities. As the name Active Directory-integrated DNS zones implies, the feature represents an alternative to the well-known primary and secondary name server designations.

As you should know by now, the primary name server processes all changes inside the applicable DNS zone, and these changes are then pulled from secondary servers. Each zone is stored as a text file, and no local changes are allowed to be made to the text files stored on secondary name servers.

When you specify a zone to be serviced by an Active Directory-integrated name server (which only can happen at a DC, which also serves as a DNS Server), the DNS records that otherwise would be stored in the zone file will be moved to the Active Directory database.

To be more specific, the DNS records will be moved to the Active Directory domain database at the DC on which the change from primary name server to Active Directory-integrated zone was specified. If you, for example, have a DNS Server implemented at a DC serving the **denmark.astonitgroup.com** domain from which you specify a change from primary to Active Directory-integrated for the **denmark.astonitgroup.com** DNS zone, you will find that all of the DNS records previously stored in the zone text file are moved to the **denmark.astonitgroup.com** domain (at the **System/MicrosoftDNS** OU, to be precise).

Note

Only DNS Servers running on Windows 2000-based Active Directory DCs can host Active Directory-integrated zones. Thus, all other DNS Services will only be able to host those zones as secondaries.

The fact that the Active Directory-integrated zone's DNS records are stored in the Active Directory domain partition means that it will be distributed automatically to all the DCs participating in that particular Active Directory domain. Because of this, any DC that has the DNS service running will have the Active Directory-integrated zone made instantly available to it.

Because of Active Directory's multi-master replication scheme, the zone is writable on any DC; therefore, the DNS service running off any of the domain's DCs will view the zone as being primary. Thus, rather than being constrained to having only one primary name server, the Active Directory-integrated zone allows you to have all DCs running as primary name servers! So, not only does the Active Directory-integrated zone feature save you some administrative overhead (because you don't have to manually define each zone on every DNS Server), it also saves you the hassle of designing, implementing, and managing a DNS replication topology. Also, it saves you some precious bandwidth (because the DNS records are updated at the local DNS Server and updated on the other servers as part of the inevitable Active Directory replications).

Additionally, the security that surrounds the DDNS records can be heightened to any level you may feel suitable, with a fairly low administrative overhead. This is because all Active Directory objects (including the DNS records being moved to the Active Directory) are

---

Watch Out for Domain Pitfall

You should take great care to understand that an Active Directory-integrated zone can only be part of one Active Directory domain. And so, this feature doesn't solve all of your issues, if you have DNS domains that span several Active Directory domains. But that doesn't mean that Active Directory-integrated zones aren't applicable in this scenario. Actually, it could turn out to be just as applicable to this scenario, because you will usually find that the majority of updates will stem from one of the Active Directory domains. In that case, you should go ahead and turn the zone Active Directory-integrated for that domain and then define secondary name servers for the zone at the applicable DNS Servers in the other Active Directory domains.

Stupid, Stupider, Event ID 4011

While the Active Directory-integrated DNS Server feature does indeed work wonders in many cases, it comes with one tremendous design blunder that you should know about. This design blunder (also known as Event ID 4011) has the very ungratifying consequence that the DNS Server isn't able to add or write an update of **_ldap**, **_gc**, and/or **gc** to the local server's Active Directory-integrated DNS zone.

This rather vital design blunder on Microsoft's part only kicks in when all of the following conditions are met:

- Your server is being registered in an Active Directory-integrated DNS zone that is using Dynamic DNS.
- The server hosts the Global Catalog, as well as the DNS Server.
- The network configuration points to the local server as being the preferred DNS Server.

Why's that? Well, it's actually quite simple: The service startup order. When the server is running as a Global Catalog (GC), some of the services that need to register with DNS will start before the local Active Directory-integrated DNS Server is ready to receive registrations. So, you should be fairly safe if you are able to avoid just one of these conditions in your environment. However, if you can't avoid any of these conditions, you're in a really tight spot. Unfortunately, there are several circumstances in which you might find yourself faced with just that. I've encountered it most often when designing for small sites in which a single server is called for, but WAN bandwidth is so scarce (or unreliable) that you need to keep all communication to the absolute minimum.

In these cases, you'll have to accept having the event log plastered with Event ID 4011 entries and make a rather risky bet on it not posing a problem with network functionality (which I for one would never do in an operations setting, as I've already heard rumors from several sources that users frequently won't be able to log on!); otherwise, you'll have to give in on your great design. I sure do hope Microsoft will wise up and find some way to fix this major shortcoming in time for ServicePack 2!

protected with an Access Control List (ACL) that allows administrators to set the security properties any way they see fit. And you really don't have any immediate downsides to turning the Active Directory-integrated zone feature on, because the DNS Servers that run off the Active Directory DCs will appear to be primary name servers to other DNS Servers. And so, you're free to define the wished-for secondary name servers on DNS Servers that aren't running off an Active Directory DC.

Oh well, there's actually one downside to the Active Directory-integrated zones that was uncovered after the release of the product. This rather serious and totally unnecessary downside is described in all its gory detail in the sidebar "Stupid, Stupider, Event ID 4011".

DHCP Integration and WINS Interoperability

The DHCP integration and WINS interoperability that are available with the technologies built into Windows 2000 Server and Windows 2000 Workstation are definitely worth mentioning, because they represent a considerable easing of the administrative chores. However, you also have to consider that this functionality is largely Microsoft proprietary technology, which means that it usually doesn't apply to non-Microsoft DNS Servers.

Stop The Presses: How to Avoid Event ID 4011

Right before this book went to the printer, I did manage to identify a workaround for having the event logs plastered with the following error (referred to as Event ID 4011; see also the sidebar "Stupid, Stupider, Event 4011") everytime the DC/GC is being restored:

- Event Type: Error
- Event Source: DNS
- Event Category: None
- Event ID: 4011

The workaround is very simple, but highly effective: You just stop the Netlogon service before the machine is restarted. I must admit that I don't know exactly why this is so, except for the fact that it's the Netlogon service that is charged with registering (and deregistering) all of the DC/GC's DNS records.

You can do this by hand (typing **NET STOP NETLOGON** at a command prompt) and rebooting the server, when its through executing that command. But even better, you can just add that very same command embedded in a shutdown script at a GPO, which is applied tot he DC/GCs in question.

The only downside to this workaround is that no Netlogon errors will be logged during a system shutdown—and so, the workaround might work to hide other errors experieinced by Netlogon during a system shutdown.

I've had the opportunity to implement this workaround at serveral different companies running Active Directory-integrated DNS. And until now, it has also worked as intended, and I kind of doubt that it will prove otherwise, no matter the installation at hand. But as this workaround isn't officially sanctioned by Microsoft, I can't guarantee that it will work in any scenario faced.

DHCP Integration

The DHCP Server functionality is largely unchanged for Windows 2000 Server compared to that found in Windows NT Server ServicePack 5. The only major change is that the DHCP client has been refurbished with some DDNS-aware code. This coding enables the client to register addresses issued by DHCP directly in the DDNS database.

By default, DHCP will take responsibility of registering down-level client computers (to be more precise: Windows clients prior to Windows 2000 that are running TCP/IP) in DNS. Provided that a computer is allowed to lease an address from the DHCP Server, the DHCP Server and DNS Server will work together to dynamically update each client's DNS host name and IP address in the appropriate DNS zone. For example, Windows 95 and Windows 98 clients will register with DNS in this way.

The functionality that allows clients to register and keep the client records up-to-date in the proper DNS zone works by letting the DDNS client register the host name of the client (in the form <computer name>.<DNS Domain Name>) and the IP address via the DHCP Server. Unfortunately, no standards currently are in existence that cover this kind of DHCP and DNS interaction, so Microsoft has been forced to invent its own.

Note

The specification of this DHCP and DNS interaction has been posted by Microsoft to the IETF for review as an Internet draft: It currently goes by the name of **draft-skwan-gss-tsig-05.txt** *and can be retrieved at* **www.ietf.org/internet-drafts/draft-skwan-gss-05.txt**.

This proprietary Microsoft DHCP and DNS interaction (defined as DHCP option 81) currently supports two modes of operation—one built for down-level clients (see Figure 7.5) and the other for Active Directory clients (see Figure 7.6):

♦ *Mode 1*—Using this mode, the client will handle the DDNS registering by tracking names and addresses, sending A RR updates straight to the name server, and asking the DHCP Server to register the corresponding PTR RR. The DHCP Server is also responsible for removing PTR RRs when leases expire, or when the address is requested to be released—and the DHCP Server, optionally, also removes the A RR, security permitting (this is highly recommended, because it will guarantee that any A records from clients that are suddenly removed from the network will be removed from the DNS Server). Mode 1 is the default mode for Active Directory-aware clients, because this will secure the A record against being overwritten by other clients. Mode 1 must always be used for multihomed computers. You might want to note that Mode 1 isn't an option for down-level clients, because of the need to update the client with functionality for registering A records at the DNS Server.

♦ *Mode 2*—All the registration work (registering of both A RR and PTR RR) is handled by the DHCP Server. This is not suitable for multihomed machines, but is great for down-level clients. However, this requires the DHCP Servers in the network to be upgraded to Windows 2000 Server, because of the need to update the DHCP Server functionality. Mode 2 is the default choice for any down-level client (defined as a client that doesn't use option 81) that contacts a DHCP Server.

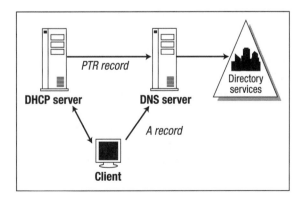

Figure 7.5
DHCP and DNS interaction, Mode 1.

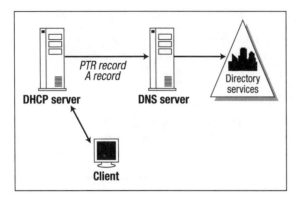

Figure 7.6
DHCP and DNS interaction, Mode 2.

You might note that, in addition to allowing legacy clients to get registered at the DNS Server, the integration between DHCP and DNS also works to keep the IP address information up-to-date, because any change implemented by DHCP automatically will be reflected at DNS.

Note

To prevent problems with stale PTR and A resource records, you can enable the proprietary feature available in Microsoft's DNS Server that allows you to specify the conditions for aging and scavenging of stale records. The administrator is allowed to enable/disable scavenging on a per-server, per-zone, and even per-record basis.

If your server or client setup doesn't give you access to use either of these two proprietary solutions—that is, when you haven't got Microsoft's own DHCP and DNS Servers in operation and the clients aren't able to register using Dynamic DNS—you have absolutely no way

---

Some Vital DHCP Interoperability Details

You should note that no security is associated with the DHCP's registering the DNS A and PTR records. In other words, if another legacy client tries to register with the same name, it will succeed and in the process wipe the former registrations. This is because the DHCP Server and the DHCP client do not share any unique identifiers that would signal such duplicate naming situations.

Additionally, you should note that the DNS records registered by the DHCP Server will be owned by that DHCP Server when registering to an Active Directory-integrated zone. In other words, only the DHCP Server is allowed to change the records. And so, you should either assign another name to the client when it's upgraded to Windows 2000 Professional, or have the DHCP Server register by using the DnsUpdateProxy Group, which will allow any authenticated user to take ownership of the records registered by DHCP Server. However, be keenly aware that registering by using the DnsUpdateProxy Group will allow any other client to overwrite the records that have been registered by the DHCP Server. So, there's really no easy solution to the DHCP question. But, at least, you should be able to make an informed decision on where to compromise.

---

to avoid the tedious and error-prone manual adding and continuous updating of A RRs and PTR RRs for all clients on the network. This alone should serve as a very persuasive reason to implement the DHCP and DNS Servers that are delivered with Windows 2000 Server.

Note

*The fact that DHCP Servers will be used for registering DNS records make them an obvious target for unauthorized users. For that reason, Active Directory will prevent DHCP Servers from joining the network until they have been authorized by the administrator. When a Windows 2000 Server DHCP Server attempts to start on the network, Active Directory is queried and the server computer's IP address is compared to the list of authorized DHCP Servers. If a match is found, the server computer is authorized and is allowed to complete the system startup. If a match is not found, the server is identified as rogue, and the DHCP service is automatically shut down. Additionally, each DHCP Server periodically tests the validity of the other DHCP Servers on the LAN, using **DHCPINFORM**.*

Additionally, you should also remember that WINS is still a required location service between down-level clients and servers, so the down-level clients still only will be able to use NetBIOS for accessing the fundamental network services. Therefore, the DHCP client should continue to register with WINS, if a WINS Server is available—and a WINS Server definitely should be available as long as you have any down-level servers and clients present on the network.

WINS Interoperability

If you still have down level/NetBIOS hosts on your network that need to be reached by the new Windows 2000-based host, you will need some sort of interoperability between DNS and WINS. In many cases, it will prove best to set up your DNS Server for querying a WINS Server (which is called WINS lookup or WINS referral), when it can't resolve a name or address. With WINS lookup, you can direct DNS to query WINS for name resolution, so that DNS clients can look up the names and IP addresses of WINS clients.

Note

WINS lookup can be enabled or disabled for each DNS zone, and you're allowed to specify multiple WINS Servers for reasons of fault tolerance. This helps prevent traffic to non-Microsoft DNS Servers that can't process requests from WINS. For more information on DNS/WINS integration, turn to the appropriate Windows NT Server 4 documentation, because the WINS lookup operates the same as in Windows NT 4.

To use WINS lookup integration, two proprietary RRs are added—the WINS and WINS-R resource records—to the forward and reverse lookup zones, respectively. These two proprietary RRs are only known to the DNS Servers delivered with Windows NT Server 4 and Windows 2000 Server.

When a DNS Server is queried for a name that it doesn't find in the authoritative zone and the zone is configured to use WINS resolution, the DNS Server queries the WINS Server specified by the WINS RR. If the name is registered with WINS, the WINS Server returns the associated record to the DNS Server.

> **Note**
>
> *If present, the WINS record only applies for the topmost level within a zone and not for subdomains used in the zone. A WINS resource record has the following syntax:*
>
> *domain class WINS [TTL] Local LookupTimeout CacheTimeout IP_address_of_WINS_server.*
>
> *The domain name where the WINS record is found is always @, and the class is always IN.*

Reverse lookups work just a little bit differently. When an authoritative DNS Server is queried for a nonexistent PTR record and the authoritative zone contains the WINS-R record, it uses a NetBIOS adapter node status query for the queried IP addresses.

> **Note**
>
> *A WINS-R resource record has the following syntax:*
>
> *domain class WINSR[TTL] Loca LookupTimeout CacheTimeoutNameResultDomain*

Due to the proprietary nature of the WINS lookup feature, it's best to make sure that all DNS Servers that are authoritative for a zone are running Windows 2000 Server or Windows NT Server 4; otherwise, you can't be sure when the WINS lookup functionality is being used. Also, you might want to note that you shouldn't try to implement lookup to the same WINS database from multiple DNS domains—in that case, odds are pretty high that DNS will get very confused, indeed. So you want to implement WINS lookup on only one DNS domain or partition per your WINS database, acording to the DNS domains, and then implement WINS lookup in each DNS domain.

> **Note**
>
> *You have to prevent the proprietary WIN-R resource records from being included in zone transfers to name servers that are based on another DNS Server implementation than those used by Windows 2000 Server and Windows Workstation 4. You can avoid these problems by creating and delegating a zone to be used exclusively for WINS queries; this zone doesn't perform any registrations or updates, but only refers DNS lookups to WINS. After you have created your WINS referral zone, you configure your DNS clients to append the WINS referral zone name to unqualified queries (that is, queries that don't specify a fully qualified domain name). The easiest way is to configure the DHCP Server to assign a connection-specific DNS suffix to all DHCP adapters on all computers in your network, which ensures that suffix is appended to unqualified queries. Alternatively, you can specify a domain suffix search list on each client. Having only one WINS-integrated zone also prevents the confusing situation in*

which DNS queries for different domain names resolve to the same WINS client name and IP address.

DNS Design in a Nutshell

You should now have a sound theoretical foundation on DNS, which is a necessary prerequisite for being able to do the actual designing and planning for DNS. Generally, when you are ready to establish the naming scheme for your Active Directory architecture, you should start with the naming standards and then move on to planning the DNS root domain, DNS zones, DNS Servers, and, finally, the DNS replication. However, because the first half of this chapter is devoted to understanding DNS, for the sake of lessening confusion, this section finishes off the very technical bits of DNS by discussing the choice of DNS Servers.

Choosing DNS Servers

The possible solutions for choosing DNS Servers can be summarized as follows:

♦ Use an existing DNS Server.

♦ Implement Microsoft DNS exclusively.

♦ Implement Microsoft DNS as a delegated subdomain.

You should *never* try to mix different types of DNS Servers when using Active Directory, because of Active Directory's reliance on RFCs that haven't been fully ratified as standards—and may not be ratified. If you try to mix DNS Servers, you are asking for trouble! The one possible exception is if you are absolutely sure that the non-Microsoft DNS Servers are 100-percent compliant with the DNS Server delivered with your ServicePack (and patch) level of Windows 2000 Server.

In other words, be keenly aware that Microsoft has made sure that the easiest path of execution regarding DNS Servers is to choose the DNS Server that is included with Windows 2000 Server. And even if you manage to track down another DNS Server that is currently on par with Windows 2000 Server's built-in DNS Server, keep in mind Microsoft's track record for adding essentially proprietary functionality to its offerings. So, if you don't have a DNS structure in place already (or have DNS only scantily implemented) or are using a previous version of Microsoft DNS Server, you should always opt for the DNS Server that is part of Windows 2000 Server.

Tip

Beware of Microsoft's muddled User Interface. Rather than having done things the easy way in regard to DNS, Microsoft seems to have chosen the worst of all directions. They've quite simply built a name server (the Microsoft DNS Service) that makes it much harder than necessary to configure and manage DNS because the user interface is quite illogical and some of the vital information is hidden behind several different property sheets. Also, in some situations, the DNS Server needs to be restarted for it to reflect the actual contents of the database files (this seemed to be fixed with

ServicePack1). The only good thing about the Windows 2000 DNS Service is that they do indeed seem to have listened to their users: A lot of the shortcomings found in the Windows NT Server 4 DNS Server have been addressed (including the stability issues).

However, if you have existing non-Microsoft DNS Servers in your environment, you need to weigh the pros and cons of staying put or migrating (parts of or all) environments to Microsoft DNS. If you are fortunate, you can avoid the worst-case scenarios in which the Active Directory namespace has to replace or be an integral part of the DNS namespace that is already in operation on non-Microsoft servers. Or, you may still have the option of placing Active Directory as a subdomain to the current namespace (which enables you to implement Microsoft DNS as a delegated subdomain).

Table 7.6 shows the advantages and disadvantages of implementing Microsoft DNS Server exclusively, Table 7.7 shows the advantages and disadvantages of implementing Microsoft DNS Server as a delegated subdomain, and Table 7.8 shows the advantages and disadvantages of keeping any current non-Microsoft DNS Servers.

Table 7.6   The advantages and disadvantages of using Microsoft DNS Server exclusively.

Advantages	Disadvantages
Not dependent on the interoperability of servers.	May require effort to replace existing DNS Servers with Active Directory.
Will co-exist with other DNS Servers.	
Interoperability with WINS for support of NetBIOS.	
Support of DHCP integration, which makes it possible to register a name in a zone on behalf of a client.	
Supports multi-master replication via Active Directory (Active Directory-integrated zone).	
Supports an extended character set (Unicode).	

Table 7.7   The advantages and disadvantages of implementing Microsoft DNS Server as a delegated subdomain.

Advantages	Disadvantages
Requires no upgrade of any existing DNS Servers.	Names will be longer and less user-friendly.
Minimizes dependence of Active Directory on existing DNS Servers.	The special needs of the added subdomain component may be forgotten.
Not dependent on the interoperability of servers.	A continued dependence on existing DNS Servers with Active Directory.
Allows you access to the proprietary functionality offered in Microsoft's DNS Server (see Table 7.6).	

Table 7.8   The advantages and disadvantages of keeping non-Microsoft DNS Servers.

Advantages	Disadvantages
Does not require replacing existing DNS Servers.	Requires integration testing.
No political changes.	The minimum requirements for your DNS Servers is support for SRV records.
	The administrative workload will increase compared to a "clean" MS DNS solution, depending on the level of compliance offered with the RFCs used by Active Directory and the proprietary features introduced with Microsoft DNS.

So, even if you already have a very thorough DNS structure implemented, you should really consider migrating all or the essential parts (that is, the name servers servicing the root domain) of the DNS Servers to Windows 2000 Server's DNS Server. If you currently employ DNS Servers that don't meet Active Directory's DDNS requirements, you can choose the path of least resistance: Implement a Microsoft DNS Server to coexist with your current DNS Server as a delegated subdomain (see Figure 7.7).

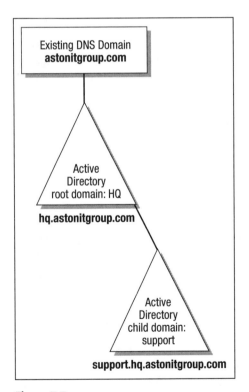

Figure 7.7
If you have an existing DNS structure that can't be migrated easily to Microsoft's DNS, you might consider delegating a subdomain for establishing a separate Microsoft DNS structure.

The Opposite of a Delegated Subdomain?

In some cases, you might want to perform the opposite of a delegated subdomain. That is, you might find it most fitting to move the root domain to Microsoft's DNS, while keeping the "old" zones at the current DNS Servers. This will usually be the case when the root domain isn't used by very many hosts.

Not only will this work to remove the only minor drawback to the delegated subdomain solution, it also removes a lot of the grunt (and error-prone) work involved in migrating to a new DNS Server infrastructure, while still removing the interoperability risks—you can still create an old-style DNS zone that can be handled by any RFC-compliant DNS Server.

The migration is quite straightforward: You just configure the new Windows 2000 Server-based DNS Server as a secondary for the root domain zone, perform a zone transfer, promote the new DNS Server to primary name server for the zone, and demote the old DNS Server. The only major drawback to this solution is that Microsoft's DNS Server is a much less battle-proven solution than virtually any version of BIND (barring the most recent ones).

Using this solution, you'll get the support needed for Active Directory (including the proprietary features that come with Windows 2000 Server's DNS service), while keeping the existing DNS Servers and namespace unaltered.

Note

However, please be aware that you need to be able to separate all the Windows 2000/ Active Directory stuff totally—meaning forward lookup zones as well as reverse lookup zones—in order to avoid the DNS interoperability troubles. So, you should remember to study the needs for reverse lookup zones carefully before you can be absolutely certain that the delegated subdomain solution is applicable to your environment.

The only minor drawback to the delegated subdomain solution is that the DNS names used will be longer than otherwise would be the case, because they inherit the name of the existing root domain name.

However, in many cases you may find yourself in a situation where you simply can't migrate to Windows 2000 Server's DNS nor devise an Active Directory design that is fully separated zone-wise from the existing DNS infrastructure. In that case, you're faced with the worst-case scenario: having to implement Active Directory on top of an existing set of DNS Servers.

In this case, you will have to bite the bullet on the level of DNS interoperability called for (see also the sidebar "A Quick Briefing on DNS Interoperability Needs"), and this usually has to be accompanied by a fair level of interoperability tests in order to ascertain that no terrible things will happen to your network infrastructure when you roll out the Windows 2000 clients and servers.

Table 7.9 outlines the feature set of a select set of other DNS Servers, courtesy of Microsoft. Microsoft also notes that Windows 2000 Server's DNS Server interoperates with those DNS

Table 7.9   The feature set found in a select set of different DNS Servers.

Feature	Windows 2000 Server	Windows NT Server	BIND 8.2	BIND 8.1.2	BIND 4.9.7
Support for SRV records	Yes	Yes (with Service Pack 4)	Yes	Yes	Yes
Support for DDNS	Yes	No	Yes	Yes	No
Support for secure dynamic updates as implemented in Microsoft's DNS Server	Yes	No	No	No	No
Support for WINS and WINS-R records	Yes	Yes	No	No	No
Support for incremental zone transfer	Yes	No	Yes	No	No
Support for UTF-8 character encoding	Yes	No	No	No	No

A Quick Briefing on DNS Interoperability Needs

To support Active Directory, your DNS Server of choice *must* support the SRV RRs defined by RFC 2052 and RFC 2782, because clients require the Active Directory services to be registered via SRV RRs—otherwise, they won't be able to log on or use the other services made available from the DCs.

If possible, your DNS Server should also support:

• Dynamic DNS (RFC 2136)

• Incremental Zone Transfers (RFC 1995)

Although implementing and running Windows 2000 Server without Dynamic DNS is possible, the network administrator's workload increases significantly, because of the work involved in manually updating DNS information. If you do not have DDNS, you need to perform updates when any of the following occur:

• Installation of an Active Directory DC (information on the RRs needed is listed in the *NETLOGON.DNS* file on the DC)

• Changes in DC name

• Changes in DC role (GC, DC, and more)

• Changes in site configuration

• Changes in DC's IP address

• Demotion of DC

Finally, you must also manually key in all the clients and their IP addresses (including their changes) or employ WINS (which means you can't put Active Directory to full use). The support for Incremental Zone Transfer is "merely" a question of keeping a lid on the replication traffic load on your network. Note that the traffic load can become quite high in a DDNS environment that has many DHCP-enabled clients (and, thus, many IP address changes).

Doing the Impossible: Implementing Active Directory on a Legacy DNS Server

While it certainly isn't recommended, it is in fact possible to implement Active Directory in a zone that is hosted by a DNS Server that doesn't support RFC 2136 nor SRV RRs. To implement Active Directory in this setting, you would need to add another DNS Server that does support RFC 2136 and SRV RRs and delegate the following zones to that server:

* _tcp.*<Active Directory domain name>*
* _udp.*<Active Directory domain name>*
* _msdcs.*<Active Directory domain name>*
* _sites. *<Active Directory domain name>*

This will allow the Active Directory DCs to create the appropriate records. Then you have to add a blank A record that specifies the IP address of each DC in the domain and an A record that specifies the host name and the IP address of each DC in the domain. And to prevent the Netlogon service at each DC from trying to dynamically register **A RR**s, you will have to add the entry **DnsRegisterARecords** of the **DWORD** type with a value of 0 to the **HKEY_LOCAL_MACHINE\ SYSTEM\CurrentControlSet\Services\NetLogon\Parameters** registry subkey at each Active Directory DC.

---

implementations mentioned. But even if you do actually employ the server versions mentioned in Table 7.9, I urge you to perform your own interoperability testing (and you should specifically remember to include the DHCP Server used in those tests). DNS is simply too important to leave anything to chance here.

When Should You Use Active Directory-Integrated DNS?

If you choose to go with the built-in Microsoft DNS Server, you still have one choice to make: whether to do a "native" implementation of Microsoft DNS Server by storing DNS data in text-based zone files (see Figure 7.8) or use the Active Directory-integrated DNS zone feature, in which Active Directory is used for storing the DNS zone data (see Figure 7.9).

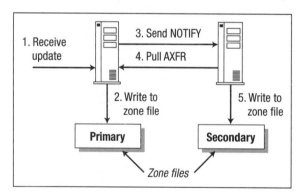

Figure 7.8
The standard zone transfer.

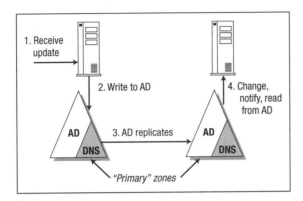

Figure 7.9
The option of using Active Directory's database as the storage container for DNS zone data.

If you choose to harness the Active Directory database as the storage container for DNS zone data, you're eligible for the following advantages:

♦ No need to manage a separate replication topology for DNS, because it will be handled by the Active Directory replication.

♦ You'll only have to create the DNS zones needed once in each Active Directory domain in order to be able to implement a DNS Server on each DC that belongs to the same particular domain.

♦ You'll eliminate the single point of failure that is inherent in standard DNS replication because of its use of single-master replication; that is, updates of the DNS database can be done only at the primary name server for the zone, whereas all DCs that have the DNS service running will be able to accept DDNS updates, because they act as a full read/write DNS authority (each DNS zone object stored in the Active Directory database acts as a primary copy for every DC in each domain). All DNS Servers running off Active Directory DCs will be considered primary name servers—and thus eligible for accepting DDNS updates. So, the local DNS is the target of DDNS updates rather than having to contact the primary name server, which is a functionality that comes in very handy given the fact that all Windows 2000 clients and servers now perform DDNS registrations by default.

♦ You can implement secure updates in the zone using the same security properties as used in the remainder of Windows 2000. This could turn out to be rather crucial in regard to avoiding "rogue" clients overwriting any entries registered by servers.

♦ You'll have full backward-compatibility with the RFC-type DNS implementations, so that you'll be able to accommodate any need to have other types (and makes) DC servers acting as secondary name servers for the zone.

If you employ the Active Directory-integrated zone functionality, you should be keenly aware that Active Directory replication is loosely consistent. That is, if you have a name-level collision in which two hosts create the same DNS name simultaneously, you encounter an attribute-level collision if using Active Directory storage, which is solved by letting the last writer win. However, this is actually very close to what will happen in a native DDNS setting, because the DDNS Server by default will allow the last writer to win. Also, you should take care to note that the Active Directory-integrated zone functionality is a Microsoft-proprietary technology. However, the proprietary nature doesn't pose any problems to DNS Servers that comply to the DNS RFCs (including the BIND implementations).

In my point of view, the improved fault tolerance alone should work to make you want to turn virtually any zone employing Dynamic DNS into being Active Directory-integrated. And the more physical locations you've got, the more persuasive the argument.

Note

Not to mention, the potential for WAN bandwidth savings because the DNS records now are replicated together with the Active Directory objects.

So, unless, you're faced with the scenario described in the sidebar "Stupid, Stupider, Event ID 4011" in the section "Getting a Handle on Active Directory-Integrated DDNS", I really do have a very hard time seeing why you should use anything but the Active Directory-integrated zone feature.

How to Pick DNS Names

Before you begin the actual namespace planning, you should spend a couple of minutes getting acquainted with the standard DNS naming restrictions. The naming requirements were introduced as part of RFC 1035, one of the core DNS standards specifications. RFC 1035 states that the characters A through Z, a through z, 0 through 9, and - (hyphen) are the only characters allowed. A full DNS name can consist of up to 255 characters (and each level in domain namespace can consist of up to 63 characters), including the periods. Note that the letters supported include only those that are available in the U.S. alphabet (ASCII).

Tip

As a general rule, always strive to keep names as concise as possible and try to limit your DNS design to somewhere between three to five subdomain levels, which should be sufficient for most applications.

As you may know, the current NetBIOS naming scheme used in previous versions of NT and Windows (as well as many other naming schemes) allows many other characters, such as / (backslash), . (dot), and _ (underscore). So, you likely are in for a rough transition to RFC 1035's more restrictive character set, regardless of your current naming standards.

Windows 2000 Server's DNS allows you to treat all the names stored in one of three ways:

♦ *Strict RFC*—Makes sure that all names adhere to the RFC 1123. If this option is chosen, you will be certain to avoid any problems with your DNS names whatsoever.

- *Non-RFC*—If this option is chosen, you'll be able to use the full set of ANSI characters. However, this entails a risk for compatibility troubles with non-Microsoft DNS Servers.

- *Multibyte*—Allows for using the full set of Unicode characters (meaning all characters found in the majority of written languages). The Unicode characters will be converted in accordance with the UTF-8 specification.

So, except when you want to use a couple of the characters available in ANSI, your only possible escape from the rather harsh restrictions found in RFC 1123 is to choose Microsoft DNS Server's Unicode option, with which the DNS Server allows a full, international character set and still provides a degree of backward-compatibility via UTF-8 character encoding (a Unicode transformation format that ensures ASCII characters are mapped to the "usual" places, and hence can be understood by non-Unicode hosts).

The UTF-8 protocol is defined in RFC 2044, which has been made obsolete by RFC 2279, which was recently moved into the draft standard category at IETF. Together, UTF-8 and Unicode (as well as the UCS-2 format of ISO/IEC 10646-1, which is a 16-bit character set that encompasses most of the world's writing systems) provide support for characters from most of the world's written languages. This allows a far greater range of possible names, allowing names to use characters that are relevant to a particular locality, while preserving the traditional ASCII data encoding. Thus, although Microsoft DNS Servers running under Windows 2000 Server are UTF-8-aware, they still remain compatible with other DNS Servers that use traditional ASCII data encoding specified by the current DNS standards.

To provide standards compatibility and interoperability with other DNS implementations, Microsoft DNS Server uses *uniform downcasing* (all uppercase characters used in ASCII are converted to their lowercase equivalents) of any received character data. Uniform downcasing behavior is needed to provide interoperability between non-UTF-8-aware DNS Servers and Microsoft DNS Servers, because non-UTF-8-aware DNS Servers are unable to perform a case-insensitive comparison of UTF-8-encoded characters. By downcasing UTF-8-encoded names before transmission, non-UTF-8-aware DNS Servers are able to receive and perform successful binary comparisons of the data and obtain the desired results.

Note

If you want to study further the finer points of data encoding in a DNS setting, consult RFCs 2181 and 1035.

However, most importantly, until the UTF-8 protocol is formally ratified as a standard, Microsoft's DNS Unicode option will be a *de facto* proprietary solution. And even if UTF-8 standardization is sorted out, the flexibility will come at a price. No problems will be present when going from non-UTF-8 servers to the Microsoft DNS Server. The UTF-8 encoding protocol adapts well to use with existing DNS protocol implementations that use US-ASCII characters, because representation of a US-ASCII character in UTF-8 is byte-for-byte identical to the US-ASCII representation. Earlier Microsoft DNS clients or other implementations that are unaware of UTF-8 characters always encode names in the US-ASCII format, and you can be sure that those names will always be correctly interpreted by Microsoft DNS Server running under Windows 2000 Server. However, you are advised to take great caution when implementing a DNS system that allows unrestricted UTF-8 character encoding, for the following reasons:

♦ While a non-UTF-8-aware DNS Server may very well accept a zone transfer for a zone that contains UTF-8 names, it may not be able to write back those names to a zone file or reload those names from the zone file. So, you should use great caution when transferring a zone that contains UTF-8 names to a non-UTF-8-aware DNS Server.

♦ Some protocols place restrictions on the characters allowed in a name. In addition, names that are intended to be visible on the Internet should be restricted to ASCII-only characters in order to avoid a very likely potential source of DNS errors.

For these reasons, you should never try to mix Unicode/UTF-8 primary name servers with other name servers. Actually, enabling multibyte UTF-8 as your preferred name-checking method on Microsoft DNS Server is a good idea only when you are operating internally within a private namespace and all zones are hosted by the current version of Microsoft DNS Server or other UTF-8-aware DNS Servers.

Note

By default, Microsoft DNS Servers use an unrestricted form of ANSI-based name checking that prevents use of multibyte UTF-8 characters. Also, DNS Server provides the capability to configure name checking that can allow or restrict the use of UTF-8 characters in DNS data. This option can be configured on a per-server or per-zone basis.

Focusing on Your Organization's Root Domain

Even though I've stressed it before, it's worth repeating many times because of its importance: Active Directory planning requires careful consideration of DNS naming, starting with the root domain for your organization.

The top domain of the corporate namespace hierarchy represents the whole organization and is known as the organization's root domain. It is from this one internal domain that all other domains that belong to the organization originate. Because every Active Directory domain is represented by a DNS domain name, the naming of the organization's root domain has vast effects on almost everything in your organization—from SMTP mail addresses to the way that users log in and define themselves in the organizational hierarchy.

Tip

The root domain name usually won't limit you on the most crucial user-focused choices. While it's much easier to reuse the existing DNS structures for SMTP mail and logon purposes, it will usually be possible to use another DNS domain for those purposes. Almost any good mail server will allow you to use an SMTP mail name that is different from the DNS domain names in use. And Active Directory does allow you to define one or multiple alias DNS domains (the so-called UPN suffixes) that applies to logon names.

Only one name should be chosen for the organization's root domain, and it should be easily recognizable. The name should not be a bizarre name and should be meaningful to everyone involved in the organization. And you should take great care in choosing the root domain name, because it won't be easy to change later on!

A Word on Root Ownership

The easiest approach to Windows 2000 Server-based deployment is to create DDNS domains that correspond to the Active Directory domains—using exactly the same names—starting from the corporate DNS root domain and all the way throughout the Active Directory forest. Note that the domain name of a client or server and the Active Directory DNS domain name don't have to be the same—actually, you don't even need to have a one-to-one relationship between the Active Directory and DNS domain names.

For example, you're allowed to use the following:

- Existing corporate DNS root—**astonitgroup.com**
- Existing Windows NT 4 domain—**sales**
- New DNS domain—**sales.astonitgroup.com**
- New DNS domain after having upgraded to Active Directory—**sales.astonitgroup.com**

In this example, a new DNS domain is created to match the new Active Directory domain. This DNS domain contains all the DNS records registered by the DCs that belong to the **sales.astonitgroup.com** Active Directory domain.

One of the Windows 2000 Professional clients participating in the Active Directory domain might be named **comp-vmortensen.sales.astonitgroup.com**. Actually, that would be likely, because computers are named as **<computer_name>.<member_domain>** by default. However, you may find that placing the clients in their own subdomains (for example, based on site membership) is useful. Actually, this is quite straightforward to implement, because you're allowed to change the domain part on individual computers or on many computers simultaneously by using a group policy. For the preceding example, a sample name could be **comp-vmortensen.london.sales.astonitgroup.com** or **comp-vmortensen.newyork.sales.astonitgroup.com**. Because both of those sample names still are subdomains to the Active Directory DNS domain, it is possible to keep them in the same DNS zone, if that should prove opportune.

But be careful to note that, even though you have the freedom to use domain names of a client or server (or just create new subdomains) other than those used by default as the Active Directory DNS domain name, you should generally refrain from doing so, unless you have a very good reason. Experience shows that the simplest viable solution (having the client and server names using the name of the Active Directory domain) always proves to be the best solution in the long run. And, specifically, you should have a very good reason for placing servers or clients in another zone than that used by the Active Directory domain.

Typically, the organization's root domain should be named after the name of the company. And regardless of whether you intend to use the domain name on the Internet, you *always* should register it on the Internet, to avoid any hassles later on (you can find the full explanation on why that is so in the section "Choosing Between Internal and External Root Names").

The following checklist should be used to determine a satisfactory root domain name for your organization:

♦ It should be easily recognizable, meaningful, and acceptable to your organization.

♦ It should be agreed upon by upper management, because of the profound political implications that this decision often has on the organization. It should also be approved by your legal department.

♦ It should be a name that will remain static.

♦ It should be a name that is available on the Internet.

♦ It should be registered immediately at the proper Internet registration authority, which secures your organization's exclusive rights to a name in the specific second-level domain on the Internet.

If your organization has an existing DNS root name that satisfies the preceding requirements, you should choose to continue to use that root name, because it likely provides consistency for the company's eventual well-known corporate Internet email names, among other things.

If you are going to use an existing DNS root name, you must determine integration and compatibility issues with existing operating systems. What DNS Servers do you currently have implemented? Will the Active Directory namespace be part of the same namespace, or will the namespace be replaced? (See "Choosing DNS Servers," earlier in the chapter, for further discussion on that all-important subject.)

Choosing Between Internal and External Root Names

Before you implement a corporate root domain, you have to ponder the situation with regard to the different needs of the internal and external corporate servers (that is, the servers on the corporate LAN/WAN and the servers on the Internet). You have the choice of two very different solutions to fulfill the need to isolate resources intended for internal users from those resources available to the Internet community:

♦ Separate internal and external namespaces

♦ The same internal and external namespace

Even if your company doesn't have a presence on the Internet now, you should plan ahead for this eventuality, because the current trend indicates that having an Internet presence sooner or later becomes a necessity for just about any organization.

Separate Internal and External Namespaces

Figure 7.10 shows an example of a company that uses separate internal and external namespaces: **corporation.com** is the name used outside the firewall (the name presented to the Internet community), and **corp.com** is the name used inside the firewall. This architecture requires that two namespaces—in this instance, **corporation.com** and **corp.com**—be reserved with an Internet DNS registration authority.

The internal name, **corp.com**, should be reserved to prevent that name from being used on the public Internet. Failure to reserve this name would prevent internal clients from accessing this namespace on the public Internet in the future, because the client would be unable to distinguish between the internally implemented DNS domain and the one that is publicly available on the Internet.

The DNS zone configuration follows a traditional format, with a zone set up to resolve resources on the public Internet for **corporation.com** and a second zone defined inside the firewall that contains the resources available to clients on the company's internal network for **corp.com**. A client is able to clearly distinguish between an internal resource and an external resource based on the Fully Qualified Domain Name (FQDN). This approach, with separate internal and external namespaces, has the advantages and disadvantages shown in Table 7.10.

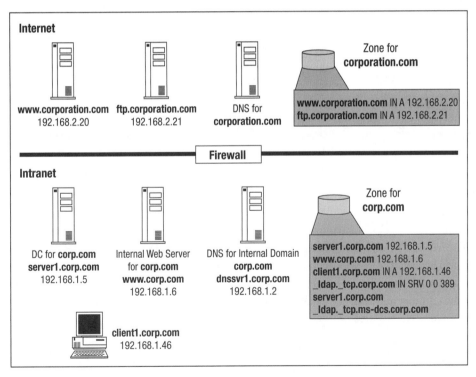

Figure 7.10
An example of different internal and external namespaces.

Table 7.10 The pros and cons of using separate internal and external namespaces.

Advantages	Disadvantages
A clear distinction exists between internal and external resources.	A user's logon name will by default be different from his or her email name (for example, Jane Smith would use the logon **jsmith@corp.com** and the external email address **jsmith@corporation.com**).
The structure is easier to manage because the disjointed namespaces can be managed separately and have no overlap.	This approach requires that the company reserve multiple names with an Internet DNS registration authority. This poses a potential problem if someone else currently owns the selected name and is unwilling to concede the name.
A simple client browser configuration (you can get by with an exception list that blocks all names that end in **corp.com** from going outside the firewall).	
A simple proxy client configuration (you can get by with an exception list that identifies all names ending in **corp.com** as internal).	

Same Internal and External Namespace

Figure 7.11 shows an example of a company that uses the same name for the internal and external namespaces: **corporation.com** is used both inside and outside the company. In this configuration, two separate zones for **corporation.com** exist:

♦ The zone file created inside the company network will usually contain the set of internal servers, as well as many or all of the servers available from the Internet, because this is the only way to enable the internal clients to contact all company resources.

♦ The zone file that resides on the DNS Servers outside the firewall will only reference the publicly accessible resources, such as Web servers, FTP servers, and mail servers. This configuration prevents clients external to the corporation from querying DNS for the internal corporate servers. Furthermore, no directory servers should reside outside the firewall, so that no Key Distribution Centers (KDCs) will be immediately susceptible to attack.

The reason for this setup is the common need for clients on the internal network to be able to access both the servers on the inside of the firewall on the intranet and the servers that reside outside the firewall on the Internet. This setup also prevents clients who are accessing the site from outside the firewall from being able to access or resolve names of internal resources, which helps protect company resources from attack.

One challenge presented by using the same namespace both internally and externally is determining how internal clients access publicly available resources. One way to ensure that corporate network clients have access to Internet servers is to mirror those services inside the corporate network. When mirrors of the applicable services are created and

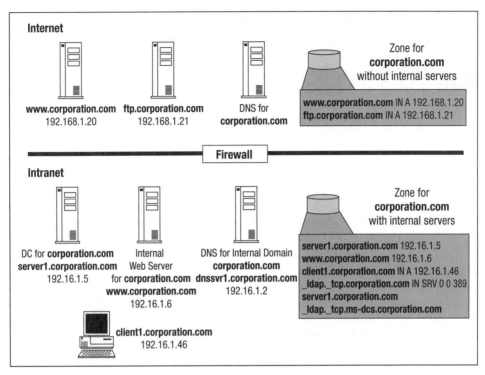

Figure 7.11
An example of having the same namespace both internally and externally.

entered in the internal **corporation.com** DNS zone, proxy client software can be config-ured to treat names ending in **.corporation.com** as internal to the corporate network and thus be just as simple as is the case with the separate namespace scenario. Mirroring has the useful side effect of making access to company Internet services from the corporate network faster than would otherwise be the case and freeing the firewall as well as the Internet servers from a fair amount of traffic. However, mirroring usually just isn't a vi-able solution because of the server hardware and administrative overhead that are added. The situation in which the namespace **corporation.com** is used both externally and inter-nally has the advantages and disadvantages shown in Table 7.11.

Please be keenly aware that the issue of whether to implement two separate namespaces or one and the same namespace for the corporate network and the Internet is subject to a lot of discussion. And so, one could go on for quite some time on this subject. But no matter what your personal preferences are, one thing is given: You should never access the Internet without a firewall (or, for the less security-sensitive, some kind of proxy server). And just for the record: Most organizations do choose separate namespaces, because it leaves less room for making serious errors that, in turn, leave a door open for uninvited guests to come from the Internet!

Table 7.11   The pros and cons of using the same namespace externally and internally.

Advantages	Disadvantages
The tree name, **corporation.com**, is consistent on the public Internet and private intranet.	Will often require a fairly complex proxy client setup, because the proxy client must understand when to send a request outside the corporate network.
The same logon and email names will be used by default.	Potential for confusion among administrators, which, for example, could lead to accidental external publication of internal-only content. Also, updating of internal and external resources must be much more in sync.
	Users must know that they will get a different view of corporate network resources, depending on the vantage point of the client. For example, when a user accesses **corporation.com** from the Internet, they can't view the internal corporate network resources.

Focusing on the DNS Zones and Replication

The last areas that need to be considered in regard to the design and planning of DNS are zones and replication.

Watch Out for This All Too Commonly Occurring Error: The DNS Server Can't Resolve Some Domain Names from the Internet

There's one error that is on the way to becoming a classic, so I just want to spend a minute on keeping you from doing it. This specific error only occurs when you've got an internal DNS Server resolving queries on Internet hosts by querying a name server on the outside of the corporate firewall for the records.

The problem—not being able to resolve some (but not all) domain names from the Internet—will occur when the Internet name server replies to the request using a different IP address from the address to which the query was sent initially by the internal DNS Server. Under these circumstances, a firewall will usually discard the reply from the external DNS Server because it isn't able to understand that it's actually an answer to a query coming from the internal network (because of the change of IP address).

You can avoid this problem in either of two ways:

- Have the DNS Server that is unable to resolve some of the domain names set the forwarders option to a DNS Server external to the firewall. The forwarders option will cause the internal DNS Server to do a recursive query to an external DNS Server, which will cause the reply to be from the same source IP address that the query was sent to.

- Set a rule on the firewall to allow any inbound traffic destined for port 53 to the IP address of the internal DNS Server. With this setting, the firewall won't drop the replies even though they are from a different source address than the query was sent to.

You might want to note that the discussion in this section applies only to the plan-
ning for standard DNS, so if you are using Active Directory-integrated DNS zones,
you might as well just skip the rest of this section.

As you may recall, DNS zones consist of sets of files that can be used to delegate or maintain authority. A DNS zone is a part of a DNS namespace in which database records are stored and managed in a particular DNS database file. The information stored in the zone is made available through several name servers that are kept up-to-date via replication (called *zone transfers* in a DNS setting).

An Active Directory domain tree always represents a contiguous namespace. And so, this namespace can be partitioned into a single zone, multiple individual zones on a per-domain basis, or any other partitioning scheme that is deemed to represent the optimum solution. Generally speaking, in a large, highly decentralized company, more zones are effective. Correspondingly, in a smaller, centralized company, fewer zones work well, because they reduce replication traffic and administrative overhead.

In other words, you can partition a namespace into multiple zones for load balancing. Establishing zones based on the physical structure of the company generally keeps the local DNS information close to the region that requires the DNS name most often—which may be a significant source of keeping a lid on the client query traffic across slow LAN/WAN links. But on the other hand, a large, centralized company that has a correspondingly large zone structure will be distributing DNS zone transfers (replication) across a much larger area, which might increase the load (coming from replication traffic) across slow LAN/WAN links.

Tip

You should understand that there's really nothing other than rules of thumbs to go
on when designing your zone and replication structures. The reason for this is the
very complexity and flexibility of the DNS design. And I urge you to put that flexibil-
ity to its fullest use when you do your zone and replication designing. The values
specified in the SOA record and the Microsoft-proprietary aging/scavenging proper-
ties are just a couple examples of the details that you're almost guaranteed to regret
not messing with.

Providing redundant sources for name resolution (having several name servers) in each of the DNS zones will work to eliminate an important single point of failure (and thus the risk of having all client queries transported across the WAN). Also, it allows you to place the DNS information close to the clients that will be using it the most. However, the more name servers, the more replication traffic. So, when you plan for DNS zones, you also have to balance the number of name servers needed for each DNS zone file with the number of zones.

Tip

Watch out for those dynamic updates. Unlike DNS, Dynamic DNS will have a fair level of updates going on. Unfortunately, the standard doesn't allow you to have the updating going on anywhere except at the primary name server. And so, you have no way of removing this all-important single point of failure, nor the bandwidth implications of having scores of updates traversing the network. Your only way of keeping a lid on the update traffic and the magnitude of the point of failure is to create more zones!

The DNS zone and name server design always entail a tradeoff between the need for fault tolerance and balancing query traffic and the need for balancing replication traffic. Ultimately, you should also remember to take into consideration that the easiest way to administer a DNS namespace is to retain authority over all the child domains in one zone only—the administrative chores will always grow with the number of zones.

Tip

You should also keep an eye on the fact that an increasing number of zones most typically also will lead to having an increasing number of queries forwarded to DNS Servers outside of the local site. A good DNS design will have taken this into account and thus avoided any decisions on the subject of zones (by having less zones, by performing a different partitioning of the domain namespace, or by having the local name servers acting as secondary name servers to the zones in question) that will prove highly detrimental to the overall network load.

But you should remember that it's really a very complex and dynamic situation you're dealing with here, in which the results can vary quite a lot between different applications (and even with different versions of the same application) and designs. So, in many cases, you'll have to trust your feelings rather than being able to base your decisions on facts.

An example of the endless complexity could be that the records for GC (Global Catalog) location and DC location by GUID only are registered in the DNS zone hosting Active Directory's top-level forest domain. While the DC location by GUID is used by replication, nobody really knows how much these records will be used—and thus, whether the queries for those records will be considered passable or if you should add the zone comprising the forest root to one of your DNS name servers at each site. (Based on my current knowledge, you should let it go; zone transfers will imply much more traffic than the queries in a bare-bones Windows 2000 environment, unless you only have a few DCs registered in the forest zone).

Don't Forget Those Reverse Lookup Zones

On the subject of zones, you should take care not to repeat one of the beginner's typical errors: to focus all the attention on the forward lookup zones and forget about the reverse lookup zones until something goes wrong! It takes just about as much effort to determine which reverse lookup zones to create and where to place them as it does to design the forward lookup zones.

While reverse lookup zones and PTR resource records aren't necessary for Active Directory to work, PTR RRs are commonly used by applications to verify the identities of clients. And you'll also need them if you want clients to be able to resolve FQDNs from IP addresses. In order to do a good job because of the reverse lookup zones, you should first gather a list of all the subnets in your network and then examine the class (A, B, or C) and type (class-based or subnetted) of each subnet.

Note

To simplify administration, create as few reverse lookup zones as possible. For example, if you have only one class B or class C network identifier, it will often be opportune to organize your reverse lookup zones along the class B or C boundaries (no matter whether you've subnetted your network or not).

And you should take great care to understand that the reverse lookup zones are part of the DNS namespace and so can—in theory—be built without any regard to the underlying TCP/IP properties of the network infrastructure. Likewise, the reverse lookup zones are totally separate from the forward lookup zones, meaning that the subdomains and forward lookup zones don't need to have their own reverse lookup zones.

Additionally, you should note that the Active Directory Installation Wizard (used for promoting a server to DC) doesn't automatically add a reverse lookup zone and PTR resource records because of the possibility that another server, such as the parent server, controls the reverse lookup zone. Actually, the DHCP Server is the only part of the Active Directory infrastructure that will automatically define PTR resource records.

WINS: Can't Do with It and Can't Do without It—A Few Words of Advice

Windows Internet Name Service (WINS) provides dynamic name resolution for the NetBIOS namespace. Before Windows 2000, WINS would generally be called for being able to keep up with all clents and servers in any large or mid-sized network environment. As mentioned earlier in this chapter, Windows 2000 clients (as well as Windows 95/98 clients that have the Active Directory client upgrade installed) no longer use NetBIOS for accessing Active Directory. And so, after you've migrated or updated all your clients and Windows NT servers, you will be able to turn the WINS Server off and remove all other NetBIOS-based compatibility measures that might be in place. Or rather, that's how the theory reads: Microsoft has stated the position that "WINS is not required in a purely Windows 2000 environment" several times during the development of Windows 2000, as well as in the Windows 2000 Server Resource Kit.

Unfortunately, this simply isn't the entire story. Windows 2000 Server still employs NetBIOS for a few things (probably due to absentmindedness on the part of a couple of the Windows 2000 developers). And so, you're still advised to implement WINS (or LMHOSTS files) in your environment so as to avoid any unfortunate events on this account.

This book doesn't include a primer to NetBIOS or WINS, because many of you already are used to working with these things and, also, they're described in every puny detail in just about any good book on Windows NT Server. However, I still feel that a few comments are called for on the subject of NetBIOS.

First of all, I will strongly advise against your implementing anything but WINS for the following reasons:

♦ You can indeed avoid all of the major issues experienced because of the NetBIOS-bound parts of the Active Directory by creating an LMHOSTS file that specifies all of your DCs and their IP addresses. However, I won't recommend your doing that because there's a high probability you would have to implement one or several NetBIOS-bound applications (there still aren't very many native DNS applications available) in your network environment.

♦ If you've only got a single LAN segment, your lazy side might take charge: After all, the NetBIOS broadcasts will work to avoid any troubles. However, please be aware that NetBIOS broadcasts can be lethal to servers and clients alike (the network equipment usually is the last one to give in). And according to my experiences, Active Directory behaves almost exactly as its predecessor (that is, it's fairly ill-behaved) in regard to the master browser election!

And yeah, I do know that WINS isn't known to be among the most stable applications devised by man. But believe me, the WINS service included with Windows 2000 Server

---

Where's NetBIOS Used?

Until now, I've only had two encounters with NetBIOS in a pure Windows 2000 environment: in the Cluster Administrator and when accessing the Schema Master and Domain Tree FSMOs. However, it also seems to be in operation at several other places, because the introduction of WINS does reduce the chat among DCs.

On top of that, you might want to note that SMS 2 is heavily dependent upon NetBIOS (actually, it's more dependent upon NetBIOS than its predecessor). Also, Exchange 2000 Server won't install at WAN locales unless it's able to resolve the NetBIOS name of the server hosting the Schema Master FSMO (probably just another consequence of the NETBIOS blunder in regard to Active Directory's forest-wide FSMO roles).

And then there's a seemingly endless number of third-party client and server applications, which also depend on NetBIOS; there's Network Neighborhood's NetBIOS-based browse functionality; and so on. So, to make a long story short: You probably won't be able to do without NetBIOS and WINS (or the *LMHOSTS* files) this time around, either. While Windows 2000 does indeed represent a good step for moving away from NetBIOS, it doesn't do away fully with the NetBIOS legacy.

goes a long way to fix the shortcomings that we've had to live with until now. Additionally, Windows 2000 Server's WINS service includes a couple of enhancements that would have come in very handy several years ago:

♦ *Persistent Connections*—Now you can configure each WINS Server to maintain a persistent connection with one or more replication partners. This increases the speed of replication and eliminates the overhead of opening and terminating connections.

♦ *Manual Tombstoning*—You are allowed to manually mark a record for eventual deletion (called *tombstoning*). The tombstone state of the record then replicates across all WINS Servers, preventing an active copy on a different server database from re-propagating the record.

♦ *Enhanced Filtering and Record Searching*—Improved filtering and new search functions go a long way toward making it easy to locate the wished-for records.

♦ *Consistency Checking*—You can now ask for the consistency among WINS Servers to be checked. And you have the choice between a full database check or two quick tests to verify consistency between replication partners. The quick test entails comparing the IP addresses returned by a NetBIOS name query of different WINS Servers (record verification) and examining the owner address-to-version number mapping tables (version number validation).

♦ *Dynamic Record Deletion*—Dynamic record deletion and multi-select allow you to delete one or multiple WINS static or dynamic entries. Now, you're also allowed to delete records that use names containing nonalphanumeric characters.

Note

The Windows 2000 Server WINS service also includes a fairly lethal option: Autodiscovery of WINS partners. Using this option, you'll have the WINS Server using multicast for locating other WINS Servers and have it adding the discovered WINS Servers as push-and-pull replication partners. As you can guess, this option should be used with the utmost care. Luckily, Microsoft feels the same way: This option is turned off by default.

So, while I do know it's nothing like you've expected, you might as well get that WINS up and running from the outset. And please remember to try to reduce your reliance on NetBIOS, because DNS is a much more capable solution and, hopefully, Microsoft as well as the third-party vendors will have done away with the remainder of "NetBIOSness" in the not-too-distant future.

The advice on reducing NetBIOS is quite simple:

♦ Use only names that adhere to the strict DNS naming standards (RFC 1123).

♦ Use DNS rather than NetBIOS name resolution wherever possible.

♦ Implement WINS lookup on your DNS zones, if possible, so that DNS is queried for NetBIOS name resolution rather than going straight to the WINS Server.

♦ Put the DHCP/DDNS integration functionality to full use.

♦ Convert your "home-grown" NetBIOS applications to WinSock.

The Recommended Steps for DNS Designing

Some of the questions that you need to answer when you start planning your company's namespace are the following:

♦ Does the company have a large existing DNS structure? If yes, what are the existing DNS Servers, and do they have support for SRV records?

♦ Is DHCP deployed?

♦ Will the Active Directory implementation assume an existing namespace?

♦ What are the current administrative boundaries?

Note

Ultimately, you should be proficient in Active Directory modeling, because the namespaces for Active Directory and DNS are interdependent—the actual level of interdependence depends on your answers to the questions outlined in this chapter.

After answering these questions, you should delve into the question of the root domain: Should it use a public root or a private root? Table 7.12 shows a comparison of the reasons for choosing one or the other.

If you choose a private root zone, be aware that it represents a private instance of a DNS tree, and because only one true DNS tree exists (the Internet tree), you should make sure that the private namespace doesn't overlap with the Internet namespace, or make sure to register the domain name used on the Internet to avoid a possible name clash later.

When you choose names for the domains and network resources, you should use Internet-standard characters. However, this often requires renaming of machines and domains in existing Windows installations, because NetBIOS allows a whole range of characters that aren't supported by DNS. If possible, you should implement this renaming before you start the Windows 2000 Server migration—or at least use only DNS-compliant names from now on.

Table 7.12   Public root vs. private root.

Public Root	Private Root
Trust the Internet for name resolution	Want full control over name resolution
Want to use the Internet root servers	No direct Internet access
Have direct Internet access	Most common in large organizations

If renaming is out of the question, you could turn to using the Unicode character set option available on Microsoft DNS Server. However, this is not a very elegant solution, because a large proportion of the DNS resolvers available today still aren't able to resolve the Unicode/ UTF-8 names. So, if you choose to use nonstandard names, you should use Microsoft DNS Server everywhere (and upgrade all the network clients to Active Directory) or make sure that the other DNS Servers (and clients) are UTF-8-compliant. Although using a one-to-one mapping of Active Directory domain names to DNS domain names is preferable, Active Directory domain names and host names don't have to be related. So, why the preference for a one-to-one mapping? Because it is the simplest solution!

This simplicity is apparent when you begin the zone planning. It's quite a bit easier to design the proper replication topology if you have a one-to-one mapping of all hosts and domain names in DNS to the Active Directory resources and domains. And if all the records for each Active Directory domain are stored in one zone, you'll be able to use the proprietary Active Directory-integrated zone option available in Microsoft DNS Server, which makes every DC in each domain appear as if it is running as a primary name server, just by adding the DNS service.

But before you may choose to venture down this path of least resistance, you need to ask yourself whether it provides the optimum fit to your organization. You may need more zones, in order to delegate along the lines of responsibility and authority, or you may need to balance the number of zones against the size of the zones in a better way. (This should mostly be an issue for ordinary DNS-type zones rather than zones in which support for RFCs 1995 and 1996 is available.) If you aren't able to harness the Active Directory-integrated zone option for some reason, you have to stick to standard DNS zone transfers and possibly create replicas to balance query traffic versus replication traffic. A summary of the most important best practices that surround your DNS design is shown in Table 7.13.

Table 7.13   Summary of the best practices for DNS design in a Windows 2000 Server/Active Directory network infrastructure.

Task	Points to Consider
Migrating non-DNS compliant naming. The NetBIOS naming scheme and many other naming schemes allow for many characters that aren't supported by the DNS standard.	Characters allowed in standard DNS include only the U.S. alphabet, numeric digits, and hyphens. Thus, a change of the current naming standards and a migration of the existing network names will be called for in most instances.
Choosing between a public or private domain.	You will need to make an informed decision as to whether the root of your DNS domain should be private or public (that is, based on the Internet domain tree). Regardless of your decision, you should always register the domain name on the Internet, to avoid any possibility of duplicate naming.

(continued)

Table 7.13   Summary of the best practices for DNS design in a Windows 2000 Server/Active Directory network infrastructure *(continued)*.

Task	Points to Consider
Choosing the correspondence between internal and external DNS namespaces.	You will have to consider whether to use separate or the same root name(s) for network resources on the intranet and the Internet. Using separate root names establishes a clear distinction between internal and external resources and makes it easier to set up and manage. On the other hand, using the same root names enables users to employ the same logon and email names by default, no matter where they reside. But, it can also be the source of more confusion among the users, because of the differences inside and outside the corporate firewall.
Choosing the name for your root domain.	You should strive to choose names for your DNS domains that are logical descriptors for your organization. Absolutely avoid names that are very cryptic or based on temporary conditions. You will learn a lot more information on the art of choosing the right domain names for your Active Directory setup in Chapters 8 and 11.
Establishing zoning strategy.	When you design the DNS zones, your basic premise should always be strict adherence to the Active Directory domains. However, remember that this is only a rule of thumb for a "standard" implementation. Many good reasons exist for implementing a different zone structure (such as minimizing query traffic across slow or heavily loaded network links).
Choosing a replication scheme.	If you choose to implement Microsoft DNS Server, you will have the choice between the usual DNS single-master replication scheme and the proprietary Active Directory-integrated zone replication. When planning for standard DNS replication, you should be sure to provide adequate redundancy, minimize traffic load, and balance the load evenly across separate WANs and name servers.
Choosing your DNS Server.	To support Active Directory, a DNS Server must support RFC 2052 (SRV RRs). Additionally, support for RFC 2136 (Dynamic Update Protocol) and RFC 1995 (Incremental Zone Transfers) will be very advantageous.

Getting Down to Business

Undoubtedly, this chapter is a tough one if you don't have any previous DNS experience. And you probably felt very overloaded if you've never worked with a hierarchical directory service—or something similar to that. But you shouldn't despair. This chapter presents a very hard (and pretty abstract) subject, and my experiences tell me that no easy way exists to fully understand DNS, which incidentally is a cornerstone of Active Directory. You have to get out there in real life and get some dirt under your fingernails before the many intricacies of DNS will dawn fully on you.

The interdependence of DNS and Active Directory means that you are at a great advantage if you fully plan the Active Directory structure before you install DNS on the network—otherwise, you run the risk of needing to introduce some unpleasant changes in the DNS setup ahead of the completion of the Active Directory implementation. Thus, I urge you to complete Chapters 8 and 11 before introducing your first Active Directory domain on the network. Additionally, companies that are currently in the process of planning a rollout of DNS or Windows NT Server 4 on their networks should also study Chapters 21 and 22 very thoroughly and establish a blueprint (however sketchy) for the transition to Windows 2000 Server, to avoid unpleasant surprises later on.

Chapter 8
Planning a Domain Structure

By now, you should have attained an intimate knowledge of Active Directory naming in general and DNS in particular. Thus, you are ready to move on to the very essence of Active Directory design: planning the domain structure.

As you may recall from earlier chapters, the Active Directory domain is the core unit of logical structure in Active Directory. The Active Directory domain is both a logical grouping of objects and a boundary for replication and security. Inside the domain, you find all the objects (user accounts, groups, computers, printers, applications, security policies, and file shares) that represent the network resources. Additionally, you will also find the Organizational Units (OUs), container objects that can be used to organize the objects into a hierarchy of logical administrative groups.

A *domain structure* is actually a domain made up of multiple OUs. When you begin planning the domain structure, you should always start with a single domain and add domains only when necessary—the simple reason for this advice is that the fewer domains, the better.

This chapter focuses on the planning that goes into building a single domain structure. Thus, regardless of whether you have to implement one or several Active Directory domains, you should study this chapter carefully. Remember, you need to design each domain in a multiple domain setting. Thus, the more domains you implement, the more important it is that you know this chapter well.

However, if you determine that you do need multiple domains, you should design the domain tree structure before you cater to the needs of the individual domains. The craft of designing domain tree structures is the topic of Chapter 11.

The structure of this book is based purely on pedagogical reasons. Grasping the domain tree structure design is much easier when you have solid knowledge of the work that you need to do and the basic concepts that go into the architecture of a single domain structure. Also, the organizational questions that need to be asked and the solution space are basically the same. So, even if you are confident that you need a multiple domain structure, please read on—you may even find yourself changing your mind midway through this chapter.

Adhering to KISS

KISS (Keep It Simple, Stupid) is a good summary for the objective of an Active Directory architecture. Because the single domain is the simplest domain structure to create and administer, this structure should always be your first consideration. And you should add more domains only when absolutely necessary.

The main reason that I'm able to pass on this rather simple advice without any kind of reservations is that the OU object really is a much more dynamic and flexible structuring mechanism than the domain. A change in the domain tree structure (such as collapses and re-creations) causes much more administrative overhead than implementing the same changes on OUs. Yet the OU still enables you to reflect your organizational hierarchy as well as allowing you to cater to a large proportion of the needs for creating administrative subgroupings.

However, you should be keenly aware that, the higher up in the OU hierarchy (remember that OUs are implemented in a tree structure) you go, the more static the structure needs to be in order to avoid confusing administrators as well as users. In other words, if you have a large OU tree structure, implementing changes on the top level OUs will prove to be almost as burdensome in terms of the "human factor" as implementing the same level of changes in multiple domains (which is the case if you have domains representing the same organizational structure as the first level of OUs). But you should note that it would still prove much easier for an Active Directory administrator to implement the same level of changes in an OU structure than in a domain structure.

If your job involves designing Active Directory implementations, you will often find that more than one domain is necessary in the following situations:

♦ *Multiple business units need to have different names*—A single domain always has one—and only one—root, which is used as the name of the particular domain (and, incidentally, also as the DNS name).

♦ *The scale of the Active Directory must be increased to accommodate well over 100,000 objects*—Microsoft and various third parties have completed a fair number of lab tests on Active Directory using all the way up to the theoretical limits for an Active Directory domain (which is somewhere between 10 and 20 million objects, depending upon which objects are being loaded into the directory and which of their properties are being used). However, experience proves that theory is a whole other realm than practice. And so, I recommend that you consider implementing more than one domain if you are approaching 100,000 objects—whether that will be today or in the coming years.

♦ *The organizational hierarchy is very deep*—At a quite early point in time, Microsoft stated a recommendation for using 10 or fewer OU levels. The reason for this is that performance degrades significantly at higher than 10 levels, eventually making the domain utterly useless from the users' point of view. I must admit that I never fully understood the underlying reasons for this recommendation (unless you start factoring in the consequences of GPOs, LDAP searches, administrative delegation, and such things, all of which differ widely among different organizations). But until further information becomes available on this, I would recommend that you start evaluating the pros and cons of using a multiple domain structure when you implement the seventh OU level. Also, you might want to keep in mind that performance actually begins degrading after you introduce the first OU level according to that same Microsoft statement; it just seems to happen at a much slower rate until you reach a certain depth in your OU tree.

♦ *Two parts of the network are separated by a link that is so slow that the level of replication traffic crossing it needs to be minimized*—Even though the site-structuring concept makes performing replications between WAN locations highly efficient, nothing can change the fact that some bandwidth is needed for replication purposes—and the larger the domain, the more bandwidth will be called for.

♦ *The network has unique security policy requirements*—Differing security policies may require separate domains, because the scope of certain base security properties are domain-wide (and thus can't vary inside a given domain). However, remember to inspect the unique parts of the security policies carefully, because you can change a fair deal of the security policies inside the OU hierarchy. If the organization doesn't need varying security policies that can only be administered at the domain level, you should still be able to use the single domain solution.

♦ *The organization is highly decentralized*—Organizationally speaking, providing someone from a separate part of the organization with grand powers over everything that resides in the corporate computing environment (including the ability to overrule all other administrators) might be quite unthinkable. However, this is what actually happens if a person from another part of the organization is holding Domain Administrator privileges in the single domain structure. This scenario is probable, because certain administrative tasks can be performed only by a person who has Domain Administrator privileges.

♦ *The organization has different users and resources that are managed by completely different sets of administrative personnel*—This type of situation might turn out to point to a multiple domain solution. As mentioned in some of the earlier items in this list, everybody in a single domain has to adhere to the same base security policies, and the Domain Administrator always hold more control than a delegated OU Administrator. Both of these things might prove unacceptable in this kind of organization.

♦ *The organization responds to political requests for finer segregation of departments, divisions, or projects*—The fact that each domain is a boundary for replication and security does prompt some organizations to insist on having multiple domains out of purely political reasons.

♦ *The organization is an international company that wants each country's users and resources to be administered locally*—International differences regarding language, business practices, or currencies might call for separate domains for each region.

♦ *You want to prevent a single point of failure*—Even though Microsoft has gone to great lengths to secure the stability of the Active Directory domain database, accidents do happen. And the larger the domain, the higher the stakes. If a centrally placed domain controller (DC) somehow goes haywire, restoring the last valid backup of the Active Directory domain database and making sure that every other DC has been "cleansed" from the corrupt data could prove to take a very long time. Furthermore, you always have to consider the worst-case scenario: a human administrative error that leads to the domain being partly or fully deleted—and this change being replicated throughout the domain before anyone notices the error. If you have several domains, the consequences of such an accident are reduced proportionally.

♦ *You want a one-to-one mapping of existing Windows NT Server domains in a migration setting*—Generally speaking, if you have more than one NT domain that is to be migrated, you will often wind up opting for implementing several Active Directory domains. The reason for this is that the easiest migration path is a one-to-one mapping of the NT domains to Active Directory domains.

Beware, however, that many good reasons exist for *not* having multiple domains:

♦ *The company wants to reflect its organization of divisions and departments rather than several quite autonomous organizations*—Remember, each domain require its own DNS domain name, which by default will be identical to the name of the Active Directory domain name.

♦ *The company wants to avoid naming domains for divisions, departments, buildings, and even floors or workgroups*—Using this type of name will prove to be quite confusing and doesn't look good in regard to the DNS names, just to name two reasons.

♦ *A good domain design should be able to withstand company reorganizations*—A reorganization shouldn't prompt a restructuring of your entire domain hierarchy.

♦ *Ultimately, you should try to resist the temptation of creating multiple domains for purely political reasons*—If you don't resist this temptation, your design probably also can't withstand political changes within the company without the need to restructure your domain hierarchy.

Much more can (and will) be said about the single domain versus multiple domain scenario. However, I won't dwell on this quite vital subject any more, because I expect you to have a fundamental understanding of the two solutions by now. And I especially expect you to be keenly aware of the common wisdom of directory services modeling: It is *not* simply a question of technical prowess, because the Active Directory structuring might ultimately grow into a fierce battleground for settling disputes regarding the organizational hierarchy, which is exactly why you should heed the advice on planning provided in Chapter 6.

The Makings of a Domain

An Active Directory "domain" is a combination of some familiar definitions and some brand new ones. The fundamental definitions on an Active Directory domain are as follows:

♦ *A unit of partitioning*—Every domain has a DNS name, and a domain's Domain Controllers (DCs) store information about the objects (such as users, applications, computers, and printers) residing in that domain. In other words, a domain is a grouping of servers and other network objects under a single name.

♦ *A unit of authentication*—To be successfully authenticated against the DCs, the user has to be known to the domain.

♦ *Manifested by DCs*—The DCs add the following properties to the domain:

  ♦ *Unit of replication*—The replication of domain information will only occur inside that domain.

  ♦ *Security boundary*—Security policies and settings (such as administrative rights, security policies, and ACLs) don't cross from one domain to another. Because a domain is a security boundary, different administrators will be able to create and manage different domains separately in your organization, if that suits your company's needs. However, please note that there are a few powerful administrative groups (Enterprise Admins and Schema Admins) that cross the domain boundaries.

  ♦ *Administrative boundary*—The administrator of a domain has absolute rights to set policies and assign permissions within that domain only.

Grouping objects into Active Directory domains enables you to reflect the corporate organizational structure in your company's computer network. Each domain stores only the information about the objects located in that domain. Thus, you're allowed to split up, or *partition*, the directory information using multiple domains, which in effect allows Active Directory to scale up to as many objects as you need to store information about on your network.

An Active Directory domain is not the same as a Windows NT Server 4 domain, as you will see from Table 8.1, which compares some of the new and exciting features found in Windows 2000 Server's Active Directory domains with their Windows NT Server 4 counterparts.

Active Directory permits you to delegate administrative control of parts of the domain to other users or groups. In other words, you are able to grant control to specific users or groups

Table 8.1   Changes to "domain" from NT Server 4 to Windows 2000 Server.

Capability	Windows NT Server 4	Windows 2000 Server
Unit of replication	Object	Attribute
Approximate maximum size	40,000 objects	More than 10 million objects
Network Naming Scheme	NetBIOS	DNS
Delegation of administration	Create new domain	Delegate within domain by using OUs or creating new domain

over a subset of the objects or properties found in the whole Active Directory domain structure or a part of the OU hierarchy. You should note that this so-called delegation of administration feature not only allows you to distribute the administrative chores to more people than possible using Windows NT Server 4, it also works to eliminate the need for granting sweeping authority over an entire domain to all administrators.

The net result of the new features of Active Directory domains (see Figure 8.1) is that an Active Directory design usually will require fewer domains than a comparable Windows NT Server 4 design. The main contributors to this domain reduction are Active Directory's ability to accommodate more objects per domain and the possibilities that Active Directory provides to delegate administration within a domain.

As described earlier, usually some of the domains found in Windows NT Server environments might just as well be collapsed into OUs. So, instead of having to use multiple domains (as will always be called for when implementing Windows NT Server 4 in a large company), you can harness the OUs to reflect the details of your company's organization, thus gaining a significant edge on future versatility, because of the easier implementation of changes inherent in OUs compared to domains. For example, after your domain structure is in place, such tasks as moving, merging, or collapsing Active Directory domains aren't trivial (exactly as is the case in NT Server-based domains).

However, there isn't such a thing as a free meal: Windows 2000 Server doesn't allow Active Directory domains to be moved or renamed (although Microsoft officials have promised on several occasions that this functionality will be included in a later release of Windows 2000 Server), and it doesn't permit the root domain of a domain tree or forest to be deleted or its role to be transferred (that is, adding another domain at the top of the domain hierarchy).

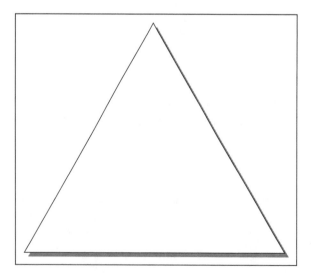

Figure 8.1
An Active Directory domain is usually represented as a triangle, whereas NT-style domains typically are shown as circles.

As you may recall, because each Active Directory domain is identified by a DNS name, a naming strategy must be applied to create a *namespace* (a bounded area in which the DNS name is translated into the objects that it contains). Consequently, you should *always* strive to use domain names that are unlikely to change—especially in regard to the name of the domain tree root(s).

Although the single domain solution is preferable from an administrator's point of view, in most medium and large organizations, implementing several domains can be necessary, as mentioned earlier in this chapter. Such multiple domain solutions can consist of one or more domain trees and/or forests. The design of domain trees and forests is the subject of Chapter 11.

Getting Down to the Basics of OUs

A domain contains various objects with relevance to the network, such as users, computers, printers, file shares, and other OUs. Many of the network objects are known from Windows NT Server 4, and the new objects seem pretty much immediately understandable, because they're just representations of things that already are found on the network—except one, the OU. Understanding the concept of OUs is even more important than you may think, because it offers a structuring mechanism for the rest of the objects that can be stored inside the domain. In other words, OUs are simply logical containers into which you can place users, groups, computers, OUs, and other directory objects.

By splitting the namespace of a domain into a hierarchy of OUs (see Figure 8.2), you no longer have to view tens of thousands of users in a flat list. And you can even use the OUs to organize the objects into a hierarchical, logical namespace tree that duplicates your organization's structure.

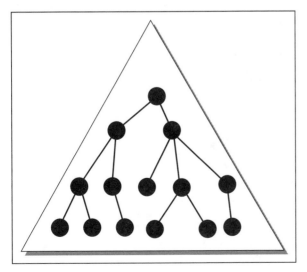

Figure 8.2
The OUs enable you to create a hierarchy inside each domain.

The following is a summary of the characteristics of an OU:

♦ Resides in a domain

♦ Is a container object

♦ Used for creating a hierarchical structure within a domain

♦ Can be easily created, moved, or removed

Because of the hierarchical nature of OUs, you can use them to create a nearly perfect mirror image of how your business is organized. And because OUs can contain other OUs, the hierarchy can be extended as far as necessary, enabling you to create any hierarchy that may be called for (which usually also will work to minimize the number of Active Directory domains needed).

OUs also can be used for creating a logical structure that maps to the way you administer the network, by delegating administrative control down to the smallest size necessary. For example, a user can be granted administrative rights for only a subtree of OUs, or even a single OU.

Windows 2000 Server's security subsystem presents you with the option of assigning fine-grained access permissions and rights to users, groups, and computers. Using a combination of OUs and Access Control Lists (ACLs), you are now able to grant permissions and rights in just about any way you may see fit the needs. The OUs allow you to define the scope of the permissions and rights (an entire domain, a subtree of OUs within a domain, or even a single OU) and the ACLs allow you to define which objects and which properties are included. Thus, you can, for example, provide a specific user or group with the rights to reset passwords within a specific OU, but not the right to modify other account attributes within that OU.

You need to understand that the DNS namespace doesn't reveal your OUs (see Figure 8.3). For example, an OU named Accounting in the **sales.example.astonitgroup.com** domain is *not* referred to by the DNS name **accounting.sales.example.astonitgroup.com**. The OU can be addressed only via one of the query methods for the directory (ADSI, LDAP, and MAPI) and via one of the many possible naming conventions. Also, any one OU is contained entirely within one domain—which also means that an OU can't contain objects from multiple domains.

Summarizing the OU Concept

OUs are containers that you can use to organize objects within a domain into logical subgroupings in a particular administrative and organizational setting. OUs can contain (but are not limited to) the following objects:

♦ Users

♦ Computers

♦ Groups

♦ Printers

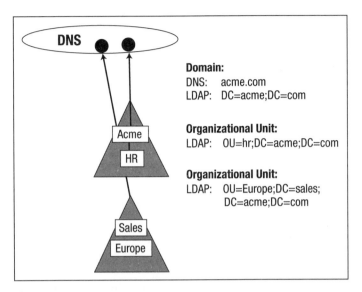

Figure 8.3
OUs are *not* part of the DNS namespace.

♦ Applications

♦ Security policies

♦ File shares

Specifically, an OU can contain other OUs, which enables you to create a hierarchy of OUs in a domain.

Typical reasons to create OUs are to accomplish the following:

♦ Delegate administration.

♦ Replace Windows NT 4 resource domains.

♦ Scope the application of one or more policies. For example, you could create different OUs for full-time and contract employees, and then create different policies for each OU, enabling you to apply the policies easily. Remember, though, that several core security policies can be defined only on the domain level.

♦ Control administration of resources. For example, instead of setting permissions on multiple file shares, you can assemble the relevant shares in an OU to allow you to set permissions on a single unit of work.

♦ Ease the administration of objects by grouping them in a consistent manner. For example, you can group objects so that objects with identical security requirements are kept together.

♦ Limit the total number of objects that appear in any one OU. This alone eases administration quite a bit in any big company because it's much faster to identify the needed object when there are fewer objects to look at.

- Hold other OUs.
- Create a static entity that is relatively stable.

The following are good reasons to create OUs (each of which is explained in depth in the upcoming sections):

- To delegate administration
- To replace resource domains
- To apply policies
- To group objects with common properties

On the other hand, you must resist the urge to create meaningless OU structures. Watch out for structure for structure's own sake!

Delegating Administration

Delegation of administration enables administrators to grant specific administrative rights for the directory objects located in containers and subtrees to other users and groups. You can define levels of responsibility (for example, to limit the administrative scope to allow only the creation of new objects of a certain type at a certain OU level). By creating a tree of OUs within each domain and delegating authority for parts of the OU subtree to others, you can delegate authority down to even the average end users of your organization, without having to make any compromises with regard to security along the way.

The scope of the administrative responsibility that you delegate is highly configurable. Generally, you can delegate permission to do any of the following administrative tasks:

- Change attributes on all objects in a particular OU (including the OU itself), such as the phone number attribute on user objects.
- Create, delete, read, and so on, child objects of a specific type within an OU, such as users, groups, or printers.
- Read and/or write specific attributes on a specific type of child object within an OU, such as the right to set passwords on user objects.

You should start delegating administration by taking current administrative groups within your IT organization and mapping their roles to the possibilities brought forward by the OUs.

After you decide how to structure your OUs and which OUs to put each directory object into, consider the hierarchy of administration. Remember, too, that you can grant an administrator access rights to manage a small subset of objects within his or her area of responsibility, while simultaneously withholding access rights to manage the same objects in other parts of the organization. Also note that the owner of an OU has the responsibility for deciding:

- Whether to inherit permissions from the parent object
- What permissions to add or change

♦ Whether to propagate access rights (that is, permissions) from the OU hierarchy to child objects

Replacing Resource Domains

In Windows NT Server, delegation of administration was achieved through resource domains (these types of domains being found in domain designs that are founded on the single master and multiple master domain models). Using resource domains is an expensive method of reducing the administrative scope, because it requires administrative personnel to manage trusts and requires additional hardware for DCs. With Windows 2000 Server, you can reduce these administrative and hardware costs by collapsing your resource domains into a hierarchy of OUs. So, if you currently employ resource domains, upgrading to Active Directory usually provides a way to reduce the number of domains in your environment, thus simplifying your network administration and network structure.

However, when you are deciding whether to upgrade a resource domain to an OU, be certain to weigh the costs of collapsing the resource domains against the costs of leaving them in place, because collapsing domains as part of the upgrade isn't a trivial task (see also Chapter 22).

Applying Policies

Active Directory introduces a new and much more versatile policy concept than is available in Windows NT Server 4-based networks. These policies, referred to as *Group Policies*, define the various components of the users' desktop environment that a system administrator needs to manage, including the following:

♦ Specifying security settings

♦ Assigning scripts (these scripts can be run at computer startup, computer shutdown, user logon, and user logoff)

♦ Redirecting files from users' desktops

♦ Making applications available to users

♦ Managing software policies

To create a specific policy configuration for a particular group of users, you use the *Group Policy MMC snap-in*. The Group Policy settings that you specify in the snap-in are contained in a *Group Policy Object (GPO)*, which in turn is associated with one or multiple Active Directory container objects—a GPO can be associated with sites, domains, and OUs.

However, you should take care to remember that each Active Directory domain also acts as a unit of domain-level policy. That is, several policies can be set up only at the domain level and, thus, apply to all users in the domain and all machines that are members of the domain (unless other policies are defined on the machines using GPOs at their OU). Account

---

Assigning Permissions: A Vital Shortcoming of OUs

Although using OUs is very logical, unfortunately, OUs aren't the answer to every server adminis-
tration task. Specifically, OUs can't be used for controlling access rights and permissions on objects.
This annoying limitation to versatility of the OUs stems from the fact that—just as in a Windows NT
Server 4 environment—the administration of access control permissions and rights can be assigned
and granted only to security principals (that is, objects that carry a Security Identifier, or SID).
Windows 2000 Server only incorporates the same set of security principals available in NT Server 4:

- Users
- Groups
- Computers

So, no matter how awkward it may sound, the simplistic group concept, which works separately
from the directory service per se, is the only viable way to apply some sort of structure to security
administration. Viewed in an administrative context, this situation is even worse than that experienced with NT Server 4: Because Active Directory introduces several new structuring concepts and
the infrastructure necessary to implement many more objects than is possible in an NT Server 4
setting, in most instances you should anticipate an even greater workload with regard to security
administration than was the case in Windows NT Server 4.

---

policies and public key policies are set on the domain level for users. To be more exact, these
policies include the following:

- Password policies (minimum length, expiration, complexity requirements, and so forth)
- Account lockout policies (threshold, duration, and so forth)
- Kerberos policies (maximum lifetime for tickets, tolerance for clock synchronization, and so forth)
- Encrypted Data Recovery agents, which specify which certificates are available for re-covering EFS-encrypted files
- Trusted certificate authorities (trusted root certification authorities and enterprise trust)

Grouping of Objects

When you create an OU, you're able to decide who is permitted to view and control objects
(and object attributes) in the OU and what level of control each person has over the objects stored in the OU. For example, you can allow certain users or groups to have full access
to certain OUs and objects, while completely restricting other users or groups from access,
so that they can't view the OU and won't even know that it exists.

Correspondingly, if you implement OUs with the relevant grouping of objects, handling
rights and permissions for these objects becomes much easier, because you will be able to
select all of these objects and assign the necessary rights and permissions in one single unit
of work.

Note

If you're able to assign permissions using the OU structure, it will be much easier for you to keep a tight grip on the security properties than when assigning permissions to individual objects.

OUs vs. Domains

By creating OUs within domains, you actually have two levels of hierarchies inside the domain tree:

♦ The hierarchy of the domains in the tree

♦ The hierarchy of OUs inside the domain

Stated another way, by using OUs you can reduce the number of domains needed to create your company's hierarchy of management, compared to the number of domains required in a Windows NT Server setting.

The two-tier hierarchy of domains and OUs introduced by Active Directory allows a great deal of flexibility in the administration of domain trees. For example, suppose an entire domain tree is managed by a central IT department. The IT department can create a set of OUs for those groups that are needed in every domain; for example, an IT department OU can be created, in which local IT department user accounts reside, or a Support OU can be created for support employees. The IT department can retain full administrative control over these common OUs.

Then, within each domain, the IT department can form additional OUs that meet the needs of users in that particular domain. For example, in a headquarters domain, HR and Sales OUs can be created. For a regional office, an OU can be created for the Office team. Thereafter, administrative rights for these particular OUs can be delegated to specific users or groups, so that these users can administer their own "realm," without involving the IT department. Furthermore, because these users have administrative rights only on their own OUs, they can't interfere with the IT department's responsibilities.

The flexibility in the logical architecture enables you to create an environment based on a centralized or decentralized model or on any combination of the two. You can provide a centralized framework with the domain structure and a general-purpose OU structure within domains—and still be able to create specialized OUs in any particular domain.

However, deciding whether to split a particular part of your network into separate domains or separate OUs is crucial, and thus requires an intimate understanding of the capabilities and shortcomings of domains and OUs. Table 8.2 provides an overview of the applicability of domains and OUs for different requirements.

Table 8.2   When to use domains or multiple OUs.

Requirement	Multiple domains	Multiple OUs
Implement different vital security policies, such as the certificate authorities that are to be trusted by users and the user password length	Yes	No
Identical user security requirements	Not needed	Yes
Different machine security policies	Not needed	Yes
Complete administrative control	Yes	Not recommended
Decentralized administrative control	Not recommended	Yes
Control of replication traffic	Good	Poor
Creation of subordinate entities that are available through DNS	Yes	No
Ability to collapse and rearrange	Poor	Good
Reducing the number of objects in each domain	Yes	No

As you can see, the primary reasons for creating a domain instead of an OU are to control replication traffic, implement different security policies on users and computers, centralize administrative control, and limit the total number of objects inside a domain.

When you are choosing between OUs and domains, you should consider the following general rules:

♦ Split the network into separate domains if you have a need for separate DNS names.

♦ Split the network into separate domains in decentralized organizations in which different users and resources are managed by completely different sets of administrative personnel. Creating multiple domains is the only way to keep high-level administrators (that is, domain administrators) from having access to parts of the network that are under another group's authority (the Domain Administrator has full access to every object in the domain).

♦ Split the network into separate domains when two parts of your network are separated by a link that is so slow that you never want complete replication traffic to cross it. However, please remember that Active Directory only will replicate the attributes that have changed since last replication, so the full domain won't be replicated except when the first DC is being installed in a new site. Additionally, Active Directory allows you to control when changes are replicated.

♦ Split a domain into OUs to reflect the details of your company's structure and organization.

♦ Split a domain into OUs to delegate administrative control over smaller groups of users, groups, and resources. The amount of administrative control that you grant can be complete (such as creating users) or limited (such as administering print queues and changing passwords).

♦ Split a domain into OUs if that particular organizational structure in your company is likely to change later. When possible, organize domains so that they won't have to be moved or split often in the future.

Designing the OU Structure

The following steps are recommended for designing the OU structure:

1. Gather information, which includes doing the following types of tasks (refer to Chapter 6 for more details):

    ◆ Identify the administrative operations that IT personnel have been performing in all areas of your organization.

    ◆ Determine whether you wish to change any aspect of the existing administrative model.

    ◆ Determine what level of administration you want personnel from the IT department to control and at what level you will delegate administration.

    ◆ Determine who will administer which users and resources.

2. Define a hierarchical OU model that matches the organization's needs.

3. Design the actual OU structure, including the development of a plan for delegating OU administration.

When you design an OU structure, you are essentially creating an administrative model that defines who in your organization is responsible for managing specific users and resources across the enterprise network. Remember that the administrative model has to make sense to the whole company, because users are confronted with this structure when they search the directory for objects with specific properties.

Although you should strive to create OU structures that are relatively static, the OU structure that you design should also have the capability to facilitate future reorganizations with minimal object movement. When you design the OU structure, the following are justified reasons to create OUs:

◆ To delegate administration

◆ To scope the application of policies or rights

◆ To replace Windows NT Server resource domains

◆ To scope visibility of objects

Generally, the OU structure is for the benefit of administrators, which is why you should ask the following three important questions before you create an OU:

◆ How will the OU be used?

◆ Who will administer the OU?

◆ What level of rights will the assigned OU administrator(s) need?

Ultimately, if you have multiple domains, after your first pass at creating the OU structure for the first domain, you should determine whether you would be able to use the model across all domains. If not, you may want to redesign the OU structure so that it is consistent across all domains, if possible.

Typical OU Models

OUs enable you to create a hierarchical structure within a domain. A hierarchical OU model provides a logical pattern for the way that OUs are designed in a domain, by defining categories of OUs and the relationships that they have with each other.

The interrelationships of the OUs in the hierarchy and the logical pattern created should be meaningful to both end users and administrators. This is usually accomplished by choosing an OU model that reflects the business practices of the organization.

The typical OU models include the following:

♦ Geographic-based OU model

♦ Department-based OU model

♦ Business unit-based OU model

♦ Project-based OU model

♦ Administration-based OU model

♦ Object-based OU model

However, many other OU models can be designed—including hybrid or mixed variants of the preceding OU models. Many real-life OU structures are in fact a mixture of the standard models in the preceding list.

Also, remember that having a well-defined OU model from the outset is among the most important factors of all for a successful Active Directory design. From that point, building the individual OU structures for each domain in a consistent manner is relatively straightforward.

If your company is built on a matrix organization, network organization, learning organization, or anything that utilizes two organizational dimensions, you should be keenly aware that you're in for some trouble, because the hierarchical structures that Active Directory is built on simply can't represent these sorts of organizational diagrams. Here, you will be faced with finding the least bad solution.

Geographic-Based OU Model

A geographic-based model structures OUs by geographic location. For example, in a multi-national company, the design often uses the first level of OUs to represent the continental boundaries, followed by the individual countries as the second level of OUs (for example, see Figure 8.4). Each succeeding level can represent smaller geographical units, such as cities, provinces, or states.

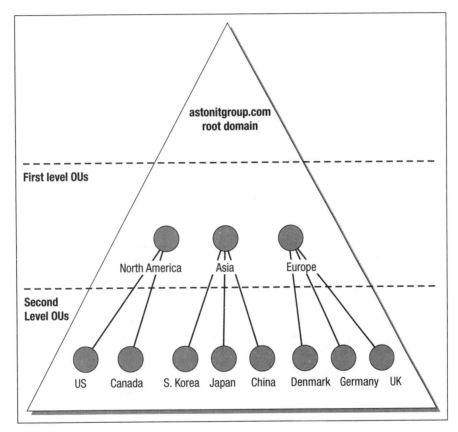

Figure 8.4
An example of a geographic-based OU model.

Department-Based OU Model

A department-based model structures OUs by department or business function. For example, in a large, multinational company, the first level of OUs could be designed to represent the different business functions, after which the second level of OUs could reflect more specific business functions (see Figure 8.5).

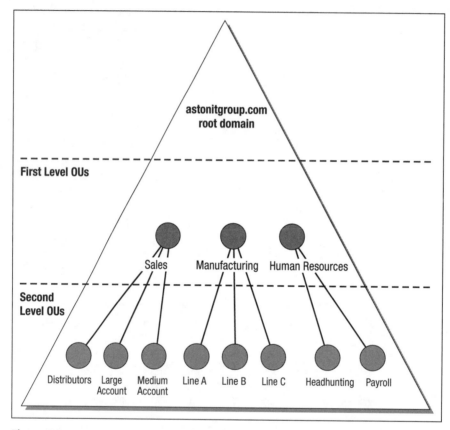

Figure 8.5

An example of a department-based OU model.

Business Unit-Based OU Model

A business unit-based model structures OUs by the divisions (typically cost centers) in which the organization must manage its operations and financial matters, independent of the rest of the organization. For example, in a large, multinational company, the first level of OUs could represent each division, and the second OU level could represent the departments that constitute each division, as shown in Figure 8.6.

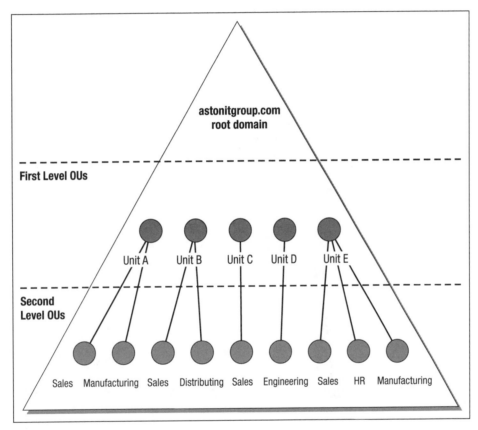

Figure 8.6
An example of a business unit-based OU model.

Project-Based OU Model

A project-based OU model structures OUs by project rather than by business function (see Figure 8.7). In this type of organizational model, individual projects often are viewed as cost centers.

You should *never* consider this OU model, unless your company is completely built on this organizational model, because the project-based OU model really can't be considered to be a static OU model, due to the inherent dynamics in such an organizational setup.

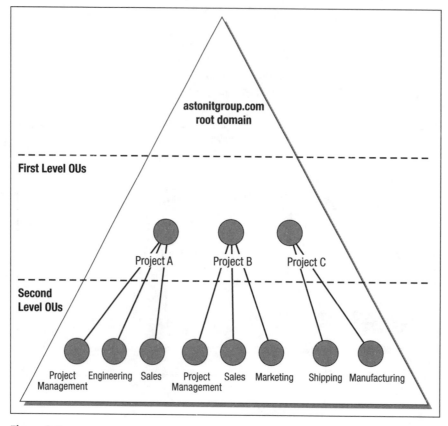

Figure 8.7
An example of a project-based OU model.

Administration-Based OU Model

An administration-based model structures OUs by how administrative control is delegated within the organization. In other words, the OU model reflects the way that the IT department maintains control over all users and resources within the organization (see Figure 8.8). For example, if the IT department works as a centralized unit, it will usually have one or more headquarters, with subordinate departments spread throughout the organization.

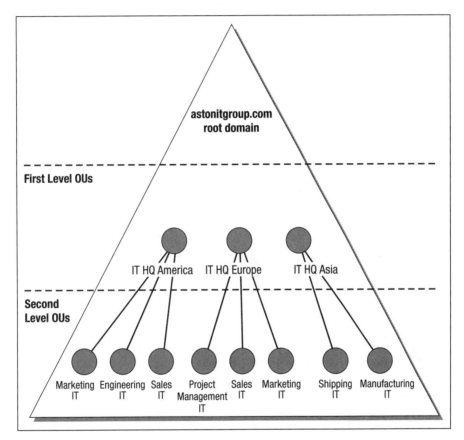

Figure 8.8
An example of an administration-based OU model.

Object-Based OU Model

An object-based model structures OUs around the actual object types. For example, a first-level OU hierarchy usually consists of each primary type of object that exists within Active Directory (users, client computers, server computers, DCs, applications, groups, printers, and so on), such as the example shown in Figure 8.9. The advantages and disadvantages to using each of these models are set forth in Table 8.3.

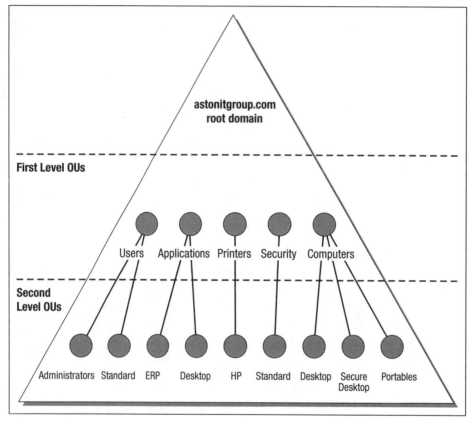

Figure 8.9
An example of an object-based OU model.

Table 8.3   Major advantages and disadvantages of the various OU models.

OU Model	Advantages	Disadvantages
Geographic-based	First-level OUs should prove to be very static, because geographical boundaries tend not to move or change names, whereas business groupings might change.	It may not match the actual organizational diagram of the business and thereby will seem highly illogical to end users. Consequently, most geographic-based OU structures represent a mixture of naming schemes.
	OU administrators can easily identify where resources are physically located.	OU administrators might have trouble identifying to which business function a resource actually belongs.
Department-based	First-level OUs should be fairly static, because business functions generally don't change.	OU administrators can't immediately identify where resources are physically located.
Business unit-based	Works well when each business unit is independent of the organization.	Users from different departments with differing access requirements may be grouped together into one OU, which makes delegation of administrative control more difficult.
		The names of the individual business units may change over time.
		OU administrators can't immediately identify where resources are physically located.
Project-based	Provides the logical method of building an OU hierarchy—if the organization really segregates objects by project.	Projects will usually have a relatively short life span, which in turn restricts the stability of the OU structure.
		Projects are generally the most volatile organizational object, thus posing the OU structure risk of being renamed more often than other OU models, resulting in end user confusion.
		OU administrators can't immediately identify where resources are physically located.
Administration-based	OU administrators can easily identify the location where resources are administered from.	Not intuitive to end users because they often don't know or need to know where they are being administered from.
	Makes it easy to achieve the desired administrative delegation inside the IT department.	Users from the different departments with differing access requirements may be grouped together into one OU, which makes delegation of administrative control outside of the IT department more difficult.

(continued)

Table 8.3   Major advantages and disadvantages of the various OU models (*continued*).

OU Model	Advantages	Disadvantages
Object-based	Makes it easy to achieve the desired administrative delegation because the OUs are designed by object type.	Not intuitive to end users because it doesn't reflect organizational structure, and end users often don't understand the object structuring principles being used.
	OU administrators can easily identify the location where resources are administered.	Users from different departments with differing access requirements may be grouped together into one OU, which could make delegation of administrative control outside of the IT department impossible.
	Makes it much simpler to create ACLs (Access Control Lists) for OU permissions, because permissions are based on containers.	OU administrators can't immediately identify where resources are physically located.
	Fewer modifications are usually required for reorganization, because the same objects are used, regardless of organization structure.	

Planning the OU Structure

An OU structure is an arrangement of OUs in a domain that reflects the details about the particular organization. The OU structure is unique to each domain, which is why you should always set out to define the overall topological properties of the OU structure for the organization by defining the OU model.

After you choose an OU model (refer to the preceding section), you begin the detailed planning by doing the following:

♦ Considering the kinds of objects to place in each OU

♦ Determining what should be on each level in the OU structure

♦ Developing a naming convention for the OUs

♦ Planning whom the owners will be and who should be able to view and administer objects within each OU

Considering Which OU Objects to Implement

OUs are logical containers that can hold objects, such as users, groups, computers, applications, OUs, and the other kinds of directory objects available. Importantly, OUs are not limited to the predefined Active Directory objects. When you define a new object, you can also place it in an OU.

Note
Remember that an OU can't span multiple domains.

You can create an OU hierarchy to customize OUs to whatever task is at hand. So, you basically have to identify where you want to put which directory objects.

When you create OUs, remember that the structure can be used only for administrative delegation, administrative groupings, and application of policies; security still has to be handled by assignment to security principals (that is, groups, users, or computers). So, the best that you can do when administrating rights and permissions is to structure all objects that belong to the same security grouping in the same OU, which will allow you to assign the needed security on those objects within a single unit of work. For example, you can

---

Some Words of Advice in Regard to Hybrid OU Models

I've encountered many more or less inventive OU models during my time. However, I really haven't seen any hybrids of the above-mentioned OU models succeed except one: When the geographic-based OU model is used for the top-level OU(s), which are then followed by one of the other OU models.

I have yet to see an example in which two other OU models are combined in another way, and one can truly prove that it brings more advantages than disadvantages to the table than all of the other options. Although I'm not totally convinced that one or two other kinds of hybrids would never prove interesting for some narrowly defined scenarios, I'm quite convinced that you will never succeed in mixing parts of the above-mentioned OU models.

I think one such example that I've encountered in real life should prove my point quite clearly: Once I was shown an OU design with departments on the first OU level followed by several OU levels based on geography and then rounded off with a couple of OU levels reflecting more specific business functions. The logic behind this OU model was that it would accommodate rather handsomely the company's specific department-based needs (that is, their usage of various GPOs that would be assigned based on department) rather than having them assign the same set of GPOs to each of the departments, which would be the case when using a geographic-based OU model combined with a department-based OU model. However, this rather special OU model was soon proved useless by considering the major strain imposed with regard to the following points:

- Implementing country-specific settings (and, potentially, the language-specific software).

- Allowing for administrative delegation on a country and/or location-based basis (the local IT people were shared between the different local departments, as is usually the case).

- Some departments weren't found at more than one or two sites.

- Some people might sometimes be performing work for more than one department (this would especially be the case at the very small sites).

- The company is experiencing rapid growth, and the probability of reorganizations was considered quite high. And so the organizational structures would most probably undergo several profound changes inside a relatively short time. However, it was expected that the preexisting sites would prevail despite many new sites were expected to be added.

Having considered the many negative implications of this hybrid OU model, it was replaced with a geographic-based OU model for the top-level OUs and a department-based OU model for the next OU levels. The need for assigning GPOs on a departmental basis was taken care of by creating a departmental group hierarchy and assigning GPOs to the domain and filtering based on the department group hierarchy instead.

place all users that have the same security privileges in one OU, select all of them, and then specify their security privileges—being able to pull off that action alone represents a huge improvement over Windows NT Server 4.

Also note that the OU structure should be beneficial and meaningful, because end users see the structure when they query the database. So, don't create structure for the sake of structure—create structure only where it makes sense.

Determining What Should Be on Each OU Level

Together, the chosen organizational model and the current administrative needs ought to identify how the OU structure in each domain should be designed. When you design the actual OU structure to be implemented in each domain, you should pay attention to the nature of the objects within each preceding OU level, and you should always be able to provide a prompt answer to the following three questions with regard to each and every OU:

♦ What is the justification for the OU (how will it be used)?

♦ Who will administer the OU?

♦ What privileges will the administrator of that OU need?

Also be aware that the closer to the domain root you get, the more static (or standardized) your OU structures should be. Because OUs are pretty "cheap" to implement (their cost is close to nothing in terms of replication or hardware costs, because you always should have a much higher number of individual directory objects than OUs), you should at least use the same first-level OUs throughout your forest for the sake of administrative and end user ease. The greater the depth of your OU hierarchy, the more important standardizing the next OU levels becomes.

Active Directory doesn't impose any theoretical limit on the number of OU levels. However, in practice, you still need to consider the performance issues of that design before you implement an OU structure. The issue is quite simple: The deeper your OU tree becomes, the more taxing it is for the servers to perform certain operations (such as queries, replication, and application of policies). According to early information from Microsoft, the performance of these operations will decrease *exponentially* as the number of OU levels increases, until the server memory limits eventually are reached.

By saying that, Microsoft effectively is declaring that a shallow OU structure (few levels, with many OUs on each level) is much better than a deep OU structure (many OU levels, with few OUs on each level).

Actually, on several occasions, Microsoft has recommended that you use 10 or fewer OU levels (usually followed by a comment such as "after that, the performance will degrade quite a lot"). I recommend that you heed its advice, because there is an exponential decrease of performance when you go from having 1 or 2 OU levels to having 10 levels—and

Microsoft seems to imply that the performance hit is even worse above 10 levels. And because Microsoft recommends 10 or fewer OU levels, I recommend that you stick to 7 or 8 OU levels for now (or perform a thorough testing of the performance in your environment).

Developing an OU Naming Convention

Because the names assigned to OUs are used internally within the domain and are seen by end users, you should use a consistent and straightforward naming convention. On the other hand, you should refrain from investing a disproportionate amount of time creating "perfect" names for all OUs—especially ones that are useful only to administrators—because most end users will only recognize the DNS name. And, as you should know by now, the DNS name refers only to the domain, because the OUs aren't part of the DNS namespace. Instead, OUs are identified by LDAP and canonical names.

The only exception to this rule (that the DNS naming is the all-important aspect in regard to the user) is when the user performs queries. However, performing queries typically is an everyday event for only a small subset of end users (if the Active Directory is designed correctly). And even when a user performs a query, he or she doesn't necessarily pay attention to the full name of the directory object.

Planning the Delegation of OU Administration

When you plan the OU structure, you should strive to define who owns each OU at its time of creation, because each OU must have a person who is responsible for performing the following tasks:

♦ Adding, deleting, and updating objects

♦ Deciding whether permissions should be inherited from the preceding OU

♦ Deciding whether permissions should be added or changed

♦ Deciding whether permissions should be propagated to the next level of OUs

♦ Deciding whether administration of the OUs at the next level should be delegated to other persons

Additionally, the Domain Administrator (who always has access to, and can step in and take ownership of, an OU) must decide what each OU should contain, its relationship to other OUs, who should have permissions to access the OU, and (most importantly) which level of control each owner has over the objects inside the OU.

Delegation of administration really is a double-edged sword: Whereas it is one of the most interesting additions to Windows 2000 Server and a vital security feature, it can wreak havoc in the hands of the wrong person. (But hey, isn't this what can be said about almost any powerful tool?)

Beware of the Big Bad Domain Administrator!

Remember that all persons belonging to the Domain Administrators group can take control of any object or OU—much like files and directories in Windows NT 4.

The Godlike power assigned to the Domain Administrator role is one reason why some organizations may want to use multiple domains—because they don't want to put any trust in administrators that are part of another section of the organization.

To avoid any trouble, security-wise, before you delegate administration of an OU, you should define whether each individual OU administrator has access to perform the following tasks:

♦ *Create, change, and delete objects within the OU*—This can be restricted to certain types of objects, such as users or groups.

♦ *Change the properties of a certain container*—For example, you can delegate the ability to change properties on the local domain policies of the domain.

♦ *Update attributes on a certain kind of object*—For example, you can delegate the ability to set passwords on user objects.

♦ *Manage a small set of objects within a specific OU region*—For example, you can delegate the ability to manage printer queues and file resources within a particular OU.

These rights are handled by setting permissions (for a group or user, as in an NT Server 4-type environment; *and thus not* by virtue of being an object within a specific OU) that grant or deny access and read/write actions on the whole OU or a select object or attribute subset of the OU. However, please remember that the permissions granted at the OU level pertain to all the objects in that OU—and, by default, all the OUs spawned by that particular OU.

All of the decisions outlined in this section emphasize the need to define a delegation plan that specifies the who, what, when, and where that govern the assignment of permissions to an OU. You should also define the type of access and the actions that are allowed on the objects for *every* OU in the domain—if you want to create something of lasting value—because previous experience with directory services shows that you need all the flexibility possible when your organization begins to grasp some of the opportunities presented by delegation of administration.

Some Advice on OU Design

Basically, you should plan your OU structure according to your company's logical organizational model. You don't need to take geography or physical location into account, unless your organizational model does so.

For example, if your company has a small North American location and a small European location, but all employees in both organizations are managed by the IT department in North America, you don't need to create North America and Europe OUs. However, if the

North America IT department administers North American users and resources and the Europe IT department administers European users and resources, then having North America and Europe OUs—or maybe even separate domains—could make a lot of sense. In this particular case, your OU structure then would follow the organizational structure of the IT department rather than the structure of the company. And please remember that you don't have to consider the physical properties of the network at all. You optimize for the physical structure by creating Active Directory sites, which are totally separated from the logical Active Directory structure (that is, the domains and OUs). A single domain can span several sites, and a single site can include users and computers belonging to multiple domains (see Chapter 11 for more information on sites).

The First Level

In a multinational company, the first level of OUs often is chosen to represent continental and geopolitical boundaries. However, in a large setting, the first layer of logical structuring usually winds up being implemented as domains, to minimize directory service replication and to provide a means for creating persistent names.

No matter the choice of structuring, you should remember that one of the main objectives on the first level is to create OUs whose names don't change. Thus, a good namespace design should be capable of withstanding most company reorganizations without the need to restructure the top level of the OU hierarchy.

The first level of OUs needs to be relatively stable and static so as to avoid any radical OU restructures. If additional OUs are needed, they should be created as child OUs under the existing first-level OUs. The naming convention for OUs (or domains) within this layer should generally be at least three characters long if using continental and geopolitical boundaries, so that they don't conflict with the ISO 3166 two-character country codes that could be used to name second-level OUs (or domains).

The Second Level

In a large company, the larger regional offices and sites could be defined as second-level or (child) OUs, which are branched off of their corresponding first-level (parent) OUs. Second-level OUs generally should be countries or cities only (the choice depends on whether your company is multinational or not). Additional OU levels can be created, if needed, off of the second-level OUs, to support a specific location within a given country or city.

If you are using countries, the naming convention that you use should be the two-character ISO 3166 standard (see Table 7.3) for all locations—no matter whether they are domains or OUs. However, you might want to make an exception for locations within the United States, and use states instead. Unfortunately, states aren't given an ISO country code and thus should be chosen to follow the two-letter U.S. postal code (see Table 11.2) or something akin to that. For ease of use, all names under the first level should be lowercase.

> **Note**
> *One of several exceptions that you might encounter with regard to the recommended U.S. naming convention is California, whose two-character postal code (CA) conflicts with Canada's ISO code; therefore, the elongated state abbreviation Calif could be used instead. Some of the other exceptions include DE, which is used for Delaware as well as for Germany; AL, which is used for Alabama as well as for Albania; and MN, which is used for both Minnesota and Mongolia.*

If you'll be using cities, the only globally unique naming convention that is up for grabs is the one used by the airport authorities. However, this might pose a problem, if your company has many locations a long way from the various airports of the world.

Additional Levels

Within most types of businesses, further organization of resources and users proves helpful in order to reflect the business's organization. However, just as it is impractical for a central IT organization to directly support all the organizational needs of various departments, it also is impractical for a central IT organization to administer all the OUs that a business-driven organization may require. Therefore, the central IT organization should directly support and define only the first level of the additional business model OUs (in order to secure a fair level of consistency among its constituents).

Because no replication or hardware costs are associated with the creation of OUs, the first layer of business organization OUs should be standardized throughout the organization, regardless of whether a particular location requires them. This provides consistency for company-wide support.

OU Design Examples

This section contains some more or less theoretical examples of how to organize your Active Directory based on the size and nature of your enterprise. For the sake of the examples, you will find that all the organizations shown are structured quite conventionally (that is, hierarchically).

However, these examples shouldn't be judged as comprising any form of reference answers (actually, in real life, some of these examples should definitely be split up into several domains). They are merely some examples of how to implement an OU design, intended to help your level of understanding and maybe provide you with a bit of inspiration for your designs.

Remember, too, that the OU structure is just the beginning. Deploying a distributed computing architecture such as Windows 2000 Server requires an organization to decide which tasks to perform centrally and which to perform locally—and, lastly: how to perform them.

A Small Organization

Suppose that you need to create a directory structure for a small organization consisting of somewhere in the range of a few hundred to a thousand employees. The sole purpose of this directory is to maintain user and group information, and you want the user and group information to be centrally managed by a group of directory administrators. The organization consists of the three main groups: Engineering, Sales, and Accounting. In that case, your Active Directory should be structured as follows:

◆ The root domain should bear the name of your organization, if possible.

◆ Three different OUs should be created that bear the actual names of the groups, so that you can cater to the individual needs of each group.

◆ Second-level OUs might be implemented later for being able to group users and resources that have uniform needs and wants, which should ease the day-to-day administrative tasks.

Figure 8.10 shows a sample Active Directory structure designed in this manner.

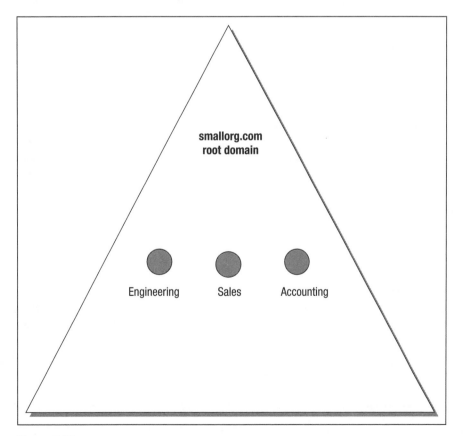

Figure 8.10
How the structure of a typical small organization could be expressed with Active Directory.

A State Government

If you are designing a directory structure for a state government, you most likely want to provide room for city and county governments, state and community colleges, and various state and local agencies to participate in your directory.

You first should try to define OU models for each type of organization that is part of the state government. You should also strive to standardize the first levels of OUs that are used for each type of organization.

Your Active Directory should be structured as follows:

♦ The root domain should bear the name of the state government, if possible.

♦ Different OUs should be created that bear the actual names of the organizational entities that are part of the state government.

♦ Second-level OUs should be created for each organization.

♦ Second-level OUs might be implemented later for being able to group users and resources that have uniform needs and wants, which should ease the day-to-day administrative tasks.

Figure 8.11 shows a sample Active Directory structure designed in this manner for an imaginary state government.

An International Corporation

Designing a directory structure for a global enterprise involves determining not only how to logically structure the various organizational parts and its users and resources, but also how to design the Active Directory to support replication on a global scale.

Your exact approach depends on several factors, including the following:

♦ The quality of the network connecting the various sites in your enterprise. If the available bandwidth is low, you should consider implementing multiple domains that are organized as a domain tree (see Chapter 11 for more details on that).

♦ The nature of your directory data and your enterprise's need to provide access everywhere to the full directory structure.

♦ Whether all the organizations in your enterprise can, or are willing to, share the same DNS name. Some enterprises, such as corporations with subsidiaries known by other names, find that creating a common DNS name across the entire enterprise is difficult or impossible. In that case, you need to employ several domain trees (see Chapter 11 for more information).

If you can make do with a single domain, your Active Directory should be structured as follows:

♦ The root domain should bear the name of the enterprise, if possible.

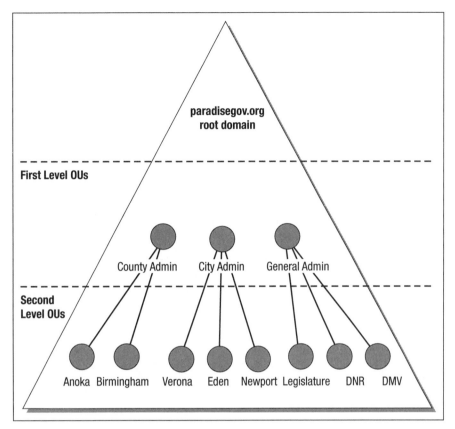

Figure 8.11
The Active Directory structure for the state government of Paradise.

♦ Optional: Different OUs should be created that bear the names of the geographical boundaries in which the enterprise is represented. This obviously isn't needed if the enterprise is limited to one geographical boundary or is located in relatively few countries.

♦ Different OUs should be created that bear the name of the country or city in which the enterprise is represented.

♦ You create different OUs that represent organizational grouping inside each country. Ideally, you will specify a range of standardized OU names for keeping things consistent across the whole enterprise.

♦ Second-level OUs might be implemented later for being able to group users and resources that have uniform needs and wants, which should ease the day-to-day administrative tasks.

Figure 8.12 shows how the Active Directory structure could look for an international corporation that is designed in this manner.

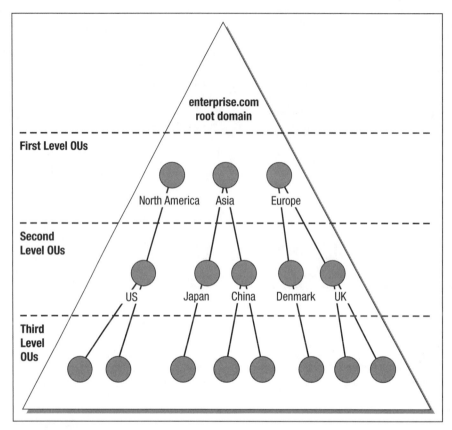

Figure 8.12
The Active Directory structure for a typical international corporation, provided that it can be restricted to a single domain.

Best Practices

When you design for Active Directory, you almost always start off with the domains, the top priorities for which are the following:

♦ Organizational changes should be accommodated, without needing to implement changes in the domain structure.

♦ The domain design must evolve as organizational needs change.

♦ Domain names must be chosen that won't change easily. One approach is to organize geographically, because geographical names rarely change.

You should always begin by creating the first domain. If you need to implement more than one domain, consult Chapter 11, which deals with the subject of designing domain trees and forests. The following are some of the reasons for having multiple domains:

◆ Too many objects (Please be aware that Active Directory has been successfully tested with several million objects in the labs.)

◆ Different user security practices

◆ Network traffic

◆ Administrative considerations

◆ Administrative model

◆ International differences

◆ Internet presence

Always strive to implement the minimal number of domains. Generally, a single domain structure has fewer administrative costs, puts less stress on computer resources, and needs less adjustment during times of growth and reorganization. Regardless of the number of domains, you always have to settle the items set forth in Table 8.4 for each separate domain (and almost always in the order given).

Table 8.4   Guidelines for planning a domain structure.

Tasks	Points to Consider
Choose the Active Directory domain name.	This name is used as the DNS name to refer to the domain. Please remember to be extra careful about the name of the root domain (that is, the domain from which other domains originate), because you can't change a root domain, and all other domains will use the root domain name as their parent DNS name.
Gather the requirements for the OU structure.	Here, you should primarily make use of the information gathered for the particular organization in question (as outlined in Chapter 6), including the following: • Identify the IT personnel and their responsibilities. • Determine the need for changes to the existing administrative model. • Determine what level of administration you want the central IT department to control, and at what level you will delegate administration. • Determine who will administer which users and resources.
Establish the right OU model.	Strive, for simplicity's sake, to use one of the "prototypical" OU models mentioned earlier in this chapter. However, if your company uses an organizational model that translates badly to a hierarchy or has similarly vital troubles with the typical OU models, you might want to consider building a hybrid OU model.
Design the OU structure.	Some of the typical reasons to create OUs are: • To enhance administrative control • To mirror the organizational structure (which could also act as a replacement for Windows NT Server resource domains) • To ease application of policies or rights • To hold other OUs

(continued)

Table 8.4   Guidelines for planning a domain structure (continued).

Tasks	Points to Consider
Delegation of administration.	When developing a plan delegation of administration, you should consider the following points: • To keep a tight grip on the environment, the central IT department often needs to provide support of the first OU level (and the second level, as well, in very shallow OU structures). • Always strive to assign control at the OU level, which provides easier tracking of permission assignments. Tracking permission assignments becomes much more complex when done on individual objects and object attributes. • Track the administrative delegation so that you can maintain precise records that enable reviewing the OU structure from any applicable angle. • Establish guidelines for delegation of administration. If you expect to implement a lot of administrative delegation, you should consider implementing guidelines on how to initiate and execute the process, too.
Ask yourself the reason for each and every OU.	Whenever you want to create an OU, you should ask yourself the following questions: • How will the OU be used? • Who will administer the OU? • What privileges will the OU administrator have?
Keep things consistent.	If you have multiple domains, you should determine whether you could use the same OU model and overall structure across all domains. If not, you may want to redesign the OU structure to achieve that objective.

You should specifically try to stay clear of the following pitfalls when you are planning the OU structure:

♦ *Creating OUs for political reasons*—Don't give in to a particular manager who wants to create an OU for no apparent reason other than office politics.

♦ *Creating structure for the sake of structure*—The OU structure must be meaningful and logical.

♦ *Creating a very deep OU tree*—The number of OU levels shouldn't exceed 7 or 8 (and never go beyond 10), because of the exponential degradation of performance experienced at this point, according to reports from Microsoft.

Ultimately, when upgrading from Windows NT Server, you have to decide among these three very different scenarios:

♦ Keep the existing domain structure as it is, without any changes.

♦ Collapse and rearrange the existing domain structure.

♦ Create a completely new domain structure.

Chapter 22 deals with the various upgrade scenarios and methods.

The Very Last Words

The many combinations made possible by domains and OUs provide you with a powerful, flexible way of organizing your network directory to reflect your organization. Creating OUs within domains enables you to reflect your organization's structure on as many levels as you want, while maintaining the benefits of creating and managing a small number of domains.

This chapter provides the foundation for designing the structure of a domain, regardless of whether you have one or many domains in your organization. Refer to Chapter 11 for a discussion of how to plan for more than a single domain.

The information previously gathered about your organization (as discussed in Chapter 6) should be used for the design of your domain structure, which organizes and connects organizational and network infrastructure elements. The variation of the design depends upon your organization's specific requirements.

After you design the domain structure, you need to develop plans to delegate administration and application of Group Policies (which is the subject of Chapter 10). These plans are usually based on the hierarchy implemented by the OUs (but might also be utilizing the site structures and/or the domain structures).

Some of the overall lessons that should have been reinforced in this chapter include the following:

♦ You can't spend too much time planning the first domain name (root domain) of your organization. This name has to make perfect sense to the particular organization.

♦ Changing the name of the root domain is the most difficult change to make, so the root domain name should be one that is very unlikely to change. This is also the reason why you should obtain upper management's approval of the root domain name.

♦ After you achieve those two objectives, you move on to settling the detailed domain structure (refer to Chapter 11) and OU structure.

Chapter 9

Planning User and Group Management

I f reading Chapter 8 convinced you that a single domain solution provides an adequate match to your needs, you may have been left under the impression that you are set to start the actual implementation project for your domain solution. However, you aren't quite ready yet. Actually, you are just off to a nice beginning of a rather long journey.

After you determine which domain structure to use (keeping in mind that you need to read Chapter 11 if your design requires more than one domain), you still have to complete the following tasks before you can be relatively certain that your domain structure will stand the ultimate test—a real-life production setting:

1. *Plan user account and group management*—Even though groups and Organizational Units (OUs) are totally separate concepts, they share one element: users. So, to create an adequate administrative solution, your group and OU structures need to be properly synchronized.

2. *Plan how to secure the objects*—Like its predecessors, Windows 2000 Server allows you to secure virtually any OS object (shares, folders, files, printers, services, etc.) from prying eyes. You're also allowed to secure all Active Directory objects using the same scheme.

3. *Plan for delegation of administration*—The base administrative delegation is attained using the OU hierarchy to set the delegation scope on the Active Directory domain partition objects. However, you will have to use ACLs for setting administrative delegation on the OS fundamentals (such as services), as well as the configuration partition and the schema partition.

4. *Plan the Group Policy strategy*—Windows 2000 Server introduces a new and very powerful successor to System Policies, *Group Policies*, which enables you to assign policies according to the position in the OU hierarchy to users and computers running Windows 2000 Professional.

5. *Plan the physical structures of sites, domains, and more*—With Windows 2000 Server, you can add Group Policies to both the site and the domain hierarchy, so you may not need to change your OU hierarchy, even though System Policies are no longer available.

6. *Test run*—Test your domain structure in a scenario that resembles the actual environment of the organization for which the system is being implemented.

This chapter guides you through Tasks 1 and 2. Tasks 3 and 4 are covered in Chapter 10, and Task 5 is covered in Chapter 12. While Task 6 is covered somewhat in Chapters 17 and 18, this task isn't covered in greater detail due to implementation testing being outside the scope of this book.

You also should be aware that Windows 2000 Server includes several advanced security options (Kerberos interoperability, PKI, EFS, etc.) that could prove very advantageous to the level of system protection. Chapter 14 goes in-depth with all of those options. Hopefully, after you complete this chapter (and the next), the domain structure that you developed according to the information in Chapter 8 will provide a good match to the job that you have before you. If not, you have no alternative but to revise your domain structure, which isn't an uncommon occurrence. Typically, a directory design is the result of numerous revisions (because you have to iterate the design). The actual number and depth of changes in each design iteration depend on the organizational complexity and the designer's Active Directory experience.

An Introduction to User Account Management

Windows 2000 security is based on the concept of the *user account*—each user's unique credential that enables them to access resources. A user account is necessary for everyone who will either regularly use the network and participate in a domain or log on to a local Windows 2000 Professional computer to access local resources.

From the user's viewpoint, user account management is central to the functionality of Active Directory. From the network administrator's viewpoint, user account management is crucial for administrative ease. Also, without proper user account management, system security could be at risk.

Basically, user account management has two very different objectives:

♦ To implement the level of security needed for the networking environment

♦ To remove as much administrative overhead and complexity as possible from everyday usage

As with other complex concepts, for user account management you first need to achieve a complete understanding of the main concepts involved before you can learn the intricacies and make decisions regarding possible tradeoffs.

Even though Windows 2000 allows you to implement security via the user account concept alone, the need for administrative ease requires introduction of the *group* concept. Just as in Windows NT Server environments, groups are the primary vehicle for implementing the security needed in Windows 2000 Server (remember, OUs can cover only the needs of administrative control and application of policies and thus not security permissions). This fact may come as a big—and rather unpleasant—surprise to directory services buffs, because the group concept isn't an integral part of the directory as is the case with OUs. In regard to a directory service, groups represent a fairly confined and annoying concept, as it isn't capable of making use of the hierarchy that has been carefully engineered to model the enterprise to the directory service.

Actually, the missing ability to assign permissions using OUs represents Microsoft's largest compromise in designing Active Directory, and I can't think of anyone who wouldn't have loved to get their hands on this functionality as an alternative to the group concept. However, you should note that the group concept shouldn't be eliminated in the process, because it represents an option of assigning permissions across the directory service hierarchy. Hopefully, Microsoft will get rid of this major blunder in a future version of Windows 2000. However, until then you have to come to terms with the fact that you're stuck with groups for assigning security permissions and thus can't make full use of the directory hierarchy.

A Quick Rundown on Security Basics

Just as in a Windows NT Server 4 environment, the user and group account information is stored in a central database (Active Directory in Windows 2000 Server's case when working as a DC and SAM in all other cases, just as you know it from NT Server 4). Regardless of whether you're running on top of a SAM or an Active Directory database, each user and group account—as well as each Windows 2000-based computer—is identified by a Security Identifier.

Correspondingly, just about any object (including all directory objects and most OS objects) features a Security Descriptor that instructs the system as to what actions are allowed to be carried out by whom on the particular object.

The SID

The *Security Identifier (SID)* is a unique number that is generated by Windows 2000 when a new account is created. The first part of the SID identifies the domain in which the SID was issued; the second part, the Relative Security Identifier (RID), identifies an account object within the issuing domain. See Figure 9.1 for the exact structure of a SID and Figure 9.2 for an example of two very different SIDs (the Administrators built-in Local Group and the Domain Admins Global Group).

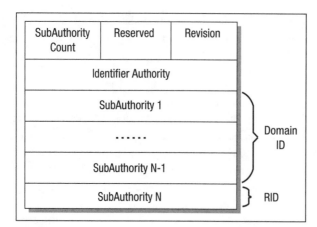

Figure 9.1
The structure of a SID.

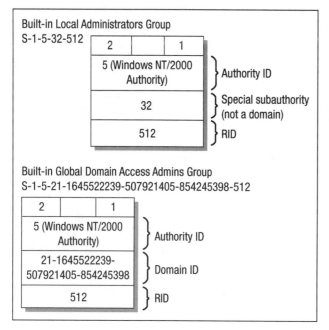

Figure 9.2
An example of two SIDs.

SIDs are never reused, so you can be sure that every account on your network will be issued a unique SID. That's also the reason why the internal processes in Windows 2000 generally prefer to refer to an account's SID rather than to the account's username or group name.

Thus, the SID, not the name that is designated by the administrator, is the actual identifier of the user, group, or computer. Consequently, you can't re-create a user, group, or computer account after it has been deleted. Even though the re-created account can be given the same name, it will be assigned a different SID that won't be recognized by any references to the old account in the domain database.

The SD

Every object has a unique header, called a *Security Descriptor (SD)*, that defines the access permissions for that given object. In other words, the SD describes the security attributes for an object and thus enables you to secure all named objects (and some unnamed objects).

An object's SD (see Figure 9.3) includes the following:

- ◆ An *owner security ID*—Indicates the user or group who owns the object. The owner of an object can change the access permissions for the object. It might help you to think of the owner as having God-like rights over that particular object.

- ◆ A *discretionary Access Control List (ACL)*—Identifies the users and groups who are granted or denied specific access permissions to the object. Discretionary ACLs are controlled by the owner of the object.

- ◆ A *system ACL*—Controls the situations for which the system should generate auditing messages and put them in the applicable log file. System ACLs are controlled by the security administrators.

The access permissions that can be granted or denied for an object depend on the type of object (see "The ACE," later in this chapter).

The ACL

The Access Control List (ACL) is a list of *Access Control Entries (ACEs)* that grant or deny to individuals or groups specific access rights or permissions to the object, by specifying the particular SID.

> **Note**
>
> *Rights provide users the ability to perform system tasks, such as changing the time on a computer. Permissions are rules that regulate which users can use a resource, such as a folder, file, or printer.*

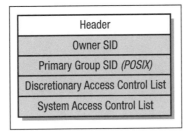

Figure 9.3
The structure of the SD.

In other words, the ACL for an object contains ACEs that apply to the object, enabling you to grant or deny, with varying levels of control, specific access rights to objects. So, when a user is given permission to access an object, such as a printer or file, the user's SID is recorded in one or more ACEs that are part of the ACL associated with the object.

Three ACE types exist: two for discretionary access control and one for system security. The discretionary ACEs are *AccessAllowed* and *AccessDenied* (see Figure 9.4). These explicitly grant and deny access to a specific user or group. No further processing of ACEs occurs when the first AccessDenied ACE that denies the user access to the resource is encountered, because an AccessDenied overrules an AccessAllowed.

SystemAudit is a system security ACE that is used to keep a log of security events (such as who accesses which files) and to generate and log security audit messages. This is used for Windows 2000's auditing features, which enable you to collect information about how your system is being used and specifically monitor events related to system security, so that you can identify any security breaches and determine the extent and location of any damage.

The ACE

As mentioned in the last section, each and every kind of permission is stored in an Access Control Entry (ACE). Although you have three very different types of ACEs seen from a functionality point of view, all ACEs are defined in the same data structure (see Figure 9.5). The multipurpose nature of ACE's makes it rather complicated to master. Because the very details of the ACE most probably won't prove to be worth anything to you—ever—I've narrowed down the discussion of this section to covering only the ACE's access mask entry.

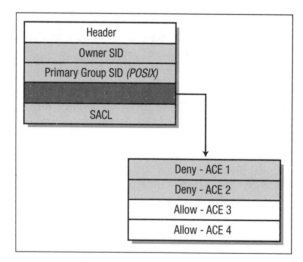

Figure 9.4
The ACL structure.

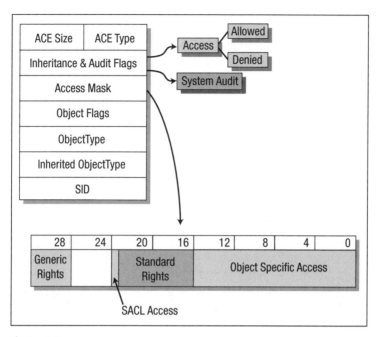

Figure 9.5
The ACE structure.

Each ACE includes an *access mask*, which defines all possible actions for a particular object type. An access mask can be compared to a menu, from which you select permissions to grant or deny. Access rights can be defined to apply at any of the following levels:

♦ To the object as a whole, which applies to all attributes of the object

♦ To a grouping of attributes defined by property sets within the object

♦ To individual attributes of an object

The specific types in the access mask include options that apply specifically to the object type. Each object type can have up to 16 specific access types. Collectively, the specific access types available for a particular object type are called the *specific access mask*. These access types are decided when the object type is defined. For example, you can specify permissions, such as Manage Documents and Print for a printer queue, and specify Read, Write, and Modify for a directory on an NTFS-formatted volume.

Turning the Theory into Practice

After having been subjected to all the many abstract and hard-to-understand elements used by Windows 2000's security subsystem, you might be surprised by the fact that these things are operated in a blatantly simple manner.

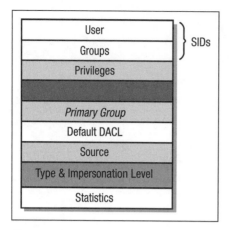

Figure 9.6
A run-down of the precise contents of the access token.

When a user logs on to a domain, the WinLogon service generates an *access token* that determines which resources the user is permitted to access. The access token (see Figure 9.6) includes the following information:

♦ The user's SID

♦ SIDs of groups to which the user belongs

♦ Privileges assigned to the user account

The GUID—Or Why You Can't Assign Security Permissions Using OUs

The rather surprising fact that OUs can't be used for assigning permissions is actually a question of Security Identifiers (SIDs) vs. Globally Unique Identifiers (GUIDs). Windows 2000 Server upholds Windows NT Server's restriction of only being able to feature SIDs in the ACEs. Unfortunately, all Active Directory objects (including the OUs) are assigned GUIDs and not SIDs, which isn't of any use in ACEs. So Microsoft will either have to start assigning SIDs to OUs, or allowing GUIDs to work as security principals in order to introduce support of permission assignments using OUs.

You might want to note that the SID concept is so deeply rooted in the whole security subsystem of Windows NT/2000 that changing it to accommodate GUIDs most probably would have demanded a total rewrite of a large proportion of the kernel and many adjacent code pieces. It would indeed be a good guess that Microsoft refrained from such a drastic step because of the very large negative effect that it might have had on the stability of the Windows 2000 platform, but surprisingly this doesn't seem to be the reason that GUIDs—and hence OUs—can't be used for assigning security permissions. According to my sources, which are very close to the Windows development team, the unfortunate event of not being able to assign security permissions using OUs stems from human error. It seems that none of the Microsoft personnel charged with designing the security permissions stuff had even thought that assigning security permissions using OUs could be of value to the users! I must admit that this represents a major blow to my perception of Microsoft being a 24/7 marketing-driven machine, because Novell NDS directory service has included this functionality right from the outset.

Now, when the user attempts to access a network object, Windows 2000 will simply compare the SIDs specified in the user's access token with the discretionary ACL for the object. If one or more of the SIDs appear in the AccessAllowed ACEs of the ACL (and isn't included on any of the AccessDenied ACEs), the user is given permissions to the object as described by the ACEs.

The User Account

Each person who will regularly use the network and participate in an Active Directory forest must have a user account in an Active Directory domain. The user account contains information about the user, including name, password, and various optional entries that determine when and how they are permitted to log on, among other things.

The user account is the fundamental entity to network security in an Active Directory environment. With user accounts, you can control how a user gains access to the domain or a local computer.

Every Windows 2000 Server or Windows 2000 Professional comes with two default user accounts:

♦ *Administrator account*—Created during system installation, it requires an initial password to be assigned to the account during setup. This account enables you to manage the

---

What Happens When a Computer Joins a Domain?

Windows 2000 computers can't simply log on to a domain and start computing. Before they are permitted access to the domain, they must be added to the domain, a formal process by which the computer is added to Active Directory's database for the domain (and thus a SID is created for the computer).

The effect of this depends on the computer's role in the domain:

• *Domain controllers (DCs)*—Fully participate in the domain security.

• *Member servers, standalone servers, and Windows 2000 Professional computers*—Each server and workstation retains its own security database (SAM) that regulates access to resources on that computer alone. And each computer has its own set of Local Groups, including Administrators, Backup Operators, Power Users, Replicator, and Users. The computers can only have Local Groups, and thus can't create Global Groups. Membership in a domain group doesn't guarantee membership in the corresponding Local Group on the various computers that participate in the domain.

After a server or workstation is added to a domain, however, administrators can administer the computer and users can use it, because when any Windows 2000-based computer is added to the domain, two group membership assignments are established:

• *Domain Admins Group*—Added to the local Administrators Group on the server or workstation.

• *Domain Users Group*—Added to the local Users Group on the server or workstation.

In this way, the server or computer indirectly participates in the core security established by the domain. And, if you need to expand on the basic security provided by the Administrators and Users Groups, you can always assign other groups to the servers or workstations.

---

server, because it is a member of the Administrators Group and thus gains complete control over the entire system operation and security. In effect, anyone who knows the Administrator account's username and password has complete power over the entire system. To avoid being locked out of the server, you can't delete or disable this account, although you can rename it (which is indeed a very wise move).

♦ *Guest account*—Used by default for anyone using the system that doesn't have a user account. Guest privileges provide very limited access to the computer's resources. Guests are denied access to any directories and files that are private. If guest privileges are allowed on a system, the administrator should set up a public directory in which to store files that are made accessible to guests. The Guest user account can't be deleted, but it can be disabled and renamed. The Guest account is disabled by default, but you can enable it to permit guest users to have limited access to your domain or server.

Note

*Several other user accounts will be found at Windows 2000 Server-based computers (the precise number depending upon the number of services running). For example, at an Active Directory DC, you will always have a user account named **krbtgt** (a service account used by the Key Distribution Center, or KDC, service) and two accounts starting with **IUSR_** and **IWAM_**, respectively (both of which are used by the Internet Information Server, or IIS).*

These two user accounts define the opposite ends of the possible access levels and can be modified by users that have sufficient privileges. These accounts never can be deleted, however.

Note, too, that you usually won't use any of the default user accounts in day-to-day use. Instead, you should create user accounts for every individual in the company and provide the necessary access privileges via groups. Even though a user account is a perfectly valid SID that can be used for assigning access permissions to objects (such as a printer or file), you should generally stay clear of that. You should instead use groups to handle permissions

Deleting the Default User Accounts

While it's possible to rename the default user accounts, it's not possible to delete them.

That limitation is really a shame from a security point of view as the SIDs of the two default user accounts won't be affected by a rename (and so the default user accounts can be identified using the public domain **user2sid/sid2user tools**).

However, you might want to note that the **passprop** utility included with the Windows NT 4 Resource Kit allows you to enable lockout for the Administrator user account (which is disabled by default to avoid you being shut out of the system) and that a very powerful low-level tool called **DelGuest** (which was recently posted at **ntsecurity.nu**) will allow you to delete the Guest account (which elsewise is impossible). Neither of these tools are available for Active Directory at present. But I sure do hope this only is a question of time.

(you can find more on groups later in this chapter) in all but a few special instances. Providing permissions on individual user accounts sooner or later leads to anarchy, and thus, in time, provides unauthorized users plenty of opportunities to exploit holes in the network security.

> ### Note
> *You must keep close at hand the Administrator account's name and password, in case of an emergency! After you create other administrators, you should also consider giving the default Administrator account an especially secure password, storing the password in a safe place, and putting the Administrator account into semiretirement. Regardless of what you do with the Administrator account, you should always change the name of the account so that unauthorized users need to guess both the password and the account name. If you are keen on establishing a high level of security, you may even create a new dummy account with the name "Administrator" that has auditing for detection of any kind of unauthorized access attempt.*

One very important issue related to user accounts is *user naming*. Here again, Microsoft has made another very annoying compromise. Even though you now are using an X.500 type of directory service, your usernames still have to be unique on a global scale (that is, across the full Active Directory forest). In other words, you should think of usernames as a flat namespace, not a hierarchical one.

Thus, even though you have moved to Active Directory, you still have to invent some type of global uniqueness for your user naming. And so the user naming will usually prove to be an even bigger nuisance than with an NT Server 4 environment, in which the well-known domain models enabled you to avoid global uniqueness (the uniqueness of usernames was limited to the local domain). However, on the bright side, global uniqueness does work to make it easier for users to log on, because they have to remember only a username. And this username can even be made identical to their email address, when using the UPN feature introduced with Active Directory.

Security principals (that is, users and groups) are furnished with three different kinds of usernames:

◆ *User Account Full Name*—Also referred to as the *Display Name* or simply *User Name*, this is the full name of the user, which, by default, is fed into Active Directory as two fields: first name and last name. However, you can change the User Account Full Name of the user into something different from the real first and last names, if needed. For example, John Smith's User Account Full Name is John Smith, by default, but could be changed to John S or something similar. The User Account Full Name has to be unique within the context in which it is present (that is, a given domain or OU).

◆ *User logon name (also known as User Principal Name or simply UPN)*—The Active Directory username, which is composed of a shorthand name for the user and a UPN suffix, such as the DNS name of the domain tree on which the user object resides. For example,

John Smith's user logon name could be **JSmith@acme.com**. The user logon name has to be unique within the forest.

♦ *User logon name (pre-Windows 2000)*—Also referred to as the *SAM Account name* or *Downlevel name*, this is the equivalent of your Windows NT Server 4 (and earlier) names. For example, John Smith's user logon name (pre-Windows 2000) could be Jsmith or acme\Jsmith. The user logon name (pre-Windows 2000) has to be unique in the domain, as in Windows NT 4.

Note

Please remember that the User Account Full Name has to be unique for the container in which it's stored (that is, a given OU or domain, depending on how the directory has been structured). I just wanted to remind you of this naming detail, because I've seen it come as a rather unwelcome surprise to quite a few people. And that works to gives you one more reason why you should always partition your directory. I might add that Microsoft isn't to blame on this one; it's a directory service axiom put forward by X.500.

When you are working out the naming convention for the user logon name and user logon name (pre-Windows 2000), you should be aware of these facts:

♦ The naming convention establishes how users are identified on the network. A consistent naming convention makes it easy for you and your users to remember usernames and locate them in lists.

♦ Usernames must be unique in some way. A User Account Full Name must be unique within its context (the OU or wherever it is located). User logon names must be unique to the forest, and user logon names (pre-Windows 2000) must be unique to the domain. Local user accounts must be unique to the local computer.

♦ The suffix on user logon names doesn't have to be related to the domain name, but Active Directory only acknowledges the pre-defined suffix names (implicitly by way of the domain names or explicitly by creating additional suffixes) in the forest. The suffix on user logon names (pre-Windows 2000) is always the user logon name (pre-Windows 2000) used for the Active Directory domain in question (which, incidentally, doesn't have to be identical to the Active Directory domain name in any way).

♦ User Account Full Name can contain an unlimited number of uppercase or lowercase characters, except for the following: " / \ [ ] : ; | = , + * ? < and >. You can use a combination of special and alphanumeric characters.

♦ User logon names can contain up to 64 uppercase or lowercase characters, except for the following: " / \ [ ] : ; | = , + * ? < and >. You can use a combination of special and alphanumeric characters.

♦ User logon names (pre-Windows 2000) can contain up to 20 uppercase or lowercase characters, except for the following: " / \ [ ] : ; | = , + * ? < and >. You can use a combination of special and alphanumeric characters.

♦ If you have many users, you will need to establish a naming convention that accommodates employees who have duplicate names. Two suggestions for handling duplicate names are the following:

   ♦ Use the first name and the last initial, and then add additional letters from the last name to accommodate duplicate names. For example, if you have two users named Dave Lang, use DaveL as one username and DaveLa for the other.

   ♦ Add numbers to the username. For example, DaveL1 and DaveL2.

♦ In large organizations, identifying temporary employees by their user account often proves useful. For example, to identify temporary employees, use a *T* and a dash in front of the username, such as T-DaveL.

Note

*Because the User Account Full Name (also known as the Display Name) will be used by Exchange 2000 Server, you might have wondered about how you can make sure that your users will indeed have forest-wide unique names. The answer to this question is quite simple: You should use the **initials** field.*

If possible, it's a good idea to use the same name for the user logon name and user logon name (pre-Windows 2000). However, you are free to choose different names. Remember, too, that if you fully migrate the whole enterprise to Windows 2000 Active Directory, you don't need to worry too much about the user logon name (pre-Windows 2000). Figures 9.7 through 9.9, which demonstrate how user John Smith would be created in Active Directory, should give you an idea of how all of these things look in real life. As an integral part of your user accounts plan, remember to include decisions on password requirements. The Create New Object (User) dialog box presents the following options (refer to Figure 9.7):

♦ *Password*—Determine whether the administrator should set a password on behalf of the user.

♦ *User must change password at next logon*—If selected, the user is forced to change the password the next time he or she logs on.

♦ *User cannot change password*—If selected, the user can't change his or her own password. This restriction is useful for shared accounts. It doesn't apply to users with administrator privileges.

♦ *Password never expires*—If selected, this user account ignores the password expiration policy set for the domain, and the password never expires. This is usually used for accounts that represent services, such as the Replicator Service. It is also useful for accounts for which you want the password never to change, such as guest accounts.

♦ *Account is disabled*—If selected, this account is disabled and can't be logged on to. It isn't removed from the database, but no one can log on to the account until you enable it again.

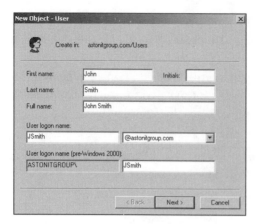

Figure 9.7
When you create the user, you first have to type the proper names for the user account.

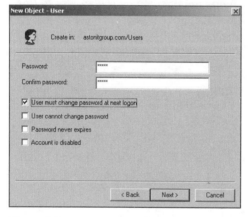

Figure 9.8
Second, you have to type the password in the New Object-User box.

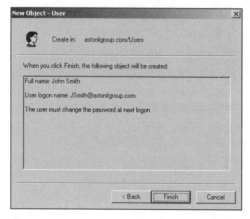

Figure 9.9
Finally, acknowledge the creation of the user with the properties specified.

When Outside of a Domain

Computers running Windows 2000 Professional standalone servers and member servers (computers running Windows 2000 Server that are part of the domain but aren't DCs) maintain user accounts separate from those of the domain, which are called *local user accounts*. The built-in accounts on such computers provide built-in rights on the computer that parallel the rights afforded by these same built-in accounts on the domain level.

However, when a workstation or member server is configured, the rights for the user accounts are confined to the local computer, because the account only exists in that computer's directory database. So, to access resources on another computer, the user must have a separate user account on the other computer. Thus, if a user needs access to more than one computer, you should refrain from implementing a local user account. You should create a domain user account instead for administrative and usability considerations.

When using domain user accounts on computers running Windows 2000 Professional and member servers, be aware that, to achieve the appropriate level of control over a workstation or member server, the domain administrator has to add the domain user accounts (or groups) to the various groups available on the local computer. Thus, the user can gain access to local resources from the local computer only by using a domain user account, if the domain administrator has added the domain user account (or the needed groups) to the local machine. This really is as simple as it sounds. But you should be keenly aware of this potential need for adding domain groups to the local computers, because this is one of the most common errors encountered in the real world.

Guidelines for Passwords

The following checklist provides the best practices for setting up passwords:

- Always assign a password to an account.
- Determine who controls the password. The following are two options:
  - Assign users unique passwords and then prevent users from changing them. This gives control to administrators.
  - Assign users an initial password and then require users to change them the first time that they log on. This way, the account is always protected and only individual users know their passwords. This gives control to users.
- In medium- and high-security networks, create random initial passwords for all user accounts.
- Determine whether an account should expire at some point. For temporary employees, set their user accounts to expire when their contract or work assignment ends.
- Educate users on ways to protect their passwords, such as selecting passwords that deter computer hackers. Windows 2000 enables you to tighten in many different ways the requirements on the sophistication level of the passwords that are allowed. You may take advantage of these features.

Hence, as an administrator, you need to contemplate which user accounts need to be able to log on from more than a single PC or need to access several PCs—and thus shouldn't be a local user account. If you're in doubt at all, it will usually pay not to use local user accounts at all.

Additional User Account Options

In addition to the core user account requirements (naming and passwords), Active Directory presents numerous options for adding more information and rules to user accounts. Also, because Active Directory is an extensible directory service, you can add more attributes to the user account class at will (see Chapter 20).

If you are going to exploit any of those options, you should set standards for when and how they are used. Reviewing all the available options here would be excessive, because you most likely won't use them all. But I recommend that you consider putting the following options to use:

- *Address*—Includes the following predefined objects: Street, P.O. Box, City, State/province, ZIP/Postal Code, and Country/region.

- *Telephone*—Includes the following predefined objects: Telephone number, Home, Pager, Mobile, Fax, and IP phone.

- *Organization*—Includes the following predefined objects: Title, Department, Company, Manager, and Direct reports.

- *Email*—States the email name.

- *Logon Hours*—Determines the hours that each user is allowed to log on.

- *Log On To*—Determines from which computers the user is allowed to log on.

- *Account Expires*—Sets a future date on which the user account automatically becomes disabled.

- *User Profile (Profile Path, Logon Script)*—Enables you to retain between logons the information regarding how to create the user's desktop environment such as program groups, network connections, screen colors, and settings determining which aspects of the environment the user can change. Also enables you to execute batch file(s) or executable file(s) automatically when the user logs on.

- *Home Folder*—Determines the location of the home folder, which is a user's default directory for the following: the File Open and Save As dialog boxes, the command prompt, and all applications that don't have a working directory defined. A home folder can prove very useful, because it provides a central location for a user's files, from which you can easily locate files to back up. You should note that the home folder also can be set for multiple user accounts using group policies.

Don't Forget Machine Naming

When you are establishing the naming standard for users, you also should establish the computer naming (the naming of the computers in your forest, both servers and clients). By default, computers are named *<computer_name>.<member_domain>*. For example, in the **acme.com** domain, a name could be **msnmktg.acme.com**. However, you aren't limited to the default. You can change the domain portion of the name at will on individual computers, or you can change it on many computers simultaneously by using a policy.

You should understand that deploying Windows 2000 doesn't force you to change the names of machines. If you already have a well-known and functional computer naming scheme at your site, you may reuse that when deploying Active Directory/Windows 2000.

However, your current naming scheme may use characters that are illegal in the DNS setting. One of the most often encountered illegal characters from a Windows NT 4 setting is the underscore (_), which isn't supported by DNS. As Chapter 7 explained, DNS allows only letters (A–Z), digits (0–9), and hyphens (-). If this is indeed the very case and you're really attached to your current computer-naming scheme, consider implementing Microsoft's proprietary unicode extension to DNS. For more information on this extension and on WINS-to-DNS name migration in general, please refer to Chapter 7.

If you decide to use any of these options, you should determine whether to make these attributes universally searchable to users in the forest. If you do make it searchable, the relevant attribute(s) must be included in the Global Catalog (see Chapter 19).

Introducing the Group Account

If opting to use the user accounts as the primary security principal (that is, if you control the access to network objects by assigning permissions to the user account SID), the administrator has to modify every user account with the relevant permissions for being able to set up the necessary accesses or restrictions. In addition to producing an almost infinite workload for administrators and related headaches from inevitable inconsistencies and errors, sooner or later, this method leads to administrative anarchy, where nobody has any idea of which permissions are given to which users. So, even though the user account is a perfectly valid SID that can be used for providing permission to access a network resource or rights on a system, generally you should avoid setting permissions on the individual user accounts. Instead, you should opt for using groups as the primary security principals. A *group* is a name—similar to the username of a user account—that can be used to refer to multiple users.

Groups provide a convenient way to assign, and then control, access to multiple users who perform similar tasks. By placing user accounts within a group, you can grant all users in that group the same abilities and restrictions. If you need to change the permissions or rights assigned to the users within the group, you have to modify only one account—the group account. Also, you can add other users to an existing group account at any time, instantly assigning them the rights and permissions granted to the group account (see Figure 9.10).

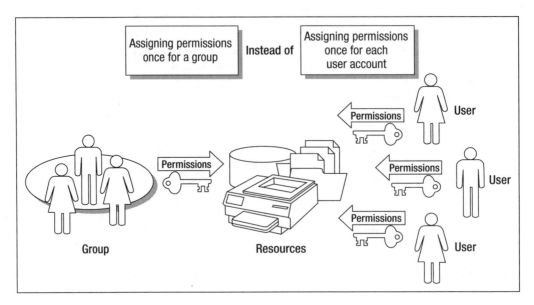

Figure 9.10
Administrators benefit by using group accounts rather than user accounts.

> **Note**
>
> *Any user who belongs to a group has all the rights and permissions granted to that group. Because the group is a list with references to user accounts, a user account can be a member of more than one group, and thus gain all the rights and permissions granted to every group to which it belongs.*

For example, if several users need to read the same folder, you simply add their user accounts to a group and assign Read permission for the folder to that group (rather than assign Read permission individually to each user account).

In a Windows NT Server 4 environment, you have two types of groups in the domain:

♦ *Domain Local Group*—Local to the domain database in which it is defined, and thus only can be used for assigning permissions and rights to objects at computers that have a copy of the domain database in which the object is located (that is, servers that act as PDC or as BDCs). However, the Domain Local Group can contain user accounts and Global Groups (but not other Local Groups) from the local domain or any domain trusted by the local domain.

♦ *Global Group*—User accounts from the local domain database that are grouped together under one group name. "Global" means that a Global Group can be used in multiple domains; it isn't restricted to the database in which it is defined. Thus, a Global Group can be used across all computers participating in the domain, even though it's defined only on the DCs. A Global Group can contain only user accounts (not other groups) from the domain where the Global Group is created. Global Groups can be given membership in Local Groups that exist on any computer in the domain or in any trusting domain. In other words, Global Groups simply are a mechanism for grouping domain users, to assign permissions, rights, and Local Group membership to computers (DCs, member servers, and workstations) inside the domain or to other computers in trusting domains. Because the scope of Local Groups is limited to the account database in which they are defined, it is recommended that you use Global Groups to ensure that groups of users are equally available (with a minimum of administration) on all Windows NT computers. However, the best practices from Microsoft calls for granting rights and permissions to Local Groups and using the Global Group as the method of adding users to Local Groups.

So, in an NT Server 4 environment, the administrator uses *Global Groups* to organize users based on the type of work they do, and uses *Local Groups* (that is, Domain Local, as well as Local Groups) to grant permissions to resources (by making the Global Groups members of the appropriate Local Groups).

This is indeed a very limited—albeit simple—way of handling rights and permissions. Fortunately, Windows 2000 Server introduces several important new group features:

♦ The Universal Group, a new and very powerful group type.

♦ Nesting of groups.

♦ Groups can be treated as distribution lists (if an Active Directory-aware email application, like Exchange 2000 Server, is installed).

♦ Groups can contain nonsecurity members (important when the group is used for both security and distribution list purposes).

♦ Security use of a group can be disabled (important when the group is used solely as a distribution list).

Note

Most of the new group features introduced in Windows 2000 Server can be used only when the domain is running in native mode, which is only possible when all DCs that participate in the domain have been upgraded to Windows 2000 Server. Until native mode is selected, the domain runs in mixed mode (default setting), which provides backward-compatibility to Windows NT Server-based BDCs.

However, Windows 2000 doesn't remedy the fact that groups are a nonhierarchical concept. Thus, as is the case with user naming, when you plan group structures, you have to struggle with a fairly simple and inflexible concept and its demands for uniqueness and interdependencies-handling, basically on a global scale. And, what may be the most confusing part, Windows 2000 consists of a combination of hierarchical and nonhierarchical concepts inside the administrative framework, thus introducing a range of new administrative chores without removing any of the old ones (which effectively raises the bar for all administrators).

In theory, groups could have been made more or less redundant by introducing the OU hierarchy as security principals (similar to what can be found in Novell's NDS directory service, where OUs are used for assigning permissions in somewhere between 80 and 95 percent of all instances). However, because this would demand some quite profound changes to the security subsystem (and thus a large part of the OS base structures), Microsoft has chosen to refrain from that.

Microsoft asserts that the use of groups (compared to OUs) is a very ingenious solution in a hierarchical directory service, because you can easily assign permissions and rights to users across OUs, a process that is usually needed because most organizations use interdisciplinary working groups.

I believe Microsoft has a very good point here. However, this just isn't a fair justification for not introducing OUs as security principals as a complement to groups (as in Novell NDS). In most cases, some 80 to 90 percent of the assignments of permissions and rights will coincide with the corporate hierarchy and thus is far easier done with OUs than with groups. So, whether you (and Microsoft) like it or not, the day-to-day handling of permissions and rights in Active Directory will demand a good deal more time and effort (not to mention the need for a lot more planning up front) than is the case with NDS, because NDS can use groups as well as OUs as security principals.

Interoperability Limitations with NT 4

Unless, you're running Windows 2000 or using the Active Directory client (available for Windows 95, Windows 98, and Windows NT 4), your clients will see Windows 2000 Server Universal Groups as Global Groups—such as clients are often referred to as *down-level clients*. When viewing the members of a Universal Group, the down-level client sees only members that conform to the membership rules of NT Server 4 Global Groups; other members are filtered out of the view. For example, when a down-level client views the members of a Windows 2000 Server Global Group, it doesn't see any other groups who are members of that Global Group.

In a Windows 2000 Server domain running in native mode, all DCs must run Windows 2000 Server. However, the domain may contain member servers that run Windows NT Server 4. These servers also see Universal Groups as Global Groups and can place them in Local Groups and assign permissions.

On a member server running NT Server 4, the administrative tools can't see Domain Local Groups of the Active Directory domain (because Domain Local Groups couldn't be granted permissions on the member servers in an NT domain). However, this might pose a problem to you, because an Active Directory domain running in native mode in fact does allow for assigning permissions to member servers using Domain Local Groups.

You can work around the issue of not being able to view Domain Local Groups on a Windows NT Server-based computer by heading for a Windows 2000 computer and focusing its administrative tools on the server running NT Server 4. You can then use these Windows 2000 Server tools to view the domain's Domain Local Groups and assign them permissions for resources on the server running NT Server 4.

Getting a Grip on the Groups

In an Active Directory setting, you are presented with three kinds of groups:

◆ *Universal Group*—The simplest form of group; can appear in ACLs anywhere in the forest and can contain other Universal Groups, Global Groups, and users from anywhere in the forest. Small installations can use Universal Groups exclusively and avoid dealing with Global and Local Groups. A Universal Group and its members appear in the Global Catalog (GC). Universal Groups are applicable only to native mode domains.

◆ *Global Group*—Can appear on ACLs anywhere in the forest. It can contain users and other Global Groups (this *nesting* of Global Groups is only available when the domain is running in native mode) only from the domain in which the Global Group exists. So, except for the option of nesting groups, it is exactly the same as an NT 4 Global Group. Global Group names appear in the GC, but their members still are assigned to the domain.

◆ *Domain Local Group*—Can be used on ACLs only at servers in its own domain; can contain Domain Local Groups from the domain in question as well as users, Global Groups, and Universal Groups from any domain in the forest. Thus, except for the intro-duction of Universal Groups and the option of nesting groups, it is exactly the same as an NT 4 Local Domain Group. Domain Local Groups are valid only in the domain in which they are defined, and thus don't appear in the GC at all.

Note

If you are used to Microsoft Exchange Server, you will notice that the Universal Group is similar to Exchange's distribution lists (DLs). Domain Local Groups can be granted permissions on both DCs and member servers in a domain. Windows NT Server (Windows 2000 Server's predecessor) did not allow granting permissions on member servers.

As Figure 9.11 shows, the new type of group—the Universal Group—is a very flexible and powerful concept. You can actually handle every security need by using Universal Groups exclusively, which is a boon to the administrator, because it eliminates the burdensome work of managing Global Groups and Domain Local Groups. However, using Universal Groups alone often isn't feasible, because the Universal Group and its members appear in the GC. Thus, every time a change is made to a group, the change has to be replicated to all GCs in the forest, which puts a heavy toll on bandwidth usage.

So, except for a small company or a company in which the entire network is on one LAN (or any other kind of high-speed network) or only consists of a single domain, you would usually need to use Global Groups to keep the replication traffic in check. Normally, this is done by using the Universal Groups as a sort of aggregate entity for Global Groups, so that the Universal Groups generally are looked to as the primary vehicle for assigning permis-sions (and thus contain Global Groups from the domains that exist in the forest) and the

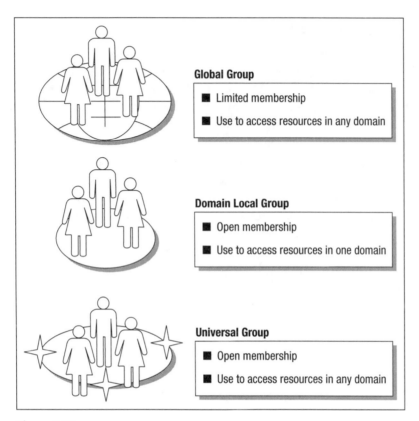

Global Group
- Limited membership
- Use to access resources in any domain

Domain Local Group
- Open membership
- Use to access resources in one domain

Universal Group
- Open membership
- Use to access resources in any domain

Figure 9.11
You have three groups at your disposal in Windows 2000.

Global Groups are used almost exclusively for holding user accounts. In that way, after the Global Groups are established, the membership in the Universal Group—and thereby the need for replication—changes infrequently, and you can still use the Universal Group to assign permissions and rights throughout the forest.

More New Group Features

Universal Groups are only one among many new features. For example, the group concept has been extended with a new class of functionality—the *Distribution Group*. Every group in an Active Directory domain is one of the following two types (see Figure 9.12):

♦ *Security Groups*—Can be listed in ACLs, which define permissions on resources and objects. This is similar to the functionality that you may be used to from NT Server 4. However, in Windows 2000 Server, Security Groups can also be used as an email entity—sending an email message to the group sends the message to all members of the group—if the administrator allows that.

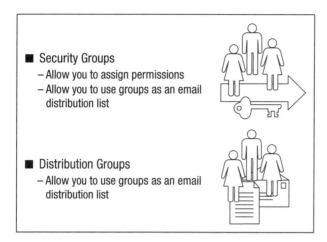

Figure 9.12
Two different types of groups are available in Windows 2000 Server: Security Groups and
Distribution Groups.

♦ *Distribution Groups*—Can only be used as an email entity (therefore, can't be listed
in ACLs).

Thus, Security Groups represent a superset of the Distribution Group functionality. So, if
you like, you could actually use a Security Group as a Distribution Group (that is, as a group
that is never used to assign resource permissions to its members, but rather is used solely for
email purposes). However, performance-wise, that isn't a very good idea, as you will see
later in "Group Strategies." Both group types can contain contacts, as well as actual user
accounts. *Contacts* are the individual-user equivalent of Distribution Groups; contacts can
only be used for email purposes, and so can't be assigned access permissions.

Contacts can appear in Security Groups and in Distribution Groups. A Security Group that
contains contacts can be assigned permissions to resources, but any contacts contained in
the group are not given those permissions. Another very interesting extension to the group
concept introduced with Active Directory is the possibility of converting between different
group types. No conversions are allowed in mixed mode domains. However, the following
conversions are allowed in native mode domains:

♦ *Global Group to Universal Group*—Allowed only if the Global Group is not a member of
another Global Group.

♦ *Domain Local Group to Universal Group*—The Domain Local Group being converted
can't contain another Domain Local Group.

Note

*A group may be converted from a Security Group to a Distribution Group, and vice
versa, at any time, if the domain is running in native mode.*

The Distribution Group Equals the Exchange DL

If you are familiar with Microsoft Exchange Server, you should be in a position to immediately understand—and love—the concept of Distribution Groups, because Distribution Groups equal (and replace) the Exchange Server Distribution Lists (DLs).

As soon as you upgrade to running your existing Exchange Server installation on top of Active Directory, the Exchange DLs can be converted to Distribution Groups with universal scope using the Active Directory Connector (ADC). Thus, the upgrade to Active Directory will in fact work to eliminate some of the duplicate user administration found in an NT 4/Exchange Server. And the new Active Directory-enabled version of Exchange Server—Exchange 2000 Server—promises to eliminate the remainder of duplicate user administration. The MAPI interface support included with Active Directory GCs enables computers running previous versions of Exchange clients to still be able to view the migrated Distribution Group in the same way as with the old versions of Exchange Server.

Also, Windows 2000 Server allows *nesting* of groups (adding groups to other groups), which, in most instances, serves to limit the negative impact of the flatness of the group concept. Although nesting is just a quick fix on an inherently flat concept, it can help reduce the number of times that you need to assign permissions.

Your nesting options depend on whether the domain is running in native or mixed mode. In native mode, the Security Groups work like this:

♦ Universal Groups can contain user accounts, Universal Groups, and Global Groups from any domain.

♦ Global Groups can contain user accounts from the same domain and Global Groups from the same domain.

♦ Domain Local Groups can contain user accounts, Universal Groups, and Global Groups, all from any domain. They can also contain other Domain Local Groups from within the same domain.

Distribution Groups have the same functionality whether the domain is running in mixed or native mode (that is, the above-mentioned functionality).

For Security Groups in mixed mode, only the usual NT 4 features are available:

♦ Global Groups can contain only user accounts from the same domain.

♦ Domain Local Groups can contain Global Groups from any domain and user accounts from the same domain.

Summarizing the Group Scopes

Table 9.1 summarizes the abilities and limits of the Security Group scopes in Windows 2000 Server, and Table 9.2 summarizes the effect of domain modes on groups.

Table 9.1   Active Directory group scopes.

	Universal Groups	**Global Groups**	**Domain Local Groups**
Domains running in native mode (no backward-compatibility with NT 4).	Can contain user accounts, Global Groups, and universal accounts from any domain.	Can contain user accounts from the domain and Global Groups from the same domain.	Can contain user accounts, Global Groups, and Universal Groups from any domain, as well as Domain Local Groups.
Domains running inmixed mode (backward-compatibility with NT 4 and DCs default settings).	Can contain user accounts.	Not available from the same domain.	Can contain user accounts and Global Groups from any domain.
Scope: When domain is running in native mode	Can be put in groups and permission lists in any domain.	Can be put in groups and permission lists in any domain.	Can be put in other Domain Local Groups and permission lists only in the same domain.
Conversion options when domain is running in native mode.	Can't be converted to any other group scope.	Can be converted to Universal Group, as long as it isn't a member of any other Global Group.	Can be converted to Universal Group, as long as it doesn't contain another Domain Local Group.

Table 9.2   The effect of domain modes on groups.

	Native Mode Domains	**Mixed Mode Domains**
Universal Group	Universal Groups are available for both Security Groups and Distribution Groups.	Universal Groups are available only as Distribution Groups.
Group nesting	Full group nesting is allowed.	For Security Groups, group nesting is limited to Windows NT 4 rules; the only allowed nesting is for Domain Local Groups containing Global Groups. For Distribution Groups, full nesting is allowed.
Group conversion	Groups can be converted freely between Security Groups and Distribution Groups; Global Groups and Domain Local Groups can be converted to Universal Groups.	No group conversions are allowed.

Understanding Domain Modes and Groups

In both native mode and mixed mode, the following are true:

♦ The Domain Local Groups of a domain are available on the member servers in a domain (please refer to the sidebar "Interoperability Limitations with NT 4" for how to do that on NT Server-based computers), as well as on the DCs.

♦ All group types can contain contacts, as well as user accounts.

Groups on Workstations and Standalone Servers

Most of the new group features, such as Universal Groups, group nesting, and the distinction between Security Groups and Distribution Groups, are available only on Active Directory DCs and member servers.

Group accounts on Windows 2000 Professional computers and standalone servers running Windows 2000 Server still work in exactly the same way as for Windows NT 4:

- Only Local Groups can be created locally on the computer.

- A Local Group created on one of these computers can be assigned permissions only on that one computer.

A Windows 2000 Professional workstation that has joined a domain will have some of the group options added from the domain. The workstation can see Global Groups and Universal Groups from that domain, as well as Global Groups and Universal Groups from all domains in the forest. You can directly assign these groups permissions for workstation resources, or place them in the workstation's Local Groups.

The Default Groups

An Active Directory domain has several default User Groups that are created by the system, at the time when the domain is created. These groups represent various levels of access to workstations and servers and are the building blocks that you usually should use for securing your network. You can always build your own groups from scratch, but if you can get your demands met by the default Built-in Groups, why bother?

However, you should take care to note that, in a high security environment or in a very decentralized environment, you will often find the scope of the default groups unsatisfying and thus will find yourself in need of building the group structures from scratch. Before doing that, you should be aware that some abilities can't be controlled directly, because they are granted only to some Built-in Groups, and the only way for you to grant a user one of these built-in abilities is to make that user a member of the appropriate Local Group. This naturally increases quite a bit the complexity of creating the group structures from scratch.

Two very different types of default groups are available in a Windows 2000 Server environment:

- *Built-in Groups*—Groups that come with the local computer. All such groups are placed in the domain's *Builtin* OU at the Active Directory DCs and in the Groups folder at all other kinds of Windows 2000-based computers. Built-in Groups are always Local Groups.

- *Predefined Groups*—Groups that come with the Active Directory domain and/or a service. All such groups are found in the domain's *Users* OU at the Active Directory DCs. The predefined groups can either be of the Domain Local, Global, or Universal Groups.

> **Note**
>
> *All the built-in Domain Local Groups automatically defined by the OS are located in the **Built-in** container, and all the default predefined groups are located in the **Users** container. You should note that the **Built-in** and **Users** containers really aren't OUs (even though they resemble them somewhat), because they can't be deleted nor have any group policies applied to them.*

In addition, Windows 2000 features a couple of other specialized group types (the built-in identities and the foreign security principals) that you should take care to understand so as to avoid introducing any security blunders into your environment.

> **Note**
>
> *You should understand that all of the default groups can be modified by users with sufficient privileges. However, the Built-in Groups can never be deleted.*

The Built-in Groups

The Built-in Groups are the only ones you'll have available from the outset at Windows 2000-based computers that aren't part of any domain and thus represent the lowest-common-denominator security functionality found in a Windows 2000 environment. Built-in Groups also are found at computers working as members of a domain (whether as a DC or a member computer). However, in that case, several new groups—the so-called predefined groups, discussed in the next section—are brought in to supplement the Built-in Groups. Also, the number of Built-in Groups will be expanded with several new groups.

Being a member of one of the Built-in Groups gives a user the rights and abilities to perform various tasks on that specific local computer (and possibly other computers on the network). The Built-in Groups are scoped for local use, regardless of the computer role used, but their exact number varies with the computer role. You aren't allowed to delete or move any of the Built-in Groups.

On Windows 2000 Professional- and Windows 2000 Server-based computers (whether they be operating in standalone mode or as members of an Active Directory domain), you will find these Built-in Local Groups (all of which are stored in the Groups folder):

♦ *Administrators*—The highest privilege level that can be assigned. If a user account is a member of the Administrators Group, the user has full control over the computer. The auto-defined Administrator account is made a member of this group when Windows 2000 Professional is installed. There's only one minor limitation to the privileges: Members of the group can't automatically access files on NTFS file systems unless the owner grants access permissions to the Administrators Group. Members of the Administrators Group can, however, take ownership of any file and thus gain access in this way.

Knowing Your Five Computer Roles

You have five different types of computer roles available when working in a Windows 2000 environment:

- *Standalone workstation*—A computer that is running Windows 2000 Professional and is a member of a workgroup (or without any network functionality).

- *Standalone server*—A computer that is running one of the Windows 2000 Server variants and is a member of a workgroup (or without any network functionality).

- *Member workstation*—A computer that is running Windows 2000 Professional and is a member of an Active Directory domain.

- *Member server*—A computer that is running one of the Windows 2000 Server variants and is a member of an Active Directory domain.

- *DC server*—A computer that is running one of the Windows 2000 Server variants and is working as a Domain Controller.

You should be aware that other variants might exist, if you're not running in a "clean" Windows 2000 environment.

♦ *Backup Operators*—Allows the user to back up and restore files on a system. Any user can back up and restore files for which they have the appropriate file-access permissions. This group overrides those permissions and allows the user to back up any and all files on a disk, regardless of the file-access permissions.

♦ *Guests*—Intended to allow anyone without an account to log on to the computer, or connect to it over the network and be granted limited abilities. These people should be instructed to log on to the Guest account (which, by default, is a member of the Guests Group, but is disabled to avoid security issues). Thus, be very careful about which rights and permissions are granted to the Security Group account.

♦ *Power Users*—Provides users with additional rights for operating the system as an end user, compared with the Users Group. Members of this group can perform system administrative functions, without being given complete control over the system. In addition to all the rights given to the Users Group, a user logged on as a member of the Power Users Group has the authority, for example, to share resources (printers and folders), manage printers, create non-Administrator accounts, manage groups (Users, Guests, and Power Users), and set the computer's internal clock.

♦ *Replicator*—Handles directory replication functions. Usually, this group account is useful only in a domain setting, where it's applied for purposes of logging on to the Replicator Services of a DC. So, you should never add user accounts representing real users to this group account.

♦ *Users*—Provides users with the necessary rights to operate the system as an end user for performing daily tasks (such as running applications and managing files). This group should include accounts for everyone who uses a computer routinely. A user logged on to a Windows 2000 system as part of the Users Group can perform the following tasks: run applications, manage files, create and manage groups, keep a personal profile, and connect to a computer over a network. You should note that the Authenticated Users and Interactive built-in identities (see the section "The Special Groups") are members of this group.

Note

When a Windows 2000 computer is being made a member of a domain, the Domain Admins and Enterprise Admins Groups (two predefined groups) are added automatically to the workstation or server's Administrators Group, the Domain Guests Group (a predefined group) is added to the workstation or server's Guests Group, and the Domain Users Group (a predefined group) is added automatically to the workstation or server's Users Group.

Please note that any Windows 2000 computer that isn't acting as a DC includes a Built-in Group—*Power Users*—that can't be found on a DC. The Power Users Group provides a user with the ability to perform system administrative functions, without giving the user complete control over the system.

If the Windows 2000 Server-based computer is running as an Active Directory DC, you have these Built-in Local Groups available (all of which are stored in the OU named Built-in):

♦ *Account Operators*—Can manage the domain's user and group accounts, but is not allowed any pilfering with groups or accounts that have any administrative privileges.

♦ *Administrators*—Granted full control over the computer. Group has only one small limitation: It can't automatically access files on NTFS file systems unless the owner grants access permissions to the Administrators Group. Administrators can, however, take ownership of any file.

♦ *Backup Operators*—Can back up and restore files on the Domain Local Group DCs and can log on to these servers and shut them down.

♦ *Guests*—Allows anyone without an account to log on to the computer or to connect to it over the network and be granted limited abilities. Guests have no rights at servers by default.

Beware: The Default Security Permissions Have Changed!

Please note that the default operations allowed for the Users and Power Users Groups have changed quite a bit compared to Windows NT 4. Much less power is allowed for members of these Windows 2000 groups compared to the NT 4 groups—actually, the Windows 2000 Power Users Group comes pretty darn close to only allowing the same system privileges as was the case with the NT 4 Users Group!

You should study the changes carefully in order to achieve the optimum level of security and flexibility—and avoid any looming incompatibility on the part of applications—for the clients used in the enterprise.

You can find a full drill-down on this subject in my book, *Windows 2000 Professional Advanced Configuration and Implementation*, also published by The Coriolis Group.

Beware of the Pre-Windows 2000 Compatible Access Group

The Pre-Windows 2000 Compatible Access Group is needed for certain old NT applications to be fully functional in an Active Directory domain. For example, you will need this group for running Windows NT 4-based RAS servers and Microsoft SQL Server-based servers running on NT-based computers (or domains).

But the group is quite dangerous, because the members of the Pre-Windows 2000 Compatible Access Group are allowed read access to all attributes on user objects that existed in Windows NT 4 (including SID, name, logon hours, and the ACL) and all group objects attributes. And so, you should try to avoid this group altogether, because it represents an added security risk: By default, it will have the Everyone Group added (meaning that every user account in the forest, including the Guest account and Anonymous, will be able to read the mentioned attributes). You should always be able to do without the Pre-Windows 2000 Compatible Access Group, if all your servers are running on Windows 2000 Server.

- ♦ *Pre-Windows 2000 Compatible Access*—Allows the system to accommodate for pre-Windows 2000 applications that require permissions that are less strict than those granted by Active Directory DCs.

- ♦ *Print Operators*—Can manage all features relevant to printers (including the ability to log on locally at DCs and shut them down).

- ♦ *Replicator*—Handles directory replication functions. Only the domain user account used to log on to the Replicator Services of the DCs in the domain should be a member of the domain's Replicator Local Group. Do not add the user accounts of actual users to this group.

- ♦ *Server Operators*—Can manage the DCs. Members of this group have many of the same powers as members of the Administrators Group, except that they can't manage security on the server.

- ♦ *Users*—Provides users with the necessary rights to operate the system as an end user for performing daily tasks (such as running applications and managing files) and so the members of the Users Group aren't allowed to perform local log ons to servers—the servers can only be accessed from the network.

The Predefined Groups

When you're constructing a new Active Directory domain, several new groups will be created by default. All of these groups will obviously be found at all Windows 2000 Server-based computers running as Active Directory DCs.

These groups—which are of the Domain Local or Global Group type (and Universal, when running in a native mode domain)—are usually referred to as the predefined groups. Table 9.3 lists the predefined groups that you will find in an Active Directory domain by default (all are stored in the OU named *Users*, which also features all your domain users, as implied by the name). You should note that other groups might be present in the *Users* OU, depending on the services running at the servers and the groups defined by the domain administrators.

Note

When you add services and server applications, new groups and/or users usually will be added for reasons of administrative convenience. For example, Internet Information Server (IIS) will add the **IUSR_<name_of_computer>** *and* **IWAM_<name_of_computer>** *user accounts to the domain and Terminal Services will add the TsInternetUser user accounts. And as you can see in the list above, the DNS Service adds the Local Group DnsUpdateProxy and the Domain Local Group DnsAdmins. DHCP and WINS will add the groups DHCP Administrators (provides you with full control over the DHCP Service), DHCP Users (provides you with view-only access to the DHCP Service), and WINS Users (provides you with view-only access to the DHCP Service).*

Table 9.3   The predefined groups that are created at the same time as the Active Directory domain.

Group Name	Explanation	Group Type
Cert Publishers	Used by computers that are running an enterprise certification authority and by renewal agents.	Global Group
DHCP Administrators	Provides administrative access to DHCP.	Domain Local Group
DHCP Users	Allows view-only access to DHCP.	Domain Local Group.
DnsAdmins	Provides administrative access to DNS.	Domain Local Group
DnsUpdateProxy	Provides access to perform DDNS updates on behalf of others.	Domain Local Group
Domain Admins	Used to group accounts that you want to be administrators in the domain.	Global Group
Domain Computers	Includes all computers joined to the domain (excluding the DCs).	Global Group
Domain Controllers	Includes all DCs in the domain.	Global Group
Domain Guests	Collects guest accounts in the domain.	Global Group
Domain Users	Collects user accounts in the domain.	Global Group
Group Policy Creator Owners	Used for grouping accounts that you want to manage group policies for the domain.	Global Group
RAS and IAS Servers	Used by computers that are running the Routing and Remote Access Services (RRAS). Members of this group are given access to the properties of User objects that apply to RRAS.	Domain Local Group
Enterprise Admins	Collects the designated administrators of the forest and allows them access to performing forest-wide changes.	Universal Group (Global Group, which exists only in the forest root domain, if the domain is running in mixed mode)
Schema Admins	Collects the administrators, who are allowed to implement schema changes.	Universal Group (Global Group, which exists only in the forest root domain, if the domain is running in mixed mode)

You are allowed to move as well as delete any and all of the predefined groups. However, you will only be allowed to move the groups to other OUs within the domain (that is, you can't move them to other domains).

Understanding the Default Groups

If you choose to follow Microsoft's best practices, you should use the predefined groups of a domain to collect the various types of user accounts in that domain (regular users, administrators, and guests). These groups are then placed in the built-in and/or predefined Local Groups on clients and servers residing in that domain (and possibly other domains) either by default, when the clients and servers are made members of the domain, or due to being added by the administrator. In most cases, the default groups not only work to make your Active Directory setup easier to understand for other administrators, they also comprise some useful collections of rights and abilities that can save you precious time in day-to-day administration.

With the predefined groups, you should be especially cognizant of the factors surrounding the following groups:

♦ *Users and Domain Users*—By default, any user account that you create in a domain is automatically added to the Domain Users Global Group at computers that are members of the domain. Consequently, you can use the Domain Users Group to represent all of the user accounts created in the domain. For example, if you want all the users in this domain to have access to a folder, you can either assign rights for the folder to the Domain Users Group or put the Domain Users Group into a group that holds the proper permissions to the folder.

♦ *Administrators and Domain Admins*—The Domain Admins Global Group will usually be used to represent the users who have broad administrative rights in the domain. Windows 2000 Server doesn't place any accounts in this group automatically, except for the built-in Administrator account, but if you want an account to have sweeping administrative rights in this domain (and possibly other domains), you can put that account into Domain Admins. Because Active Directory supports administration and delegation of authority, you shouldn't have to grant these broad administrative rights to many users. By default, the Domain Admins Group in a domain is a member of the Administrators Local Group on computers participating in the same domain.

♦ *Schema Admins and Enterprise Admins*—The forest root domain's default Administrator user account also is added to the Schema Admins Global Group and the Enterprise Admins Universal Group.

♦ *Guests and Domain Guests*—By default, the Domain Guests Global Group is a member of the Guests Local Group on computers participating in the same domain, and contains the domain's default Guest user account.

You should understand that the Domain Admins, Domain Guests, and Domain Users built-in Global Groups have no inherent authority; they receive authority by being made a member of a Local Group. Likewise, the Built-in Domain Local Groups of a domain are used primarily to assign default sets of permissions to users who will have some administrative control in that domain. For example, the Administrators Group in a domain carries a broad administrative authority over all user accounts and resources in the domain from the outset.

The Special Groups

In addition to the Built-in Groups listed in Table 9.3, Windows 2000 includes a set of so-called built-in identities that behave quite differently from the groups. These special identities don't have specific memberships that you can modify (in other words, they can't be assigned any members, because they apply to any account that is using the computer in a specified way) and they don't refer to the privilege level of a user, but instead refer to accessing computer resources; thus, they represent the set of users online at different times, depending on the circumstances.

Windows 2000 includes the following built-in identities:

♦ *Anonymous Logon*—Any user that has logged on anonymously.

♦ *Authenticated Users*—All logged-on users that have been authenticated by the local system. You can, for example, use this group instead of Everyone to prevent anonymous access to a resource.

♦ *Batch*—Any batch process (such as the task scheduler) that is logged on to the computer.

♦ *Creator Group (only on an Active Directory DC)*—A placeholder in an inheritable ACE. This identity is only used by the POSIX subsystem.

♦ *Creator Owner (only on an Active Directory DC)*—A placeholder in an inheritable ACE. When an ACE listing this SID is inherited, the system will replace the Creator Owner SID with the current owner's SID. For a directory, if permissions are granted to the Creator Owner Group, the creator of a subdirectory or file is granted those permissions for that very subdirectory or file. For a printer, if permissions are granted to the Creator Owner Group, the creator of a print job is granted those permissions for that print job.

♦ *Dialup*—Any user logged on to the computer using dial-up networking.

♦ *Everyone*—All users logged on to the computer, including users that are logged on using the Guests Group and users from other domains.

The Additional Identifiers

Windows 2000 includes yet another bunch of identities, which are used only by the security subsystem—and so they aren't available, when assigning permissions and rights. However, you should know about their existence in case you should ever see a funny-looking SID featured on an ACL. The identities available to the security subsystem (as well as to programmers) are: Null Authority, Nobody, World Authority, Local Authority, Creator Authority, Creator Owner Server (not used at present time), Creator Group Server (not used at present time), Nonunique Authority, NT Authority, Logon Session, Enterprise Controllers, and LocalSystem. The SIDs for the identities mentioned here (as well as the built-in identities and the Built-in Groups) are listed in Microsoft Windows 2000 Server Resource Kit's Table E.1.

- ◆ *Interactive*—All users that have logged on locally at the computer (as opposed to users who have logged on over the network).

- ◆ *Network*—All users that have logged on the computer over the network (as opposed to users who logged on locally).

- ◆ *Proxy (only on Windows 2000 Server)*—Not used by Windows 2000 at present.

- ◆ *Restricted (only on Windows 2000 Server)*—Not used by Windows 2000 at present.

- ◆ *Self (only on an Active Directory DC)*—A placeholder in an ACE on a user, group, or computer object in Active Directory that the system will replace with the actual SID. So, when using Self, you are in fact granting the security principal represented by the Active Directory object permissions to the object. Self is also known as principal self in some quarters.

- ◆ *Service*—Any account that has logged on as a service.

- ◆ *System*—The operating system.

- ◆ *Terminal Server User*—The users who have logged on to the local server's Terminal Services (formerly known as Terminal Server).

You can't modify or view the memberships of these identities, and you don't even see them when you administer the Local Computer or Domain Groups. However, they are available for use when you assign rights and permissions.

On the Issue of Service Accounts

When you're installing or enabling a service, you have the choice between two security contexts: The so-called LocalSystem account and a Windows 2000 user account (which should be referred to as a service account and used for that purpose only).

The LocalSystem account is already used by many of the built-in system services, which is why many people will just choose this without thinking further about it for any other third-party service that may be installed on the system. However, I urge you to think a little harder than that. Otherwise, you might be in for a rather big (and unwelcome) surprise.

LocalSystem is a special, predefined local account available only to system processes—the LocalSystem account doesn't have a password, which makes it much easier to work with in operations than the usual service accounts (you will need to change password on each service account at least two or four times a year in order to uphold the security level intended).

The Localsystem account is a regular user account, although it has a flag that states that it is used only by the computer. The password is generated randomly and is stored on the DC, when the new server joins a domain. The password for this account automatically changes every seven days.

Although the LocalSystem account has a token to allow authentication against the domain, it doesn't have user credentials associated with it. In Windows NT4, this meant that the LocalSystem acccount couldn't be used for authentication between two servers. However, this doesn't apply to Windows 2000 Server, due to it using Kerberos, rather than NT LAN Lanager (NTLM) authentication. As a result, services on two different member services are allowed to authenticate to each other without special account.

The advantages of moving away from a special account are as follows:

- The system adminstrator does not need to change the password for a logon account.

- A separate Service account password could come under attack because it isn't feasible for the sistem administrator to lock the account after a certain number of failed attempts (locking the account would result in the applicable services being unable to authenticate with one another, which could cause services to be denied).

- The password is more secure because it consists of a random string of characters.

- The password automatically changes every seven days, making it very resistent to attack.

On computers running Windows 2000, a service that runs in the context of the LocalSystem account uses the credentials of the computer when accessing resources over the network and has full access to local resources. In other words, a service that runs in the context of LocalSystem on a DC has full access to the directory, because the DC hosts a directory replica and LocalSystem has complete access to local resources. So you should never run a service under LocalSystem on a DC, if you can avoid it.

The security context under which the service runs affects the access rights that the service has on the computer and on the network. So, if possible, you should always run each service under a separate service account on any system, regardless of its role. However, running a service in the context of a service account has two disadvantages:

- The account must be created before the service can run.

- Service account passwords are stored on each computer on which the service is installed.

With all that said on service accounts, you should note that, although the user interface in the Services MMC Snap-in allows you to change the Log on properties for a service to an account other than the Local System account, certain services (including DNS Server and DHCP Server) should only run on the Local System account, because Microsoft doesn't support using an ordinary service account.

The Trusted Domain Groups

Windows 2000 includes yet another type of groups, when trust relationships are established with domains outside of the Active Directory forest.

Note

No matter whether such trust relationships are going to Active Directory domains or Windows NT domains, these trust relationships will always be defined using ordinary NT 4-style one-way trusts.

These groups are found in the OU named *ForeignSecurityPrincipals*. This very OU will stay empty until the first trust relationship has been created. When that is the case, you will find the following two groups:

- NT Authority\Authenticated Users
- NT Authority\Interactive

As you can see, both of these groups are really Special Groups. Thus, you should note that the Authenticated Users and Interactive users Special Groups also will feature users from trusted domains, if applicable.

User Rights

Another very interesting thing about the Built-in Groups is that some of them are assigned so-called *user rights* to perform some actions on the system. A user right is authorization to perform an operation that affects an entire computer (such as backing up files and directories, logging on to a computer interactively, or shutting down a computer system) rather than a specific object on the computer. User rights are divided into two categories:

♦ *Logon rights*—Control who is authorized to log on to a computer and how they can log on. So logon rights control how human users and other security principals are authorized to access a computer—at the keyboard, through a network connection, as a service, or as a batch job.

♦ *Privileges*—Control access to system resources and whether a given user is allowed to override the *permissions* that are set on a particular object on the computer. So privileges control which users are authorized to manipulate system resources—by setting the computer's internal clock, by loading and unloading device drivers, by backing up or restoring files and folders, or by doing anything else that affects the system as a whole.

Unlike permissions, which are granted by an object's owner, user rights are assigned as part of the *security policy* for the computer. Unless the computer is a DC, user rights are computer-specific policies. If the computer is an Active Directory DC, the same user rights will be used on all DCs in the domain.

Note

To view the user rights assignment for a computer, log on using an account that has administrative authority, open the Administrative Tools folder in the Control Panel, and then start Local Security Policy.

User rights can be assigned to individual user accounts, but are usually (and more efficiently) assigned to groups. The predefined (Built-in) Groups have a set of user rights assigned, and many services will also be adding some of their own groups to several of the user rights.

Note

The special account LocalSystem has built-in capabilities that correspond to almost all privileges and logon rights. Processes that are running as part of the OS as well as the core system services are associated with this account, because they require a complete set of user rights. Although you can configure other services to also run under the LocalSystem account, it's recommended that you do so with care.

Table 9.4 shows the default user rights held by the Built-in Groups in an Active Directory domain, as well as the user rights for a Windows 2000 Professional-based workstation or Windows 2000 Server-based member server.

Table 9.4 Default user rights assigned to the Built-in Groups of the Active Directory domain.

User Right	Allows	Group Assigned this Right on a DC	Group Assigned this Right on Non-DCs
Access this computer from the network	a user to connect to the computer over the network.	Administrators, Authenticated Users, Everyone	Administrators, Backup Operators, Power Users, Users, Everyone
Act as part of the operating system	a process to perform as a secure, trusted part of the OS; some subsystems are granted this right. This right should be carefully watched, because it allows the process to request additional privileges to be added to the access token and to build an anonymous token, which can't be audited.	Not configured	Not configured
Add workstations to domain	adding up to 10 computers to a domain (and thus won't apply to anything but DCs). The behavior of this privilege is duplicated by the Create Computer Objects permission available for OUs; therefore, you have to set this permission in order to be able to add new computers to the domain.	Authenticated Users	Not configured
Back up files and directories	a user to back up files and directories. This right goes before the file and directory permissions, but only when using the NTFS backup API (otherwise normal file and directory permissions apply).	Administrators, Backup Operators, Server Operators	Administrators, Backup Operators
Bypass traverse checking	a user to change directories and to access files and sub-directories, even if the user has no permission to access parent directories. In other words, this privilege only allows the user to traverse directories, not list the contents of a folder.	Administrators, Authenticated Users, Everyone	Administrators, Backup Operators, Power Users, Users, Everyone
Change the system time	a user to set the time for the internal clock of the computer.	Administrators, Server Operators	Administrators, Power Users
Create a pagefile	a user to change the size of the pagefile.	Administrators	Administrators

(continued)

Table 9.4 **Default user rights assigned to the Built-in Groups of the Active Directory domain** *(continued).*

User Right	Allows	Group Assigned this Right on a DC	Group Assigned this Right on Non-DCs
Create a token object	a process to create access tokens. The LocalSystem account can do this, so you should use this account for processes that need this privilege. This right should be carefully watched because of its inherent security risks.	Not configured	Not configured
Create permanent shared objects	a user to create special permanent objects, such as \\ Device, that are used within Windows 2000.	Not configured	Not configured
Debug programs	a user to debug any process and low-level objects, such as threads.	Administrators	Administrators
Deny access to this computer from the network	nothing; rather, it blocks the "Access this computer from the network" right.	Not configured	Not configured
Deny logon as a batch job	nothing; rather, it blocks the "Logon as a batch job" right.	Not configured	Not configured
Deny logon as a service	nothing; rather, it blocks the "Logon as a service" right.	Not configured	Not configured
Deny logon locally	nothing; rather, it blocks the "Logon locally" right.	Not configured	Not configured
Enable computer and user accounts to be trusted for delegation	a user to change the Trusted for Delegation setting on a user or computer object in Active Directory (provided that the user also has write access to the account control flags on the object in question). This setting is what allows the implementation of multitier client/server applications, where a front-end service use the credentials of a client for authenticating with a back-end service.	Administrators	Not configured
Force shutdown from a remote system	a user to shut down a remote computer.	Administrators, Server Operators	Administrators
Generate security audits	a process to generate entries in the security log.	Not configured	Not configured

(continued)

Table 9.4   Default user rights assigned to the Built-in Groups of the Active Directory domain (continued).

User Right	Allows	Group Assigned this Right on a DC	Group Assigned this Right on Non-DCs
Increase quotas	a process to increase the processor quota assigned to another process (however, it's only allowed to do it on processes to which it has write property access).	Administrators	Administrators
Increase scheduling priority	a process to boost the execution priority of another process (however, it's only allowed to do it on processes to which it has write property access).	Administrators	Administrators
Load and unload device drivers	a user to install and remove Plug and Play device drivers. Please note that this privilege doesn't apply to non-Plug and Play drivers; such drivers can be installed by Administrators. This right should be carefully watched because of its inherent security risks (device drivers run as trusted programs).	Administrators	Administrators
Lock pages in memory	a user to lock pages in memory so that they can't be paged out to virtual memory. Microsoft dubs this privilege as obsolete, which unfortunately doesn't tell us whether or not it still works.	Not configured	Not configured
Log on as a batch job	a process to register with the system as a batch job.	Not configured	Not configured
Log on as a service	a process to register with the system as a service.	Not configured	Not configured
Log on locally	a user to log on at the computer from the computer keyboard.	Account Operators, Administrators, Backup Operators, Print Operators, Server Operators	Administrators, Backup Operators, Power Users, Users, Everyone
Manage auditing and security log	a user to specify what types of resource access (such as file access) are to be audited, and to view and clear the security log.	Administrators	Administrators
Modify firmware environment variables	a user or process to modify system environment variables stored in nonvolatile RAM on systems that support this type of configuration.	Administrators	Administrators

(continued)

Table 9.4 **Default user rights assigned to the Built-in Groups of the Active Directory domain** *(continued).*

User Right	Allows	Group Assigned this Right on a DC	Group Assigned this Right on Non-DCs
Profile single process	a user to perform profiling performance monitoring) on a non-system process using the built-in tools for doing that.	Administrators	Administrators, Power Users
Profile system performance	a user to perform profiling (performance monitoring) on a system process using the built-in tools for doing that.	Administrators	Administrators
Remove computer from docking station	a user to undock a computer by clicking Eject PC on the Start Menu.	Administrators	Administrators, Power Users, Users
Replace a process-level token	a process to replace the child process's security-access token. This is a very powerful (and thus dangerous) right that should be used with the utmost care by the system.	Not configured	Not configured
Restore files and directories	a user to restore backed-up files and directories (including their permissions). This right goes before the file and directory permissions, but only when using the NTFS backup API (otherwise normal file and directory permissions apply).	Administrators, Backup Operators, Server Operators	Administrators, Backup Operators
Shut down the system	a user to shut down Windows 2000.	Account Operators, Administrators, Backup Operators, Print Operators, Server Operators	Administrators, Backup Operators, Power Users
Synchronize directory service data	a process to provide directory synchronization services. This is only of relevance to DCs.	Not configured	Not configured
Take ownership of files or other objects	a user to take ownership of files, directories, printers, and other objects on the computer. This right goes before the permissions protecting objects.	Administrators	Administrators

For the most part, conflicts between privileges and permissions occur only in situations where the rights required to administer a system overlap the rights of resource ownership. When rights conflict, a privilege overrides a permission!

For example, one common administrative task is backing up files and folders. In order to do its job, backup software must be able to traverse all folders in an NTFS volume, list the contents of each folder, read the attributes of every file, and read data in any file that has its archive attribute set. And these rights are exactly what you get by using the *Back up files and directories* privilege.

The ability to take ownership of files and other objects is another case where an administrator's need to maintain the system takes priority over an owner's right to control access. Normally, you can take ownership of an object only if its current owner gives you permission to do so.

Note

Owners of NTFS objects can allow another user to take ownership by granting the other user Take Ownership permission. Owners of Active Directory objects can do the same thing by granting another user Modify Owner permission.

If the current owner gives you permission and you do take ownership, you can do whatever you want with the object. You can even deny the previous owner access to it. For this reason, owners are understandably reluctant to give Take Ownership or Modify Owner permission to anyone.

However, the *Take ownership of files or other objects* privilege allows you to step in and take ownership, if needed—regardless of the current owner's permission. So, used correctly, it will for example allow an administrator to take ownership of an abandoned resource and then transfer ownership by granting another user Take Ownership or Modify Owner permission. But, used incorrectly, this very privilege might very well prove to be a big void in your security setup.

Group Strategies

Generally, a user or computer needs access to many resources. If a group has been provided with the rights to access a resource, you can control access by adding the user or computer to, or removing it from, the group, rather than changing the permissions on the resource. Setting permissions for an individual user or computer does not override permissions granted to the user or computer through groups to which the user or computer belongs (except when it denies permissions).

Basing security policies and account management on groups rather than users or computers reduces your cost of ownership. Administration at the account or resource level can then be limited to exceptional cases. A group can also have members that are other groups. You can use this to create an appropriate range of group contexts for assigning rights. For example, you may have a Production Group that encompasses manufacturing, packaging, and shipping responsibilities. You could create Manufacturing, Shipping, and Packaging Groups, assign appropriate rights to each, and make all of these groups members of the Production Group. Now, the rights that you assign to the Production Group also applies to all of its member groups.

To implement a group-based strategy:

1. Establish a comprehensive set of Security and Distribution Groups. In many cases, you should find it helpful to make use of the group-nesting functionality offered with Active Directory native mode domains.

2. Determine what you need to accomplish: network responsibility, assignment of permissions to resources, or creation of mail lists.

3. Use Built-in Groups wherever possible (unless you're building a high security environment; in these cases, you would usually build your own security hierarchy from the ground up). Determine whether an existing group is suitable for the task at hand.

4. Add the groups needed. When adding a group, you are asked to provide a group name. Keep the following in mind when you do so:

   ♦ The group name must be unique to the computer being administered (Local Groups), to the domain being administered (Domain Local Groups and Global Groups), or to the forest (Universal Groups).

   ♦ A Universal or Global Group name can contain up to 64 characters, including any uppercase or lowercase characters, except the following: " \ ; = , + < and >. But, if the domain is running in mixed mode (and for user logon names (pre-Windows 2000)), the following limitations apply: Can contain up to 20 characters, including any uppercase or lowercase characters, except the following: " / \ [ ] : ; | = , + * ? < and >. A Universal or Global Group name can't consist solely of periods and spaces.

   ♦ A Local Group name can contain up to 256 characters, including any uppercase or lowercase characters, except the backslash character (\).

   ♦ You need to establish where the group should be located in the Active Directory hierarchy. Placing a group in the correct place in Active Directory will work to ease any needs for delegation of administration, as well as improving your general overview of the environment.

5. Assign rights to the Security Groups before you create user or computer accounts. The best practices for creating and using Security Groups, outlined by Microsoft, are as follows:

   ♦ *Within the domain*—Make the domain's Security Group a member of a Local Security Group and assign rights and resource permissions to the Local Security Group; or

   ♦ *Within and between domains*—Make the domain's Global or Universal Security Group a member of a Local Security Group and assign rights and resource permissions to the Local Security Group; or assign rights and resource permissions to a Universal Security Group.

Note

While the best practices from Microsoft call for granting rights and permissions to Local Groups and adding Global or Universal Groups for adding users to Local Groups, you might note that you can in fact assign Global, as well as Universal Groups directly to your resources. So I would suggest that your choice depends more on what will be looked to as the simplest and most manageable solution, rather than on Microsoft's best practices.

6. If a domain contains a hierarchy of OUs, nesting groups that contain user accounts can be useful. Nesting enables you to add a group as a member of another group. The nested groups can be thought of as a *hierarchical node*, in which each individual group is referred to as a *leaf*. Routine account maintenance can then be performed on the individual (leaf) group.

7. Assess whether you need to change the user rights for the new or Built-in Groups.

8. Delegate administration of groups to the appropriate manager or group leader.

9. Make the appropriate users members of the built-in or newly created groups, for domain-wide access. The following are the best practices outlined by Microsoft for the usage of Security and Distribution Groups:

   ♦ *Security Groups*—Assign domain user accounts to the domain's Global (only applicable to users within the same domain as the Global Group) or Universal Security Groups as applies.

   ♦ *Distribution Groups*—The general strategy for creating Distribution Groups is to either:

      ♦ Assign domain user accounts to the domain's Global (only applicable to users within the same domain as the Global Group) Distribution Groups or Universal Distribution Groups; or

---

Performance: Why to Use a Distribution Group Rather than a Security Group

When a user logs on to the network, Windows 2000 Server determines the groups in which the user is a member and then creates a security token that is assigned to the user. The security token lists the user's account ID and the ID of all Security Groups in which the user is a member.

This token is sent to any computer that the user accesses, so that the target computer can determine whether the user has any rights or permissions at that computer, by comparing all the IDs contained in the token against the permissions listed for any resources at that computer. This is how the user gets access to resources when permissions for the resources have been granted to a Security Group that the user is a member of.

If the user is a member of any Distribution Groups, these groups are ignored when Windows 2000 builds the token. Thus, using Distribution Groups rather than Security Groups, when no permissions will be assigned using that particular group, will work to improve the performance during logon and reduce the size of the token—which also improves performance, because the token is sent to the various computers that the user accesses.

♦ Assign domain user accounts to the domain's Global (only applicable within the domain) Security Groups or Universal Security Groups.

These strategies apply to all kinds of domains, whether they be a single domain, multiple domains that are part of a tree, or multiple domain trees that form a forest.

When you design your group structures, you should be keenly aware of the one major drawback to the group implementation chosen by Microsoft: The group membership attribute has been implemented as a multivalued attribute in Active Directory rather than each membership being implemented as a separate attribute.

This design choice in effect makes group memberships an exception to the rule of having Active Directory only replicate the actual attribute-level changes imposed on it (as opposed to the whole object, as is always the case with the SAM). That's indeed a very displeasing design choice, because it means that any change to the group membership is dependent on the whole set of group members being replicated, and thus a single change (whether be it a delete or an addition of a group member) will either succeed or fail as an operation on the whole group.

The usage of a multivalued attribute has two very unfortunate side effects on your group design:

♦ You need to assess how many people will be administering each of the intended groups and from where. The simple reason for this is that you should avoid having several people changing the same group at the same time (that is, before the Active Directory is fully replicated to the DCs on which the group is being administered), because only the last writer will prevail (please look to Chapter 12 for the detailed discussion on how replication collisions are handled).

♦ You need to estimate how many members each group eventually will entail. Because all the members of each group are replicated whenever a change happens, you will find yourself subjected to heavy replication traffic if the groups grow too big.

No 5,000-User Limit

There have been a lot of rumors that Microsoft has put some limitations to how many users each group can hold. I just want to put these rumors to rest: There's no limitations whatsoever for 5,000 users or anything of that sort in regard to any groups.

The 5,000-user limit is merely a design *recommendation* on the part of Microsoft. You might note that the 5,000-user design recommendation is a rather vague and unclear recommendation that you shouldn't base your full group design on. Unless you're dealing with a group where memberships are only replicated inside a LAN (or a high-speed LAN with plenty of bandwidth) and all the people administering the group are assembled at this very LAN, you should keep your groups much smaller than 5,000 members due to the multivalued attribute issue mentioned here.

Guidelines for Group Nesting

When you add groups to other groups, you should do the following:

- *Minimize the nesting levels*—Nesting can reduce the number of times that you assign group memberships and permissions/rights. However, nesting comes at a price: The tracking of permissions becomes more complex with multiple levels of nesting. So remember, less is better.

- *Always document group memberships*—You should *always* develop comprehensive documentation of the group memberships and their use in a nested environment, to avoid security hiccups and the like.

Note

If you're working with Security Groups, the last-writer situation might not only turn out to become an administrative pain, but a major security problem, when administering groups that deny permissions. On the positive side, you should note that the earlier group changes that are discarded by the Active Directory replication engine aren't gone forever. They're actually stored in the LostAndFound container inside the domain.

For this reason, you should strive to design your groups based on the following simple, but hard-to-follow, guideline: Each group with more than 50 users should follow the site boundaries.

You might notice that the group design is really not a question of the exact number of users, but how often the group needs to be changed, how fast replications are happening inside the scope of the group, and how much bandwidth is used for replicating the group with each change. If the scope of your groups covers several sites, you should especially want to keep abreast of what will happen when the line is down at a site: In the case where administration of the same group happens during the downtime and at several sites, only the last group changes will prevail when the link is up again.

You should note that the need for implementing smaller groups than what you might be used to with Windows NT Server really isn't that big a deal, if you're able to switch to Active Directory native mode (which by the way also is a best practice). As soon as you're running in native mode, you'll be able to implement group nesting and thus remedy just about the worst effects of Microsoft's very unfortunate Active Directory design decision.

The Limitations

From an administrative standpoint, you should always prefer Universal Groups over Global Groups. Universal Groups are much more powerful and versatile than Global Groups, because they support the possibility of spanning users from several domains.

If you are *running native mode* on your domains and *have no slow links* (or bandwidth bottlenecks) on your network, you can use Universal Groups for all of your needs (see Figure 9.13) and forget all about the customary Global and Domain Local Groups strategy from Windows

Figure 9.13
This is by far the simplest way of implementing groups in an Active Directory setting, regardless of whether you have a single domain or a complex forest.

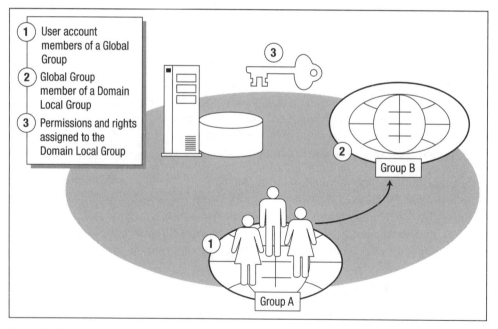

Figure 9.14
This is the Microsoft best practices approach for using Global Groups in a single domain, which is also used in Windows NT Server. Please note that you are, in fact, allowed to assign the Global Group straight to the resource as shown in Figure 9.13.

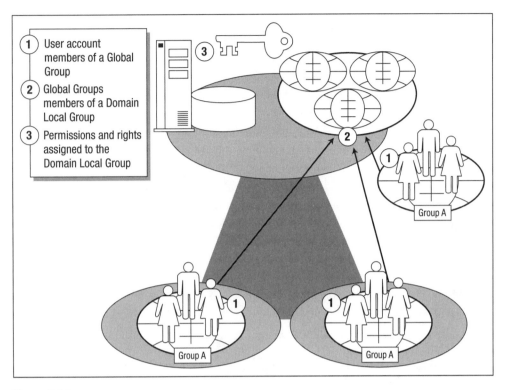

1. User account members of a Global Group
2. Global Groups members of a Domain Local Group
3. Permissions and rights assigned to the Domain Local Group

Figure 9.15
One of two common approaches to using groups in a forest.

NT Server (see Figure 9.14). However, if those two conditions don't describe your situation, you should move forward with caution in regard to the all-out Universal Groups approach.

If you have any domains in mixed mode, they *must* use Global Groups (and thus Local Groups, if you stick to Microsoft's best practices); which you definitely should want to do in a multiple domain scenario, but might want to skip for simplicity's sake in a single somain scenario. But, after you are over the transitional period regarding the DCs—and thus can convert to native mode—you can convert those groups to Universal Groups.

The outlook is much more grim if you have slow or oversubscribed links on your network. In such a case, you will positively need Global Groups to define your organization's functional groups because of the need for minimizing network traffic (see Figure 9.15). However, you will be able to tap some of the power of Universal Groups if you build your Universal Groups so they won't have frequent membership changes; the main problem with Universal Groups is that membership changes cause excessive traffic, because their members will be replicated across the network to all Global Catalog (GC) servers. Thus, you should never use Universal Groups for handling groups in which frequent membership changes will be the norm.

Note

Universal Groups and their members are listed in the GC. Global and Domain Local Groups are also listed in the GC, but their members are not. Thus, using Global Groups instead of Universal Groups reduces the size of the GC and dramatically reduces the replication traffic needed to keep the GCs up to date.

Also, you should ponder when and how you want to use Universal Groups for user account validation. Using Universal Groups as the basis for rights or permissions will cause the user's access token to contain all the user's Universal Groups, which can become a liability if many of the Universal Groups aren't used in each domain.

Thus, in many cases, the best way to achieve minimum bandwidth usage while still tapping into the potential of Universal Groups is to add Global Groups to Universal Groups (for having all users in the forest placed in the same group), add the user accounts to the Global Groups (to allow fast user account validation and less bandwidth usage), and maybe use Domain Local Groups or Local Groups to define access policies that apply to resources within each domain (for creating a more manageable permission infrastructure). You should take a look at Figure 9.16 for an example of how this works.

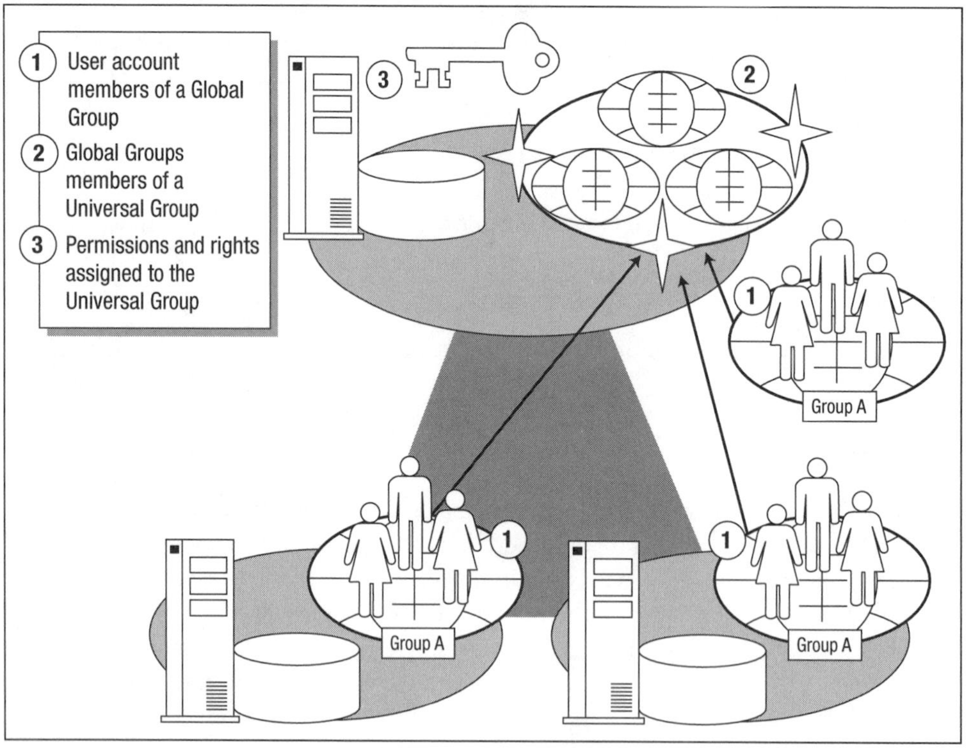

Figure 9.16
The other common approach for using groups in a forest.

Don't You Go Forgetting about Ownership—Ever!

When you're building your security, you'd better take proper care of the ownership attribute (also known as Creator Owner). If you don't take great care in who will be set as the owner of each and every file, folder, and object, you might very well wind up with a huge hole in your security here. Also, you should remember to carry out a thorough evaluation of who is assigned the *Take ownership of files or other objects* user right. This is a very powerful privilege and thus should be handled with the utmost care.

For example, the group **all-sys-admins** in the domain **sales.astonitgroup.com** should be defined as a Universal Group, containing the Global Groups **sys-admins** from **northamerica.sales.astonitgroup.com**, **sys-admins** from **europe.sales.astonitgroup.com**, and so on. Each of these Global Groups would contain the individual system administrators from each domain. In that way, the Global Groups are involved in daily maintenance activities, because they contain accounts; and their membership changes don't cause GC changes, because they are Global Groups. The membership of the Universal Group is represented in the GC, but the membership changes very rarely. Membership in the Universal Group should change only when the domain structure changes. Stated another way, if you use Universal Groups only for widely used groups that seldom change and use Global Groups (and possibly Domain Local Groups) for the rest, you minimize the bandwidth demands of the environment.

Best Practices

One of the very profound lessons of this chapter is that Active Directory's paradigm still contains a lot of "flatness," because of heavy use of some old NT Server 4 concepts. Apart from that, recognize that you always have to settle the issues listed in Table 9.5 on a global scale before you venture into the implementation of Active Directory.

Table 9.5 Summary of best practices.

Task	Points to Consider
Develop a user naming scheme.	Ensure that the usernames are globally unique. Remember that it will make it much easier for users to have the same logon and email names—the only exception to this rule is security (having the same names will make it easier for third parties to compromise security).
Develop a policy regarding user account properties.	Decide which of the many possible user account properties to set—and, maybe even more important, which not to use. Note which properties would be relevant to your users for searching the forest, and refer this data to the people designing your GC setup. Please note that the user account properties decisions usually will have an impact on the messaging system and all other Active Directory-aware applications that you may implement now or later.

(continued)

Table 9.5 Summary of best practices *(continued).*

Task	Points to Consider
Avoid the application of security assignments to user accounts.	User accounts will lead to inconsistencies and ultimately anarchy, which in turn can lead to holes in the overall security setup. So you should strive to use groups for security permissions instead.
Develop a plan of where to locate users in the OU structure.	This has a profound impact on the way that the user is presented to the computer, if you are using group policies.
Design a suitable group model.	You have two kinds of groups (Distribution Groups and Security Groups) and three very different types of Domain Groups (Domain Local, Global, and Universal) to choose from. Groups is a nonhierarchical concept by nature, unlike the domain and OU structures used elsewhere. Take your time when hammering out the group model; this may well be the single most important design task in securing the actual day-to-day use of the environment. The use of Universal Groups could be an important contributor to total bandwidth usage throughout the WAN, depending on the implementation strategy chosen.
Design a group structure.	Because of the crudeness of groups, you should strive very hard to establish a group structure that is both very powerful and easy to use. Also, develop a naming scheme for groups that enables administrators to grasp easily the intended audience for every group—and understand when not to make a new group if the application is covered by one or more existing groups. Use Built-in Groups whenever possible.
Analyze the reason for each group.	After you design your group structure, you should revise it very carefully with an eye to the following questions: • Have you properly identified users with common job responsibilities and common resources? • Which group scopes are used and which groups might as well be folded into other groups or implemented as nested groups? • How will the group be used, and how should it not be used? • Who will administer the group?
Keep things consistent.	If you have multiple domains, you should determine whether you can use the same group model and group structure across all domains. If not, you may look into redesigning the group model and/or structure.
Develop a policy for the creation of new groups.	Because groups are the heart of network security, make sure that the design is properly documented and easily accessible for all administrators in the forest. A vital part of this documentation should specify who creates new groups and how, and which permissions and users are to be assigned to each group. If possible, you should always make sure that the policy states that no single administrator is allowed to create a new group without authorization from some sort of administrators council—and that less-knowledgeable administrators aren't capable of doing it by themselves. In any case, never give access to the creation of Universal Groups to anyone but a very few administrators that understand the full implications of creating Universal Groups.

(continued)

Table 9.5   Summary of best practices (continued).

Task	Points to Consider
Decide who can create and administer groups.	Be very careful with the delegation of group administration privileges, because the groups are destined to become the backbone of your security setup.
Decide where to put groups.	You should invest a lot of effort into settling on where to place each group in the OU hierarchy, because this can provide added understanding of the scope and proper usage of each group, when done right.

Users and Groups in Short

This chapter provides you with the necessary means to handle the many facets of user and group management. And, as you probably now recognize, this will prove to be a very arduous undertaking by any measure. Actually, the work involved in executing a suitable user and group design could end up being the most demanding task of them all. And, as always, if your designs provide the perfect match to the organization in question, this effort won't be very well recognized by most people as anything but a series of obvious choices!

To recap a bit, here's a quick rundown on the user naming scheme that users see and that, thus, you will wish to handle with the utmost care in your design.

Users have the following:

♦ User logon names

♦ User logon names (pre-Windows 2000)

♦ Email names

Groups have the following:

♦ User logon names (pre-Windows 2000)

♦ Email names

Computers have the following:

♦ DNS names

♦ NetBIOS names

So while the all-important topic for the administrators is to create a rugged and manageable user and group design, you should never forget that the naming structures will prove of the utmost importance as well, because users now are able to search the directory. With that said, it's time to move on to the next big undertaking—the design of group policies and the Delegation of Administration—which in many cases will wind up demanding the same amount of work as is the case for getting the user and group structures just right.

Chapter 10

Planning of Group Policies and Delegation of Administration

I guess it's about time you get a demonstration of how to reap some of the rewards of all the work you have to put into designing your OU, user account, and group account structures (the subject of the two preceding chapters). The rewards detailed here primarily deal with two of the most exciting features introduced with Active Directory that hinge upon the OU structure you've defined (and a wee bit on the user and groups accounts). These two features are delegation of administration and Group Policies.

Delegation of administration will prove a major boon to any mid-sized or large company that has had to deal with the painstakingly simple administration role structures found in Windows NT Server. Using the delegation of administration feature, you'll be able to single out just about any operation (and its scope) and delegate the right to perform it to one or more persons.

Group Policies are just as big an improvement over the past as the delegation of administration feature—actually, you might very well find Group Policies to include everything plus the kitchen sink. Using Group Policies, you will be able to control all of the system properties previously controlled by using System Policies. You'll also find a lot of new features that formerly could only be controlled by implementing one or more highly advanced scripts that would require you to spend a lot of time on development. Additionally, the Group Policies feature makes it very simple to get those policies implemented (meaning much simpler than was the case for System Policies). I like to refer to Group Policies as "system policies on steroids" to convey an image of the level of improvement found here.

But, well, enough talk. Let's get down to business, because there's plenty more to talk about in this chapter, which strives to tell you how to really put the delegation of administration and Group Policies features to work and—maybe even more importantly—how to plan for them.

Note

*You should note that this book stops short of listing and commenting upon the several hundreds of settings brought forward with the Group Policies; I feel such a listing lies outside the scope of this book, due to it being a thing that one usually works with, when implementing Active Directory, rather than something one plans for. For that you might want to refer to my other book—*Windows 2000 Professional: Advanced Configuration and Implementation, *also published by The Coriolis Group—or other material. However, you might want to note that Chapter 14 covers some of the security settings in greater detail.*

Delegation of Administration

As many of you probably know, Windows NT Server doesn't offer very many choices between being a power user and the almighty Administrator that commands everything. And even worse: There's really no way of creating the oft-needed fine-grained role system when using Windows NT Server, because virtually all of the system tasks really can't be delegated to anything but the Built-in groups.

This fact of life is very unsettling for two reasons:

♦ The overall security of the environment is compromised a great deal if you have a lot of people able to control everything (including clearing all Event logs, even the security log).

♦ The stability of the environment is at stake if many people carry all-encompassing power to control everything in the environment.

Note

Also, the first step to securing your system is to give full control only over the objects that the person needs to manage.

So you should want to keep the number of members of the Administrators and Domain Admins built-in groups to a minimum. However, on the other hand, quite a lot of people have to be assigned the all-encompassing administrator role if they are to be able to carry out their jobs, because many routine tasks demand that you carry the Administrator privilege.

In sum: The lack of a system of relatively fine-grained administrative roles and the option to build it yourself work to make your system much less secure and stable than might otherwise be the case. And maybe worse: It hampers you from being able to delegate most of the administrative chores to anyone outside of the "glass house."

Many people who have felt the restraints of the Windows NT Server concepts for themselves will be happy to hear that Windows 2000 Server and Active Directory do remove most of them.

Note

One of the very few things that Active Directory doesn't address is the oft-heard wish of being able to separate the power of configuring the auditing features from that of configuring the administrative features, and, optimally, being able to separate the setting up of when and what to log from the ability to control the contents (including the viewing) of the logs.

Active Directory's delegation of administration capability is indeed a highly valuable instrument that can be put to use by your organization for confining the relevant bits of administration powers to subsets of the entire organizational domain. Using delegation of administration, you can grant privileges to manage a small set of users or groups within an area of responsibility and, simultaneously, withhold permission to manage irrelevant account properties or accounts in other parts of the organization. For example, large organizations typically depend on many individuals or groups to secure and manage the network account infrastructure. Such organizations will be able to profit a lot from the ability to grant rights for specific operations—such as resetting user passwords or disabling accounts—to specific persons, without also having to grant permission to create new accounts or change other properties of user accounts.

One of the most important aspects of Active Directory's delegation of administration feature is that it usually will enable you to reduce the number of Domain Administrators (and other administrator types) that hold sweeping authority over a large part of the Active Directory. And so, even when you don't wish to delegate administrative power to persons outside of the IT organization, you should *always* take time to look into the options for implementing a much stricter control with the administrator roles in the organization by using the delegation of administration feature for assigning only the rights needed for each person to carry out their responsibilities.

Tip

You will often find that first-level and second-level supporters and administrators can carry out their job responsibilities with very few rights. And now, you can put this knowledge to use via the delegation of administration feature.

The Base Delegation of Administration Features

As was described in Chapter 8, delegation of administration is always defined at the OU level (including the root of the OU tree, which represents the whole domain). Generally speaking, you can scope the delegation of administration responsibilities in three different ways:

- Delegate specific permissions (that is, Full Control, Delete, or Modify) to manage properties on a particular container (OU), such as the Computers OU.

- Delegate specific permissions to manage child objects of a specific type (such as Users, Groups, or Printers) in a particular container (OU).

- Delegate specific permissions to manage specific properties on child objects of a specific type in a container (OU)—for example, the right to Reset Passwords on the user accounts, which are held in the Users OU.

Tip

Chapter 18 includes an example of how to use the Delegation of Control Wizard (that is, the wizard that is used for performing delegation of administration).

In other words, you're able to set up the delegation so that persons with administrative privileges inside one OU aren't able to manage anything for other OUs within the domain. However, you may also choose to have permissions defined at higher levels in the OU tree, thus applying to several OUs in the domain and even to the full domain using inheritance.

After you've designed the most suitable OU structure for your domain—based on the information given in Chapter 8—you just need to figure out the appropriate structure for your members of each of the intended delegation of administration scopes.

Note

You should always consider locking down your OUs and containers. For example, you will often find that objects of a specific type should only be creatable in designated OUs and by a more narrow set of people than will be assigned these powers by default.

As is true for regular user administration, using groups rather than individual user accounts to assign delegation of administration responsibilities usually proves to be the best solution. To understand why, simply consider the number of changes in titles and responsibilities of users throughout the enterprise. Also consider that at least two persons usually retain the same delegation of administration responsibilities, because of holidays, business trips, and other things that preclude an individual from performing their administrative duties at any given time. Also, you should take a serious look at the feasibility of the group nesting feature. If the security hierarchy parallels the corporate hierarchy, you might be able to develop a group nesting structure that equals the delegation of administration structure that you're implementing.

Tip

Active Directory's group nesting features are, of course, helpful only if they apply to the delegation of administration structure—That is, if the delegation of administration structure is hierarchical in nature.

The Prototypical Delegation of Administration Assignments

These are the most often seen uses for Delegation of Administration:

- Create, delete, and manage user accounts.
- Reset passwords on user accounts.
- Read all information in user objects.
- Create, delete, and manage groups.
- Modify the membership of a group.
- Manage Group Policy Links.

Actually, these uses are so common that Microsoft has included a shortcut to performing these kinds of delegation in the Delegation of Control Wizard.

In addition to the above-mentioned uses, you will most probably also need to delegate the management of one or more of the office-based properties included with each user object. However, because the properties in question are unique to the task at hand, you'll have to step through all of the Wizard pages to achieve this kind of delegation of administration.

In addition to these uses, here is a list of some frequently occurring delegation of administration scenarios on computer objects:

- *Install computers*—Typically needed by installers; in less security-conscious environments, this may even be delegated to all users. Achieved by way of the Create computer objects property. Alternately, you can use the Add workstations to domain user right. You might note that one often doesn't want the creators of the computer objects to be owners, in which case you will need to take ownership after the computer object has been created.
- *Manage computer accounts*—Typically needed by managers. Achieved by assigning Full Control permissions on computer objects and possibly the Create computer objects property.
- *Manage location property*—Typically needed by logistics. Achieved by assigning Write permission to the property or properties in question.
- *Reset computer account*—Typically needed by support personnel. Achieved by way of the Reset password property.

However, if the security hierarchy doesn't parallel the corporate hierarchy, you are simply out of luck, because you have no way to match the group concept to the hierarchical OU/delegation of administration structure, and you will be forced to design at least two different group structures (one for handling the routine user administration and one for delegation of administration), which in turn will work to increase the administrative workload and the potential for errors. But remember that you might still be able to reap some benefits from the group nesting features.

Finally, you might want to note that, although it's perfectly possible to delegate authority to the physical resources, it will prove a bit harder than outlined here for all the objects that reside in the configuration-naming context (that is, the objects stored in the sites and services containers) or outside of the Active Directory (DHCP, WINS, RRAS, Terminal

Services, etc.). The Delegation of Control Wizard does work in the Configuration Partition, but you will have to resort to local assignment of permissions for all objects residing outside the Active Directory.

Understanding Group Policies

With Group Policies, Active Directory introduces yet another radical improvement in reducing administrative tasks via standardized User and Computer Configurations. Simply stated, Group Policies enable administrators to make a one-time declaration of one or more rules about the state of their users' environment, and then rely on the system to enforce that set of rules. Or, from another perspective, Group Policies bring the administrator and end users closer to the goal of an administration-free desktop than ever before. Group Policies are in fact one of the cornerstones of Microsoft's much vaunted IntelliMirror (or ZAW) concept.

To understand the Group Policy framework, you must know the difference between a profile and a Group Policy:

♦ *Profile*—A collection of user environment settings that the user is at liberty to change. Profiles may or may not follow the user if he chooses to log in to another computer, and their settings are stored in many locations, including the Registry, Desktop, Profiles directory, My Documents, and so forth.

♦ *Group Policy*—A collection of user environment settings, specified by the administrator. A Group Policy is stored in a central location and always affects the users or computers covered by the policy.

System Policies, introduced with Windows NT Server 4, gave administrators the ability to create a policy file that contained Registry settings written to the user or local computer portion of the Registry. Although the Group Policy model is based on many of the underpinnings of System Policies, it represents much more than a simple extension of the System Policy model. Actually, System Policies could be described as a simplistic predecessor to Group Policies.

Windows NT 4 (and Windows 9x) includes 72 system policy settings, which have the following general properties:

♦ Limited to properties that can be controlled via configuring Registry settings; thus, they primarily are of use to lock down desktops.

♦ Persist in users' profiles until the specified policy is reversed or the Registry is edited.

♦ Extensible, by using ADM files.

♦ Aren't secure; they can be changed using Registry Editor (**regedit.exe**).

In comparison, a Group Policy enables organizations to handle the following:

♦ *Software Installation*—Administrators can selectively assign and publish applications to desktop systems, based on the policy settings.

- *Application Assignment*—Upgrade or remove applications automatically on the client computers or provide users with a shortcut that represents a connection to an application that the users can't delete by accident.

- *Application Publishing*—The applications appear in the list of components that a user can install via Add/Remove Programs in the Control Panel. These applications can also be installed by activating a document that is associated with the application.

- *Security Settings*—Access to certain files, folders, Registry keys, and system services can be restricted. These settings enable you to manage Local Computer, Domain, and Network security settings.

- *Administrative Templates*—Full compatibility with the old-style administrative templates that enable administrators to customize the Registry settings that provide the personalized management of various system services, desktop settings, and application settings—in other words, Registry settings that are written to the **HKEY_LOCAL_MACHINE (HKLM)** and **HKEY_CURRENT_USER (HKCU)** trees.

- *Folder Redirection*—Allows files that represent the user's desktop to be placed in folders on the server, or allows special folders, such as My Documents, to be redirected to a network location. The files are delivered to the desktop at user logon. Administrators can use this feature to establish true roaming.

- *Logon/Logoff, Startup/Shutdown Scripts*—Scripts to be run by the computer at startup and shutdown or when the user logs on or off the computer. These scripts enable you to easily implement functions that are specific to certain users, groups, or machines. For example, a logon script may connect to a specific file or print share, or a logoff script may be used to remove environment variables, set a process in motion, or alert a system that you are shutting down. Windows 2000 Server supports the use of any Windows Scripting Host (WSH) scripting tool (Visual Basic, JavaScript, and so forth), as well as WMI and ADSI scripting interfaces, to develop scripts.

Note

Group Policies technology doesn't provide support for Windows NT 4, Windows 95, or Windows 98. In other words, to reap the benefits of Group Policies, you need a "pure" Windows 2000 environment that extends to clients and servers. So, for controlling your Windows NT 4 and Windows 95/98 clients, you still have to make do with the well-known System Policies and use the native tools available for implementing System Policies for those environments.

In addition to providing much more functionality and usability to the work of setting policies (compared to System Policies), Group Policies take full advantage of Active Directory in the following respects:

- Provide greater granular control

- Can be applied at the site, domain, or OU level (which Microsoft abbreviates as *SDOU*) of the directory

- Can be hierarchically inherited or filtered with Security Groups

These levels of control minimize the need for the Administrator or Help Desk engineer to visit each desktop physically when a configuration change or setting is needed. Table 10.1 shows a comparison between Windows NT 4 System Policies and Windows 2000 Group Policies.

Essential Group Policy Concepts

A Group Policy defines the various components of the user's desktop environment that a System Administrator wants to manage. That is, you add the wished for policy settings to a Group Policy Object (GPO), which in turn is associated with one or more SDOU (remember: site, domain, or OU) objects.

Note

Group Policy Objects also apply to a local or remote computer. Please be aware that you're left with less functionality in this situation. The software installation and folder redirection features aren't available, and fewer options are found inside several areas. However, the discussion of Group Policies for individual computers is outside the scope of this book (refer to Windows 2000: Advanced Configuration and Implementation Black Book *from Coriolis for more on that subject).*

Defining the GPO

The *Group Policy Object (GPO)* contains the Group Policy settings that you specify. GPOs store Group Policy information in two locations (see Figure 10.1):

♦ *Group Policy Container (GPC)*—Used for Group Policy data that is small in size and changes infrequently. GPCs are stored in Active Directory.

♦ *Group Policy Template (GPT)*—Used for Group Policy data that is larger in size and may change frequently. The GPT is a folder structure that is stored in the system volume folder of DCs (Sysvol). Just like any other directory object, the GPO gets assigned a GUID, when it's created. GPT is stored in a folder using the GUID as its name, and SDOUs referencing the GPO will be basing their reference on the GUID.

Table 10.1   Windows NT 4 System Policies vs. Windows 2000 Group Policies.

System Policies	Group Policies
Policy is applied to Domains and may be further controlled by user security group membership.	Group Policy may be associated with site(s), domain(s), and OU(s). By default, a Group Policy membership affects all computers and users in the specified container, but it may be further controlled by user or computer security group membership.
Aren't secure, and they "tattoo" (make permanent changes to user's profiles).	Are secure, and default policies don't "tattoo" the Registry.
Policy capabilities are limited to "desktop lockdown."	A Group Policy is the primary method for enabling centralized administration. A Group Policy may be used for expanded "desktop lockdown" and to enhance the user environment.

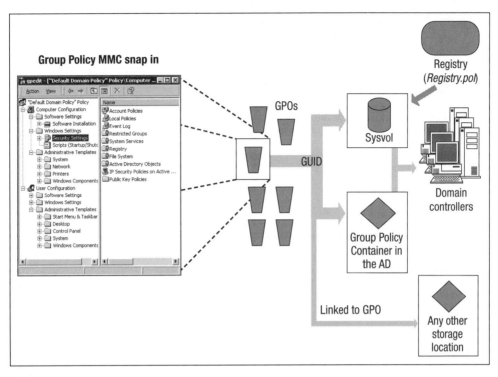

Figure 10.1
The GPO actually is stored in two locations, which are handled by different replication mechanisms (see Chapter 12).

Defining the GPC

The *Group Policy Container* is an Active Directory object that stores GPO information; it includes subcontainers for Machine and User Group Policy information. The GPC contains the following properties among other things:

♦ *Version information*—Used to ensure that the information is synchronized with the GPT information.

♦ *Status information*—Indicates whether the GPO is enabled or disabled.

The GPC stores the Class Store information for software installation. The *Class Store* is a Windows 2000 Server-based repository for all applications that supports for application publishing and assigning.

Defining the GPT

The *Group Policy Template* is a folder structure that includes all the Group Policy information for a particular GPO that is input by you. The GPT contains information for all policy, script, file, and software installation. The GPTs are stored in the system volume folder of DCs (that is, \%*SystemRoot*%*SYSVOL**sysvol*\<*domain name*>, where %*SystemRoot*% represents the folder in which Windows 2000 Server is installed) in the Policies folder.

The GPT folder contains the following subfolders:

♦ ADM—Contains all the ADM files used by the GPT. By default, this folder will include *conf.adm* (Netmeeting policy settings), *inetres.adm* (Internet Explorer policy settings), and *system.adm* (the base Group Policy settings, excluding the security policies).

♦ MACHINE—Includes a *Registry.pol* file that contains the Registry settings to be applied to computers. During the computer's start-up sequence, the *Registry.pol* file is downloaded and applied to the Registry. The MACHINE folder contains the following subfolders:

   ♦ *Applications*—Contains the files used by the OS-based Windows Installer Service.

   ♦ *Microsoft\Windows NT\SecEdit*—Contains the security policy settings that can be implemented using a security template. By default, this folder contains a file named *GptTmpl.inf*.

   ♦ *Scripts*—Contains all of the scripts and related files used by clients in this GPT. Scripts comprise a Startup and a Shutdown folder.

♦ USER—Includes a *Registry.pol* file that contains the Registry settings to be applied to users. When a user logs on to a computer, the *Registry.pol* file is downloaded and applied to the Registry. The USER folder contains the following subfolders:

   ♦ *Applications*—Contains the files used by the OS-based Windows Installer Service.

   ♦ *Documents and Settings*—Contains the hidden file *fdeploy* specifying the folder redirection settings (which is specified in the Folder Redirection folder in the Group Policy MMC).

   ♦ *Microsoft\IEAK*—Contains files to be added to the Internet Explorer configuration (which is specified in the Internet Explorer Maintenance folder in the Group Policy MMC).

   ♦ *Microsoft\RemoteInstall*—Contains the oscfilter.ini file specifying choice screen options for the Remote Installation Service (which is specified in the Remote Installation Service folder in the Group Policy MMC).

   ♦ *Scripts*—Contains all of the scripts and related files used by clients in this GPT. Scripts comprise a Logon and a Logoff folder.

There's a *gpt.ini* file in the GPT's top folder, and there's also a *gpt.ini* file that specifies the version number of the GPT.

When you create a GPO, the directory name that is given to the GPT is the *Globally Unique Identifier* (GUID, a 128-bit integer that looks like this: 47636445-af79-11d0-91fe-080036644603) of the GPO. For example, if you modified a GPO associated with an Active Directory domain called Sales, which is part of **astonitgroup.com**, the resulting GPT folder would be named as follows (provided that the GPO's GUID is the one mentioned in the last sentence):

```
%systemroot%\SYSVOL\sysvol\astonitgroup.com\Policies\{47636445-af79-11d0-91fe-
080036644603}
```

Note

You can find out a GPO's GUID by opening the GPO in the Group Policy MMC snap-in, right-clicking on the policy (shown at the very top of the scope pane), and choosing Properties. The resulting property sheet will show the GUID of the GPO in the "Unique name" field. You can achieve the same thing by selecting the applicable GPO and pressing the Properties button at the Group Policy tab shown in the property sheet of the domain that holds the GPO.

You might want to note that the Links tab on this very property sheet also allows you to find out which sites, domains, and OUs are currently using the GPO in question.

Note that the second sysvol also is used as a share named SYSVOL. The sysvol folder is automatically created when an Active Directory DC is installed. A multi-master replicated copy of the system volume resides on each DC (see Chapter 12 for more information on the replication bit).

Defining Administrative Templates (ADM Files)

The policy settings available have to be defined. Most of these settings are provided in an ASCII file referred to as an *Administrative Template* (files that have the .adm extension)— however, you can also create an MMC extension snap-in.

Each ADM file consists of a hierarchy of categories and subcategories that, together, define how the settings are displayed in the administrative interface (the Group Policy Editor). Each entry in the ADM file also indicates the Registry locations where changes should be made if a particular selection is made, specifies any options or restrictions (in values) that are associated with the selection, and, in some cases, specifies a default value to use if a selection is activated. The ADM files are stored in the GPT.

Note

The Windows NT 4 System Policy Editor likewise uses files called Administrative Templates (ADM files) to determine which Registry settings you can modify, by presenting a namespace for those settings in the System Policy Editor. However, Windows 2000 ADM files include several new features, such as Explain text (shown on the Explain tab of each policy) and Unicode support.

Although you can add any NT 4-style ADM file to the namespace, this is strongly discouraged by Microsoft, because an ADM file from a previous version of Windows either won't have any effect on Windows 2000 Professional (because of the changes in the Registry imposed by Microsoft) or will mark (or tattoo) the Registry with these settings. That's also the reason why only the Windows 2000-compliant policies are shown in the Group Policy snap-in by default. You can view the NT 4 System Policies by unchecking the Show Policies Only checkbox under the View button. In that case, all the "true" Group Policy settings appear in blue, and System Policy settings appear in red.

On the Issue of Duplicating Existing GPOs

Until now, I have encountered at least one instance where a detailed understanding of GPCs and GPTs comes in handy. And that's when you have several domains using common Group Policies. If you've got plenty of bandwidth and stable links between the domains, you might just settle for defining the GPO(s) only once and linking to the applicable GPO(s) from the other domains. However, this will prove to be a rather bandwidth-intensive task, because the GPO will be requested every time it needs to be applied.

But the bandwidth load added by GPOs might prove to be inadmissible if the reason for having several domains was to cut down on the bandwidth usage in the first place. And what do you do then? Well, you can always duplicate the GPOs (that is, recreating the same GPOs manually) in each domain and impose strict guidelines for securing that the duplicate GPOs are kept up-to-date, whenever a policy change is being implemented by an Administrator.

However, although guidelines are good, control and automation always prove much better in the long run. And so, you will probably be looking for a way to copy or duplicate GPOs across several domains. Unfortunately, you're totally out of luck at present, because this is not supported by Microsoft. The official response given by Microsoft Premier Support is quite dismissive: "The ability to have enterprise-wide GPOs and the ability to copy GPOs will be considered for the next release of Windows 2000 Server."

This is quite surprising, because it really isn't that hard to implement a copy function. Conceptually speaking, you would basically need to create a new GPO in each domain and overwrite the GPT in the newly defined GPO with the GPT (bar the *gpt.ini* file) of the original GPO from the source domain.

Due to how Active Directory works, it's straighforward to have the GPT being overwritten every time the source GPTundergoes a change. However, you do face at least one little snag with regard to making this overwriting procedure work as intended: Having the version number (the **versionNumber** attribute)—as well as the USN (**uSNChanged** and the **whenChanged** attributes)—being changed in order to reflect that the GPO has undergone a change. The version number is stored in the GPC (in the **versionNumber** attribute) as well as in the GPT (in the *gpt.ini* file). For this very reason (and the problem with duplicate GUIDs), you should never try to use the available tools to back up GPOs for duplication purposes.

You'll have to do a bit of researching on how to change the version number correctly (the USN is easy; it will be changed as soon as you write something to the GPC) for getting the copying functionality implemented. I still have to find out exactly how Active Directory does this, because it doesn't just increment the version number for every change.

And when you've figured that one out, you might as well go all the way by creating the GPC yourself. In that case, you might want to note that the GPC is found in the domain at **CN=System,CN=Policies** using its GUID as its name. And you link a GPC to an OU by specifying its full LDAP name at the **gPLink** attribute (please note that, because of the static inheritance scheme used by Active Directory, all applicable GPCs, whether linked directly or through inheritance, are stored in this attribute).

However, before you do decide to create the GPC yourself, you should be aware that a long range of attributes seems to be set when the GPO is created. The attributes that need to be set include **whenChanged**, **whenCreated**, **canonicalName**, **cn**, **displayName**, **distinguishedName**, **name**, **objectCategory**, **objectGUID,** and so forth.

Please note that the concepts outlined in this sidebar haven't been implemented in a production environment yet; hence, you might find a thing or two that you need to patch in addition to the things noted here. But that you should be able to grasp the base concepts involved in this very important issue in case you should find a pressing need to perform this operation. And you might want to swing by my Web site (**www.strunge.com**) to see if I've made any progress on this issue since writing the book. Hopefully, I'll be ready with a small shareware application that does the trick when you read this—if not, you're welcome to add a bit of gentle pressure by asking me for an update.

Group Policies in Depth

Group Policies take advantage of Active Directory, because their settings are contained in GPOs that, in turn, are associated with directory containers (SDOUs). You can apply Group Policy settings from multiple GPOs to each SDOU, and vice versa. See Figure 10.2 for an illustration of the full set of options.

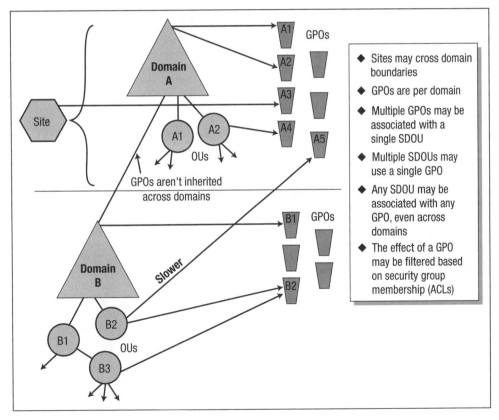

Figure 10.2
An educative illustration of a Group Policy scenario.

> **Note**
>
> *For standalone computers that aren't members of a domain, a Group Policy can be set and applied to the local machine. Optionally, you can exempt some computers from inheriting Group Policies from the domain to which they belong, via a Registry switch. In this case, the computer functions as if it were a standalone computer, with respect to Group Policies.*

A Group Policy is applied hierarchically, from the least restrictive container group (site) to the most restrictive container group (OU). Child containers inherit a Group Policy from parent containers by default. This means that, if you assign a specific Group Policy to a high-level parent container, that Group Policy applies to all containers beneath the parent container. However, if you explicitly specify a Group Policy for a child container, the child container's policies will override Group Policies set in the parent container in case of overlaps.

Optionally, you can enforce a Group Policy on child directory containers, and you can prevent inheritance of a Group Policy from parent directory containers. Note that you should use these options only as an exception, because they make it very hard to understand exactly what occurs when Group Policies are processed.

By default, a Group Policy affects all computers and users in a selected directory container. Although some settings are user interface settings, they can also be applied to computers. For example, you can apply the background bitmap and the ability to use the Start menu's Run command to computers. If a conflict arises between User and Machine settings, the default is to apply the User Configuration (due to the order the Group Policy settings are applied in).

You can filter the effects of a Group Policy based on users' or computers' group memberships (or, more theoretically speaking, one or more user accounts) and by setting ACL permissions. This is a very efficient and meaningful way to modify the scope of GPOs, because doing so provides an improvement of logon performance. Also, you can delegate access to managing the individual GPOs in the same way.

> **Note**
>
> *Although you can filter a Group Policy via membership to security groups (which can include users and computer accounts as well as other groups) and by setting ACL permissions, you can't associate a Group Policy directly to a Security Group.*

Finally, notice that Active Directory introduces an ACE named *Apply Group Policy*. The Read and Apply Group Policy permissions are required for having the GPO applied to the system—consequently, you need to set Deny On Apply Group Policy to not having a GPO applied to the applicable users(s) or computer(s).

> **Note**
>
> *The default ACL settings for GPOs are set up in such a way that Group Policies can be applied by any user except Local System and the members of the Domain Admins and Enterprise Admins Groups, to avoid any unfortunate side effects. Domain Admins and Enterprise Admins are assigned Full Comtrol for the Group Policies.*

Default Domain Policies

Each Active Directory domain comes with a Default Domain Controllers Policy assigned to the domain. This GPO includes some Group Policy settings that are enforced (they can't be blocked) on all DCs in the domain to assure that they will apply to all user and computer accounts. These settings (account policies and public key policies) can only be applied on the domain level.

To be more exact, you're dealing with the following settings that have to be the same throughout a domain:

- *Password policies*—Minimum length, expiration, complexity requirements, and so forth.

- *Account lockout policies*—Threshold, duration, and so forth.

- *Kerberos policies*—Maximum lifetime for tickets, tolerance for clock synchronization, and so forth. Please note that some of these settings are accessible only from a security template.

- *Several security options*—To be precise, it's the Automatically log off users when logon time expires, Rename administrator account, and Rename guest account settings.

- *Encrypted data recovery agents*—Specifies which certificates are available for recovering EFS-encrypted files.

- *Trusted certificate authorities*—Trusted root certification authorities and enterprise trust.

If multiple GPOs are linked to the domain, application of the Group Policy objects starts with the GPO at the bottom of the list and ends with the GPO at the top (the GPO at the top taking precedence over the others). The resulting set of settings will be applied on all Active Directory DC, and thus, become domain-wide settings.

The policy settings consist of two separate configuration types (which, coincidentally, is also how they are presented in the Group Policy Editor):

- *Computer configuration*—Includes policies that specify OS behavior, desktop appearance, application settings, assigned applications, security settings, and computer startup and shutdown scripts. Computer-related Group Policies are applied when the OS initializes—thus, they apply to all users of those computers that are covered by the GPO.

- *User configuration*—Includes all user-specific information, such as OS behavior, desktop settings, application settings, assigned and published applications, folder redirection options, a security setting, and user logon and logoff scripts. User-related Group Policies are applied when the user logs on to the computer.

All of the available in the Group Policy settings are structured in the following three containers (or topics, if you prefer):

- *Software settings*—Includes the subtopic of software installation.

- *Windows settings*—Includes the following subtopics: Internet Explorer Maintenance (only available in User Configuration), Folder Redirection (only available in User Confiiguration), Scripts (Startup/Shutdown for Computer Configuration; Logon/Logoff for User Configuration), and Security Settings.

On Group Policy Extensions

Group Policy Extensions are components that are clients tot he Group Policy infrastructure. Each of them have a server-side and client-side component.

The administrator uses the server-side component and the Group Policy MMC snap-in to define the policy. When a Group Policy is being applied to a user or computer, the client component—also known as Group Policy client-side extensions—interprets the policy and makes the appropriate changes to the environment.

You might need to identify the client-side extension, when faced with various troubleshooting scenarios. The client-side extensions are identified by GUID.

The standard client-side extensions and the GUIDs are the following:

- *Folder Redirection*—GUID: 25537BA6-77A8-11D2-9B6C-0000F8080861
- *Microsoft Disk Quota*—GUID: 3610EDA5-77EF-11D2-8DC5-00C04FA31A66
- *Component: Scripts*—GUID: 42B5FAAE-6536-11D2-AE5A-0000F87571E3
- *Component: Security*—GUID: 827D319E-6EAC-11D2-A4EA-00C04E79E83A
- *EFS Recovery*—GUID: B1BE8D72-6EAC-11D2-A4EA-00C04F79F83A
- *Application Management*—GUID: C6DC5466-785A-11D2-84D0-00C04FB169F7
- *Internet Explorer Settings*—GUID: A2E30F80-D7DE-11D2-BBDE-00C04F86AE3B
- *Component: Registry Settings*—GUID: 25537BA6-77A8-11D2-9B6C-0000F808061
- *ID Security*—GUID: E437BC1C-AA7D-11D2-A382-00C04F991E27

Any other client-side extensions added to the system will be registed in the following rgistry location: HKLM\Software\Microsoft\WindowsNT\CurrentVersion\Winlogon\GPExtensions.

The knowledge of client-side extensions will prove worthy, when faced with having to decipher event log entries and log files, as well as logging through the GPO history (that is, the order in which GPOs are read and applied when the computer starts, or when a user logs on). The GPO history is specified in the following:

- **HKEY_LOCAL_MACHINE\Software\Microsoft\Windows\CurrentVersion\GroupPolicy\History—** For GPOs applied to the local computer.
- **HKEY_CURRENT_USER\Software\Microsoft\Windows\CurrentVersion\GroupPolicy\History—** For GPOs applied to the currently logged on user.

♦ *Administrative templates*—In Computer Configuration, includes these subtopics: System, Network, Printers, and Windows Components. In User Configuration, includes Start Menu and Taskbar, Desktop, Control Panel, Network, System, and Windows Components.

Software Settings—Software Installation

You use *Software Installation* to manage software distribution centrally in your organization. Or to be more precise you can install, assign, publish, update, repair, and remove software for users and computers using the features.

Software Installation Best Practices

The software that you install from a Group Policy isn't included in the GPT; rather, it's stored at a software distribution point. You should keep these best practices in mind when creating your software distribution points:

- You should use Distributed File System (DFS) to provide a single share point for all published applications. This will work to simplify the process of deploying applications across the enterprise, because you can take advantage of DFS redundancy and load-balancing features (see Chapter 12 for more on DNS).

- You should create a separate folder (using the name of the application) for each application that includes the .msi package file and all required installation files. Even though you can store the .msi package file separately from the application installation files, it will simplify administration to store all files in the same location.

- You might want to use a hidden shared folder (for example, *packages$*), to prevent users from browsing the contents of the software distribution folder.

Note

You can use Software Installation only on applications that adhere to the Microsoft Installer (MSI) technology, which is the new transaction-based application installer responsible for managing application installations or the ZAW Down-level application packages (.ZAP) file format. You can repackage legacy applications with an MSI repackager tool, such as VERITAS WinINSTALL (Limited Edition), which is found on the Windows 2000 Server CD-ROM.

You should *assign* an application when you want everyone coverd by the GPO to have the application installed on his or her computer. When you assign an application from the Users Configuration, you are actually advertising the application on all the users' desktops, which means that the application shortcut appears on the user's Start menu and the Registry is updated with information about the application, including the location of both the application package and the source files for the installation. Thus, the application appears to be installed from the user's viewpoint, but it won't be actually installed until the user tries to activate the application (from the Start menu shortcut or by clicking a document associated with the application).

A user can't delete an assigned application. If a user attempts to do this, the assigned application is advertised again the next time the user logs on. Thus, the application is resilient, and the administrator can be sure that every user can always get the applications that they need.

You *publish* an application when you want the application to be available to people managed by the GPO. Each person can then decide whether or not to install the published application. When you publish an application, no shortcut to the application appears on users' desktops and no local Registry entries are made. That is, the application has no presence on the users' desktops. Published applications store their advertisement information in Active Directory. To install a published application, users can either use the Add/Remove Programs tool, which includes a list of all published applications that are available for them to use, or activate a document, pertaining to the applications, just as it's called for.

Windows Settings—Security Settings

You use *Security Settings* to define a security configuration for computers operating within the scope of a GPO. A *security configuration* consists of settings applied to each security area supported for the Windows 2000 Professional or Server. This configuration is included within a GPO and then applied to computers as part of the Group Policy enforcement.

Security Settings define an engine that can interpret a standard security configuration and perform the required operations automatically in the background, thus complementing existing system security tools. You can continue to use existing tools to change specific settings whenever necessary.

The security areas that can be configured for computers include the following:

♦ *Account Policies*—Computer security settings for Password Policy, Lockout Policy, and Kerberos Policy in an Active Directory domain.

♦ *Local Policies*—Include security settings for Audit Policy, User Rights Assignment, and Security Options. A Local Policy enables you to configure who has local or network access to the computer and how events are being audited locally (if at all).

♦ *Event Log (can only be managed from the Security Template)*—Controls security settings for the Application, Security, and System event logs.

♦ *Restricted Groups (can only be managed from the Security Template)*—Refers to the memberships of Built-in Groups that have certain predefined capabilities. Restricted Groups settings affect which accounts are allowed to be members of these groups. Examples of restricted groups are Local Groups (such as Administrators, Power Users, Print Operators, and Server Operators) and Global Groups (such as Domain Administrators).

♦ *System Services (can only be managed from the Security Template)*—Control configuration settings and security options (ACLs) for system services, such as network services, file and print services, telephone and fax services, Internet/intranet services, and so on. The Security Settings extension directly supports all general settings for each system service, including Startup mode and permissions.

♦ *Registry (can only be managed from the Security Template)*—Used to configure and analyze settings for Security Descriptors (including object ownership), including the ACL, and auditing information for each Registry key. When you apply security on Registry keys, the Security Settings extension follows the same inheritance model that is used for all tree-structured hierarchies in Windows 2000 Server. That's why Microsoft recommends that you specify security only at top-level objects, and redefine security only for those child objects that require changes to the inherited security setup. This approach greatly simplifies your security structure and reduces the administrative overhead that would result from a needlessly complex access control structure.

♦ *File System (can only be managed from the Security Template)*—Used to configure and analyze settings for SDs (including object ownership), including the ACL, and auditing information for each object (volume, directory, or file) in the local file system.

♦ *Public Key Policies*—Used to configure and analyze settings for the trusted root certification authorities, enterprise trust, automatic certificate request settings, and encrypted data recovery agents.

Active Directory allows you to control the security settings imposed on all client computers by imposing one or more different security profiles (known as *Security Templates*) on a GPO. The security templates, as well as the available security settings, are discussed in more detail in Chapter 14.

Microsoft supplies a set of predefined security templates for common security scenarios:

♦ Typical workstation settings (**idealws.inf**)

♦ Secure workstation settings (**securews.inf**)

♦ Secure DC settings (**securedc.inf**)

♦ Sample workstation settings (**sample.inf**)

♦ Sample DC settings (**sampledc.inf**)

You can use these or other security templates as the basis for your security settings and then edit the settings according to your requirements.

Windows Settings—Folder Redirection

You use the Folder Redirection extension to redirect to an alternate location (such as a network destination) any of the special folders that represent the user's desktop. Special folders are those located under the %winroot%\profiles folder (where %winroot% is the Windows 2000 root folder), and they include such folders as My Documents, Start menu, Desktop, and Favorites.

The Folder Redirection that you specify is delivered to the user's desktop upon user logon (because it is located in the User Configuration container), regardless of which computer the individual logs on to.

Tip

You should always implement Folder Redirection on the My Documents folder, unless you've got a very good reason for not doing so. Not only does Windows 2000 place a My Documents shortcut on the desktop, but it's the default location for the File Open and Save As commands.

Because My Documents is the default location where users store their personal work data, it's a good thing to get this data stored on a server, where backups are done regularly. Also, given time, the amount of data in the folder can grow quite large and so it will prove highly advantageous not to have the data in this folder contained in a roaming user profile, but in a separate folder on a server, instead.

Windows Settings—Scripts

With the *Scripts* extensions, you can assign scripts to run when the computer starts or shuts down or when users log on or off. For this purpose, you can use Windows Scripting Host, which is a language-independent scripting host for 32-bit Windows platforms that includes both VBScript and JScript scripting engines. You also can use the good old BAT- and CMD-type batch files. The names of scripts and their command lines (in the form of Registry keys and values) are stored in the *Registry.pol* file.

Note

You should note that startup scripts are hidden and run synchronously (meaning that each script must complete or timeout before the next one starts) by default, whereas logon scripts are hidden and run asynchronously (that is, multiple scripts can be executed at the same time) by default. Also, if there are other logon scripts associated with a specific user account, these scripts run after the Group Policy logon scripts have finished executing.

Administrative Templates

Administrative Templates include all Registry-based Group Policy information (the information controlled by the NT 4 System Policies). Administrative Template settings include policies for the Windows 2000 OS and its components and for applications. The settings are written either to the User or Local Machine portion of the Registry database. Administrative Template settings that are specific to a user who logs on to a given workstation or server are written to the Registry under **HKEY_CURRENT_USER (HKCU)**, and computer-specific settings are written under **HKEY_LOCAL_MACHINE (HKLM)**.

Administrative Templates save information in the Group Policy Template (GPT) in ASCII files, referred to as *Registry.pol files*, which contain the customized Registry settings that you specify to be applied to the Machine or User portion of the Registry. Please note that the format and features available in the *Registry.pol* files differ from that of Windows NT 4 and Windows 9x.

What It's All about: Planning

To tell you the truth, it's quite easy to get lost at first in all the policy settings available. The vast number of different policies—you've got approximately 500 policies to work with right from the outset—and the incredible variety will prove overwhelming to anybody.

As mentioned earlier, this book has no intention of trying to document all of these policies. That's simply too far off the scope of this book. And really, there's no substitute for the real thing on the policies: You have to step through all of the policies to find which you need and which you don't. But that's really not the worst part of Group Policies. The worst part is that, just like any other powerful tool, the Group Policies feature is a double-edged sword: On the one hand, it can ease the administrative workload tremendously, but on the other hand, it can grow over time into an administrative nightmare previously unseen to anyone. Which of the two scenarios that will prove true in your organization depends largely on the people responsible for planning and administering the Group Policies.

The more you use the Group Policy features, the larger the challenge becomes of keeping the looming chaos in check. The following list includes the things that you should understand, at the very least, regardless of whether or not you are involved in planning the Group Policies:

◆ Group Policies can be used to define virtually anything about a user's workspace: access to applications, resources, administrative privileges, desktop settings, and much more.

◆ The Group Policy settings that you specify are contained in a GPO, which in turn is associated with the applicable Active Directory objects. You can also set a Group Policy for computers that are not members of a domain. To set a Group Policy for a selected Active Directory object, you must have Read and Write access to Sysvol and Modify rights to the currently selected directory object.

◆ Group Policies are processed hierarchically in the following order: site, domain(s), and OU(s)—also known as SDOU.

◆ A Group Policy is applied at the SDOU level of Active Directory. The Group Policy can be further scoped to apply to specific user accounts, groups, or computers.

◆ When a Group Policy is applied to a container (such as an OU), the policy affects all computer and user objects within that container, as child containers will inherit the policy from the parent containers. A Group Policy doesn't affect any container objects other than computers and users.

  ◆ Group Policies that don't conflict are cumulative, which means that all Group Policies that affect an object (such as a user account) are combined. An object receives all Group Policies that are applied anywhere above the object in the Active Directory hierarchy. Note that this is the default setting; you can prevent policy inheritance further down in the hierarchy.

  ◆ If two policies conflict, the one applied closest to the object prevails. Group Policies conflict only when they are in direct disagreement with each other. This rule enables administrators to set policies that affect large groups of objects at the top of the Active Directory hierarchy, and then to fine-tune for exceptions wherever they may be needed. Note that this is the default setting; you can force a policy to override conflicting settings from a policy that is closer to the object.

  ◆ There are two exceptions to the rule of competitiveness: IP Security and User Rights management (both use "last writer wins").

◆ Group Policies for computers (the settings stored in the Computer Configuration container) are applied at the computer's startup, whereas Group Policies for users (the settings stored in the User Configuration container) are applied when the users log on. Please note that Group Policies assigned to users don't affect the computer's configuration (that is, the Computer Configuration container isn't of any use for GPOs assigned to users), and Group

Policies assigned to computers don't affect the user's configuration (that is, the User Configuration container isn't of any use for GPOs assigned to computers).

♦ Computer policies take precedence over user policies. This has actually given rise to one of the "classic" troubleshooting situations, where nobody can understand what happens because a setting that is established for the user is overridden by a setting that is established for the computer that they are using.

♦ Be careful about doing any inferences based on the SDOU hierarchy, because you are allowed to either mark a GPO as one whose policies can't be overridden, or block policy inheritance (negate all GPOs that exist higher in the hierarchy, rather like starting with a clean slate).

♦ By default, Group Policies assigned to users don't apply to members of Domain Admins, Enterprise Admins, and the Local System. If you want to change this, you will have to access the security descriptor for the GPO and add the Apply Group Policy permission to the applicable group.

Take care to understand exactly what a Group Policy Object is. A GPO is an Active Directory object that can be assigned to one or more SDOU containers, and multiple GPOs may be associated with a single SDOU container. That is, a GPO is an object that comprises the specifications on some policies, which then can be assigned to one or more SDOU containers—and vice versa.

A Group Policy is a very flexible tool that can be used in various combinations, allowing it to meet a variety of business requirements. The overriding caution is to use the simplest possible combination of these capabilities and to plan their use carefully. When you plan for Group Policies, you should at least have settled on some very precise guidelines for the scopes of management—whether to use a centralized management model, delegated management model, or a combination of both. This work also includes decisions regarding delegation of authority and separation of administrative duties. The next section focuses on these topics.

Scope of Management

When designing Active Directory and selecting methods for using Group Policies in your organization, you should consider and decide on how the following factors are to be handled:

♦ Central versus distributed administration

♦ Delegation of authority

♦ Separation of administrative duties

♦ Design flexibility

♦ Performance impact

The first four factors can be turned into questions of how you want to settle the following fundamental design points:

- Whether to do a layered or monolithic design
- Whether to use a single-policy type or multiple-policy type design
- Whether to use functional roles or team design
- Whether to use OU delegation with centralized or distributed control

Layered or Monolithic Design?

When deciding the overall GPO design, you basically have a choice between creating GPOs based on a layered approach (separate GPOs applied at each level of the SDOU hierarchy) or creating GPOs based on a monolithic approach (a single GPO for each directory container that encompasses most of the policies concerning the objects located in the given container).

A layered design (see Figure 10.3) provides more flexibility and detailed security—because most policy comes through inheritance and thus usually needs to be changed

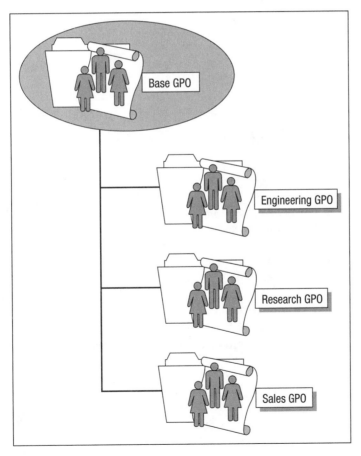

Figure 10.3
In a layered GPO design, you have GPOs at several—or all—levels of the SDOU organization.

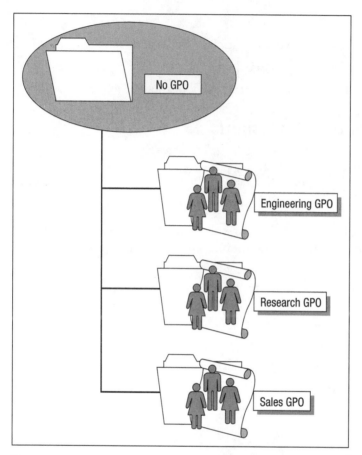

Figure 10.4
In a monolithic GPO design, instead of using inheritance, you ultimately have a separate GPO for each SDOU, with common settings repeated in each GPO.

only in one place—whereas a monolithic design (see Figure 10.4) is easier to understand and faster to process.

In a layered GPO design, you first create a base GPO to be applied to the domain that contains the common policy settings for the users and computers in the domain. You can then create additional GPOs that are tailored to the specific requirements of each functional unit (OU).

With a layered GPO design, you have to change only one or a few GPOs to enforce a change. Thus, administration is simplified at the expense of logon time and at the risk of losing oneself in the details. Also, you can delegate administrative authority of GPOs to local administrators.

In a monolithic GPO design, you strive to place all Group Policies in as few GPOs as possible (ideally, only one). This design offers minimum logon time, because less GPOs are processed for each user. The disadvantage lies in its relative inflexibility, because you generally aren't able to delegate authority. This also works to make it harder to institute corporate-wide policy changes and keep in check the anarchy that always lurks behind the corner of any installation (by way of the inherent risk of instituting different changes in GPOs pertaining to the same sort of objects, as well as the danger of seeing an explosion in GPOs designed to support exceptions at the OU level).

Single-Policy Type or Multiple-Policy Type Design

When choosing the policy application design, you can choose either a *single-policy type design* or a *multiple-policy type design*. A single-policy design (see Figure 10.5) provides the means for centralization and fine-grained administrative delegation, whereas a multiple-policy design (see Figure 10.6) facilitates fast processing and easy troubleshooting.

In a single-policy design, you put only one type of policy in each GPO. For example, the software installation policies would have a different GPO than script policies. With a single-policy design, you can limit the access to each GPO to fewer administrators (because different

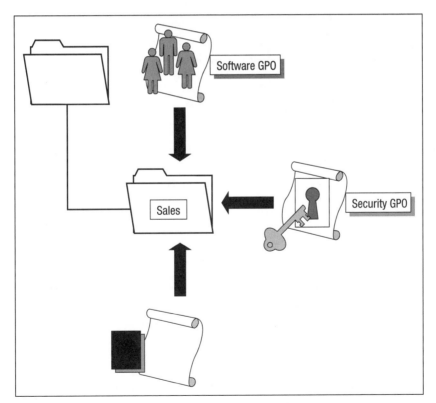

Figure 10.5
In a single-policy design, you have one type of policy in each GPO.

Figure 10.6
In a multiple-policy design, you have all applicable policies in each GPO.

people often handle different policies). But the result is longer logon times and harder trouble-shooting, because of the larger number of GPOs.

In a multiple-policy design, ideally you place all policies in the same GPO—in practice, how-ever, you usually end up creating two GPOs: one for users and one for the computers. For example, the software installation policies would be in the same GPO as the script policies.

With a multiple-policy design, you can ease troubleshooting and provide shorter logon times because of the limited number of GPOs. However, you also face administrative complications, because all administrators have to work on the same GPO, which is not very well supported today (a last writer wins method is used for handling cases of GPO replication collisons).

Functional Roles or Team Design?

The fact that every organization can be divided into several hierarchies, in which each child has only one parent, is perhaps the most deeply rooted assumption for a directory service. If this assumption proves to be wrong (which may be the case in some organizational models), you will have trouble attaining the ease of administration and delegation of authority promised by Microsoft.

When settling on the Group Policy design for an organization that adheres to the directory services assumption (in which the functional roles are mirrored by the domain and OU structures), you likely will choose to leverage the Active Directory structure—a functional role design (see Figure 10.7). However, if the OU architecture doesn't reflect the way that the organization is structured (for example, in matrix- or project-based organizations), you might choose to use a Group Policy design that is more dependent on the security groups—a team design (see Figure 10.8).

In a functional role design, you take advantage of the fact that your Active Directory hierarchy reflects the organizational roles, by constructing your Group Policies around the existing Active Directory containers. The potential disadvantage of the functional role design is that it could be rather complex in some organizations, because of a high number of roles.

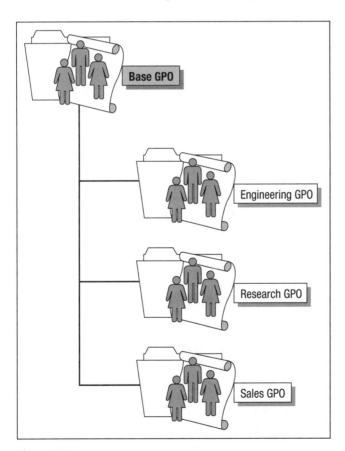

Figure 10.7
In a functional role design, you take advantage of the Active Directory hierarchy.

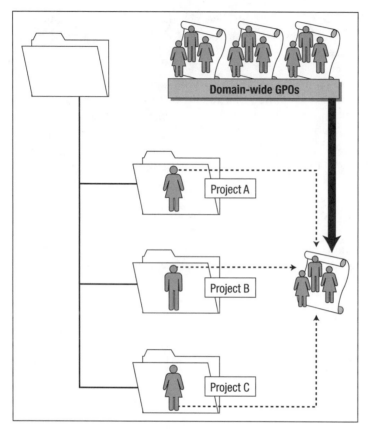

Figure 10.8
In a team design, you see the world as being flat—which doesn't go well with Active Directory.

In a team design, you won't be able to provide a good match to the actual organizational roles by mapping your GPOs to Active Directory containers. Instead, you might choose to rely mostly on domain-wide GPOs that use the capabilities for security group filtering when building your Group Policy design. Such a design is very simple, but it could also grow to be harder to keep a grip on, if the organization has many teams and roles.

OU Delegation with Centralized or Distributed Control?

The final thing that you need to consider regarding the overall GPO design is how to design the flow of control. Here, you can either choose a centralized control design or a distributed control design (see Figure 10.9).

In a centralized control design, you allow administrators to force the rest of the GPOs that are processed in the SDOU to inherit one or more policies, which are applied earlier, regardless of the needs and wants of the other GPOs. This is done by using the Force Policy Inheritance option. This design is well suited to organizations that choose to delegate administration of

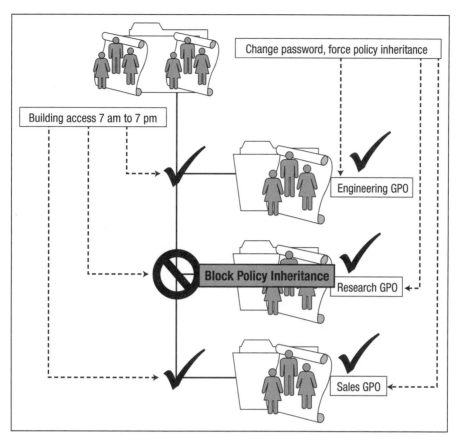

Figure 10.9
You have the choice of doing OU delegation with centralized or distributed control.

Group Policies, but need to enforce certain key policies on a large scale. However, note that the use of the Force Policy Inheritance option makes determining how the policies are applied more difficult, if its use isn't limited to a very few instances.

In a distributed control design, administrators are free to implement an implicit or explicit block of the policy inheritance. Implicit blocking of inheritance occurs when administrators specify another policy on their level; explicit blocking of inheritance occurs from utilizing the Block Policy Inheritance option. Although this is potentially the most flexible method of policy administration, it also involves more complexity in troubleshooting—especially if the Block Policy Inheritance option is widely used.

On a More Practical Note

You need to be familiar with a couple of fairly advanced topics to be able to put the Group Policies to their fullest use (and avoid troublesome experiences). First of all, you should be aware that Group Policies for client computers are refreshed every hour and a half, by default.

However, GPOs are refreshed every five minutes at DCs and member servers. In other words, you should be aware that changes to a Group Policy won't be fully implemented at the computers and users that were already logged on at the time when the Group Policy was put in operation until after at least two hours (depending on the number of DCs in the site and the Intersite replication setup).

Note

Remember to make the rather hefty time lag very clear to your Help-Desk personnel, because otherwise this can be a source of a lot of confusion. Also, please note that the refresh for the client computers uses a randomized time offset in an effort to avoid having many client computers contact the DC at the same time.

However, the processing of software installation and folder redirection settings in a Group Policy occurs *only* when a computer starts or when the user logs on, rather than on a periodic basis.

So, you should be very cautious when deleting Group Policies that include software, unless you want to risk having the application not be removed from all of the client computers covered by the Group Policy. This very situation will occur if you haven't asked for the application(s) to be removed before deleting the Group Policy or haven't allowed enough time between marking the application for removal and deleting the Group Policy (some users may not have logged on and some computers may not have restarted). Also, remember that GPOs can't be directly assigned to security groups, users, or machines. GPOs can only be applied to sites, domains, or OUs (as well as locally to a given machine), and then security groups (which can include users, groups, and computer accounts) can be used to filter the policies.

Note

You can't link GPOs to the default Active Directory containers (Users, Computers, and Built-in). Although these containers exist within Active Directory, they are not OUs. So, if you need to grant policies to objects that are stored in these containers, you must create a new OU and move these objects there.

To access a Group Policy, you simply need an appropriate Active Directory tool (such as Active Directory Users and Computers) focused on the SDOU container that you want to access. Then, access the context menu of the container, select Properties, click on the Group Policy tab, and select the needed GPO.

Note

Please note that the GPOs are processed in the reverse order listed on the Group Policy tab. In other words, higher GPOs override lower GPOs.

To set a Group Policy on a selected Active Directory object, you must have a Windows 2000 DC installed, **Read/Write** permission to access the system volume on the DC (Sysvol folder), Modify rights to the currently selected directory object, and the Manage Group Policy links permission (**Read/Write gPOptions** and **gPLink**).

To access a Group Policy that is scoped to the local computer (or any remote computer that you have permissions to access), you should load the Group Policy MMC snap-in and tell it which computer to contact. Two major reasons exist for these differences in regard to gaining access to the different types of Group Policies:

♦ Sites, domains, and OUs may have multiple GPOs per directory folder; this requires an intermediate property page to manage them.

♦ A GPO for a specific computer is stored on that computer, *not* in Active Directory.

If a server is upgraded to Windows 2000 Server, down-level clients (Windows 95/98 and NT Workstation) still only receives NT Server 4-style policies, because Group Policies can't be understood by down-level clients. As clients are upgraded to Windows 2000 Professional, they will continue to get NT 4-style policies, in addition to Group Policies, until the Group Policy "Disable 4.0 Style Policies" is enabled.

Precedence for the processing of policies is L4SDOU, which means Local Group Policies, the NT Server 4-style System Policies, Site Group Policies, Domain Group Policies, and OU Group Policies. Thus, the processing of local policies takes precedence over NT 4 policies, which in turn take precedence over SDOU policies. Please also note that you will also have a processing hierarchy inside each site, domain, or OU, if you've got more than one Group Policy assigned to each of them.

Standard GPO Inheritance Rules

First of all, please understand that unconfigured Group Policy settings can be ignored, because they are not inherited down the tree; only configured settings are inherited.

You're facing four possible scenarios across different objects, each carrying a Group Policy (remember that the rankings used are SDOU):

• A higher ranked Group Policy has a value for a setting for which the lower ranked one has no setting—the value will prevail when the Group Policies are run.

• A higher ranked Group Policy has a value for a setting, and the lower ranked one has a nonconflicting value for the same setting—both values will prevail.

• A higher ranked Group Policy has a value for a setting, and the lower ranked one has a conflicting value for the same setting—the lower ranked one's value will prevail, because the lower ranked one is being run last.

• The setting is disabled at one of the Group Policies—The disabled setting will prevail. In other words, the disabling of a setting takes precedence over the other values and so will always be inherited down the hierarchy (just as is the case with the Deny permission).

Please note that the scenarios are resolved in the same way when you have more than one Group Policy assigned to the same site, domain, or OU. However, you should just remember to keep track of which Group Policy is the higher ranked one (that is, which Group Policy is assigned first) and whether any of the GPOs are set to force or block.

And, finally, you might want to stay aware of the fact that there's a variation—called the Loopback Processing Mode—on how Group Policy settings are applied. Normally, the Group Policies assigned to the computer and the Group Policies assigned to the user are being applied (with the user's policies taking precedence, because they're assigned after the computer's).

However, the Loopback Processing Mode allows you to apply the computer's settings to any user that logs on to it, which can prove highly beneficial at computers placed in public places (classrooms, libraries, etc.), where you want the computer to determine which policy settings apply. Loopback Processing Mode can either be run as "replace" (all the settings specified in the computer's Group Policies replace the settings specified in the user's Group Policies) or "merge" (the settings specified through the Group Policies for the computer and the user are combined; however, the settings specified in the computer's Group Policies will always take precedence over the settings specified in the user's Group Policies).

Note

*The loopback processing mode is configured using the **User Group Policy Loopback Processing Mode** setting, found in the Computer Configuration\Administrative Templates\System\Group Policy container. Please note that, for loopback to work, the computer account as well as the user account must both reside in Active Directory DC.*

Staying Clear of Bandwidth Overload and All Its Consequences

You will do wisely to avoid Group Policy assignments, as well as roaming user profiles, over slow network links. You can control what should be considered a slow link using three Group Policies (that is: Computer Configuration\Administrative Templates\System\Group Policy\Group Policy slow link detection, User Configuration\Administrative Templates\System\Group Policy\Group Policy slow link detection, and Computer Configuration\Administrative Templates\System\Logon\Slow network connection timeout for user profiles). The default slow link setting for Group Policies is 500Kbps.

Note

*The link speed for the Group Policies (as well as roaming user profiles, unless the user profile comes from a non-IP server, in which case it instead checks the file system's response time) is determined by using a rather complicated algorithm that goes approximately like this: If the server pings faster than 10ms, then you've got a fast link. If not, a **Ping** with 4KB data is sent to the server and the speed is calculated. This test is being run three times, after which the average transfer speed is calculated, unless the server pings faster than 10ms.*

Individual Group Policies determine whether Group Policies (Computer Configuration\Administrative Templates\System\Group Policy) or roaming user profiles (Computer Configuration\Administrative Templates\System\Logon), respectively, should be applied over the slow link at all (and in the case of the Group Policies, which parts of the Group Policy should be applied).

The default settings for the Group Policies over slow links for computers are as follows:

♦ Administrative Templates and Security Settings: ON (this can't be turned off), Scripts: ON, Software Installation: OFF, Folder Redirection: OFF.

In other words, if a slow network link is encountered, the software assigned to the computer won't get installed and the folders won't be redirected. You can change these settings (using the settings found in the Computer Configuration\Administrative Templates\System\ Group Policy container), but before you start doing that, please remember that the computer isn't able to service the user until the last GPO has been executed.

You should also try to limit how often each Group Policy is updated, because updates require replication of the Active Directory database as well as the Sysvol folder. The updates will either involve all DCs in the domain (in the case where the GPO is assigned to a domain or an OU) or the forest (in the case where the GPO is assigned to a site). Two simple ways of lowering the Group Policy update frequency are, first, to institute the use of test GPOs that are limited to a separate Active Directory forest that is running in the lab and, second, to minimize the number of administrators that are allowed to edit the live GPOs.

Tip

You should also be careful about assigning GPOs to sites, because the GPO resides in one domain only, and clients in the site will read the GPO from that domain as required. This obviously is fine if a DC from the domain is present in the site, but it will add a lot of load on your WAN if that's not the case.

Finally, you should limit the use of cross-domain linking (that is, applying GPOs across domains) for domains that cross WAN links as much as possible, because the GPO and GPT are transferred from the source domain every time the policy is being applied to a user or computer.

Performance Optimization

In many cases, the logon time on the client will prove even more important than the network load. And so, you should always strive to minimize the number of GPOs that a given computer or user has to process, because computer startup and user logon time are affected by the number of GPOs that are applied.

By default, the GPOs use synchronous processing, which effectively means that all GPOs are executed simultaneously. However, the computer still won't be available until the last GPO is finished processing—and, by default, the time out for scripts is set to 600 seconds, which means that in a worst-case scenario, the processing of all the Group Policy scripts

---

How Many Group Policies Should You Use?

Although it's easy to answer a question on how many Group Policies you *can* use, it's very hard—if not impossible—to answer the question of how many Group Policies you *should* use (and how they will impact the startup and logon performance on your client machines).

Although it's obvious that each policy you apply will cause a slowdown in the startup and logon at the system, currently no good guidelines exist for how many policies can be applied. And you really shouldn't be too optimistic that any usable guidelines will arrive soon, because the time spent on each Group Policy depends almost entirely upon the settings used in that given Group Policy, making it very hard to avoid having the guidelines be either overly simplistic or highly theoretic.

So really, I would advocate that you go ahead and test the impact of your specific Group Policies on your specific client machines in a lab setting rather than waste time trying to look for some rules of thumb that don't exist. However, you should remember that it will no doubt take more time to execute five policies of 20 settings each than to implement a single one with all 100 settings.

And what was the answer to the easy question (how many Group Policies you can apply)? That's 1,000 Group Policies. It's highly unlikely that you'll hit that ceiling any time soon, but you might want to note that a Group Policy will fail whenever a user has Read access to more than 1,000 Group Policy objects stored in one domain.

---

included with the Group Policy will take more than 10 minutes at the client computer, if a faulty script is included.

One way to optimize performance is to utilize security groups (ACLs) to filter the effect of Group Policies. This reduces the real number of GPOs that a computer (at startup) or user (at logon) must process. This reduction is done very efficiently, because deciding whether to apply each GPO simply requires a comparison of the SIDs in the access token to the GPO's ACL.

Another way to optimize performance is to limit the scope of each GPO. That is, reduce the use of cross-domain GPO associations, because each of the GPOs has to be retrieved from another domain, which takes more time (and potentially could be *very* slow, depending on the WAN setup). In the same vein, you should be very aware of which GPO is associated with which sites, to reduce the number of GPO associations that stem from DCs that aren't available at the site (see Figure 10.10). Also, remember to disable unused portions of each GPO; if the version number for User Configuration or Computer Configuration is zero, it is skipped, thus decreasing the time spent on applying the Group Policy in question. Finally, you might want to change the default settings on the Group Policy refresh interval if you don't need to have the client nor the DC refresh every one-and-a-half hour and five minutes, respectively.

Note

Please note that you especially don't want to refresh Group Policy too often if you are using a laptop computer, because each refresh resets the hibernate timer, so choosing too short an interval, will in effect, cause the computer never to hibernate.

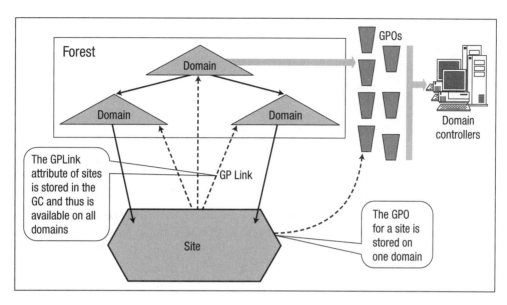

Figure 10.10
When planning your GPOs, recognize that a GPO is stored in a domain.

Administrative Optimizations

When planning for Group Policies, always strive to limit the use of the following:

♦ Block Policy Inheritance

♦ Force Policy Inheritance

♦ Cross-Domain GPO Assignments

This results in ease of management. If you need to use any of these capabilities, avoid using more than one at a time, because each adds more complexity—and thereby makes the administration of the Group Policies more error-prone. Likewise, you should always use revision numbers for User Configuration and Computer Configuration as a hint to their usage, because this makes it easier for the administration to keep the GPO selection neat and tidy.

You should also create the minimal number possible of GPOs that contain Administrative Templates settings. Because there are so many of these settings, it will soon prove impossible to manage user environments properly, if you create many GPOs with these settings.

Note

Remember to always test GPOs that contain Administrative Templates settings before setting them in production. Believe me, if you are going to lock down user desktops, you will always want to ensure you have the correct settings configured unless you want to risk having your whole world come tumbling down in a matter of minutes because you inadvertently disrupted all users' ability to work.

Likewise, you should always prefer to assign your User Configuration settings to users rather than computers—except for the very special situations, where Loopback Processing Mode applies—because you should want to control what users can do regardless of which computers they log on to.

Note

Also, remember that the settings assigned to the user in the User Configuration container always will override the ones assigned to the computer.

Finally, you should remember to put the option for prioritizing Group Policies to full use. In many instances, the possibility of controlling the ordering of the application of policies will allow you to cut down on the complexity of the individual Group Policies because you are able to cater to the exceptions without having to resort to making totally separate Group Policies—in other words, you just reset the "damage" done by the higher-ranked Group Policy, which is usually applied to the majority of users or computers.

Note

And ultimately: Be careful how the Group Policies are administered. Unless you instill some common sense about how to administer the Group Policies, you might risk having one administrator inadvertently overwriting the changes done by another administrator because of the simplistic "last writer wins" method used for Group Policies.

For example, if a person opens a Group Policy (for editing) that another person is already working on, you will face this very problem when the two persons save their work. The same thing might happen if the administrators don't allow the system to fetch the Group Policy from the DC currently holding the PDC Operation Master role, but just ask for it to be loaded from the nearest DC.

Best Practices

I sure do hope that you've found a fair deal of very profound lessons in this chapter—especially with regard to the Group Policy feature. And I urge you to recognize that you'll always have to settle the issues listed in Table 10.2 on a global scale before you venture into the implementation of Active Directory.

Table 10.2   Summary of best practices.

Task	Points to Consider
Develop a plan of where to locate users and computers in the OU structure.	This has a profound impact on the way that the user is presented to the computer, if you are using Group Policies.

(continued)

Table 10.2   Summary of best practices *(continued).*

Task	Points to Consider
Delegate administration.	Take advantage of the Active Directory hierarchy for fine-grained delegation of administration. This could well prove to be an invaluable tool for organizations to confine the different parts of security administration very precisely to each person's job responsibilities. The best practices for delegation of administration are: • Assign control at the OU level whenever possible. Tracking permission assignments becomes more complex when you assign permissions to specific objects and object attributes rather than OUs. • Use the Delegation of Control wizard. The wizard assigns permissions only at the OU level, and it simplifies the process of assigning object permissions by stepping you through the process. • Track the delegation of permission assignments. Tracking assignments allows you to maintain records for reviewing security settings.
Establish the right Group model.	Strive to take full advantage of the Active Directory domain Policy and OU structure for simplicity's sake. If you have trouble doing that, consider reverting to the Active Directory design stage to iron out the reasons for the difficulty.
Implement the Group Policy structure.	The following are reasons to create Group Policies: • Automate software installations • Manage security settings • Customize Registry settings • Redirect folders to the server • Implement scripts GPOs are linked to Active Directory containers, allowing multiple relationships as well as prioritization. The usual applications for GPOs are as follows: • Organizations with a flat Active Directory structure may apply GPOs at a granular level by making use of the capabilities for security group filtering. • Organizations with a deep Active Directory structure should be able to leverage the hierarchy for GPO assignment and may use security groups for handling exceptions—that is, to further refine the targeting of the GPO.
Determine the scope of Group Policies management.	Delegation of authority, separation of administrative duties, central versus distributed administration, and design flexibility are important factors that you need to consider when designing a Group Policy framework and selecting which scenarios to put to use in your organization. Whether you implement Group Policies in a modular and structured fashion will be determined by the administrative requirements and roles in your corporation.
Keep things simple and straightforward.	If you have multiple domains, you should determine whether you can use the same GPO structure and overall structure across all domains. If not, you may want to redesign the Active Directory design or GPO structure. Also, try to avoid overriding the default GPO behavior characteristics, make use of the inheritance property, and minimize the number of GPOs applied to each user or computer.

(continued)

Table 10.2   Summary of best practices *(continued)*.

Task	Points to Consider
Make the most of Group Policies.	Several hundred Group Policies are available right from the outset, and many more will be added, if you're using Microsoft Office or other policy-controllable applications. There's really no other way of getting into Group Policies than the hard way: Evaluating each and all of the policy settings! So there's quite a lot of time to be spent here, before you are truly mastering Group Policies.
Optimize for speed.	You should always remove the Read permission to the Group Policies that doesn't apply to certain computer, user, or group accounts, because this will work to minimize the computer's startup time and the user's logon time. Likewise, please note that you're allowed to disable unused parts of a Group Policy (that is, the User Configuration or Computer Configuration node), which also helps expedite logon sessions for users and computers.
Make the Group Policies easy to administer.	Follow these best practices to avoid making a total mess of your Group Policies: • Limit the use of blocking, forcing, and cross-domain linking GPOs. Each one of these introduces a further level of complexity. • Group related settings in a single GPO. A GPO that is used to publish Microsoft Office 2000 should also contain any Registry-based Group Policy settings for Office 2000. • Limit the number of users to whom you delegate control of a GPO to one or two. This limits the possibility of having multiple administrators make changes to Group Policy settings at the same time.

You should want to note that the Windows 2000 Server Resource Kit includes a couple of very interesting tools:

♦ *Group Policy Migration Utility*—Allows you to migrate settings from earlier version policy files to the Windows 2000 GPO structure.

♦ *Group Policy Object Utility*—Allows you to check the consistency and replication of the Group Policy objects on the Active Directory DCS.

♦ *Group Policy Results*—Allows you to see how Group Policy works on a particular computer and its logged-on users.

Group Policies in Short

Group Policies are most certainly proving themselves to be one of the very significant features in Windows 2000 Server from the network administrator's viewpoint. Consequently, the Group Policies design should be recognized, well understood, and deeply scrutinized by all administrators early on. And I sincerely hope that you are convinced by now that investing the necessary time and effort to execute the Group Policy planning will prove beneficial. Also, you should be aware that when you plan your Group Policies, it will become apparent whether or not you've done a good job planning the Active Directory hierarchy, because the ways that a Group Policy can be applied depend on the Active Directory structure at hand.

If you have done a skillful Active Directory design (which, by definition, demands some Active Directory experience), with Group Policies in mind, you should be able to implement as well as administer Group Policies in a very simple and straightforward way. And remember: Don't despair if you didn't get it right the first time—that's how experience is derived.

In most cases, you will find that you have to fiddle somewhat with the Active Directory design before everything falls into place—and you should be prepared to do that occasionally as the Group Policies and the use of Active Directory evolve. Regardless of how many changes you implement to the Active Directory hierarchy today or in the future, you should never give up. Remember, a plan is only as good as you make it, and anyway, implementing even rather profound changes to the OU hierarchy is fairly easy. Domains and sites are a whole other story, though. These areas are the subject of Chapter 11 and 12, respectively.

Chapter 11

Planning of Domain Trees and the Forest

N ow that you have survived the challenges of defining OU hierarchies, putting the Group Policies to use, as well as the perplexing experience of having to deal with groups rather than the "beautiful" hierarchical structures defined in Active Directory and the other more mundane tasks (most of which were also present in Windows NT Server 4), you should be ready to tackle one of the more important tasks of Active Directory design: planning domain trees and forests.

Recall from earlier chapters that you can create another hierarchy on top of the Organizational Unit (OU) hierarchy; that is, the domain hierarchy. However, before you invest a lot of effort working through this chapter, first you should again consider that, in many cases, a single domain will prove to be sufficient. And, if that is true for your situation, you really should go with that single-domain design. Regardless of whether you look at it from an administrative standpoint or from a functional standpoint, the fewer domains, the better.

However, many situations do require multiple domains. If you require more than one domain, you have to figure out exactly how to structure the relationship among these domains. This chapter focuses on the planning that is required to build a multiple-domain structure, whether it be a domain tree, multiple domain trees, or multiple forests. Designing the domain tree and/or forest structures should prove to be a somewhat simpler task than designing the first domain—however, you should keep in mind that you still must design every single domain present in the domain tree or forest setting, following the advice given in Chapter 8.

Thus, even if you have established that your structure requires multiple domains, you still need a thorough knowledge of single-domain planning. So, if you are somewhat hazy on the information provided in Chapter 8, you should at least review the checklist at the end of that chapter. You'll need to keep most of the information presented in Chapter 8 handy in order to create a proper domain tree or forest setup.

Going after the Single Domain

Recall from earlier chapters that the domain is the core unit of logical structure in Active Directory. The Active Directory domain is both a logical grouping of objects and a boundary for replication and security. Inside the domain, you find all the objects (user accounts, groups, computers, printers, applications, security policies, file shares, and so on) that represent the network resources. These objects can be arranged in logical administrative groupings using OUs.

In short, a domain consists of numerous directory objects that can be ordered hierarchically through the use of OUs. And, as I've mentioned several times (because of its vital importance), you should always strive to keep things as simple as possible. So, if you can make do with a single domain, you should do so, because it is the simplest domain structure to create and administer.

Your initial goal should always be to achieve a single-domain structure. Consequently, you should add more domains only after you have determined that doing so is absolutely necessary. And, you likely won't reach that conclusion as a result of hitting the ceiling regarding the capacity of Active Directory, because each Active Directory domain can hold at least 10 million objects in its Active Directory store (actually, a third party has already set up and tested an Active Directory domain with up to 16 million objects). The theoretical limit for the database is as much as 17 terabytes, which generally should prove to be enough storage for all but the very largest companies.

Nonetheless, you may encounter many situations in which implementing a single domain is out of the question, such as the following:

♦ You have multiple business units that, for political reasons, need to have different names.

♦ Two parts of your network are separated by a link that is so slow that you want to minimize the level of replication traffic crossing it.

♦ You haven't got IP connectivity between two or more areas of the network.

♦ You have unique security policy requirements.

♦ You have a highly decentralized organization or an organization in which different users and resources are managed by completely different sets of administrative personnel.

♦ You want to prevent all single points of failure in the design—however unlikely their occurrence may be.

♦ You want a one-to-one mapping of existing Windows NT Server 4 domains in a migration setting.

These are just a few examples from a wide range of good reasons for implementing multiple domains (if you don't understand the implications of one of the preceding reasons, you should go back to the beginning of Chapter 8, which explicitly states the reason for having several domains in each of these situations).

Conversely, the following are two very bad reasons for creating multiple domains:

♦ *To reflect your company's organization of divisions and departments*—You should always avoid naming domains for divisions, departments, buildings, floors, and groups. A good Active Directory design will withstand company reorganizations without the need to restructure your domain hierarchy.

♦ *For political reasons*—A good design will withstand political changes within the company without the need to restructure your domain hierarchy.

Introducing the Domain Tree and the Forest

Regardless of whether you need a domain tree or a forest, you should understand the following concepts, because you will be asked to provide this information by the Active Directory Installation Wizard when installing a domain controller (DC):

♦ *Domain tree*—A hierarchical organization of domains with contiguous names. The minimal tree is a single domain, so even if you have only a single domain, strictly speaking you still have a domain tree that consists of that domain. The domains in a domain tree:

  ♦ Connect by trust relationships

  ♦ Share a common schema

  ♦ Share configuration information

  ♦ Share a Global Catalog (GC)

  ♦ Use the name at the root of the domain tree to refer to that particular domain tree

♦ *Forest*—A set of one or more domain trees that don't form a contiguous namespace (the domain trees have their own unique namespaces, which are referred to as *discontiguous* or *disjoint namespaces*). The minimal forest has a single domain tree, so even if you have only a single domain tree, strictly speaking you still have a forest, which consists of that domain tree. The domain trees in a forest:

  ♦ Connect by trust relationships

  ♦ Share a common schema

  ♦ Share configuration information

  ♦ Share a Global Catalog (GC)

  ♦ Use the name at the root of the first domain tree in the forest to refer to that particular forest

Thus, the concepts of the domain tree and the forest enable you to make your network resources more globally available, by enabling you to join domains together into domain trees and to associate multiple domain trees into one forest. Ultimately, you can create several forests, if you want total segregation of some domains.

Combining the concepts of the domain tree and the forest provides you with the flexibility of both contiguous and discontiguous naming conventions. This can be useful, for example, in companies with independent divisions that must each maintain their own DNS names. To make the resources in a domain or domain tree universally available to users, you simply join the domain to a domain tree, or create two domain trees that are part of the same forest.

When a domain joins a domain tree, a *transitive trust* is created between the joining domain and its parent domain. When two domain trees are created in a forest, the trust is created between the root domains of each domain tree. Because domains and domain trees are linked together by transitive, two-way Kerberos trusts, users have access to resources in any domain in the entire forest or domain tree.

Note

Using the Active Directory Installation Wizard (aka, DCPromo) to join a domain to a domain tree, or to joining a new domain tree to a existing domain tree in the same forest, creates a transitive, two-way Kerberos trust. The trust relationships are created transparently to the administrators, and thus no management of the trust relationships is really necessary—which is a nice change from the trust nightmares that have haunted Windows NT Server administrators for many years.

Domain Trees Explained

When you need more than one domain, you should usually link domains into a domain tree. All domains within a single domain tree share a hierarchical naming structure. The first domain in a domain tree is the *root* of the tree. Additional domains in the same domain tree are referred to as *child* domains. Domains immediately above other domains in the same domain tree are called *parent* domains. Because the concept of domain trees is based on a contiguous namespace, the domain name of a child domain is the relative name of that child domain, added to the beginning of the name of the parent domain. For example, **headquarters.acme.com** would be a child domain of the **acme.com** domain. Figure 11.1 shows an example of a domain tree that consists of three subtrees (organizations), each internally contiguous, joined into a single, contiguous domain tree.

Domains in a domain tree are transparently joined together through two-way, transitive trust relationships. Because these trust relationships are two-way and transitive, a domain joining a tree immediately has trust established to all other domains in the tree. The transitive trust relationships enable users to be authenticated in one or more of the domains and granted access throughout the entire domain tree. This effectively makes the resources in

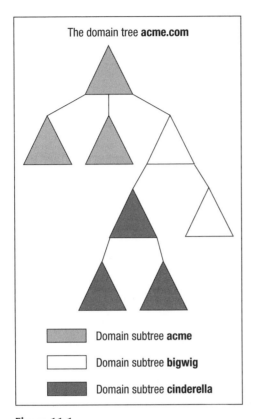

Figure 11.1
An example domain tree structure. Because the domain tree's root name is **acme.com**, the root
domains of the subtrees are **bigwig.acme.com** and **cinderella.bigwig.acme.com**, respectively.

all the domains of the tree available to users and computers in all other domains in the
domain tree.

However, as you may recall, the domain is a security boundary, and administrative rights in
a domain tree aren't shared between the individual domains (except for the Enterprise
Admins and Schema Admins Groups). So when you create a separate domain in a domain
tree, you are effectively adding an additional layer of security by limiting the scope of domain administrative rights between the domains.

Forests Explained

A *forest* consists of one or more domain trees. Because a forest is based on disjointed naming, the domain trees in a forest don't share a common root. For example, the two domains
acme.com and **netlog.dk** have no relationship to each other in the domain namespace—
this also is true with the domains **acme.com** and **astonitgroup.com**, because the **.com** belongs
to the Internet domain authorities and thus can't be utilized for a common parent Active

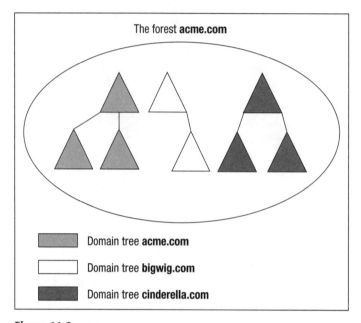

Figure 11.2
The same organizational structure used in Figure 11.1 expressed as a forest. Note the changes to the naming of the subtrees.

Directory domain in which the two domains could intersect. Figure 11.2 shows an example in which the same company shown in Figure 11.1 is implemented as a forest in which each domain tree is distinct.

A particular company can, of course, have an Active Directory structure that consists of more than a single Active Directory forest. In that case, by default, no relationship whatsoever exists between these forests. Thus, if you really need a relationship to exist between two corporate entities, you should *always* implement them inside the same forest (either as domain trees or as domains in an existing domain tree). Remember, however, that Active Directory enables you to define the old-style directional trust relationships between separate enterprises, so you can still define a limited form of relationship between two separate forests—keep in mind that its not really a very practical solution for anthing, but to connect two separate enterprises, as any NT Server administrator can attest to.

Getting It Right—Right?

I must admit that initially I had some difficulty understanding the exact meaning of the forest and domain tree concepts, which is why I am going to try to explain them in another way—by an example that is related to the way that you actually implement the domains in Windows 2000 Server (that is, via the Active Directory Installation Wizard tool).

Creating an Active Directory domain is always the very first thing that you will do when you set out to implement the Active Directory structure that you have architected. When you create your first domain, you are implicitly creating a domain tree, as well as a forest. So, if you start out by creating the **acme.com** domain, you actually create the Active Directory structure shown in Figure 11.3.

As Figure 11.3 shows, when you create the first Active Directory domain, you also create a domain tree (the minimal domain tree is a single domain) and a forest (the minimal forest is a single domain tree), which both use the same name as the first domain's name—in this instance, **acme.com**. The next step is to add two new domains, which are defined as child domains of the **acme.com** domain. At this point, your domain tree starts to take form (see Figure 11.4).

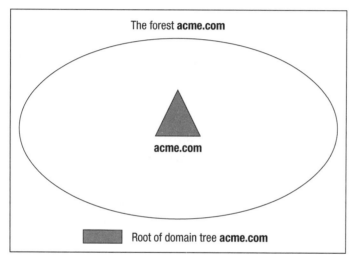

Figure 11.3
When you create your first domain, you actually also start a domain tree and a forest.

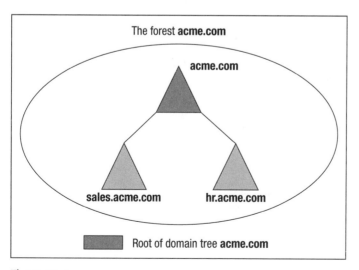

Figure 11.4
A domain tree must always have a name. However, you don't make the implicit domain tree into a "real" domain tree until you start adding child domains to the initial domain.

Recall that a domain tree is a set of one or more Active Directory domains sharing a common schema, configuration information, and Global Catalog (GC), joined together to form a *contiguous* namespace (that is, the children of **somedomain.com** are always children of **somedomain.com** in the DNS namespace—for example, **child1.somedomain.com**, **child2.somedomain.com**, and so forth). All domains in a particular tree trust each other through transitive, hierarchical Kerberos trust relationships.

As Figure 11.4 demonstrates, the domain tree name is the DNS name of the root of the domain tree—which always is the first domain implemented. Also, you should understand that this naming issue is one of the main reasons that Active Directory won't allow you to put another domain on top of the **acme.com** domain.

Finally, you might have to cater to the needs of the bigwig company (**bigwig.com**), which has just been acquired by your company. This acquisition may create the need to implement some domains, which have no bearing—namespace-wise—on your current **acme.com** domain tree. When you execute this implementation, your forest starts to take shape (see Figure 11.5).

Again, per definition, a forest is a set of one or more domain trees that form a discontiguous namespace. All domain trees in a forest share a common schema, configuration information, and GC, and trust each other through transitive, hierarchical Kerberos trust relationships.

Unlike domain trees and domains, the forest doesn't need a distinct name, per se, because a forest exists as a set of cross-referenced objects and Kerberos trust relationships known to the member domain trees. Domain trees in a forest form a hierarchy for the purpose of

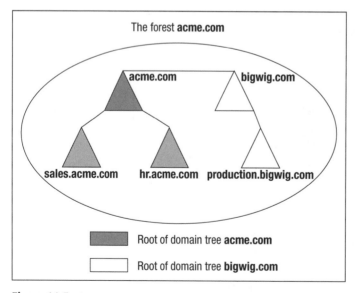

Figure 11.5
When you add another domain tree to your current **acme.com** domain tree, you make the implicit enterprise into a "real" forest.

Kerberos trusts; that is why, by convention, the name of the domain tree at the root of the trust tree is used to refer to a particular forest.

So, what really is the difference between a domain tree and a forest? Theoretically speaking, the difference is that a forest doesn't require that the member domains always form a tree (which, in turn, is reflected in the DNS naming of the individual domains). Therefore, in a forest, you can arbitrarily join together disjointed subtrees. This can prove valuable, because you're able to eliminate the confusing situation caused by forcing disjointed namespaces into an arbitrary, contiguous tree structure.

This rather small difference between a domain tree and a forest requires the relationships to be represented differently. Whereas the relationships in a domain tree are simply Kerberos trusts between the adjacent domains, in the forest approach, it's the domain trees that have a peer relationship.

Note

The trust hierarchy within a domain tree follows the naming hierarchy, which is both intuitive and easy to implement. The trust hierarchy in a forest is an arbitrary graph. By default, the trust hierarchy of the forest is formed in the order the domain trees are joined to the forest—that is, the "top" is the root domain of the first domain tree, and subsequent domain trees trust the top of the domain tree that was joined last. The trust hierarchy is exposed to the administrator only for management purposes and is only significant as to performance; users don't know or care what the trust tree looks like.

This small, albeit noticeable, difference has but one effect in practice: the LDAP search behavior. In a domain tree, the behavior of LDAP is intuitive; search operations will flow down throughout a domain tree following the trusts (this is achieved by automatically searching through every subordinate reference given by each domain). In a forest, the search behavior is just as intuitive: An LDAP search operation is restricted to the domain tree in which it was initiated.

However, with that said, also note that the GC can help you to do forest-wide searches. If the attribute for which you are searching is available in the GC (recall that the subset of attributes from each domain replicated to the GC is specified by the administrator), a forest-wide search takes place in the GC. Thus, the GC will ensure that the relevant attributes are retrieved regardless of where they are located in the domain trees that comprise the forest.

Setting Out to Design the Domain Structure

When you set out to design your Active Directory domain structure, you should take the following steps:

1. Start with one domain tree.

2. Pick a domain to be the root:

   ♦ This domain is to become the root of both the forest and the domain tree.

   ♦ Assign a DNS name to the domain (which can be unrelated to the current domain name, if upgrading an existing Windows NT Server domain).

3. Add subsequent domains as children to the root domain:

   ♦ Assign each domain a DNS name.

   ♦ The DNS name of the child domain can be only one label longer than the parent because it inherits the DNS name of the parent.

4. Create additional domain trees—and thus take advantage of the forest feature of Active Directory—if you have business units that require distinct DNS names.

5. Create additional forests:

   ♦ To isolate schema, configuration information, and GCs.

   ♦ You connect domains across the forests using explicit one-way trusts (that is, Windows NT Server-style trusts).

As repeated several times, you should always strive to keep the domain structure as simple as possible, and ultimately settle for a single domain, whenever possible. The way to achieve the simplest domain structure is to start out with a single domain on the drawing board and thereafter demand specific justification for each additional domain (examples of sufficient justification are: isolating replication, a requirement for unique domain-level policy, or providing for an in-place upgrade of the current NT Server 4 domains).

Also, when you are doing your design work, you should be keenly aware of the limitations that apply to the current version of Windows 2000 Server. Microsoft has postponed the following flexibility features to a later version of Windows 2000 Server:

♦ Moving or renaming domains

♦ Merging domain trees

♦ Splitting domain trees

♦ Moving directory objects across forests (however, this is remedied by the Active Directory Migration Tool, which is discussed in Chapter 22)

♦ Merging schemas between forests

Domain Structure Design Unwind

When designing a domain architecture, you should first and foremost consider the following criteria:

♦ Replication traffic requirements.

♦ The need to accommodate organizational changes without expensive domain changes.

♦ The ability of the Active Directory design to evolve as organizational needs change.

A Word on Domain Tree and Forest Management

One of Active Directory's primary design goals was to provide easy administration and flexibility of the resulting domain trees and the forest. For example, if a newly formed company designs its domain trees and forest to suit its initial size and company structure, this first implementation is unlikely the best long-term solution. As the company grows, its needs and its organization will change. The IT department may require a refined naming convention later, or the hierarchy of the domains and domain trees may cease to match the organizational structure.

For that reason, Active Directory implements a set of operations that allow renaming and restructuring of objects in the directory. This set of operations includes the following:

- Easy addition of domains
- Easy deletion of domains
- Renaming of domains

Of these operations, the easiest is the addition of a domain. An Active Directory domain can join a domain tree when its first DC is being installed. The DC must be pointed to an existing Active Directory domain as its parent domain. This establishes the transitive Kerberos trusts and allows the domain to join the tree.

A domain "deletion" isn't really a deletion; it merely removes a domain from a domain tree. Active Directory allows removal of domains from a tree at any time. However, the domain must not have any child domains that are supposed to remain in the tree. Removing parent domains breaks the trust relationships between the parent of the domain to be removed and the child domains of the domain to be removed. If the child domain is to be removed together with the parent, a recursive deletion is possible.

Any object in Active Directory can have several names—a common name, a relative name, and so forth. The only object identifier that can never be changed is the object's *Globally Unique Identifier (GUID)*. The GUID is a large number that is created by the DC. The algorithm used for GUID creation ensures that a GUID can never be created twice. By using this unique identifier as the only identifier that can never be changed, Active Directory allows all other names to be changed. For this reason, you can rename any object or domain in Active Directory without side effects—however, the current version of Windows 2000 Server doesn't support renaming of domains (probably due to the inherent risks in regard to the DNS naming and the trust relationships). Microsoft has promised that this functionality will be implemented in a later release or version of Windows 2000 Server.

In theory, GUIDs should also allow objects (including domains) to be moved inside the directory tree or forest. One of the main reasons for that is that the GUIDs are included in the subset of object properties stored at the GC. So if an object is moved, the GCs should prove able to use the GUID for locating the object, and thus constructing the distinguished name of the object by using the object's new relative ID (RID) and the LDAP path to the domain in which the object now resides.

Determining the Number of Domains Your Organization Requires

Basically, you should plan your domain structure according to your company's logical, organizational model. You don't need to take geography or physical location into account unless your organizational model does so. You specifically shouldn't ever base your network model on your current physical structure, because that can usually be handled by creating Active Directory sites, which are unrelated to the domain structure. Site structure and domain structure are separate and flexible; a single domain can span geographical sites, and a single site can include users and computers belonging to multiple domains. (Sites are covered in more detail in Chapter 12.)

Although planning a good domain structure is indeed very important, the question of what is "good" is highly subjective and based on the specific needs of your organization. Actually, the best domain structures are those that are able to anticipate (or adapt to) future changes in the organizational structure.

Trying to Settle for a Single Domain

Every Active Directory namespace design includes at least one domain. Each domain has one or more servers that serve as DCs. Each DC stores a complete copy of the domain's directory database (and the schema and configuration partitions) and enables you to manage changes and updates to the directory. When you perform an action that results in an update to the directory, the DC automatically will replicate, or copy, the information to all other DCs in the domain.

For slow links that can handle replication traffic on a less frequent schedule, you can configure a single domain with multiple physical sites. So, one domain really is sufficient for most organizations, and administering and maintaining one domain will always prove to be much easier than multiple domains.

Deciding on Adding More Domains

For some enterprises, you will need to create additional domains, for any of the following reasons:

♦ You have two or more groups in your organization that have unique, domain-level policy requirements.

♦ You want to prevent a single point of failure.

♦ Two parts of your network are separated by a non-IP connection link so slow that you never want complete domain replication traffic to cross it.

♦ You want optimum control of replication, regardless of the administrative and hardware costs involved.

♦ You have a decentralized organization in which different users and resources are managed by completely different sets of administrative personnel (this will usually pose a demand for being able to segregate the security administration quite a lot between the different parts of the organization).

♦ Your organization responds to political requests for entirely autonomous administration of departments or divisions.

The Placeholder Domain Structure: Everything You Need to Know

One very distinctive kind of domain structure has grown quite popular in some places. I've felt compelled to comment on it several times. And now, I have the perfect excuse for it: Making sure that you know something about what it is—and, maybe even more importantly, about what it isn't.

In this very special domain structure, you create a domain tree with a dummy domain at the root (the so-called placeholder domain) with no users or computer accounts, apart from two or three DCs, and a completely static name (usually a name that isn't known to the Internet, such as *root.local*). When it comes to installing new domains or upgrading existing ones, they will simply link in to the placeholder domain that you've created.

Why should you want to do that? Well, I've heard three reasons until now:

- To isolate the forest-wide groups in order to avoid any tampering with these all-powerful groups.

- To avoid being faced with the current Active Directory limitations (that the forest root can't be deleted or renamed, its role can't be transferred, and other domains can't be represented above this domain) in case a need for a domain restructure should arise.

- For being able to implement Active Directory in a part of an enterprise before a full Active Directory design is in place.

While I do understand the rationale of the first reason in a security-sensitive environment, I must admit that I don't really understand the rationale of the other two.

Although it does take some time to do an Active Directory design, it's foolish not to spend the time doing it right the first time. As for the Active Directory limitations: Well, usually it won't make much difference if you have a placeholder domain or not. Also, Microsoft now delivers a very powerful tool for domain restructures (Active Directory Migration Tool, which is discussed in Chapter 22) and has pledged to remove most of the current limitations in a later-coming release of Windows 2000. To be precise, Microsoft has pledged to add mechanisms for renaming, splitting, and merging forests (it's still too early to judge whether it will come with the planned "Whistler" release targeted for the second half 2001 or the release coming after that).

Actually, I've heard one more reason for implementing a placeholder domain: To make it straightforward to break off a domain in case it's being divested from the enterprise (you "just" put in a couple of extra DCs at the placeholder domain and move those DCs as well as the actual domain out on its own). Please promise me that you never will do a buy-in on this being possible. Doing so is *not* supported by Microsoft nor anybody else because of the indeterminate consequences in regard to trust relationships, FSMOs, replication topology, and many other vital parts of the Active Directory environment. I haven't spent any time trying such a crazy thing, because I'm quite convinced that you'll be left with an insurmountable level of trouble in both the initial forest and the new one; I just don't know exactly how badly things will turn out.

- ◆ You have an international company and want each country's users and resources to be administered in the local language (this will often call for creating separate domains for each language region).

- ◆ Your current Windows NT Server 3.51 or 4 environment has more than one domain and you want to upgrade to Windows 2000 Server, using a one-to-one mapping of domains.

♦ You anticipate that your domain will contain more than one million directory objects (this should prompt you to add more domains in most cases, despite the fact that the lab tests show fine results with much higher numbers of objects).

However, you should resist the temptation to create domains for political reasons (for example., some business managers insisting on getting their own "kingdom" to separate them from the pack rather than out of a real need). These types of domains are costly, and they tend to change more often than domains that you create for practical, business-driven reasons. Adding more domains is sure to increase server hardware costs, because doing so requires that you add more DCs. Additionally, changes in the overall domain architecture, such as domain consolidation and re-creation, can be an IT-intensive support proposition.

Arranging the Domains in a Tree

If your current organizational structure lends itself to implementation as a contiguous DNS namespace, you should set up all of your domains in a single domain tree (see Figure 11.6). An advantage to maintaining a single-tree namespace is that searching for objects within one tree is easier.

The following are some rough guidelines for determining which parts of your organization you should consider turning into domains instead of OUs:

♦ Offices that have a staff of more than 1,000 people

♦ Offices that have a sufficient number of DCs (at least two) and plenty of LAN bandwidth

♦ Offices that are connected with low WAN bandwidth

♦ Offices that operate autonomously

♦ Offices that have local technical IT support personnel

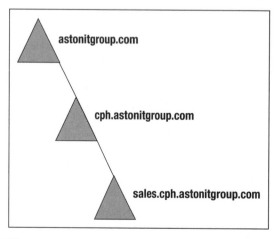

Figure 11.6
An example of how your Active Directory structure may look if you add three domains.

Arranging the Domain Trees in a Forest

A forest is a set of one or more domain trees that don't form a contiguous namespace. In other words, each domain tree in a forest has its own unique namespace, so you can accommodate distinct DNS names. For example, you might have subsidiaries that each require a separate namespace (see Figure 11.7).

Because the number of domain trees should be kept to a minimum, you should use a forest only when you positively can't operate within the confines of a single domain tree. The following are some good reasons for having a forest:

♦ Your company acquires or merges with another company.

♦ Your company has subsidiaries that require separate namespaces.

♦ Your company needs tight integration with suppliers, customers, and other parties. (Please note that this very requirement in some cases will lead to establishing two separate forests.)

You should refrain from building a forest for political reasons or to reflect your company's organization of divisions and departments.

Typically, a forest should be used only for conglomerates, for organizations with highly autonomous suborganizations, or for organizations that are deeply involved in joint ventures and partnerships. Also, a forest sometimes provides the easiest upgrade path from a complicated NT Server 4 domain structure.

Creating Additional Forests

You should create additional forests only for organizations that your company works with in a business partnership or for other limited "trust" situations.

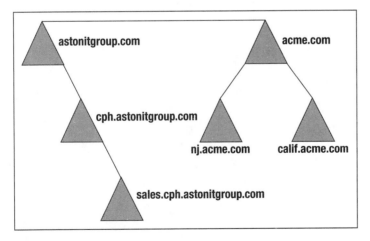

Figure 11.7
An example of how your Active Directory structure may look as you add an additional domain tree to the forest.

> **Note**
>
> *You might also want to employ separate forests in order to prevent changes in the configuration and schema naming contexts from propagating through the enterprise. For this very reason, your test lab should always be set up as a different forest from the production environment.*

For example, if your company conducts business with partners or with joint venture organizations and gives them access to your namespace, you may want to operate with several forests in your namespace. This enables you to tailor carefully the access rights for these entities. You need to set up an explicit one-way trust relationships between the domains involved from each forest.

You might also want to note that these explicit one-way trusts supported by Active Directory enable domains that are members of another Active Directory forest as well as old Windows NT Server 3.51 or 4 domains to gain access to a particular Active Directory domain. The one-way trust relationship limits the scope of authenticated access to the member domain that is explicitly trusted, because one-way trusts are not transitive.

Defining the Domain Namespace

Be careful when you define the naming scheme for the domains in the forest. As a good benchmark, check each name that you choose against this short list:

- The name is easily recognizable and meaningful to your organization.
- Appointed individuals within your organization can agree on the name.
- The name will remain static.
- Your legal department has approved the name.

Choosing a name for your domain namespace might appear to be an easy task at face value, but this often proves to be one of the more political and iterative tasks encountered during the course of your Active Directory design phase.

The naming convention for domains and top-level OUs basically should be treated the same, because this allows an OU to be promoted to a domain with as little user impact as possible and vice versa. The need to be very careful about naming is especially true for domains. Because of the lack of support for domain renaming in the current version of Windows 2000 Server, you need a naming scheme for the domains that is unlikely to change, no matter how your organization may evolve in the coming years.

A good namespace design should be capable of withstanding company reorganizations without the need to restructure the domain hierarchy. So, by all means, you should try to avoid naming your domains for divisions, departments, buildings, floors, or groups. The life of a domain is usually three to seven years, whereas divisions, departments, and groups could be renamed and reorganized many times in that time frame.

Highly Decentralized Organizations Could Call for Multiple Forests

Even though it could prove to be an exception to the rule of never implementing more than a single forest inside each enterprise, you should know about one case that will almost surely call for implementing multiple forests inside a single enterprise. This seldom-occurring situation is found inside decentralized enterprises in which the different constituents won't accept any trust in people outside their own organization.

Because of Active Directory's need for the Enterprise Admins and Schema Admins Groups (see also Chapter 9), you won't be able to get away with implementing a single forest in this particular case. However, you should understand that the multiple forest case represents a dramatic break with the whole directory services concept and so will prove to have some rather dramatic consequences to the overall functionality of the IT environment (for example, you won't be able to make do with a single Exchange 2000 Server Organization when you have multiple forests; you need one Organization for each forest). So even though the IT people might not want to put any trust in other parties from the outset, it will most certainly prove a worthy investment to put a lot of effort into considering whether a looming multiple forest situation can be avoided in any way.

The most commonly occurring "workaround" on the trust problem is implementing a placeholder domain, which nobody has access to for day-to-day routines. This also effectively means that the Enterprise Admins and Schema Admins Groups will be secured.

> **Note**
>
> *Even when Windows 2000 Server eventually does include support for domain renaming, your main objective for domain naming will still be to create domains whose names don't change. Changes in the overall domain architecture, such as domain collapses and re-creation, pose an arduous and potentially IT-intensive support proposition, regardless of the tools that you have at your disposal.*

When you define the naming scheme, always remember to specify whether the names are to be put in uppercase or lowercase (it can be quite confusing to look at different capitalization schemes). Remember, too, that long names usually cause a lot of grief to the people who use the Active Directory structure regularly.

The following subsections provide a quick rundown on the underlying reasoning that you should employ when defining the namespace, whether you have a single-domain structure or a forest consisting of several domain trees.

The Root

The first domain created in the forest hierarchy represents the whole organization and is known as the *forest root domain*. If you have several domain trees in your forest, you will also have several domain tree root domains (which usually are referred to simply as root domains). Thus, the first domain created will become the forest root domain as well as being the root domain of the first domain tree.

The name that you choose for all root domains should be easily recognizable and related to your company's registered Internet name. Only one (relatively short) DNS name should be used. Choosing a root domain name in this manner reduces the costs associated with maintaining DNS names and provides consistency for user logon names and (optionally) the company's corporate Internet email names. Also, remember to choose a name that can't easily be made obsolete by organizational restructuring, because the current version of Windows 2000 Server doesn't support renaming of domains.

The First Layer

The first layer of domains (or OUs), which is branched off the root domain, should be highly stable and not susceptible to change. If additional domains (or OUs) are needed, they should be created as child domains under one of the existing first-layer entities. The naming for the first layer of domains (or OUs) under the root domain should be very stable. Microsoft recommends using a naming scheme in which the first layer is represented by continental and geopolitical boundaries (that is, continents or countries), because those names are unlikely to change unless you're dealing with politically unstable regions.

If your company is operating in many countries, you should use a naming convention that is at least three characters long (as shown in Table 11.1), so that the names don't conflict with the ISO 3166 two-character country codes that Microsoft recommends using to name second-layer domains or OUs.

If your company operates in only a few countries, you should consider using the ISO 3166 two-character country codes listed in Table 7.3. Even if your company is operating in a single country, you might want to stick to the applicable ISO 3166 two-character country code for the first layer, unless you are extremely confident that the company won't open offices in other countries.

Table 11.1   An example of how first-layer domains could be expressed in a multinational organization.

Domain	Definition
Corpit	Company IT Headquarters
Noamer	United States of America and Canada
Soamer	Mexico, Central America, and South America
Nopac	Hong Kong and locales north of Hong Kong (Hong Kong, China, Korea, and Taiwan)
Sopac	Locales south of Hong Kong, including the Indian subcontinent, reaching through (but not including) Afghanistan
Europe	All locales on the European continent, including the U.K.
Meast	Israel, Saudi Arabia, Turkey, and United Arab Emirates
Africa	Africa
Partners	Business partners
Jvt	Joint ventures

The Second Layer

The second layer of domains (or OUs), which is branched off the first-layer domains or (OUs), should also be relatively stable by design. Microsoft recommends using countries for the naming of the second-layer domains (or OUs). If you already used countries as the naming scheme for the first layer, you should consider counties or cities for the naming scheme of the second layer.

When using countries for the naming scheme, you should use the ISO 3166 two-character country codes (see Table 7.3). The two-character ISO 3166 standard can be used for all locations. If your company is pervasive in a certain country (typically, the company's country of origin), you might very well want to make an exception to the rule of using countries as the naming scheme for every entity on the second layer. In this situation, you would substitute a number of locations inside that country for the specific country. Obviously, the locations don't have an ISO country code, so you should instead follow the most common abbreviation system used for locations in that country (which usually is the postal codes or airport codes).

So, for example, if you are working for a company based in the United States, you might choose to place your U.S. locations on an equal level with the other countries on the second layer. In that case, you should use the two-letter U.S. postal codes (see Table 11.2).

Note

One of several exceptions that you might encounter to the two-letter U.S. postal codes naming convention is California, whose two-character postal code (CA) conflicts with Canada's ISO code; therefore, the elongated state abbreviation calif or something of that sort should be used instead. Some of the other exceptions include DE, which is used for Delaware as well as for Germany; AL, which is used for Alabama as well as for Albania; and MN, which is used for both Minnesota and Mongolia.

Table 11.2   The two-letter U.S. postal codes are suitable for naming locations inside the U.S.

Postal Code	State
AL	Alabama
AK	Alaska
AS	American Samoa
AZ	Arizona
AR	Arkansas
CA	California
CZ	Canal Zone
CO	Colorado
CT	Connecticut
DE	Delaware
DC	District of Columbia
FL	Florida
GA	Georgia

(continued)

Table 11.2   **The two-letter U.S. postal codes are suitable for naming locations inside the U.S.** *(continued)*.

Postal Code	State
GU	Guam
HI	Hawaii
ID	Idaho
IL	Illinois
IN	Indiana
IA	Iowa
KS	Kansas
KY	Kentucky
LA	Louisiana
ME	Maine
MD	Maryland
MA	Massachusetts
MI	Michigan
MN	Minnesota
MS	Mississippi
MO	Missouri
MT	Montana
NE	Nebraska
NV	Nevada
NH	New Hampshire
NJ	New Jersey
NM	New Mexico
NY	New York
NC	North Carolina
ND	North Dakota
OH	Ohio
OK	Oklahoma
OR	Oregon
PA	Pennsylvania
PR	Puerto Rico
RI	Rhode Island
SC	South Carolina
SD	South Dakota
TN	Tennessee
TX	Texas
UT	Utah
VT	Vermont
VA	Virginia
VI	Virgin Islands
WA	Washington
WV	West Virginia
WI	Wisconsin
WY	Wyoming

If you'll be using cities, the only globally unique naming convention that is up for grabs is the one used by the airport authorities. However, this might pose a problem, if your company has many locations a long way from the various airports of the world.

Third Layer and On

Often, a company finds that it wants to organize its resources and users beyond the two layers discussed up to now, in order to reflect its business organization. You should be keenly aware that OUs, per definition, always are the most appropriate vehicle for achieving that, because administering changes within and between OUs is relatively simple, and you can extend the level of granularity as far as necessary by extending the OU hierarchy. Also, much of the administration of OUs can be delegated without risk of any unwanted side effects.

Because creating OUs entails no replication or hardware costs, you might even choose to allow a wide range of people in the organization access to creating OUs. Consequently, I've already heard people recommend that the central IT organization should directly support and define only the first level of the business model's organizational OUs. The reasoning behind this recommendation is that, just as having a central IT organization directly support all the organizational needs of various departments is impractical, having the central IT organization administer all the OUs that a business-driven organization may require is impractical, too. However, I suggest that the IT department keep a tight grip on every part of the OU layers, because of the need for consistency and administrative ease (remember, OUs can be used for assigning group policies and administrative delegation). You can delve much deeper into the subject of OU hierarchies in Chapter 8.

A Domain Design Example

To place everything into perspective, this section shows some examples of the design options for the fictitious major multinational company "Telltale," which has three major locations (London, Tokyo, and New York) and four business units that are distributed among the three locations. In an Active Directory setting, Telltale could be implemented as a single domain, a domain tree, and a forest, respectively. This section analyzes each of these options and provides a short table of the pros and cons of each particular domain structure, so that management can decide which domain option to choose—which isn't a trivial decision.

Single-Domain Solution

For the single-domain solution (see Figure 11.8), the first layer of OUs is based on the business units, because this is the structure that makes the most sense to users at Telltale. However, you might find a geographic structure to be a better fit to the organizational needs in case the company frequently undergoes reorganizations. You should note that a geographic structure really wouldn't make sense for any other reasons, because you still have all the domain replication occurring across the WAN between the three locations. The pros and cons of using the single-domain solution shown in Figure 11.8 are listed in Table 11.3.

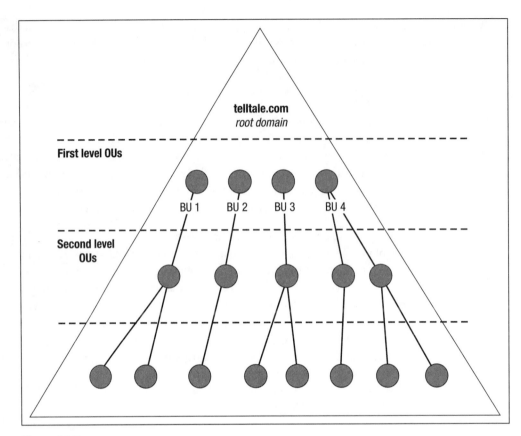

Figure 11.8
Telltale structured as a single domain.

Table 11.3 The pros and cons of using a single domain.

Pros	Cons
Uses organizational domains instead of geography.	If you later need to implement multiple domains, multiple DCs will be needed at the sites.
Allows administration of any OU level.	Reorganization issues may harshly affect the first OU layer in the domain.
	High bandwidth usage for replication.

Domain Tree Solution

In the *domain tree solution* (see Figure 11.9, for example), the first layer of domains is based on the geographical properties, because this reduces the bandwidth usage. (Please note that you might as well have chosen to use the ISO 3166 two-character country codes instead of the non-standard city abbreviations used in this example.) Table 11.4 sets forth the pros and cons of implementing a domain tree solution.

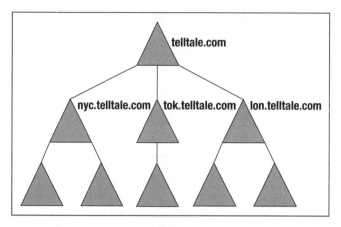

Figure 11.9
Telltale structured as a domain tree.

Table 11.4   The pros and cons of employing a domain tree solution.

Pros	Cons
Highly scalable design.	Organization prefers business units.
Regional site administration is easily achieved.	Once committed, difficult to change course.
Medium bandwidth usage.	Several DCs at each location.
	Eliminates the risk of a single point of failure.

Forest Solution

When you implement the forest solution (see Figure 11.10, for example), the domain trees are based on the business units, because the need to use business unit-based domain trees is the only valid reason for using the forest solution in this scenario.

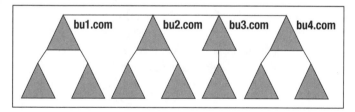

Figure 11.10
Telltale structured as a forest.

Note

Remember that you should only implement a forest if you're dealing with a discontiguous namespace.

Table 11.5 lists the pros and cons to implementing the forest solution at Telltale.

Table 11.5   The pros and cons of implementing a forest solution.

Pros	Cons
Uses organizational domains instead of geography.	Administrative headache (no straightforward option for regional administration).
Supports the business units' desire for independence.	A high level of bandwidth usage because the business units are present in all three geographical locations.
Eliminates the risk of a single point of failure.	A very high number of DCs at each location.
	Potential trouble with forest-wide searches (i.e., if a given attribute isn't replicated to the GC, all domains won't get searched).
	Reorganization issues across business units will usually prove harsh to the forest structure.
	A high potential for "computing anarchy" inside each domain tree.

Best Practices

The best practices for designing your domain structure are the following: KISS (Keep It Simple, Stupid). There are really two reasons for that, the first being that the simplest solution almost always will be the easiest to implement and manage. And the other reason is that the future might have something in store for you that you didn't anticipate; and if something that you haven't prepared for does happen, it may very well bring mayhem to the domain structure. For a detailed analysis of some key points in domain structure design, consult Table 11.6.

The Final Cut

A vital part of planning for Active Directory entails deciding on the number, scope, and relationship among your domains, domain tree(s), and forest(s). These decisions have a major impact on replication traffic, security, administration, usability, extensibility, and—ultimately—system responsiveness. As you have seen, your Active Directory installation can range from a very simple (and highly recommended) single domain tree holding a single domain to complicated, multiple forests, each with many domain trees.

To make the hard decisions on what to do in a specific organization, you should have a clear and deep understanding of the differences and similarities between domains, domain trees, and forests. The following list summarizes the main points regarding the domain concept:

♦ The core unit of logical structure in Active Directory

♦ A logical grouping of objects

♦ A unit of partitioning (a boundary for replication and a scope for complete administration)

♦ A unit of authentication

Table 11.6   Key tasks in domain structure design.

Task	Points to Consider
Gather the requirements for the domain structure.	You should primarily use the soft (organizational diagram, work delegation, and so on) and hard (bandwidth, WAN connectivity, and more) information on the organization, when following the scheme outlined in Chapter 6.
Determine the name of the first Active Directory domain.	This name will be used to refer to the domain, domain tree, and the reference to the forest, so you'd better make it good!
Add domains to the domain tree.	Several reasons exist to expand the domain tree with new domains. However, your overriding goal is to use as few domains as absolutely possible, because this makes your domain structure easier and cheaper to plan, build, run, and ultimately migrate.
Add domain trees to the forest.	If you have to use a discontiguous namespace, you are forced to implement several domain trees inside your forest. Beware: This increases hardware and administration costs and makes forest-wide searches harder. A query based on an attribute that is indexed in the GC can search the entire set of domains in the forest, whereas a search based on an attribute that isn't included in the GC searches only the domain tree from which the user or application is performing the search.
Question the reason for each domain.	Whenever you want to create a new domain, first ask yourself whether you can meet the needs by using the existing domain(s).
Create more than one forest.	If you need to isolate one or more domains because of security reasons (which represents just about the only valid reason for creating more than one forest), you need additional forests in which the domains are connected via explicit one-way trusts. But, again, try to avoid that scenario by finding some suitable alternative whereby the resources and users can be stored in the existing domain(s).
Keep naming standard consistent and intuitive.	Settle on a naming standard that is concise, easy to relate to the company, highly stable, and consistent. You should always try to use a location-based and standardized naming scheme, because this will prove to be the best way to uphold a stable and consistent naming scheme and avoid naming clashes. Ultimately, you should be able to use a common naming scheme across all domains at each layer (and use the same scheme for other domain trees); but, in some instances, you might have to settle for less.

♦ A unit of domain-level policy (a boundary for security)

♦ Manifested by DCs

The new domain tree and forest concepts can be summarized as follows:

♦ *Domain Tree*—One or more domains with contiguous names that share a common schema, GCs, and site and service configuration.

♦ *Forest*—One or more domain trees, in which all domain trees share a common schema, GCs, and site and service configuration.

Remember that two domains within a domain tree and two domains in different domain trees in a forest have the same relationship. Both have resources stored in the same GC, and users from each domain can access resources in the other. The primary difference lies in their DNS name structure and search capabilities. As a final note, when comparing domain trees to forests, consider the facts put forward in Table 11.7.

With that said, you should almost be ready to go into the real world and start designing for Active Directory. However, be aware that the planning of multiple domains often requires that you take into account the effects of trusts, DCs, and GCs—the subject of the next chapter.

Table 11.7 Domain tree versus forest.

Domain Tree	Forest
Easier to browse and understand, because trusts follow the tree hierarchy.	More complicated, due to the nonintuitive trust hierarchy, but not very much slower than a domain tree in practice.
Ideal for companies that are centrally controlled and only have one DNS root.	Ideal for companies with truly independent units that use separate DNS roots.
A deep search from the root domain flows down to all the domains in the domain tree by following a chain of subordinate references.	A deep search is restricted to the domain tree in which the search is initiated. However, if the search attribute(s) are available in the GC, you still get results that encompass the whole forest.

Chapter 12
Planning the Physical Structures

In Active Directory, the logical structures (how the network objects are represented to users and administrators) have been separated from the physical structures (how servers behave on the LAN and WAN). This is a great improvement over Windows NT Server 4, in which the design of the domain structure is the only way of accounting for the underlying properties of the network.

The new approach in Active Directory finally, and effectively, enables administrators to model the logical directory structures based on the organization's needs and then take the necessary steps to produce the performance levels required on the underlying physical properties—in terms of logon time, bandwidth utilization, and so on.

The chapters subsequent to Chapter 6 have dealt exclusively with designing the logical structures. So now, you ought to be ready to delve into the intricacies of modeling the physical structure of Active Directory, which is done through the domain controller (DC), Global Catalog (GC), and site concepts. In addition to these three obvious components that need to be considered when planning your physical structure, you also need to ponder how replication is going to be carried out.

Although Microsoft finally has segregated the logical and physical structures, you shouldn't let that trick you into believing that you are able to design your logical structures in Active Directory without any regard to the physical aspects. You may be able to get by with such an approach in a few situations, but the much more probable situation is one in which the physical properties of the current infrastructure place some weighty restraints on the modeling of the logical namespace. Thus, you must deal with the likely prospect of having to either change the physical properties or redesign the logical structure to accommodate the physical limitations of the current infrastructure. So, in most cases, you do still need a solid understanding of the physical structures in Active Directory to be able to do a complete Active Directory design.

Introducing DCs, GCs, and Sites

The three essential concepts governing the physical properties of Active Directory—DCs, GCs, and sites—are somewhat intertwined, so this chapter begins with a high-level introduction to each of them. Please study this introduction carefully, because it will prove highly beneficial to your overall understanding of both the physical behavior of Active Directory and how that behavior is affected by each of the three major concepts—observed in isolation and as part of the whole physical structure.

The Domain Controller

Each Active Directory domain has one or more servers that function as domain controllers (DCs). Each DC stores a complete copy of the Active Directory domain—the domain naming context, as well as the two other naming contexts (or partitions, if you like) that form the Active Directory—and is involved in managing changes and updates to the directory.

The Active Directory information stored on a DC is, in turn, used by clients both to obtain authentication and to access the data stored in the Active Directory domain. So, if you want fast logon performance, you should situate a DC close to your computers.

When a person performs an action that causes an update to the Active Directory, the change must be copied—or *replicated*—to the other DCs. Thus, a DC is the physical target for replication of Active Directory data to and from the other DCs in the domain. Consequently, a steady flow of replication traffic occurs wherever a DC is situated, and you must take this into account when planning the physical network layout.

Essentially, everything involved in Active Directory's DC setup resembles a Windows NT Server 4 setup; thus, any base knowledge that you have regarding the primary domain controller (PDC)/backup domain controller (BDC) concepts in NT Server 4 will prove relevant in a Windows 2000 Server setting. However, it's only the DC fundamentals that stay the same: The details are very different from that of Windows NT Server 4 due to Active Directory being a directory service and using a multi-master replication scheme.

The use of a multi-master scheme is a rather large change from NT Server's single-master scheme. In a single-master scheme, changes must be made only to the PDC, which then replicates the updated information to all other servers in the domain. However, if the PDC stops working, the entire network grinds to a halt with regard to doing any updates to the directory database (including password changes). In the multi-master scheme, replication continues even if any single server stops working, which has the benefit of providing the users as well as the administrators with a much greater level of fault tolerance with regard to doing directory updates.

The Global Catalog

The Global Catalog (GC) has no parallel whatsoever in the Windows NT Server 4 environment. The GC has been introduced into the Active Directory setting to ensure fast, forest-wide search performance. The GC also caters to some of the new features introduced with Windows 2000 Server and Active Directory, which means that the GC is used during a user login.

Warning

The GC is just as important to being able to log on as the DC is. In other words, Active Directory presents you with two single points of failure with regard to user logins: the DC, as well as the GC. In comparison, only a DC was needed to be able to log on in a Windows NT Server 4 domain.

As you know by now, the Distinguished Name (DN) of an object includes enough information to locate a replica of the partition that holds the object. Often, however, the user or application knows neither the DN of the target object nor which partition might contain the object. The GC enables users and applications to find objects in an Active Directory forest simply by providing one or more attributes of the target object—and enables them to find the objects much faster than is possible by traversing the domain tree.

To accomplish this feat, the GC contains a partial replica of every domain in the forest in addition to a copy of the schema and configuration naming contexts used in the forest (due to the fact that you can only add the GC functionality to DCs). This means that the GC basically holds a replica of every object available in the forest, but with only a small number of their attributes.

Note

For simplicity's sake, you might want to think of GCs as DCs that contain partial replicas of information from all domains in the forest. However, remember that the replica stored on a GC is a read-only copy of some of the information from each Active Directory domain in the forest.

The attributes that the GC contains are those most frequently used in search operations (such as first and last names, login names, and so on) and those required to locate a full replica of the object (the DN and the GUID). With these strategic attributes contained in the GC, a user can quickly find an object of interest even if the user doesn't know in which Active Directory domain the object is held and even if the object is not part of the same contiguous namespace as the user.

The GC is built by the Active Directory replication system, and the GC replication topology is generated automatically. The attributes being replicated into each GC include a base set defined by Microsoft. Administrators can specify additional attributes that need to be included in the GC to meet the needs of their installation.

The Site

Briefly stated, a *site* is a location on the network specified by one or more TCP/IP subnets (see Figure 12.1). To be more exact, a site is one or more well connected TCP/IP subnets, where "well-connected" means network connectivity is highly reliable and reasonably fast. In this context, "reasonably fast" means that the networking infrastructure is fast enough to transmit within a reasonable timeframe the replication payload needed inside that site.

Defining a site as a set of TCP/IP subnets enables administrators to quickly and easily set up the Active Directory access and the Active Directory replication topology to take advantage of the physical network infrastructure. Also, a Windows 2000 computer acting as a client to the domain uses the site information to locate a nearby Active Directory DC and a GC—connectivity-wise. When users log in, their workstations will always have a preference for an Active Directory DC and a GC that are located in the same site. Because computers in the same site are close to each other, in network terms, communication between these computers

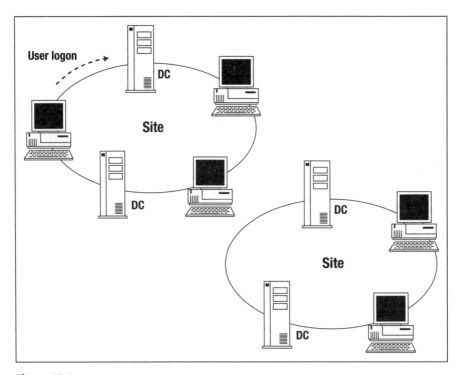

Figure 12.1
An example of two sites.

Replication: Find and Implement the Right Tradeoff

Ideally, users and services must be able to access directory information at any time from any computer on the network. To make this possible, information that is added or changed at one DC must be transferred to all other DCs.

Using a hypothetical scenario, this means that if a user changes her mail address and telephone number attributes in the New York office, the new information should be available for anyone allowed to view it in the London office as soon as possible to avoid errors. And even more important: If the password is changed, it should be reflected throughout the enterprise to avoid any lockouts, if the user moves to another location.

Realistically, administrators must always strive to optimize network performance, and constant directory replication is far from being the optimum solution seen from the performance perspective, because such directory updates would tend to monopolize computing and network resources. Active Directory enables you to implement a replication scheme that supports your decisions on how to balance these competing interests. However, due to the importance of avoiding lockout situations, Active Directory will always perform an immediate replication of a password change to a particular DC in the domain; that DC is used as a tiebreaker in case of a user trying to log on using another password than currently registered at the local DC.

should prove to be reliable, fast, and efficient. Determining the local site at login time is easy, because the user's workstation already knows which TCP/IP subnet it is on, and subnets translate directly to Active Directory sites. Note that the domain structure and site structure are separate and flexible. Thus, a single domain can span several geographical sites, and a single site can include computers belonging to multiple domains.

Replication in Depth

Replication traffic likely is the single biggest contributor to bandwidth usage in an organization's Active Directory infrastructure (excluding actual use of the network services made available to users). Therefore, delving deep into the "ugly" details of replication will prove very useful and necessary.

Active Directory is built on multi-master replication, which means that no single DC is the master; instead, all DCs within a domain are equivalent (or *peers*, if you prefer). Multi-master replication provides several advantages:

- ♦ No single point of failure exists in the DC structure (if a failure occurs, no master DC must be replaced for directory updates to resume).

- ♦ All DCs are capable of making changes to the domain, which makes updating the domain information a much faster (and somewhat less bandwidth-intensive) proposition. Also, this decentralization of information updating can potentially alleviate some of the pain of sizing the bandwidth for an organization's HQ.

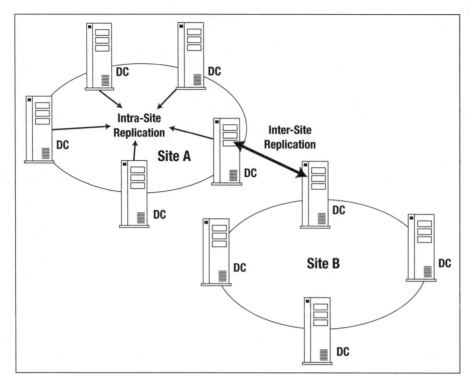

Figure 12.2
The two types of replication: intra-site and inter-site.

Two types of replication are available in Active Directory (see Figure 12.2):

♦ *Intra-site replication*—Occurs between DCs within the same site.

♦ *Inter-site replication*—Occurs between DCs in different sites.

When you plan a site structure, you must know the differences between these two types of replication—from both the administrative and network traffic perspectives.

Intra-Site Replication

Replication of directory information within a site is done frequently and automatically. Active Directory automatically generates the replication topology that allows it to exchange directory information. Active Directory will establish a topology that provides at least two network connections to every DC, so that if one connection becomes unavailable, directory information can still reach all online DCs. Active Directory does this by generating a ring topology for replication among the DCs within the particular site.

Active Directory automatically evaluates and adjusts the replication topology to meet the changing state of the network. For example, when a DC is added or removed from a site, the replication topology is adjusted to incorporate this new change efficiently. Directory replication within a site is always performed via the remote procedure call (RPC) protocol.

Replication vs. Synchronization

You really should know the difference between replication and synchronization when venturing into the world of directory services. *Directory replication* is the process that occurs directly between peers (such as DCs in an Active Directory setting) when changes occur to the directory. Generally, replication requires a high degree of trust and homogeneity between systems.

Directory synchronization is the process that occurs between different directories (such as Active Directory and NDS) exchanging information. An agent that acts as a buffer between the two parties performs the necessary mappings that make the parties understand each other.

Because directory synchronization is much harder to set up, administer, and maintain than directory replication, a lot of research and development have been invested recently toward finding ways to provide replication instead of synchronization between different vendors' systems. A breakthrough in this area likely will occur through the IETF LDAP working group.

But for now, you have to make do with directory synchronization, using the so-called MS DirSync technology or using Microsoft Metadirectory Services (MMS). MS DirSync is put to use by Active Directory Connector (ADC) (included in Windows 2000 Server), which provides directory synchronization between the Exchange Server directory and Active Directory. You can find more information on the current and future plans for DirSync and MMS in Chapter 23. Also, the features found in ADC and MMS are discussed in depth in Chapters 15 and 16, respectively.

Note

You can override the automatically generated replication topology, if necessary, but this is strongly discouraged by Microsoft because it can result in significant replication problems and does work to add a lot of administrative overhead. So, you should ponder to configure the intra-site replication topology manually only if you have a highly compelling reason for doing so.

Inter-Site Replication

An administrator will always need to set up inter-site replication more or less manually. This involves the following decisions:

- Which sites (and servers) should be linked to one another?

- At what intervals should replications be performed and at which times of the days in the week?

- What cost should be assigned to each replication connection defined, so that Active Directory can choose the cheapest routes available in each replication cycle?

The only time that Active Directory will automatically do some of the work for you with regard to generating links between sites is when you install a DC in a site with other DCs (prompting the DC to be added automatically to the intra-site replication topology), and then move the DC to another site. When you do this, a link is automatically established between the site in which the DC was created and the site to which it has been moved. However, although a DC that is moved to a new site is automatically connected to an

---

Pull vs. Push Replication

Active Directory builds on pull replication. In pull replication a destination replica requests information from a source replica. The request specifies the information that the destination needs. When the destination receives information from the source, it applies that information (bringing itself more up-to-date).

Push replication is the alternative to pull replication. In push replication, a source sends information to a destination unsolicited, hoping to bring the destination more up-to-date. But that's a very problematic scheme, because it's difficult for the source to know what information the destination needs.

---

existing DC, only one link is created, at most. So, in most cases, you don't want to leave this automatically defined site link alone.

In all but the most special cases, you would want to customize the connections between sites, create more links to enable connections between specific sites, and specify how and when directory information should be replicated. Also, you might want to take advantage of the fact that you have two different replication protocols to choose from—RPC and SMTP—with regard to inter-site replication.

How Replication Is Done

Although users may not realize it, due to multi-master replication, when they apply changes, they update a single instance of the Active Directory database. After a copy of the directory database is modified at a DC, all other DCs must be notified of the changes so that they can update their directory database correspondingly. Therefore, although the DCs need the latest directory information, to be efficient, they must limit their updates to only those times when new or changed directory information exists. Indiscriminately exchanging directory information with other servers can quickly turn out to be an overwhelming task to many networks. That's why Microsoft has invested much time and effort in designing Active Directory to optimize the replication process. Active Directory strives to ensure that the most up-to-date changes are distributed as efficiently as possible, by doing the following:

♦ Identifying changes to replicate

♦ Preventing unnecessary replication

♦ Resolving conflicting changes

Note that, regardless of which type of replication (intra-site or inter-site), or replication connector used, the replication scheme is exactly the same. Furthermore, you aren't allowed to modify any of the change-control and conflict-resolution mechanisms.

Identifying Changes to Replicate: Update Propagation

DCs keep track of how many changes they have made to their copy of the directory, as well as how many changes they have received from every other DC to which they are linked. For example, if the DC in site A discovers that it doesn't have all the changes from the DC in site B, the DC in site A can request the new changes—and only the new changes—from the DC in site B. This system greatly simplifies the task of updating a server that, for example, has been disconnected from the network, because identifying which directory information has changed—and thus needs to be replicated—is quite straightforward.

Tip

You should take care to note that each replication is always one-way—that is, a DC request changes from another DC. It's very important that you understand this detail when you try to fast track the usual replication speed by doing them manually. Otherwise, you might be mightily surprised by the fact that some parts of the replications won't be delivered after you've forced the replication between multiple DCs.

Some directory services use timestamps to detect and propagate changes. In these systems, keeping the clocks on all directory servers synchronized is very important, but time synchronization in a large networked (and possibly geographically wide-spread) environment is quite difficult. Even with very good network time synchronization, the time at an individual directory server may still be incorrectly set, which can lead to that directory server losing changes.

Microsoft has addressed this problem quite well by using a numerical sequence called *Update Sequence Numbers (USNs)* to track changes, instead of using timestamps. Correspondingly, with USNs, a precise synchronization of clocks among all the DCs in the forest is less vital, because time isn't used as the primary means for update propagation. Actually, Active Directory uses timestamps only when settling who wins a replication collision, if the USNs don't provide the answer.

Warning

You should be aware that the Kerberos authentication used by Active Directory (see Chapter 14) is heavily reliant upon the correct time, because timestamps are an integral part of the Kerberos tickets that are issued whenever a user or resource is authenticated. As a consequence of that, you're still faced with a pressing need for keeping the clocks fairly well synchronized across the enterprise.

A USN is a 64-bit number maintained by each Active Directory DC (and thus has meaning only locally to that DC). Each object and property in the directory actually has two USNs—an object has USNcreated and USNchanged, and a property has USNchanged and OrgUSN.

When a client performs any kind of changes at an Active Directory DC, the property's USN is advanced and stored with the property written. This operation is performed *atomically*—incrementing and storage of the USN and the write of the property succeed or fail as a single unit of work.

Each DC maintains a table—called the *high-watermark vector*—that lists the highest USNs received from each of the DC's replication partners. Each DC then periodically notifies the other DCs in the domain that it has received changes and sends its current USN to them.

Each DC that receives this message checks its USN table for the last USN it has received from the sending DC. If changes have occurred that the DC hasn't received, it requests those changes to be sent, by requesting all changes with USNs greater than the current value stated in its high-watermark vector. This replication methodology is a very simple, yet highly efficient, approach that doesn't depend on the accuracy of timestamps.

The following three tables show some examples of what can occur in Active Directory's replication methodology. In Table 12.1, a new object is created on DC1, which has a USN of 5710 before this change. Consequently, the USN for both DC1 and the object's properties are changed to 5711. All values in italic are changed at the time of the write to DC1's directory.

Table 12.2 shows what occurs when property P2 in the existing object from Table 12.1 is modified on DC1, which has a USN of 5720 before the modification is committed. Again, the USN for both the DC and the object's properties are changed to 5721. All values in italic change at the time of the write to DC1's directory.

Table 12.3 shows what occurs when a new object is created through replication from DC2 to DC1, whereby the USN before replication is 5710 for DC1 and 3291 for DC2. Again, the USN for both the DC and the object's properties are changed to 5711. However, apart from that change, only the timestamp is changed compared to the "original" object coming from DC2. All values in italic change at the time of the write to DC1's directory.

Table 12.1 A new object is created on DC1.
For the Object: USNcreated=5711 and USNchanged=5711

Property	Value	USN	OrgUSN	Version No.	Timestamp	Org. GUID
P1	Value1	5711	5711	1	Time of write	DC1 GUID
P2	Value2	5711	5711	1	Time of write	DC1 GUID
P3	Value3	5711	5711	1	Time of write	DC1 GUID

Table 12.2 Property P2 is modified on DC1.
For the Object: USNcreated=5711 and USNchanged=5721

Property	Value	USN	OrgUSN	Version No.	Timestamp	Org. GUID
P1	Value1	5711	5711	1	Time of write	DC1 GUID
P2	Value2	5721	5721	2	Time of write	DC1 GUID
P3	Value3	5711	5711	1	Time of write	DC1 GUID

Table 12.3 The result of a new object's creation via replication from DC2 to DC1.
For the Object: USNcreated=5711 and USNchanged=5711

Property	Value	USN	OrgUSN	Version No.	Timestamp	Org. GUID
P1	Value1	5711	3291	1	Time of write	DC2 GUID
P2	Value2	5711	3291	1	Time of write	DC2 GUID
P3	Value3	5711	3291	1	Time of write	DC2 GUID

Because the USN stored in the high-watermark vector is updated atomically for each update received, recovery after a failure is also simple. To restart replication, a DC simply asks its partners for the changes that have USNs greater than the last valid entry in its high-watermark vector. Because the high-watermark vector is updated atomically as the changes are applied, an interrupted replication cycle always resumes exactly where it left off, with no loss or duplication of updates. You can find an example of the update propagation scheme "in action" in Figures 12.3 and 12.4.

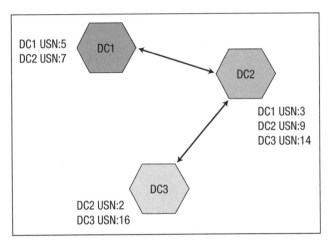

Figure 12.3
A sample high-watermark vector prior to contacting the DC's replication partners.

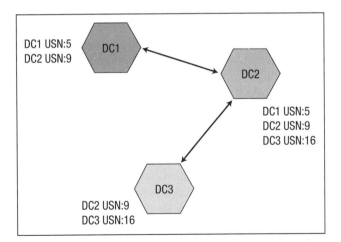

Figure 12.4
The same high-watermark vector after contacting the DC's replication partners (for DC2, at least twice). This is an imaginary example. With real life, DCs very seldom are totally in sync.

Preventing Unnecessary Replication: Propagation Dampening

Active Directory replicates data through the intra-site and inter-site replication connections specified in the directory. Active Directory's replication system allows *loops* in the replication topology (and thus makes it possible to define virtually unlimited redundant replication connections). Using loops enables administrators to configure a replication topology with multiple paths among the servers, to secure the level of performance and fault tolerance sought.

However, allowing loops also requires Active Directory to ensure that a single change is not replicated multiple times to the same DC as a result of traversing different replication paths. For example, after the DC at site A applies a change received from the DC at site B, the DC at site A must indicate that its new information shouldn't be replicated back to the source of the change—the DC at site B. If a cycle of replication such as this isn't prevented, theoretically, it could continue indefinitely, ultimately bringing your network to a halt.

Active Directory's replication system includes a *propagation-dampening* scheme that prevents changes from propagating endlessly, and eliminates redundant transmission of changes to replicas that are already up-to-date. This propagation dampening is performed simply by tracking which attribute changed in the updated object and how many times the object has been changed directly (as opposed to indirectly via replication). The propagation-dampening scheme employs an up-to-date vector and originating writes to track this information.

An *up-to-date vector* for a specific DC consists of a list of USN pairs that states the highest USN for an originating write thus far received from each of the DCs in the domain that has performed any originating writes. While an *originating write* is a change that indicates a modification that has been made to the object at a given DC (as opposed to a modification that has occurred due to replication among DCs). Property writes caused by replication are not originating writes and don't advance the version number. For example, when a user updates his or her password, an originating write occurs and the Property Version Number is advanced. Replication writes of the changed password at other servers don't advance the USN in their up-to-date vector.

When a replication cycle begins, the requesting DC sends its up-to-date vector to the sending DC. The sending DC uses the up-to-date vector to filter changes sent to the requesting DC. If the highest USN for a given originating write is greater than or equal to the originating write USN for a particular update, the sending DC doesn't need to send the change; the requesting DC is already up to date with respect to the originating write.

Stated another way, when the DC at site B is notified that an object in the DC at site A has changed, it checks whether the change is a new originating write. If it isn't, no replication change is necessary for the DC at site B. A simple example of replication is shown in Figures 12.5 and 12.6. However, for a more realistic example, take a look at Figures 12.7 through 12.14. For the sake of not getting lost in the details, the example shows only the full vectors residing on DC2.

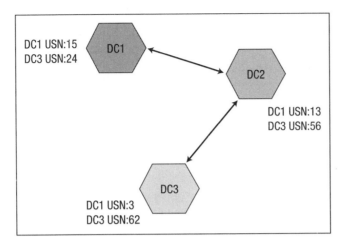

Figure 12.5
A sample up-to-date vector prior to replication. No originating writes have occurred on DC2.

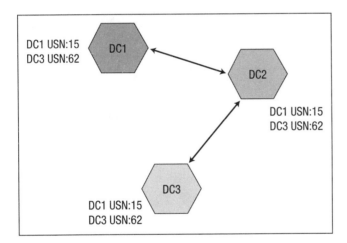

Figure 12.6
The same up-to-date vector replication between all the replication partners in the domain.

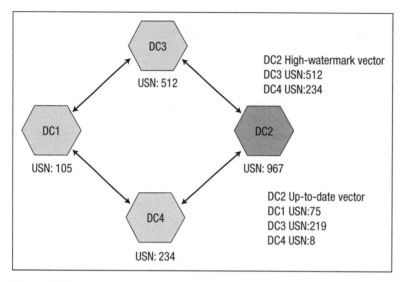

Figure 12.7
Initial situation on the four DCs that are part of the domain, showing the replication topology between the DCs and the fact that the DCs are synchronized across the board.

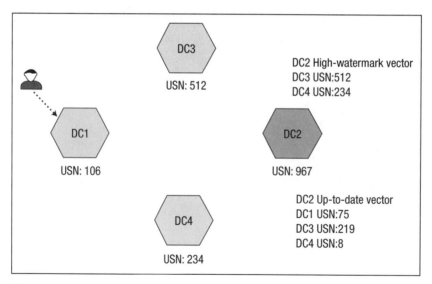

Figure 12.8
A user is added to DC1.

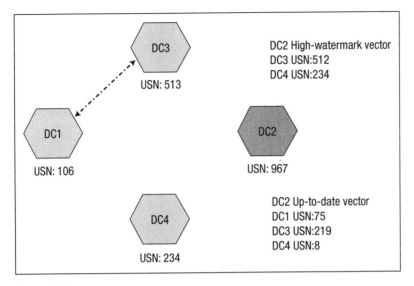

Figure 12.9
The user created at DC1 is replicated to DC3. Note that the handshaking going on between DC2 and DC1 is not shown here.

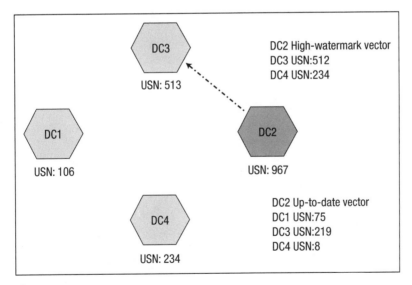

Figure 12.10
DC2 initiates replication with DC2 by sending some replication information that includes the up-to-date vector of DC2.

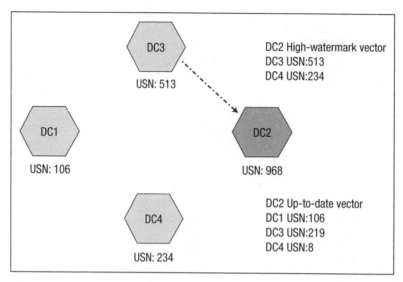

Figure 12.11

DC3 replicates the new user to DC2. Here, DC3 replies by sending its USN, the new user object, and its up-to-date vector, because it realizes—by comparing DC2's up-to-date vector with its own—that DC2 hasn't received the latest object added at DC1. Correspondingly, DC2 updates its DC1 entry in the up-to-date vector, the DC2 entry in the high-watermark vector, and its own USN.

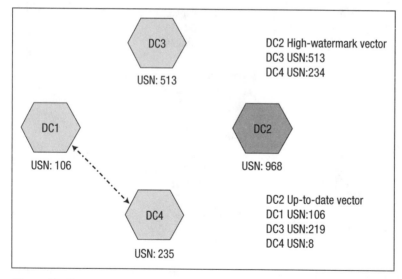

Figure 12.12

The user created at DC1 is replicated to DC4. Note that the handshaking going on between DC4 and DC1 is not shown here.

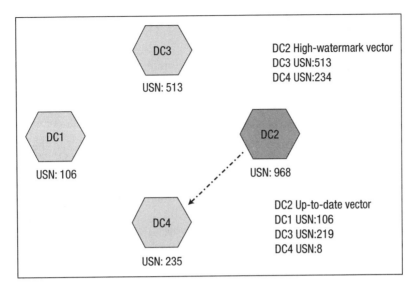

Figure 12.13
DC2 initiates replication with DC4 by sending some replication information that includes the up-to-date vector of DC2.

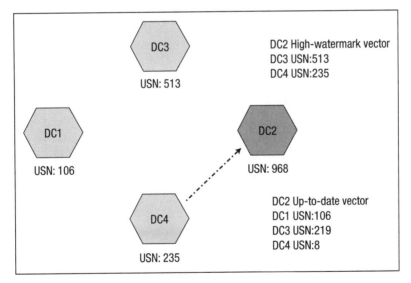

Figure 12.14
By comparing DC2's up-to-date vector with its own, DC4 has determined that DC2 is already up to date, so it sends only its own USN and its up-to-date vector. Correspondingly, DC2 updates its DC4 entry in the high-watermark vector.

Resolving Conflicting Changes: Collision Detection

Although rather unlikely, two or more different users can make changes to the exact same object property and have these changes applied at two different DCs before replication of either change is completed. When a property changes in a second (or third, fourth, and so on) replica before a change from the first replica has been fully propagated, a *replication collision* occurs.

Collisions are detected through the use of *Property Version Numbers (PVNs)*. Unlike USNs, which are server-specific values, the PVN is specific to the property on an Active Directory object. When a property is first written to an Active Directory object, the version number is initialized, and only originating writes (remember, it's a write to a property at the system initiating the change) advance the property's PVN. A collision is detected when a change is received via replication in which the PVN received is equal to the locally stored PVN, and the received and stored values of the property are different.

When a replication collision occurs, the DCs involved decide which of the attributes should be kept in the directory's database, based on the following order of priority:

1. *On the basis of the PVN.* Active Directory always chooses the attribute with the highest PVN (assuming that the attribute with the lowest PVN is obsolete). So, when the received PVN is lower than the locally stored PVN, the update is presumed stale and thus discarded. If the received PVN is higher than the locally stored PVN, the update is accepted. Of course, this might not always prove to be the correct solution. But at least it is a deterministic decision-making method.

2. *On the basis of the timestamp.* If the PVN of the property is the same and the values of the attribute differ, the DC uses the timestamp to decide which property is the "winner." So, when this situation occurs, the receiving system applies the update if it has a later timestamp. This, in fact, is the only situation in which time is used by Active Directory replication. Obviously, the clocks on all the DCs have to be synchronized for this solution to function as intended. And even when they are synchronized, the timestamp still isn't guaranteed to provide the correct solution. Nevertheless, it is a sensible and deterministic method with which to solve a replication collision.

3. *On the basis of the buffer size.* In the extremely unlikely instance that the PVN and the timestamps are identical, the DC performs a binary memory-copying operation and compares the buffer sizes. The biggest buffer size is the winner. If two buffers generate the same result, the attributes are completely identical—so discarding one of them shouldn't be a problem.

With that said, note that all decisions on solving replication collisions are logged, and the administrator has the option of restoring the attributes that were rejected by the tie-in scheme.

A Note on Active Directory's Replication Model

Actually, the replication model used by Active Directory is called *multi-master loose consistency with convergence*. In this model, the directory can have many replicas; and the replication system propagates the changes made at any given replica to all other replicas.

The replicas aren't guaranteed to be consistent with each other at any particular point in time ("loose consistency"), because changes can be applied to any replica at any time ("multi-master"). Thus, it's not possible to guarantee complete knowledge of the current or future state of the replicas, because the information on state changes must be propagated, and propagation takes time, during which time more state changes may occur.

This is actually an axiom of distributed computing! Loosely coupled systems such as Active Directory deal with uncertainty simply by tolerating it. A loosely coupled system allows the nodes to have differing views of the overall system state and provides algorithms for resolving conflicts. However, you should note that if the system reaches a steady state in which no new updates are occurring and all previous updates have been completely replicated, all replicas are guaranteed to converge on the same set of values ("convergence").

That Little Exception to the Multi-Master Replication Rule: FSMOs

Certain changes—such as the addition or deletion of a domain or changes to the directory schema—have consequences for the entire forest or for very important domain properties. Such critical operations can't easily be resolved by using multi-master replication; they require some lockout mechanism to ensure that the change is correctly propagated prior to when the next critical change begins.

Active Directory addresses this lockout requirement via the *Flexible Single-Master Operation (FSMO)*, which is called Floating Single-Master Operation or simply Single Masters of Operation by some. (Most Microsoft people that I've met simply pronounce FSMO as "fizmo.")

The FSMO is always used as a lockout mechanism. Depending on the actual use of the FSMO, its scope includes either the Active Directory domain or the whole Active Directory forest. Therefore, only one DC in the domain or forest, respectively, can serve as the FSMO at any point in time. At different times, different DCs can assume this role. And, if the DC that has the FSMO role fails, another DC can be promoted (manually) to take over this role.

In Windows 2000, the FSMO is used in five variants, which Microsoft refers to as "roles":

♦ *Schema Master (a.k.a. Schema Operations Master)*—Its scope is the forest, and it belongs to the DC that is allowed to make schema changes. By default, the first DC installed in the forest will become the schema master. To perform a schema update at a given DC, that DC must be the current schema master. If the DC isn't currently the schema master, it must ask the current schema master to transfer that power.

♦ *Domain Naming Master (a.k.a. Domain Naming Operations Master)*—Its scope is the forest, and it belongs to the DC that controls changes to the domain namespace (in other words, for adding and removing domains or adding or removing cross-references to external directory services).

♦ *PDC Emulator (a.k.a. PDC DC or PDC Advertiser)*—Its scope is the domain, and it belongs to the DC that has assumed the PDC role for down-level BDCs (NT 4- or 3.51-based BDCs) and down-level clients. Essentially, the PDC Emulator is a role used for down-level compatibility. However, it still retains one very crucial function in a native mode Active Directory domain: Password changes performed by other DCs of the domain are replicated preferentially to the PDC Emulator so that it can perform a second check before reporting a fail, when authentication fails at a DC because the user has provided the wrong logon credentials.

♦ *RID Master (a.k.a. RID Operations Master)*—Its scope is the domain, and it belongs to the DC that manages the Resource Identifiers (RIDs) pool, which is needed to create a security principal—that is, a new SID for a user, group, or computer. RIDs are part of the Security Identifier (SID) and are allocated to each DC in pools of 512 RIDs. So, the DC needs to contact the RID Master only once for every 512 security principals created. The RID Master also is needed to move an object from one domain to another, because this involves a change of SID.

♦ *Infrastructure Master (a.k.a. Infrastructure Master Demon)*—Its scope is the domain, and it belongs to the DC that maintains reference to objects in other domains (so-called *phantoms*). It is used to ensure instant consistency of objects for interdomain operations; for example, to make sure that a rename of a user is reflected in all groups that the user belongs to. Note that this FSMO shouldn't reside on a GC, unless you have only a single domain.

Tip

See "The FSMO Story" in Chapter 18 to learn how to find and move the five FSMO roles among the Active Directory DCs.

PDC Emulator, RID Master, and Infrastructure Master often are referred to as *Operations Masters*.

Although you don't have to direct much planning attention to these five FSMOs in your design, they're crucial to the well being of Active Directory and thus must be understood at least by the administrators. Likewise, although the FSMOs won't be of interest for daily routines, you must be aware of their presence if you are going to perform fault-finding on the Windows 2000 Server infrastructure.

Also, if you are designing a large-scale Windows 2000 environment, you should plan the placement of FSMO roles to match the replication and network topologies. Typically, you would place both the RID Master and the PDC Emulator roles on the same DC, unless the

DC is already overloaded—in that case, you should put these two roles on separate DCs. Likewise, the Schema Master and the Domain Naming Master should be placed on the same DC—and that DC should be close to whoever is responsible for schema updates and the creation of new domains. The Infrastructure Master should be placed on a DC that has close proximity to some GC server (preferably, the one housing the RID Master and the PDC Emulator).

Yet Another Exception: Urgent Replication Triggers

Although a clear majority of the Active Directory objects and properties will be governed by the replication scheme discussed until now, a select set of objects changes will prompt immediate replication. Under one, the mechanism used for handling those object's changes is known as an *urgent replication trigger*.

The following events will trigger immediate replication between Active Directory DCs:

♦ Replicating a newly locked out account

♦ Changing a Local Security Authority (LSA) secret

♦ RID Manager state changes

If the domain is running in mixed mode, the following events will trigger an immediate replication from the Active Directory DC holding the PDC Emulator role to all Windows NT 4 BDCs:

♦ Replicating a newly locked out account

♦ Changing an LSA secret

♦ Inter-domain trust passwords (trusts between domain A and B)

Additionally, changes to user account passwords (thus, machine account password changes are excluded) performed on an Active Directory DC will trigger an instant replication to the Active Directory DC holding the PDC Emulator role for the domain. This is done to avoid lockouts for users because a password change has not reached the DC that they've contacted for logging in. So when a lockout is generated on the grounds that the password is

---

Comparing to Windows NT Server 4 Domains

In Windows NT Server 4 domains, the following events will trigger an immediate replication:

• Replicating a newly locked out account

• Changing an LSA secret

• Changing the account lockout policy

• Changing the domain password policy

• Changing the password on a machine account

---

wrong at any Active Directory DC, it will retry the request on the PDC Emulator role to make absolutely sure that the lockout isn't due to a password change having been performed at another DC (see also the "Knowing Your Passwords" section in Chapter 20).

Note

Clients that aren't Active Directory-aware will always contact the Active Directory DC holding the PDC role when making a password change, because this is how password changes are done in Windows NT Server 4.

DCs and GCs in Depth

Now that you've gotten intimate with the replication scheme used by Active Directory—and its pros and cons—you should be ready to go more in depth with the Active Directory DCs and GCs. And you should definitely want to spend a bit of time studying the details of DCs and GCs because both of them are absolutely crucial to your clients. Also, the DCs and GCs will allow you to gain a much better overview of how Active Directory operates "out in the wild."

The Client Logon: A Few Pointers?

When a computer or user requests access to Active Directory, an Active Directory DC is located by a mechanism called the domain controller locator (or simply Locator). Locator is an algorithm that runs in the context of the Netlogon service. Because the Windows 2000 Locator is shared code with the Windows NT 4-compatible Locator, both DNS clients and NetBIOS clients are supported. Thus, Locator can find DCs by using DNS names or by using NetBIOS names.

During a search for a DC, Locator attempts to find a DC in the site "closest" to the client. If the domain that is being sought is an Active Directory domain, the DC uses the information stored in Active Directory to determine the closest site. That is, when DNS is used, Locator searches first for a site-specific DNS record before it begins to search for a DNS record that isn't site-specific (thereby preferentially locating a DC in that site). When the domain being sought is a Windows NT 4 domain, DC discovery occurs at client startup and the first domain controller that it finds will be used, just as is the case in Windows NT Server 4.

If an Active Directory-aware client is placed in a new location, it will contact a DC in its home site, which is not the site to which the computer is currently connected. In that situation, the DC looks up the client's site and returns the name of the site closest to the client. The DC stores site information for the entire forest in the configuration naming context. The DC uses the site information to check the IP address of the client computer against the list of subnets in the forest. In this way, the DC ascertains the name of the site in which the client is assumed to be located, or the site that is the closest match, and returns this information to the client.

In a native mode Active Directory domain, the Key Distribution Center (KDC) on the DC that is responsible for authenticating the user's logon request locates and communicates with the GC to enumerate the Universal Groups the user is a member of, and it adds the SIDs of those groups to the user's token. And so, the GC will prove just as crucial for performing a user logon as a DC (and thus, you will in fact have two single points of failure with regard to logon to an Active Directory domain).

However, you might want to note that there's an important exception to this rule: If the user is an administrator, Windows 2000 allows the logon to take place even if no GC is available.

In a mixed mode domain, Universal Groups can't be created, so the KDC doesn't need to contact the GC. However, other domains may be operating in native mode and Universal Groups may have been created that contain the user as a member. And so, when an attempt to use resources in another domain occurs, the computer hosting the resource contacts a DC for that domain. The DC adds the SIDs of the groups local to that domain (which may include Universal Groups of which the user is a member) to the user's token.

This stems from Microsoft's decision to store the Universal Group memberships in the GC. If Microsoft had chosen to allow logons to proceed without Universal Groups, you would have faced two problems:

- Users would see inconsistent behavior; sometimes they can access a resource and other times not, because the required Universal Group is not in the token.

- Users may be able to access a resource that has been denied access via a Universal Group (and it would not be practical to implement a rule that Universal Groups aren't able to occur on denied ACEs). This would constitute a security leak, which clearly isn't acceptable.

In other words, the GC requirement is imposed so as to secure a complete logon in which all group memberships (including Universal Groups) of the user are added to the access token. This isn't as bad as it may sound, when you consider that, in the case of Exchange 2000 Server (and probably many more applications to come), the GC will provide your address book—and thus will become quite indispensable.

Finally, you should remember that the UPN suffixes are stored in the GC. And so, if your user opts for UPN logons, she has, in effect, made the GC vital to the logon process. Chapter 20's "The Client Logon Situation" provides a more detailed rundown on the individual steps taken in the client logon process.

Understanding the DCs

DCs don't require much discussion. The following list sets forth what you really should understand about the DC concept:

- Each DC can be assigned to one, and only one, Active Directory domain. Likewise, to exist, each domain has to exist on at least one DC (and preferably two to avoid any single point of failure).

- The DC provides the user with the means to log on to the domain.

- The DC can handle all queries to the domain that it is part of. For example, the DC enables you to search the domain for any object or property.

- The DC enables you to create, delete, or edit the current objects and properties in the domain.

- If you have more than one DC in a domain, you need to distribute the changes made on each DC to all other DCs in the domain, via replication. The replication used in Active Directory is bidirectional, by default (but can also be set up to be unidirectional), and you are allowed to define one or multiple replication paths between each pair of DCs.

Also note that a DC holds at least three naming contexts. A *naming context* (a.k.a. partition), which is a contiguous subtree of the directory, is the *unit of partitioning* (the replicable unit) in Active Directory. The three naming contexts being:

♦ *The Schema Naming Context*—Definitions of the objects that can be created in the directory.

♦ *The Configuration Naming Context*—The replication topology and related forest-level metadata. This is also referred to as the *site and service configuration*, because it includes the site definitions and the forest-wide service configurations.

♦ *One or more Domain Naming Contexts (a.k.a. the User Naming Contexts)*—The subtrees/domains containing the actual objects in the directory. The current version of Active Directory allows storage of only one domain (user naming context) on each DC. Microsoft has promised that this "one DC, one domain" limitation will be removed in a future version of Windows 2000.

Each domain naming context is replicated to all DCs belonging to the same domain. The schema and configuration naming contexts are replicated onto every DC in the forest.

If you don't want your Windows 2000 server to work as a DC, you can have it installed as either of the following:

♦ *Standalone server*—A computer that is running Windows 2000 Server and *is not* a member of an Active Directory domain.

♦ *Member server*—A computer that is running Windows 2000 Server and *is* a member of a domain, but isn't a DC. Member servers don't receive copies of the directory, because they typically are dedicated to application services or resource services.

Any standalone or member server can be promoted to the role of DC (using the Active Directory Installation Wizard). Likewise, any DC is allowed to be demoted just as easily to the role of a standalone or member server.

Two features built into Active Directory help minimize and optimize replication traffic (which is needed for keeping all DCs up to date) over the network:

♦ Only changed properties are replicated. For example, if an existing user's phone number is changed, only the new phone number is replicated (and the object's PVN), because the rest of the information stored in the user account hasn't undergone any changes.

♦ You can schedule how often replication occurs both within each geographical site and between sites.

Because of these features, you don't need to create separate domains for every geographical site that you have. Instead, you can configure inter-site replication to happen infrequently, such as once a day. Then, you can keep the multiple sites as part of one domain and gain the many benefits of that.

However, it is widely acknowledged that the size and number of domains that you want to configure should be gauged by the volume and nature of directory replication traffic. If, for example, your network has any existing WAN links that are already saturated by network traffic, you may not want to replicate Active Directory across these links. So, even with the features offered, you still may decide to divide your network into multiple domains in order to lessen replication traffic across extremely slow or oversubscribed links.

Understanding the GCs

Even though the Global Catalog (GC) is a new concept, it seems to require even less explanation than the concept of the DC. But don't be fooled into believing that. The GC concept includes more than meets the eye.

The following is what you really should understand about the GC concept:

♦ The GC is a data repository meant for queries. It contains a partial replica of every user naming context in the forest, as well as the schema and configuration naming contexts.

♦ The GC holds all objects from all the domains in Active Directory and a subset of each object's attributes. The attributes replicated to the GC are those most frequently used in search operations (such as a user's logon name), which are needed to locate the actual object.

♦ Because the GC holds all objects in the forest, executing a forest-wide query is straightforward, whereas an ordinary LDAP query has its scope limited to a domain tree. All queries are executed on the flat view that is presented by the GC, which translates into regular LDAP searches that don't return LDAP referrals.

♦ Clients find GCs by using DNS.

♦ Universal Groups and their members are listed in the GC. Global and domain local groups are also listed in the GC, but their members are not.

♦ A GC can be created anywhere in the domain tree. Only DCs can serve as GCs, however.

♦ Usually, at least one GC should exist per site.

♦ The GC can be accessed through MAPI and LDAP. A GC is needed for users to be able to log on to the Active Directory domains.

Note

*GCs contain the most commonly searched attributes from all Domain Naming Contexts in the forest. Many attributes are replicated to the GC by default. You're allowed to change the default settings, because an attribute will be included in the Global Catalog. That is, if the **partialAttributeSet** property of the attribute is set to TRUE in the Schema Naming Context (see Chapter 19 for more information), the attribute will be replicated to the GC.*

*Please note that if the **partialAttributeSet** property is blank, the attribute isn't included in the GC. If the **partialAttributeSet** property is set to FALSE, the attribute is marked to be removed from the GC. The Knowledge Base article Q230663 provides a recipe for finding out which attributes are being replicated to the GC.*

Watch Out: It's Become Much Easier to Delete Your Critical Computer Objects by Mistake

One of the more unfortunate effects of Active Directory is that the Active Directory Users and Computers MMC and the AD Sites and Services tools actually make it much easier for any administrator to impose a major disaster on the enterprise.

The easiest way of creating a disaster is if the administrator inadvertently deletes one or more critical directory objects. In an Active Directory setting, the two most critical objects are the machine account representing the Active Directory DC (which is mostly used for authentication between two domain controllers) and the NTDS Settings object assigned to the Active Directory (which is used for locating other DCs and determining enterprise Active Directory replication topology). However, you might want to note that several other critical objects are vulnerable to mishaps, including DHCP authorization objects, FRS subscription objects, and just about anything else stored in the System OU.

So although it was a common troubleshooting procedure to delete certain objects in Windows NT Server 4's Server Manager in an attempt to re-synchronize a Backup Domain Controller (BDC) with the Primary Domain Controller (PDC), this will have some very nasty effects in Windows 2000. There's no easy way to recover a deleted DC's machine account, because it includes specific authentication data; much the same goes for the NTDS Settings object. Deleting any of those objects will probably orphan the Active Directory DC from the enterprise replication topology, resulting in changes to the Active Directory that is orphaned right along with the DC and, therefore, causing client logon failures.

If a backup is available, it may be possible to perform an authoritative restore of the deleted machine account object to another nearby DC and then try to "kick start" the DC by stopping the KDC service on the nearby DC and forcing a replication from the nearby DC to the troubled DC. If no backup is available, you might want to try your luck at issuing the command **dcdiag /s:localhost /repairmachineaccount** on the DC (Windows 2000 Support Tools must be installed at the local machine) if you're logged on with Domain Admins privileges. In most cases, it won't help a bit—but you might as well try it, because you're already in deep water.

Even if you are able to recover the machine account, a demotion and re-promotion of the server are called for in most cases to ensure that all data is correctly written back to the account. For example, some services (including FRS) keep information under the machine account.

In the event that the NTDS Settings object is deleted, you should be able to manually create a new object and a replication link to another DC in order to reintroduce the DC to the replication topology. This will trigger replication so that the critical objects can be replicated to at least one other DC and the Active Directory replication can propagate that object to other DCs. After time, the KCC on every other DC should notice the new server object and adjust the replication topology accordingly.

At present, the administrator won't be prompted when deleting machine account objects that represent an Active Directory (however, Microsoft has stated that they're working on modifying the MMC tools so this will be the case). The same thing holds true for the NTDS Settings object—though you won't be allowed to delete this object under some circumstances. Note, however, that Microsoft has no plans to restrict the more powerful administrative tools—including ADSIEdit and LDP—with regard to performing such operations.

You can find more information on how to recover a deleted Active Directory DC machine account in the Knowledge Base article Q257288. The Knowledge Base article Q216498 outlines the corresponding procedures for getting all traces of an old Active Directory DC deleted from the directory.

To summarize: Maintaining information in the GC allows fast queries of all objects in the entire forest. If you have multiple domain trees, or just multiple domains in your forest, queries are much more efficiently handled by the GC, because you don't need to traverse several domains—or, in the worst-case scenario, several domain trees—to perform a complete query. Additionally, GC searches are faster than regular LDAP searches, because GC searches have a dedicated port (3268).

Note

In the event that the Active Directory forest only has a single domain, all DCs contain the same data, so there is no reason for not promoting all DCs to also being GCs. This won't add any more replication load to the network, because the GC will get the data from the local copy of the DC database. But it will prove advantageous to the domain logins, for searches and for applications making use of the GC (such as Exchange 2000 Server).

Also, in many cases the user or application doesn't even know which domain contains the object, much less the actual placement of the object in the OU hierarchy. This fact doesn't pose any problem with a GC, because it enables users and applications to find objects in an Active Directory domain tree simply by providing one or more attributes of the target object. And, as a measure of security, the access rights of objects are included by default in the GC. This reduces the obvious security risk posed by the GC, because if a user doesn't have rights to access an object, the user's query fails. Thus, from a security perspective, the GC doesn't pose a point of risk exposure.

However, nothing is perfect, and the following list describes the four main shortcomings of GCs:

♦ *GCs introduce more replication traffic inside and between sites.* Parts of the domain actually are replicated twice (once each for the DCs and the GCs), and you face a further increase of replication load stemming from Universal Groups and other elements that are part of the GC.

♦ *You can base queries only on the attributes that are stored in the GC.* Consequently, you will encounter a wide range of situations in which a GC search returns empty-handed, even though one or more objects that have matching attributes are available in the forest.

♦ *The GC is separated from the domains.* As a result, the GC never provides referrals to domains, because it isn't even aware of them.

♦ *Generally, you need at least one GC inside each site.* A GC must be available, because user authentication requires global knowledge of each user's group memberships, to compute all the groups to which that user (directly or indirectly) belongs and, thus, be able to establish all relevant Allow and Deny permissions and rights. Also, the GC very likely will be used by other server applications, thereby becoming even more indispensable. For example, Exchange 2000 Server uses the GC to generate the Global Address List as well as other address book views.

Tip

*You can eliminate the need for a GC to be present for user logons by adding the **IgnoreGCFailures** key to the Registry at **HKLM\System\CurrentControlSet\Control \Lsa** (it doesn't matter what value the key gets, because only the presence or absence of this key is being tested). Before you do that, you should understand that setting this key adds a potential security vulnerability, if any Deny permissions are set using Universal Groups.*

So, although you usually shouldn't employ this key in the general case, you might want to use it to avoid implementing GCs (thus adding to the bandwidth needed for replications) in very small remote sites. However, you might want to note that you could be faced with another application (for example, Exchange 2000 Server) that builds on the GC later on.

Finally, you should note that the replication topology for GCs is generated automatically and that GCs are built by the Active Directory replication system.

Sites in Depth

Sites enable you to provide information about both the structure of your network and how you want to replicate directory information. Sites also enable you to take advantage of a network's physical topology to provide fault tolerance, resource availability, and improved performance for the Active Directory organization.

Simply put, you should view a site as being the following:

♦ A collection of machines that are interconnected using some kind of fast and cheap communication link

♦ A structure that is totally independent of the domain structure

♦ A concept that is used both for determining replication and for locating the resources available closest to a particular machine

♦ A physical organization that provides fault tolerance and performance for the logical organization

The Definition of a Site

A *site* is an area of the network where connectivity among machines is assumed to be very good. Typically, you can think of sites as areas of the network that are connected using some kind of LAN technology—or, in a very few cases, by some high-bandwidth WAN technology. Areas of the network that are separated by WAN technologies, slow or oversubscribed links, or low- or medium-performance routers should be defined as separate sites (and thus should be allocated a TCP/IP subnet that is separate from the areas of good connectivity).

Warning

You should be careful to allocate all TCP/IP subnets that may include clients and servers to a site. If a client contacts a given DC and the IP address can't be found in the subnet-to-site mapping table, the client will simply keep on using that DC.

In practice, the network area utilized in the site concept is defined by a mapping of one or more IP subnets, based on the assumption that computers that have the same subnet address are connected to the same network segment. So, when you create each Active Directory site from the AD Sites and Services MMC tool, you specify a group of one or more IP subnets that belong to the site. Each of these IP subnets can belong to only one site, because each site object holds references to the subnet objects that define it, and Active Directory needs to be able to make a "reverse lookup" of the site by specifying an IP subnet.

Understanding Site Coverage

Best practices call for having at least one DC and GC for every domain that applies to each site, but you might be in a position where it simply isn't possible—or, more probably, isn't economically feasible.

For this reason, an Active Directory DC will advertise itself (registers a site-related SRV record in DNS) in any site that does not have a DC available for that domain and for which its site has the lowest-cost connections—this is usually referred to as site coverage. By doing so, it is ensured that every site has a DC that is defined by default for every domain in the forest, even if a site does not contain a DC for that domain.

To be precise, the site coverage algorithm adheres to these rules during registration of SRV records in DNS (for every DC in the forest):

- Build a list of *target sites*: sites that have no DCs for the domain hosted by the DC.

- Build a list of *candidate sites*: sites that also include DCs that support the same domain.

- For every target site, follow these steps:

  1. Build a list of candidate sites that have the domain as a member. (If none, do nothing.)

  2. Of these candidate sites, build a list of sites that have the lowest site link cost to each of the target sites. (If none, do nothing.)

  3. If more than one, break ties (reduce this list to one candidate site) by choosing the site that has the largest number of DCs.

  4. If more than one, break ties by choosing the site that is first alphabetically.

  5. Register target-site-specific SRV records for the DCs for this domain in the selected site.

The sites added to the DC's site coverage are stored in memory, and a new list is assembled each time the Netlogon service starts. While Netlogon runs, it updates this list at an interval specified by the value stored in the **HKLM\SYSTEM\CurrentControlSet\Services\Netlogon\Parameters\DnsRefreshInterval** (**REG_DWORD**) Registry key, which is specified in seconds and set to 1 hour by default. After a successful registration, Netlogon re-registers the DNS name after five minutes have passed. The interval between each subsequent registration is doubled until the interval reaches the value of **DnsRefreshInterval**. Thereafter, Netlogon re-registers DNS names when the value of **DnsRefreshInterval** expires.

If you want to control the assignment of DCs to sites that don't have their own DC, you can input the sites that a given DC should register itself to (in addition to the site in which the DC resides) in the **HKLM\SYSTEM\CurrentControlSet\Services\Netlogon\Parameters\SiteCoverage** (**REG_MULTI_SZ**) Registry key—and you can do the same for GCs by way of the **GcSiteCoverage** key. Also, you can deny a DC permission to add itself to any other site than its own by setting the **HKLM\SYSTEM\CurrentControlSet\Services\Netlogon\Parameters\AutoSiteCoverage** Registry key to 0.

You should note that automatic site coverage detection also applies to sites that already have one or multiple DCs present, but where the local DCs have been out of order for some two hours. So you should put some thought into assigning the costs on each site link.

If a computer requests a DC at a time when all DCs in its local site are offline, the Locator will return a reference to a DC in a different site. The location of this domain controller is stored in the client cache, whose lifetime is controlled by the **CloseSiteTimeout** Registry entry (which is set to 15 minutes by default). The implications of the **CloseSiteTimeout** setting are that if the time-out value is too large, a client never tries to find a local DC if there isn't one available at startup, and if the value of this setting is too small, secure channel traffic is unnecessarily slowed down by discovery attempts. The Netlogon service will only attempt to find a DC in the local site again if either of the following events occurs:

- An interactive logon process uses pass-through authentication on the secure channel.
- The **CloseSiteTimeout** value has elapsed since the last attempt, and any other attempt is made to use the secure channel (for example, pass-through authentication of network logons).

The **CloseSiteTimeout** is specified in seconds and is stored in **HKLM\SYSTEM\CurrentControlSet\Services\Netlogon\Parameters** as a **REG_SZ** type key. A fair amount of caution is advised in changing this value. If this value is too high, the requesting client might be delayed significantly; if this value is too low, repeated attempts to find a better DC could create excessive network traffic.

You might also note that the **HKLM\SYSTEM\CurrentControlSet\Services\Netlogon\Parameters\SiteName** Registry key (**REG_SZ** type) does allow you to specify which site a member server or client is part of. The site specified here will always override any site that is dynamically determined by Netlogon.

The Implications of a Site

To be very precise, sites are used to control the following:

♦ *Authentication*—When a user tries to log on to an Active Directory-aware workstation that is part of an Active Directory domain, it will attempt to find a DC (and later, a GC) that resides in the same site as the workstation. This attempt to always use DCs and GCs that are located in the same site is intended to consolidate network traffic and increase the efficiency of the authentication process—and represents a very powerful and very welcome change compared with Windows NT Server 4.

♦ *Replication*—When a change occurs in Active Directory, the site setup governs how and when the change is replicated to the other DCs and GCs. The DCs/GCs that reside in the same site receive the change almost immediately (the delay depends on the number of DCs found in the site), whereas you have a range of options for controlling how and when replication is performed to the DCs and GCs in other sites.

♦ *Active Directory services*—You can (and are supposed to) have such information as service bindings and configurations made available through Active Directory, because this will make administration and use of network resources easier and more efficient. These services can be made site-aware and can take actions based on what site you're in. Actually, one such service is already available out of the box: *Distributed File System (DFS)*.

Thus, sites enable you to balance the need for up-to-date directory information and fast logon with the limitations of your network resources. Also, sites aren't tied in any way to the logical Active Directory namespace, so you can mix and match DCs from different domains and sites in any way that you may see fit for your needs—in other words, DCs for a particular domain can reside on many sites, and a site may contain DCs for several domains.

When you plan your site structure, you should also be aware that this structure will likely influence the way in which you can later set up third-party server applications, because many independent software vendors (ISVs) apparently are already taking advantage of the site definitions for their own applications. Some ISVs merely use the site structure to decide where good connectivity does and does not exist, whereas other ISVs also are inclined to use the option to store specific information for their own use, along with the site structure.

Intra-Site Options in Depth

Within a site, a process called the intra-site *Knowledge Consistency Checker (KCC)* automatically generates a ring topology for replication among the DCs that are part of the same domain. Readers familiar with Microsoft Exchange Server should already know a lot about the KCC, because the Windows 2000 Server team adapted KCC from Exchange Server. However, Exchange folks shouldn't skip this section, because the Windows 2000 Server KCC has become a bit more sophisticated in the transition process.

The topology generated by the intra-site KCC defines paths for directory updates to flow from one DC to another, until all DCs have received the directory updates. The ring structure created guarantees that at least two replication paths exist from one DC to another, ensuring that if one DC is down, replication continues to flow to all other DCs.

To avoid very big rings (and thus avoid the potential for very long-winded replication cycles inside the site), the intra-site KCC creates additional connections between DCs so that any update won't need more than three hops from where it originates to reach any other DC in any direction. To ensure that this occurs, the magic number is seven DCs. Where seven or more DCs exist, the intra-site KCC creates random direct routes to maintain the three-hop rule. For example, in Figure 12.15, A can get to D either through B and C or through F and E. In the example where seven DCs exist, A to D is four hops, when going through G, F, and E, so the KCC creates a direct route from A to D. The same result occurs when the intra-site KCC checks the route from B to E, C to F, and so forth.

Know Your Locator Service

When Active Directory-aware clients log on, they check the Active Directory DC to determine rules for site membership, match those rules to the internal configuration of the computer, and then make the appropriate changes. For example, if a user based in Munich, Germany, travels to New York, her computer will determine that it is now in New York and set the site assignment to reflect that fact when it logs on. Thus, any applications that are site-aware will be able to perform such smart things as running any application components needed from a server in New York, and more.

On the basis of parameters passed to Netlogon, the process of locating a DC proceeds in one of two ways:

- *The IP/DNS-compatible Locator is used if the domain name is a DNS-compatible name.* The Netlogon service on the client looks up the name in DNS by using SRV records. If the client site name is known, the client DNS query specifies the site and DNS will return the IP addresses of DCs that match the DNS query (sorted by the priority and weight properties specified in the applicable SRV records). If the site isn't known, Netlogon will attempt to find a DC in the site of the client or the site closest to the client. The client pings each IP address in the order returned (the ping being a UDP LDAP query to port 389). After each ping, the client waits one-tenth of a second for a response to the ping (or to any previous ping) and then pings the next DC, ensuring a basic level of load balancing. The first DC to respond to a ping will be chosen by the client. If the client specifies a site that isn't consistent with its IP address (which happens when a computer has been moved), the contacted DC will look up the client site on the basis of the client IP address by comparing the address to the sites that are identified in Active Directory and will return the name of the site that is closest to the client. The client then updates the information in the registry.

- *The Windows NT 4-compatible Locator is used if the domain name is a NetBIOS name (or if IPX and NetBEUI are the only transports available).* The Netlogon service on the client sends a transport-specific logon request (using a mail slot message) to locate a DC in a particular domain. The specific name resolution mechanism and datagram delivery mechanism that are used will be transport-specific. The client uses the first DC that responds to the message.

An Active Directory-aware client that is using the Windows NT 4-compatible Locator will always inspect the answer from the DC to determine if it's communicating with a DC from the same site. If that isn't the case, the client will try to find a DC in the site once more. If no better DC can be found, the original DC returned will be used.

Note

The intra-site KCC runs on every DC in the site and periodically analyzes the replication topology to ensure that it is efficient. So, if a DC dies, the intra-site KCC automatically generates a new route the next time the replication cycle runs. If a DC is added or removed, the intra-site KCC reconfigures the topology to reflect the change. The KCC calculates routes every 15 minutes, by default.

The KCC goes through the same process for creating the replication topology for each naming context:

1. It makes a list of all master-naming contexts that are hosted on the DC.

2. It builds a list of all the DCs in the site.

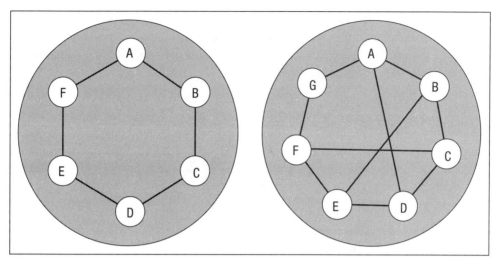

Figure 12.15
If seven or more DCs exist, the KCC makes sure that getting from one DC in a site to another in any direction requires no more than a maximum of three hops.

3. *It sorts this list of DCs by their GUIDs.*

4. *It determines which DCs in the list are fit for being used as replication partners for the particular naming context (that is, which other full copies of the particular naming context that exist).*

5. *The list of DCs are then consolidated by removing all DCs that haven't been able to replicate lately.*

6. *Now you're left with a set of DCs that are deemed worthy of acting as valid source servers. The KCC then builds a replication topology between these DCs.*

The GC is generated following the same process, except that it will also include partial replicas (that is, other GCs) in the list of possible servers and the GC replication topology is superimposed over the replication topology already created between the DCs, so that additional connections only are being created, if they're not already present in the DC topology.

Besides checking on the topology, the intra-site KCC automatically creates the connection objects that it deems necessary, based on the above-mentioned rule set.

Note

You can disable the intra-site KCC altogether (which is not recommended, unless you know exactly what you are doing) at each site. This rather delicate operation (which also allows you to disable the inter-site KCC in a given site) is specified in Knowledge Base article Q242780. You also can change the time interval for recalculation of routes via the Registry (which likewise isn't recommended).

If, by chance, you aren't satisfied (which is unlikely) with the intra-site KCC's manner of generating and sustaining a replication topology inside a site, you can add your own connections manually—and, ultimately, disable the intra-site KCC altogether and define your own custom-made replication topology.

Adding connections manually to change the default replication topology is done by defining so-called *connection objects*, which represent a replication connection between two DCs by defining the two end points for replication. You should understand that a connection object is unidirectional (requiring two connection objects to replicate in both directions) and, thus, identifies incoming replication from its partner—so, if a connection object is created on server A and points to server B, server B will replicate changes to server A. For all practical purposes, this means that you will need to define two connection objects for each replication link.

You are allowed to schedule the use of each connection object by configuring how many times per hour (none, once, twice, or four times) you want replication to occur and during what hours and what days of the week it is allowed. Generally, you should let the intra-site KCC define all connection objects in the site, because this will save you precious time for other chores and usually will prove more efficient (because the definition of additional connection objects increases both the network load spent on replication and the load on

---

Duplicate Connection Objects

The KCC will attempt to build a spanning tree for all naming contexts (domain, schema, and configuration). Generally, the spanning tree algorithm strives to have one inter-site connection between any two pair of sites.

However, the KCC or an administrator may create duplicate connection objects between a given pair of Active Directory replication partners in the same domain by accident. The KCC manages duplicate connection objects in the following manner:

- It favors administrator-created (manual) connection objects over automatic connection objects.

- If more than one manual connection object exists, it uses the last one (newer over older).

- If more than one connection object exists with the same create time and type (manual or automatic), it arbitrarily selects one (with manual connections favored over KCC-generated connections).

If these connections are generated by the KCC, the redundant connection is eventually removed following this scheme:

- Sort the connections by GUID in ascending order.

- Sort by newer connections versus older connections.

- Remove duplicates based on the sort order (that is, remove duplicates that are lower in list).

Manual connections that are created by an administrator won't be deleted by the KCC.

While the KCC will look to see that the replication of the three naming contexts will work correctly, regardless of duplicate connection objects, FRS will stumble if multiple connections exist between two DCs. FRS will simply treat duplicate connections as an invalid configuration, skipping both connections and halting outbound replication on the server(s) that are experiencing duplicates! Much the same goes for DFS, except that it's running off a separate topology that is hidden under the covers of Active Directory.

---

the two servers defined in the connection object). So, to make a long story short: You should *not* define connection objects manually unless you have a very good reason to do so.

If you still are inclined to create additional connection objects, you should know the following rules that apply to manually created connection objects (as opposed to the connection objects defined by the intra-site KCC):

♦ The intra-site KCC never deletes a manually created connection object.

♦ If you create a connection object that is identical to one that the intra-site KCC would define, the intra-site KCC won't create an additional connection object.

♦ If replication within a site ever should become impossible or the replication topology makes up a single point of failure, the intra-site KCC steps in and establishes the connection objects needed.

Inter-Site Options in Depth

Inter-site replication occurs only between sites. So, an Active Directory design that has only a single site can use intra-site replication only. Just as is the case with intra-site replications, Active Directory includes an inter-site KCC that is charged with keeping the replication topology between the individual sites (see the "Optimizing for Different Scenarios" section for more information) up and running.

Note

You've got one DC in each site that works as Inter-site KCC (being referred to as the Inter-site Topology Generator Role Owner), which by default is the oldest DC in each site. This so-called Inter-Site Topology Generation being performed by the KCC will perform the following process for each naming context that is hosted in the site:

• *Determine the other sites that host replicas of the applicable naming context.*

• *Determine the possible connectivity paths for all transports available between the applicable sites (in contrast to the intra-site topology generation case, the assumption of any server being able to replicate to any other server, can't be made for replication between sites).*

• *Evaluate the minimum cost path for each of the connection paths.*

• *Reduce the number of connections, if possible, making sure that all sites are connected.*

After that, each of the connection object remaining is set up for replicating every naming context possible.

After you establish multiple sites, you need to consider how replication information should be exchanged between those sites. You have two instruments for defining that exchange:

♦ Site links

♦ Site link bridges

Inter-site replication is, for all practical means, manually administered—that is, if you haven't defined any site links for a given site, it won't be added automatically by the Active Directory. Because there's no notification going on between the replication partners, each of the applicable naming contexts must be checked for changes in every replication cycle. This in turn makes the replication traffic slightly higher for the inter-site case than the intra-site case—and on top of that you will find that a fair amount of traffic will be generated for setting up the connections; this doesn't apply to the intra-site replications, where the connections are kept open. On the other hand, you are provided with the possibility of controlling when the replication is performed.

Site Links

A *site link* connects two or more sites together (just as you might know it from an Exchange connector). A site link is unidirectional and nontransitive (paralleling Windows NT Server 4's trust relationships; but here it used solely to define the replication topology), so in all but the most special cases, you need to establish a site link in both directions and between all the sites in the forest.

Note

Active Directory automatically creates site links when the first Active Directory DC is added to a new site. However, you need to fine-tune or supplement the initial site link configuration for all but the simplest situations, because Active Directory automatically creates only one link between a new site and an existing site. Although a single site link is sufficient, you'll usually want to supplement your network's inter-site replication topology by creating additional site links, in order to create a more reliable replication system (to avoid any single point of failure for inter-site replications).

In addition to defining the sites to be included in the link, you can also configure the following components for each site link:

◆ *Transport*—The networking technology used to transfer the data being replicated. You have a choice between RPC and Simple Mail Transfer Protocol (that is, mail-based replication using SMTP that is handled by the IIS component found in Windows 2000 Server).

◆ *Cost*—The cost value set is used by the inter-site KCC to determine which site link is the most efficient connection available between sites, if multiple site links exist between the two sites. Active Directory always uses the available site link that has the least cost for replication between two sites. You should make it a habit to configure site link costs for all site links as part of the process of providing Active Directory with information about available inter-site connections.

◆ *Frequency*—The frequency value, specified in minutes, determines how often the connection is used to check for replication updates.

◆ *Schedule*—The times when replication can occur on the link. The schedule specifies the time periods during which the site link is available on a weekly basis—this is specified on an hourly basis from Monday through Sunday.

On the Choice of Inter-Site Transports

Although you have no choice but to use RPC for intra-site replications, you actually do have a choice with regard to inter-site replications. The choice stands between SMTP and RPC. However, you should note that the RPC option is compressed, which makes it very efficient for reducing the bandwidth needed compared with the uncompressed RPC used for intra-site replications (though at the cost of the CPU cycles used for compression at the sending and receiving DCs).

Unfortunately, you won't be able to employ SMTP for all your inter-site replications, because SMTP only applies to replication of GC, schema, and configuration naming contexts—rumor has it that the underlying reason for not including the domain naming context is the fact that the File Replication Service (FRS) doesn't yet support an asynchronous transport for replication. Also, you should note the fact that you will need to install a Microsoft Enterprise Certificate Authority (CA) to be able to make use of SMTP replications—the good bit being that all SMTP messages are encrypted using public key certificates in order to avoid anyone tampering with the replication traffic.

In other words, SMTP replication is primarily of use for GC replication. And you will definitely always need direct IP-connectivity to all DCs participating in the same domain. Consequently, you will need separate domains in areas for which direct IP-connectivity doesn't exist.

The default settings for a site link are a cost of 100 and a replication schedule of every 180 minutes (24 hours a day, 7 days a week). A simple example of three sites connected by four site links (two in each direction) is shown in Figure 12.16. Due to the nontransitiveness of the site links in this scenario, site A has no knowledge of site C, so if site B is down, no replication traffic flows from A to C.

Site Link Bridges

Site link bridges mend the nontransitiveness of site links (and thus are similar to transitive trusts, but only in terms of replication) so that, from the perspective of replication, all the sites connected by the bridge know about each other even though one site is down. For example, in Figure 12.17, site A knows about site C, which wasn't the case in Figure 12.16.

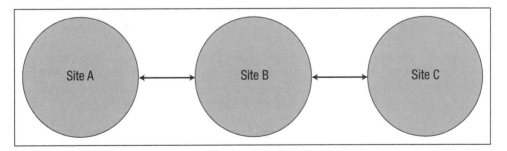

Figure 12.16
A simple example of site links used between three sites.

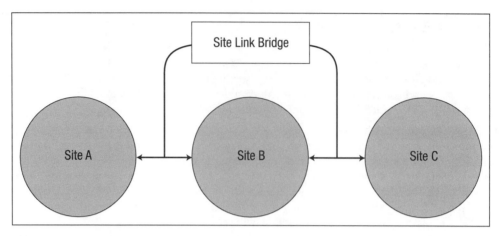

Figure 12.17
If you define a site link bridge, you won't need to explicitly define a site link between sites A and C. Although this won't make much of a difference for a small set of sites, as the number of sites grows, the administrative savings increase.

A site link bridge represents a set of site links, all of which can communicate through some transport. If you know a thing or two about networking hardware, you may want to think of the site link bridges as routers and the site links as hard-wired links. Multiple site link bridges for the same transport work together to model multi-hop routing.

Any network that can be described by a combination of site links and site link bridges can also be described by site links alone. However, site link bridges work to ease the replication setup work quite a bit, and thus make it easier to maintain, because you don't need to create site links for every possible path between pairs of sites.

Note
Even though the site links and site link bridges only allow you to define the sites between which replication is to occur, replication is done by some specific servers. These bridgehead servers are usually the first Active Directory DCs installed in each site (but can be specified by the administrator). If no server is assigned as the bridgehead server (for example, when the first server created in the site is down, demoted, or moved to another site), the server that has the lowest Globally Unique Identifier (GUID) is named the bridgehead server by the inter-site KCC. You can have a different bridgehead server for each transport. You can determine the GUID of an Active Directory GUID by looking in your DNS, because the GUID also is used as a reference point by Active Directory to locate a DC. However, it will usually prove faster to get the GUID from the Active Directory Replication Monitor (REPLMON) utility found in the Windows 2000 Support Kit. See also the Knowledge Base article Q224544.

Actually, you also could opt to mend the nontransitiveness of site links when they are created, because Windows 2000 allows you to have all site links defined for a certain transport to be transitive (the name of the checkbox, which is found on the Properties sheet of the transport, is simply Bridge all site links). This, in turn, makes the creation of site link bridges automatic. The term used most often by Microsoft to make the site links transitive is link transitivity.

The cost of a site link bridge is the sum of all links included in the bridge. For example, if a site link bridge contains two site links, one with a cost of three and another with a cost of four, the cost of the site link bridge is seven.

Connection Objects

Apart from using site links and site link bridges to define the replication topology, you are also allowed to define connection objects (see the prior section, "Intra-site Options in Depth") across sites in exactly the same way that you can define them inside a site. The major difference between a connection object and site links/site link bridges is that a connection object provides a definition of which two DCs should communicate (albeit a unidirectional communication channel), whereas site links/site link bridges define only the sites involved in the communication (without defining which DCs are responsible for handling the actual communication; this is decided by the inter-site KCC, which figures out which connection objects should be created by the system).

A connection object is set up a bit differently from a site link. A connection object provides you with the choice of both the transport and the schedule. The schedule that you set actually determines the site link's frequency and schedule, because it specifies when replications occur on a weekly basis—that is, Monday through Sunday, with four choices (none, once, twice, or four times) inside each hour.

Basically, connection objects, site links, and site link bridges, respectively, give you the following three options for creating an inter-site replication topology:

♦ *Manually*—Create all the needed connection objects by hand (and maybe even disable the inter-site KCC altogether).

♦ *Fully automated*—Enable site link transitiveness on all transports.

♦ *Automatic with preferences*—Leave some site links nontransitive and add site link bridges to enforce certain routes.

Fully automated is the recommended solution with regard to administrative overhead. If your goal is minimum use of inter-site bandwidth on a more advanced setup, you should choose Automatic with preferences. As with intra-site replication, the manual option generally isn't recommended, but you might find yourself pressured into doing just that if you have a lot of sites and/or domains (see the section "Optimizing for Different Scenarios," later in this chapter, for more information).

Choosing a Replication Topology

As you know by now, sites are the primary vehicle for defining the replication topology. When people informally discuss sites and replication topologies, they usually assume that only one topology exists for each domain in a site.

Unfortunately, this assumption is wrong. Active Directory usually winds up creating two or more separate replication topologies (as bidirectional rings) inside each site:

♦ One to cover the configuration naming context and schema naming context

♦ One for each Active Directory domain naming context

♦ Possibly one to cover the replications to the GC

Actually, each of the naming contexts (schema, configuration, and user) can have its own replication topology. However, in the intra-site case, the schema and configuration naming contexts will share the same topology by default, because their information is replicated to all DCs within the site. The domain naming context has its own topology, because it is replicated to all DCs (and GCs) in the site that are participating in the particular domain.

If all DCs in a site participate in the same domain, all three naming contexts can share the same replication ring. You will have more than one replication topology if a site comprises multiple domains. The same holds true for the inter-site case, for which a *spanning tree topology* is automatically built between the sites.

So, if you want to plan all the connection objects yourself (and disable the KCC), you have to consider the needs of both replication topologies. Figures 12.18 and 12.19 demonstrate the work required to plan the connection objects and should give you an appreciation of the work done by the KCC—and a reason never again to consider disabling the KCC.

Note, too, that GCs embrace the replication topology used for domains, so if you have an instance of several domains inside one site, Active Directory also defines connection objects from DCs belonging to other domains to the DCs that also act as GCs (see Figure 12.20 for an example).

Tip

The key to understanding which replication topologies are being created is the fact that each Active Directory DC/GC only is able to replicate the naming contexts stored locally. In other words, if you have an Active Directory DC, you'll be able to use it for:

• *Feeding any other DC with the schema and configuration-naming contexts*

• *Feeding the domain naming context to other DCs that are part of the same domain*

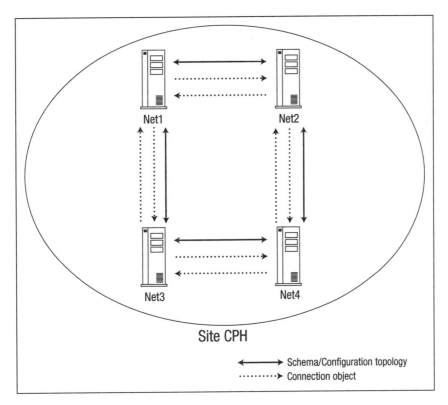

Figure 12.18
A "typical" domain with four DCs.

- *Feeding the domain naming context to any other GC that needs to retrieve a partial set of attributes from that very domain*

If you have an Active Directory DC/GC, you will be able to use the GC for: Feeding the partial domain naming contexts to any other GC.

You can build the replication topology by hand just by using those simple rules and keeping in mind that each DC/GC always will try to minimize the number of servers it's replicating to (so a DC will always want to replicate its schema and configuration naming context with the server that is supplying the domain naming context).

The Time Service: Don't Overlook It

On a whole different note, you should also know a bit about the Time Service, which is charged with making sure that all DCs, member servers, and clients participating in the forest will be using the same time and date. Although time isn't used as the primary means for resolving replication collisions, it will still be called for if you're faced with a tie on the USNs. And, even more important: The new authentication protocol (Kerberos) is heavily

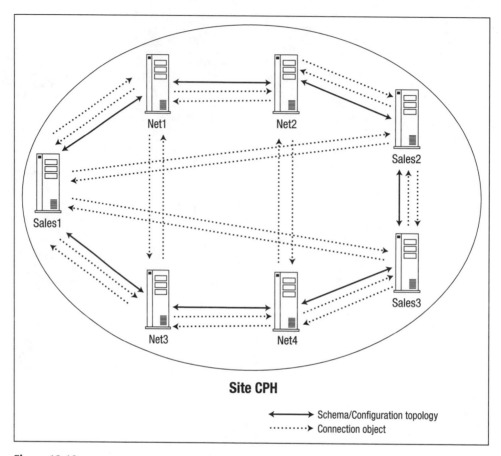

Figure 12.19
The domain from Figure 12.18 after adding three more DCs from another domain in the forest.

reliant on having time properly in sync across the domain, because it uses the time as part of the authentication ticket generation process. In other words, time synchronization is quite important to Active Directory's well being.

Windows 2000's Time Service is an implementation of one of the lesser known RFCs—RFC 1769, the *Simple Network Time Protocol (SNTP)*, which isn't a standard at present time. As is implied by the name, SNTP is a simplified version of the Network Time Protocol (NTP).

This is a rather unfortunate choice on the part of Microsoft, because SNTP is rather scantily documented compared with NTP and, even more important: It's not a standard. Serving to further underscore the absurdity in the choice stands the fact that the RFC specifically states that, for reliability, an SNTP client should never be dependent upon another SNTP client for synchronization—rather, it should rely on the more advanced NTP protocol.

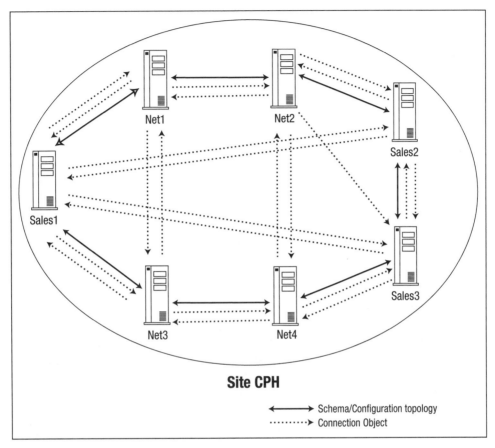

Figure 12.20
Development of the situation in Figure 12.19 after the Sales3 DC has been promoted to a GC. A connection object was added between Sales3 and Net2, due to the three-hop rule.

And so, the fact that Microsoft has implemented SNTP across the board in all Windows 2000 variants really doesn't sit well with the RFC.

I will encourage you should want to comply as closely as possible with the recommendation made in the RFC. At the very least, you should have the Active Directory DCs that are deployed in the data center synchronize their clocks from a reliable NTP server(s) located in close proximity.

Note
*Microsoft's reason for choosing SNTP over NTP isn't known to me, so it's likely that they're just sticking to the well known, because Microsoft has already done some of the code needed in connection with the **TimeServ** and W32Time Resource Kit tools for Windows NT 4.*

On Windows 2000 Professional clients, the Time Service (a.k.a. W32Time or Windows Time Service) works in the following way:

1. The workstation contacts the authenticating DC. They exchange packets to determine latency of communication between the two machines, and the workstation determines the time that it should converge to.

2. The local time on the workstation is adjusted. If the target time is ahead of local time, local time is immediately set to the target time. If the target time is behind local time, the local clock is slowed over the next 20 minutes to align the two times, unless local time is more than two minutes out of sync; in that case, the time is immediately set.

3. After that, the workstation will perform periodic checks on its time settings. Initially, this is done by asking the authenticating DC every eight hours. If local time is off from target time by more than two seconds, the interval check period is divided in half, and so forth (until the interval frequency gets down to 45 minutes). If accuracy is maintained within two seconds, the interval check period will be doubled again, up to a maximum period of eight hours.

Note

The act of joining a domain enables the Windows 2000 Time Service, so that it automatically starts at boot. When a computer communicates with other Windows 2000 computers, time packets are secured with a signed hash of the time information. Security is based on the secure channel, and signature key is determined by the machine account of the client.

The Windows 2000 servers are handled in the following ways:

♦ All member servers follow the same procedure as the clients.

♦ All DCs in a domain nominate the PDC FSMO to be the partner that they synchronize their clocks against (using the same rule set as the clients).

♦ All PDC FSMOs follow the domain's hierarchy in the selection of their time partner.

Note

Please note that time synchronization uses Universal Time Coordinate (UTC), which is time zone independent. SNTP defaults to using UDP Port 123, so if this port is not open across your forest, you won't be able to synchronize your server to any Internet SNTP servers.

So, when you follow the default Time Service settings for the Active Directory hierarchy, the PDC FSMO at the root of the forest becomes authoritative for the enterprise; therefore, this machine should reference an external time source—or be kept under tight observation with regard to its time. This fact is actually logged in the System log as Event ID 62 on the computer holding the PDC FSMO at the root of the forest.

Unfortunately, the Time Service can't be managed from anywhere in the MMC toolset. The Time Service is controlled by using the **NET TIME** command and/or configuring the Registry.

*You can change the default configuration of the Windows Time Service by manually editing the Registry on the machine. You provide the changes to the default NTP server definitions by adding the **REG_SZ** value named **NTPServer** to the **HKLM\SYSTEM\CurrentControlSet\Services\W32Time\Parameters** Registry key; a data value is the list of servers listed as DNS names or IP addresses, with each of those entries separated by semicolons. You also need to change the Type Registry key from "Nt5DS" to "NTP" to signify that you are not making use of the default Windows 2000 time hierarchy any more, but will be making use of the NTP server specified by you. You can find more Registry tweaks in the Knowledge Base article Q223184.*

*Administrators can configure the Windows Time Service at the PDC role holder at the Active Directory forest root to recognize an external Simple Network Time Protocol (SNTP) time server as authoritative, using the following **NET TIME** command: **net time /setsntp:<server list>**.*

DFS and FRS: Those Other Replication Topologies

Windows 2000 Server includes two other services—Distributed File System (DFS) and File Replication Service (FRS)—which will create yet another kind of replication topology.

Because DFS employs FRS as its replication engine, the two services work in much the same way. However, their scope is quite different:

- *FRS*—Used for replicating file data (that is, all data that isn't stored in the Active Directory database) between Active Directory DCs. The scope of FRS is limited to an Active Directory domain.

- *DFS*—Used for creating distributed file systems. You can have a DFS file share span several servers, shares, and files. Also, DFS can be used to create replicas of a given share on other servers. Consequently, you might want to think of DFS as a technology that does for servers and shares what the file systems and RAID do for hard disks.

Getting a Feel for the FRS

Microsoft has focused all of their attention on the engine for replicating Active Directory objects. And so, virtually no information exists on the other and just as vital part of the replication story: the File Replication Service (FRS), which is used on all DCs.

As the name implies, FRS takes care of the file replications in an Active Directory setting, and thus it replaces the flaky **NT LMREPL** service that everybody has learned to hate. Chances are good that people will be more satisfied with the FRS. FRS is used to replicate the contents of the Windows 2000 System Volume (SYSVOL), which is built during creation of the Active Directory DC. SYSVOL can be located on any local NTFS 5 volume available to the Active Directory Installation Wizard when the DC is created. The default path suggested by the Active Directory Installation Wizard is WinNT\SYSVOL, where SYSVOL represents a user-defined path. The SYSVOL directory and SYSVOL Server Message Block (SMB) share are located under the user-defined path, defaulting to WinNT\SYSVOL\sysvol.

SYSVOL is really a tree of folders containing the following:

- SYSVOL share
- NETLOGON share
- Directories to store user logon and logoff scripts
- Directories to store GPT (Group Policy Template) objects
- FRS's own staging directories
- Other files that need to be available and synchronized between DCs in a domain (such as profiles)

Note

Consider placing SYSVOL on a different partition than the OS, if you replicate large amounts of data.

The main reason that SYSVOL has to be located on an NTFS 5-formatted disk is that the FRS uses one of the new NTFS features—USN Journal. This feature provides FRS with the ability to track the changes made to files (in other words, any attribute change done to a file or directory, except for the Archive bit, last file access time, and the NTFS compression bit attribute), to assess which files need to be replicated.

It's crucial that you understand that the content of SYSVOL is replicated to all other DCs in the domain. In other words, the scope of FRS is the domain (you will need to use DFS for moving beyond the domain).

The SYSVOL replication is done by using the FRS replication engine, which is a replacement for the LAN Manager Replication Service (LMREPL) used by Windows NT Server 4. Some of the many new features offered with FRS are the following:

- Multi-master replication.
- Use of the same replication topology as defined for the Active Directory DC/GC replications.
- Multithreaded operation, so that several files may be replicated simultaneously between two partners.
- ACLs are included in the replication.

Understanding the SYSVOL Contents

You will probably find some of the following directories present on your DC:

- *\SYSVOL*—The path defined when promoting a server to DC. Defaults to WinNT\SYSVOL.

- *\SYSVOL\sysvol*—Root of the SYSVOL tree and physical path for the SYSVOL SMB share.

- *\SYSVOL\sysvol\<domain name>\scripts*—Contains login scripts for legacy clients (Windows NT 4 and Windows 9x). The contents of the Netlogon share (System32\REPL\Export\Scripts) will be moved here during an upgrade from Windows NT Server to Windows 2000 Server.

- *\SYSVOL\sysvol\<domain name>\Policies*—Contains Group Policies for Windows 2000 Server clients and System Policies for all legacy clients (Windows NT 4 and Windows 9x). Each policy is stored in a separate directory expressed as long strings shown in the Policies folder. The long strings represent the GUID for the individual policy object.

- *\SYSVOL\staging*—Used by FRS to stage inbound and outbound information to other DCs.

Note that no shell extensions or utilities exist to distinguish junctions in the SYSVOL tree from physical paths. However, the DOS **DIR** command displays reparse points as "junctions" instead of "directories." So, if you want to understand these details, you can either browse the UNC path for a given DC or the FQDN for the machine's domain from a Windows 2000 machine on the network.

Note

There's no way to deny file sharing or enforce file locking between two users writing the same file on two different FRS (or DFS) replicas. To implement single master replication, the administrator must ACL the root of the replica tree to limit write access appropriately, then establish a policy that a specific computer is the "master" replica.

Also, FRS is site aware. FRS uses RPC and adheres to the replication topology defined for the Active Directory DCs. FRS doesn't employ compression, no matter whether we're talking intra-site or inter-site replications. So you will have exactly the same amount of data flowing over the WAN as on the LAN—the only difference is that you can specify the number of DCs involved in replications going across sites.

FRS operates at the file level. And so, changing a single character in a 10MB document will cause the entire file to replicate!

Note

FRS is also used to replicate any DFS volumes residing on the servers. However, the DFS replication properties are governed by separately defined DFS connection objects, which are found in the DFS MMC snap-in.

Simply said, the replication algorithm used by FRS works as follows:

1. A file is changed, which is noted by the system as soon as the file is closed as a function of the USN Journal feature of Windows 2000 Server.

2. FRS monitors the journal for changes that it cares about and moves the appropriate entries into its own journal.

3. FRS generates a staging file of the file change(s) and updates the outbound log.

4. FRS holds onto changes until the replication is scheduled to commence. At this point, a notification of changes is sent to the replication partner:

   ♦ Each time a Windows 2000 server is started or the FRS service is started, the computer object in the Active Directory is polled in eight short intervals followed by eight long intervals, provided no configuration changes take place. Thus, long polling intervals occur only after eight short polling intervals have finished without change.

   ♦ The FRS service waits two polling intervals, short or long, before replication takes place.

   ♦ With each FRS reset event, the eight short and eight long polling cycle is invoked again. Events that reset the polling interval include DC added, DC deleted, connection added, connection deleted, schedule changed, and file or folder filter changed.

5. The replication partner, in turn, pulls the staging file and applies the specified changes to its own SYSVOL share.

SYSVOL Troubleshooting

If you experience trouble with the core FRS functionality, you should do the following (which isn't too rewarding an experience, because Microsoft hasn't developed a GUI for FRS yet):

• Check the File Replication Service folder in the Event Viewer for events that might shed some more light on what's wrong. Remember to use common sense in case of trouble: Is the file or folder locked? Does the computer or connection object exist in Active Directory? Are you out of free disk space on one of the replication partners? And so on.

• If you've just promoted the server to DC status, you should take a peek at the *NtFrsApi.log* file (in the WinNT\DEBUG directory) for SYSVOL-specific errors. FRS writes to this log, when the SYSVOL directory is established by the Active Directory Installation Wizard.

• Look closer at the *NtFrs_xxxx.log* files, which show any errors, warning messages, and milestone events from FRS. Over time, these files tend to get long, so you might want to search for the strings "error", "warn", and "fail" in the log file, to save some time. Always start with the last log file, if the problem has just begun. And, when checking the file entries, understand that the following are "normal" errors not worth looking into:

   • "jet attach db - 1811. Db not found" should be expected when using Active Directory Installation Wizard.

   • "Sharing violations" (which has a 0x00000043 status code) shows that a user or process has a lock on a file.

If you still aren't able to pinpoint the source of the problem, you might want to pilfer with some of the following Registry keys (which are all located in **HKLM\System\CurrentControlSet\ Services\NtFrs\Parameters**):

• *Debug Log Severity (REG_DWORD)*—Controls the verbosity level of the *Ntfrs_000x.log* files in the %SystemRoot%\Debug folder. Severity levels are assigned to different debug print statements in the code. 0 is minimum and 5 is maximum. 4 is the default value.

- *Debug Log Files (REG_DWORD)*—The number of active log files that record FRS service transactions and events. Logs are written on a first-in-first-out (FIFO) basis with the highest number containing the most recent events. Logs one through "Debug Log Files" are created in sequential order. Once Debug Maximum Log messages are written to the last log (*Ntfrs_0005.log*), the lowest log (*Ntfrs_0001.log*) is deleted and the version number for the remaining logs gets decremented. 0 is minimum and there's no maximum. 5 is the default value.

- *Debug Maximum Log Messages (REG_DWORD)*—The number of lines stored in a single *Ntfrs_000x.log* file. There's no minimum and no maximum. 10000 is the default value, which will amount to a log file size of between 1.5 and 2.5MB.

- *DS Polling Short Interval in Minutes (REG_DWORD)*—The interval with which FRS polls the Active Directory at service startup or after configuration changes. FRS performs eight short polling intervals and then switches to long polling intervals, if not interrupted by configuration changes that cause the short polling sequence to start over. 1 minute is minimum and there's no maximum. 5 minutes is the default setting for DCs as well as member servers.

- *DS Polling Long Interval in Minutes (REG_DWORD)*—The interval with which FRS polls the Active Directory for configuration changes after eight short polling intervals have finished without interruption. 1 minute minimum and there's no maximum. 5 minutes is the default setting for DCs and 60 minutes is the default setting for member servers.

- *Staging Space Limit in KB (REG_DWORD)*—The maximum amount of disk space to allocate to files held on disk until retrieved by all downstream replication partners. This should be less than the amount of free disk space. If set to large numbers, staging space may consume all available drive space if downstream replication partners do not pick up changes because of link failures or operating system problems. There's no minimum or maximum. 660MB is the default value.

- *Working Directory (REG_DWORD)*—By default the FRS database (Ntfrs.jdb) will be located in %SystemRoot%\Ntfrs. You can move the FRS database to any NTFS 5-formatted volume. But you should remember to stop the Ntfrs service before you move the database.

Finally, if you exhaust your list of possible causes and can live with not being able to pinpoint the source of the error, you have this rather harsh option for recovery:

- Stop FRS on all DCs, and change the value of the BurFlags entry found at **HKLM\System\ CurrentControlSet\Services\NtFrs\Parameters\Backup/Restore\Process at Startup** to D4 (which means that this DC is authoritative for FRS data) on the DC that you trust to be in the best shape, FRS-wise. Change the BurFlags value on all other DCs to D2 (which means the that DC is nonauthoritative as pertains FRS data). Start FRS on the "good" DC and then go on to start the FRS on the remainder of the DCs.

This should cause all DCs with BurFlags set to D2 to replicate from the DC with BurFlags set to D4. And so, FRS will be reinitialized on all the DCs and the FRS contents will be restored from the trusted DC to all the other DCs. This usually is the only solution if FRS replication has halted on all DCs and you can't find the source of the error.

Finally, keep in mind that FRS depends on the same replication topology as the DC and GC replications. Thus, if your DC and GC replications don't work (for instance, due to some connection objects missing), you will most probably also be at odds with FRS. The same goes if you've got duplicate connection objects between two DCs.

Some of the key points of this process are that only unlocked files will be replicated and that a simple, last-writer-wins algorithm is used (that is, the last update on any replica becomes authoritative). File version, size, and any user effort are totally ignored by FRS when performing the replication, which means that you should use FRS only for relatively static data that has a low risk of collisions occurring or employs some kind of collision-avoidance technique (which is the case, for example, with Group Policies, in which the updates, by default, will take place only on the PDC FSMO, making it impossible to have different writes being made on multiple DCs).

But you might want to note that FRS doesn't replicate files or folders with the following attributes:

♦ Folders that fall outside the trees managed by FRS (that is, SYSVOL)

♦ Files with a .bak or .tmp extension, or files that begin with ~. The file and folder filters can be modified

♦ EFS-enabled files and folders

♦ Changes to a file or folder's last access time

♦ Changes to a file or folder's Archive bit

♦ NTFS mount points

Note

You can exclude more files and folders from the FRS replications by following the advice given in Knowledge Base Q221110.

Also, FRS is utterly incompatible with the old LAN Manager Replication Service used by Windows NT Server, so you have to either do a swift migration to Windows 2000 Server and get used to the fact that the Windows NT Server BDCs and the Active Directory DCs aren't talking with regard to file replications, or implement some kind of batch file to replicate the appropriate files to a Windows NT 4 Server (see Chapter 22 for more information on how to bridge **LMREPL** and FRS).

Unfortunately, uncertainty still exists regarding FRS replication efficiency and robustness, as well as the implementation details (including the load properties, although everything indicates that FRS is disk-, network-, and processor-dependent). However, FRS should prove fairly robust, because it uses the Jet Database Engine. And FRS can't be any worse than the **LMREPL** service, which isn't very popular with Windows NT Server administrators.

Don't Overlook that Nifty DFS Feature

The FRS file replication engine is also used for replicating files that are stored in Distributed File System (DFS). Although DFS also has file replications as its scope, it's very much different from FRS. The leading principle of DFS is actually quite simple: Group together partitions or volumes from many different servers to act as an unbroken logical drive. In doing so, DFS breaks with the time-honored principle that a disk partition or volume should always appear as a logical drive to be readily accessible to users.

This change is most welcome, because problems already exist in the larger settings, as a result of having had all the drive mappings that a user may need grow beyond the 22 possibilities of assigning drive letters. The improvements to the environment delivered by DFS are shown in Figures 12.21 through 12.23. Figure 12.21 shows how a company's data can be spread out over many unrelated shares in a networked environment, leading to a lot of confusion when looking for files or collecting data.

Figure 12.22 shows the same set of shares assembled in a single share by way of DFS, which will prove to be much easier to grasp for just about any user.

Figure 12.23 shows the physical implementation of the logical structure shown in Figure 12.22. This figure also goes to demonstrate how several servers, each containing one or multiple shares, can be made a part of a DFS root. And you should note that the servers can even run on different OSs—according to Microsoft, DFS will allow you to add server shares from any OS for which a redirector to Windows 2000 Server is in existence.

To state it in another way: DFS takes the shape of a single hierarchical file system whose contents can be distributed across the servers that comprise the Active Directory forest. Further, DFS provides a logical tree structure for file resources that may be physically located anywhere on the network. Because the DFS tree is a single point of reference, users will have an easier time gaining access to network resources: They won't need to know the exact name of the files as well as the file servers needed.

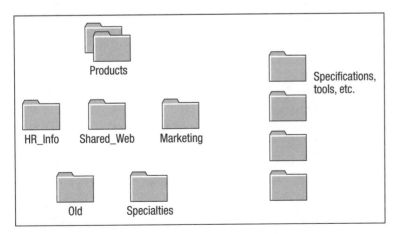

Figure 12.21
The data in everyday use is often spread out among many different shares.

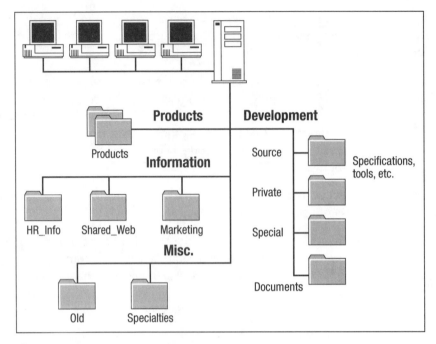

Figure 12.22
Collecting all the shares and disk partitions from Figure 12.21 into just one share using DFS will most certainly work to improve the user's situation.

The highlights of DFS are the following:

♦ *Organizing file and folder resources in a tree structure*—DFS organizes shared folders that can reside on different servers. A DFS share uses a tree structure that contains a root and child nodes. Each DFS root can have multiple child nodes beneath it, each of which points to a shared folder. The child nodes of the DFS root represent shared folders that can be physically located on different file servers.

♦ *Simplified network navigation*—DFS provides users with easy navigation to shared folders, because the users only need to know the name of the folder (avoiding the need for knowing the name of the server on which the folder is shared). When users are connected to a DFS root, they can browse and gain access to all file resources below the root (provided that they have permissions for it), regardless of the location of the server on which the resource is located.

♦ *Improved network administration*—DFS makes it easier to administer multiple shared folders. If a server fails, you can move a child node from one server to another without users having to know anything about the change. All that is required to move a child node is to modify DFS to refer to the new server location of the shared folders—the users will continue to use the same path for the child node, unless it's changed by the administrator in the process.

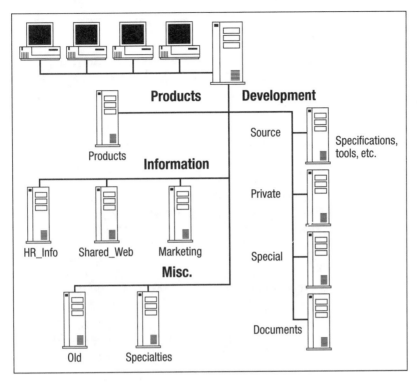

Figure 12.23
The individual shares and partitions making up the DFS share can be spread among several servers. And these servers don't even have to be running Windows 2000 or Windows NT!

- *Preserves network permission*—DFS doesn't get in the way of the permissions set on the shared folder or the files being stored there. So the user won't see any changes to his permissions, no matter whether he's working directly on the local server's shared folder or via DFS.

The DFS root represents the topmost part of the DFS topology; therefore, it forms the starting point for the hierarchy of shared folders that make up a logical namespace. Although you may have any number of DFS roots running in your company, each server can only host one DFS root.

You have two kinds of DFS roots to choose from:

- *Standalone DFS root*—Stores the DFS topology on one computer. This type of DFS provides no fault tolerance, in case the computer that stores the DFS topology, or any of the shared folders that DFS uses, should fail. And there's no load balancing (being able to choose between multiple servers for accessing the individual files) or root-level fault tolerance to be found, because it's working in the Windows 2000 Server context and doesn't make use of Active Directory. Only one server can host each standalone DFS root and a single level of child nodes. And so, you really shouldn't implement this option for anything but backward-compatibility with the earlier versions of DFS.

♦ *Fault-tolerant DFS root*—Stores the DFS topology in Active Directory. You are able to host each DFS root on multiple servers, allowing for load-balancing, as well as adding fault tolerance (the fault-tolerant DFS root continues to function even when a server hosting the root fails, provided that you have a new one waiting to take over). Because fault-tolerant DFS is integrated with Active Directory, all the information about the logical namespace is maintained in Active Directory.

Tip

You can create additional replicas of a fault-tolerant DFS root (called root replica members), allowing you to remove a single point of failure with regard to the DFS root. Additional root replica members need to be hosted on computers in the same domain.

Further, you can expand a DFS tree by adding multiple child nodes to the DFS root (this feature only applies to servers running Windows 2000 Server and using an NTFS-formatted partition for storing the child node). Each of these child nodes can be hosted on multiple servers through the use of replicas, thus removing any single point of failure here. Because DFS is site-aware, the multiple replicas will also reduce the network traffic, because the DFS client will attempt to connect to the replica closest to the user.

If you configure multiple replicas of the same child node, you need to ensure that each replica contains the same data. You can do this by manually synchronizing the contents of multiple replicas, or by using FRS to replicate files between all replicas of the child node. To keep the contents of the replicas synchronized as changes to one or more of the replicas occur, you should configure replication between the replicas. Because this file replication may take several minutes or longer, multiple replicas of the same node really only apply to read-only data. By default, the replicas are synchronized at 15-minute intervals.

And the beauty of all this is that the user won't notice a thing, provided that he's using a PC that is equipped with a DFS client. The user just accesses the DFS share using a Universal Naming Convention (UNC) name, specifying *server**share**path*: the *server* being the name of the server or domain hosting the DFS root, the *share* being the name of the DFS root, and the *path* being the name of the child node and any folders within it.

Note

DFS clients exist for Windows 95, Windows 98, Windows NT, and Windows 2000.

With regard to Active Directory use, you should be most keenly aware of the capabilities of having a DFS root replicated to other servers—but having the data being registered and accessed using exactly the same UNC name (this being *domain**share**file*). This is a great solution for software distribution using GPOs, where you are prompted for a path to the .MSI file in question (and DFS allows you to use the same path throughout the enterprise, despite the fact that you will be accessing local servers for the data).

Warning

DFS only supports 32 replicas of each DFS root. So if you have a lot of locations, the DFS solution might not prove fully adequate.

How to Design for the Physical Properties

You define your network's site structure purely to optimize the behavior of Active Directory for your network's physical structure. Site containers contain only computer objects and connection objects that are used to configure inter-site replication, whereas computers and users are grouped into domains and OUs.

When you design the physical properties for Active Directory, you should always start with the site design, because the DCs and GCs can be considered "helper servers" to Active Directory. The number and placement of these helper servers is based on the physical properties that are uncovered when you do the site design. Also, each major site really should have at least one DC and GC available, which is more easily accomplished when you know the site design up front.

Introductory Site Design

The definition of a site as one or more TCP/IP subnets is based on the assumption that computers within one subnet address are connected to the same network segment (that is, an area of good connectivity). If this assumption isn't true for your network design, you should consider either redesigning the TCP/IP addressing used on your network as soon as possible or acknowledging that the introduction of Windows 2000 on your network could very well trigger some large capital outlays on higher bandwidth levels across your WAN connections.

The preceding redesign suggestion shouldn't be regarded simply as an unfortunate side effect of Active Directory. Actually, a good TCP/IP network design (by today's standards) always has each LAN and WAN segment cover one or more dedicated subnets. This is the only way to ensure swift and efficient handling of TCP/IP packets by the intelligent network hardware components (routers, switches, and so forth). So, you shouldn't blame Microsoft if you have computers within one subnet address that aren't connected to the same network segment; your network designers should bear the blame for not mapping the TCP/IP properties correctly to the network.

If you are in the unfortunate situation of having one or more subnets that are used across slow WAN links, you should start to redesign the TCP/IP network design immediately. Remember, too, that this redesign almost certainly will limit the traffic traveling across the slow link and, thus, should save you money in the process.

> **Tip**
>
> *You should also be very careful to note any potholes on the TCP/IP network (that is, areas that can't be contacted using IP, because they will most probably demand a separate Active Directory domain), as well as any firewalls or other kinds of filtering devices on the internal network. (Active Directory uses a fair number of different ports as well as dynamically assigned ports, which might prove to be a problem).*
>
> *Please note that Knowledge Base article Q224196 outlines how to restrict Active Directory replication traffic to a specific port (as opposed to using dynamically assigned ports).*

Reviewing the Locations

Your first step in planning the site structure is to examine all the locations in which the company has offices and then determine whether each location requires a DC. When doing that, consider the tradeoffs, as described in Table 12.4.

Determining Connectivity and Available Bandwidth

Because sites are defined as one or more subnets with good connectivity, you must con-sider connectivity when you plan the sites. Available bandwidth also is a very important consideration, to avoid creating a site plan that turns out to be a heavy user of an already oversubscribed line.

When you consider how to group subnets into sites on your network, remember to combine only those subnets that have a "fast, cheap, and reliable" network connection with each other. To be considered "fast," a network connection should be at least 512Kbps. An avail-able bandwidth of 128Kbps or higher should be sufficient for all but the largest and most special cases.

> **Note**
>
> *A multihomed computer with subnet addresses in different sites can belong only to one of the sites, not to several or all of them. Assigning all the subnet addresses for a multihomed computer to belong to the same site is a good idea, if possible.*

Table 12.4   Determining the need for a DC.

No DC at Location	One or More DCs at Location
No replication traffic to and from the location	Replication traffic to and from the location
Logon traffic to and from the location from locations with DCs	No logon traffic crossing the site boundary, except for in a disaster situation (all DCs or GCs down at location)
No need to make this location a separate site	Need to determine whether the location should be made a separate site

As is true for domain design, when you plan for sites, you should always start with the simplest site structure and then add sites as the constraints of bandwidth and connectivity dictate.

Setting up the Site Structure

How you set up your site structure affects Windows 2000 Server in two main ways:

♦ *Workstation logon*—When a user logs on, Windows 2000 tries to find a DC and a GC in the same site as the user's computer.

♦ *Replication*—The way in which you configure the schedule and path for Active Directory replication can be different for replication between two or more sites than it is for replication within a single site.

Generally, the objectives of a site structure are to avoid sending workstation logons over the WAN and to keep the directory replication in check by containing and controlling it. Furthermore, always follow this assumption when planning the site: Network traffic within a site will be much higher than traffic between sites, due to logon and search traffic, as well as uncompressed replication traffic flowing between the DCs and GCs inside the site.

Typically, your site planning will require some compromise between the need to control workstation logons and the need to control replication. Thus, you initially must determine the appropriate balance between controlling workstation logons and controlling replication. You are on the way to accomplishing that if you have carefully examined each of the network links between locations and determined whether the individual links should be used for logon traffic or for replication traffic. This choice applies only to each domain, which means that you could have both types of traffic flowing on the WAN if your choices differ between different domains available at the same location.

Configuring each geographical location as a separate site generally is the best practice. Even in situations in which you want inter-site and intra-site replication to occur with equal frequency, configuring separate sites will provide you with more flexibility. By creating separate sites, you can configure them with more than one replication connection (for example, a high-bandwidth line as the default connection and a dial-up backup connection). And, in the case of multiple redundant connections, Active Directory always chooses the connection with the least cost assigned, so the cheaper connection will be used if it is available. Also, be keenly aware that bandwidth almost always is the most important practical consideration when choosing sites.

Planning Sites to Control Workstation Logon

When you plan your sites, consider which DCs each workstation should use. At logon, a workstation attempts to find a DC in its local site and needs to access a GC. Consequently, you might want to limit the area covered by each site. Designing a site structure for a network that consists of a single LAN is simple. LAN connections typically are fast, so the entire network can be a single site.

> **Tip**
>
> *Although you can define multiple sites within one well-connected location, this choice has potential drawbacks. For example, when a user attempts to log on, if no DC is available in the same Active Directory site, the client searches for alternative DCs anywhere on your network. This can result in connections (and bandwidth usage) that are less than optimal, because Active Directory doesn't try to determine which other site is "nearest" in terms of connectivity. Furthermore, each site defined usually ends up "costing" you at least one (and typically two) server that is used to provide DC and GC services.*

Designing a site structure for a network that consists of multiple locations is more difficult. You must first decide whether each of the locations even needs a DC or a GC. If a location has neither a DC nor a GC, no replication traffic goes to that location, and workstations use the WAN connection to log on to a DC and a GC. This approach might be acceptable if the location is at the end of a very fast and reliable connection to one or more other locations, but the relatively slow logon process might be inconvenient.

Generally, the solution with no local DC (or GC) is acceptable only for very small locations that have only a few workstations. Larger locations should have one or more local DCs and GCs and should be configured as separate sites, so as to eliminate the possibility of having workstations log on to DCs and GCs located on the other side of the WAN connection.

> **Tip**
>
> *At logon, a workstation attempts to find a DC in its local site. If you care only that a workstation be able to find a DC over a fast, reliable connection, then you can simply define your sites to mirror your topology of fast network connections. If a workstation logs on and no DCs are available on the same Active Directory site, the workstation uses some other DC on your network. Availability and traffic containment are the main reasons that you will want multiple DCs within a site: When you or your users need a DC, you have a better chance of being able to access one quickly onsite than you do by going to another site.*

Planning Sites to Control Replication Traffic

The other major consideration that goes into site planning is how and when replication should occur. Sites should be used to control replication across slow, expensive, or unreliable connections.

Between sites (inter-site replication), you have the option of controlling the following:

◆ In which time slots is inter-site replication allowed to occur?

◆ How frequent are the connection checks for replication updates?

◆ Which network transport should you use?

◆ Which connection (if more than one exists) is preferred?

When you plan for replication traffic, you should focus on determining how much replication traffic will actually take place on the network. Fortunately, even if you have a large directory, Active Directory provides ample help in minimizing and optimizing replication traffic over the network, through the following features:

♦ *Replication of revised attributes and objects only*—Active Directory only replicates objects and attributes that have recently been updated. If you update an existing user's telephone number, the directory replicates the new phone number to all other DCs. Any other information related to that user isn't replicated, minimizing traffic on the network.

♦ *Compression of replication traffic*—Inter-site replication is compressed, regardless of the transport used. Although compression does cost some CPU cycles at the bridgehead server, it is easily worth it, because inter-site replication traffic at its best can be brought down to some 10 to 15 percent of comparable intra-site replications. (See Chapter 16 for more information.)

Warning
Remember that a promotion of a server to DC will prompt a replication of the complete domain naming context, schema naming context and configuration naming context (this will also happen, if the DC has been without connection to the rest of the Active Directory infrastructure for longer than the tombstone time, which is 60 days by default). This might prove a major problem, if you're running off very little bandwidth. Also, promoting a DC to a GC will add a full replication of a subset of all the available domain naming contexts in the forest.

When you plan for replication, you should try to determine how many attributes and objects are changed (added, deleted, or edited) per day/week/month. If your company utilizes a large directory, be especially aware of recurring changes (for example, new passwords) and determine whether they occur at exactly the same time or are approximately evenly spread out over the password expiration interval. Also consider whether you might experience some replication "explosions" when you add new domains or DCs to the network.

Finally, to organize your sites effectively, check out the replication requirements and available connectivity inside the sites. Strive to find a balance that ensures DCs in the same site are sufficiently well connected to handle frequent exchange of directory information, but do not exact what you consider to be excessive costs (such as high financial expense or compromised network performance).

Determining Site Properties

After you establish multiple sites, you need to consider how information should be exchanged between sites. Active Directory automatically creates site links when DCs are added to new sites. However, you should review, fine-tune, or supplement the initial site link configuration and properties in correspondence with your WAN topology.

A Mature RPC Transport

If you've been subjected with RPC-based solutions from Microsoft, you should want to note that Active Directory's built-in RPC transport should prove to work much better than what you are expecting. Not only is it quite rugged (that is, it won't start doing a full retry when encountering the first packet error), but it's surprisingly stable to slow links. Actually, it will prove to work fine with the default settings on 19,200 bps connections, whereas timeouts will start to occur at 9,600 and 2,400 bps. However, if you do a little bit to optimize things (see Chapter 20), you can get the RPC transport to function over a 2,400 bps link provided that no other traffic is there and the 9,600 bps link will work fine—albeit very slow—as long as it's not oversubscribed! Consequently, you shouldn't need to employ the SMTP alternative, except in a few very special cases.

When you plan the inter-site replication, make the effort to attach some well-defined costs to each site link, because this is the only way to ensure that replication traffic flows optimally around the network. When you assign costs to the site links, you should (at a minimum) differentiate between the following types of connections (the precise definitions depend on your settings):

♦ 100Mbps or higher

♦ 10Mbps

♦ High-performance WAN (for example, T1/E1)

♦ Medium-performance WAN (for example, smaller leased lines, frame relay with a relatively high CIR, or heavily used high-performance connections)

♦ Low-performance WAN (for example, leased lines with a low bandwidth, frame relay with a low CIR, or oversubscribed high-performance connections)

Use increments of site link costs of at least 10 for each connectivity level (where the lowest performance is assigned the highest cost). If you have a large WAN setup, consider using an exponentially growing site link cost for each connectivity level, to avoid suboptimization on shortcuts in your infrastructure (that is, very slow connections that connect large locations situated a long way from the network's "main roads"). Remember, that the cost of a site link bridge is the sum of all links included in the bridge. Also, consider implementing site links only (no site link bridges) for each pair of sites that cross a slow WAN connection. This ensures that the connection is never burdened with replication traffic going between other sites. If you have connections that are oversubscribed or more expensive at certain times of day (or all weekdays), you might also want to implement schedules on these site links.

You also should choose which transport (RPC or SMTP) to use on each inter-site link. GC, schema, and configuration containers are the only naming contexts that can be transported by SMTP, so a DC in one site can't talk to a DC in another site via SMTP. Thus, SMTP replication is primarily used for GC replication. Also be keenly aware that SMTP ignores the scheduling (that is, you have no upper bound on the delivery time of delivered data or messages or ability to ensure the order of delivery), because it assumes that the underlying SMTP messaging system takes care of the routing.

Additionally, invest some time determining how to create your inter-site replication topology:

♦ *Manually*—Create all the needed connection objects by hand (and maybe even disable the KCC). Not recommended for anything but the most extreme cases.

♦ *Fully automated*—Enable site link transitiveness on all the transports utilized. Whenever possible, use this option.

♦ *Automatically, with preferences*—Leave some site links nontransitive and add site link bridges to enforce certain routes. Use this option if you are faced with a partitioned network.

The second option is the one that you should try to stick to, whenever possible. However, if you are faced with a partitioned network, you really want to go with the third option. The first option isn't recommended for any but the extreme cases.

Finally, review your site link topology to determine, if applicable, whether or not you can avoid having only one link going out from each site. Although a single site link is sufficient, to create a more reliable replication system, you must provide Active Directory with at least two site links.

Note

You also should establish the worst-case scenario with regard to convergence in your site setup: How long could a change that is being implemented at one end of the Active Directory structure take to reach the last DC or GC in the forest?

If you know that the worst-case propagation delay within a site is 15 minutes, you know that the bridgehead servers in each site will receive an update no later than 15 minutes after it is delivered to a DC or GC in that site, if the inbound and outbound bridgehead servers are different.

If the inter-site replications are taking place every 15 minutes, you also know that if the change arrives at the outbound bridgehead at the start of its 15-minute interval between inter-site replication cycles, a delay of 15 minutes will occur before the change is propagated to the next site. And so the end-to-end delay in this Active Directory setup will be the number of sites times 15 minutes, plus 15 minutes for each inter-site connection.

Determining Where to Place DCs and GCs

When you plan your sites, placement of DCs and GCs is also of importance. The following are the general guidelines for DC placement:

♦ A DC must be able to respond to requests in a timely manner.

♦ For best logon performance, each site should contain at least one DC from each domain that has members (be they users or computers) in the site.

♦ Consider how the DC has to be configured with regard to the number of objects supported. For example, should the DC be capable of supporting several thousand, tens of thousands, hundreds of thousands, or upwards of one million objects? You are destined to add new objects and attributes from third-party application developers (and perhaps more objects for suiting the corporate needs) in the years to come, so try to avoid underestimating this figure.

♦ Adding a DC increases the amount of data to be replicated to and from the site, as well as inside the site.

When you consider where to place DCs for a particular domain, one approach is to place at least one DC in each physical site that contains users or computers of that domain. This enables you to get the best network performance. Also, for most medium or large sites, you should implement at least two DCs, to provide the necessary guarantee against single point of failure situations.

The theory behind this approach is based on a "99 percent query and 1 percent update" model. This means that 99 percent of your Active Directory network traffic will be query and retrieval, from users, administrators, and applications requesting information about objects on the network. Updates to the directory, which cause directory replication traffic, will occur much less frequently.

If you place a DC at each site, all users have a local computer that can service update, retrieval, and query requests without requiring slow-link traffic. You can configure DCs at smaller sites to receive directory replication updates only during off hours, to help optimize traffic flow. However, placing a DC at every site where users and groups from the domain are present can potentially be a rather expensive proposition, because each DC can service only one domain. So, you might want to settle for less.

The following are the general guidelines for GC placement:

♦ A GC should be dimensioned so that it has the capacity to hold all objects from all domains in the forest. The initial GC configuration should have the capacity to support the current number of objects in your Active Directory, with ample room for future growth (you really should base that estimate on the estimates that you do for each domain when deciding on DC placement).

♦ The best logon and query performance is achieved when you place a GC at every site where you have a DC, enabling the GC to fulfill queries about objects in all Active Directory domains that are part of the same forest without actually having to put out the query to servers in other sites.

♦ Place a GC in each major site (at least), where a "major site" could be either of the following:

  ♦ A regional IT hub

  ♦ A location on your WAN where a large collection of users and resources intersect

♦ Not every DC should be a GC. A GC adds some load to the server; except for large sites, you really should need only a few GCs to accommodate your needs for executing fast forest-wide searches and logon requests.

Watch Those Nonlinked Multivalued Attributes

When planning a very large setting, you should also keep a keen eye on the data being stored in non-linked multivalued attributes—which include the list of authorized DHCP servers and DNS servers. The problem is the fact that the nonlinked multivalued attributes have a limited storage facility. Approximately 850 DHCP servers can be authorized before the limit is exceeded, and the following error is displayed: "Administration limit for this request has exceedeed." So this will only prove a problem to the very largest of enterprises.

Currently, the only way to work around this problem is to reduce the number of DHCP and/or DNS servers. Microsoft doesn't seem intent on fixing this shortcoming before the next minor release of Windows 2000 Server, Whistler.

♦ Adding a GC increases the amount of data to be replicated to and from, as well as inside, the site.

Basically, you should consider the same factors for placement of both DCs and GCs. However, you don't need a GC server at all sites. A GC server might be better placed in each major site or regional IT hub, because it adds a rather high replication load and it is less bandwidth-intensive with regard to the typical client usage.

Placing Those FSMOs

Because these FSMOs are crucial to Active Directory's well being and may be the reason for a lot of grief if placed less than optimally, you are well advised to decide on where to place the different FSMO roles when you do the implementation planning for Active Directory.

Generally, you should follow these guidelines when planning the placement of FSMO roles:

♦ The FSMO role holders should be direct replication partners and well connected to each other.

♦ Clearly identify the possible "standby" FSMO DCs that can be used to hold FSMO roles temporarily during failure at the FSMO role-holder DCs.

♦ Keep all FSMO roles on as few machines as possible and only move them if the load added by the FSMO role causes performance problems.

Table 12.5 lists implementation strategies for the five different FSMO roles.

After the desired DCs are allocated to these five FSMO roles, any changes should be very rare, and should be required only if one of the following situations occurs regarding one of the FSMO role-holder DCs:

♦ Hardware failure or replacement of DC

♦ Decommissioning of DC

♦ Starkly reduced network connectivity to some of the FSMO role-holder DCs

♦ Addition of GC to the DC holding the Infrastructure Master role

Table 12.5   Strategies for the five FSMO roles.

FSMO Role	Description	Important Implementation Advice
Schema Master	The DC that hosts the Schema Master is the only machine allowed to make changes to the Active Directory schema. If unavailable, no schema changes are allowed.	The Schema Master and Domain Naming Master should always be placed on the same DC, and that DC should be placed in close proximity to the people responsible for schema updates and creation of new domains.
Domain Naming	You must connect to the DC holding this role to add or remove a domain to/from a forest. If unavailable, you can't add/remove domains.	See the advice given for the Schema Master FSMO role.
RID Master	When creating new users, computers, and groups at a DC, the new accounts are assigned a Security Identifier (SID), part of which actually includes a Relative Identifier (RID), which is allocated by the RID Master in blocks of 512. When 100 RIDs are left, the DC contacts the RID Master for another block of RIDs. If the RID Master is unavailable, the DC won't be able to create new accounts when its current RID pool is exhausted.	Usually, you should place the RID Master and PDC Emulator roles on the same DC. However, in large domains, you may need to separate these on two different DCs.
PDC Emulator	The DC holding this role acts as PDC for all domain members that are running older versions of Windows (such as NT 4). If the PDC Emulator is unavailable in a mixed mode domain, users won't be able to change passwords, and the event logs on NT BDCs will show failed replication attempts. In a native mode domain, password changes are replicated preferentially to the PDC Emulator, because it is used to resolve password failures. So, although unavailability in a native mode domain won't impact the base functionality, it might affect newly created accounts (by returning password failures) trying to log in to a DC in which replication of their credentials are pending.	See the advice given for the RID Master FSMO role. Note that the Group Policy Editor uses the PDC Emulator FSMO role to ensure uniqueness when editing a GPO. Thus, you should place the PDC Emulator FSMO role on a DC that is close to those people who are responsible for GPO management.
Infrastructure Master	Responsible for fixing up the group-to-user references between domains (interdomain).	If you have several DCs in a domain, the DC possessing this role must not be a GC or it won't be able to resolve the object references. So, place the Infrastructure Master on a DC that isn't a GC. However, note that the DC chosen must have good connectivity to a GC that is located in the same site as the DC.

Windows 2000 Server will add the three domain-specific roles to the first DC installed in each domain and the two forest-wide roles to the first DC installed in the forest. This placement might prove fine for a setting with few DCs (unless the first DC in each domain is also a GC, in which case the Infrastructure Master has to be moved to another DC that isn't a GC, which will be flagged in the Event log as error 1419). However, if you have many DCs, the default placement is unlikely to be the best match to your network.

Optimizing for Different Scenarios

You should account for several special situations in your planning for different scenarios. The first special situation that calls for some attention is actually caused by a bug. As mentioned earlier, DCs from other sites will be assigned to cover a site that doesn't have any DCs online (including when a local DC is down). Unfortunately, the DCs that have registered DNS SRV records to cover a given site won't eliminate their entries if a local DC is brought online. And so, you might find a fair proportion of the users and machines in the local site connecting to a remote DC. It's very likely that this bug will be fixed with Service Pack 2. Until then, you will have to take this into consideration in your design and operational planning.

Optimizing Replications for Large Networks

In some very large settings, you might find yourself in a position where the inter-site KCC executes much too slowly and consumes too much CPU and memory. And that's clearly not a pleasant experience, because the inter-site KCC is running on one DC in each site.

Generally, you will find yourself in this situation when the following proves true: $(1 + <number\ of\ domains>) * <number\ of\ sites>^2 > 100,000$. So you will find yourself in the danger zone, for example, as soon as you have more than 100 sites and 9 domains, or 180 sites and 3 domains.

To further elaborate on this, Microsoft supplies the data shown in Table 12.6 that lists the execution times and memory consumption figures for an inter-site KCC running in a variety of hub-and-spoke configurations. Each site contains a DC for a single domain and a GC with domains equally dispersed across the sites and automatic site link bridging enabled. And, worst of all, the measurements were made on an Intel Pentium III Xeon at 500MHz with 1GB of memory, which is probably more than what you will be using for your DCs and GCs in most cases. Execution times are roughly doubled when using a Pentium II 200MHz server.

Based on the numbers shown in Table 12.6, Microsoft has found the execution time to be: $(1 + <number\ of\ domains>) * <number\ of\ sites>^2 * 0.0000075$ minutes in each satellite office. And that's on an Intel Pentium III Xeon at 500MHz with 1GB of memory!

You can check how long the inter-site KCC runs by determining which DC is acting as inter-site KCC (a.k.a. Inter-site Topology Generator, or ISTG) and the time the execution of the Check Replication Topology is available when right-clicking on the NTDS Settings object.

424 Chapter 12

Table 12.6 The fairly scary performance figures quoted for the inter-site KCC by Microsoft in a variety of scenarios.

Location	Number of Sites	Number of Domains	Time Elapsed (h:m:s)	KB Memory Used
Satellite	125	1	0:00:12	11748
Hub	125	1	0:00:21	12256
Satellite	250	1	0:00:41	45660
Hub	250	1	0:01:05	44820
Satellite	500	1	0:02:56	173216
Hub	500	1	0:04:34	174752
Satellite	1000	1	0:15:23	685596
Hub	1000	1	0:17:34	688568
Satellite	1000	1	0:15:54	685604
Hub	1000	1	0:17:51	689668
Satellite	125	10	0:00:59	58520
Hub	125	10	0:01:19	58536
Satellite	250	10	0:04:00	228304
Hub	250	10	0:04:47	227508
Satellite	500	10	0:21:32	815916
Satellite	500	10	0:19:41	823808
Hub	500	10	0:21:18	828484
Satellite	125	50	0:04:49	266088
Hub	125	50	0:05:54	264024
Satellite	250	50	0:20:19	831924
Hub	250	50	0:22:49	841536

*Alternately, you can monitor the execution time of the KCC on an on-going basis by changing the **HKEY_LOCAL_MACHINE\SYSTEM\CurrentControlSet\Services\NTDS\Diagnostics** Registry key value to 3. In that case, the KCC will log events 1009 and 1013 to signify the beginning and end of the check.*

As you can see, some of these scenarios call for some serious optimization given the fact that, by default, the KCC is run every 15 minutes.

The way you should go about optimizing on this situation is to cut down on the use of site link bridges. In a typical hub and spoke configuration, you will find it easy to reduce the number of potential routes between sites by implementing fewer site link bridges. You might want to note that site link bridges are necessary only if a particular site contains a DC of a domain that is not present in any adjacent site, but another DC of that domain does exist in other sites in the forest. If the KCC is unable to directly or transitively connect all the sites containing DCs of a particular domain after you disable automatic site link bridging, the KCC will log event 1311.

In most instances, this will be enough to get some sensible KCC results. However, you might still be faced with needing to add a lot of site link bridges (almost offsetting the idea) or simply being confronted with a much too large network. If you're able to shy away totally from any transitiveness and site link bridging, you will still be faced with performance numbers approximating 10 percent of the data shown in Table 12.6.

The formula for the execution time for satellite sites is: $(1 + <number\ of\ domains>) * <number\ of\ sites> * 0.0006$; the formula for hub sites is: $(1 + <number\ of\ domains>) * <number\ of\ sites> * 0.0015$.

If this is indeed the case, you should change the KCC's setup to postpone its running during peak hours, or you could disable the KCC altogether and build your own configuration using connection objects (which should only prove viable in the largest enterprises or the simplest settings). In both scenarios, you will be disabling the inter-site KCC. However, in the former case, you will be running some kind of script (see an example of that in Knowledge Base article Q244368) at specific times of day, which sees to that the inter-site KCC is disabled and enabled as apply.

Note

If the inter-site KCC is disabled for a particular site, that site will not respond to changes happening outside of the site. And so, if one or both replication partners for all inter-site connections that replicate a given domain are unavailable, no KCC automatic adaptation to a new source or destination will occur until the DCs come back online or the inter-site KCC is run again.

However, neither of these choices is ideal, because you will have to come to terms with either getting more single points of failure or adding more replication load to your WAN (due to defining redundant connections). If you disable the KCC altogether, you will also find yourself faced with a fair amount of planning of the replication topologies, because it takes a bit of thought to get all the required naming contexts loaded to each site and to keep a sensible load at the various DCs and GCs in the forest. And not to mention the worst part: Having to keep everything in working order by accurately reflecting any changes in the environment that will most probably happen every day of the year because of the size of the environment.

Taking Your Network Properties into Account

As mentioned earlier, the KCC will automatically rebuild the replication topology if it recognizes that a DC has failed or is unresponsive.

The criteria used for a DC to be declared unavailable by the KCC are as follows:

♦ The requesting DC must have made *n* number of attempts to replicate from the target DC.

♦ For replication between sites, the default value is 1 attempt.

♦ For replication within a site, the following distinctions are made between the two immediate neighbors (in the ring) and the optimizing connections:

   ♦ For immediate neighbors, the default value is 0 failed attempts. (Thus, as soon as an attempt fails, a new server is tried).

- For optimizing connections, the default value is 1 failed attempt. (Thus again, as soon as a second failed attempt occurs, a new server is tried.)

♦ A certain amount of time must pass since the last successful replication attempt.

♦ For replication between sites, the default time is 2 hours.

♦ For replication within a site, a distinction is made between the two immediate neighbors (in the ring) and the optimizing connections:

- For immediate neighbors, the default time is 2 hours.

- For optimizing connections, the default time is 12 hours.

However, you might find yourself in a situation where the default settings simply don't cut it. This might be because you're working in a very stable setting in which the maximum functionality and uptime are called for (in which case the default settings might be reduced) or because you're building on an unstable network environment (in which case the default settings might need to be upped a bit).

You're got the following parameters (all found in the **HKEY_LOCAL_MACHINE\ SYSTEM\CurrentControlSet\Services\NTDS\Parameters** Registry key using the **REG_DWORD** data type) to tune:

♦ *Inter-siteFailuresAllowed*—Number of failed attempts for inter-site replications. Default value is 1.

♦ *MaxFailureTimeForInter-siteLink (secs)*—Time that must elapse for inter-site replications to be considered stale. Default value is 7200 seconds/2 hours.

♦ *NonCriticalLinkFailuresAllowed*—Number of failed attempts for intra-site replications. Default value is 1.

♦ *MaxFailureTimeForNonCriticalLink (secs)*—Time that must elapse for intra-site replications to be considered stale. Default value is 43200 seconds/12 hours.

♦ *CriticalLinkFailuresAllowed*—Number of failed attempts for intra-site replications for immediate neighbors. Default value is 0.

♦ *MaxFailureTimeForCriticalLink (secs)*—Time that must elapse for intra-site replications for immediate neighbors to be considered stale. Default value is 7200 seconds/2 hours.

Optimizing Your DFS Replication Topology

While FRS is using the same replication topology as the Active Directory DCs, the DFS builds a separate replication topology automatically. The DFS replication topology is full mesh between all Windows 2000 computers being part of a DFS replica set. So the default replication topology is similar to a fully trusted domain model, in which the connection objects are analogous to two-way trusts. Consequently, the number of default connection objects can be determined using the well known one-way trust formula: $(N*(n-1))$, where N is the number of Windows 2000 servers participating in the DFS namespace.

Understanding the DFS Connection Objects

For a domain controller in the A.COM domain hosting a fault-tolerant DFS root namespace named "DFSFT" and a child node replica named "TOOLS," the path in the Active Directory is: **CN={59ec0127-ccdf-11d2-8fd1-00c04f8f4f54},CN={d42a1614-cd9e-11d2-8fd2-00c04f8f4f54},CN=DFSFT | tools,CN=DFSFT,CN=DFS Volumes,CN=File Replication Service,CN=System,DC=a,DC=com**

Where:

- **DC=A,DC=COM** is the **A.COM** domain.
- **CN=DFSFT** is the root of the DFS namespace and **NTFRSReplicaSet**.
- **CN=DFSFT | tools** is the DFS root name and tools is a DFS child node.
- **CN={d42a1614-cd9e-11d2-8fd2-00c04f8f4f54}** is the GUID for the NTFRS member.
- **CN={59ec0127-ccdf-11d2-8fd1-00c04f8f4f54}** is the GUID for the **nTDSConnection**.

You might want to note that the GUIDs for DFS connection objects belong to the NTDSConnection object class.

As such, it will most certainly prove a slap in the face to your detailed design work, if it's focused on keeping the network load to a minimum. To make matters worse, Windows 2000 doesn't provide a tool for modifying the connection objects defined for DFS replicas.

Luckily, you're able to modify the default DFS replication topology manually, if you just follow this method:

1. Click Advanced Features on the View menu of the Active Directory Users and Computers MMC tool.

2. Navigate to the System \ File Replication Service \ DFS Volumes \ DFS Root folder.

3. Now, you will find the automatically defined connection objects displayed in the right pane for each level of the DFS namespace. You are allowed to do anything to change the replication topology to fit your needs.

The DFS snap-in lacks the functionality of the Active Directory Knowledge Consistency Checker (KCC) to evaluate and generate new connection objects to re-enable connectivity. If the replication topology is significantly modified, perhaps to the point of a single point of connectivity, the failure of a critical link, computer, or system could prevent, or seriously delay, replication between two computers and their dependents until the problem is resolved. Thus, you will have to stay alert to the fact that any customization of the DFS replication topology does add more responsibility to the administrator. However, this proves a great feature, as you can be sure that your customizations will stay exactly as you left them.

Tip

However, you should be keenly aware that additional pruning will most probably be required as new Windows 2000 servers are added to a DFS replica namespace, because DFS will continue to build a full-mesh topology for the new computer.

If things prove to go haywire, you might want to note that you have DFS restore the full mesh connectivity by simply disabling replication for all servers in a given namespace from the Distributed filesystem MMC snap-in, just by enabling the replication a few seconds later.

Some Examples

To place everything into perspective, this section shows some alternative design options for the fictitious multinational company "Telltale," which has three major locations (London, Tokyo, and New York) and four business units distributed among the three sites. To limit the scope of these examples to a reasonable length, a full discussion regarding site properties (attaching cost to each WAN link and adding site links, site link bridges, and/or connection objects) has been omitted, because this would involve too many possibilities.

The most probable scenarios for the actual communication links are London-New York, New York-Tokyo, and Tokyo-London, which should be implemented as three site links with a cost attached, depending on the available bandwidth and the cost of the connection. The Tokyo-London link probably is the most expensive, and if the company HQ is based in New York, this link might be intended as a backup (with a frame relay that has a very low CIR, or even a few multilinked ISDNs), and thus should be given an extremely high cost estimate.

On WANs stretching such long distances (or expensive communications circuits), you generally should do some very detailed evaluations of the consequences of adding site link transitiveness on all the transports used, or maybe a somewhat smaller study on implementing a site link bridge between two of the major sites. Furthermore, you may choose to refrain from adding anything but the needed site links, to keep traffic flow under the tightest reign possible—after all, nobody knows just how bad the replication traffic could become when using Active Directory with a host of Active Directory-enabled server applications.

In an Active Directory setting, Telltale could be implemented as a single domain, a domain tree, and a forest, respectively. The following description for each of these options is accompanied by a short list of the consequences to the site structure, so that the management can decide on which site structure/domain structure option to choose—by no means a trivial decision.

Single Domain Solution

The single domain solution (shown in Figure 12.24, and in Figure 10.8 in Chapter 10) has a site structure that is fairly obvious: two DC/GC servers at each location, to avoid single point of failure situations. If small offices exist, you need to evaluate whether to allocate a DC/GC server in their sites.

> **Note**
>
> *When deciding whether to implement DC/GC servers in the smaller offices, weigh your options carefully. If you decide not to implement DCs and GCs (and consider the office part of the closest major site), no replication traffic goes to the office, and*

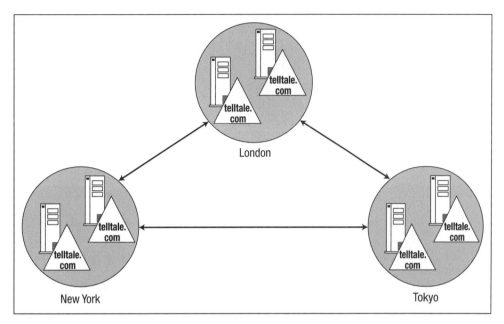

Figure 12.24
With Telltale implemented as a single domain, you likely would choose to implement at least two DC/GC servers at each major site.

workstations must use one of the connections to the closest major location to log on, perform queries, and work with the directory objects. This is acceptable if a fast and reliable connection is available. However, a connection to a distant, major office usually is relatively slow and/or unreliable, so you face the risk of having the work-stations be unable to log on and access the directory in case of an overloaded or broken connection.

If you decide to implement DC/GC servers in the smaller offices, you face a rather large capital outlay for server hardware, configuration, and administration, as well as some mind-bending exercises to determine whether the current connections are adequate. And, if you implement only one DC/GC server and it fails, you face the risk of having to have users log on at sites other than the closest major site.

Depending on the size of the domain, you could face some trouble regarding bandwidth between locations, because domain replication occurring across the WAN could be rather high.

Domain Tree Solution
The domain tree solution (shown in Figure 12.25 and in Figure 10.9 in Chapter 10) has its first layer of domains based on geographical properties. Consequently, implementing this structure with two DC/GC servers for the domain belonging to the locations is a fairly straightforward task.

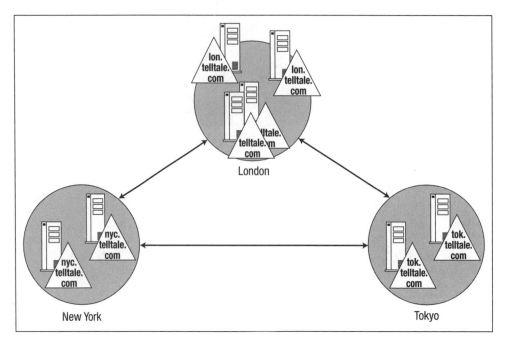

Figure 12.25
With Telltale implemented as a domain tree, you most likely will choose this implementation.

However, you have to decide how to handle the top-level domain. You need at least one DC server (preferably two) to accommodate this domain, so the question is whether you should simply add one or two DC servers to one of the sites or add one or two separate DC servers in each site (this depends on whether or not the DC will be used so seldom that you can live with having to cross the WAN to log on and access the directory objects). Also, you need to determine whether your WAN will be able to accommodate logons and directory accesses from the other locations if needed.

You could be heading into big trouble if your smaller offices include people and resources that belong to a variety of the domains or, even worse, have their own domains, because this immediately triggers an investment of one (likely two) DC/GC servers. If these situations don't apply, you are faced only with the problems discussed in the first example.

Forest Solution

The forest solution (shown in Figure 12.26 and in Figure 10.10 in Chapter 10) has domain trees based on the business units, with a *lot* of DC servers at each site. If the business units are fairly evenly distributed among the physical locations, you need to contemplate acquiring at least four DC servers (and possibly eight, to avoid single point of failure situations) for each site.

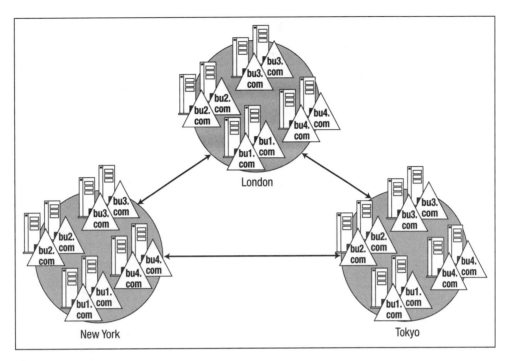

Figure 12.26
With Telltale implemented as a forest, you face a plethora of DC servers and what will most likely amount to a worst-case scenario on replication traffic.

Except for a very large company, this is an expensive proposition that is made even worse by a virtually endless flow of replication traffic passing between all the sites. This situation is aggravated further if the company chooses a business unit view for its smaller offices and this doesn't fit with the situation in each of the locales. To afford the forest setup, the company apparently would have to settle for having either geographical domains under-neath the business units or no additional domains and no DC/GC servers at smaller sites.

Best Practices

Regardless of the size of your organization, you almost always have to go through the follow-ing tasks shown in Table 12.7 (and almost always in the order presented in this chapter).

Note
Watch out for the site coverage bug, which is mentioned earlier in this chapter.

Table 12.7   Summary of the best practices regarding the handling of the physical properties.

Tasks	Points to Consider
Check that the network design is synchronized with the site concept.	If you don't have a one-to-one mapping on each of the LAN segments (in other words, network segments with good connectivity) to one or more TCP/IP subnets, you should immediately start contemplating whether to do an all-encompassing redesign of the TCP/IP network.
Examine site locations.	The first step in the actual planning of a site structure is to examine all the locations in which the company has offices and determine whether each location requires a DC (and maybe a GC).
Determine connectivity and available bandwidth.	Locate the areas of good connectivity (and check that the lines aren't already oversubscribed), which should be described by locations and by the TCP/IP subnets used.
Specify the sites.	Each of the IP subnets that include good connectivity should be mapped to separate sites. Take great care to limit the number of sites in your environment to what's strictly necessary, and remember to consider the availability of services for each site.
Plan sites to control workstation logons.	Your site structure setup affects Windows 2000 in two main ways, one of which is workstation logon. When a user logs on, Windows 2000 tries to find a DC and a GC in the same site as the user's computer. You should contemplate whether or not you want a DC/GC in each site.
Plan sites to control replication traffic.	The second way that your site structure setup affects Windows 2000 is in directory replication. You can configure the transport, schedule, and path(s) for replication of Active Directory differently for replication between two or more sites (inter-site replication) versus replication within a single site (intra-site replication). Additionally, you can also opt to enable notification between sites. By default, replication between sites occurs on a scheduled basis in contrast to the replication that occurs between DCs within a single site (which use change notification every five minutes). Site notification enables an administrator to specify (on a site link by site link basis) that certain sites function like one large site with regard to replication, but not for client login and DFS.
Establish a method for the site structure.	Determine a method to use to assign costs to each site link. Even more important is your decision on how to handle inter-site replication: • *Manually*—Create all the needed connection objects (and maybe even disable the KCC). • *Fully automated*—Enable site link transitiveness on all transports used. • *Automatically, with preferences*—Leave some site links nontransitive and add site link bridges to enforce certain routes.
Site link properties.	The site plan must document how site links are named (usually specified as ***site_name–site_name***), the schedule that site links are on (the default is 180 minutes), and the cost model that is used. The cost model default for a site link is a value of 100. It is recommended that you first create a matrix of values based on connection speed.
Determine where to place DCs and GCs.	Decide which sites will have DCs and/or GCs by weighing the costs of having them versus not having them. Also, implement at least two DCs and GCs in the sites in which you want to provide an optimum level of availability. Remember to decide which servers should be used as bridgehead servers.

(continued)

Table 12.7   Summary of the best practices regarding the handling of the physical properties (continued).

Tasks	Points to Consider
Evaluate the physical design to the logical design.	Finish the physical design by reviewing it in context with the logical design. Evaluate whether you can reduce the number of domains and thus realize savings on the number of DCs needed for the design—or perhaps revise the domain structures in a way that better reflects the physical structure and thus saves some DCs. However, be careful to avoid destroying all the advantages derived with Active Directory for the sake of a few DCs!
Have an eye on the future.	When designing your site plan, be keenly aware that some of the up-and-coming Active Directory-aware Microsoft BackOffice releases (including Exchange Server) will use the site concept, and more third-party applications are destined to follow. So, before you end your site planning, try to get a grip on how your mainstream and mission-critical server applications intend to use the Active Directory site structures.

The Final Words

This chapter has focused on presenting how to balance network speed, available bandwidth, and the ruggedness of the infrastructure with the need to control workstation logons, the need for replication, and the need for availability through the design of the Active Directory structure as it pertains to the physical network properties (that is, sites, DCs, and GCs).

Additionally, you've also been subjected to a rather detailed drill down into one of the less talked-about details of Active Directory: the relatively unknown File Replication Service (FRS). FRS constitutes a very important part of the Active Directory infrastructure, so it's really surprising that it has been subjected to little discussion up until now. By now, you should have a solid working knowledge on sites, DCs, and GCs—and how to plan for them.

Also realize that, even though the physical aspects of Active Directory have been separated from the logical aspects, they still have a high level of interdependence. For example, having a single domain in the forest ensures that you need only one DC at any one site, whereas having 40 domains in the forest—in the worst case—will require 40 DCs at any one site (which will grow to 80 DCs when you factor in the need to secure availability). Likewise, decisions regarding the number of objects, use of Universal Groups, and much more have an impact on the replication load.

Essentially, your decisions at the logical level still have a lot of effects on the physical level, despite the lack of a direct interrelationship. For example, you might find that you need more than one domain, simply on the basis of having a too narrow (or unreliable) bandwidth available between the corporate locations. However, that should be the exception, because Active Directory isn't very bandwidth hungry, after all (see Chapter 16).

Patience Is Now a Major Virtue

You should be keenly aware that Active Directory introduces a new virtue: patience. And to tell you the truth: The more patient you are, the better the probability that you won't get in trouble.

The need for patience arises out of the fact that it can take a long time before a change in the Active Directory has been replicated throughout the enterprise—how patient you need to be depends on the size of your Active Directory, how often replications are performed, and the uptime (and available bandwidth) offered by the WAN lines connecting the various parts of the enterprise. And so, you should be very careful not to make any assumptions on the state of a given Active Directory DC—best practices call for you to always check out the actual state of a given DC before you move ahead and implement any changes on the DC.

If you aren't a patient person by heart, you should remember that it's possible to force replications by choosing the Replicate now option on a given connection object and by using the Replication Monitor utility (see the "Forcing the Replications" sidebar in Chapter 18 for the full explanation on that one). You should also note that Replication Monitor allows you to check whether or not anything is waiting to be replicated between any given two DCs—which will prove tremendously important for troubleshooting purposes.

If you want to force replications, you should take great care to understand that you need to ask for replications in both directions; practice has shown that Active Directory's replication scheme needs that to work correctly.

Usually, the logical structuring decisions of Active Directory wind up taking precedence over the physical structuring decisions—and so you will instead have to face the tolls of increased bandwidth usage and the need to secure reliable connections between locales. However, skillful Active Directory architects can detect such problems early (and many others of that sort) and shortcut the process by proposing an alternative that represents the compromise most fit to a particular company. So, even though the physical structure should be the very last thing that you decide upon in the "core" Active Directory planning, this doesn't mean that you should wait until the last moment to start thinking about it!

Chapter 13
Assessing the Results

Y ou now have passed the first major test on becoming an Active Directory architect. Having made it this far, you should be proficient in all the major parts of Active Directory, and thus should be on the brink of starting your first real designing assignment. This chapter strives to lay out the broad guidelines for planning and designing for Active Directory by recapitulating the design fundamentals. Best practices and checklists aren't repeated in this chapter, because that would simply involve cutting and pasting from the earlier chapters—so, if you have questions regarding a specific subject, you should return to the end of the chapter on that subject to inspect the checklist.

If you have a full understanding of the subjects discussed in this chapter, chances are good that you possess the sound theoretical foundation that is necessary for you to be able to design an Active Directory structure from scratch. However, I urge you to complete the book before you try to finish your first Active Directory design, because you usually will want to implement some of the more advanced features from the outset and will need to perform a smooth migration from the existing environments (whether they are based on NT Server 4 or on competing OSs) to the new one. And you definitely will need to get a pilot successfully up and running before your Active Directory design can be considered complete.

Understanding Directory Services

One of the most significant benefits of network computing is the ability to make the resources from one system available to users on many systems. In fact, this is one of the core concepts of a distributed computing environment. However, making resources available on a network doesn't make access to the resources simple or intuitive. Without some sort of reference information, knowing what resources are available and how to access them can prove quite difficult.

Note

A directory is an information source that is used to store information about interesting objects, just as a telephone directory stores information about telephone subscribers, and a file system directory stores information about files. The primary function of a directory service is to provide a means of presenting the network resources in an understandable and cohesive format. The directory service differs from a normal directory in that it serves as both the information store and the service that makes the information available and usable to users. You might want to think of the directory service as a place that enables you to locate and access any available network resources.

For example, a distributed computing system or a public computer network (such as the Internet) includes many objects—such as printers, fax servers, applications, databases, and other users—that each user will want to be able to locate and use, and that administrators need to manage. Doing just that is quite simply the working order of a directory service.

Additionally, a directory service should be used for securing those resources that allow the administrator to tailor access privileges to the needs of individuals and groups. So, a directory service is really both a management tool and an end-user tool. And, because the number

Microsoft ADSI

One of the most ambitious objectives of Active Directory is to provide a platform through which the most common directory service products appear to be integrated into a common directory. And the need is definitely there, because virtually all directories and directory services are sporting their own proprietary interface protocols and authentication mechanisms.

Active Directory Service Interface (ADSI) aims to provide that common interface by presenting a single, consistent, open set of interfaces for the management and use of directories (see Figure 13.1). You might also want to note that a separate variant of ADSI allows accessing the Exchange Server 5.5 directory service. ADSI accomplishes this task by abstracting the capabilities of a directory service. ADSI provides a set of predefined objects that ensure directory-service manipulation is uniform across some of the most popular namespaces. This set of objects, in turn, represents persistent objects in the underlying directory service.

ADSI objects are divided into two groups (see Table 13.1): directory service leaf objects and directory service container objects. By evaluating ADSI compared to its alternative, LDAP, you will see that ADSI adds value over LDAP by being a higher-level API set, and thus should prove easier to use than LDAP. Although LDAP supports the full set of C APIs, ADSI supports multiple high-level languages, such as Visual Basic, Perl, Java, REXX, and C/C++.

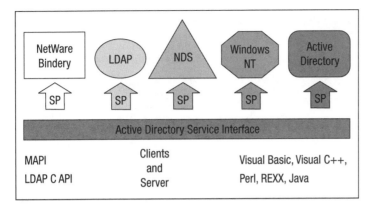

Figure 13.1
Microsoft is betting on ADSI to provide the means for making Active Directory the heart of the network.

Table 13.1   The predefined ADSI objects.

Object	Type	Hierarchical Level
Namespace	High-level container	Directory Provider
Country	High-level container	Geographic Location
Locality	High-level container	Geographic Location
Organization	Mid-level container	Organization Structure
Organizational Unit	Mid-level container	Organization Structure
Domain	Mid-level container	Security Authentication
Computer	Low-level container	Security Authentication
Group	Low-level container	Security Authentication
User	Leaf object	Security Authentication
Alias	Leaf object	Security Authentication
Service	Leaf Object	Resource
Print Queue	Leaf Object	Resource Identification
Print Device	Leaf Object	Resource Identification
Print Job	Leaf Object	Resource Consumer
File Share	Leaf Object	Resource Identification
Session	Leaf Object	Resource Consumer
Resource	Leaf Object	Resource Identification

of objects found in most networks are on the increase, the directory service should turn out to become ever more essential to end users and administrators alike.

Because of the nature of the distributed environments, a well-thought-out directory service should, at a minimum, provide the following:

♦ *Location transparency*—The ability to find information about a user, group, networked service, or resource without knowing the full address information.

♦ *Information on people and services*—The ability to store user, group, organization, and service information in a structured way.

♦ *Rich query*—The ability to locate objects of interest by querying based on one or more object properties.

♦ *High availability*—The ability to have several replicas of the directory at different locations for reasons of performance and/or availability.

In effect, the directory service is the hub around which a large distributed system turns, which is why a directory service also should be able to do the following:

♦ Enforce security defined by administrators to keep information safe from intruders.

♦ Distribute the directory across many physical network sites in an efficient manner.

♦ Partition the directory into multiple stores, to allow storage of an almost infinite number of objects.

Active Directory is indeed a well-thought-out directory service that provides all of these capabilities, and many more.

Understanding Active Directory

Like any other directory service, Active Directory really is a store for just about every possible type of object (such as users, groups, computers, domains, OUs, security policies, and services) that can be found on the network. However, this doesn't imply that you have to keep the information for all objects on the network in one physical store—you can partition the store using multiple Active Directory domains. Each domain has its own directory store that holds the information for all objects of that domain. No matter whether you've got one or multiple Active Directory domains, the information on global objects—such as the complete list of all domains and domain trees in the forest, the location of all services, and the schema—will still be available locally in each domain.

Remember the Schema?

The *schema* is the formal definition of which objects can be created in the directory and what attributes can be assigned to those objects. Active Directory includes a default schema, which defines the well-known types of directory objects, such as users, groups, computers, domains, OUs, and security policies.

Administrators and programmers can extend the schema by defining new object types and their attributes and by defining new attributes for existing objects. This can be done either with the Active Directory Schema MMC snap-in or by addressing the Active Directory directly via ADSI programming. The Active Directory schema is implemented and stored within the directory itself, enabling it to be read by applications. The schema can be updated dynamically; that is, you can create new object types and attributes while the system is running, and then start using them immediately. Like every other object in Active Directory, schema objects are protected by ACLs, ensuring that only authorized users may alter the schema. The same Active Directory schema is replicated and used on all DCs that belong to the same forest.

It is of vital importance that the Active Directory designer realize that the logical structuring in Active Directory doesn't need to mirror in any way your network's physical structure (the physical location of workstations and computers and the speed of connections between them). Actually, Active Directory goes to great lengths to separate the logical and physical properties from each other.

The Core Active Directory Concepts

Before you begin architecting your Active Directory structure, you need to understand the core definitions of the following Active Directory concepts and terms (see Figure 13.2):

- DDNS
- Domain
- OU
- Domain tree
- Forest
- Group
- DC
- Site
- GC

Dynamic DNS

In recent years, TCP/IP has rapidly gained ground as the universal networking protocol, and so Windows 2000 Server also installs TCP/IP as its default protocol. And although other networking protocols may be used, TCP/IP is required to harness Active Directory. One of the reasons for this requirement is that Active Directory uses the newer, dynamic version of the Domain Name System (DNS) for name and location services. DNS enables you to use hierarchically structured "friendly" names to easily locate computers and other resources on TCP/IP-based networks and on the Internet. In other words, DNS is used to translate an easily readable name, such as **www.astonitgroup.com**, to a numeric TCP/IP address.

Because Active Directory uses DNS as its location service, Active Directory domain names are also DNS names. For example, **headquarters.bigwig.com** could simultaneously be a DNS name and an Active Directory domain name. Also, Active Directory supports the DNS hierarchical naming structure, so that **headquarters.bigwig.com** can be assumed to be a child domain of **bigwig.com**.

DNS naming is used for other objects as well. **CarlPerkins@bigwig.com** can be both an Internet email address and a Windows 2000 username. To be more precise, Windows 2000 Server uses a relatively new DNS standard, called *Dynamic DNS (DDNS)*. DDNS enables

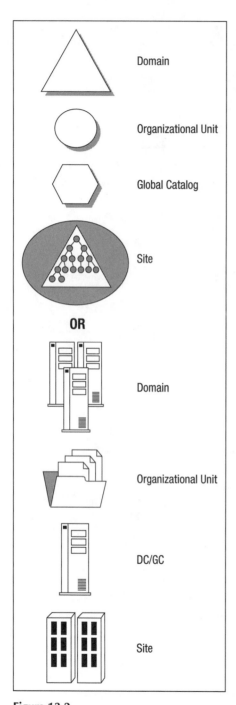

Figure 13.2
Some of the core Active Directory terms and the two different sets of icons commonly used to illustrate them.

clients with dynamically assigned addresses to register directly with the DNS server and update the DNS table dynamically. Prior to DDNS, administrators had to configure manually the records stored by DNS servers.

The use of DDNS eliminates the need to use other name services, such as Windows Internet Naming Service (WINS). So, even though a new version of the well-known WINS Service is included with the Windows 2000 Server product, it is to be regarded as a legacy solution.

Domain

Active Directory consists of one or more domains. An Active Directory *domain* is a grouping of servers and other network objects under a single name (the domain name). Domains give you several benefits:

♦ Grouping objects into domains can help you to reflect your company's top-level organization in your computer network. Usually, you will want to model the detailed properties of the organization using OUs.

♦ Each domain is a partition of the network directory, storing only the information about the objects located in that domain. By splitting the directory store this way, Active Directory scales up to a virtually unlimited number of objects (and certainly as many as you may need to store information on your private network).

♦ Each domain is a *security boundary*, meaning that security policies and settings (such as administrative rights, security policies, and ACLs) don't cross from one domain to another by default. The administrator of a domain has rights to set policies and permissions within that domain only.

Because a domain is a security boundary, different administrators can create and manage different domains in your organization, if that suits your company's needs. Each administrator would have power only within his or her particular domain. Access control lists (ACLs)—or permissions—are cumulative within a domain (unless explicitly denied), but don't flow out of the domain to child domains. Also, domains are *units of replication*—that is, a single domain can span multiple physical locations and still work as one single logical unit.

Providing the Location Service

Active Directory servers publish their DNS addresses in such a way that clients can find them even if they know only the domain name. This small trick is done by publishing Active Directory servers using the *Service Resource Records (SRV RRs)* in DNS. The SRV RR is a DNS record used to map the name of a service to the network address of a server offering that service. The name of a SRV RR appears in this form: **_service._protocol.domain**.

Active Directory DCs offer the LDAP service over the TCP protocol, so that published names are **_ldap._tcp.domain**. Thus, the SRV RR for locating the DCs being part of the **astonitgroup.com** Active Directory domain is **_ldap._tcp.astonitgroup.com**.

Organizational Unit

Organizational Units (OUs) are but one type of directory object contained within domains. An OU is a logical container into which you can place users, groups, computers, and even other OUs for structuring purposes. Any one OU is contained entirely within one domain, so that an OU can't hold objects from multiple domains.

OUs should attract more attention than many of the other directory objects, because an OU is the main element used for partitioning the logical namespace (that is, imposing a logical hierarchy inside the domain). By using OUs within each of the domains that are found in your organization, you can create a hierarchical, logical namespace tree to model your company's organizational properties.

OUs often are used to mirror the departments within a company. Their hierarchical nature enables you to represent the relationship between departments and enables you to discover the organization by browsing the tree of OUs. Because OUs can contain other OUs, the hierarchy can be extended as far as necessary. Thus, OUs enable you to create a hierarchy that could have been expressed in NT Server 4 only by using the same number of domains.

Windows 2000 Security

The security elements in Windows 2000 Server (see Table 13.2) are essentially unchanged from those found in Windows NT Server. The main difference is that the domain security information now is located in Active Directory; it was previously stored in the Registry (SAM). Storing the security account information in Active Directory means that the security principals—users, computers, and groups—are represented among other objects in the directory.

All objects in Active Directory are protected by an ACL, which defines the access permissions users have. The ACL of an object lists who can see or access the object and what specific actions are allowed. Because none of the new Active Directory concepts (such as OUs or domains) can be used as security principals, you still have to make do with the computer, user, and group elements in regard to setting security permissions.

Active Directory supports both inheritance and delegation of authority:

- *Inheritance*—Propagates a permission set on an object to all its child objects (including the child containers and their objects).

- *Delegation of authority*—Enables the administrator to grant security principals the ability to administer an entire domain, specific containers or subtrees inside the domain, objects inside a specific container, or attributes on certain objects inside a specific container. This is done by using a combination of OUs and ACLs.

In other words, delegation of authority enables the administrator to grant administrative rights with just about any granularity, ranging from all the objects in the domain all the way down to granting permissions on the per-user, per-object property level. For example, a user can be delegated the right to reset passwords on user objects within a specific OU, but not to modify other account information in that OU.

Table 13.2   Windows 2000 security elements.

Elements	Short Description
User Accounts	Login information that defines a specific user to the OS and establishes the level of access granted to anyone using the account. A user account can be used as a security principal.
Groups	Associations of multiple user accounts (and other groups) that share some specific access privileges within the domain. A group can be used as a security principal.
Computers	Information about specific systems that have been included as members of an Active Directory domain, including some specific access privileges. A computer can be used as a security principal.
X.509 Certificates	Public key certificates issued by a trusted certificate authority that can be used to authenticate users and machines and to define access privileges for users and systems.
Kerberos Keys	Shared-secret keys that define access privileges; used to authenticate users and computers accessing the system. The Kerberos authentication mechanism replaces Windows NT's NT Lan Manager (NTLM) authentication mechanism.
Trust Relationships	Arranged agreements between two or more domains that allow either domain or both domains to trust the domain security information from the other party. For example, defining a trust will work to enable users from the first domain to be able to access resources in the other domain.
Access Control List (ACL)	Consists of a list of the security principals that are allowed (or denied) to access the resource protected by the ACL. The ACL also defines how the resource may be used by those granted access.
Security Identifiers (SIDs)	Unique identification numbers assigned to all security principals. The SID identifies the security principal to the system, and thus is used to define privileges at the ACL. The SIDs are relative to the domain—and thus unique inside that scope.

Note

All Active Directory objects are assigned a GUID at time of creation. Each of these GUIDs is guaranteed to be unique inside a forest to allow improved searching. The GUID is one of an object's properties that is published in the GC, and so, searching the GC for any object by Object-GUID will prove to be the most reliable way of finding the object you want to find as the values of other object properties can change, whereas the Object-GUID never changes. Please take great care to note that Globally Unique Identifiers (GUIDs) aren't a security principal; you can assign permissions to a GUID, but not use it for assigning privileges to other objects. And so, your OU hierarchy only works to improve the flexibility of the administrative model.

Even more importantly, OUs help you to provide a finer-grained administrative model. Administrative rights can be granted to a user for only a subtree of OUs, or even a single OU. Such a user has no administrative rights for the contents of other OUs in the domain. The combination of domains and OUs provides you with a powerful, flexible way of organizing your network directory to reflect your organization. Creating OUs within domains enables you to represent your organization's structure to as many levels as you want, while still having the benefits of creating and managing a small number of domains. Note that OUs are not exposed in the DNS namespace. So an OU named **accounting** in the **sales.bigwig.com** domain is not referred to as **accounting.sales.bigwig.com**. In fact, the OU is only addressable from LDAP or ADSI.

Domain Tree and Forest

To make your network resources globally available, you can join domains together into domain trees, and you can associate multiple domain trees into one or more forests in your organization.

A *domain tree* is a hierarchical organization of domains. All the domains in a domain tree are transparently joined together through two-way, transitive Kerberos trust relationships. Because these trust relationships are two-way and transitive, a domain joining a tree immediately has trust relationships established with every domain in the tree. These trust relationships make all the objects in all the domains of the tree available to all other domains in the tree. For example, a user or group in any domain can be granted permissions for any object in other domains in the tree. This also enables a user to access any part of the network via a single network logon.

All domains within a single domain tree share a hierarchical naming structure. Following DNS standards, the domain name of a child domain (for example, **sales.astonitgroup.com**) is the relative name (**sales**) of that child domain, appended with the name of the parent domain (**astonitgroup.com**).

A forest consists of one or more domain trees that don't share a naming structure, but still need to have the same properties as domains that are part of the same domain tree. Correspondingly, if you want to isolate two domains completely from each other, you should place them in separate forests. The combination of the domain tree and the forest concepts provides you with a flexible naming structure—both contiguous and disjointed DNS namespaces are allowed inside the same forest. This can prove very useful, for example, if one company acquires another and wants to combine both companies' directory structures into one unified structure, while keeping the existing publicly known DNS names of the acquired company.

Groups

Groups are Active Directory or local computer objects that can contain users, contacts (that is, entities that only are defined for email purposes and thus are not defined as security principals), computers, and other groups. Groups can be used to do the following:

- Control user and computer access (that is, permissions) to shared resources, such as Active Directory objects and their properties, network shares, files, directories, printer queues, and so on.
- Create email distribution lists.
- Filter group policies.

Creating One-Way Trusts

When needed, you can explicitly configure NT-style one-way trusts between domains or domain trees. A one-way trust with a domain in a forest provides access only to the domain specifically named in the trust relationship, not to other domains in the forest. To provide access to other domains in the forest, additional trust relationships must be created for each domain.

With a one-way trust, users in the trusted domain can be granted access to resources in the trusting domain. Creating these kinds of trust relationships might be useful when less-permanent relationships between separate entities are needed. For example, this might be useful if two companies take part in a joint venture. In that case, explicit one-way trusts can be created between the involved domains of the two companies, enabling the sharing of necessary resources without creating a permanent link between the two companies or exposing each company's entire forest.

Groups are distinct from OUs in that, where OUs are useful for creating a hierarchy for administrative delegation or setting group policy, groups are useful for granting permissions and creating distribution lists.

Groups and OUs also differ in regard to the domain boundaries to which they are applied. You can create groups to contain users, computers, or shared resources on a local server, a single domain, or multiple domains in a forest. OUs represent a collection of objects (including group objects) only within the context of a single domain.

Each Security and Distribution Group has a scope:

♦ Domains from which members can be added to the group

♦ Domains in which the group can be used for granting permissions

♦ Groups in which the group can be a member

Table 13.3 summarizes the three group scopes that are available in an Active Directory native mode domain.

If you have multiple forests, users from one forest can't be placed in groups in another forest, and groups from one forest can't be given permissions in another forest unless you've defined the necessary one-way trust relationships. Also, a domain must be running in native mode for you to be able to utilize the following new group features introduced by Active Directory:

♦ *Universal Security Groups*—Universal Groups are a new type of group that can be created and used in any domain in the forest.

♦ *Nesting Security Groups*—The option of creating a hierarchy of groups paralleling the hierarchies used to create OUs and domains for load-balancing and high-availability.

♦ *Conversion of groups*—Provides you with the possibility of converting an existing group to another group scope.

Table 13.3   **The three available domain group scopes in a native mode domain.**

Scope	Members	Grant Permissions	Member of Other Groups
Universal	From any domain in the forest: Universal Groups; Global Groups; users, contacts, and computers.	In any domain in the forest.	Can be a member of Local Groups and Universal Groups in the forest.
Global	Only from the domain containing the group: users, contacts, and computers.	In any domain in the forest.	Can be a member of Global Groups, Local Groups, and Universal Groups in the forest.
DomainLocal	From any domain in the forest: Universal Groups; Global Groups; users, contacts, and computers from any domain in the forest. Domain Local Groups from the domain containing the group.	Only on the domain containing the group.	Can be a member only of Local Groups in the domain containing the group.

Domain Controller

Each domain has one or more servers that serve as *Domain Controllers (DCs)*. Each DC stores a complete copy of the domain directory and helps manage the changes and updates to the directory. When a user or administrator performs an action that causes an update to the directory, they don't need to know which servers are the DCs. They simply make the update using the proper MMC-based tool, which then transparently has the change written to a nearby DC. The change must then be replicated to the peers (other DCs) in the domain. This replication is also automatic and transparent to everybody.

Active Directory uses *multi-master replication*, in which no single DC is the master; instead, all DCs within a domain are equals. Multi-master replication provides the following advantages for Active Directory over the single-master model used by Windows NT Server 3.51 and 4:

♦ No single-master DC exists that, in case of a crash, must be replaced for directory updates to resume.

♦ DCs capable of making changes to the directory can be distributed across the network and thus exist at multiple physical sites.

Note

You should note that a few exceptions to the rule of multi-mastering exist in Active Directory. These exceptions are handled using the so-called FSMOs (see Chapter 12 for a more in-depth review of them).

Site

By defining sites, you can take advantage of your network's physical organization to provide the needed level of fault tolerance, availability, and performance for your logical organization. A site is defined as one or more IP subnets. When you designate a site, all computers within that site should be connected together by high-speed network links (typically a LAN). Areas of your network that are separated by a WAN, routers, or other low-bandwidth links should be defined as separate sites. The DCs for any given domain can be distributed among many different sites, and one site can contain DCs from many different domains.

Note

But each DC can be a member of one site only when seen from the Active Directory Sites and Services MMC tool. However, as mentioned in Chapter 12, exceptions to this rule do exist.

Applications can use site information to direct requests from one computer to be fulfilled by another computer at the same site (see Figure 13.3). For example, when a workstation logs on, Active Directory will use the TCP/IP address of the workstation—along with the site information that the administrator has already defined—to locate a DC and a GC residing in the local site. The local DCs and GCs are used to service the workstation's requests from there on.

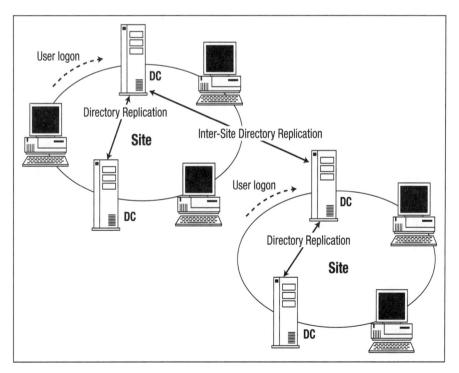

Figure 13.3
The essential function of sites: controlling logons and replication.

Searching Across Domain Trees

If your company has multiple domain trees (that is, a forest), the way in which information queries work depends on the attributes being used to query. A query based on an attribute that is indexed in the GC can search the entire forest of domain trees. However, a search based on an attribute not in the GC searches only the domain tree in which the user or application is performing the search. Therefore, to improve search efficiency, you should group your entire company into a single domain tree, if possible.

Site topology is also used to optimize the replication of directory updates between DCs. Sites are separate from, and are not represented in, the Active Directory domain namespace, because this namespace is purely logical.

Global Catalog

The *Global Catalog (GC)* is a service and store that contains directory information from all domains in your forest. The whole point of the GC is to enable users to find and retrieve an object easily, regardless of the domain in which it is located, by being able to search for a match on one or multiple attributes. Also, the GC is needed when performing authentication, because it manages universal groups and UPN suffixes.

The GC is designed to answer queries about objects located anywhere in the forest—across domain trees, with optimum speed, and with the least network-traffic generation possible. Because the GC contains information about objects that reside in different domains, a query that is resolved by the GC doesn't generate requests to multiple domains to find the objects.

The GC contains a partial replica (in the form of a read-only copy) of every domain partition. It contains an entry for every object in the forest, but does not include all the attributes of each object. Instead, it contains only the attributes that are likely to be used as search properties—for example, the first name and last name of a user. The properties deemed to be of most interest to users can be configured by the administrator.

The GC is kept on specific servers throughout the forest. Only DCs can serve as GC servers. Active Directory automatically generates the contents of the GC from the domains that comprise the directory via the normal replication process.

Planning: Getting It Wrong to Get It Right

Before venturing into the Active Directory design phase, you should have a clear understanding of your organization's business structure and operations. This includes determining whether the company has a centralized structure (typically characterized by a strong IT department that defines the network structure and implements that structure down to the smallest detail) or a very decentralized structure (lacking a single department in the corporation that can control or even begin to manage all IT resources).

Always remember that deploying a distributed computing architecture such as Active Directory requires an organization to decide which tasks it will perform centrally and which it will perform locally. Many factors dictate the answer to this question, such as geography, business requirements, and technology infrastructure. For example, data integrity and capacity planning may be performed centrally, but each branch office may be responsible locally for end-user assistance. Refer to Chapter 6 for a complete explanation of the core informational needs and handling of the preplanning phase. A short introduction is given in Table 13.4.

When you do the design work, always follow the preceding order, starting with the DNS and domain namespace plan and ending with the site topology. Also, remember to factor in a lot of time for obtaining upper management's buy-off of your DNS root namespace, domain structure, and naming standards.

After you complete each of the steps previously outlined, you should step back and examine the plan and ask yourself such questions as the following:

♦ Are all the domains, OUs, and sites really necessary?

♦ Who is responsible for administering each domain and OU?

You should understand that, more often than not, the planning of each of the main Active Directory structures (domains, trees and forests, OUs, and so on) is a highly iterative process, looking somewhat like this:

1. Document the current environment (point A).
2. Create a "Nirvana" design (point B).

Table 13.4   Major elements in Active Directory design.

Design Element	Considerations
DNS Namespace	Do you need one or more DNS namespaces? Will you use the same DNS namespace internally and externally? How will DNS be deployed—as a separate structure or using the proprietary Active Directory-integrated feature? Will you be using Windows 2000 Server's DNS or another brand of name server?
Domain Namespace	How many domains will there be? How will the domains be arranged? How will the domains be named? What are the security policies governing each domain? How will computers be named?
OU Structures	How will the OUs be arranged? Will the same OU structure be used throughout all domains?
Group Structures	How will the users be named and arranged? How will the groups be named and arranged? Which group policies will be implemented and how will they be arranged?
Physical Topology	Which sites and where? How many DCs and where? How many GCs and where?

3. Analyze the work involved to travel from point A to point B.

4. Weigh long-term savings at point B versus the cost of the trip.

5. Repeat again from Step 2 utill you're satisfied with the result.

And believe me, you won't get it right the first time. So, you should expect to make many revisions and comparisons of alternative designs. Simply stated, the design experience should approximate the following: Iterate, iterate, iterate, and then iterate some more.

Ultimately, although you don't necessarily have to plan every little aspect of your Active Directory structure in advance of deployment, your life will be much easier if you complete all the planning phases prior to deployment. Furthermore, you should *always* have a clear plan for your root namespace, domains, and groups (changing your OU structure and site structure later on is much easier) before you start to do anything in practice.

Planning Active Directory Logical Structures

When you design for Active Directory, always start out doing the domains, unless a very good reason exists for not doing so. When you plan the domain structures, the following are the top three priorities:

♦ The domain design must evolve as organizational needs change.

♦ Organizational changes must be accommodated without requiring expensive domain reorganizations.

♦ Domain names must not change. One approach is to organize geographically, because geographical names rarely change.

Planning Your DNS Structure

How you should set up your DNS architecture with Active Directory depends on your current DNS environment. When you design a new DNS namespace, the simplest approach is to place all hosts in a DDNS zone, which corresponds to each Active Directory domain. The Active Directory DNS integration should be enabled so that all DNS data will be stored and replicated in the domain partition. After the DNS zone is stored in Active Directory, any DC that is part of the same domain can act fully as a read/write DNS authority. Not every DC needs to be a DNS server, but you are recommended to have at least one DNS server at every site containing a DC.

If you have an existing, complex, heterogeneous DNS environment, you do not have to redesign your DNS namespace when you implement Active Directory. Even if you have an environment in which client domains don't relate to Active Directory domains, you can operate by using standard DNS zone transfer mechanisms. Here, you just have to decide whether you want Windows 2000's built-in DNS server to reduce administrative overhead, total cost of ownership, and the need for compatibility testing.

Note that a relationship doesn't have to exist between the DNS domain name of a client or server and the name of the Active Directory domain. However, having domain names and DNS names that are alike will usually prove quite helpful.

You should always start with a single domain and try to keep it that way. The single domain structure should always be your first consideration, because one domain is, by far, the simplest domain structure to create and administer.

You can use OUs within a single domain to model the detailed organizational properties and thus reduce the number of domains needed to create your company's management hierarchy. Actually, whenever you need to reflect the details of your company's organization, you should always prefer OUs to domains. Using OUs in your design is good practice because it will allow you to:

♦ Scope the application of policy. The policy precedence used by Group Policies is SDOU (Site, Domain, and OU).

♦ Make administration of objects easier.

♦ Delegate administration.

♦ Control administration of resources. For example, instead of setting permissions on multiple shares, you can set permissions once by selecting all the shares that are included in a given OU.

♦ Replace Windows NT Server 4 resource domains.

♦ Limit the total number of objects that will appear in each directory container.

Users will often see the OU structure when they query. Therefore, don't create structure for the sake of structure; rather, create structure where it will be meaningful. Furthermore, even though the OU hierarchy within a domain is independent of the structure of the OU hierarchy in other domains—which provides you with the freedom to implement a different OU hierarchy for each domain—always strive to design an OU model that can be duplicated across all the domains.

Domains vs. OUs

When considering whether to split a particular part of your network into separate domains or separate OUs, you should consider the following guidelines:

• If you have a decentralized organization, in which different users and resources are managed by completely different sets of administrative personnel, you might want to opt for separate domains.

• When two parts of your network are separated by a link so slow that you never want complete replication traffic to cross it, you should opt for separate domains.

• To reflect the details of your company's structure and organization, you should choose to use OUs.

• To delegate administrative control over smaller groups of users, groups, and resources, you should choose to use OUs.

• If your company's particular organizational structure is likely to change later, you should choose to use OUs.

Finally, when you create each OU, consider (and document) who will:

♦ Administer the OU.

♦ Be able to see the OU.

The great OU features notwithstanding, sometimes you will need to create a design that comprises more than one domain. Some reasons for having more than one domain include the following:

♦ To control where certain data is replicated.

♦ If differing domain-level security policies are needed.

♦ If multiple business units need to have different names.

♦ To provide a one-to-one mapping of Windows NT Server 4 domains.

♦ To prevent a critical single point of failure, however theoretical.

♦ To attain the highest possible level of security in a decentralized organization, in which different users and resources are managed by completely different sets of administrative personnel.

Conversely, at least one bad reason exists for having multiple domains—to reflect the company's organization of divisions and departments. Also, you should *always* avoid naming domains for divisions, departments, buildings, floors, and groups, because a good domain design should be able to withstand company reorganizations. The same is true regarding the creation of domains for political reasons. Also, because each domain can contain more than one million objects, needing more domains on that account is highly unlikely.

When you need multiple domains, you should always prefer to hold them in a single domain tree (see Figure 13.4 for a rough sketch of a domain tree), instead of using several domain trees in a forest. The use of the forest concept should be kept to a minimum. However, the following are a few reasons to have a forest (see Figure 13.5 for a rough sketch of a forest) with multiple domain trees:

♦ A business need exists for discontiguous namespaces; for example, when one company buys another company or when dealing with subsidiaries that require a separate namespace.

♦ For joint ventures and partnerships.

Actually, as far as I've been able to establish, Compaq ended up with a very simple design (see Figure 13.6), which reinforces the most important rules of Active Directory design: Keep it simple and avoid building a forest, if you've got the chance.

Best practices for planning groups are the following:

♦ *Universal Groups*—If you are building a simple distributed system with native mode-only domains on a single LAN or in a well-connected campus setting, you might want to opt for using Universal Groups for all permission assignments, because they are much easier

Planning Your Delegation Model

By creating a tree of OUs within each domain and delegating authority for parts of the OU subtree to others, you can delegate authority down to the lowest level of your organization, without having to create numerous domains. Additionally, you eliminate most of the need to have people who regularly do administrative work log on to accounts that have sweeping authority over the entire domain.

Although you still have an Administrator account and the Domain Admins and Enterprise Admins Groups, with administrative authority over the entire domain and entire forest, respectively, you can keep these accounts reserved for occasional use by a select number of highly trusted administrators. So, when deciding how to structure your OUs and in which OUs to put each user, remember to consider the hierarchy of administration.

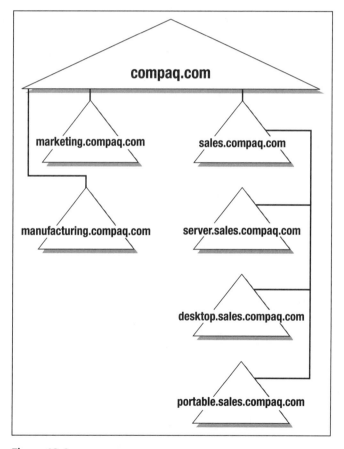

Figure 13.4
A quick layout of the Active Directory domain tree for the intended Windows 2000 Server deployment at Compaq.

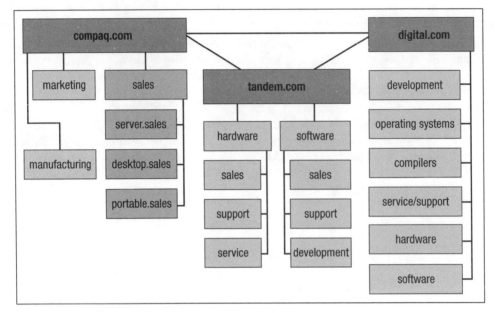

Figure 13.5
A forest with multiple domain trees.

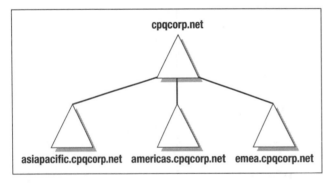

Figure 13.6
Compaq allegedly ended up with a very simple Active Directory design comprising a tree with four domains.

to understand and use than are Global and Domain Local Groups. For larger systems with slow connections, you generally only should use Universal Groups to define functional groups that span domains. To do this, you nest Global Groups within Universal Groups and thus make the majority of membership changes confined to the Global Groups.

♦ *Global Groups*—Generally, membership maintenance (adding and removing users) should occur within Global Groups. And, if a domain contains a hierarchy of OUs and administration is delegated to administrators at each OU, nesting Global Groups may prove to be a very simple and efficient solution to all your needs.

Checklist for Your Design

When you design the logical Active Directory structure, consider the answers to the following questions:

- Does the design cover naming standards for all objects in the directory?
- Will the design be able to withstand reorganizations?
- How does the design handle different business partitions?
- How does the design provide for network bottlenecks?
- How does the design map to the physical topology?
- Will the physical topology change in the future?
- How will the design be administered?
- How will the design handle the administration model?
- Do different corporate areas have different models of administration?
- How easily understandable are the main properties of the design for the user community at large?
- How does the design deal with any special needs posed by different users?
- How effectively does the design deal with the administrative needs?
- How effectively does the design deal with permissions and rights?
- How does the design tackle disaster recovery?
- Does the design properly take into account the advantages or disadvantages of directory partitioning?
- Does sharing of work occur in the environment?
- Does the design promote the sharing of resources between divisions and departments?

The answers to these questions should help you to check that the Active Directory design is indeed well-adapted to the needs of your environment.

- ◆ *Domain Local Groups and Local Groups*—Should be used for defining access policies on resources within a domain. Depending upon the situation, Domain Local Groups will contain Global Groups, Universal Groups, individual accounts, other Domain Local Groups, or a mixture of these.

Also, because groups can be used for security purposes (such as access control and policy) or grouping purposes (such as distribution lists), when you create a group, always specify explicitly whether it will be used for security purposes or not. Likewise, choose a naming scheme in which the differences between groups' purposes are immediately visible, to avoid security hiccups.

Planning Active Directory Physical Structures

Defining your network's site structure enables you to optimize the behavior of Active Directory for the physical structures of your network. Generally speaking, network traffic stemming from Active Directory should be much higher within a site than between sites. How you set up your network's site structure affects Windows 2000 in two main ways:

♦ *Workstation logons*—When a user logs on from a computer running Windows 2000, it will try to find a DC (and shortly thereafter a GC) that is located in the same site as the user's computer, to service the user's logon request and subsequent requests for network information via the LAN rather than via a WAN.

Note

Remember that only Windows 2000-based clients are site-aware.

♦ *Directory replication*—You can configure the schedule and path for replication of a domain's directory differently for inter-site replication than for intra-site replication. Generally, inter-site replication should be set to occur less frequently than intra-site replication, although both are configurable by administrators.

Sites aren't part of the domain namespace; consequently, when you browse the logical namespace, computers and users are grouped only into domains and OUs, not sites. The site structure is kept in a separate directory partition (the configuration naming context).

When planning for sites, you should be aware of the following:

♦ Sites enable you to map replication traffic to your physical infrastructure. Remember, though, that you can only control—not reduce—the traffic needed. However, the data transferred between sites (inter-site replication) is compressed.

♦ A site is one or more well-connected TCP/IP subnets. Each site should only include a network area that is connected using LAN or other high-speed networking technologies.

♦ Site topology is orthogonal to domain namespace: Multiple sites may span a domain, and multiple domains may span a site.

♦ You must recognize that inter-site replication is controllable (by scheduling, frequency, cost-based routing, and choice of transport), whereas intra-site replication generally can't be as rigidly controlled.

♦ The administrator defines the connection properties between sites (inter-site replication) with the following Active Directory features: using site links and site link bridges and possibly by setting site link transitivity on transports or by creating connection objects.

♦ You can use RPC or SMTP (inter-site only) as your transport.

When planning your sites, also ponder which DCs and GCs you want each workstation to use. Generally, the best network performance is obtained by having at least one DC and GC in each physical site that contains users or computers of that domain.

The theory behind this approach is based on a "99 percent query and 1 percent update" model. That is, 99 percent of your Active Directory network traffic will be query-related, as users, administrators, and applications request information about other objects on the network. By having a DC at each site, updates to the directory—which cause directory replication

Replication Planning: Knowing Your Connectors

When you plan the sites, you should also specify which connectors should be used, for which you have the choice between the following:

Connector	CPU Usage	Network Traffic	Latency	Installation Ease
Intra-site	Low	High	Good	Light/No installation
RPC	High	Low	Scheduled	Light
SMTP	High	Medium	Depends on connectivity	More complex

The preceding table can be translated into the following general rules:

- For high-speed network connections and fast client logon, use one site (which utilizes the intra-site connector).

- For low-speed network connections with fairly stable network connections, use several sites connected by RPC connectors.

- For an unreliable network or a non-IP network, use the SMTP connector.

The following are the most important guidelines for site planning:

- Limit the number of sites in your environment, because each site entails a certain amount of administrative overhead.

- Consider the availability of services (DCs, GCs, and other core application services) in each site created.

traffic—occur much less frequently. Also, all users will have access to a local host that can service query requests without requiring network traffic traversing a slow and possibly oversubscribed link.

Consider the following guidelines for placing DCs in your company:

◆ A DC must be able to respond to client requests in a timely manner.

◆ DCs should be configured so that they are capable of supporting many more objects than currently necessary, to prepare for increased future use.

◆ At best, you would have several DCs in each major site, for purposes of availability.

◆ The best query performance happens when you have a DC and a GC in the same site.

Generally, the best network performance occurs when the DC at a small site is also a GC server, enabling that server to do logon authentication and fulfill queries about all objects in all domains on your network.

Consider these guidelines for placing GCs in your company:

◆ A GC server must have the capacity to hold all objects from all other domains in the forest—today and in the future. Therefore, the initial GC should have the capacity to support at least twice as many objects as you deem probable today.

Knowing Your Way Around Replication

Even though Microsoft has been quite preoccupied with replication of the core Active Directory data structures (schema, configuration, and domain-naming contexts), you will actually find more replication going on in a real-life Active Directory setting.

When Active Directory is up and running, you will at least have the following kinds of replication going on:

- Active Directory domains (domain-naming contexts)
- The schema (schema naming context)
- The physical namespace (sites and services; the configuration naming context)
- Files that are stored in the SYSVOL folder (the GPT part of the group policies, login scripts, and more)
- DNS

Replication for the first three items listed is taken care of by the much-vaunted multi-master replication architecture, whereas replication of the fourth item is done by the File Replication Service (FRS). So, you are urged to get a grip on FRS well before your first replication problem occurs. You can find much more detailed information on replications and other network traffic in Chapters 12 and 20.

♦ If sensible, you might place several GCs in each major site, for purposes of availability.

Don't Forget about Security

When you deal with a grand new concept such as Active Directory, security can tend to get relegated to a secondary position (and, in the worst case, added on as an afterthought). As is the case with NT Server 4 roll-outs, you might choose to divide the security area into three different scopes:

♦ Physical security surrounding your service providers (servers that provide services to the network)

♦ Logical security surrounding your service providers (users, groups, GPOs, IPSec, certificates, and other security features)

♦ Auditing of the security system (audit policies)

Windows NT Server 4 security planners delving into Active Directory's security aspects should feel fairly at ease (more so than for other aspects of Active Directory), because Windows 2000 Server is built on the same security subsystem (and thus the same security concepts) used in NT Server 4.

In Active Directory, every object in the directory has a *security descriptor*, which describes the access-control information associated with an object. And one still uses an ACL consisting of a list of ACEs for specifying the access rights to define what abilities a security principal has when it attempts to perform an operation on an object. Actually, even the security principals used in Active Directory are exactly the same as before (users, computers, and groups). The beginning of Chapter 9 provides a more detailed look at Active Directory security fundamentals.

Active Directory opens up a whole new world of possibilities, because it provides more-granular access control for objects than before (by using OUs for grouping objects), introduces a range of new built-in groups (because of the inclusion of new functionalities), and makes day-to-day administration of the security properties much easier (via the consolidation of the security-specific settings into the Security Templates MMC Snap-in and its range of predefined configurations). However, things are more or less the same as far as the core security concepts.

A lot can be said about Microsoft's decision not to go all the way in regard to Active Directory security (and Chapter 9 states about all that needs to be said on that subject). However, this means that NT Server 4 professionals shouldn't be too worried about security planning for Windows 2000 Server, because although its security aspects look a bit different, are located in a different place, and are complemented by a lot of new features (see also Chapters 10 and 14), most of the differences really are only skin-deep. However, you should note that the Active Directory adds a lot of new objects that need to be secured (as well as the many new security features) into the equation, so there's no doubt that more time needed to be allocated for security planning.

The Very Last Cut

By now, you should be familiar with the four major components of the Active Directory namespace:

♦ Domain namespace

♦ DNS namespace

♦ OU namespace

♦ Site topology

Users generally aren't exposed to namespaces (except for results of searches). That is an administrator-only experience.

Also, you should always remember the following:

♦ Domains are for partitioning.

♦ OUs are for delegation of administration and application of policies, not for assigning permissions.

♦ Sites are for DC/GC selection by clients and for replication control.

♦ DNS is the domain and computer locator.

But, even though you have a hierarchical structure in Active Directory, be keenly aware that the user logon name has to be unique within the forest and that you won't need to use suffixes that are related to actual domain names.

When doing the designing of Active Directory, remember the three words that really define the Active Directory experience (and any other directory service, for that matter): Iterate, iterate, iterate. Remember, too, that all good designs are based on accomplishing the right compromises. Except in the most simplistic of settings, you will always confront divisiveness regarding which needs and wants are more important—and thus you must determine which tradeoffs to make. After you implement your design, if you feel that you have achieved a high degree of satisfaction within the organization and the IT department and haven't found any serious shortcomings regarding all the things mentioned in the preceding chapters, then your design is more successful than most.

If you feel perfectly comfortable with the facts presented in this chapter, you should be ready to either initiate an Active Directory design team, delve into the material on migration and coexistence, or simply continue onwards with a discussion on some of the advanced parts of your Active Directory experience. To begin your design venture, refer to Appendix A for advice on how to handle the project and refer to Appendix B for some detailed case studies on Active Directory designs. To attain an understanding of migration and coexistence, study Chapters 21 through 23.

Finally, before you move on, note that this book supplies only the information that is necessary to plan the Active Directory aspect of a Windows 2000 Server setup. Although this is the core planning needed to realize a Windows 2000 Server environment, it isn't all that you need to do in order to achieve a successful completion of your implementation. Actually, after you execute the Active Directory design that is detailed in the previous chapters, you still have to determine the following (and probably some other things, too):

♦ Whether to use Windows 2000 Server, Windows 2000 Advanced Server, or Windows 2000 Datacenter Server on the servers in question.

♦ How to confiugre your servers hardware-wise (such as the file system configuration, LAN configuration, dial-up networking, and more including clustering).

♦ How to set up DHCP (and WINS, for backward-compatibility).

♦ Which network protocols to use and how to configure them.

♦ Which optional Windows 2000 services to use (for example, Indexing Service, Admission Control Service, Remote Installation Services, and Terminal Services) and how to configure them.

♦ Which licensing mode to use (per seat or per server).

♦ What to use for each server as far as backup software, antivirus software, and other add-on software options.

♦ How the file shares should be structured (namespace, as well as permissions-wise). You might also want to take advantage of the many new functionalities offered with Windows 2000—such as DFS, Disk Quotas, and Disk Defragmenter.

- How network printing should be done (in regard to sharing, publishing, security, priorities, and printer pools). You might also want to take advantage of the new functionalities offered with Windows 2000—such as improved PostScript support and Internet Printing System.

- What resources should be presented to the client at logon time (for example, using roaming user profiles, mapping shares using login scripts, and so on).

- What level of overall security is needed and which properties (including the auditing) need to be set to ensure that level—on servers as well as clients.

- Whether existing server applications are compatible with Windows 2000 Server, and what to do in case of incompatibilities.

- When and why to upgrade existing Windows NT servers on the network.

- How, when, and why to migrate other existing network servers.

- How to test, pilot, and ultimately roll out Windows 2000 Server in your environment.

- How your environment is going to be managed (tool-wise and people-wise).

- How Windows 2000 Professional should be set up on clients.

- How, when, and why to upgrade the clients on the network.

- Whether existing client applications are compatible with Windows 2000, and what to do in case of incompatibilities.

Please understand that this list of configuration decisions aren't covered in this book—apart from the thorough introduction to the planning activities regarding migration and coexistence—because of space limitations, and due to me considering them quite implementation-near as oppsed to the core design tasks that are the main focus of this book. Also, you should find most practically-oriented Windows 200 Server books to include the facts needed for resolving these issues.

Part III
Advanced Design Topics

Chapter 14

Advanced Security Topics

S ecurity is something that never goes out of fashion. And given the many new and exciting security features introduced with Active Directory, you're certain to have your hands full for some time to grasp the many details found inside this important area.

The major new security features found in Windows 2000 Server/ Active Directory include the following:

- ◆ *Kerberos v5 authentication*—This is Active Directory's default authentication method. Kerberos is an industry standard, which allows for much simpler management of trust relationships, and a more secure and robust authentication method than the one used by Windows NT 4 (NTLM). Kerberos shares secret keys with devices on network via a central server and, so, acts as a third-party certifier/arbitrator.

- ◆ *Encrypting file system (EFS)*—Enables you to encrypt the data on your NTFS partitions, protecting them from unauthorized access from anyone who might gain physical access to the computer or hard disk.

- ◆ *IPSEC*—Enables you to create secure end-to-end communications across IP networks.

- ◆ *Public key infrastructure (PKI)*—Public key cryptography enables you to securely exchange information with others across insecure connections, such as the Internet.

- ◆ *Smart Card support*—Smart Cards enable the portability of security credentials and other private information in a secure manner. Users can use the Smart Card to authenticate in a more secure manner than is the case, when specifying a username and a password.

This chapter includes an in-depth introduction to all the new security features garnered with some hard-earned, real-life experiences with each of these technologies.

Note

Due to the complexity of this area and the many new and very advanced security options, I won't dare to suggest this being more than an in-depth introduction to the security features. While you will indeed be able to customize the security features to your needs, you should definitely want to refer to other material, if you are charged with configuring a security-sensitive environment or a large PKI solution. For getting in-depth with all the "dirty" configuration details, I recommend the Windows 2000 Server Resource Kit.

Security Infrastructure Fundamentals

By definition, any security infrastructure builds on two cornerstones:

♦ *Security protocol(s)*—The protocols define exactly how a user is able to prove to the system that he or she really is who is claimed (authentication), and keep the communication between the user and the system secure.

♦ *Encryption algorithm(s)*—Allows the security protocol to protect the data exchanged between the user and the system from prying eyes.

Windows 2000 proves no exception to this rule (just as is the case with Windows NT).

As the years have passed, it has become more and more clear, that no one security protocol and encryption algorithm is able to accommodate the varied needs faced in an enterprise setting. And so, you are truly faced with a plethora of security protocols and encryption algorithms in real life.

For Windows 2000 Server and Active Directory, Microsoft has sought the very best standards for each security area and added them to the product specification sheet in order to make the product more interoperable. As a consequence to that, Windows 2000 Server includes support for such protocols as Lightweight Directory Access Protocol (LDAP), Kerberos, Public Key Cryptography Standard (PKCS), and IP Security (IPSEC), in addition to the old set of proprietary protocols (NTLM, Secure RPC, and PPTP). Much the same can be said in regard to encryption, which now include DES, 3DES, RSA, RC4, and a couple of more well-known algorithms.

In order to avoid having to "hardwire" applications for a specific security protocol and encryption algorithm—thus reducing flexibility and/or adding to the application development costs, when more than one protocol or algorithm need to be supported—Windows 2000 (as well as Windows NT) bases its support of security protocols and encryption algorithms on these two elements:

♦ *Security Support Provider Interface (SSPI)*—An API that shields the applications from the available security mechanisms available and vice versa.

♦ *CryptoAPI*—An API that shields all applications and services from the available encryption methods and vice versa.

Both elements take the shape of APIs, allowing the developers to reuse services provided by the OS and avoid any costly "hardwiring." Abstracting applications from the provider also protects the applications from obsolescence, because you are able to update and enhance provider components as technology progresses without affecting the application and, in most cases, allow old applications to tap into new security protocols and encryption algorithms.

SSPI

Security Support Provider Interface (SSPI) is a system API that applications and system services (including Microsoft Internet Explorer, Internet Information Services and Certificate Service) use to tap into security mechanisms, while hiding the complexity inherent in any network authentication security protocol from the applications.

Beside isolating applications on one side and application-level protocols on the other side from the intricacies of the applicable network security protocols, using SSPI ensures consistent security in the Windows-based environment, as is demonstrated in Figure 14.1. Additionally, SSPI provides a generic abstraction to support multiple authentication mechanisms based on shared-secret as well as public-key protocols.

Applications using integrated Windows 2000 security take advantage of the modularity provided by SSPI by calling the SSPI routines directly or by using the higher level network connection management protocols provided by authenticated RPC or DCOM.

Note

The SSPI communicates with a Win32 API based on the Generic Security Services Application Program Interface (GSS-API) and provides similar interface abstraction for security context management. You might want to check out RFC 1508 (Generic Security Services Application Program Interface) for more information on GSS-API.

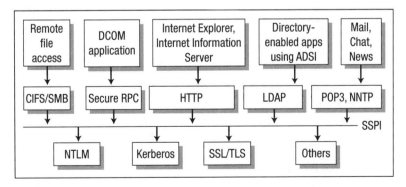

Figure 14.1
SSPI sits between the security protocols and the processes that use them, and thus helps reduce the application-level code needed to support multiple authentication protocols.

It's thanks to SSPI that your applications (as well as yourself) are being provided with a very rich set of authentication options:

♦ *Windows NT LAN Manager (NTLM)*—The authentication protocol used by Windows NT. NTLM continues to be supported by Windows 2000. It is, however, a legacy solution that is meant for pass-through network authentication, remote file access, and authenticated RPC connections to earlier versions of Windows NT only.

♦ *Kerberos Version 5*—The authentication protocol that has replaced NTLM as the primary security protocol for access to resources within or across Active Directory domains. The Kerberos authentication protocol is a mature industry standard that presents you with several major advantages (such as mutual authentication of both client and server, reduced server load, and support for delegation of authorization/impersonation) compared with NTLM.

♦ *Distributed Password Authentication (DPA)*—An authentication protocol used by some of the largest Internet communities, including MSN and CompuServe.

♦ *Public key-based protocols*—Authentication protocols using public-key certificates to authenticate clients and servers for privacy and reliability over the Internet. SSL has turned into a *de facto* standard today for connections between Web browsers and Web servers. But the IETF standard protocol definition (which is based on SSL3) known as the Transport Layer Security Protocol, or TLS, is a strong comer.

Windows 2000 allows the use of NTLM and Kerberos, as well as public key-based protocols for authentication against the Active Directory.

CryptoAPI

The goal of *CryptoAPI* is as simple as it's powerful: to provide one-stop shopping for low-level cryptographic services to all applications and OS components. As such, CryptoAPI allows application developers to avoid having to implement cryptographic code themselves and thus avoid having to redesign applications whenever the various encryption algorithms change.

Tip

The CryptoAPI is conceptually close to the well-known ODBC standard, which allows an application access to many different databases through the same ODBC interface. And just as is the case with ODBC, the CryptoAPI does allow you to develop custom CSPs. Unfortunately, you aren't allowed to add custom-built CSPs to the system before the CSP has been digitally signed by Microsoft (which entails a fair amount of paperwork and delivering the CSP's source code).

CryptoAPI achieves this goal by way of installable cryptographic service providers (CSPs), which are implemented as DLLs. CSPs provide key generation, signatures, encryption, hashing, and certificate services through a standard interface.

Encryption Primer

The word "encryption" originates from the Greek words *kryptos* (to hide) and *logos* (word), so encryption is far from a new phenomenon. Examples of encryption have been found as far back as the Egyptians' days of glory, 4,000 years ago, where some of the monuments' inscriptions are encrypted. Two thousand years later, Julius Caesar himself used a simple form of encryption, too.

But it was only in connection with World War II that encryption grew to become vital. At that time, the importance of encryption had grown in parallel with the rapid progress inside the computer and communications fields, due to encryption being the most appropriate way to protect sensitive information against unauthorized persons.

The three central concepts in the encryption field are:

- *Encryption*—Transformation of data, which cause the meaning of the data to become unintelligible.

- *Decryption*—Transformation of the encrypted data back to the original, readable form.

- *Key*—A collection of characters from which the encryption is being done. Most often the same key must be used again to perform a successful decryption.

In the professional context, DES or RSA are the most commonly used encryption algorithms. DES and RSA are widely acknowledged to be among the commercially-grade algorithms that on one hand are of practical use and on the other hand prove sufficiently complex to make it infeasible to start a brute-force attack on each encrypted message. In other words, DES and RSA can be broken, but in most cases the cost of breaking the code quite simply is higher than the value of the unencrypted data, which is why such algorithms are regarded as secure.

Opposite the *practically secure* algorithms are *theoretically secure* encryption algorithms that, unfortunately, have always proved to be too impractical to use on a day-to-day basis. The mathematician C.E. Shannon has, among other things, proved that an encryption key chosen completely by random and of the same length as the document to be encrypted, is theoretically secure, provided the key is used only once. In his demonstration, Shannon even used an encryption method that is as simple as anything can be—Vernam encryption—where only the **XOR** operation is used for the physical encryption.

According to the former British agent Peter Wright and his book *Spycatcher*, the Russians were using such a theoretically secure encryption key during the Cold War. However, it was broken by the British, because the Russians had more or less ignored the fact that the key, in order to be secure, can only be used once. The Russians were using the same key in different parts of the world.

Windows 2000 is delivered with the following set of CSPs:

♦ *Microsoft Base CSP*—Comprises a broad set of sensible commercial-grade, encryption algorithms. The Base CSP is featured in all versions of Windows 2000.

♦ *Microsoft Enhanced CSP*—Comprises all the encryption algorithms found in Base CSP with improved key lengths, as well as a couple of additional algorithms. Until the softening of the rather tight American export regulations governing encryption, the Enhanced CSP was available only in products sold in North America (that is, the U.S. and Canada). The Enhanced CSP is now available as a separate download from Microsoft, which definitely should be added to any solution built outside of North America for improved security.

♦ *Microsoft DSS CSP*—Adds support for data signature and signature verification using the Secure Hash Algorithm (SHA) and Digital Signature Algorithm (DSA). The DSS CSP is featured in all versions of Windows 2000.

♦ *Microsoft Base DSS and Diffie-Hellman CSPs*—An extension of the DSS CSP, which includes support for Diffie-Hellman key exchange, hashing (message digests), data signing, and signature verification using SHA or DSA. Until the softening of the rather tight American export regulations governing encryption, the Enhanced CSP was available only in products sold in North America (that is, the U.S. and Canada). These CSPs are now available as a download from Microsoft.

♦ *Schannel CSP*—Comprises a set of diverse cryptoalgorithms that are needed for data integrity, exchange of session keys, and authentication in connection with safe Web communications based on the SSL and TLS protocols.

The Two Base Encryption Techniques

There are two basic techniques for encrypting information:

• *Symmetric encryption*—Also known as secret key encryption.

• *Asymmetric encryption*—Also known as public key encryption.

Symmetric encryption is the oldest and best-known technique. A secret key (which can be a number, a word, or just a string of random letters) is applied to the text of a message to change the content in a particular way. This might be as simple as shifting each letter by a number of places in the alphabet. As long as both sender and recipient know the secret key, they can encrypt and decrypt all messages that use this key.

The problem with secret keys is exchanging them, because the security stands or falls with your being able to prevent them from falling into the wrong hands—and so, you generally aren't able to pass the keys over the Internet, you need some sort of "secure channel" to do it from—as anyone who knows the secret key is able to decrypt the message.

The need for a secure channel is obliterated, when using asymmetric encryption, which does encryption and decryption from two separate (but related) keys—these two keys are commonly referred to as a key pair. Typically, the public key of the key pair is made freely available to anyone who might want to send you a message. A second, private key is kept secret, so that only the owner of the key knows it. Asymmetric encryption does away with the worries for how to pass keys, because one of the two keys is supposed to be public.

Any messages that are encrypted by using the public key can be decrypted using the same algorithm used for the encryption, but by using the private key in the public key's place. Oppositely, any message that is encrypted by using the private key can be decrypted, only by using the matching public key.

In the age of the Internet, asymmetric, or public key, encryption really proves a much superior choice. And the only reason why public key encryption hasn't overtaken symmetric encryption by now is the fact that it's much slower—that is, it requires far more processing power to both encrypt and decrypt messages using asymmetric encryption than is the case with symmetric encryption—making it unsuitable for encryption of data streams and other kinds of online and near-online contents.

Algorithm	Base CSP	Enhanced CSP
RSA public key signature	Key length: 512 bits	Key length: 1,024 bits
RSA public key exchange	Key length: 512 bits	Key length: 1,024 bits
RC2 block encryption	Key length: 40 bits	Key length: 128 bits
		Salt length: Settable
RC4 stream encryption	Key length: 40 bits	Key length: 128 bits
		Salt length: Settable
DES	Not supported	Key length: 56 bits
3DES (2-key)	Not supported	Key length: 112 bits
3DES (3-key)	Not supported	Key length: 168 bits

Table 14.1   The contents of the Base CSP and Enhanced CSP at a glance.

Table 14.1 shows the encryption algorithms included with the Base CSP and Enhanced CSP. You should want to take note of the fact that public keys, which are used for digital signatures, are allowed to have a length of up to 16,384 bits. However, public keys, which are used for encryption and key exchanges (that is, to protect secret keys), are limited to 1,024 bits for the Base CSP and 16,384 bits for the Enhanced CSP.

As any security buff will be fast to point out, the CryptoAPI is the do-or-die proposal on generating real security in Windows 2000. Unfortunately, thus far Microsoft hasn't been able to come up with a real explanation of why we shouldn't expect the National Security Agency (NSA) to have added their very private back doors to the CryptoAPI. After all, why should Microsoft insist on keeping a very rigid authorization procedure in place for custom-built CSPs, if that wasn't the case? But, if nothing else, I guess it's better to "just" have the NSA listening in than the whole world.

The Base Authentication System: Kerberos

If one moves in the mythological Greek underworld, Hades, one would be wise to show great respect for Kerberos. Kerberos being the three-headed dog guards Hades with six watchful eyes and plenty of sharp teeth.

Luckily, the Kerberos of the real world is a somewhat more peaceful creature, whose task it is to guard the entrance to Active Directory. Kerberos, which replaces NT LAN Manager (NTLM) authentication as the default authentication mechanism used, is a well established industry-standard protocol that has been developed with the specific goal of supporting authentication in distributed systems.

Instead of three heads, the computer version of Kerberos offers a three-sided authentication process with shared-secret keys, which let the users, as well as the resources, prove their identity to each other over the network without compromising the security. The Kerberos security is based on two fundamental concepts:

♦ *Shared-secret keys*—The concept of shared-secret keys means that the two parties involved share the secret key, which proves that the user is indeed who he or she claims to be.

Kerberos' Source

Kerberos was developed by scientists from MIT in the 1980's. Kerberos was designed with a keen eye to all the needs found in a distributed environment. The source code for the original Kerberos implementation has been accessible to the public via the Internet for many years.

The first three Kerberos versions were used only for development and testing, which is why Kerberos 4 is the first version that ever gained a foothold outside MIT. Kerberos 4 has been implemented in many Unix and Internet-oriented systems, because Kerberos was chosen as one of the core components in the DCE framework (Distributed Computing Environment).

As it is often seen with new systems, Kerberos 4 turned out to have a fair number of trouble spots. The feedback on Kerberos 4 from the field led to the development of Kerberos 5, which among other things present you with the option of using triple DES encryption or other encryption algorithms for securing the communications. Kerberos 5 has been adopted as an IETF standard (Internet Engineering Task Force) in the form of RFC 1510.

Even though many Kerberos 4-based products are still in use, the vast majority of the current products incorporating Kerberos are based on version 5.

♦ *Three-sided authentication*—The three-sided authentication process means that the process for authentication involves three components:

  ♦ The client (or the client application), which represents the user. The client will want to make sure that each resource accessed is legitimate to avoid any security breaches by way of Trojan horse attacks.

  ♦ The resource (typically a server) that is accessed by the user. Each resource will wish to make sure that the client is legitimate.

  ♦ A central repository with information about the users and resources, which is referred to as the Key Distribution Center (KDC) service. The KDC database contains the identities and master keys (passwords) of all users and resources that belong to the given administrative area.

Tip

In Kerberos terminology, each administrative area (or domain) is called a realm. In order to secure against unauthorized access to the database, all master keys are encrypted with the server's private master keys, which in their turn are protected by the administrator's local KDC password. It is essential to understand that a physically secure KDC is an essential condition of an effective Kerberos security system.

Kerberos was designed from the ground up for using Data Encryption Standard (DES) shared-secret key encryption (see Figure 14.2) to authenticate clients in unsecured environments (that is, networks that contain clients who aren't physically secured). As such, all Kerberos communications transmitted on the network always will be in encrypted form.

Know Your DES

DES was released to the public all the way back in 1977 by the American Bureau of Standards. DES is a 64-bit block encryption algorithm. This means that the algorithm encrypts 64 bits of the information at a time using a 64-bit encryption key (in fact the key only has 56 bits, because 8 of the bits are used to generate a checksum).

According to the American standard, 16 encryption transformations (also called rounds) are carried out. Each encryption transformation consists of relatively simple transpositions and substitutions in groups of 4 bits. During each transformation only 48 of the key's 64 bits are used, but the 48 bits are chosen at random.

DES's working method means that the individual bits in each block of 64 bits depend on the others, which make it impossible to decrypt only parts of the encrypted data, even if a part of the password is known. Additionally, DES was specified in such a way that the number of possible combinations of encryption keys would be sufficiently large to make it highly unlikely that anyone should find the right encryption key, unless commanding a powerful computer for that purpose. So far, the mathematicians have found no other, or better, methods than the exhaustive search process—which in the worst case means that it is necessary to go through all 72.058 trillion (2^{56}) possibilities. However, due to the rapid rise in computer power from then to now, DES has become more manageable to break, by today's standards.

Adding to DES's problems is the fact that DES isn't always DES. Several of the DES programs use less than the prescribed 16 transformations. And that is a very unsettling thought, because the security in DES depends on how many transformations the original information has undergone. Already, in the early 1990s, Professor Adi Shamir demonstrated that it is possible to break DES-encrypted documents that have undergone six and eight transformations. On an ordinary PC it took three seconds and three minutes, respectively, to break the encryption. The only further condition was that the encrypted data be written in English.

Fortunately the standardized DES of 16 transformations is cryptographically essentially different from eight transformations. But Shamir's attack on DES makes it abundantly clear that the current "default" encryption key length of 64 bits should be increased to at least 128 bits by today's standards. Furthermore, Shamir's example shows that buyers of programs and hardware for DES encryption should make sure that it at least follows the American standard.

It is important to realize that even though DES is a very effective encryption technique, it's by no means foolproof. Actually, it has already been the target of several successful break-ins. And that's why Kerberos v5, as mentioned, offers the opportunity to implement other encryption algorithms, including triple DES.

The General Working Method

The fundamental security element in Kerberos is the so-called ticket. Tickets are used by clients for setting up sessions with servers or services. A ticket is a certificate issued by the Kerberos service, which proves that the client is whom he claims to be and is allowed to set up a more or less specific session to another party.

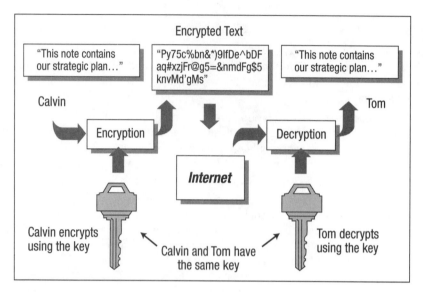

Figure 14.2
Kerberos is a secret key encryption algorithm (sometimes called shared-key) based on the use of the same password by sender and recipient. This is why the password must not be known by other parties, if security is to be maintained.

In addition, you have a very important kind of ticket named "TGT"—which is an abbreviation of Ticket Granting Ticket. The TGT removes the need to go through a full authentication of the client with the KDC every time a ticket has to be issued (that is, for each client request to access a new network resource).

When the KDC is done authenticating the user at the time of logging into the client system, a TGT is returned. As mentioned, this TGT can be used for "cutting some corners" in the authentication of the client, when it requests a ticket for a given network resource. This is done by sending the TGT to the KDC, in conjunction with the request for accessing the network resources.

If the TGT is proven valid, the server will return the requested ticket to the client without further ado. As such, the TGT not only works to simplify the authentication for a resource, but it also eliminates the need to send passwords over the network. And Kerberos escapes the risk of man-in-the-middle attacks, because only the rightful owner of the ticket will be able to make use of the ticket issued by the KDC (due to the KDC encrypting the ticket with the user's password, the ticket will only be of any use to the local client).

Tickets (and especially the TGT) must be handled properly in order to avoid other parties using them for unauthorized access to network resources. To bolster security further, Kerberos demands setting an upper limit to the validity of a given ticket. This upper limit is configurable and you are encouraged to carefully consider whether the default setting does work for your environment—or if you will need to reduce the duration a ticket's validity for improved security.

Note

You're allowed to control the time of expiration for the tickets by setting up a security template and adding it to the default domain Group Policy. The standard expiration for tickets is eight hours. If a ticket expires during an active session, the client will automatically renew the ticket without troubling the user using the TGT.

How Kerberos Secures the Local Area

When a client wishes to access information on a server within the same realm (that is, the client and the server belong to the same Active Directory domain), the client as well as the server must be authenticated. In practice, the authentication can be divided into a sequence of events happening between the client and the KDC and between the client and the server, respectively.

Note

Each Active Directory domain translates into a Kerberos realm. Consequently, all DCs inside each domain work as KDCs; therefore, the KDC is using Active Directory as its user database.

Kerberos uses messages to provide each Kerberos component with the necessary information during the authentication process. As mentioned, many of these messages are encrypted, as well as including timestamps to secure against man-in-the-middle attacks (that is, someone picking up the network communications going on between the client and the KDC with a protocol-sniffing device and playing the client communications back at a later time in a bid to authenticate themselves).

The following is an explanation of the usual sequence of events (see Figure 14.3), when a client needs to gain access to a given server (or service):

1. The client sends a plain-text message to the KDC, where it asks for a ticket that allows it to communicate with the KDC from then and on. The message from the client contains the user's name, the name of the KDC, and a timestamp.

2. The KDC returns an encrypted message to the client. The message is encrypted with the client's password, and contains a timestamped session key to be used with the KDC and a general ticket—the Ticket Granting Ticket (TGT)—which the client can use to obtain future tickets for specific services within the realm of the KDC.

3. The client sends an encrypted message to the KDC in which it requests the right to communicate with a given server or service. The client encrypts this message with the session key that it has just received from the KDC. The message contains the name of the desired server or service, a timestamp, and the TGT. When the KDC receives the message, it can be certain that the request indeed came from the client, because the message can only be decrypted by means of the client's session key. The KDC then produces a shared session key, which is to be used by both the client and the server. The KDC also produces a specific ticket that accommodates for the needs at the server. This

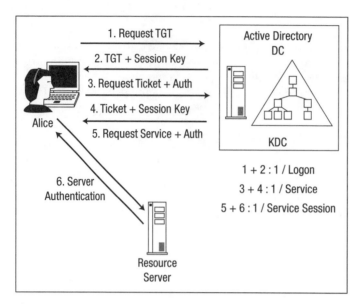

Figure 14.3
This is how the Kerberos authentication of the client against a given server takes place.

specific ticket contains the session key, the name of the client, the address of the client's network interface card, the ticket's period of validity, and a timestamp.

4. The KDC sends a message to the client that contains the encrypted shared session key and the encrypted ticket. The shared session key is encrypted with the client's session key; the ticket is encrypted with the server's session key.

5. The client sends a message to the server to inform it that it has the right to communicate with the server (whether or not the client can have its subsequent requests carried out is of course up to the client authentication being performed at the server's security system). The message contains the encrypted ticket that the client received from the KDC and a timestamp authenticator, which is encrypted with the shared session key. The server uses its own password to decrypt the ticket, which contains a copy of the shared session key and a few other vital pieces of information about the client. The server uses the shared session key to decrypt the timestamp authenticator to check when the client sent the message. If the client sent the message within the ticket's period of validity, and if everything else is in order, the server will accept the client's request.

6. When the server has approved the client, it will send an encrypted message, telling the client that it accepts the request to communicate. The message contains the timestamp authenticator that the client sent to the server in Step 5. The timestamp authenticator is still encrypted with the shared session key.

7. And now the communication between client and server can finally begin.

Tip

Your Windows 2000 Professional client will, in fact, only be performing all the seven steps mentioned for Kerberos authentication, when it logs on to the Active Directory. In this case, the user will be allocated a TGT at soon as he or she has entered username and password. The TGT is then stored with other user logon information at the cache on the client.

When the client wishes to communicate with a service, it looks for a valid ticket to the resource. If a ticket isn't available, the client sends a TGT to the KDC, and carries out the procedure from Step 3 onward.

You should note that Kerberos serves exclusively as an authentication protocol. And so, it doesn't cover the access control component, which is still handled by means of the SID (Security Identifier), ACL (Access Control List), and SD (Security Descriptor), as discussed in Chapter 9.

You should note that the first two of the six events are superfluous if the client wishes to get access to another server or service later on (see Figure 14.4), because the client can reuse its TGT, until it expires.

How Kerberos Secures the Global Area

The authentication of clients across Kerberos realms does, in fact, not differ very much from the authentication within a realm. As you know from the earlier discussions, each Kerberos realm is equipped with its own KDC and ticket-issuing service. But rather than having to

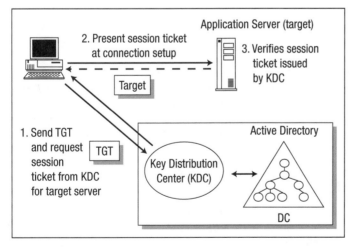

Figure 14.4
The Kerberos authentication opens up the possibility to effectively use resources from several different servers. The client can either ask the KDC for a ticket to the desired server as outlined in Figure 14.3 or let a server (to which the client already has a ticket) handle the authentication work.

open a separate account in each realm for the same user, Kerberos allows for realms to approve each other's users, and thus let users get access to servers and services within both realms—exactly as you might be used to from Windows NT when working across multiple domains that trusts each other.

When authenticating across two realms, two additional steps are carried out, before reaching Step 3 in the client authentication (as described in the last section). In other words, the events mentioned below will either replace events 1 and 2 (provided the client already has a TGT for the local realm) or be inserted between Step 2 and 3:

1. The client sends an encrypted message to the KDC. This message contains a request for a session key, which makes it possible to communicate with the KDC in the other realm.

2. The KDC sends the client an encrypted message, which contains a ticket to the KDC server in the other realm. Now it is possible for the client to contact the other KDC server directly and ask for a ticket to the desired server or service.

Naturally, the above applies only if the KDC in the client's own realm has a session key for the desired KDC—which requires that a more or less manual registration between the two KDC's has taken place.

If the client wishes to get access to a realm that doesn't prove to be accessible directly from the local KDC, this is in fact also made possible in an Active Directory setting. Active Directory's Kerberos implementation can handle a hierarchy of realms, so that the client can contact a realm that has access to another realm, and so on. This stepping through the hierarchy will continue, until the client has located the desired KDC, or reached the top of the hierarchy. As you might have guessed, the hierarchy of realms is of course based on the Active Directory domain tree.

> **Note**
>
> *The fact that Active Directory's KDC is using SIDs for access control adds a rather big limitation on the part of cross-platform interoperability. But that's really not just Microsoft's fault. The problem stems from the fact that the implementations of Kerberos on different platforms will be operating on different security fundamentals (usually the underlying operating system's base identifiers and access control mechanisms). And because of that, it will usually prove necessary to set up local user accounts at the local KDC for each user coming from other systems needing to access the services offered in that particular realm.*
>
> *However, it's definitely also worth noticing that Microsoft and the other major Kerberos providers are all cooperating with the IETF CAT Work Group (Internet Engineering Task Force Common Authentication Technology) in order to finish an expansion of the Kerberos RFC 1510, which opens up the possibility of using private/public key encryption methods. Provided that this project is successful, it will become possible for a KDC to determine the authentication of a request from a*

client by means of his public key—and subsequently to return an answer in a secure way. Please note that Chapter 23 delves further into the subject of Kerberos interoperability.

Nobody Is Perfect

In Greek mythology, the three-headed dog was bypassed on some occasions in spite of its deterrent nature. On one occasion, Hercules pulled the dog from the underworld to the surface of the Earth, and on another occasion Ulysses succeeded in bribing the dog with cake.

The same is true of the computer version of Kerberos. Even though the Kerberos technology must be said to be an optimum solution to the security challenges faced in distributed environments, it is by no means a completely watertight solution. The biggest and most obvious risk is for Kerberos to fall prey to a password dictionary attack (that is, an attack based on going through a number of ordinary passwords) because the user has chosen a far too simple and common password.

Another obvious weakness of Kerberos is that the KDC must be physically secured. Improper handling or inadequate security measures around the KDC will cause a major reduction of the security surrounding the client authentication. And then there is of course the greatest risk of them all: the human element. Experience shows that the vast majority of cases of computer fraud are actually carried out by the company's own trusted staff members. Against the company's own staff members, any security system will prove insufficient.

But if nothing else, Kerberos is definitely the best current offer for a secure and easily administered security authentication system for distributed environments. And in any case, it is considerably better than the NTLM authentication, which was the prevailing authentication method in Windows NT Server. For example, Kerberos includes support for mutual authentication (that is, the clients will get proof that a server is what it claims to be and vice versa), transitive trust, and delegation, and it introduces a time limit in the client's access to servers across the network. And, besides all that, Kerberos is an acknowledged standard, offering a fair level of interoperability with many other systems.

Tip

I guess that most people reading this still remember NTLM. And that's quite lucky, because you most probably will need to keep your NTLM skills handy for a while longer.

For example, you won't be able to perform an automated join of machines to the domain, unless you have NTLM access enabled! So, although Kerberos is taking over from here on, you really can't avoid NTLM altogether—not even in a pure Windows 2000/Active Directory environment. And so, it will make a lot of sense for you to make use of the options offered in the Security Template for controlling which NTLM variants that are allowed in the domain.

The Alternative: PKI and Smart Cards

As mentioned earlier, asymmetric or public key encryption does prove a very interesting alternative to symmetric encryption, which is used by Kerberos and NTLM, in these Internet times. On the face of it, the symmetric encryption algorithms are best at securing the confidence and the integrity inside the enterprise, because they prove faster and more efficient than the asymmetric ones (and here, Kerberos is definitely a great step forward compared to NTLM). But public key encryption is clearly the most qualified encryption method for communications outside of the company's private network due to the symmetric encryption algorithms' problem with sharing keys over an inherent unsecured medium.

> **Note**
>
> *You might also want to note that public key encryption is the only suitable answer to handling electronic documents correctly. In the nonelectronic world, the integrity problem was often solved by entering the information in such a way that it was difficult to add or erase information without leaving traces. The authentication was defined by the signature (provided, of course, that it was a one-page document).*
>
> *When you're dealing with electronic documents, it makes no sense to talk about masters and copies, the only thing that matters is determining whether a given document in fact does come from the alleged person and that it hadn't been tampered with. In the age of electronic documents, it has not been possible to ensure that a given document really came from a given recipient, and hadn't been changed, before the introduction of public key encryption.*
>
> *Before the advent of public key encryption, making changes in the contents of a document (or distributing a forged document) has only been a question of pressing a few keys, because a change doesn't leave any noticeable traces in the document.*

Understanding Public Key Encryption

As mentioned public key encryption is based on creating two keys:

♦ A *private key*—The private key is issued to a certain person or entity and should be kept private to that person.

♦ A *public key*—At the time of the private key being issued, a public key is generated. This key is to become publicly accessible.

Public key encryption applies to the following usage scenarios:

♦ *Nonrepudiation*—A service (proof of origin) that allows the recipient of a message to verify the originator of the message. In this case, the sender will use his private key to encrypt the information, and the receiver will then be able to use the sender's public key to decrypt the message. This scheme allows the recipient to be certain, right away, that the sender really is who he claims to be.

♦ *Confidentiality*—A service that creates confidence a message can be read only by those for who it is intended. In this case, the sender will encrypt the message using the receiver's public key to secure it against prying eyes.

♦ *Integrity*—A service that allows the recipient to verify that the message has not been altered since it left the originator. This can be done in several ways using the public and private keys.

You might want to note that you are able to combine these scenarios at will. For example, you should want to ensure the integrity **and** nonrepudiation for a contract (see Figure 14.5).

As a consequence of that, public key encryption has been adopted as the standard method for digital signatures. Digital signatures make it possible to create an electronic copy of a master document that can't be changed without this being evident and, at the same time, demonstrably won't lose its link to the creator—which means that possible claims based on the contents of a document can hold water in a court of law. These claims are met because anyone in possession of the public key from the sender can read the document—and so, indirectly, make sure that the alleged writer did indeed create it. But the document can't be re-encrypted without the writer's secret key. Currently, most countries are in the process of adding provisions for digital signatures in their laws, for putting them on an equal footing with the traditional, manual signatures. RSA is the preferred encryption algorithm in connection with public key encryption.

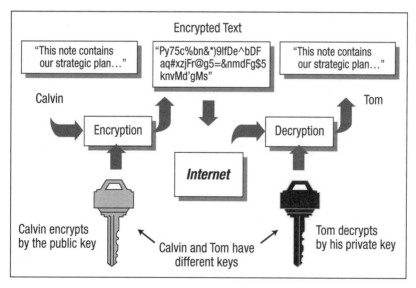

Figure 14.5
Public key encryption is based on the use of so-called asymmetrical keys.

A Bit about RSA

RSA (the initials of the names of the inventors: Rivest, Shamir, and Adleman) is a so-called public key encryption system. A public key encryption system carries the advantage that the encryption key can be published without compromising the data security.

RSA is almost obligatory when it comes to, for example, the authentication of data, which is becoming more and more necessary as business deals and bills are becoming electronic. The RSA system is a so-called asymmetrical encryption algorithm (see Figure 14.5). This means that different keys are used for encryption and decryption. One of the keys must be kept secret; whereas the other key can (and should) be made publicly accessible.

The public key consists of the pair (**e,n**) and the secret key of the pair (**d,n**). Here **n** denotes the encryption key, which is the product of two suitably large prime numbers **p** and **q** (that is, **n=p×q**). **d** and **e** must meet the requirement that **d×e/(p-1)×(q-1)=1** as well as **e** nor **(p-1)×(q-1)** being divisible by any number. The entire security in RSA depends on keeping **p**, **q**, and **d** secret.

If **M** is plain text, the encryption process is defined by the transformation **C=Me modulus n**. The transformation back to plain text is defined as **M=Cd modulus n**.

The high degree of security of the RSA method is primarily based on the special properties of the prime numbers used in connection with computers. While it is relatively easy to find large prime numbers with a computer, it's a very computationally-intensive task to split up a large number into its prime number factors **p** and **q**.

It's possible to improve the security by choosing so-called strong prime numbers, which is a prime number **p**, where **p-1** has a large prime number factor, **r** and **p+1** has a large prime number factor. Also, **r-1** must have a large prime number factor and **s-1** a large prime number factor.

Public encryption algorithms use much longer encryption keys than is the case with the symmetric encryption algorithms—and, consequently, they work considerably more slowly. Typically, each of the prime numbers **p** and **q** consists of 100 digits. Still, the most commonly used digit length in RSA (150 digits) has already fallen victim to the development inside the computer field.

What's in PKI?

To use asymmetric encryption, there must be a way for people to discover other public keys. The typical technique is to use a digital certificate (also known simply as a certificate), which is a package of information that identifies a user or a server and contains such information as the organization name, the organization that issued the certificate, the user's email address and country of origin, in addition to the user's public key.

In order to make the certificates generally available and have a trustworthy third-party vouch for the authenticity of the certificates, you need to set up a so-called Certificate Authority (CA). When you have a system of digital certificates, CAs, and other registration authorities that verify and authenticate the validity of each party involved, you are said to have a Public Key Infrastructure (PKI). Or, to state it in another way: A Public Key Infrastructure (PKI) provides the capability to use, manage, and retrieve certificates.

Also, if you're in doubt as to whether you'll need a CA solution in the near future, please take a look at this rather persuasive list of the immediate uses for certificates:

♦ Securing email communications using Secure/Multipurpose Internet Mail Extensions (S/MIME)

♦ Performing secure transactions and communications using Secure Sockets Layer (SSL) or Transport Layer Security (TLS)

♦ Signing executable code for delivery over public networks

♦ Providing Internet Protocol security (IPSEC) authentication for clients that can't use the Kerberos protocol or shared-secret passwords

♦ Encrypting files using Windows 2000 Encrypting File System (EFS)

♦ Supporting local or remote network logon using Smart Cards

The Windows 2000 PKI Solution

Windows 2000 Server allows you to implement a full-blown PKI solution in concert with Active Directory. The standard certificate format used by Windows 2000 certificate-based processes is X.509v3. An X.509 certificate includes information about the person or entity to which the certificate is issued, information about the certificate, and optional information about the certification authority issuing the certificate.

In order to allow you to implement PKI without depending on an external Certificate Authority (CA), Windows 2000 Server includes a component called Certificate Services to create and manage CAs. Certificate Services is integrated with Active Directory and distributed security services.

A CA is responsible for establishing and vouching for the identity of certificate holders. A CA also revokes certificates if they should no longer be considered valid and publishes Certificate Revocation Lists (CRLs) to be used by certificate verifiers.

The simplest PKI design has only one root CA. In practice, however, the majority of organizations deploying a PKI will use a number of CAs, organized into trusted groups known as *certification hierarchies*.

Note

In a secure system, the root CA should actually be taken offline in order to ensure against attacks that allows a perpetrator to gain access to the keys that validate the authenticity of the CAs that are available to the general public.

A separate component of Certificate Services is the CA Web enrollment pages. These Web pages are installed by default when you set up a CA and allow certificate requesters to submit certificate requests using a Web browser.

Additionally, the CA Web pages can be installed on Windows 2000-based servers that do not have a CA installed. In that case, the Web pages are used to direct certificate requests to the CA, which you don't want requesters to access directly. If you choose to create custom Web pages for your organization for accessing a CA, the Web pages provided with Windows 2000 Server should prove a good starting point.

To make it easy to deploy public key security, the steps for enrolling for the certificates used by computers, as well as by users, can be automated within the Windows 2000 infrastructure by way of Group Policies. That is, by using Group Policies, computers will be aware of the fact that they can obtain a certificate and will automatically obtain one when needed, and users will automatically be provided one. This will save the users and administrators for having to go through a series of manual steps to enroll certificates for computers and/or users.

Windows 2000 Server's Certificate Services can operate in either of two modes:

♦ *Standalone mode*—Makes the CA work as any other standard implementation of the CA functionality, which means that each machine and user has to apply for a certificate (by default, using a Web page) and wait for the CA administrator to approve their application to get the certificate registered.

♦ *Enterprise mode*—Extends the CA with proprietary functionality that allows all participants in the Active Directory infrastructure to automatically get assigned the wished-for certificates using Group Policies, thus relieving the administrators from a rather large work burden, as well as making it possible to have certificates ready in a matter of seconds rather than hours or days.

Warning
Please note that a lot of administration will be added to the administrator's plate by implementing a CA. And that's why the proprietary Enterprise CA option will prove so important to getting public key infrastructures in place in most enterprises. However, you should remember that the Enterprise CA might not be applicable to all scenarios, because it currently demands you having a pure Windows 2000 environment that is using Kerberos and includes full network connectivity. In other words, the Enterprise CA doesn't apply to users that are working off other OSs than Windows 2000, as well as mobile users whose machines aren't registered in the domain!

And believe me: The Windows 2000 Server Certificate Services component works great. So, unless you need to store and service millions of certificates, I really can't see the point in implementing another CA.

Smart Cards for Logon
Active Directory includes support for a very interesting application for certificates: Using them for logging on. In this case, you will need to have the certificate stored on a Smart Card in order to make the private key portable. And so, instead of entering a user name and a

password, the user simply will be charged with inserting the Smart Card into a reader attached to the PC and entering the card's PIN (just as you know it from any other credit card).

Note

Microsoft's public key extension for Kerberos, which allows the use of certificates instead of the usual user/password combination, simply adds the user's X.509 certificate to Active Directory (see Figure 14.6).

When the client requests a connection, the Kerberos service is able to authenticate the client by means of the public key as the client will be using the private key for encryption purposes. After authenticating the user, the KDC issues the desired ticket and encrypts it with the client's public key, which secures that only the correct recipient can have access to the ticket. From this point on, additional connections the user makes during the session use Kerberos authentication in exactly the same way as described earlier in this chapter.

Smart Cards, which are typically the size of a credit card, provide tamper-resistant storage for protecting user's certificates and private keys. And the PIN works to protect the information stored on the Smart Card from abuse, if the card should be lost. In this way, Smart Cards provide a very secure means of user authentication and interactive logon (as well as the many other applications for certificates mentioned earlier). So Smart Cards will not only relieve the user from having to remember a password, they will also increase the overall security of the network resources: Any unauthorized person can't "just guess" the name of a user and his password.

The Smart Card contains a chip that stores the user's private key, logon information, and public key certificate used for various purposes, such as digital signatures and data encryption. Smart Cards enhance software-only authentication by requiring a user to provide both a physical object (the card) and required knowledge (the card's PIN number) before being able to access a resource.

This requirement for presenting both the card and the PIN is referred to as *two-factor authentication*. Using a Smart Card to authenticate users is ideal for situations where additional security is deemed important, such as for people accessing your payroll application.

Smart Cards are more secure than passwords for several reasons:

♦ A physical object, the Smart Card, is needed to authenticate the user.

♦ The card must be used with a personal identification number (PIN), helping to ensure that the proper person is using the card.

♦ The risk of an attacker using a stolen credential is effectively eliminated, because it is physically impossible to extract the key from the card.

♦ Without the card, an attacker cannot access Smart Card-protected resources.

♦ No form of the password or any reusable information is transmitted over the network.

Note
Smart Card functionality is viewed as being so important to Microsoft that a model has been published of how to connect and use Smart Card readers with Windows 2000. The model is based on PC/SC specification (Personal Computer/Smart Card) and on Windows 2000's built-in SCard COM implementation, which is a collection of COM interface objects that can be used to build high-level interfaces or applications that use Smart Cards.

Microsoft rightly expects the Smart Card logon to become an important feature used by still more companies in the future. In practice, you might want to start taking Smart Cards to heart for improving the security on the most sensitive user accounts (especially the all-powerful administrators accounts, because this will also help ease the need on the part of the administrators to remember several passwords) and for users logging on from outside the organization.

You should take great care to note that Smart Card logon still is in its infancy. And for that reason—as well as the delicate nature of the Smart Card login—you should be careful to choose only Smart Card readers that are stated in the Windows 2000 Hardware Compatibility List (HCL). And, most importantly: You should check whether the Smart Cards chosen need to add an additional CSP to the systems supporting the Smart Card readers in order to be able to work, because this might prove a lot of work, depending upon the number of systems involved and their setup.

Tip
At present time, Windows 2000 includes support only for Gemplus, GemSAFE, and Schlumberger Cryptoflex Smart Cards. Thus, you'll be faced with adding a CSP for any other Smart Card!

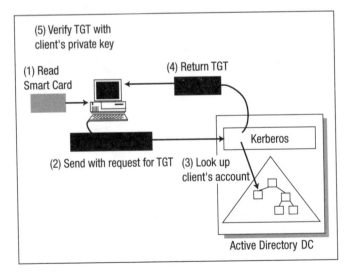

Figure 14.6
Smart Cards integrate quite effortlessly in a Windows 2000 Kerberos setting.

Network-Level Security: IPSEC

As the name indicates, IP Security (IPSEC) opens up the possibility of defining security policies that relate to the network communication layer. IPSEC is a suite of Internet-standard protocols that allow secure, encrypted communications between two computers over an insecure network. The encryption is applied at the IP network layer, which means that it is transparent to most applications that use specific protocols for network communication as well as the underlying network hardware.

Further, IPSEC provides end-to-end security, meaning that the IP packets are encrypted by the sending computer, are unreadable en route, and can be decrypted only by the recipient computer. For further safety, the process uses pre-existing keys (stemming from either Kerberos, public keys or a preshared key) for generating a single symmetric encryption key that is used at both ends of the connection in order to avoid having the key being passed over the network.

IP Security is completely independent of the other kinds of security measures implemented in the enterprise, because it works on the network layer rather than on the application layers. Thus, IP Security can be used to improve on the general security level in the entire organization or selected parts of it, in addition to what is achieved using the other security options discussed in this chapter.

IPSEC in Use

IP Security (IPSEC) allows you to set up Windows 2000 to automatically decrypt and encrypt IP network packages that go to and from the system—and, thus, secure the communication against eavesdropping and the like. IPSEC can be installed to cover all or some of the machines on the IP network, as well as selected TCP/IP ports and addresses. The scope and setup of IPSEC is controlled using Group Policies—thus, it can be assigned to a local machine as well as a set of machines.

Warning

Understand that IPSEC can't be assigned to users, but only to machines. And because the IPSEC policy settings are imposed late in the processing of the machine's Group Policy, the data sent across the network as part of the authentication of the computer (including any machine Group Policies) isn't and can't be encrypted!

You might also want to note that the opportunities present in IPSEC don't become less fascinating by the fact that they are completely invisible to the user and can be administered centrally—this means that in practice there will hardly be any additional administrative costs incurred by the introduction of IPSEC on the network!

The IPSEC implementation includes three pre-built IPSEC policies:

♦ *Client (Respond Only)*—In this case, the Windows 2000 machine will negotiate IPSEC security with any computer that supports IPSEC, but it won't start a security negotiation on its own. Thus, in the ordinary case, this policy really only applies to client computers.

◆ *Secure Server (Require Security)*—States that all IP communication to, or from, the policy target *must* use IPSEC. In this case, "all" really does mean all communications to and from the machines, and everything else that uses an IP connection either has to use IPSEC or it'll be blocked. In most cases, this might not be what you want, because very few organizations will be able to implement an all-IPSEC network.

◆ *Server (Request Security)*—A combination of the two other policies in that it will instruct the machine to always attempt IPSEC, by requesting it when it connects to a remote machine and by allowing it when an incoming connection requests it. However, if the other machine doesn't support IPSEC, it won't bring the communications to a halt.

Note

The IPSEC implementation does include a few notable exceptions to the IP communications covered: Broadcasts, multicasts, Kerberos, RSVP, and ISAKMP/IKE. Although all of these things make great sense to actually keeping the IPSEC implementation usable in the real life, you should stay alert to this fact for avoiding any misunderstanding.

You are allowed to customize the pre-built policies, as well as creating your own. Based on my extensive experiences with IPSEC, I have to say that there's a lot more to IPSEC than meets the eye. Thus, you should expect to spend a lot of time to get things exactly right. And you should always want to start out softly, using the pre-built IPSEC policies rather than building your own. Once you have compatible IPSEC policies assigned to two or more computers, you should spend some time coming to terms with the consequences of running IPSEC and the IPSECMON tool that allow you to see what's going on. Only after you've gotten IPSEC to work and have dabbled around a bit with it, should you move forward in building your own customized policies.

Warning

You should understand two not-so-great details about IPSEC. First off, the way that Microsoft has chosen to implement IPSEC means that it doesn't apply to Active Directory DC/GCs, because IPSEC client login isn't supported. So IPSEC really only applies to servers that are working as member servers or standalone servers! However, while this isn't supported by Microsoft, you are indeed able to tweak things to make IPSEC work for Active Directory DC/GCs (I know because I've done that), except in regard to clients doing the initial join to the domain.

Additionally, IPSEC does add a sizable performance hit, because all data has to pass the CPU for encryption and decryption. This especially doesn't sit very well with high-performance servers, which have been optimized for network-to-disk communications. Depending upon the exact circumstances (that is, the number of concurrent users, and the choice of protocol and encryption algorithms), you should expect your CPU load on the server to grow by some 50 to 90 percent, when IPSEC communications are employed.

Table 14.2 **Performance results seen, when running a variety of different scenarios, where one client is communicating with a server. All the IPSEC traffic is ESP with 3DES encryption.**

Communication Setup	Server Networking Adapter	Client Networking Adapter	Data Sent from Client	Data Sent from Server	Time (Minutes)	% Processor	Bytes Tot/Sec
Clear-text traffic	Ordinary	Ordinary	277MB	0MB	1:44	9.0	2,903KB
Clear-text traffic	Ordinary	Ordinary	277MB	277MB	3:53	14.2	2,687KB
Clear-text traffic	IPSEC	Ordinary	277MB	0MB	1:48	9.1	3,053KB
Clear-text traffic	IPSEC	Ordinary	277MB	277MB	2:20	24.3	4,592KB
IPSEC traffic	Ordinary	Ordinary	277MB	0MB	04:55	26.3	1,089KB
IPSEC traffic	Ordinary	Ordinary	277MB	277MB	12:51	12.1	847KB
IPSEC traffic	IPSEC	Ordinary	277MB	0MB	02:55	11.8	1,991KB
IPSEC traffic	IPSEC	Ordinary	277MB	277MB	04:17	13.6	2,472KB
IPSEC traffic	IPSEC	IPSec	277MB	0MB	02:25	15.3	2,205KB
IPSEC traffic	IPSEC	IPSec	277MB	277MB	02:43	26.4	4,389KB

Table 14.2 includes a practical demonstration of this rather scary picture, including the fact that the server will spend a lot longer on getting the data moved due to the time spent on IPSEC encryption and decryption. And that's only with just one client running. However, you should note that this is really a worst-case scenario, due to 3DES adding the most load to the CPU. Also please be sure to note that not only does the processor load grow a fair bit when IPSEC is added, but the time spent also increases a fair amount for most of the scenarios.

Due to this very harsh performance hit, you should always employ IPSEC network cards that are able to offload the CPU somewhat (limiting the performance hit to some 20 to 50 percent). Also, you might want to add an extra CPU to relieve the added load.

IPSEC Options

IPSEC can be configured to perform one or more of the following security functions:

♦ Ensure the integrity of the IP data packets that are transmitted over the network.

♦ Encrypt all data that is sent over the network with full confidentiality.

♦ Hide the originating IP addresses while they are *en route*.

Note

You should note that Windows 2000's IPSEC allow you to authenticate the sender of IP data packets on the basis of Kerberos authentication, digital certificates, or a shared-secret key (password).

The support for digital certificates is based on the PKCS extension for IPSEC, which isn't fully standardized at present. Also, my experience is that it really isn't fully ready for prime time, because it sometimes acts a bit flaky.

The integrity bit is handled using a protocol called Authentication Header (AH). To be more precise, AH digitally signs the entrie contents of each packet, protecting your network against three kinds of attacks:

♦ *Replay attacks*—This is when an attacker captures packets, saves them until later, and resends them to impersonate another machine on the network. The AH protocol prevents replay attacks by including a keyed hash of the packet, so no one will be able to resend the packets.

♦ *Tampering*—The keyed hash mechanism employed by AH provides assurance that no one has changed the contents of a packet after it was sent.

♦ *Spoofing*—Provides two-way authentication, so the client and server can both verify the other end's identity.

In other words, the AH secures the integrity and authenticity of the network packets. It works by adding an authentication header to each packet. This header contains a keyed hash, which is computed across the entire packet, so any change to the underlying data will render the hash invalid—that provides integrity protection. AH uses either HMAC-MD5 or HMAC-SHA encryption algorithms.

Note

Hash Message Authentication Code (HMAC) is a secret key algorithm, where a secret key is combined with a hash function. The hash function can either be HMAC-MD5 (Message Digest function 5) or HMAC-SHA (Secure Hash Algorithm), which produces 128-bit and 160-bit values, respectively, which are used as a signature of a given data block.

Although the AH protocol protects your data against attacks on the integrity and authenticity, it doesn't do anything to keep people from reading your traffic off the wire. For getting that bit covered, you need to use the Encapsulating Security Protocol (ESP).

ESP basically encrypts the entire contents (or payload) of each IP packet. To be precise, the application data is encrypted and the ESP header and trailer, along with the application data, are signed to prevent spoofing. There's also a separate ESP authentication payload tacked onto the end.

Like the AH packet, this ESP packet is encapsulated inside a regular IP packet. As such, ESP secures the integrity, authentication, and confidentiality of the packages; people commonly refer to ESP as being IPSEC. ESP uses the HMAC-MD5 and HMAC-SHA algorithms to ensure integrity and the DES-CBC to perform the actual encryption.

> **Note**
>
> *DES-CBC (Cipher Block Chaining) is a secret key algorithm, where a random number is generated and used with the secret key in connection with the encryption of the data. You have the choice between the DES and 3DES algorithms.*

You should note that you have to choose between ESP and AH—you can't use them both. Also, any IPSEC packet is always encapsulated within an ordinary IP header. This makes IPSEC able to freely pass anywhere ordinary IP traffic can, which in turn makes it easier to deploy than previous network security protocols.

IPSEC Behind the Scenes

IPSEC establishes an end-to-end channel between two computers. And so, a scheme is needed for each two IPSEC computers to agree on a common set of security settings. And, even more importantly, there must be a way for those two machines to securely exchange a set of encryption keys to use for their connection.

This chore is being handled by the Internet Security Agreement/Key Management Protocol (ISAKMP). Thus, ISAKMP provides a way for two machines to build a security association (SA). The SA encodes a policy agreement between the computers that specifies which algorithms and key lengths they'll use, as well as the actual encryption keys themselves.

Actually, there's more than one SA:

1. The two computers start by establishing an ISAKMP SA, which specifies which encryption algorithm they'll use (DES, 3DES, 40-bit DES, or none at all), what hash algorithm will be used, and how connections will be authenticated.

2. ISAKMP isn't used for key negotiation; that process belongs to the Oakley protocol. After the ISAKMP SA is built, the Oakley protocol is used to negotiate a master key that can be used to secure further IPSEC negotiations. When Oakley has done its thing, the two machines are finally able to negotiate the actual IPSEC settings to be used for the connection; that is, whether AH and/or ESP will be used and which algorithms they will be using.

3. When the negotiations are complete, IPSEC can establish two new SAs to link the machines: one for inbound traffic, and one for outbound traffic.

4. Once the new SAs are built, Oakley is again put into service to negotiate session-specific keys. You can control the lifetime over which these session keys remain valid in terms of time as well as number of bytes having gone through IPSEC.

> **Note**
>
> *IPSEC is always using symmetric keys for ESP, as well as AH, because of the performance implications. However, you are free to choose between using public keys, Kerberos, or a pre-shared key to establish trust between the two computers and to exchange the symmetric keys used by ESP and AH—this is commonly known as the secret key.*

You should note that IPSEC isn't limited to the Windows 2000 machines on the network, because it's based on IETF RFC standards (RFCs 1825, 1826, 1827, 1828, 1829, 1851, 1852, 2085, and 2104) and as such will grow to become a checkmark item for all other TCP/IP protocol stacks. However, you're faced with a rather heavy authentication problem with regard to implementing IPSEC across multiple platforms, because public keys (PKCS) aren't supported by very many systems at present and Kerberos works to limit the interoperability options quite drastically. So you're faced with having to use the pre-shared key option for achieving interoperability for the most instances.

Disk-Level Security: EFS

As is implied by the name, Encrypted File System (EFS) represent Microsoft's attempt to protect the data stored on the computer. EFS lets you encrypt designated files or folders on a local computer merely by selecting a checkbox for the applicable files and folders; as such, it is particularly useful for protecting data on computers that easily can fall victim to being tampered with, such as a laptop.

Note

*EFS is controlled from the **Advanced Attributes** dialog box accessed from the **File Properties** dialog box.*

When you enable EFS for a file or folder on an NTFS file system (NTFS) volume, EFS automatically encrypts the file when it is saved and decrypts it when the user opens it again. So the encryption protects files even if someone bypasses EFS and uses low-level disk utilities to try to read information. Even if the file can be stolen, over the network or physically, it cannot be decrypted without first logging on to the network as the appropriate user. And because it can't be read, the file also can't be surreptitiously modified.

Note

A perpetrator is sure to notice a difference, when EFS is being added to the equation, because he won't be able to read the encrypted file as easily as before. Prior to EFS, it was possible to bypass NTFS security simply by removing a physical storage volume, mounting it on another system, and having the administrator of the second system take ownership of all data; or, NTFS security could be bypassed by using some of the public-domain utilities for accessing NTFS from DOS.

EFS encrypts a file using a symmetric encryption key unique to each file. The symmetric encryption key is based on DESX (Data Encryption Standard X). The North American version of Windows 2000 uses a key length of 56 bits, whereas the other versions are using a 40-bit key length (which can be brought up to 56 bits by downloading Microsoft's Enhanced CSP, as discussed earlier).

Then it encrypts the encryption key as well, using the public key from the file owner's certificate. Because the file owner is the only person with access to the private key, that person is the only one who can decrypt the key and, hence, the file.

EFS also includes a file recovery certificate feature for properly handling emergencies, or when an employee leaves your organization. When EFS is used, a separate recovery key is created automatically by the system (that is, the encryption key is encrypted using the public key from the administrator's EFS file recovery certificate). Consequently, an administrator can use the private key from that certificate to recover the file, should the need arise.

Figure 14.7 provides a schematic of the encryption process. The user's plain-text file is encrypted using a randomly generated encryption key. This file-encryption key is stored along with the file, encrypted under a user's public key in the DDF, and encrypted under the Recovery Agent's public key in the DRF. Note that although Figure 14.7 shows only one Recovery Agent, EFS supports multiple Recovery Agents with independent keys.

Because EFS handles encryption and decryption with complete transparency to the user and the application program, you are able to use it for protecting any and all application data. But you aren't able to utilize it for OS files as EFS won't be in effect until NTFS and the user certificate are operational—and, thus, there's no replacement for the various schemes for full encryption of the computer's hard disk for high-security scenarios.

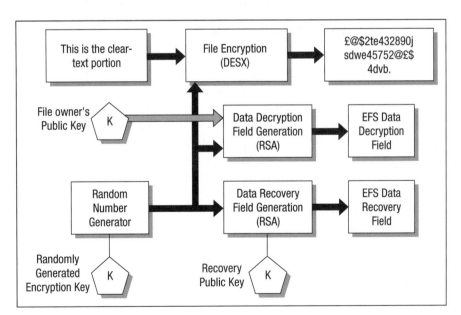

Figure 14.7
The EFS encryption process.

Also, the version included with Windows 2000 doesn't apply to file sharing. EFS is theoretically able to handle file sharing, but it seems that Microsoft simply wasn't able to finish this feature for the Windows 2000 release date. However, Microsoft has promised to include support for file sharing in a later release (this most probably being the Whistler release, scheduled for the second half of 2001).

Note

You should note that the missing support for file sharing also means that EFS does't apply to applications and application data stored locally that should be accessible to more than one user.

Finally, you should be keenly aware of the fact that, despite the fact that EFS employs a moderate bit length for file encryption (which also means that security can be broken, given enough time), it will detract a lot from file system performance. Based on my experience, you should expect a performance hit in the 20 to 40 percent range.

Warning

Because EFS is handled by NTFS, you should be careful to note that data will be passing between clients and network servers in clear text. Thus, you will need to complement EFS with IPSEC to ensure end-to-end encryption of your network files.

Watch Out for the Obvious EFS Pitfalls

The EFS technology can make it very hard for unauthorized users to gain access to your critical files and folders, and it really won't get in your way, which most other tools and techniques for heightening security have a habit of doing. But, EFS might as well be left unused if you aren't careful about where you store the private keys that can be used to discover the initial file-encryption key and thus decrypt the EFS-protected file or folder. If EFS is to provide any real security, you need to keep the security-critical private keys separated from the information that EFS is meant to secure, by moving those keys somewhere else. To be precise, you need to export the certificates and the private keys for the Data Recovery Agents, secure the certificates and keys in a safe place, and then delete the data recovery certificates located on the local computer (see Chapter 19 for how to export a certificate and its private key). In this way, the only person who can recover data for the system is the person who has physical access to the data recovery certificate.

By taking these precautions, you can avoid being susceptible to any back-door-type attacks that can exploit the fact that the keys that enable you to open every encrypted file or folder on the local computer are floating around on a poorly protected hard disk. The need to keep the private keys separate from the encrypted files and folders should especially be emphasized in regard to standalone computers, because the data recovery certificates are stored on the local computer by default. On a standalone computer, you have to remove the private keys for the Recovery Agents if you are to reap the full security improvement rewards brought to the table by EFS. Unfortunately, this means that you'll need to reinstate the Recovery Agent certificate if you need to recover a file or folder. Thus, in regard to a standalone computer, securing the platform is somewhat difficult.

But, even in a domain setting, you still need to make sure that the data recovery certificates aren't located on the local machine, to ensure a proper protection level. On computers that are members of a domain, the handling of the certificates and private keys is set in the Public Key Policies | Encrypted Data Recovery Agents Group Policy folder. Here, make sure to allow only domain administrators to function as Recovery Agents—not the local administrator. That in turn ensures that a successful attack will require two computers to be compromised—the machine that contains the target data, and the machine that contains the Recovery Agent's key. This significantly increases the difficulty of the attack. Also, attacking the machine with the Recovery Agent's key will be much more difficult, because domain servers can be properly protected against physical attacks.

However, if you want the best possible protection, you obviously have to remove the certificates from the domain administrators to some kind of offline media (typically, on floppy disks that are put away in a safe) in the same way as mentioned earlier. Finally, even though the Recovery Agent certificates are moved to other computers on the LAN, EFS won't be able to raise the protection of your files and folders beyond the security level provided by the login (that is, the username and password combination; and, if the last logged-on user is displayed at the login prompt, this is already reduced to identifying the password) used by those in possession of keys that can unlock the EFS protection. So, you should consider the many trouble spots in regard to the login, such as using SYSKEY for improved protection of SAM, the Registry, and other information.

Implementing Security

As mentioned in earlier chapters, defining the security behavior of Windows 2000/Active Directory is much easier than what you might be used to from Windows NT. In the earlier Windows NT versions, security was set in several places. Now, with the advent of the Group Policy, you can set up security from a single point of administration.

Just as importantly, you now can define several different security profiles (known as *security templates*) that can be applied to various classes of computer or used interchangeably on the same computer. Windows 2000 contains several predefined security templates appropriate to various levels of security and to different types of clients and servers on the network. But, if you're part of a large network, you will probably find it worth your while to extend those security templates with your own preferences.

That's Just the Way It Is

You might find yourself in a situation where you want to customize the current security system for suiting the needs of a high-security environment, or you simply would like to cut down on the powers vested in the administrators.

Unfortunately, you will find this to be impossible (or exceptionally hard to do) in most cases, as most of the more delicate permissions and rights for managing the OS can only be controlled from the built-in and predefined groups. And Windows 2000 won't let you do anything to change that as the problem stems from a lot of this security being "hardwired" to the Administrator Local Group on the servers (which the Domain Admins and the Enterprise Admins are members of by default), as well as the clients. And so, in most cases, you are faced with a choice of adding a lot of rights to the individual administrator, or limiting them so severely that it doesn't make any sense.

The only major exception to this is Active Directory, which allows you to customize the security almost as much as you want, by using the Delegation of Administration features (or by removing the predefined permissions assigned to the various groups). By default, the Enterprise Admins Global/ Universal Group is assigned full control for the whole domain and configuration naming contexts. But the Administrators and Domain Admins Groups do also carry a lot of weight in these two contexts, only stopping short of full control and—in most cases—deletion rights.

Another new feature is the Security Configuration and Analysis MMC snap-in, which offers the capability to compare the security settings of a computer to a given security template, view the results, and resolve any discrepancies revealed by the analysis.

Understanding the Security Configuration Tool Set

The overriding goal of the Security Configuration Tool Set is to provide a single point of administration for Windows 2000-based system security. To meet that goal, the tool set enables administrators to do the following:

♦ Configure security on one or more Windows 2000-based computers

♦ Perform security analysis on one or more Windows 2000-based computers

♦ Complete the preceding two tasks from an integrated and uniform framework

The process of configuring security in a Windows 2000-based network can be rather overwhelming in terms of the system components involved and the level of change that may be required. Therefore, the Security Configuration Tool Set is designed to enable you to perform configuration at a macro level. In other words, the Tool Set enables you to define several configuration settings and have them implemented in the background. Thus, you can group and automate the configuration tasks for one or several Windows 2000-based computers.

Importantly, the Tool Set wasn't designed to replace the existing system tools that address different aspects of system security. Rather, the Tool Set's goal is to complement them by defining an engine that can interpret a standard configuration file and perform the required operations for configuring the security settings automatically in the background. Administrators can continue to use existing tools (or their newer versions) to change individual security settings whenever necessary.

To address the security-analysis gap that exists when using the traditional security administration tools, the Tool Set provides security analysis at a micro level. The tool set is designed to provide information about all system aspects related to security, and to let the security administrators view the information and perform security risk management for either a subset or their entire system environment.

Note
Microsoft has promised that a future version of the analysis capabilities of the Security Configuration Tool Set will be able to create reports and perform specialized queries.

The Tool Set comprises the following components:

♦ *Security Configuration Service*—The core engine of the Security Configuration Tool Set, it runs on every Windows 2000-based system and is responsible for all security configuration and analysis functionality provided by the Tool Set. This service is central to the entire infrastructure.

♦ *Setup Security*—Performs the initial security configuration done during setup, using predefined configurations that ship with the system. This creates an initial security database, called the *Local Computer Policy database*, on every computer with a clean installation of Windows 2000.

♦ *Security Templates*—This standalone MMC snap-in tool enables you to define computer-independent security configurations (*security templates*), which are saved as text-based INF files.

♦ *Security Configuration and Analysis*—This standalone MMC snap-in tool allows you to import one or more saved configurations to a security database (it may be the Local Computer Policy database or any private database). Importing configurations builds a machine-specific security database, which stores a composite configuration. You can apply the composite configuration to a computer, as well as analyze the current system configuration against the stored composite configuration stored in the database.

♦ *Security settings extension to the Group Policy*—This snap-in tool represents an extension to the Group Policy MMC snap-in, which allows you to define a security configuration as part of a Group Policy Object.

In addition, the Tool Set contains a command-line utility, **Secedit.exe**, which enables administrators to run configuration and analyses as part of a script.

Understanding Security Templates

To provide comprehensive security administration and information, the Security Configuration Tool Set allows you to configure and analyze all of the following on Windows 2000 computers:

♦ *Account Policies*—You can use the tool to set access policies, including local Password Policy and local Account Lockout Policy.

♦ *Local Policies*—You can configure local Audit Policy, User Rights Assignment, and various Security Options, such as control of floppy disks, CD-ROMs, and so forth.

♦ *Event Log*—You can configure the base settings for the three event logs (security log, application log, and system log).

♦ *Restricted Groups*—You can assign group memberships for built-in groups, such as administrators, server operators, backup operators, power users, and so on, as well as any other specific group that you would like to configure. This should not be used as a general membership management tool—only to control membership of specific groups that have sensitive capabilities assigned to them.

♦ *System Services*—You can configure security for the different services installed on a system, including network transport services, such as TCP/IP, NetBIOS, printing, and so on. These can be configured as startup options (automatic, manual, or disabled) or you can also set access control on these services—grant or deny access to start, stop, pause, and issue control commands.

♦ *Registry*—You can use the Tool Set to set the security on system Registry keys.

♦ *File System*—You can use the Tool Set to set the security and permission settings for locally attached volumes, directories, and files provided they're using the NTFS file system.

And, as mentioned earlier, the Security Configuration Tool Set allows you to define security configurations (security templates) that include settings for security attributes in each of the areas just outlined. By using these security templates, you can configure the system. You can also perform security analyses on the system by using these security templates as recommendations.

Note
The security templates can be saved (in text-based INF files).

The Tool Set includes a set of predefined security templates. You can choose to use these configurations as shipped, or you can use them as starting points for building your own customized configurations. The Tool Set's configuration editing tool, called the Security Configuration and Analysis MMC snap-in, provides this capability.

Using the Security Templates

As mentioned earlier, the security templates are key to managing the security settings in a controlled and cost-effective way, no matter whether you have one or several thousand clients to administer. The security templates are handled from the Security Templates MMC snap-in. After you've got the security template configured to your liking, you can implement the security features by importing the template into the applicable Group Policy. The rest of this section will provide you with a brief introduction to the various security settings available in a template.

The following are the four different kinds of templates supplied by Microsoft:

♦ *Basic*—Applies the Windows 2000 default access control settings (except for User Rights and Restricted Groups). The primary application of the Basic template is to a Windows NT machine that has been upgraded to Windows 2000, because this will bring the upgraded machine in line with the Windows 2000 default security settings (these settings are applied only to clean-installed machines). The Basic templates can also be used to revert back to the defaults after making any undesirable changes.

♦ *Compatible*—Some companies might not want to make their users members of the Power Users group just for making it possible for the users to run applications that aren't compliant with the Windows 2000 application specification. Power Users have additional capabilities (such as the ability to create shares) that go beyond the relatively liberal access control settings necessary to run legacy applications, which is why some companies may prefer not to give users that status. For customers who do not want their end users to be Power Users, the Compatible template "opens up" the default access control policy for the Users group in a manner that is consistent with the requirements of most legacy applications. For example, Office 97 SR1 will run successfully as a Power User or as a User under the Compatible configuration. However, Office 97 will not run successfully as a clean-installed User. A machine that is configured with the Compatible template should not be considered a secure installation.

♦ *Secure*—Modifies settings (such as Password Policy, Audit Policy, and Registry Values) whose impact is more likely to be on the operational behavior of the OS and its network protocols than on application functionality. The Secure template provides recommendations that are distinct from the defined default access control policy. The Secure template does not modify any ACLs, but it does remove all members of the Power Users group.

♦ *Highly Secure*—Increases the security defined by several of the parameters in the Secure template. For example, whereas the Secure template might enable SMB packet signing, the Highly Secure template would require SMB packet signing. Likewise, whereas the Secure template might warn about the installation of unsigned drivers, the Highly Secure template would block the installation of unsigned drivers. In short, the Highly Secure template configures many operational parameters to their extreme values without regard for performance, operational ease of use, or connectivity with clients using third-party applications. Like the Secure template, the Highly Secure template also removes all members of the Power Users group.

When you open the Security Templates snap-in, you'll find the following major predefined templates:

♦ *basicsv*—The basic template for stand-alone and member servers.

♦ *basicdc*—The basic template for Active Directory DCs.

♦ *basicwk*—The basic template for client computers.

♦ *compatws*—The compatible template for client computers.

♦ *DC security*—Default security settings for an Active Directory DC.

♦ *hisecws*—The highly secure template for client computers.

♦ *hisecdc*—The highly secure template for Active Directory DCs.

♦ *securews*—The secure template for client computers.

♦ *securedc*—The secure template for Active Directory DCs.

♦ *setup security*—The out-of-box security settings of Windows 2000 Professional.

Account Policies

A domain's Account Policy defines how strong the passwords have to be, the password history, account lockouts, and so on. You can define all of these attributes from the security configuration for local accounts.

Note

A fair number of the options provided here (including the Kerberos Policy) only apply to the whole domain.

Local Policies

Local Policies, by definition, are local to a computer, with no distinction made between different types of computers. Local Policies include the auditing policy, user rights and privilege assignment, and various security options that may be configured locally on a particular Windows 2000-based computer.

The Local Policies tree includes the following:

♦ *Audit Policy*—Enables you to configure which security events are set in the security log on that computer.

♦ *User Rights Assignment*—Enables you to control to whom rights and privileges on a given system are granted.

♦ *Security Options*—Enables you to control who has access to items, such as the floppy drive and CD-ROM drive.

Event Log

Event Log enables you to control the policies on the information stored in the event logs. That is, you can use Event Log Policies to control the settings of the application, system, and security event logs on local computers. For example, you can specify maximum log sizes, how long logged events are maintained, and log retention methods.

Restricted Groups

The Restricted Groups area enables you to manage and enforce membership of built-in or user-defined groups that have special rights and permissions. These groups can include built-in groups, such as Administrators, Power Users, Print Operators, Server Operators, and so on (as well as domain groups, such as Domain Admins, if applicable). You can also add groups that you consider sensitive or privileged to the Restricted Groups list, along with their membership information, which allows you to track and manage these groups as part of your system security configuration or policy.

In addition to group members, the Restricted Groups area tracks and controls reverse membership of each restricted group in the Members Of column (which is found in the same dialog as where you input the group membership). This field lists other groups to which the restricted group can belong. You can use this field to control exactly which groups your restricted group members can join—you can also use this feature to limit a group of users to one group and prevent them from joining any others.

When you apply the configuration, you can be sure that group memberships are set as specified in the template file. Groups and users that are not specified are removed from the restricted group, and the Reverse Membership Configuration option ensures that each restricted group is a member of only those groups specified in the Members Of column.

System Services

The System Services folder enables you to define the startup mode and assign permissions to all the services running on the system (such as network services, file and print services, and telephony and fax services).

Because of the breadth and diversity of this area, the Security Templates MMC snap-in's System Services area is designed to be extendable by third parties. The Security Templates MMC snap-in includes support only for the general settings for each system service, which are service startup mode (Automatic, Manual, or Disabled) and security on the service.

Registry

You can use Registry Policies to configure security and control security auditing for Registry keys and their subtrees. For example, you can use Registry Policies to do the following:

♦ Ensure that only administrators can change certain Registry keys, by granting administrators full control over the Registry keys and their subtrees and granting read-only permission to other users.

◆ Prevent certain users from viewing portions of the Registry.

◆ Audit user activity in the Registry of the computer, when auditing is enabled. You can specify which users and which user events are logged for both failed and successful events.

Because Windows 2000 supports a dynamic inheritance model for all object providers, when applying security on Registry keys, the Security Templates MMC snap-in follows the same inheritance algorithm as the directory tree.

File System

You can use File System Policies to configure security for files and folders and to control security auditing of files and folders. For example, you can use File System Policies to do the following:

◆ Ensure that only administrators can modify system files and folders, by granting administrators full control over system files and folders and granting read-only permission to other users.

◆ Prevent certain users from viewing files and folders.

◆ Audit user activity affecting files and folders, when auditing is enabled. You can specify which users and which user events are logged for both failed and successful events.

File System Policies treat all volumes as part of a single tree, with first-level nodes as the root directory of each volume. This is similar to the directory and Registry security configuration insofar as the templates file contains a list of fully qualified file or directory paths and security descriptors for each volume. The dynamic inheritance model is supported on NTFS files, also.

How to Configure and Analyze the Security Settings

Unlike other operating system features, security is a characteristic of the system as a whole. Almost every component of the system is responsible for some aspect of system security. Therefore, questions such as "Is my computer secure?" or "Is my network secure?" become extremely difficult to answer. Typically, a system administrator must examine many different system components and use many tools in an attempt to answer these questions.

The goal is for the Security Configuration Tool Set to be the resource for answering security-related questions, whether they are general or very specific. And this goal is indeed well-served by the Security Configuration and Analysis MMC snap-in.

Note

Security Configuration and Analysis might look a bit obnoxious when you launch it for the very first time, because it doesn't include anything but an empty console tree and a bit of explanatory text in the results pane. But, that initial impression will soon pass no matter whether you want to configure the security settings or analyze the current security settings.

A Truly Great Solution with Few Flaws

Virtually everyone has an angle on security nowadays, because a fair level of security is a fundamental precondition for enterprise computing. And these years, more and more home users are starting to follow suit as a result of the inherent risks of being increasingly online and the ever-recurring virus scares.

So, the only thing that's really up for discussion is what level of security will be called for in each given scenario. And the answer to that question depends on the corporate risk profile, as well as the general sentiments on security in the upper echelons of the company.

Windows 2000 is a great example of this tendency. This product alone introduces more new security features than have been delivered from Microsoft in the last five years. And, although Windows 2000 admittedly is a very fine solution that leaves Windows NT 4 in the dust, Microsoft still has a couple of major issues that need to be addressed before it can compete with the top-of-the-line secure OSs. These issues include the following:

♦ *Making it possible to separate the rights for viewing the security logs and those for managing them*—It's very unsettling that you can't be assigned permissions to security logs without also being able to change the very same logs. Ideally, the two roles will be separated from the "ordinary" administrator roles.

♦ *Creating more (and varied) predefined security roles*—This would go a long way toward making it possible for many more people to perform their jobs without needing a God-like account (such as Enterprise Admins, Domain Admins, or Administrators).

♦ *Adding options for customizing the permissions and rights to the resources existing on the individual servers*—Currently, you have no feasible way of limiting a person to only being able to administer the core server features found on an Active Directory DC (but not the actual directory), and vice versa.

♦ *Removing a lot of the rights and permissions that are assigned to certain predefined or built-in groups*—In Windows 2000 a lot of the important rights and permissions are "hardwired" to the built-in Administrators Group account (just as you know it from Windows NT), which Domain Admins and Enterprise Admins then are made members of. There's an urgent need for getting some better-qualified choices in this area.

♦ *The dawn of the really customizable security setup*—Microsoft definitely has some work ahead of them for making it easier to customize the security settings. This work includes removing a fair number of the rights and permissions that are assigned to the Administrators account by default, no matter which client or server you're working on, as well as making it less complicated to add new default object ACLs to the Active Directory schema than is the case currently.

But again, please remember that this is the wish list for creating an "out-of-this-world" security system. Windows 2000 Server is most definitely a very competent solution, security-wise, especially compared with its predecessor. And with that said, I'll leave you on your own to figure out how to map Active Directory's security attributes to the domains faced.

Chapter 15

How to Design with Exchange Server in Mind

If you have just one Microsoft server application running, all bets are that it is Exchange Server, which is Microsoft's most popular server application—besides their network operating OSs (NOSs), Windows NT Server 4, and Windows 2000 Server. And more often than not, Exchange Server will be viewed as being more important than the NOS, no matter its name and version number. After all, who can live without email nowadays?

Because of these facts, and Exchange Server 4/5 including a fairly advanced directory, it represents a near-perfect case for discussing directory coexistence. But there's actually much more sense to it than what meets the eye. Chances are that those of you running some version of Exchange Server sooner or later will be charged with upgrading to the latest version of Exchange—Exchange 2000 Server—which is the first example of an application that is fully integrated with Active Directory. That is, Exchange 2000 Server doesn't include its own separate directory anymore; rather, it is using Active Directory for that.

Note

Exchange 2000 Server is the very first native Active Directory application coming out of the labs at Redmond, Washington. It remains to be seen when (or whether) more applications will follow in the footsteps of Exchange.

Exchange 2000 Server's reliance on Active Directory means that you can't design either one in isolation. Thus, you should at the very least want to take Exchange 2000 Server's directory properties into account, when doing your Active Directory designing—and at best, you should want to do the Active Directory and the core parts of your Exchange 2000 Server design more or less concurrently.

Interoperating with Exchange Server

It's fairly tough to migrate servers running Exchange Server 4/5 from Windows NT Server to Windows 2000 Server. Additionally, because the fact that Exchange Server 5.5 takes the shape of a standalone application, you will be hard pressed to find good reasons to upgrade from Windows NT Server to Windows 2000 Server. The only valid reasons that I've seen until now are the following:

♦ A need to migrate due to Exchange Server's being hosted on a PDC or BDCs that need to be upgraded due to the move to Active Directory.

♦ A wish to standardize fully on Windows 2000 Server throughout the enterprise.

♦ A belief that the current Exchange installation will be able to benefit from the improved stability and scalability offered in Windows 2000 Server compared with those in Windows NT Server.

Tip

Specifically, being charged with upgrading to Exchange 2000 Server doesn't necessarily comprise a valid reason for moving your current Exchange environment to Windows 2000 Server. Please see "Moving to Exchange 2000 Server," later in this chapter, for an in-depth discussion on that subject.

In other words, no convincing universally applicable reasons exist for migrating a well-established and stable Exchange Server environment to Windows 2000 Server. But you might still find that it makes a lot of sense in your specific scenario. Even in those cases where you might profit somewhat from a move to Windows 2000 Server, you should weigh the pros and cons of upgrading very carefully—especially because you actually stand to lose some functionality from upgrading to Windows 2000 Server (see "Keeping the Directories in Sync," later in this chapter).

Moving from Windows NT Server to Windows 2000 Server

First of all, the only available upgrade path is from Exchange Server 5.5 Service Pack 3 (SP3) or later. That is, Microsoft supports only an in-place upgrade from Windows NT Server to Windows 2000 Server for Microsoft Exchange Server version 5.5 Standard Edition SP3, and Microsoft Exchange Server version 5.5 Enterprise Edition SP3.

So you're in for some additional work, if you're not already upgraded to the Exchange Server 5.5 platform. But you might want to note that the upgrade to Exchange Server 5.5 really isn't that bad, because you can upgrade to Exchange Server 5.5 from Exchange Server 4.0 SP2 or higher (except in a single-server organization) and Exchange Server 5.0 (any Service Pack level will do).

Additional Exchange Server 5.5 Upgrade Info

For more discussion on the practicalities of the upgrade to Exchange Server 5.5, I recommend the "Microsoft Exchange Server 5.5 Upgrade Procedures" whitepaper (available at **http://support.microsoft.com/support/Exchange/Content/Whitepapers/upgrade.asp?LN=EN-US&SD=gn&FR=0**) and the Knowledge Base article "Considerations When Upgrading from Exchange Server 4.0/5.0 to 5.5" (Knowledge Base article ID Q179258, which is available at **http://support.microsoft.com/support/kb/articles/Q179/2/58.ASP?LN=EN-US&SD=gn&FR=0**).

However, you might yet find some additional work in the fact that all Exchange Server 5.5-based systems have to be running Windows NT Server 4.0 SP3 or higher. Also, it might take quite a while to perform the upgrade, depending upon the database size. Microsoft quotes the following rates on a typical dual processor server with 256MB of RAM and RAID5 subsystem:

♦ Exchange Server 4.0 to Exchange Server 5.5 Upgrade: 500MB per hour

♦ Exchange Server 5.0 to Exchange Server 5.5 Standard Upgrade: 700MB per hour

♦ Exchange Server 4.0 to Exchange Server 5.5 Fault Tolerant Upgrade: 1.2GB per hour

Warning

You will most likely be faced with a host of complicated decisions, if you need to upgrade a server that currently acts as a PDC or BDC (see Chapter 22 for a more in-depth discussion on what it takes to migrate your NT PDC/BDCs). And much the same goes for promoting any server(s) running Exchange Server 5.5 to an Active Directory DC.

First, you need to determine the appropriate edition of Windows 2000 Server for each server that you're upgrading. The possible in-place upgrade paths from Windows NT Server to Windows 2000 Server are listed in Table 15.1. Also, please remember that you're only able to upgrade a localized version of Windows NT Server to the corresponding localized version of Windows 2000 Server.

Table 15.1   The upgrade paths supported when moving from Windows NT Server to Windows 2000 Server.

Upgrade from	Windows 2000 Server Retail Edition	Windows 2000 Upgrade Edition	Windows 2000 Advanced Server Retail Edition	Windows 2000 Advanced Server Upgrade Edition	Windows 2000 DataCenter Server
Windows NT Server 3.51	Yes	Yes	Yes	No	No
Win NT Server 3.51 with Citrix	No	No	No	No	No
Win NT Server 4.0	Yes	Yes	Yes	No	No
Win NT Server 4.0 Terminal Services	Yes	Yes	Yes	No	No
Win NT Server 4.0 Enterprise Edition	No	No	Yes	Yes	Yes

Second, you need to determine the order in which you are upgrading the computers running Exchange Server. This choice will most probably prove crucial to the organization, because it will decide who will have their mail services interrupted at which time—and, in case something goes terribly wrong, who will be left without mail services while you restore the server(s) from backup. Generally, you should always postpone the upgrading of each site's local mail server until last—thus, upgrading the bridgehead server(s) and the gateway server(s) first—because this will minimize the down time experienced by the user.

Finally, you should review the following Knowledge Base articles (**http://support.microsoft.com**), if any of them applies to the scenario faced:

♦ "Upgrading to Windows 2000 Upgrades Existing Novell Client" (Q218158)

♦ "XCON: TP4 Transport Protocol Not Supported Under Windows 2000" (Q242157)

♦ "XCON: X.25 Support for SAT Cards" (Q169668)

♦ "XCON: X.25 Support for CIREL Cards" (Q169667)

♦ "XIMS: Cannot Open IMS Dial-Up Connections Tab" (Q236910)

Then, you should be ready to perform the actual upgrade by running the Windows 2000 Server Setup program (after you've ensured that a valid and functional backup exists and the proper recovery procedures are in place). After the upgrade is through, you should be careful to ensure that DNS is properly configured as this represents the far most common upgrade problem.

Keeping the Directories in Sync

A lot of Exchange Server 4/5 installations have made use of the fact that Exchange Server 4/5 sports a fairly close integration between the Exchange directory and the Windows NT Server 4 Security Accounts Manager (SAM) database. That is, when a user account is being created in Windows NT Server's User Manager for Domains, you are prompted to create a mailbox for that user while you're at it, and vice versa.

Note

With Windows NT Server 4, the Exchange installation installed an extension, called MAILUMX.DLL, to User Manager for Domains. For that reason, the Exchange Administrator and User Manager programs appeared to be linked together.

The close integration between Exchange directory and the SAM is really a very crude kind of directory synchronization. Because of the shortcomings of SAM (it is a user database rather than a full-blown directory service), the directory synchronization covers only a few directory attributes.

Because Windows 2000 Server uses a different administration architecture, the "linking" to Exchange Server 4/5 that prompts you for creating a mailbox at the same time as you create user accounts in Active Directory Users and Computers MMC tool simply isn't there anymore. And no way exists that you can get this cherished functionality back.

Additional Windows 2000 Server Upgrade Info

You should note that it's actually a bit harder to install Exchange Server 5.5 from scratch on Windows 2000 Server than it is to upgrade from Windows NT Server 4. You can read more on this subject, including a run-down of the many minor details that might apply to you when performing a Windows NT Server to Windows 2000 Server upgrade in the "Migrating Exchange Server 5.5 to a Windows 2000-Based Computer" whitepaper (available at **www.microsoft.com/Exchange/techinfo/ upgrade2000.htm**).

But you'll still be able to add user accounts to the Active Directory from the Exchange Administrator program. However, in that case, only two fields will get populated:

♦ *Display name*—Set to the mailbox display name.

♦ *User logon name (pre-Windows 2000)*—Set to the selected logon name.

In other words, the user won't even get the user logon name field filled in. This in turn means that users won't be able to log in by specifying a UPN name (the SMTP-alike name) until the administrator steps in to fix that from the Active Directory Users and Computers MMC tool.

Along the same lines, you may notice that the Active Directory contains absolutely no information about Exchange. This is disappointing, to say the least. Now that you're finally faced with a great directory in the OS (Active Directory, that is) that allows you to include all the information previously found in Exchange Server 5.5's directory and much more than that, you're actually faced with having a worse integration between the two directories than was the case with Windows NT Server 4's SAM and the Exchange directory. Fortunately, there's a great solution to be found for eliminating this rather disappointing lack of support for integration between Active Directory and the Exchange directory. That solution is called the Active Directory Connector (ADC).

If you want Active Directory to recognize the very existence of an Exchange Server installation, the ADC should be installed. The ADC represents a very fine piece of engineering that will allow you to synchronize just about any directory attribute(s) that you may want to be kept in sync between the two directories.

Actually, you'll start to see the positive effects of the ADC as soon as you have it installed— that is, even before you start configuring the many options presented by the ADC—because the ADC will appear in the Active Directory Sites and Services Manager and all Active Directory User and Contact objects will have two new configuration options added:

♦ Email Addresses tab

♦ Create Exchange Mailbox tab

Note

Please note that these two objects can only be seen when the Active Directory Users and Computers MMC tool has Advanced Features view enabled.

And when you create new user objects, the "New Objects-User" pages will now prompt you to create an Exchange Mailbox (although without configuring the ADC further, these options will be grayed out).

It should be noted that the new options available after having installed the ADC only are found on the Active Directory DCs that have the ADC installed locally.

So for all practical purposes, you will need to get in deep with the ADC to reap the rewards of directory synchronization between the Exchange directory and Active Directory. And you should be forewarned: The ADC is a very powerful tool that will need a lot of work before you can get the job done exactly the way you want it.

Due to the complexities inherent in the configuration of ADC, you might want to think twice about implementing it in a simple setting with relatively few users. But you might also note that you need ADC in most Exchange 2000 Server upgrade scenarios—so if you're intent on migrating to Exchange 2000 Server in the next couple of years, you might as well bite the bullet now in order to reap the ample directory synchronization rewards in the meantime.

Note

You can find a more in-depth discussion on the different Exchange 2000 Server upgrade scenarios in "Moving to Exchange 2000 Server," later in this chapter.

ADC in a Nutshell

Active Directory Connector (ADC) is designed specifically for allowing enterprises to keep their address lists and configuration settings in sync between the Active Directory and the Exchange 4/5 directory. In other words, you should always want to install and configure the ADC if you want to synchronize between these two directories.

The applications for the ADC include the following:

◆ *Leveraging the user data already found in your directories*—You can replicate the information stored in the Exchange directory to Active Directory and vice versa in order to avoid duplication of data and avoid inconsistencies between the two directories. This might in fact save you some work in a Windows 2000 Server/Active Directory implementation project, because a lot of organizations have already added quite a lot of the wished-for information to the Exchange directory.

◆ *Regaining the Windows NT-to-Exchange synchronization in an Active Directory environment*—The link that exists between Exchange Administrator and Windows NT's User Manager for Domains, which prompts you to create a mailbox when making a new user object, is lost when you use Windows 2000 Server. ADC will allow you to bring this functionality back.

♦ *Making management of both Active Directory and Exchange directory possible from one place—* You will be able to define mailboxes and similar options from Active Directory Users and Computers, which is then replicated to Exchange Server 5.5. Or you can define a mailbox in Exchange Administrator and have that information replicated to Active Directory.

♦ *Enabling servers running Exchange 2000 Server to be deployed in the existing Exchange Organization—*If you want your Exchange 2000 servers to coexist with previous versions of Exchange, you will need ADC. *This applies to the Exchange 2000 ADC only.*

Two different versions of ADC exist: one version is supplied on the Exchange 2000 Server CD-ROM (referred to as Exchange 2000 ADC) and another version is supplied on the Windows 2000 Server CD-ROM (referred to as Windows 2000 ADC).

Although the Windows 2000 ADC works fine to replicate objects from the Exchange directory site-naming context (such as the contents of recipients' containers), it has less functionality than found in the Exchange 2000 Server one. First and foremost, the version of ADC that ships with Windows 2000 Server can't replicate the Exchange configuration data from the Exchange 5.5 directory to Active Directory. This in turn means that you won't be able to deploy Exchange 2000 Server in the pre-existing Exchange Organization, when using the Windows 2000 ADC.

Additional improvements to the Exchange 2000 version of the ADC include a new Public Folder Connection agreement, an inter-organizational option, and improved performance. Additionally, the Exchange 2000 Server ADC is a prerequisite for deploying Exchange 2000 Server into an existing Exchange Organization. So you should never install the Windows 2000 Server ADC if you have a need—or anticipate a need—for coexistence between Exchange 2000 Server and the previous versions of Exchange. And who will dare claim that unless the organization has chosen to migrate away from Exchange altogether?

Tip

You should never use the ADC supplied with Windows 2000 Server, but always prefer Exchange 2000 Server's ADC instead. And I'm not just saying this to be on the safe side. Microsoft has made it blatantly clear that the Windows 2000 ADC version isn't supported under any circumstance, if you use it to connect different Exchange Server 5.5 organizations, if you add Exchange 2000 servers to your existing organization, and so forth.

And even more importantly: No future versions of the Windows 2000 ADC are planned. Moving forward, there will be only one version of the ADC: the one now supplied with Exchange 2000 Server.

In other words, you'll gain a heap of advantages in addition to securing version upgrades (and the better support from Microsoft that always follow from that fact) for a long time to come for a meager single server license of Exchange 2000 Server. Who can turn such an offer down?

The Usage of the ADC Term Probably Won't Expand in the Future

On several occasions, Microsoft has said that it probably would expand the scope of the ADC technology from the current Active Directory-to-Exchange Server integration to also cover synchronization to other directories, such as Netscape Directory Server and generic LDAP directories. Also, they've also been pondering using ADC as the future model for directory synchronization with such messaging systems as Lotus cc:Mail, Novell GroupWise, and Lotus Notes. However, these plans have most probably been scrapped as a consequence of Microsoft's purchase of the metadirectory product that has become Microsoft Metadirectory Services (MMS), which is discussed in Chapter 16.

And so, despite this being a Windows 2000 Server book, you will only find Exchange 2000 Server's ADC discussed here. However, you might want to note that, except for the added functionality, everything does have the same look and feel in the Windows 2000 ADC.

ADC Fundamentals

Connection Agreements are the very essence of the ADC, because each Connection Agreement defines the synchronization between Active Directory domain(s) and Exchange site(s). Or, to be more precise, the Connection Agreement provides a definition of the Active Directory domain containers (the OUs) and the Exchange site recipient containers in which synchronization occurs.

Note

To establish a relationship between an Exchange site and an Active Directory domain, one or multiple Connection Agreements have to be configured. The Exchange servers accessed by Active Directory Connector (ADC) must run Exchange 5.5 with Service Pack 1 or later, when the server is running Windows NT Server 4, and Exchange 5.5 with Service Pack 3 or later, if running on Windows 2000 Server.

Besides defining the source and target containers, the Connection Agreement also defines which objects to synchronize, the synchronization schedule, which two servers to contact for replication (the so-called bridgehead servers, which are targeted for performing the actual synchronization), whether the synchronization is unidirectional or bidirectional, and many other details.

Each ADC server can host multiple Connection Agreements covering multiple Exchange sites and/or multiple Active Directory domains. Each Connection Agreement can provide either unidirectional or bidirectional synchronization between the Exchange directory and Active Directory.

Note

The Microsoft Active Directory Connector (ADC) takes the shape of a service (MSADC) and an MMC snap-in. The MMC snap-in is used to configure the service and the Connection Agreements.

Each Connection Agreement points from one or multiple Active Directory OUs to one or multiple recipients container(s) (such as Recipients) inside a single Exchange site. In other words, you have to define at least one Connection Agreement for every Exchange site that you want to synchronize with. The reason for having an architecture in which at least one Connection Agreement must be defined for each site is to avoid directory loops.

The exact number of Connection Agreements required is dependent upon your Active Directory structure and the number of containers inside each Exchange site that need to be replicated. You need one Connection Agreement each time you want to replicate one or more Exchange containers to a specific OU in Active Directory and vice versa.

The ADC provides three different types of Connection Agreements:

♦ *Recipient Connection Agreement*—Used for replicating recipient objects between the Exchange directory (here, the recipient objects are mailboxes, distribution lists, and custom recipients) and Active Directory (here, recipient objects are mail-enabled users, groups, and contacts). These agreements allow you to replicate directory data you want available throughout the enterprise. The Recipient Connection Agreement is the commonly occurring kind of Connection Agreement, so you should take it for granted that this sort of Connection Agreement is meant, unless it is explicitly stated otherwise.

♦ *Public Folder Connection Agreement (for Exchange 2000 use only)*—Used to synchronize the various public folders (that is, the public folder names; not the actual public folder content) found in the Exchange Server 4/5 Organization to Active Directory. Unlike Exchange Server 5.5, public folders don't need a directory object to represent them, but if the Active Directory/Exchange 2000 Server users are to be able to send mail to a public folder, a mail-enabled object referencing the public folder needs to be present.

♦ *Configuration Connection Agreement (for Exchange 2000 use only)*—Used to replicate Exchange-specific configuration information between the Exchange sites and the Active Directory. These agreements are needed for being able to add an Exchange 2000 server to a site where one or multiple Exchange 4/5 servers already are present.

You are faced with several choices on how to set up each of your Recipient Connection Agreements:

♦ You can have one Exchange Recipients container synchronizing one way or two way with one Active Directory OU.

♦ You can have multiple Exchange Recipients containers synchronizing one way with one Active Directory OU.

♦ You can have multiple Active Directory OUs synchronizing one way with one recipients container.

♦ You can have multiple Exchange Recipients containers synchronizing one way with multiple Active Directory OUs.

♦ You can have multiple Active Directory OUs synchronizing one way with multiple Exchange Recipients containers.

It's crucial that you understand that it's only possible to define two-way synchronizations between a single Active Directory OU and a single Exchange recipients container for consistency reasons (else, the ADC wouldn't know which container/OU that is supposed to be the target of the various objects being replicated).

Also, you should be very careful in establishing what you want to achieve, before you decide the setup of your Connection Agreements (see Figure 15.1):

♦ *If you want to upload your existing Exchange Server directory information to your Active Directory, you should choose From Exchange to Windows (that is, a one-way Connection Agreement).* From this choice it will follow that you should continue to administer your current recipients objects from Exchange Server 4/5.

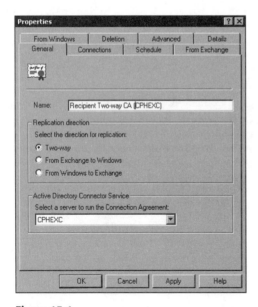

Figure 15.1
The General tab at the Connection Agreement's Properties sheet allows you to define the replication direction among other things.

ADC: Two Simple Examples

If, for example, you have two containers—Recipients and DL—in an Exchange site, and you want to replicate all objects from these containers to a single OU in Active Directory, only one Connection Agreement is required (see Figure 15.2). You might want to note that you will also be able to keep only one Connection Agreement, even if the containers come from two different sites, due to the fact that the full Exchange directory is being replicated between all Exchange servers. However, before you do that, you should want to note that you'll be depending on the Exchange replications to deliver the changes to the bridgehead server used by the Recipients Connection Agreement (and thus might have to wait a fair while before the changes made in the remote container are available in Active Directory).

If you have an Active Directory structure in which the contents of Recipients and Distribution Lists are placed in separate OUs, you need to define two Connection Agreements to the Exchange site (see Figure 15.3).

♦ *If you want to download the information stored in the Active Directory to the existing Exchange Server directory, you should choose From Windows to Exchange (that is, a one-way Connection Agreement).* From this choice it will follow that you want to administer the recipients from the Active Directory.

♦ *If you want to synchronize information between the existing Exchange Server directory and the Active Directory, you should choose Two-way.* From this choice it will follow that you can administer all recipients objects from Active Directory as well as from Exchange 4/5 (please note that you'll still be subjected to the limitations of the administration tools available on the platforms involved).

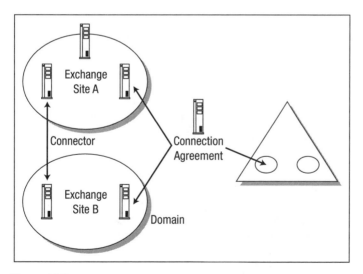

Figure 15.2
How to replicate objects between an Active Directory OU and two Exchange containers from the same site.

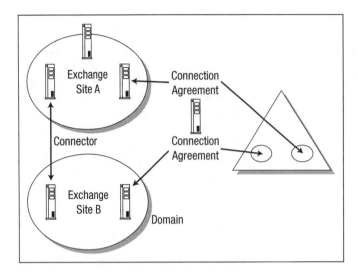

Figure 15.3
How to replicate objects between two Active Directory OUs and two Exchange containers.

Finally, you should take care to understand that it's not a simple task to calculate the exact number of Connection Agreements required in advance, because this number depends upon your Active Directory structure at hand (that is, domains and OUs), the number of Exchange sites, and the number of containers inside each Exchange site that need to be replicated to a unique Active Directory OU and vice versa.

ADC in Depth

As you can see, the ADC and Connection Agreements fundamentals are fairly simple. And so, you might be deceived into thinking that it will prove relatively easy to get the Connection Agreements configured to your needs. While you might be correct in that assertion, chances are that you will be proven very wrong.

There's a wealth of tiny details hiding under the covers of the ADC that apply to the scenario faced. A fair deal of these details will most definitely apply, when you're setting up ADC for any large or complex Exchange installation.

Note

While the many details found in the ADC make it possible to adapt it to almost any coexistence situation, it does also work to make it quite hard to configure the ADC. So while ADC on one hand does look quite straightforward, you might find it very difficult to master this feature—and it's definitely very hard to get that invaluable breadth of view in regard to this feature.

As I definitely could go on for a long while about the many tiny details and the subtle points of ADC configuration, I will stop short of covering each option in depth. But I've included a run-down on the most important—and complicated—examples of those options on each tab. Combined with the online help included with the MMC console and some trial and error, this should allow you to get the ADC properly configured for most cases. But you should definitely want to refer to a much more in-depth discussion on the ADC than found here for the very large or very complex Exchange scenarios.

Before moving into the features and functions offered on the ADC's eight tabs, you should acquaint yourself with how the individual objects are mapped between Active Directory and the Exchange directory, which is shown in Table 15.2.

The General Tab

Besides being the place where you decide the replication direction, the General tab (see Figure 15.1) includes the Active Directory Connector Service option. This option allows you to decide which ADC server will be handling the Connection Agreement, if you have more than one ADC server running in your Active Directory forest.

You should most definitely want to check the settings on this option, when having more than one ADC server running, because it might prove crucial to the load imposed on your WAN links (if possible, you should always want to have the ADC server running on the same LAN as the Active Directory DC and Exchange 5.5 server specified), as well as the overall functionality (ADC demands direct-IP connectivity to the Active Directory DC and Exchange server being used by the Connection Agreement).

The Connections Tab

The Connections tab (see Figure 15.4) allows you to specify which Exchange Server 5.5 and Active Directory DC, respectively, the ADC should connect to when it performs its work. You should be very careful which authentication method you choose, because you need to log on with a user account that carries a fair deal of permissions in one or both directories. In a two-way replication, the user account specified must be able to read and write to both Active Directory and the Exchange directory. In a one-way replication, it will only need read permissions to the source directory and write permissions to the destination directory.

Table 15.2 How objects are replicated between the two directories.

Active Directory Object	Exchange Object
Mailbox-enabled User	Mailbox in the correct container
Mail-enabled User	Custom Recipient in the target container
Non-mail-enabled User	Not replicated
Mail-enabled Contact	Custom Recipient in the target container
Non-mail-enabled Contact	Not replicated
Mail-enabled Group (type: Distribution)	Distribution List in the target container
Mail-enabled Group (type: Security)	Distribution List in the target container
Non-mail-enabled Group (type: Distribution)	Not replicated
Non-mail-enabled Group (type: Security)	Not replicated

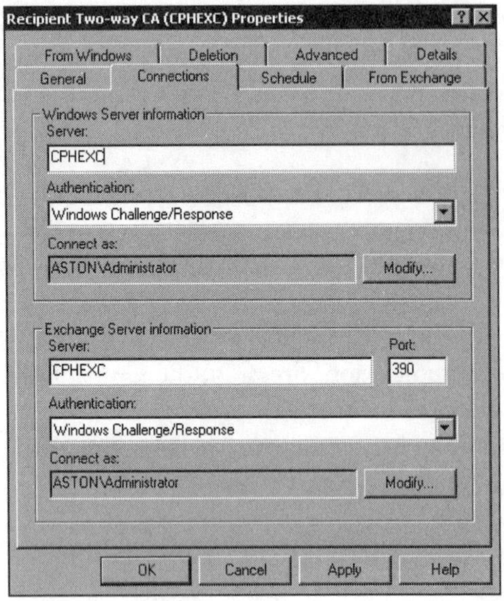

Figure 15.4
The Connections tab allows you to configure the precise properties of the connections to the Exchange server and the Active Directory DC accessed by the ADC.

Also, you should just take a minute to ensure that the Exchange server specified does use the default LDAP port (389). For example, this will not be the case if the Exchange server doubles as an Active Directory DC, because Active Directory also runs off port 389.

The Schedule Tab

In addition to allowing you to control when the Connection Agreement is run, the Schedule tab (see Figure 15.5) also includes the quite useful "Replicate the entire directory the next time the agreement is run" checkbox. Here, the words "entire directory" of course refer only to the objects and containers covered by the Connection Agreement.

By default, the "entire directory" is only replicated the first time you run the Connection Agreement. After that, it's only the directory changes that are replicated. This makes perfect sense as long as everything works as intended, but you might very well find yourself in a position where you want to start from scratch—in that case, this option will prove very worthwhile.

The From Exchange and From Windows Tabs

The Default destination option is found on the From Exchange (see Figure 15.6) as well as the From Windows tab (see Figure 15.7). The Default destination option is used to specify the destination for the objects (coming from Exchange and Active Directory, respectively) that are being replicated for the first time. Please note that any source objects that correspond to objects that already exist in the target directory (that is, the Active Directory and Exchange directory, respectively) will continue to replicate to the pre-existing objects, even if they are located somewhere other than the default destination specified.

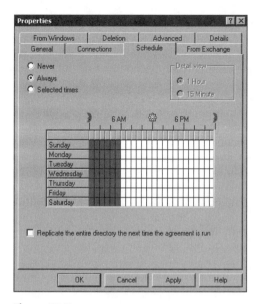

Figure 15.5
The Schedule tab allows you to configure the scheduling of the replications, which might prove important, depending upon your settings.

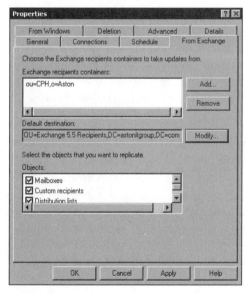

Figure 15.6
The From Exchange tab allows you to define which container(s) and objects to replicate and which Active Directory OU to add them to. The precise set of options available in this tab varies.

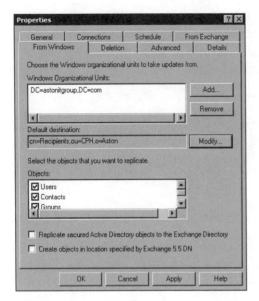

Figure 15.7
The From Windows tab allows you to define which OU(s) and objects to replicate and which Exchange container to add them to, plus a few other neat things. The precise set of options available in this tab varies.

You should also want to take note of the "Replicate secured Active Directory objects to the Exchange Directory" option on the From Windows tab. By default, secured Active Directory objects—that is, Active Directory objects that contain an explicit Deny ACE—aren't replicated to the Exchange directory, because Exchange Server 4/5 doesn't allow Deny permissions. Using this option, you can allow secured Active Directory objects to be replicated to the Exchange directory in spite of the security problems this may rise.

Also, the "Create objects in location specified by Exchange 5.5 DN" on the From Windows tab can prove crucial to the implementation of some scenarios, because it will allow you to fix some of the shortcomings of one-way replications from Active Directory to the Exchange directory that may be encountered, if you have Exchange 2000 Server running in your Exchange Organization.

Note

*The problem fixed by "Create objects in location specified by Exchange 5.5 DN" applies to the situation in which you create an Exchange 2000 mail-enabled user object in Active Directory. When you create a mail-enabled object, the default recipients container specified is inserted into the **legacyExchangeDN** attribute (which stores the X.500 Distinguished Name). Therefore, if the destination of the Connection Agreement is configured to some other container than the default recipients container, the Distinguished Name specified in the **legacyExchangeDN** attribute will prove to be incorrect. Because you're not doing two-way replications, this error will never be corrected and, thus, Exchange Server 5.5 won't be able to deliver mail to the Exchange 2000 mailbox.*

The Deletion Tab

The Deletion tab (see Figure 15.8) allows you to specify how the ADC should go about replicating object deletions. You should consider the consequences of replicating deletions very carefully, because it might not be what you want—and will work to worsen the effects of any mishaps in one or the other directory. So if you are in any doubt whatsoever, you shouldn't allow the deletion of objects to ripple to the other directory, because this might wreak some serious havoc. You should instead choose the other option, which keeps the deleted items and stores the deletion list in a CSV file.

The Advanced Tab

The Advanced tab (see Figure 15.9) brings together a number of very different configuration options. The most important of these options are "This is a primary Connection Agreement for the connected Exchange Organization" and "This is a primary Connection Agreement for the connected Windows Domain." This is because the primary Connection Agreements are allowed to create new directory objects in the connected Exchange Organization and Windows domain, respectively.

Thus, if you define multiple primary Connection Agreements replicating from the same Active Directory OU to the same Exchange Organization (or multiple primary Connection Agreements replicating from the same Exchange container to the Active Directory domain), this will result in duplicate recipient objects! Needless to say, you're advised to handle this setting with the utmost caution.

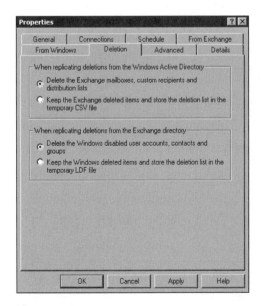

Figure 15.8
The Deletion tab allows you to specify how deletion of objects from either directory is to be handled by the ADC.

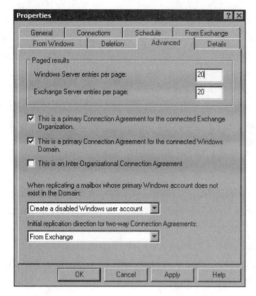

Figure 15.9
The Advanced tab allows you to configure a variety of interesting options.

Note

Microsoft advises that you only have one primary Connection Agreement defined for each Exchange Organization and Windows domain, respectively. However, this advice might not be correct, depending upon the scenario faced. One of the commonly occurring scenarios in which you need multiple primary Connection Agreements is when you're setting up separate Connection Agreements for separate OUs in which you want new objects replicated to the Exchange Organization (or have separate OUs for separate Exchange containers in which you want new objects replicated to the Active Directory). As you can see, this scenario doesn't present you with any problems as long as you don't set up multiple primary Connection Agreements asking ADC to replicate from the same Active Directory OUs or Exchange containers to the same Exchange Organization or Active Directory forest, respectively.

Conversely, you should be keenly aware that a nonprimary Connection Agreement would never attempt to create an object. And so, if no Active Directory user object (or Exchange recipients object) exists that corresponds to a given Exchange recipients object (or Active Directory user object), the changes discovered by ADC that apply to that object won't be replicated to the other directory.

The Advanced tab also includes a checkbox that allows you to designate a Connection Agreement to work as an Inter-Organizational Connection Agreement, which allows the ADC to replicate objects between two separate Exchange Organizations. You aren't allowed to define two-way Inter-Organizational Connection Agreements—you are only allowed to replicate one way from Exchange Server 5.5 to Active Directory, or vice versa.

Most people don't know much about the Inter-Organizational Connection Agreement feature, because Microsoft has been unusually quiet about it. And that's quite unfortunate, because it is one of the niftiest features found in the ADC. An educated guess as to the reason for that is that Microsoft might be a bit afraid that people will be using this option to keep separate Exchange Organizations in sync rather than migrating to Exchange 2000 Server. This is further collaborated by the fact that Microsoft asks us to view Inter-Organizational Connection Agreements as an intermediate—not a permanent—step in developing an Exchange infrastructure.

Warning

*Microsoft states that the ADC isn't supported under any circumstances, if you use it to connect different Exchange Server 5.5 Organizations together. The only exception to that rule is when you first deploy Exchange 2000 Server into the Active Directory forest or if you run Exchange 2000 Server **ForestPrep** before enabling the first Inter-Organizational Connection Agreement. And it seems that you should take this warning very seriously. According to Microsoft, you won't be able to deploy Exchange 2000 Server in that forest, if you configure an Inter-Organizational Connection Agreement before you add your first Exchange 2000 Server to the Active Directory forest (either directly or by running **ForestPrep**).*

Microsoft's prototypical example of when the Inter-Organizational Connection Agreement will be called for is when you need to replicate recipients objects between an existing Exchange Server 5.5-based Organization and a new Exchange 2000 Organization (which now uses Active Directory as its directory).

Before you venture into the Inter-Organizational Connection Agreement, you should be keenly aware that it initiates an irreversible process. As soon as the Connection Agreement becomes an Inter-Organizational Connection Agreement, it begins linking objects in the Active Directory forest to facilitate inter-organizational synchronization, and there's really no way back. Or, to be more precise:

- If you clear the This is an Inter-Organizational Connection Agreement checkbox, the changes implemented by the Connection Agreement won't be eliminated.

- If you delete and re-create the objects in the Active Directory forest, the earlier changes replicated to Exchange won't be eliminated and vice versa.

- If you delete the Connection Agreement, the changes to the directories by the Connection Agreement won't be eliminated.

Although most people won't ever need to make use of the Inter-Organizational Connection Agreement feature, there is no doubt that some of you will be very thrilled about its existence. If nothing else, it's currently the only way of migrating into another Exchange Organization without employing any third-party tools.

> **Note**
>
> *You might want to note that Microsoft has promised to extend Microsoft Metadirectory Services (which is discussed in Chapter 16) with a wizard that is targeted for synchronizing users, contacts, groups, and containers across two or more Active Directory forests. At face value, the toolkit primarily will prove of interest to Active Directory or Exchange 2000 Server administrators who need to synchronize this type of information across forests. But who knows, it might also apply to synchronizing Exchange 5.5 Organizations. Currently, Microsoft expects the so-called Interforest Toolkit to ship some time in the second quarter of 2001.*

Finally, the Advanced tab also includes an option for controlling how ADC is handling mailboxes for which no user accounts are to be found in the Active Directory domain. The "When replicating a mailbox whose primary Windows account does not exist in the Domain" option offers you these three choices:

- *Create a disabled Windows user account*—Creates a user account that doesn't permit logons. This is the default choice.

- *Create a new Windows user account*—Creates a new user account in Active Directory that includes the default group memberships and permissions assigned to a user.

- *Create a Windows contact*—Create an account that acts as a pointer to the Exchange Server 4/5 mailbox.

Which of the three choices is preferable depends on the precise scenario at hand. But you should note that it usually will prove more advantageous to put some effort into getting all the missing user accounts transferred to Active Directory before the Connection Agreement is initiated than having the ADC create them.

Attribute-Level Control

You should be aware that the ADC actually also allows you to specify which attributes should be replicated from Exchange and from Active Directory, respectively, and to specify how these attributes should be mapped (and possibly converted in the process) between the two directories—a functionality known as *attribute mappings*.

Additionally, you are able to define object matching rules, which are the rules governing replication of directory objects (that is, which attributes should be mapped to which attributes in the other directory to decide whether each object is new to the other directory or already in existence). The Active Directory Connector Manager MMC snap-in allows you to control which attributes that should be replicated and the object mapping rules from Active Directory Connector Management's Property sheet. However, you will only be able to define the attribute mappings (as well as any conversions needed) by use of schema map files. You can find more information on the subject of schema map files in the Microsoft Knowledge Base (**http://support.microsoft.com**) articles Q253832 and Q253834.

Tip

You can find more information on how to copy or move existing Windows NT Server domain user accounts to Active Directory in Chapter 22.

ADC Performance Issues

Finally, you should want to note that the ADC server, the Active Directory DC, and the Exchange servers may be exchanging a lot of data—especially when performing the initial rounds of replications—and so, the servers involved should be able to handle the additional load (with regard to CPU and RAM) and be placed somewhere with good network connectivity (preferably the same LAN).

Tip

You should be able to save a fair bit of WAN load by making use of the knowledge that all data from the whole Exchange Organization can be read from any Exchange Server 5.5. However, you should remember to take into account the additional replication delays imposed by doing so.

Likewise, you're able to write (as well as read) all data for a given Exchange Organization to any local Exchange 2000 Server running SRS. Also, if you are faced with the decision of either placing the ADC close to the Exchange server or close to the Active Directory DC, then it is usually best to go with the former option. Usually, the ADC will generate more data to the Exchange server than the Active Directory DC—in part because the GC takes a fair share of the load. Please note that this will be the case, even when comparing the traffic between the ADC and the Exchange server with the traffic between the ADC and the DC as well as the GC.

The need to be careful regarding the dimensioning of these machines can't be emphasized enough, because the ADC server, by default, polls its partners (that is, the bridgehead servers for Active Directory and Exchange Directory, respectively) for changes every five minutes. And, although the network load usually is small (because most of the ADC cycles won't replicate any data), the processor load will be quite high inside each replication cycle.

As a general rule, Microsoft recommends that each ADC server will have no more than some 50 to 75 Connection Agreements running at any one time. Likewise, if you'll be synchronizing more than 20,000 recipients at a single Connection Agreement, you should seriously consider spreading the load across multiple Connection Agreements (or even separate ADC servers) for performance reasons. Thus, in enterprise environments, you may very well want to deploy multiple ADC servers.

The exact number of Connection Agreements supported depends on the server's hardware specifications (CPU power and memory). Each Connection Agreement will spawn a thread while processing, and, by default, each thread will be allocated a minimum of 1MB of memory.

Note

Although installing ADC on a local DC/GC will work to reduce the network bandwidth consumed, doing so generally isn't recommended, because of the ADC's rather heavy load of the CPU.

Microsoft quotes the expected resource usage for small servers (that being a 200MHz Pentium-class server with 128MB of memory) running a single Connection Agreement to be as shown in Table 15.3. Microsoft also quotes the expected resource usage for medium-size servers (this being a 450MHz Dual Pentium II-class server with 256MB of memory) running a single Connection Agreement to be as shown in Table 15.4.

As you can see from Tables 15.3 and 15.4, you should be a bit careful with which server you choose to place the ADC on as well as which bridgehead servers that are used. And I guess that you'll be inclined to endorse another general rule: that you should move the ADC service to a dedicated (member) server, if you need to run more than 10 Connection Agreements.

Introducing Exchange 2000 Server

Exchange 2000 Server represents quite a departure from Exchange Server 5.5. Microsoft has chosen to take the integration with Active Directory offered by Exchange to a previously unseen level by removing the Exchange directory altogether, adding all directory information to the Active Directory instead. In other words, information about users, mailboxes, servers, sites, custom recipients, and so forth is now stored in the Active Directory.

So, whether you like it or not, you won't be able to make the switch to Exchange 2000 Server unless you have a Windows 2000 Server *and* Active Directory up and running. No Active Directory equals no Exchange 2000 Server! Further, the differences between Exchange Server 5.5 and Exchange 2000 Server are so great that all Exchange Server 5.5

Table 15.3 The typical resource usage on small servers when working with just a single Connection Agreement.

Server Usage	CPU Usage Inside Every Synchronization Cycle
Server running the ADC	8–24%
Active Directory DC	6–66%
Connecting Exchange Server 5.5 bridgehead	0–91%

Table 15.4 The typical resource usage on medium-size servers when working with just a single Connection Agreement.

Server Usage	CPU Usage Inside Every Synchronization Cycle
Server running the ADC	1–12%
Active Directory DC	0–30%
Connecting Exchange Server 5.5 bridgehead	20–36%

administrators are in for some heavy retraining. The tight integration with Windows 2000 Server and Active Directory offered by Exchange 2000 Server constitute the primary reason for a large number of the major changes found in Exchange 2000 Server compared to Exchange Server 5.5.

Making Good on the Active Directory Promise

The move on Exchange 2000 Server's part of integrating all directory data in the Active Directory rather than a separate, proprietary directory provides you with the following advantages:

♦ *Easy Implementation*—Because Exchange 2000 Server has Active Directory as its native directory, you remove a fair number of the planning chores, due to a fair amount of the Active Directory structures and objects are now being put to use by Exchange. For example, the mailbox properties will be added to the user objects, the distribution lists are replaced with mail-enabled groups, and so on.

♦ *Smooth and Centralized Administration*—Because Exchange no longer carries a separate directory, you'll be able to administer the more mundane parts of Exchange and Active Directory at the same time. That is, the administration of users, groups, mailboxes, distribution lists, and so on is now happening from the Active Directory Users and Computers MMC snap-in. However, you should note that you'd still have to go to the Exchange Administrator MMC snap-in to administer the configuration of the Exchange server(s).

♦ *Real Security Integration*—Exchange 2000 Server has inherited the Active Directory security fundamentals. This means that Exchange users are authenticated by the Active Directory, and that permissions for objects are also handled by the Active Directory. This does go a long way toward reducing the daily administration, because you now can administer only one user account and a single set of groups in order to assign permissions for both environments.

♦ *Property-Level Security*—Exchange 2000 Server now allows setting permissions on the attribute-level of the directory objects (unlike Exchange Server 5.5) as well as the whole directory object.

♦ *Much-Improved Security Performance*—Active Directory applies all permissions directly to every object. So, rather than cycling through a hierarchy to check on a user's access to a certain piece of data (as is the case in Exchange Server 5.5), the object itself knows whether a user has access to its particular piece of information. This feature not only results in greater performance, but also alleviates the need for administrators to consider the wide-reaching hierarchical implications that can result when setting permissions on certain directory objects.

♦ *Advanced Search Capabilities*—All users (as well as the administrators) are able to perform powerful searches on all of the Active Directory objects as well as their attributes. This allows for much more flexible (and fast) searches than what you're used to from Exchange Server 5.5.

◆ *Schema Extensibility*—Whereas Exchange Server 5.5 comes with a dozen attributes that could be used for specialized purposes, Active Directory allows you to add an unlimited number of new objects (or extend existing objects with new attributes). Actually, the schema extensibility is how Exchange 2000 Server itself gets into Active Directory. When you install the first Exchange 2000 Server, some 158 objects and 854 attributes are added to Active Directory.

◆ *Per-Property Replication and Reconciliation*—Whereas Exchange Server 5.5 replicates the whole object every time something is changed in it, Active Directory replicates only changed properties. For example, if the office location of a user is changed, only the new office location attribute is replicated to other servers, rather than the entire user object. Needless to say, this property-specific updating results in significant reductions in the replication traffic volume within and between sites.

◆ *Improved Replication Model*—Although the Active Directory was built from the replication engine used by Exchange Server 5.5, it does improve quite a bit on the one found in Exchange. For example, Active Directory supports any replication topology including a ring topology, which allows for multiple replication paths to different sites, so that the system isn't prone to a single point of failure.

◆ *Full LDAP Support*—Active Directory is a native LDAP store, which means that it provides full support of the latest LDAP standards (currently version 3). By contrast, Exchange Server 5.5 only provides base-level compatibility with LDAP.

◆ *Building on a native TCP/IP Infrastructure*—Active Directory is built from the ground up for TCP/IP-based networking infrastructures. The Exchange team has capitalized on this by doing the same to Exchange 2000 Server.

Further, you should also note that Exchange 2000 Server taps into a fair number of Windows 2000 Server features. First and foremost, all client access protocols (except MAPI) now are run as part of Internet Information Services (IIS), which has become the protocol engine.

Incorporating the protocols into IIS both serves to add some new exciting TCP/IP-based features to Exchange 2000 Server and enables almost endless scalability because the protocol, storage, and directory now can be hosted on different servers. For example, you now are able to design an Exchange 2000 Server solution that consists of a number of front-end and back-end servers—here, the front-end servers take care of directory lookups and handling the supported protocols, whereas the back-end servers are used to store messages and collaboration data.

Note

Exchange 2000 Server has a lot of other new and improved features not found in Exchange Server 5.5. However, going into an in-depth discussion of those is clearly outside the scope of this book. So you'll have to refer to specialized Exchange 2000 Server books for full coverage on that part.

Points of Integration

To be precise, Exchange 2000 Server features the following points of integration with Active Directory:

♦ *Domain Naming Context*—Domain objects include Exchange 2000 Server recipients objects (users, contacts, distribution lists) and public folder definitions.

♦ *Configuration Naming Context*—All Exchange 2000 Server information not specific for recipient objects is stored in the configuration partition. The Exchange 2000 Server data stored in the configuration partition includes the message routing topology (routing groups), Exchange servers, connectors, protocols, Administrative Groups, and the settings of any additional Exchange services (such as Instant Messaging) of the Exchange 2000 organization. The Exchange 2000 configuration is stored under the following path in the configuration partition: **CN=Microsoft Exchange, CN=Services, CN=Configuration**.

♦ *Schema Naming Context*—The schema is extended with all the new objects and attributes introduced by Exchange 2000 Server. There are so many new objects and attributes added to the schema partition that it is approximately doubled in size. To be precise, Active Directory contains 142 object classes and 827 attributes by default, and the installation of Exchange 2000 Server adds another 158 classes and 854 attributes to the schema. In addition, in excess of 250 additional attributes are added to the Global Catalog.

♦ *Global Catalog (GC)*—Because the GC holds all domain partition objects found in the entire forest (and a partial set of the attributes), Exchange 2000 Server uses it for holding the Global Address List. As such, you will find the load on the GCs to grow quite a deal with the introduction of Exchange 2000 Server.

♦ *Security*—The security fundamentals of Windows 2000 Server and Active Directory now applies to Exchange 2000 Server, removing major parts of the separate security system found in the earlier versions of Exchange Server. However, you will still encounter the old MAPI permissions in a couple of places, most notable for setting mailbox permissions.

As should be evidenced by the many points of integration to Active Directory (and Exchange 2000 Server's extensive usage of each of them), you should expect to find quite substantial changes compared with Exchange Server 5.5, almost no matter where you look (see Figure 15.10).

You should especially take note of the fact that more than 250 additional attributes will be marked for replication to the GC. So your GCs are set to grow quite dramatically when Exchange 2000 Server is installed—and thus be the target of more replication traffic for the future. And since all Outlook clients will target the GC, you should expect some fairly major increases on the load on the GCs as well.

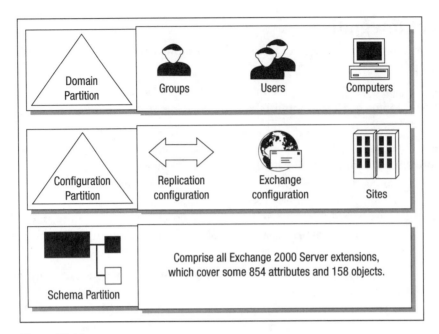

Figure 15.10
Exchange 2000 Server uses all three Active Directory partitions.

The New Primary Directory Objects

As a result of the change from using Exchange's own directory service to using Active Directory, object classes and terms have changed as of Exchange 2000 Server. Table 15.5 compares the base directory objects from Exchange Server 5.5 to those of Exchange Server 2000.

Moving to Exchange 2000 Server

The amount of work that you're being faced with in moving to Exchange 2000 Server will in large part be dependent on where you're coming from messaging-wise. Best case, you'll "only" be charged with designing and implementing a new Exchange 2000 Server-based messaging solution. And worst case, you'll be charged with migrating to Exchange Server 2000 from Exchange Server 5.5.

> **Note**
> *Actually, you might also be charged with the worst of all cases—migrating from another messaging system than Exchange Server. However, this scenario won't be covered here.*

Exchange 2000 Server now operates as an integral part of Windows 2000 Server/Active Directory, so you will find that a fair number of the design decisions also are somewhat dependent upon your Active Directory design and vice versa. Thus, you should definitely

Table 15.5 A comparison of the base directory objects in Exchange Server 5.5 and Exchange 2000 Server.

Exchange Server 5.5	Object	Equivalent Exchange 2000 Server Object Comments
Mailbox	Mailbox-enabled user	A mailbox-enabled user is a special instance of an Active Directory user account that includes a mailbox on an Exchange 2000 server. This type of user gets a number of additional property pages (with Exchange 2000-specific configuration options) compared to a standard user account.
Custom recipient	Mail-enabled contact	Mail-enabled contacts aren't security principals in Active Directory (meaning that one can't log on by specifying a mail-enabled contact). Thus, a mail-enabled contact really is a mail account (an SMTP address) with a couple of configuration options, just as you're used to from using custom recipients with Exchange Server 5.5.
Distribution list	Mail-enabled group	The distribution list functionality is implemented using groups. You now have two kinds of groups: • Security Groups. A group that works as a security principal, meaning that it can be used for assigning permissions. A security group can either be mail-enabled (making it possible to use it as a distribution list, too) or not. • Distribution Groups. A group that is identical to a distribution list in functionality, meaning that it can't be used for assigning permissions. Just as is the case for using groups (see Chapter 9) for security assignments, you should ponder which group scope to use (Local, Global, or Universal). The fact that you're now using groups will in many instances prove a boon to administration, because you'll be able to use the already implemented security groups for distribution list purposes.

want to do some of your Exchange 2000 Server designing concurrently with the Active Directory designing in order to avoid any major hiccups here. And that's exactly, why it does make a lot of sense to delve a bit more in-depth on Exchange 2000 Server in this book.

Tip

No matter what migration scenario you face, migrating should prove tough for the administrators. Exchange 2000 Server is so different from Exchange Server 4/5 that a large part of the existing Exchange Server knowledge will be rendered useless.

Exchange 2000 Server Designing

The major areas where you'll find the Exchange 2000 Server design to be somewhat inter-dependent with Active Directory are the following:

♦ *Active Directory Forest*—The first and most important Active Directory concession is the fact that you can only have one Exchange Organization inside each Active Directory forest and vice versa (see Figure 15.11). In other words, Exchange 2000 Server can't span multiple Active Directory domains from separate forests as is the case with Exchange Server 4/5. The reason for this is that the Active Directory forest now *is* the Exchange Organization.

♦ *User Principal Name (UPN) and Simple Mail Transfer Protocol (SMTP) Addresses*—A user is allowed to log on to the Active Directory using the so-called UPN, which is a forest-unique logon name that allows users to log on to their domain from anywhere in the forest. UPNs use the same notation as SMTP addresses, so what would be more logical to the users than to use the same SMTP addresses and UPNs, ensuring that all users will be using the same name for logging on to the network and for email—thus giving each user only one identification to remember and providing some relief to the administrators with regard to inventing different unique naming schemes? However, you should be aware that this imposes a bit of work on your part, because the SMTP addresses and the UPNs are separate entities.

♦ *Active Directory domains*—Generally speaking, Exchange 2000 Server won't affect your domain solution and vice versa. Therefore, you can focus solely on the business require-ments and the Active Directory technicalities for the Active Directory domain design. But you should understand that, although the domains in themselves won't have much of an impact on Exchange 2000 Server, there are a lot of the things inside the domain that will prove of consequence to Exchange 2000 Server. The domain structuring does have a relevance to Exchange 2000 Server as the recipients objects (users, contacts, and groups) will depend upon the same OU structures and security rights and permissions. So you should ponder the applicability of your current group and OU hierarchies to Exchange 2000 Server. Likewise, you should remember to make sure that the current security boundaries (and administrator privileges) are consistent with the ones needed by (and assigned by default) by Exchange 2000 Server.

Figure 15.11
You can only have one Exchange Organization inside each Active Directory forest and vice versa.

♦ *Domain Controllers (DCs) and Global Catalogs (GCs)*—Exchange 2000 Server as well as the messaging clients need to get in contact with the DCs and GCs quite often for doing name queries and resolving the group members. There's a requirement to have a GC configured for each domain where Exchange clients have been deployed, because Outlook clients always use the GCs to resolve their queries. Exchange 2000 Server always uses LDAP to access the directory information stored on the DCs and GCs. Although the recent versions of Outlook are able to use LDAP, all the Outlook clients available at present will be using MAPI to obtain directory information, such as address list information—hence the reason that the Outlook clients always are accessing the GCs (DCs don't support the MAPI protocol). Because of the load added to the DCs and GCs from Exchange 2000 servers and messaging clients, the recommendations call for having one DC for every four Exchange 2000 servers. Microsoft also states that Exchange 2000 servers should be installed as member servers in the domain rather than as DCs or GCs, because of performance implications.

♦ *Sites*—The messaging clients as well as Exchange 2000 Server take advantage of the Site knowledge set up in Active Directory to locate the nearest DCs and GCs, just as in Windows 2000. Also, the servers have a level of intelligence built into them that enables requests from clients to be load balanced between the local GCs. Besides that, there's no connection between the Active Directory site topology and Exchange 2000 Server design—but in many cases you will find that the Exchange 2000 Server routing structure winds up mirroring that of the site topology. The current set of recommendations from Microsoft call for having two GCs in every Active Directory site. This is because the messaging servers and client make heavy use of GCs, which in turn makes it crucial that all Exchange 2000 servers have fast, local access to a GC. So you should definitely never want to have a Windows 2000 site that doesn't include at least one GC unless some very persuasive reasons exist for not doing so.

♦ *Active Directory Stability and Scalability*—The fact that Exchange 2000 Server now uses Active Directory means that Exchange 2000 Server relies entirely on the replication topology to replicate Exchange directory information. In other words, the well being of the Exchange 2000 Server infrastructure is now fully dependent upon that of the Active Directory. And so, you should never implement Exchange 2000 Server before you're fairly convinced that the Active Directory structure is stable.

The rest of the Exchange 2000 Server design doesn't depend on the Active Directory configuration.

Migrating to Exchange 2000 Server

Things do tend to get a bit more complicated when you're faced with migrating from Exchange Server 5.5 to Exchange 2000 Server. That's largely because you'll need to work a fair bit to ensure a proper level of interoperability between the two platforms unless you're able to switch to Exchange 2000 Server in a matter of hours or days.

It's true that you can indeed encounter many quite different scenarios in which coexistence between previous versions of Exchange Server and Exchange 2000 is necessary or highly beneficial, but you are basically faced with two conceptually different situations:

♦ Adding Exchange 2000 servers to the same Exchange Server 5.5 Organization.

♦ Implementing Exchange 2000 servers in a new, separate Exchange Organization.

In most cases, you'll be able to choose (more or less) freely between the two scenarios. And, although the first scenario arguably will be the prevalent one, some very good reasons exist for carefully pondering the pros and cons of both scenarios.

In the Same Organization

Having the new Exchange 2000 servers running in the same Organization as the old Exchange servers introduces some limitations on the part of Exchange 2000 Server (which is a consequence of the so-called Exchange mixed mode). But worst of all, you will most probably need to invest a fair bit of time in preparing the Exchange Organization for having Exchange 2000 servers added and setting up the ADC's Connection Agreements so that the Exchange Server directory and the Active Directory are kept in sync.

Some of the issues that you absolutely will want to take care of, before adding the first Exchange 2000 server to your Organization, are the following:

♦ Making sure that DNS is working correctly between the servers that are part of the Exchange Organization as well as between the Exchange servers and the Active Directory servers.

♦ Removing characters that are invalid in Active Directory from the Exchange Organization and/or Site display names.

♦ Identifying Exchange 5.5 connectors that have a locally scoped address space and fix any routing issues that the locally scoped address space may give rise to.

♦ Using the **NTDSNoMatch** tool to identify multiple mailboxes that are mapped to the same Windows NT account (often referred to as resource mailboxes) and avoiding that duplicate user accounts are created when the ADC is started.

♦ Running DS/IS consistency adjust on all servers in order to get rid of any "zombie" permissions found on mailboxes and public folders.

After that, you should be set to implement and configure the ADC in order to get your Active Directory populated (provided that the Active Directory is in place and that all pre-existing directory objects have been moved, copied or cloned to the Active Directory in advance of this). However, it might take a fair bit of time before you reach this standing, depending upon the state of your migration to Active Directory (see Chapter 22 for more information on how to migrate from Windows NT Server to Windows 2000 Server) and the inherent complexities of the current messaging solution.

You have to install at least one instance of the Exchange 2000 ADC in your Active Directory forest to be able to add Exchange 2000 servers to your current Exchange Organization. This is because Exchange 2000 ADC's Configuration Connection Agreement provides replication of the site-specific configuration information between Exchange Server 5.5 and Exchange 2000 Server/Active Directory.

And then you're off to implement Exchange 2000 Server in your current Exchange Organization. This can be done in a variety of ways, the most common being:

♦ *In-place upgrade*—Upgrading an existing Exchange server by way of the Exchange 2000 Server Setup program.

♦ *Move mailbox*—Installing Exchange 2000 Server on a new server in the same site and moving mailboxes and public folders to the new server.

♦ *Swing*—A fairly novel combination of the in-place upgrade and move mailbox methods that allows you to keep the existing server.

♦ *Leapfrog*—Yet another combination of the in-place upgrade and move mailbox methods that likewise allows you to keep the existing server.

♦ *Parallel upgrade*—Moving your Exchange data to a new Exchange 2000 Server Organization.

In a Separate Organization

If you have a separate Exchange 2000 Organization and a separate pre-Exchange 2000 Organization, you will be able to make good on all of the features found in Exchange 2000 Server right from the outset (due to being able to run it in native mode). However, on the other hand, having two Exchange Organizations will most probably also entail some additional planning and implementation (as well as a somewhat higher potential for various problems), depending on the precise implementation scheme chosen.

No matter what the precise requirements that have prompted you to create two Exchange Organizations, you're very likely to be faced with the same two needs. That is, integrating the address lists across the two Exchange Organizations and allowing users in both Exchange Organizations to mail one another. Bringing these things to life will demand a fair amount of additional work on your part compared with the single organization scenario.

If you need to implement the ADC to gain the necessary level of coexistence between two Exchange Organizations, you should stay aware of the fact that a separate Exchange 2000 Server has to be found in either the source or the target Organization in order to comply with the requirements for Inter-Organizational Connection Agreements.

Why You Don't Want to Have Multiple Exchange Organizations

The major side effects of having more than one Exchange Organization are as follows:

- You can't include all Exchange servers in the same set of sites (or Administrative Groups or Routing Groups) and, thus, won't be able to administer all servers from a focal point.
- You can't replicate calendar information between users in the various Organizations.
- You will have more than one GAL (as well as address lists). You will find it possible to implement some sort of directory synchronization to fix this. However, the recipients from other forests will always have to be created as mail-enabled contacts/custom recipients, not mailboxes/mail-enabled users.
- You can't exchange routing information going between multiple Organizations.

Also, the message routing between multiple Exchange Organizations is similar to configuring coexistence to external messaging systems.

Depending upon your requirements, having two separate Exchange Organizations might also present you with the following hard-to-solve issues:

- How to integrate non-Exchange address lists.
- Finding out which part of the infrastructure should handle the connections to outside email systems (such as the Internet) and how to accomplish that.
- How to make public folders accessible across the two Exchange Organizations.
- How to make Exchange-based applications and templates coexist in both Exchange Organizations without inflicting a reduction in functionality.
- How to go about bringing coexistence to the custom-built solutions that integrate to the current Exchange Organization.

Best Practices

You should be aware that Exchange 2000 Server and Active Directory are somewhat interdependent in the areas mentioned in Table 15.6. Therefore, you should take a fairly detailed look at those issues and settle them as early as possible in the process—preferably when you're designing your Active Directory structures.

If you face the need of having to keep the Active Directory and the Exchange directory synchronized, you should be helped immensely in your ADC planning if you start out by answering the questions brought forth in Table 15.7.

Tip

You will always need to install the ADC when you have to add Exchange 2000 servers to an Exchange Organization running off Exchange Server 4/5. However, you won't necessarily need to implement Connection Agreements. Whether or not you need an ADC depends on your stance to the four possible applications of ADC put forward in "ADC in a Nutshell," earlier in this chapter.

Table 15.6   Exchange 2000 Server depends on a fair number of your Active Directory design points.

Area	Comments
The Active Directory Forest	You can only have one Exchange Organization inside each Active Directory forest and vice versa.
User Principal Name (UPN) and Simple Mail Transfer Protocol (SMTP) Addresses	You should consider whether or not you can use the same SMTP addresses and UPNs for all users employing the same name for logging on to the network and for email.
Active Directory domain object structures	Exchange 2000 Server depends upon how Active Directory implements users, contacts, and groups as well as the OU structure and the security rights and permissions.
Domain Controllers (DCs) and Global Catalogs (GCs)	Exchange 2000 Server as well as the messaging clients depend on the DCs and GCs for performing quite a lot of tasks. And so, they are adding a sizable load to these servers as well as depending on being able to access them at any time.
Active Directory Sites	Currently, Microsoft recommends that you have two GCs in every Active Directory site.

How you will migrate to Exchange 2000 Server depends upon the scenario faced and the state of (and method used in) your migration to Active Directory. If you're faced with a Windows NT to Active Directory migration concurrently with having to implement Exchange 2000 Server, you can narrow the choices down to the following four commonly used ones:

♦ *Performing an in-place upgrade to Windows 2000 Server followed by implementing ADC—* The "straight" choice. However, be forewarned that this scenario looks much easier than it really is. Also, it only applies to environments where you're able to upgrade all existing Windows NT Server domains before moving further in the rollout of Exchange 2000 Server.

♦ *Implementing ADC and postponing the full migration to Windows 2000 Server/Active Directory to a later time—*The fastest way to Exchange 2000 Server is to just go ahead and implement a couple of Windows 2000 servers/Active Directory running in the existing Windows NT Server domain(s)—usually by way of in-place upgrading. However, please stay alert to the fact that you are merely postponing the worst part of the platform upgrade until later on, complicating matters a bit more.

♦ *Implementing ADC and postponing the cloning of user accounts to a later time—*Just as fast as the previous scenario; you'll have to perform approximately the same work before implementing Exchange 2000 Server (installing a couple of Windows 2000 servers running Active Directory). But it will usually prove easier to get to the finish line using this scenario because it eliminates the requirement of performing in-place upgrades of the current domains.

Table 15.7   The questions that you will need to answer before designing and configuring your ADC setup.

Question	Comments
How do you take inventory of your Exchange sites?	You will need to know how many you have, how they are managed, and whether they are candidates for synchronization. For those sites to be synchronized, you will need detailed information on their recipient containers and the objects to be synchronized.
How will you manage objects in Exchange Directory?	ADC enables you to manage Exchange Directory through Active Directory's tools. However, the easiest solution clearly is to accept that Exchange Administrator should still be used to manage the Exchange environment, because this enables you to create most of the Connection Agreements as one way to Active Directory. This is the least expensive solution regarding the performance hit on the ADC server and the network as well as the planning involved.
How many (and what size) Active Directory Domains do you have?	For total flexibility and replication capabilities, you need to place an ADC server in each Active Directory domain. Although you might decide to deploy an environment in which smaller domains don't have separate ADCs (in that case, another ADC has to take on this workload), remember that IP connectivity is needed between the ADC server and the Exchange sites. Exchange sites may contain mailboxes that are associated with Active Directory accounts from multiple domains, so you should remember to watch out for Exchange servers holding objects across multiple domains.
Do any Windows NT Server 4 Domains remain?	Usually, each Exchange 4/5 mailbox is mapped to a Windows NT Server user account. You can move these user accounts to Active Directory by upgrading the PDC to Windows 2000 Server/Active Directory in each of the domains or you can clone the user accounts to Active Directory by using a tool (such as Active Directory Migration Tool, discussed in Chapter 22). Otherwise, you must decide which Active Directory objects (Contact, User, or Disabled User) the mailboxes should be mapped to. By default, the mailboxes are mapped to Active Directory as mail-enabled Contacts. However, this is not recommended as you'll be facing chaos when upgrading the NT Server domain to Active Directory, because the user account objects already exist within Active Directory.
How does the container structure look?	By default, an Exchange site has only the Recipients container. Some customers have created other containers for different types of objects (such as Distribution Lists and Custom Recipients). However, encountering containers for business units or departments is relatively uncommon, because moving objects between containers is quite difficult. Hopefully, your organization hasn't deployed a lot of containers, because you must create a separate Connection Agreement for each container that you need to replicate to a separate OU in Active Directory.
How will you map Exchange objects?	Many organizations have a multi-master domain topology where user accounts exist in more than one domain. You should identify where users' mailboxes reside in each domain. ADC automatically does the following: • Maps each Exchange mailbox to the corresponding user account (thus making it a mailbox-enabled user and merging all Active Directory and Exchange directory attributes for that object in both directories). • Has Exchange Distribution Lists appear as domain local distribution groups (and makes these groups mail-enabled in the process).

(continued)

Table 15.7   The questions that you will need to answer before designing and configuring your ADC setup *(continued).*

Question	Comments
	• Has Exchange Custom Recipients appear as Contacts (and makes these Contacts mail-enabled in the process). Thus, you need to decide, for example, how to handle user accounts that, instead of having mailboxes, have their email addresses defined as Exchange Custom Recipients. Also, you should heed the advice given in the previous entry "Do Any Windows NT Server 4 Domains Remain?" regarding users still on NT Server domains.
What should you do when you encounter deletions?	Be very careful with the way you handle object deletions. For example, are you really certain that you want to have the user or mail-enabled Contact deleted when the Custom Recipients object is deleted? Also, do you want to have the user account deleted when you delete the mailbox? By default, objects that are deleted from each directory aren't propagated to the other directory. Instead, the deletions are recorded in a file on the ADC server. This is a very sensible setup, so you should closely consider all the effects of changing the default before you do so.
How do you determine a schedule for directory synchronization?	You can set up individual Connection Agreements to perform synchronization at specific times of the day or night. Each Connection Agreement has its own associated schedule. As a rule of thumb networks with a large number of users may require synchronization more frequently than a smaller network, and some networks may require specific objects to be synchronized more frequently than other objects.
Where should you install ADC?	Selecting the right server(s) to run ADC depends very much on the size of your Exchange environment, the number of Windows 2000 Server domains and the number of Connection Agreements. Generally, ADC can consume a lot of processor time—depending on the replication schedule and the number of Connection Agreements. Although installing ADC on a DC reduces the network bandwidth consumed (given that the Connection Agreements defined in the ADC all involve the domain that the DC is holding), doing so generally isn't recommended, due to ADC's rather high CPU load. For the best performance, ADC should be installed on a member server in the Active Directory domain. If, however, you are positive that the server hardware can accommodate the extra processing load, you can opt to put the ADC service on a DC or GC. Ultimately, you can deploy as many ADC servers in your installation as you like, wherein each server takes care of a separate set of Connection Agreements (currently, no way exists to deploy more servers for adding fault tolerance to the ADC solution, because you can't define duplicate Connection Agreements).
When do you introduce Connection Agreements?	When you implement a Connection Agreement (either two-way or one-way) to Exchange, the ADC server modifies and adds some attributes to each Exchange directory object inside its scope. This, in turn, instigates a replication of all the directory objects (because Exchange lacks attribute-level replication) throughout the Exchange Organization. Therefore, you must plan to set the major Connection Agreements in production at times when plenty of network bandwidth is available throughout the Exchange Organization.

♦ *Cloning or copying user accounts to a new Active Directory infrastructure and implementing ADC*—This scenario represents the cleanest break with the current environment and thus will allow you much more flexibility in building the Active Directory infrastructure of choice. This solution will often prove to be the least labor-intensive proposition. However, you'll be tasked with doing the platform migration upfront.

Tip

It's without doubt much easier to get Exchange 2000 Server installed in your Active Directory forest when you do it from scratch. Unfortunately, this really isn't an option in most enterprise environments because of the immense consequences that will be wrought on end-user functionality due to the distinct lack of any kind of interoperability with the current Exchange environment.

Exchange Is It!

I sure hope that you now see why it makes very good sense to take a closer look at Exchange Server from the Active Directory perspective. Exchange Server 4/5 is a great—and very real—case of directory coexistence in a lot of scenarios, and Exchange 2000 Server provides you with some insight on what a fully integrated Active Directory application should look like.

Exchange 2000 Server really makes good on the promise of the immense operational benefits that can be achieved from applications that are fully integrated with Active Directory. Hopefully, Exchange 2000 Server will grow into being the reference point that any application—whether it's from Microsoft or third parties—is compared to, when running Windows 2000 Server/Active Directory. However, you should be keenly aware that Exchange 2000 Server probably will be one of very few applications that deliver native Active Directory support for a long while. For one, it doesn't seem that Microsoft or the third parties have a lot of native Active Directory applications up their sleeve for now. Secondly, as you've seen from this chapter, there are quite a lot of things that need to be done in order to migrate from a standalone directory to the Active Directory-integrated solutions.

The reason you won't see very many native Active Directory applications along the lines of Exchange 2000 Server for some time to come is that it represents a very big bet on the part of the software developer: It doesn't seem probable that a native Active Directory application will be picked up by enterprises that aren't willing to bet fully on Active Directory at present time. Additionally—and probably most important of all—the software developers will be held hostage to the future developments (including the changes brought to the table by Microsoft) inside the Active Directory area, if they opt for a close integration. That's why you might as well start reading your way into the next chapter, which presents you with the rundown on the more limited kinds of Active Directory integration and the options for implementing some sort of synchronization between Active Directory and other directories.

Chapter 16

How to Design with Other Active Directory-Aware Applications

As mentioned in the introductory chapters, directory services are a whole new ball game compared to the user database known from Windows NT Server. One of the very interesting things about the introduction of Active Directory is that you're faced with a new set of previously unheard-of options with regard to integrating your other applications and services running in the enterprise. And while it's most likely that only a fraction of the Independent Software Vendors (ISVs) will make good on the directory services promise in the course of the coming years, you should consider the possibilities that it may bring you in order to be able to benefit from it when you have the chance—or else accept the fact that you really won't be able to profit from these options.

Who knows? You might find that this integration will provide you with so many advantages that it will pay a handsome dividend to arrange for that integration yourself by using some kind of directory synchronization engine. Or even better, you might find yourself in a position to put some gentle pressure on your current application solution providers to add a new checkmark item saying "Active Directory-enabled" or something along these lines.

However, Active Directory integration is not an either-or proposition, as you are soon to see from the in-depth discussion on directory integration in this chapter. Like so many other things, the pledge for integration ranges over a very wide solution space and, thus, it may just as well be used for something very trivial as for something that will have profound consequences to you and your enterprise. It's my hope that this chapter will help you dodge the unimportant stuff and get a handle on how you can reap the rewards of Active Directory that apply to your enterprise, as you move forward.

What's in Integration?

You might be able to think up a lot of very different integration scenarios, but Microsoft has already established some sensible baseline criteria for independent software vendors (ISVs) that you should become acquainted with.

From the lowest level of integration to the highest, you have:

♦ Service Connection Point (SCP)

♦ Existing directory objects

♦ Service principal name (SPN)

♦ Single sign-on

♦ Full or partial directory integration

Note that the first two integration levels are required for meeting the "Application Specification for Microsoft Windows 2000 Server, Advanced Server & Datacenter Server, version 1.3," which allows the ISVs to stamp their products with the coveted Certified for Windows 2000 logo.

> **Note**
>
> *The ISVs only need to use Service Connection Points if their "application is comprised of multiple components that run on different machines" and there are "client components" that request services from "server components." Likewise, the demand for using existing directory objects only applies to situations where "the customer maintains authoritative information in Active Directory and your application uses this type of information."*

Service Connection Point (SCP)

Service publication governs the creation, storage, and maintenance of information in the Active Directory database of the services found in the third-party applications. The information published to Active Directory can be used by network clients and network administrators for finding, connecting to, and managing a service. In addition, Active Directory enables clients and administrators to view the distributed network as a collection of services in addition to "just" being a collection of individual computers (which is the only option found in non-directory-service environments).

To publish a service in Active Directory, the service must store, as a minimum requirement, its binding information in the directory. *Service bindings* are the information a client uses to connect, or bind to, an instance of a given service. The information needed to bind to a service includes the service name and its location. For example, a Web browser binds to a

Web server by using a uniform resource locator (URL) in just the same way as you bind to a file service by using Uniform Naming Convention (UNC) names.

A specific service can publish itself one or more times in Active Directory. Each instance of the service running on one or multiple computers in the network can create connection point objects in Active Directory. As such, a connection point represents one or more instances of a service available in a network. For example, if a service such as Microsoft Certificate Server for Windows 2000 Server is installed and running on two computers in the network, there can be two connection point objects—one for each instance of the service running on each computer.

Similarly, a service that has multiple instances installed on a single computer can create separate connection point objects for each instance. It is also possible for multiple instances of a replicated service to publish themselves using a single connection point in Active Directory. In this case, the connection point contains information that enables a client to select and bind to a replica.

The Active Directory schema defines a variety of object classes for use in publishing a service. All objects representing resources that accept connections are derived from the object class **Connection Point**. Examples of such objects include **Volume**, **Print Queue**, **RPC**, **Windows Sockets**, and **serviceConnectionPoint**.

Service Connection Points are used by services that need to explicitly publish themselves in Active Directory, rather than use an existing abstraction (such as RPC Name Service or RnR). A service that uses a Service Connection Point should provide an abstraction layer to hide service location details from client applications. This abstraction can be implemented as a dynamic-link library (DLL) or as part of the client application. The abstraction queries Active Directory for a connection point object representing the service requested by the client application and uses the binding information from that object to connect the client application to the service.

A client application finds the Service Connection Point objects that represent the services that the application wants to use by searching the directory for keywords. The keywords attribute of a Service Connection Point is included in the GC, so clients can simply search the GC to find the applicable Service Connection Points anywhere in the forest. For this reason, it won't matter to the client where the Service Connection Points are being published (that is, which domain the Service Connection Points are being published to). The client then selects one of those objects and uses the binding information from that object to connect to the service.

Note

COM-based services do not use Service Connection Point objects to advertise themselves. These services are published in the class store. The Windows 2000 class store is a directory-based repository for all applications, interfaces, and APIs that provide for the publishing and assigning of applications.

To know where to publish services in Active Directory, you should understand and observe the following guidelines:

♦ A service should publish its information in the domain-naming context, and never in the configuration-naming context. Publishing service information to the configuration-naming context doesn't make the service more available or easier to access. It does, however, cause extra replication traffic. Also, if a client is able to access a computer running a service, that client should be able to access a replica of the domain containing that computer. Therefore, it's sufficient for a service to publish information to the domain that contains the computer running the service.

♦ A service should create service-specific objects in the same domain as the computer that is running the service and in locations that are convenient for the administration of the service and maintenance of those objects. The recommended location is the computer object on which the service is installed.

Service-related objects can exist in three containers in the domain-naming context:

♦ Computers

♦ OUs

♦ The system container or one of its children

Figure 16.1 shows part of the default container hierarchy for a domain partition to give you an idea of where the Service Connection Point objects might be placed.

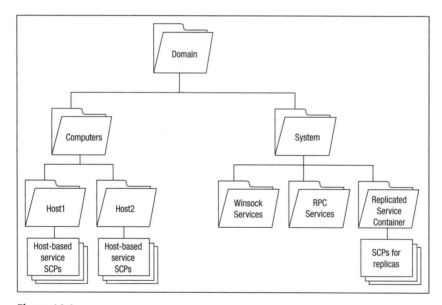

Figure 16.1
Where to place the Service Connection Points.

Using the Existing Directory Objects

It's definitely beneficial if applications that use information about network elements—such as users, machines, or devices—can extract this information from Active Directory rather than having to create a separate directory that includes a fair amount of duplicate information. Microsoft recommends that you meet this need in one of the following two ways:

♦ *Have the applications obtain the information directly from Active Directory*—It follows that the Active Directory schema might have to be extended with several objects and attributes that are needed by the application, but aren't included in the default schema. See also the section "Full or Partial Directory Integration."

♦ *Maintain a duplicate copy of the information found in Active Directory*—In that case, the application must provide a way to synchronize its local directory data with that in Active Directory, either by offering a synchronization mechanism from within the application or by exposing APIs (or something along those lines) that enable an external metadirectory or directory synchronization product to keep the information stored in the application's directory consistent with that of Active Directory's.

Service Principal Name (SPN)

Windows 2000 and, thus, Active Directory provide support for the so-called service principal names (SPNs), which are a key component for doing mutual authentication. An SPN is a unique name that identifies an instance of a service. SPNs are associated with the security principals (that is, a user or computer account) in whose security context the service executes. Each security principal can have many service principal names—that is, you might want to use a single security principal for handling multiple services so you can confine the power vested in the services to very few accounts in order to keep them on a tight leash.

Establishing Mutual Authentication

The central principle of mutual authentication is that neither party can "trust" the other before identity has been proven. This means, in practical terms, that the server must be able to determine who the client is without asking the client, and the client must be able to determine who the server is without asking the server in order to avoid spoofing attacks.

In other words, mutual authentication is a security feature in which a client process must prove its identity to a service, and the service must prove its identity to the client, before any application traffic is sent over the connection between client and service. The ability of a client to authenticate the service to which it is connecting is important in client/server applications that support delegation of the security context to the client.

Identity can be proven through a trusted third party and can use shared secrets, as in Kerberos, or it can be proven through cryptographic means, as with a public key infrastructure. Each party is identified by a *principal name*.

Services Security Basics

Services can execute in one of two security contexts:

• LocalSystem account

• An ordinary Active Directory account, which typically is referred to as a *service account*

The security context under which the service runs affects the access rights that the service has on the local computer and the network.

LocalSystem is a special, predefined local account that is available only to system processes. The big advantage of this account is that it doesn't have a password, so you won't need to go through the tedious routine of changing passwords from time to time, which is the case for a service account (all of you coming from Windows NT Server will no doubt be used to this).

On computers running Windows 2000 Server, a service that runs in the context of the LocalSystem account uses the credentials of the computer when accessing resources over the network and has full access to local resources. A service that runs in the context of LocalSystem on a DC has full access to the directory, because the DC hosts a directory replica and LocalSystem has complete access to local resources. Thus, you might very well find that you'll be granting too many powers to the service, when using the LocalSystem account.

The biggest drawback to using the LocalSystem account is that when a service runs under the LocalSystem account on a system that is a domain member, that service runs under the context of the computer account when accessing domain resources—including Active Directory—but computer accounts typically have very few privileges outside of the local system and don't belong to very many groups.

On the other hand, running a service in the context of a service account has these two major disadvantages:

• The account must be created before the service can run. If the service setup creates the account, the setup must run from an account with sufficient privileges to create accounts in the directory service.

• Service account passwords are stored on each computer on which the service is installed. If the password for a service account on a computer is changed, the service cannot start on that computer until the password is set to the new password for that service.

As a general rule, all services should run under a separate service account on any system, regardless of role, if you want to create a secure setup—and you should definitely always adhere to this rule for handling third-party services on DCs; otherwise, you will bestow too much power to the service.

The syntax of an SPN is: *<service type>/<instance name>:<port number>/<service name>* where the elements of the syntax have the following meanings:

♦ *service type*—Type of service, such as "www" for World Wide Web service or "ldap" for Lightweight Directory Access Protocol.

♦ *instance name*—Name of the instance of the service. Depending upon the service type, it is either the name or IP address of the host running the service.

♦ *port number*—Number of the port used by the service on the host, if it is different from the default for the service type.

♦ *service name*—Name of the service. The name may be the DNS name of a host, of a replicated service, or of a domain or it may be the distinguished name of a Service Connection Point object or of an **RPC service** object.

If *service name* and *instance name* are the same—as they are for most host-based services—then a service principal name can be abbreviated to two components: *<service type>/<instance name>*.

A service (or an administrator on behalf of the service) registers its SPN or SPNs in Active Directory when it's being installed.

Clients establish a local security context, either by executing in a previously established context—for example, in the session of a logged-in user—or by explicitly presenting credentials to the underlying security provider.

The client authenticates with the server by composing an SPN based on information it already knows about the service, which is then presented to the security system, demanding that the server prove it can authenticate using the presented SPN. The client refuses further communications with a server that can't authenticate the SPN. When using Kerberos to authenticate to a server, the client requests a session ticket for the specified SPN. When using certificate-based authentication, the SPN is validated against the contents of the "SubjectName" field of the certificate of the server.

Single Sign-On

It makes sense for everybody to have applications tapping into the security infrastructure that are already configured in the Active Directory domain for authorization purposes. The prototypical example of this situation is when an application allows the administrator to map Active Directory accounts to the security principals or roles used by the application. In that case, the administrator will be able to put his existing Active Directory configuration (this usually means the groups) to use for assigning the application permissions needed to the applicable subset of users—and save some administrative work in the process as well as secure a more transparent security setup. And the users will profit hugely from this, too, as they'll be getting single sign-on functionality, which saves them the hassle of keeping track of multiple user accounts and passwords.

Full or Partial Directory Integration

The very last—and most advanced—level of directory integration is attained when the following statements are true:

♦ *The application uses Active Directory for storing all its directory objects*—As a consequence of that, all the mundane object administration chores can be handled by working on the Active Directory database. For most applications this will usually entail making use of the existing objects and attributes as well as adding new attributes and objects to the domain naming context and/or configuration naming context. Also, an MMC snap-in will typically be needed to provide the administrator a "native" view of the objects and attributes belonging to that particular application (just as it's the case for Exchange 2000 Server).

♦ *The application relies on Active Directory for security services*—This means that no additional load will be put on the administrator for working a separate directory, which usually would entail creating a whole new set of user accounts, user grouping, etc., needed for assigning the proper permissions. Rather, the administrator will be able to just add the applicable permissions to the pre-existing security principals in Active Directory. As you can imagine, this makes a world of difference in regard to the initial configuring as well as the daily management of the application.

Note

Microsoft demands that the administration be done from an MMC snap-in in line with the "Application Specification for Microsoft Windows 2000 Server, Advanced Server & Datacenter Server, version 1.3," which allows the ISVs to stamp their products with the coveted Certified for Windows 2000 logo. However, it doesn't make any difference whether the object administration is performed from the standard MMC tools or from an application-specific MMC tool.

At this level of integration, the application should also prove to be Active Directory Site-aware, if applicable.

The Current Standing

The marketing of the Microsoft .NET Enterprise Servers could easily lead one to believe that all these server applications are operating on the highest Active Directory integration level (that is, the full or partial directory integration). Unfortunately, that isn't the case at the present time. Actually, the support for Active Directory varies quite a bit between the major individual Microsoft .NET Enterprise Servers:

♦ *Exchange 2000 Server*—Full directory integration. Exchange 2000 Server does away with its own directory and uses Active Directory's instead. Exchange 2000 Server includes all the features discussed in the last section. To avoid overloading the Active Directory Site concept, it introduces its own definition of sites (called Routing Groups), which is used for handling message routing. You should head to Chapter 15 for an in-depth discussion on Exchange 2000 Server (as well as its predecessor, Exchange Server 5.5) used in combination with Active Directory.

♦ *SQL Server 2000*—Provides single sign-on functionality as well as support for SCP and SPN. The single sign-on functionality is available when you are running SQL Server in the Windows Authentication Mode, in which case the administrator is allowed to create mappings from the existing Active Directory security principals to SQL Server's roles. SCP is used to publish an instance of SQL Server 2000, including information on replication, publications, databases, and SQL Server Analysis servers.

Microsoft SMS

The current version 2.0 of Microsoft Systems Management Server (SMS) only include scant support for Active Directory. That is, with Service Pack 2, SMS 2.0 support the Windows 2000 platform (clients as well as servers) and most of the integration offered with Windows NT Server 4 is also available. However, SMS really don't look at Active Directory as anything but another kind of SAM database, so we're really not talking any Active Directory integration.

But Microsoft have promised that the next version (currently referred to as Emerald) will feature pervasive Active Directory integration (possibly bringing it to the highest level of directory integration), including support for Add/Remove Programs.

- ♦ *Host Integration Server 2000*—Provides single sign-on functionality for 3270 and 5250 emulation sessions (APPC and CPI-C), as well as support for SCP and SPN.
- ♦ *Internet Security and Acceleration (ISA) Server 2000*—Full directory integration. ISA Enterprise Edition allows you to leverage Active Directory to provide scalable and centralized administration of ISA Access Policies and ISA Server Configuration information from within Active Directory. Also, permissions can be assigned to Active Directory users and groups. Please note that ISA 2000 Server was only available in the RC1 edition as of this writing, so these things are still subject to change.

Currently, Microsoft is far ahead of the pack in terms of Active Directory integration. Just about any server applications that I've encountered until now (except for a couple of the tools built for migration to and management of Active Directory) only include support for the SCP and possibly the SPN features. And judging from the current lack of firm statements of direction on Active Directory from the ISVs, it should prove fairly safe to presume that this picture won't be turned upside down in the short term.

Tip

*You can gain an overview of the applications that are Certified for Windows 2000 at **www.microsoft.com/windows2000/upgrade/compat/certified.asp**. You can find VeriTest Certification reports at **www.veritest.com/mslogos/windows2000/ certification/ServerApps.asp**. Please note that the reports are pretty basic, so you really aren't able to discern the applications' precise Active Directory integration level from these reports; but they do provide you with a fine starting point for doing so.*

You might also want to note that client and server applications aren't the only areas from which you'll be able to reap some major integration rewards. There are also a fair deal of integration rewards to be found when it comes to managing your network.

For instance, chances are that you will have introduced a separate user database, if you've implemented a Virtual Private Network (VPN) solution based on networking hardware. And much the same goes for any Quality of Service (QoS), Virtual LAN (VLAN), and advanced firewall solutions that you may have—or might be planning for the future. You should want to note that your options will depend on your choice of network equipment manufacturer:

♦ Nortel Networks (formerly Bay Networks) currently provides very little specific integration with Active Directory. That is, the support offered is limited to what is offered through the reigning standards, including L2TP, IPSec, and RSVP and DiffServ (both QoS). As of this writing, Nortel Networks hasn't announced any intentions to improve on the Active Directory integration offered in the near future, except for the next version of Optivity Policy Services (Nortel's QoS manager), which promises to include some Active Directory integration. It does, however, seem that Nortel Networks is intent on opening their products using LDAP, which you might be able to profit from by using MMS (see next section).

♦ Cisco Systems has been working closely with Microsoft, right from the very beginning of Microsoft's long journey toward the finished Windows 2000 product. And while Cisco still is working on implementing all the integration features promised, it's already lifted the covers on a fair deal of interesting integration points including VLANs, QoS, VPN, and firewall management, as well as Cisco's own DHCP, DNS, and PKI solutions. However, the Active Directory integration features are still a work in progress, so you will be wise in going in-depth with the actual features available at the time of your implementation.

Note

The market has been rife with rumors that Cisco was ready to do an about-face on Active Directory integration due to it having received a lot of flak from having focused on Active Directory at the expense of other directory services. While Cisco has been quietly backing away from this exclusive support, saying it will integrate a variety of directory services into its switches, routers, and policy-management products, Cisco isn't backing off the tight Active Directory integration promised. Cisco has merely put on hold plans to develop a version of Active Directory for Unix, which many people had a hard time understanding in the first place.

You should be forewarned that it usually will prove a bit demanding to bridge the wide gaps between the Active Directory and network infrastructure people—not because of unwillingness to talk to each other, but because they see the world from very different points of view. But it's imperative that these two groups are brought to a common understanding, before you start planning the future integration between Active Directory and the underlying networking infrastructure, for the sake of avoiding hiccups in this crucial area. You also want to make sure that your enterprise makes the most of the many possibilities for reducing the mundane administration chores related to users and their computers in the networking infrastructure.

General-Purpose Integration

Microsoft's integration strategy builds on a desire to persuade companies to place Active Directory as the hub of the enterprise (for holding user accounts and any other relevant information in order to provide integration to third-party applications, networking hardware, and potentially other OSs). That is, Microsoft wants to position Active Directory as the heart of the network—as a *metadirectory*.

As mentioned earlier, it will probably be some time until a fair number of Active Directory-integrated applications are available—depending upon the success of Windows 2000 Server/Active Directory and the willingness and pressures placed on the third-party developers by Microsoft as well as the customers. Additionally, you definitely won't find support for Active Directory in all the existing applications that have been running in the back office for more than a year.

Note

A metadirectory is a dedicated enterprise directory solution that joins (or merges) information between the various existing directory systems and programs used within an enterprise, and then provides access to the consolidated information. This gives customers a platform for managing diverse information and reduces the growing cost of directory management. You might want to think of a metadirectory as a sort of general-purpose tool for creating any-to-any directory connectivity.

The current state of affairs obviously doesn't sit particularly well with Microsoft's wishes. Having acknowledged that, Microsoft has introduced a general-purpose tool for establishing directory synchronization between Active Directory and other directories: Microsoft Metadirectory Services (MMS).

MMS allows you to solve just about any need you may have for providing integration to other directories. Some of the major reasons seen for introducing directory integration in your current infrastructure include the following:

♦ *Global address book applications*—Synchronizing mailbox information between different email directories used within a company.

♦ *"Hire & fire" solutions*—Propagating information about newly hired employees quickly to all systems that require identity data, and performing the same processes quickly in reverse when employees leave.

♦ *Single sign-on initiatives*—Managing user name, password, and access rights information in a single place.

♦ *E-commerce applications*—Synchronizing information such as digital certificates for suppliers and extranet users with e-commerce directories that reside outside of firewalls.

But the above-mentioned reasons barely scratch the surface. Most enterprises are ripe with directory synchronization opportunities that will show a healthy return in terms of Return on Investment (ROI) as well as improve overall security.

Tip

MMS is available from Microsoft at no charge. However, just like any other meta-directory product, MMS does demand some fairly specialized skills for successful deployment. For that reason, MMS currently is available only via a select number of authorized partners as part of the purchase of consulting time.

A broad MMS training program has been underway from Microsoft for some time (it was delivered in the shape of a Microsoft Official Curriculum course in mid-2000) and continues to establish a channel of trained enterprise service providers who can deliver the MMS product and related services. Therefore, it's likely that MMS will become more known to the public (as well as the consulting hordes) in the near future.

MMS is targeted to become an integral part of Active Directory a bit further down the road and constitutes the best possible choice for building directory synchronization with Active Directory. Additionally, MMS should prove a bargain because Microsoft is providing it free of charge to authorized MMS partners.

MMS in Brief

Like any good metadirectory, MMS provides the capabilities that address these identity management challenges:

♦ *Connectivity*—Enabling the sharing of identity information between different directory services, databases, and applications.

♦ *Brokering functionality*—Distributing changes made in one directory or application to other identity repositories in the enterprise that are affected by the change. The brokering capability is completely "elastic," which means that identity information can be pieced together from multiple sources.

♦ *Integrity mechanisms*—Ensuring that related information remains consistent throughout the enterprise, observing ownership and referential integrity rules. An attribute can be "mastered" anywhere, meaning that changes can occur in different source directories. For the most part, MMS supports both full and delta updates to and from the connected directories.

♦ *Business rules and logic*—Providing customers the capability to decide how metadirectory information is constructed in their environment.

Tip
MMS isn't just another new product from Microsoft that needs to go through a couple of iterations before being ready for prime time. MMS is actually just a repackaging of one of the best metadirectories (Zoomit VIA) currently available; Microsoft acquired Zoomit Corporation in June 1999.

To achieve consistency with other product names, Microsoft changed Zoomit VIA to Microsoft Metadirectory Services (MMS) and released a new version in December 1999.

MMS does these things in a rather convincing way. More than 100 customers (constituting more than 1 million directory entries) were using Zoomit VIA at the time of Microsoft's purchase. MMS also work at the attribute level and includes support for bi-directional synchronization and flexible scheduling options. And most importantly, Zoomit VIA doesn't require additional software on the connected directory systems.

At the current time, MMS allows you to integrate directory information from all the most popular platforms, including:

♦ Banyan VINES

♦ GMHS (BeyondMail, DaVinci)

♦ Lotus Notes and Domino

♦ Lotus cc:Mail

♦ Microsoft Exchange

♦ Microsoft Mail

♦ Microsoft Windows NT

♦ Microsoft Active Directory

♦ Netscape Directory and Meta-Directory Server

♦ Novell 3.x/bindery

♦ Novell GroupWise

♦ Novell NDS

♦ A variety of ODBC/SQL databases

♦ X.500 directories from a variety of vendors (including ISOCOR, ICL, and Control Data) that are accessible via LDAP

♦ Other "metadirectory" products such as Netscape, Control Data, and ISOCOR

MMS Fundamentals

The core functionality delivered by MMS comprises a joined namespace and directory-enabled provisioning:

♦ The joined namespace allow you to manage objects and attributes across multiple isolated directories as if they were one (and have MMS keep track of which isolated directory owns which attribute).

♦ Directory-enabled provisioning is about life-cycle management of identity information. For example, you might want to have changes within an HR application distributed to other directories based on a set of business rules that execute within MMS.

Stated more simply, MMS allows directory information (that is, objects and attributes) to flow in both directions between connected directories and the metadirectory based on a set of rules that are configured by you (by configuring the applicable management agents and the metadirectory namespace).

In the MMS model, the enterprise metadirectory structure consists of one or more servers, management agents, and connected directories (see Figure 16.2). To be more precise, MMS introduce the following terms:

♦ *Metadirectory Namespace*—Although the metadirectory contents usually will be presented as a single tree structure, it really consist of two logical namespaces:

   ♦ *Connector space*—This portion of MMS is charged with linking each connected namespace with the metadirectory. The connector space is the place where the connected directory entries are first imported.

   ♦ *Metaverse*—This portion of MMS presents the global view of the union of entries stemming from the various connected directories. MMS joins the metaverse entry to one or multiple connected directory entries through the connector objects, which are held in the connector space.

♦ *Connected Directory*—A connected directory is essentially any directory that you want to integrate into the metadirectory. The only requirement is that the directory contents be organized into some minimal hierarchical structure and that a method exists for extracting the directory information in it. The information extracted from the connected directory is imported into the metadirectory using a management agent. Optionally, you may want to export information from the metadirectory into the connected directory.

♦ *Management Agent*—The management agents are charged with the actual importing (and exporting) of connected directory information, and therefore, determine what information (objects or attributes) has changed in a connected directory. The directory data is imported into the connector namespace and, where desired, merged with entries in the metaverse. The management agents keep the directory information synchronized by allowing attributes to flow bi-directionally. You will have one management agent for each connected directory.

MMS comes with a set of predefined management agents that are designed to integrate information from specific external directories. The predefined management agents cover the following directories:

♦ Banyan VINES

♦ Lotus cc:Mail

♦ Lotus Notes and Domino

♦ Microsoft Active Directory

♦ Microsoft Exchange (LDAP-based)

♦ Microsoft Exchange (MAPI based)

♦ Microsoft Windows NT

♦ Netscape LDAP

♦ Novell Groupwise API

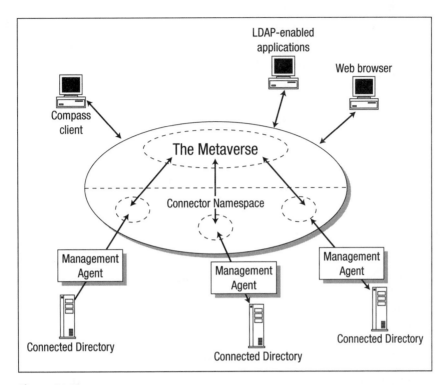

Figure 16.2
The MMS constituents.

♦ Novell NDS (LDAP-based)

♦ Novell NetWare bindery

Note

MMS also include a generic management agent, which is a great place to start from if you have to build your own management agent from scratch.

Be aware that some of these directories are handled using a generic management agent (for example, the support of NDS, Netscape, and Exchange Server 5.5 all come from a generic LDAP agent). Although the generic management agents are indeed able to import and export directory information, they might prove inefficient at importing data (for example, the generic LDAP agent must read the entire directory contents to infer that changes have occurred in an LDAP-based directory) and thus not always practical in large directory environments. But, then again, you really can't have everything.

Five primary methods exist for accessing the MMS from a client or an application:

♦ *Compass client*—A standalone client with the most complete features and most efficient interface of the MMS clients. Can be used to manage the directory.

♦ *Active Compass client*—An ActiveX implementation of the Compass client that runs within any browser that supports ActiveX technology. Can be used to manage the directory.

♦ *Java Compass client*—A Java-based tool that provides read and write access to the directory. It doesn't allow you to manage the directory.

♦ *LDAP-compliant user agent*—Allows you to use any LDAP-compliant application for accessing the directory (read-only access).

♦ *HTML-compliant user agent*—Allows you to use any HTML-compliant application for accessing the directory (read-only access).

There's much more to say on the subject of MMS, but this introduction should prove sufficient for now.

Tip

MMS also applies to replicating Active Directory objects between multiple Active Directory forests. Thus, MMS carries a lot of potential with regard to allowing an enterprise to provide interoperability (and consolidation) between separate Active Directory forests, which works to remedy one of Active Directory's major shortcomings.

This Is (Hopefully) Only the Beginning

As I mentioned at the very start of this chapter, chances are that you won't start seeing a lot of third-party applications that are closely intertwined with Active Directory until a major part of the current Windows NT Server installations has been (or is in the process of being) migrated to Active Directory. And even at this stage, it's hard to guess what will happen, because this will be the first time that a major piece of the network OS (NOS) market might be moving into a certain directory service. So, whether the directory services potential will ever be met still remains to be seen (see Chapter 3). However, Microsoft's very bold move on Exchange 2000 Server's part instills hope that we will indeed be in for some very interesting times in the coming years.

As a former NDS neophyte, I personally hope that Microsoft will be able to pull it off with Active Directory. After all, the directory services do hold the very persuasive promise of consolidating user and resource information (see Figure 16.3) that will be sweet music to the ears in any enterprise.

In order to avoid Active Directory stifling competition and future progress inside this very important area, one can only hope that the major vendors will be able to agree on how different directories should be placed together. There have been several unsuccessful attempts at doing that in the past, but it might turn out that the Directory Services Markup Language (DSML) will fit the bill because a lot of the major players have been involved in its development.

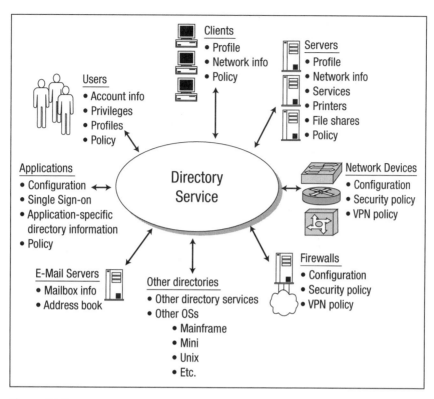

Figure 16.3
The directory services sweet spot, which Microsoft hopes that Active Directory will grow to fill.

The DSML 1.0 standard is an XML-based standard for sharing information among directories and applications that has been developed as a collective effort by Bowstreet, IBM, Microsoft, Novell, Oracle, and the Sun-Netscape Alliance. After the completion of the DSML 1.0 specification, it was turned over to a nonprofit organization named the Organization for the Advancement of Structured Information Standards (OASIS), and sent to review by the World Wide Web Consortium (W3C).

However, the DSML 1.0 standard is not the means to an end because it is limited to defining the schema for data in directories. So even if DSML turns out to become a *de facto* or *de jure* standard, we're still short of a standard query language for directory entries and standards for defining access control. So it seems that there'll be plenty of reasons for coming to grips with a metadirectory such as MMS for years to come.

Part IV

Testing

Chapter 17
Implementing Active Directory

N ow that you have been subjected to 16 chapters of Active Directory planning, you probably are itching to lay your hands on the actual Windows 2000 Server product. That time has finally arrived. This chapter guides you through installing Windows 2000 Server and implementing your first Active Directory (one domain), including configuring DNS and populating the domain with objects (users, OUs, groups, and so on).

> ### Note
> *The Windows 2000 Server setup outlined in this chapter isn't meant as a primer for setting up all aspects of your Windows 2000 Server infrastructure. Rather, its scope is limited to providing you with the essential skills to do a "quick and dirty" setup of your Windows 2000 Server structure, for the sake of "proof of concept." This chapter focuses on the differences between Windows 2000 Server and Windows NT Server 4, so it doesn't go into much detail on the topics that are already familiar to NT Server 4 administrators. To study the basic NT Server concepts, and for a complete and detailed explanation of how to implement Windows 2000 Server for pilot testing and the subsequent rollout, you should consult additional resources.*

This chapter narrows the focus to the implementation skills that are essential for establishing your Windows 2000 Server implementation. Chapter 18 covers the more advanced topics, such as how to set up sites, handle the Flexible Single Master of Operations (FSMO) roles, and perform administrative delegation, as well as implement Group Policies.

Installing Windows 2000 Server

Much of the process of setting up Windows 2000 Server should be familiar to anyone who has set up previous versions of Windows NT Server. When you factor out the potential hardware trouble spots (complying with the minimum requirements for running Windows 2000 Server and implementing the correct drivers and patch levels for your various hardware components), installing Windows 2000 Server really is a straightforward procedure. Basically, you need a Windows 2000 Server CD-ROM and the ability to answer the questions in Table 17.1.

> **Note**
>
> *The default selections on additional components have DNS Server disabled, even though Active Directory requires the availability of a DNS server, either locally or remotely.*

In my experience, you should adhere as much as possible to the default settings for the items listed in Table 17.1. You can always change your setup options after Windows 2000 Server is up and running. Likewise, for proof of concept, you don't need a perfect setup; instead, you need a bare-bones implementation that enables you to start testing.

> **Note**
>
> *Remember, chances are high that you will install Windows 2000 Server quite a few times during the proof-of-concept phase, so you really don't want to waste too much time fretting about minor details in the Windows 2000 Server installation at this point.*

If you really want to start with a server that adheres to the precise settings that you intend to roll out, you should develop some kind of automation of the Windows 2000 Server installation; otherwise, you risk having to repeat the same keystrokes numerous times. You can design this automation either via some kind of cloning tool (preferably one that is used in conjunction with the Microsoft System Preparation Tool, *SysPrep*) or via the answer file parameters for unattended installation that are built into Windows 2000 Server (also known as an *unattend.txt* file). When in doubt, always opt for the answer file solution, because this alone provides a majority of the needed documentation, whereas you should view the cloning solution more as an intrinsically ad hoc solution (unless the person doing it is a hard-nosed documentation person who has an extremely well-organized working method).

> **Note**
>
> *If you already are accustomed to doing answer file solutions for Windows NT Server 4, you will find the unattended setup provided by Windows 2000 Server to be very familiar. Apart from the addition of numerous genuinely useful options and a few minor changes and corrections, it's actually exactly the same as used in the Windows NT Server 4 unattend.txt.*

Table 17.1   Issues in installing Windows 2000 Server.

Topic	Questions to Answer
Language	What is the primary language and region? Do you need additional character sets installed?
Default setup	Do you want to copy files to or from a nondefault location during the setup procedure?
Accessibility	Do you need a specialized setup regarding any of the means for system I/O?
Upgrading to NT File System	Do you want to upgrade to NTFS when installing Windows 2000 Server?
Customization of regional options	What are the preferred language settings, keyboard layout, and appearance of numbers, currency, time, and date?
Name and organization	To which individual and organization is the copy of Windows 2000 Server licensed?
Licensing mode	Per seat or per server licensing? With per seat licensing, each computer that accesses Windows 2000 Server requires a separate Client Access License (CAL), which enables a particular client computer to connect to any number of Windows 2000 Servers. With per server licensing, each concurrent connection to a server requires a separate CAL. Per seat licensing is the most commonly used licensing method for companies with more than one Windows 2000 Server. If you aren't sure which mode to use, choose per server, because you are allowed to change once from per server to per seat at no cost.
Computer name and administrator password	What is the computer name? Although it can be as many as 63 characters, pre-Windows 2000 computers recognize only the first 15 characters of the name. Also, using only Internet-standard characters in the computer name is highly recommended, to avoid interoperability troubles later. What password will be used for the built-in Administrator account that has administrative privileges for managing your computer's overall configuration?
Additional components	Do you want to install any of the multitude of additional services and tools that are part of Windows 2000 Server?
Date/time and time zone	In which time zone is your company located? Is the current date and time information on the computer's internal clock set correctly for your region?
Network settings	Do you want to start with the typical network setup, defined by Microsoft, or configure the network settings yourself?
Domain membership	Do you want to install Windows 2000 Server as a standalone server (if you choose to join a workgroup) or as a member server (if you choose to join a domain)?

Regardless of your choice of automation techniques, be keenly aware that this kind of work rightfully belongs to the pilot test phase and thus will add time to your proof-of-concept phase. Despite this added time, however, doing the automation from the outset might be a good idea, because if you need to make a lot of adjustments to the default settings presented

---

When Hosting Multiple Windows 2000 Installations on the Same Machine

If you need to install several instances of Windows 2000 (or Windows NT 4) on a machine to make a dual-boot between these installations, you must use a different computer name for each installation if the computer participates in an Active Directory domain.

---

by Windows 2000 Server's setup routine, the automation may actually save you more time in the proof-of-concept phase alone than what is spent in doing the automation.

Selecting the Right File System

Just like its predecessor, Windows 2000 Server supports both File Allocation Table (FAT) and NT File System (NTFS). Additionally, Windows 2000 Server has support for the new FAT32 file system (which is supported only on Windows 95 OSR2, Windows 98, and now Windows 2000).

FAT vs. NTFS

As with NT 4, NTFS is the recommended solution for Windows 2000, because it provides the following advantages over the FAT file system:

♦ File security

♦ Disk compression and encryption

♦ Better scalability to large drives

NTFS is available only on the Windows 2000/NT breed of OSs. In other words, only Windows 2000 and Windows NT can read directly from local NTFS volumes that reside on the local computer. However, any operating system can read from NTFS volumes when accessed over a network. Thus, you generally should use FAT or FAT32 only to sustain backward-compatibility with OSs other than Windows 2000 and Windows NT that are running on the same machine. Having a dual-boot configuration on a server system is highly unusual, so you probably won't ever have to make this trade-off. In short, use NTFS for your Windows 2000 servers.

Setting up NTFS

Your choices of how to set up NTFS on your server are limited. If you are upgrading from a previous version of NT (versions 3.51 and 4) that includes locally attached NTFS-formatted volumes, the Windows 2000 setup routine upgrades these volumes automatically to Windows 2000's native NTFS format—NTFS 5. This upgrade takes place after the graphical portion of the Setup routine, when you first restart your computer.

Also, any NTFS volumes that are removed or powered off during the installation or upgrade process are upgraded to NTFS 5 automatically when the drives are mounted. Likewise, removable media that is formatted using NTFS 4 is upgraded automatically after the installation or upgrade process or when the media is inserted and mounted in Windows 2000.NTFS 5 sports the following new major features (compared to its predecessor):

♦ *Encryption*—NTFS can automatically encrypt and decrypt file data as it is read and written to the disk.

♦ *Disk quotas*—Administrators can limit the amount of disk space that users can consume on a per-user, per-volume basis. The three quota levels are no limit, warning, and limit.

♦ *Distributed link tracking*—Helps to preserve shortcuts when files are moved from one volume to another or to another computer.

♦ *Reparse points and volume mount points*—Applications can trap open operations against objects in the file system and run their own code before returning file data. This feature is used by Windows 2000 to extend file system features. One of the applications of reparse points is *volume mount point functionality*, which enables you to redirect data read and written from a folder to another volume or physical disk. *Volume mount points* are file system objects in the Windows NT internal namespace that represent storage volumes. Mount points provide you with the option of grafting new volumes into the namespace, without requiring additional drive letters. This removes the limitation that you can create only the same number of volumes as you have drive letters—and also makes bringing data online and offline less painful.

♦ *Volume extension without rebooting*—Gives you the option of adding unallocated disk space without having to restart the computer.

Note that the volume used for storing Active Directory's SYSVOL folder (the folder used by File Replication Service to replicate files and policies between DCs) must be NTFS 5-formatted. One of the major reasons for this requirement is the new USN Journal feature in NTFS 5, which enables you to track changes made to files by way of a log or change journal—which is crucial for assessing whether or not you need to perform a replication.

Note

If you want to switch a FAT volume to NTFS 5, you need to use the command-line tool **convert** *with the proper arguments—for example,* **convert c: /FS:NTFS** *converts the C drive from FAT to NTFS.*

Storage: Basic vs. Dynamic

With NTFS 5, you have to decide which of two types of storage to use:

♦ *Basic storage*—The traditional format from prior OSs that uses partition tables. A disk initialized for basic storage is called a *basic disk*, which can hold primary partitions, extended partitions, and logical drives.

♦ *Dynamic storage*—A new type of storage introduced with Windows 2000. Dynamic storage gives you the option of extending the space on the volume without invoking a reboot. On a dynamic disk, storage is divided into volumes rather than partitions. A disk initialized for dynamic storage is called a *dynamic disk*, which is allowed to hold simple volumes, spanned volumes, mirrored volumes, striped volumes, and RAID-5 volumes. With dynamic storage, you can perform disk and volume management without having to reboot.

Stating the difference in another way, whereas a basic disk uses *partitions*—portions of the disk that function as physically separate units—a dynamic disk divides storage into *volumes*, storage units made from free space on one or more disks (which can be formatted with a file system and assigned a drive letter).

Volumes on dynamic disks can have any of the following layouts:

◆ *Simple*—Uses free space from a single disk. Can consist of a single region on a disk or multiple, concatenated regions. Can be extended within the same disk or onto additional disks. If extended across multiple disks, it becomes a *spanned volume*.

◆ *Spanned*—Made from free disk space that is linked together from multiple disks (up to a maximum of 32 disks). Can be extended onto additional disks, but can't be mirrored.

◆ *Mirrored* (also known as *RAID-1*)—Fault-tolerant volume whose data is duplicated on two physical disks—all the data on one volume is copied to another disk, to provide *data redundancy* (if one disk fails, the data can be accessed from the remaining disk). Can't be extended.

◆ *Striped* (also known as *RAID-0*)—Data is interleaved across two or more physical disks, allocated alternately and evenly to each of the physical disks. Can't be mirrored or extended.

◆ *RAID-5*—Fault-tolerant volume whose data is striped across an array of three or more disks. Parity is also striped across the disk array. If a physical disk fails, the portion of the RAID-5 volume that was on that failed disk can be re-created from the remaining data and the parity. Cannot be mirrored or extended.

Storage types are separate from the file system type; that is, a basic or dynamic disk can contain any combination of FAT, FAT32, and NTFS 5 partitions/volumes. A disk system can use any combination of storage types. However, all volumes on the same disk must use the same storage type.

Table 17.2 provides a summary of the tasks that you can perform on basic and dynamic disks. As you can see, dynamic disk storage performs quite a few more feats than basic disks (primarily because some of the functionality found in NTFS 4 isn't available for basic disks anymore). Really, the only major downside to the new dynamic disk storage type is that it renders the entire local disk unreadable to OSs other than Windows 2000.

Which type of disk storage you choose will probably depend on the application. But, undoubtedly, dynamic disk storage comes as a very welcome addition to disk management on volumes that store user data, because of the ease of adding more space. Generally, you should opt for dynamic storage for multiple-disk storage solutions—for example, if you want to create simple volumes on the disk or plan to share the disk with other disks, to create a spanned, striped, mirrored, or RAID-5 volume. Correspondingly, you should select basic storage only if you want to create partitions and logical drives on the local disk (which usually is advantageous only if you want to enable other local OSs to use the disk).

Table 17.2 Tasks that can be performed on basic disk storage and dynamic disk storage.

Task	Basic Disk Storage	Dynamic Disk Storage
Create and delete primary and extended partitions	Yes	No
Create and delete logical disks	Yes	No
Format a partition and mark it as active	Yes	No
Delete a volume set, stripe set, and mirror set	Yes	No
Break a mirror from a mirror set	Yes	No
Repair a mirror set or a stripe set	Yes	No
Upgrade a basic disk to a dynamic disk	Yes	No
Create simple, spanned, striped, mirrored, and RAID-5 volumes	No	Yes
Extend a volume across one or more disks	No	Yes
Remove a mirror from a mirrored volume or split the volume into two	No	Yes
Repair a mirrored or RAID-5 volume	No	Yes
Reactivate a missing or offline disk	No	Yes
Check disk properties	Yes	Yes
View volume and partition properties	Yes	Yes
Make and change drive-letter assignments for volumes or partitions	Yes	Yes
Create volume mount points	Yes	Yes
Set or verify disk sharing and security arrangements for a volume or partition	Yes	Yes

Planning a Dual-Boot Configuration between NT and Windows 2000

If you need to keep a working copy of Windows NT on a system on which Windows 2000 is installed, you should heed the following advice:

- Each OS should be installed on a separate drive or disk partition.

- You can't access NTFS 5 volumes from any OS other than Windows NT 4 with Service Pack 4 (SP4) or higher, because SP4 includes a new NTFS.SYS driver that supports limited interoperability between NT 4 and Windows 2000. However, Microsoft has clearly indicated that SP4 NTFS.SYS is provided for evaluation and testing purposes only. It doesn't constitute a long-term, dual-boot solution, because of several limitations of the SP4 solution, such as the following:

  - You only have read-only access to NTFS 5 volumes.

  - No support for **Chkdsk.exe** on NTFS 5 volumes.

  - Any files saved in Windows 2000 using the advanced features of NTFS 5 (reparse points, encrypted files, and the like) are not available to users of Windows NT.

  - You shouldn't use any of the previous NT disk utilities on an NTFS 5 volume; this is almost certain to corrupt the data, because of the changes brought forward in NTFS 5.

So, although you can use the SP4 functionality if you're in a pinch, you really should opt to use FAT for dual-boot configurations. Although using NTFS in a dual-boot configuration is supported on NT4 SP4, it includes too many shortcomings to be recommended.

Installing Your First DNS Server

If no DNS server is available on the network, Microsoft recommends that you install the Microsoft DNS Server on the server that is to become the DC, before you initiate the domain-promotion process. Based on my experience, I think that installing the Microsoft DNS Server as part of the domain-promotion process is easier.

If you still have doubts regarding the dynamic disk versus basic disk question, you may want to choose basic storage at first, because you can quite easily upgrade a basic disk to a dynamic disk (you can do so from the Disk Management MMC snap-in at any time). However, there's no way of downgrading it—except by doing an all-out reformat of the disk.

Readying the Server for Active Directory

After you complete the Windows 2000 Server Setup program, you have a server that is installed as either a member or a standalone server—which is a departure from Windows NT Server 4, in which you had to choose between PDC, BDC, and member/standalone server in the Setup Wizard.

This departure from the old setup principle is caused by Windows 2000 Server's capability to change server roles without requiring you to reinstall the entire OS. So, for Windows 2000 Server, you have to take an additional step if you want to promote the server to a domain controller (DC) for an Active Directory domain.

As mentioned several times in earlier chapters, DC promotion is done via the Active Directory Installation Wizard (formerly known as Domain Controller Promotion Wizard, or DCPROMO, which the executable still is named) located in the system root directory. The next section describes this Wizard in detail. Before you run the Active Directory Installation Wizard, verify base functionality discussed in Table 17.3.

Table 17.3 Pre-Active Directory Installation Wizard checklist.

Verify	More Information
Server has at least one NTFS 5 partition.	Active Directory's SYSVOL folder can't reside on anything but an NTFS 5 partition. Use the command-line tool **convert** to turn a FAT volume into an NTFS volume.
The TCP/IP protocol is correctly installed on the computer; network connectivity is established.	This is most easily done by using the IPCONFIG /ALL command (see Figure 17.1 for an example) to view all current TCP/IP network configuration values. If the IP Address, Subnet Mask, Default Gateway, DNS Servers, and Primary Domain Name (that is, the DNS Domain) fields of the applicable network adapter look correct, try out the TCP/IP functionality by using the **PING** command (for instructions, see the next section, "Testing the Basic Network Configuration").

(continued)

Table 17.3   Pre-Active Directory Installation Wizard checklist *(continued)*.

Verify	More Information
Static IP address (check when verifying the TCP/IP network configuration values).	Never use dynamic allocation of IP addresses (DHCP enabled) for a server; instead, implement static TCP/IP addresses (which, unfortunately, aren't used when you choose the typical network setup defined by Microsoft).
Necessary DNS functionality.	Except for the installation of the very first DC (and thus the creation of Active Directory), you should have the DNS functionality in place. To verify this, use the **NSLOOKUP** command (for instructions, see the section "Testing the Basic Network Configuration").

```
Windows 2000 IP Configuration

Host Name . . . . . . . . . . . . . : cphsv0002
Primary DNS Suffix . . . . . . : astonitgroup.com
Node Type. . . . . . . . . . . . . : Hybrid

IP Routing Enabled. . . . . . . : No

WINS Proxy Enabled. . . . . . : No

DNS Suffix Search List. . . . : astonitgroup.com

Ethernet adapter Local Area Connection:


Connection-specific DNS Suffix . :
Description . . . . . . . . . . . . : Compaq NC3161 Fast Ethernet NIC
Physical Address. . . . . . . . : 00-50-8B-A8-5F-4B

DHCP Enabled. . . . . . . . . . : No

IP Address. . . . . . . . . . . . : 10.1.10.12

Subnet Mask. . . . . . . . . . . : 255.255.0.0

Default Gateway. . . . . . . . : 10.1.1.254

DNS Servers. . . . . . . . . . . : 10.1.10.12
                                    10.1.10.10
Primary WINS Server . . . . : 10.1.10.10
```

Figure 17.1
An example of the results of the **IPCONFIG /ALL** command.

Note

*IPCONFIG is a command-line utility that prints out the TCP/IP-related configuration of a host. When used with the /**all** switch, it produces a detailed configuration report for all interfaces, including any configured serial ports (which are used for RAS). See Figure 17.1 for an example.*

If you experience trouble with any of the previously mentioned network functionality, note that the TCP/IP configuration (including the pointers to the DNS domain servers serving the computer and the DNS domain name of the computer) is controlled from the Network and Dial-up Connections tool. The configuration of a DNS server, on the other hand, is controlled from the DNS MMC tool (found in Programs | Administrative Tools) or the Computer Management MMC.

Testing the Basic Network Configuration

You should test for the presence of the following three core functionalities on your server before you initiate the DC promotion process:

♦ Name and address resolution

♦ Network connectivity

♦ DNS resolution

You can verify the first and second functionalities by using the **PING** command and verify the third functionality by using **NSLOOKUP**.

When you work with TCP/IP, familiarize yourself with *Packet Internet Groper (PING)*, the foremost tool for testing the base TCP/IP functionality on every kind of system. Although the **PING** command provides for testing only of the most simple IP functionality, nonetheless, it is the most important command.

The **PING** command sends an Internet Control Message Protocol (ICMP) echo request to a target name or IP address, which in turn makes easy the testing and verification that TCP/IP is installed and working properly. In the case of Windows 2000, first try pinging the server to see whether it responds, because this is the simplest test. If that succeeds, then try pinging the name. **PING** uses Windows sockets-style name-to-address resolution; therefore, if pinging by address succeeds but pinging by name fails, the problem lies in name resolution, not network connectivity.

If those two **PING**s work as intended, **PING** the default gateway (and possibly a computer connected on the same network segment and a computer connected to another network segment) to test that everything surrounding the network connectivity is in order.

The following example illustrates how a successful **PING** to another host on the same network segment looks:

```
Pinging 10.1.2.2 with 32 bytes of data:
Reply from 10.1.2.2: bytes=32 time<10ms TTL=128
Reply from 10.1.2.2: bytes=32 time<10ms TTL=128
Reply from 10.1.2.2: bytes=32 time<10ms TTL=128
Reply from 10.1.2.2: bytes=32 time<10ms TTL=128
Ping statistics for 10.1.2.2:
  Packets: Sent = 4, Received = 4, Lost = 0 (0% loss),
Approximate round trip times in milli-seconds:
  Minimum = 0ms, Maximum =  0ms, Average =  0ms
```

By default, **PING** waits one second for each response to be returned before timing out. If the remote system being pinged is across a link with a big delay, responses may take longer to be returned. Use the **-w (wait)** switch to specify a longer timeout. Computers using **IPSec** may require several seconds to set up a security association before they respond to a **PING**. You can see all the command-line options available for **PING** by typing **PING -?**.

Although most people haven't noticed, a command for DNS testing exists, **NSLOOKUP**, that is almost as ubiquitous as **PING**. **NSLOOKUP** is used to view and verify that you can obtain and resolve DNS names on a particular computer. When you start **NSLOOKUP** without providing any parameters, it shows the host name and IP address of the DNS server that services the local system and then displays a command prompt. If you type a question mark, **NSLOOKUP** shows the different commands that are available.

To look up the IP address of a host being registered in the DNS, type the host name and press Enter. **NSLOOKUP** defaults to using the DNS server that is configured for the computer on which it is running, but you can focus it on a different DNS server by typing "server *name*" (where *name* is the host name of the DNS server that you want to use for future lookups).

When you use **NSLOOKUP**, you should be aware of the domain name devolution method. If you type just a host name and then press Enter, **NSLOOKUP** appends the domain suffix of the computer (such as **yoursubdomain.yourdomain.com**) to the host name before it queries the DNS. If the name isn't found, then the domain suffix is "devolved" by one label (in this case, **yoursubdomain** is removed and the suffix becomes **yourdomain.com**) and the query is repeated. Windows 2000 computers only devolve names to the second level domain (**yourdomain.com** in this example), so if this query fails, no further attempts are made to resolve the name. If an FQDN is typed (as indicated by a trailing dot), then the DNS server is queried only for that name, and no devolution is performed. So, to look up a host name that is completely outside of your domain, you must always type an FQDN that is terminated with a trailing dot.

When testing the DNS functionality of your Windows 2000 computer, first try to look up the host name and IP address of your computer (that is, test that forward and reverse lookups are implemented correctly for the host in question). Generally, if that works as intended, you should be in the clear. If you already have an Active Directory DC running, try an

NSLOOKUP of it, too, by writing the name of that DC (**servername.yourdomain.com.**), to check whether other hosts will be able to locate it.

The following example illustrates how a successful **NSLOOKUP** of the local host name (**test.astonitgroup.com**) appears:

```
Server:   win2kdom.astonitgroup.com
Address:  10.1.2.200

Name:     test.astonitgroup.com
Address:  10.1.2.1
```

You could experience some problems regarding the **NSLOOKUP** when you are using a Microsoft DNS Server and aren't connected to the Internet. As mentioned in Chapter 7, Microsoft DNS Server comes with the name servers for the top-level domains preloaded (via the *cache.dns* file, which can be easily edited to reflect your network surroundings). The **NSLOOKUP** might force the DNS Server to look for these name servers, consequently producing an error.

Also be aware of the **NBTSTAT** command, which is used to view and verify that you are able to obtain and resolve NetBIOS names on a computer; although the need for NetBIOS is reduced dramatically in a pure Active Directory environment (a setup in which all clients, servers, and applications are set up to use DNS for name resolution), you will definitely find it very handy for environments in transition from Windows NT to Windows 2000.

Tip

*Please note that you should take the Network Connectivity Tester (**netdiag.exe**) and Domain Controller Diagnostic Tester (**dcdiag.exe**) command-line tools, included on the Windows 2000 CD-ROM as part of the Windows 2000 Support Tools, for a test drive. Both tools are discussed in Chapter 18.*

A Word on DNS

If you don't have any DNS functionality in place already, when you're ready to promote the first server in the enterprise to an Active Directory DC (thus, prior to creating the Active Directory) and you want to implement the needed DNS Server functionality on the future DC, I urge you to postpone that task until after the DC promotion process is completed. The reason for that recommendation is that if no DNS Server is available, when the server is promoted to become a DC, the Active Directory Installation Wizard (hereafter referred to as **DCPROMO**) will notice this and ask whether it should install the Microsoft DNS Service on that particular server—to save you the hassle of manually installing the DNS Service. Also, as part of the promotion process, **DCPROMO** inserts most (if not all) of the needed information in the Microsoft DNS Service. In my opinion, relying on **DCPROMO** to do most of the "dirty" DNS work is far easier than doing it yourself.

*Evidence suggests that the **DCPROMO** does in fact include a small bug that in some cases will result in having the DNS Service left in a less-than-perfect state. For this reason, some people swear to yet another variant of how to install DNS with the least effort:*

- *Install the DNS Service (found at Add/Remove Programs|Add/Remove Windows Components|Networking Services|Domain Name System (DNS)).*

- *Create the zone for your root domain at the DNS Server.*

- *Change the computer's DNS properties to point to itself.*

- *Change the name (the computer name field featured at the Control Panel|System| Network Identification tab|Properties button) of the computer to a fully qualified domain name (FQDN) in which the domain suffix matches the DNS root zone.*

*The most daring use will actually perform this delicate procedure while **DCPROMO** is running. The less daring people will perform less or none of this concurrently with **DCPROMO**.*

However, you most likely will need to do some additional configuration after the **DCPROMO** completes its work. For example, **DCPROMO** doesn't automatically create all the *reverse lookups* (mapping IP addresses back to names, as opposed to *forward lookups*, in which names are mapped to IP addresses) needed at the DNS Server, because reverse lookups aren't a strict requirement for Windows 2000 or Active Directory to function correctly. However, reverse lookup will prove very useful for translating IP addresses into computer names when you debug network problems. Furthermore, reverse lookup is required by several Internet services (including many firewalls) and TCP/IP applications.

Reverse lookup is configured separately from forward lookup. Chapter 7 discusses how to implement reverse lookup. Basically, it is done by defining one or more zones in the Reverse Lookup Zones folder for the particular IP address segment and then creating PTR records that map the IP addresses of the hosts to the DNS names of the hosts.

If you configure the DNS Server before the DC promotion process or want to use a DNS Server other than Microsoft DNS Service, remember to choose a Dynamic DNS Server and set it to allow for dynamic updates, before you run the **DCPROMO**.

Please remember to implement Windows 2000 Service Pack 1 on your computer before you start to rely on the DNS Service in questions, because SP1 eliminates a very serious memory leak in the DNS server that you might otherwise be faced with.

Setting Up Active Directory DCs

As the prior section noted, when you create a DC in Active Directory, an additional installation step is required, compared to Windows NT Server 4. This step covers the promotion of a Windows 2000 Server to an Active Directory DC, which you do via the Active Directory Installation Wizard, started by typing **DCPROMO** at the Start | Run prompt.

Separating the setup of the core server OS and the DC role enables you to promote standalone servers to the DC role without having to reinstall the OS from scratch—and, correspondingly, enables you to demote a DC to standalone or member server without having to perform the very painful task of reinstalling the OS. By imposing that separation, Microsoft has achieved a near-perfect level of flexibility regarding the Active Directory DC role for the lifetime of the Windows 2000 servers.

Note

*Actually, if you are upgrading a Windows NT PDC/BDC, **DCPROMO** is initiated after you complete the OS upgrade and reboot the server (also, when using an unattended script installation, you have the option of performing the DC promotion as part of the OS installation). Whether do everything at once or wait on running **DCPROMO** until the base installation is completed (which is my recommendation, if this is one of your first times working with Windows 2000 Server), you will face the same choices with regard to the DC promotion process (and thereafter).*

Before you begin the DC promotion process (by running **DCPROMO**), you should review Table 17.4. The actual domain promotion process is a breeze. After you initiate the Active Directory Installation Wizard (via the **DCPROMO** command), you are greeted with the window shown in Figure 17.2.

Table 17.4   Pre-DCPROMO checklist.

Task	Information You Need
Create the first DC in the enterprise (thus creating a new domain tree and forest).	Full DNS name of new Active Directory domain (check whether this domain name already is registered with the relevant Internet domain name registration authority). The down-level domain name (the NetBIOS domain name, which is used by non-Active Directory—aware clients, servers, and applications).
Create a new domain to become a child domain in a current domain tree.	Full DNS name of parent Active Directory domain.
	DNS name of new Active Directory child domain. Down-level domain name for new child domain (the NetBIOS domain name, which is used by non-Active Directory-aware clients, servers, and applications).

(continued)

Table 17.4   Pre-DCPROMO checklist *(continued).*

Task	Information You Need
	Account name and password of an Enterprise Administrator (or an Administrator for the root domain).
Create a replica DC for an existing domain.	Full DNS name of Active Directory domain.
	Account name and password of Domain Administrator (or an Enterprise Administrator).

Figure 17.2
The opening screen of the **DCPROMO** on a server that currently doesn't function as an Active Directory DC.

Your first choice is whether to join an existing domain or create a new domain (see Figure 17.3). If you have an existing Active Directory domain in place, you may want to join that domain and thus create a replica DC for that domain (in that case, choose Additional domain controller for an existing domain). If no Active Directory domain exists, choose Domain controller for a new domain instead.

Note
Please read the information given in Figure 17.3 to avoid any unfortunate events caused by the upgrade.

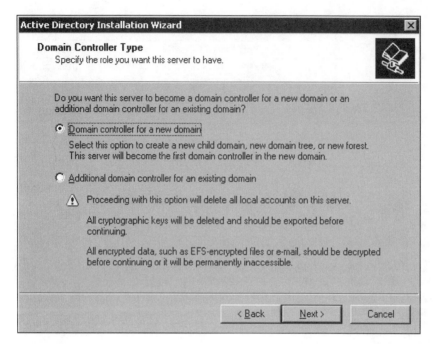

Figure 17.3
The first choice is whether to create or join an Active Directory domain.

If you elect to create a new domain, **DCPROMO** enables you to join an existing domain tree (Create a new child domain in an existing domain tree) or create a new domain tree (Create a new domain tree), as shown in Figure 17.4. A domain tree consists of multiple Windows 2000 domains combined into a logical, hierarchical organization, with parent domains and child domains. For example, if you are installing the first DC for the first domain in your company (or, more likely, for your test or pilot site), you need to choose Create a new domain tree.

If you elect to create a new domain tree, you must choose either to make the new domain tree part of an existing forest (Place this new domain tree in an existing forest) or have **DCPROMO** create a new forest (Create a new forest of domain trees), as shown in Figure 17.5. If you opt for an existing forest, then you are asked to specify the name of the forest that you want the domain tree to join.

If you elect to create a new forest, **DCPROMO** asks you to provide the fully qualified DNS name of the new domain (see Figure 17.6) and the down-level domain name (see Figure 17.7).

Note

Active Directory's security settings dictate that domain naming has to come from a central Administrator authority (a member of the Enterprise Administrators Group). If you want to avoid promoting the local administrator to be a member of the Enterprise Administrators Group, an Enterprise Administrator can add a new domain name to the

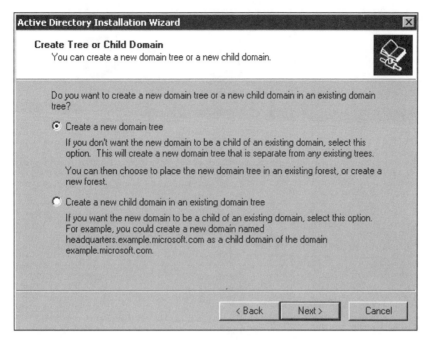

Figure 17.4
The next **DCPROMO** choice is whether to create or join an Active Directory domain tree.

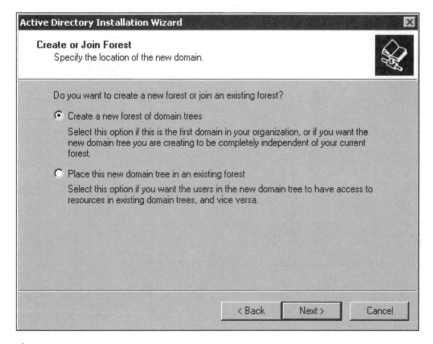

Figure 17.5
Choose whether to create or join an Active Directory forest.

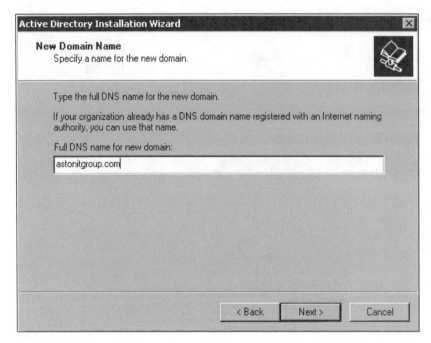

Figure 17.6
Provide the full DNS name of the new domain.

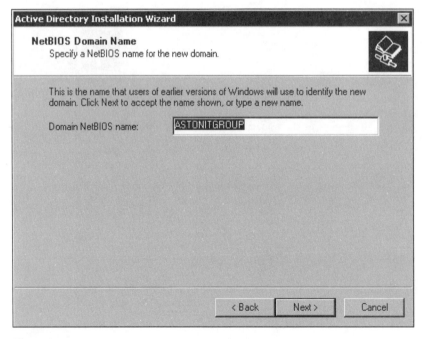

Figure 17.7
Specify the NetBIOS domain name that is needed to provide backward-compatibility.

*configuration container (in other words, add a cross-reference object) via the **ntdsutil** command-line utility, using the Domain Management option. This enables local administrators who aren't part of the Enterprise Administrators Group to create a DC (because the domain name already exists), but doesn't enable them to create a new name for the domain (because they don't have the appropriate rights).*

DCPROMO's final request is for you to specify where to store the following vital elements of Active Directory:

♦ *Active Directory database*—The default location for the database and database log files is \WINNT\NTDS (see Figure 17.8). As with Microsoft Exchange, you experience an increased performance (as well as bettering the odds for swift recoverability in case of a disaster) if you place the database and log files on separate disks—that is, physically different disks, not just different volumes. The reason for the increased performance is quite simple: Every write to the Active Directory database also results in a write to the log file—thus, two writes compete for disk access if you aren't using volumes that have physically separate disk storage.

♦ *Shared system volume (SYSVOL folder)*—The default location for the shared system volume is \WINNT\SYSVOL\Sysvol (see Figure 17.9). The SYSVOL folder can be stored only on an NTFS 5.0-formatted volume, and thus you must have at least one NTFS volume on your DC servers.

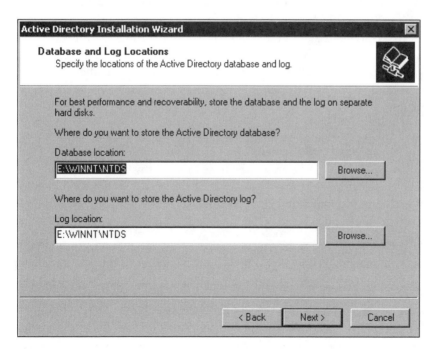

Figure 17.8
Decide where to store the Active Directory database and log files.

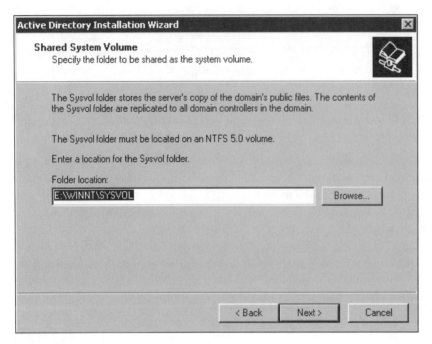

Figure 17.9
You must have an NTFS 5-formatted disk, where the SYSVOL folder can be placed.

If no DNS server is found on the network, **DCPROMO** will display a text box with a warning. After that, **DCPROMO** will ask you whether you want it to autoinstall a DNS server or you want to do it yourself (see Figure 17.10). As mentioned earlier in this chapter, I usually opt for letting **DCPROMO** perform that rather mundane task—and it usually will pan out quite fine.

After that, you will be asked whether **DCPROMO** should loosen the security a bit or not (see Figure 17.11) by implementing permissions that are compatible with pre-Windows 2000 servers. You will need to make an informed decision on this and should refer to Chapter 9 for a detailed discussion on the pros and cons of allowing this compatibility ("Beware of the Pre-Windows 2000 Compatible Access Group").

Then, you will be asked for a Directory Service Restore Mode Administrator Password (see Figure 17.12). As the name suggests, this account will be implemented in a mini-SAM database, which is used if you need to start the computer in Directory Service Restore Mode.

DCPROMO next provides a summary, so that you can confirm your choices before entering the actual DC promotion process (see Figure 17.13). Click Next to begin transforming the server into an Active Directory DC. When you click the Next button, the Configuring Active Directory dialog box appears, showing you the progress through each step of the promotion process. This process takes several minutes and shouldn't be interrupted for any reason.

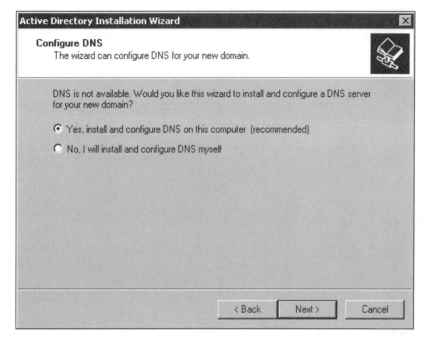

Figure 17.10
If no DNS server can be found, **DCPROMO** will prompt you for what to do. Please note that **DCPROMO** can't proceed without a DNS Server.

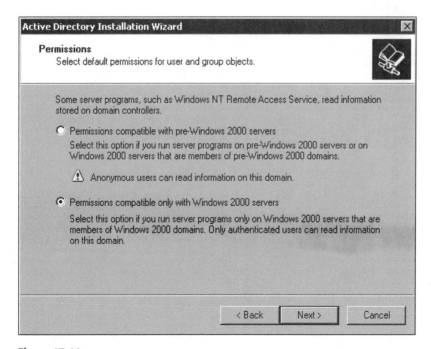

Figure 17.11
You might need to loosen the security a bit to allow your current server applications and services to continue working.

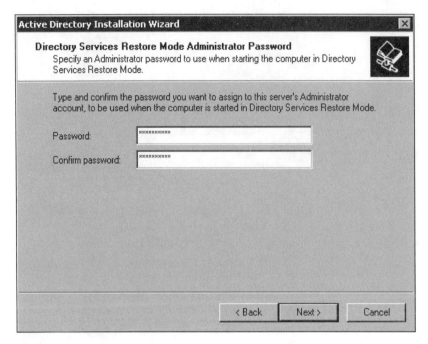

Figure 17.12
You need to specify the Administrator password that is used, if you should ever be in the unfortunate situation of having to boot this computer in Directory Services Restore Mode.

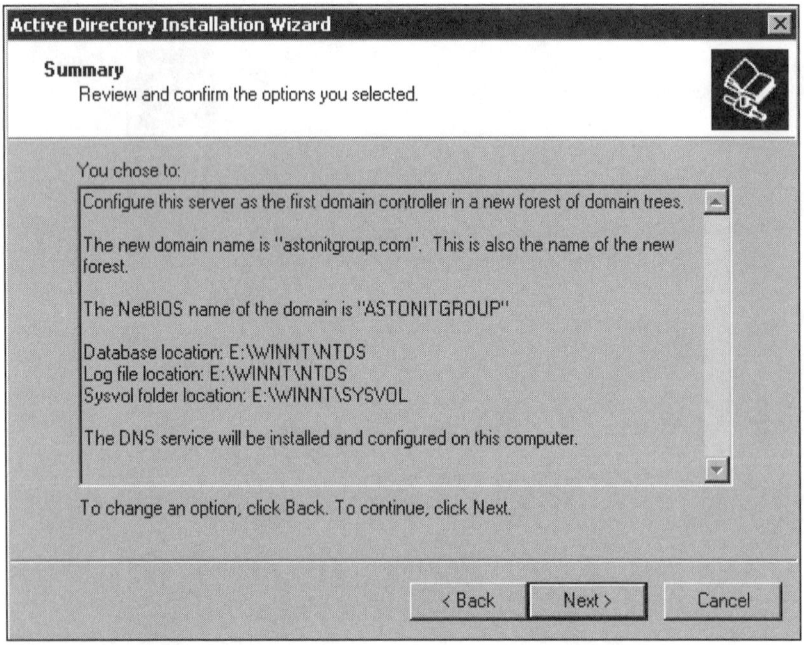

Figure 17.13
Summary of the options chosen in the Active Directory Installation Wizard.

Finally, the Active Directory is completed, and you can close **DCPROMO** by clicking Finish (see Figure 17.14). After the machine reboots, you are still able to log on using the Administrator account with the same password that you used before the machine was promoted. At this point, you can either continue to promote more servers to DCs or begin experimenting with Active Directory.

Also, as promised earlier, demoting a DC is a breeze. With **DCPROMO**, you simply have to be careful when you provide the information requested and decide what the password should be for the demoted server's Administrator account (just take a look at the work that is needed to complete the demotion, shown in Figures 17.15 through 17.18). The following steps explain how to demote a DC by using **DCPROMO**:

1. Start the Active Directory Installation Wizard by typing **DCPROMO** at the Start | Run prompt. If the server already functions as a DC, **DCPROMO** states that the only course of action is to demote the server (see Figure 17.15). Click Next.

2. **DCPROMO** asks whether the DC is the last in its domain (see Figure 17.16). If that is indeed the case, place a check in the checkbox and click Next. Remember to read the text offered in this window carefully to avoid any unwelcome surprises after the demotion has been brought to completion.

3. **DCPROMO** will ask for an account with Enterprise Administrator privileges, which is needed to remove a domain from the domain tree (see Figure 17.17). Enter the information requested and then click Next.

Figure 17.14
After the server reboots, you have an Active Directory DC implemented.

Figure 17.15
When the Active Directory Installation Wizard is instigated, it will tell you up front if the server already works as a DC and, thus, if the wizard is good only for demoting the server.

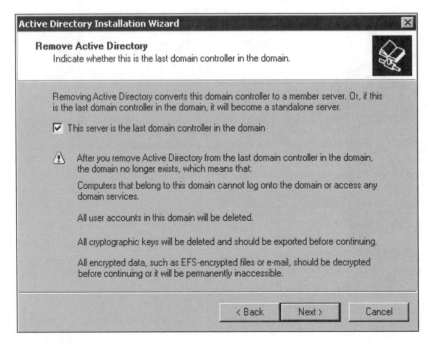

Figure 17.16
And then it will ask whether or not the DC is the last in its domain.

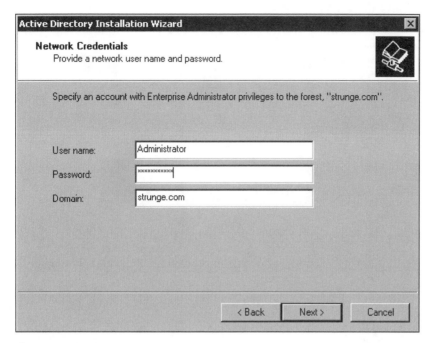

Figure 17.17
If the server is indeed the last DC in the domain, it will ask for an account with administrator privileges on the parent domain (which is needed for removing the domain from the domain tree).

4. **DCPROMO** asks for the password to be assigned to the new Administrator account on the former DC (see Figure 17.18). Enter and confirm the password and then click Next.

Remember, demoting a server removes it from both the forest configuration and DNS. Demotion removes the directory and all security principals from the server and replaces it with the default security database, Security Accounts Manager (SAM). This database is the same as the one that is installed with a new Windows 2000 Server installation—or with a Windows NT Server 4 server, for that matter. Also, demoting the last DC in a domain effectively removes that domain from existence. However, the root domain of a forest can be removed only if it is the last domain in the forest.

Completing the Final Details of DNS

After the **DCPROMO** Wizard is completed, the DNS server should be operational and fully configured, other than a few details, such as reverse lookup. To verify the DNS server's availability, perform a reverse lookup on the server itself, by running the following command: *NSLOOKUP the_server's_ip_address 127.0.0.1*. If the server is up and running, the name *localhost* will be returned.

If you experience problems with the DC functionality of the newly promoted server and the DNS server's base functionality seems to be in place, verify whether you have all the needed DNS entries registered in the applicable DNS zone (especially if you are using a third-party

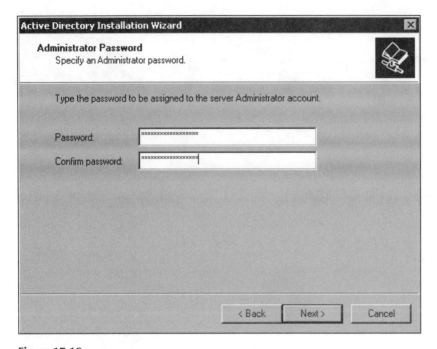

Figure 17.18
And then it will ask for the password for the new Administrator account on the former DC.

DNS server). To identify the DNS entries that should exist for your DC, look in the *netlogon.dns* file, located in WINNT\system32\config.

To use **NSLOOKUP** to verify service records registered for DCs:

1. Run **NSLOOKUP** on a command prompt.

2. Type "**set type=SRV**" to set the DNS query type to filter for Service Resource Records (SRV RRs) only.

3. Type the full SRV RR that you want to check out; doing this will send off a query for the registered SRV RR. For example, you might type "*_ldap._tcp.FQDN_for_Active_Directory_domain*" to send a query for the SRV RRs registered by the DCs that are available in the Active Directory domain.

Occasionally, you may see several timeouts reported during this procedure. This should occur only when reverse lookups haven't been configured for the domain.

Note

If you are using a DNS server that isn't capable of using DDNS, your clients won't be able to locate your DC and other Active Directory services until you have manually inserted the entries listed in the netlogon.dns file. Remember, for this to work at all, your DNS server must at least support the SRV RR type.

Don't Panic if the DNS Doesn't Work at First

I've performed many installations using the automated installation of the DNS Service from **DCPROMO**, so you really can believe me when I say that letting **DCPROMO** install and configure DNS really does work.

However, it can take a little while for the new DC to register the required SRV records. So don't panic if you:

- Find that a lot of RRs are missing when you inspect the DNS server.

- Find, when running **DCPROMO**, that what is to become the second DC can't contact the first DC in the domain that you have just installed.

This will often be because the first DC still hasn't completely registered with DNS. To correct this, you can either wait a while (typically 15 minutes) or simply run the **ipconfig /registerdns** command (which forces the DNS registration) on the first DC, and then retry the operation that failed.

Adding Member Workstations and Servers

Windows 2000 clients and servers are joined to an Active Directory domain in the same manner as in Windows NT 4 (machine accounts can be created in the domain ahead of time, or a machine account can be created when the computer initiates the join operation). That is, you join the domain from the client via the Network Identification tab in System:

1. Click the Properties button to change the membership of the computer (or choose Network ID if you prefer to use a wizard).

2. In the highlighted text box, enter the new fully qualified computer name (for example, "**testwks.astonitgroup.com**").

3. In the Member Of area, select Domain and enter the full DNS name of the domain that you want to join (for example, "**astonitgroup.com**").

4. Click OK.

5. Enter the name and password of a domain account that has sufficient privilege to join this computer to the domain. If you created a machine account for this computer ahead of time, enter the credentials of the user to whom you assigned that machine account. If you want to create a machine account on the fly, enter the credentials of a user who has Create permissions in the default Computers container. In either case, Domain Administrator credentials will be sufficient.

6. Click OK.

Remember, however, that because of the departure from the old NetBIOS protocol standards, Windows 2000 computers have to be seeded with the IP address of at least one DNS server, so that they can locate the applicable Active Directory DCs in the join process.

Down-level clients and servers (Windows NT and Windows 9x) still use WINS (or NetBIOS broadcasts) to locate DCs, so you must run WINS or use LMHOSTS files if you want those machines to participate in the domains in which no DCs are available on the local subnet.

A Brief Introduction to the Core DNS Entries

Active Directory DCs must register several DNS records to enable other Active Directory-aware clients and servers to find the services offered (including the Netlogon service). These DNS records all are prefixed with **_ldap._tcp** and are SRV RRs.

In the following descriptions of the DNS SRV records that Windows 2000 DCs can register, *Domain* refers to the FQDN specified when the Active Directory domain was created, and *Domain_Tree* refers to the FQDN of the root Active Directory domain tree:

- **_ldap._tcp.*Domain***—Allows a client to find the DCs located in the *Domain*. Each DC registers to this record.

- **_ldap._tcp.*Site.*_sites.*Domain***—Allows a client to find the DC that is part of the *Domain* and also in the *Site*. Each DC registers to the record for the appropriate site.

- **_ldap._tcp.pdc._msdcs.*Domain***—Allows a client to find the DC acting as a primary domain controller (PDC) for down-level machines using the *Domain*. Only the DC holding the PDC role for the Active Directory domain will register this record.

- **_ldap._tcp.gc._msdcs.*Domain_Tree***—Allows a client to find a GC server. Only servers serving as GCs for the *Domain_Tree* register to this record.

- **_ldap._tcp.*Site.*_sites.gc._msdcs.*Domain_Tree***—Allows a client to find a GC that is in the *Site*. Only servers serving as GCs for the Active Directory *Domain_Tree* that is in *Site* will register to this record.

- **_ldap._tcp.*DomainGUID*.domains._msdcs.*Domain_Tree***—Allows a client to find a DC in the *Domain_Tree* based on its Globally Unique Identifier (GUID).

- **_ldap._tcp.dc._msdcs.*Domain***—Allows a client to find a DC in the *Domain* that holds a modifiable copy of Active Directory in the *Domain*.

- **_ldap._tcp.*Site.*_sites.dc._msdcs.*Domain***—Allows a client to find a DC that holds a modifiable copy of Active Directory in the *Domain* and in the *Site*.

One exception exists to the rule of using only SRV RRs for registering Active Directory services. The Netlogon service also registers the following DNS A (Host) record:

- *Domain*—Allows a non-Windows 2000 client to find a DC in the *Domain* via a normal A (Host) record lookup.

You are allowed to disable the publishing of A RRs of DCs in DNS, because lookup by Active Directory-aware clients and servers is done via the SRV RRs.

If you have any legacy NetBIOS applications or machines in your environment, you might also want to implement the proprietary WINS Lookup Integration feature of Microsoft DNS Service. This feature instructs the name server to use WINS to look up any requests for hosts in the root zone that aren't registered in the DNS zone database. You will usually want to use the proprietary WINS lookup feature only if you don't want to use WINS on your Windows 2000 machines or if you have non-Microsoft-based TCP/IP clients that need to be able to resolve NetBIOS host names to IP addresses. You should refer to Chapter 7 for more information on WINS.

Likewise, after you promote the first server to an Active Directory DC, you might want to take advantage of a certain Active Directory feature. This first Active Directory application might be to move the DNS zone files into the Active Directory store (the so-called Active Directory-integrated feature)—an operation that obviously can't be done until the first Active Directory DC (and Active Directory) is created.

Using Active Directory-Integrated DNS

If you are using the DNS Service that is supplied with Windows 2000 Server, you can configure Microsoft's proprietary Active Directory-integrated DNS feature, which enables you to store DNS zone data in Active Directory instead of in files on the disk. Active Directory-integrated zones are replicated among Active Directory DCs and thus can be loaded by any DNS server that is running on a DC for that domain. This eliminates the need to handle the DNS zone files separately and coin a separate DNS replication structure. Also, using Active Directory-integrated zones provides DNS with the benefit of Active Directory's multi-master dynamic update (instead of using the single-master operation used by standard DNS), and includes some other "minor" features, such as relieving you of having to add the applicable zones manually to each Active Directory DC—the DNS servers automatically load zones that are stored in the applicable Active Directory domain.

In short, if you are using a "pure" Windows 2000 Server environment with regard to DNS servers, I recommend that you use Microsoft's proprietary Active Directory-integration feature (please see Chapter 7 for more details on the Active Directory-integrated DNS feature).

To configure an Active Directory-integrated DNS zone rather than a standard DNS zone, follow these instructions (see Figure 17.19):

1. Point to the specific DNS zone (in the DNS Server that is acting as primary name server for the zone).

2. Right-click and choose Properties from the Context menu.

3. On the General tab of the Properties dialog box, click the Change button, which presents the Change Zone Type dialog box.

4. Change the zone type to Active Directory-integrated and click OK.

Depending on the size of the zone, the conversion may take a few minutes to finish. You need to repeat this process for each forward lookup zone and reverse lookup zone that you want to store in Active Directory. You should do this conversion for all the forward lookup zones and reverse lookup zones, and for the root zone.

If you use Active Directory-integrated DNS, you also gain access to the Secure Dynamic Update feature. When you use this feature, only the computers that you specify are allowed to make new entries or modify existing entries in a zone.

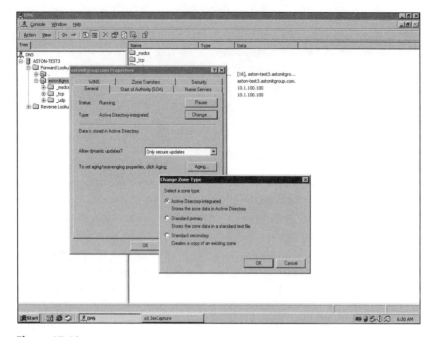

Figure 17.19
How to go from a standard DNS setup to using Active Directory as the store for one or more DNS zones.

By default, all authenticated computers in a forest can make new entries in a zone and change existing entries. Secure Dynamic Update enables you to introduce ACL control of RRs and thus prevent unauthorized computers from adding RRs or overwriting existing RRs. With the help of the Secure Dynamic Update feature, you can ensure that only the machine that registered an RR can modify it, thus preventing the name theft that occurs when another computer tries to register the name of a computer that is currently down or offline.

Warning

You should be careful as to which RRs you've got stored in the applicable zone (possibly testing things out in the lab first). Unless you do that, you might find yourself confronted with all kinds of problems with your DNS.

You can enable Secure Dynamic Update on as many or as few Active Directory-integrated zones as you want, as follows (see Figure 17.20):

1. Point to the specific Active Directory-integrated zone.

2. Right-click, then choose Properties from the Context menu.

3. On the General tab of the Properties dialog box, select Only Secure Updates from the Dynamic Update drop-down list.

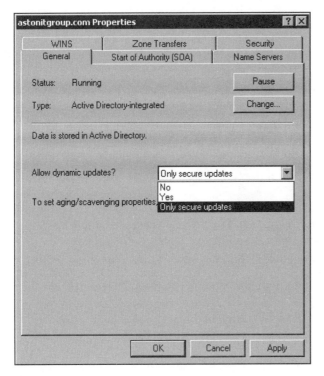

Figure 17.20
Enabling secure dynamic updates on an Active Directory-integrated zone.

Completing the Final Details of Active Directory

After you check the DNS functionality, you may want to review the results of the Active Directory promotion process. You can do so by looking at the log files (found in \WINNT\DEBUG) that list the results of each step in the installation procedure.

Although you shouldn't need to delve deep into these log files (unless the promotion process went haywire, which should be blatantly clear from **DCPROMO**'s completion message), you may want to do it out of curiosity—which incidentally may enhance your understanding of the Active Directory internals, because these log files actually are somewhat readable.

You also may want to check that the DHCP Server functionality is in place on the server, because the role that DHCP plays for the base functionality of Active Directory is even more important than it was for Windows NT Server. Used in the default setup, the DHCP Server will register the PTR record in the DNS server on behalf of each client (the A RR is still registered by the client) and make sure that both the A and PTR records are deleted upon lease expiration. For legacy clients, the DHCP Server registers both the A and PTR records and performs any necessary cleanup action.

Perhaps the most important configuration detail regarding DHCP is that, as a defense against "rogue" DHCP Servers (unauthorized providers of the DHCP Service), you have to specify which DHCP Servers are allowed by Active Directory. If you forget to configure this authorization, it will look like the DHCP Server is at fault from the client's point of view because the DHCP Server doesn't answer the request for a DHCP address. Therefore, you should always remember to check this authorization before you start to do any other troubleshooting on your DHCP Server setup. I've faced this error more than a few times.

Note

Actually, DHCP authorization is one of the worst things to forget, because it is darned hard to locate the source of the problem when coming from a Windows NT 4 environment—I've seen many people spend more than a day's work trying to figure out why the DHCP functionality wasn't working, despite everything looking right. What makes this error even more frustrating is that performing the needed authorizing of a DHCP Server actually is very easy. You simply start DHCP Manager, select the computer operating as a DHCP Server that you want to have added as an authorized server in Active Directory, and then choose Authorize on the shortcut menu. This action has to be done by someone with the necessary administrative privileges (full rights to the DHCP Server container object, which is stored in the Active Directory Configuration container). From the outset, the only persons with those privileges are the members of the Enterprise Admins Group, but the right can be delegated to others.

Finally, if you aren't using any down-level DCs in your domain (NT 3.51/4-based BDCs) and won't be needing any, you should consider moving to Active Directory's native mode.

When **DCPROMO** is creating a new Active Directory domain, it always makes it a mixed mode domain, because native mode domains can only include Windows 2000 DCs. But, if you are creating a Windows 2000-only domain, you might as well take immediate advantage of the additional functionality offered by native mode.

Follow these steps to change your Active Directory domain to native mode (see Figure 17.21):

1. Point to the specific Active Directory domain (by using either the Active Directory Users and Computers tool or the Active Directory Domains and Trusts tool).

2. Right-click, then choose Properties from the Context menu.

Setting up a DHCP Server

Often, the DC is used to provide the DHCP Service to clients and other servers. This is done by installing the Microsoft DHCP Service, which you can find in the Optional Networking Components Group, included among the many optional Windows components (choose Settings|Control Panel|Add/Remove Programs|Add/Remove Windows Components).

Thereafter, the configuration is straightforward compared to Windows NT 4. Microsoft includes some improved wizards that make configuring the basics of the DHCP scopes a breeze.

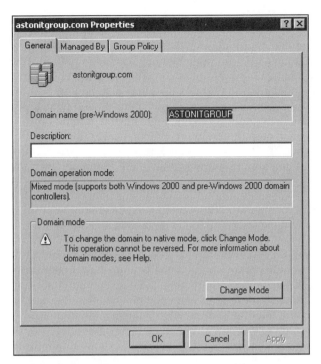

Figure 17.21
You can change from operating your Active Directory domain in mixed mode to native mode in a few seconds. However, you could experience a time lag caused by the need to replicate the change to all other DCs in the domain.

3. On the General tab of the Properties dialog box, click the Change Mode button.

Warning

Going into native mode is a one-way operation: After you choose native mode, you can't revert to mixed mode. So, make sure that you want to make this change before you complete it.

Administering Active Directory

After you work a bit with Windows 2000 Server—and Active Directory in particular—you'll discover four crucial tools on the Administrative Tools menu (choose Start | Programs | Administrative Tools). Listed in order of importance, these four tools are the following:

♦ *Active Directory Users and Computers*—The main management console used to administer and publish information in Active Directory. It enables you to do such tasks as add, delete, and move users, computer accounts, and groups within Active Directory OUs; modify specific properties, such as the security properties of user and computer accounts and the properties of groups, OUs, and network resources; and publish the available network resources, such as printers and shared folders.

- *Computer Management*—Helps you to manage local or remote computers, using a single, consolidated desktop tool that combines several of the core administrative utilities, such as Device Manager, Disk Management, DNS, Event Viewer, Services, and Shared Folders.

- *Active Directory Domains and Trusts*—Provides a graphical view of all the domain tree hierarchies in the forest. With this tool, you can request to manage a domain that is participating in the forest, manage trust relationships between domains, configure the mode of operation for each domain (native or mixed mode), and configure alternative User Principal Name (UPN) suffixes to be used in the forest.

- *Active Directory Sites and Services Manager*—Used to administer sites and replication between sites, as well as the configuration of network services and the replication properties of the configuration naming context.

This section presents recipes for creating the fundamental Active Directory objects, and so the Active Directory Users and Computers tool is used almost exclusively (except in one instance in which the Computer Management tool is used). So, you have to wait until the next chapter to get a real feeling for the three other tools.

As mentioned in Chapter 2, all the administrative tools available in Windows 2000 are Microsoft Management Console (MMC) snap-ins, which is a new management interface. MMC is essentially an empty shell into which so-called snap-in modules are plugged, to provide whatever specific management information and controls the user desires. Without snap-ins, the MMC console provides no functionality worth mentioning.

This new interface means that all the tools have gotten a common look and feel, because all the snap-ins have to be loaded into the same console. Further, it means that you can mix and match the available MMC snap-ins to create one or more MMCs that cover the needs of your job function (or combine the tools needed to perform certain tasks). So the tools available on the Administrative Tools menu really refer to the preconfigured MMCs (one or more MMC snap-ins shelved together) that Microsoft has provided for you.

Before you review the details on how to perform the most common administrative chores, you should understand a few key definitions regarding the MMC console:

- *Scope pane*—The left console window, which shows all the container objects.

A Few Words on the Computer Management Tool

Unlike Windows NT, Windows 2000 doesn't include a Devices tool to start and stop devices in the Control Panel. Instead, you can view and manage all hardware and software device drivers from the Device Manager, which is a snap-in that is included in the Computer Management tool (here, you find it in the System Tools folder). Device Manager enables you to troubleshoot devices, disable or uninstall devices, view driver details, update drivers, and view or change resources assigned to devices.

The Disk Management utility also is part of the Computer Management tool. Disk Management enables you to create partitions or volumes and initialize or upgrade disks—on the local system as well as on any remote system that runs NT 4 or Windows 2000. Likewise, all other kinds of disk management (such as Disk Defragmentation and Disk Quotas) can be initiated from Disk Management.

◆ *Results pane*—The right console window, which shows all the objects contained within the selected object in the scope pane.

◆ *Console toolbar*—The toolbar above the scope and results panes, which shows the standard options of an MMC console.

◆ *Snap-In toolbar*—The toolbar above the results pane on the right side, which shows the options associated with the MMC snap-in currently in use.

Creating an OU

When the first Active Directory domain is created, four OUs are automatically created:

◆ *Users*—The default location for domain user objects and the predefined groups in the domain.

◆ *Computers*—The default location for the client computer objects in the domain.

◆ *Domain Controllers*—The default location for DC objects in the domain.

◆ *Built-in*—The default location for local group objects.

Three of those OUs—Built-in, Computers, and Users—belong to a special category of OUs (sometimes referred to as containers by Microsoft) that can't be moved or deleted. Thus, you really shouldn't think of them as being OUs.

If you want to add a new plain vanilla OU to the domain, open the Active Directory Users and Computers tool and follow these steps (see Figure 17.22):

1. Right-click the domain object that is to become the parent of the new OU.

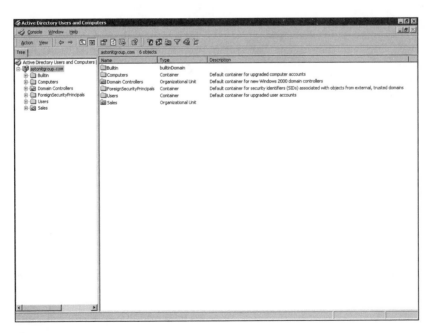

Figure 17.22
The Active Directory Users and Computers tool, after the Sales OU has been added to the
astonitgroup.com domain.

2. Either select New and click Organizational Unit or use the New Organizational Unit toolbar button.

3. Type the name of your new OU (for example, Sales, as in Figure 17.22).

Creating a User

To create a new user account, open the Active Directory Users and Computers MMC tool and follow these steps (see Figures 17.23, 17.24, and 17.25):

1. Right-click the OU in which the user should reside, click New, and then click User; or click the New User toolbar button.

2. Enter the First name, Last name, Full name, User logon name, and User logon name (pre-Windows 2000), as shown in Figure 17.23. You should turn to Chapter 9 for more information on the syntax and semantics of these fields. Click Next.

3. Type the password, confirm the password, and then select the appropriate account options by checking the corresponding checkbox(es) (see Figure 17.24).

Note that you have a lot of additional user account options available for each user, which you can fill out by doing the following (see Figure 17.26):

1. Right-click the user object and click Properties.

2. Add more information about the user in the applicable tabs of the Properties dialog box for the user object.

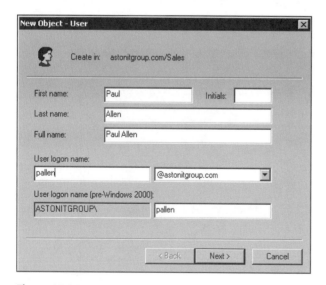

Figure 17.23
For creating the user Paul Allen in Sales OU, you will first have to fill in the appropriate information.

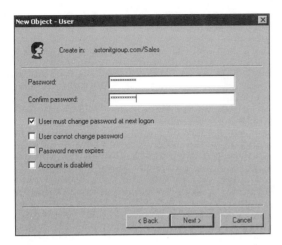

Figure 17.24
And for completing the creation of the user, you will have to provide a password and select the applicable account options.

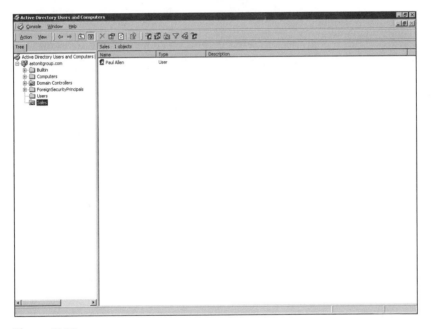

Figure 17.25
And then the user is ready for use in the Sales OU.

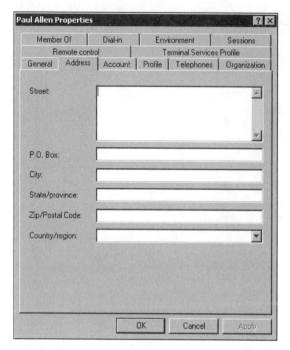

Figure 17.26
Various additional user account options are available. Remember, too, that you can add any other options that you need by extending the schema (turn to Chapter 19 for more details).

Creating a Computer Object

A computer object is created automatically when a computer joins a domain. You can also create a computer object in advance of the computer's joining a domain by following these steps (see Figure 17.27) in the Active Directory Users and Computers MMC:

1. Right-click the OU in which the computer object should be created, click New, and then click Computer.

2. In the Computer name text box, type the computer's FQDN DNS name and in the Computer name (pre-Windows 2000) text box, type the computer's NetBIOS name. You're also able to specify a user or group that is allowed to join the computer to the domain and to specify whether or not the computer can be running OSs other than Windows 2000.

After the computer has been put online, you may want to manage it remotely; for example, so you can diagnose services running on it, look at the event viewer, and so forth. To configure the computer for remote management, follow these steps in the Active Directory Users and Computers MMC after the computer has joined the domain:

1. Right-click the computer object and click Manage at the Context menu.

2. The Computer Management snap-in will start for the selected computer.

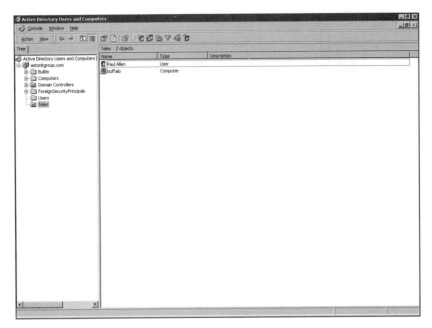

Figure 17.27
The Active Directory Users and Computers tool, after the buffalo computer object has been added
to the Sales OU in the **astonitgroup.com** domain.

Creating a Group

To create a new group, open the Active Directory Users and Computers tool and do the
following (see Figures 17.28 and 17.29):

1. Right-click the OU in which the group object should be created, click New, and then
   click Group; or click the Create New Group button on the toolbar.

2. In the New Object-Group dialog box, enter the name of the new group, enter the pre-
   Windows 2000 name of the new group, and then select the Group type (indicates whether
   the group can be used to assign permissions to other network resources, such as files and
   printers) and the Group scope (determines the visibility of the group and what type of
   objects may be contained within the group as shown in Figure 17.28). For more information on the syntax and semantics of these fields, turn to Chapter 9.

3. Click OK.

Note that the particular set of Group scope choices available depends on whether the Active Directory domain is running in mixed mode or native mode. Additionally, if you are
running in native mode, you have the option of using nested groups, which are easier to
manage and thus can reduce administrative overhead. You implement this option via the
Member Of and Members tabs of the specific group. Likewise, you can add a user to a group
by clicking the Members tab of the group.

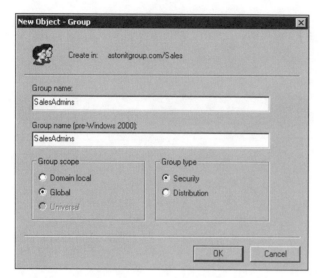

Figure 17.28
To create the Global Group SalesAdmins in Sales OU, you first have to fill in the New Object-
Group dialog box.

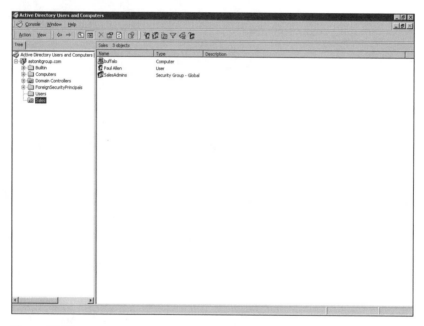

Figure 17.29
And then the new group is ready for use in the Sales OU.

Publishing Network Resources

Of paramount importance, you *must* understand that you need to publish your network resources (shared folders and printers) in Active Directory—so users can retrieve needed resources in a more user-friendly way than in Windows NT Server's case, and turn off the legacy NetBIOS protocol. If you remove the NetBIOS protocol without publishing the resources in Active Directory, users simply won't have any easy way to locate the resources.

Any shared network folder, including a Distributed File System (DFS) folder, can be published in Active Directory. However, creating a shared folder object on a Windows 2000 Server doesn't automatically share the folder: You first must share the folder, and then you can publish it in the directory.

You share a folder in exactly the same way as in Windows NT Server 4:

1. Use Windows NT Explorer, the command line, or some other file viewer to create a new folder on one of your disk volumes.

2. In Windows Explorer or My Computer, right-click the folder name, click Properties, click the Sharing tab, and then click Shared As.

3. In the Share Name text box, type the name of this share.

You publish the shared folder in Active Directory by opening the Active Directory Users and Computers MMC and following these steps (see Figures 17.30 and 17.31):

1. Right-click the OU in which the shared folder object should be created, then click New | Shared Folder.

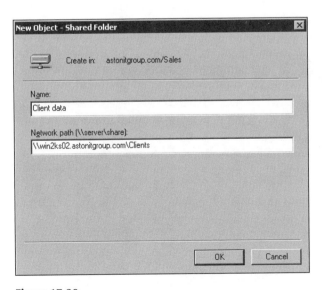

Figure 17.30
When publishing the share, this is what you specify if your shared folder is named Client data and is located on the **win2ks02.astonitgroup.com** server.

A Guide to Publishing Non-Windows 2000 Printers

Active Directory allows you to publish printers shared by systems other than Windows 2000. The optimum way to achieve this is to use the ***pubprn*** script (located in the system32 directory), which publishes all the shared printers on a given server.

The syntax for ***pubprn*** is **cscript pubprn.vbs *server dspath [trace]***.

So, for example, if you want to publish all the printers on the server with the UNC path of \\prnsrv1 and you want to have all the printers placed in the Sales OU of the **astonitgroup.com** domain, you would write

```
Cscript pubprn.vbs prnsrv1 "LDAP://ou=sales,dc=astonitgroup,dc=com"
```

If you run *pubprn* again, it will update (rather than overwrite) existing printers. Be advised, however, that the script only registers the following subset of the printer attributes: Location, Model, Comment, and UNC Path. You can add other attributes by using the Active Directory Users and Computers snap-in.

The only immediate alternative to utilizing the ***pubprn*** script is as follows:

1. Open the Active Directory Users and Computers tool and right-click the OU in which the printer object should be created.

2. Click New, then click Printer.

3. In the Name field, type the name that you want the printer to be known by in Active Directory.

4. In the UNC Path Name field, type the path to the printer.

Although defining the printer via the Active Directory Users and Computers tool might look a bit easier, it really isn't, provided that you have more than one printer attached to a server or want to avoid manually typing all the relevant attributes of the printer.

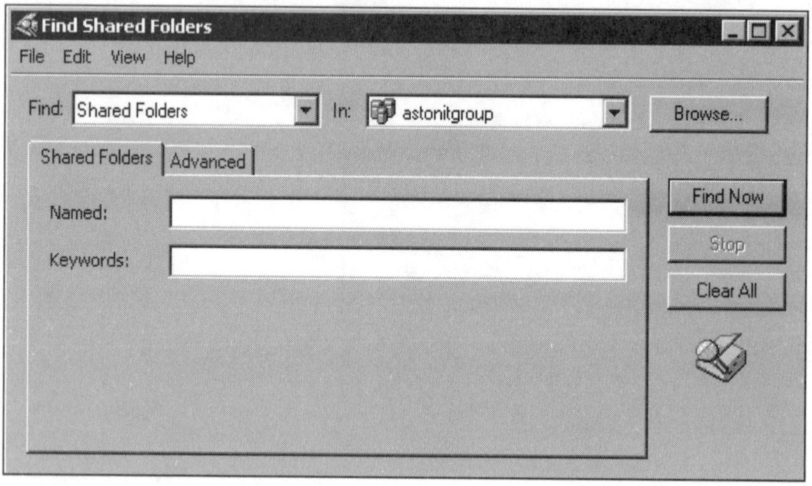

Figure 17.31
User now will be able to locate the shared folder when browsing or searching the directory, as well as from the usual tools (for example, using Network Neighborhood, which has been renamed My Network Places in the transition to Windows 2000).

2. In the Name text box of the New Object-Shared Folder dialog box, type the name of the shared folder as shown in Figure 17.30.

3. In the Network path text box, type the UNC name of the share.

As is the case for shared folders, you need to publish the printers in Active Directory. In all but the most special cases, you should definitely want to publish all of your available network printers in Active Directory, because this enables users to search for printers with a given set of properties, browse for printers, submit jobs to those printers, and even install the needed printer drivers directly from the server after locating the printer in Active Directory.

A printer shared by a computer running Windows 2000 is published by using the Sharing tab of the printer's Properties dialog box (see Figure 17.32). By default, the List in the Directory option is enabled (which means that the shared printer will be published in Active Directory, by default).

Note
Although you can search for the printer and its properties (see Figure 17.33), the printer object is not immediately available in the Active Directory Users and Computers tool (unlike other directory objects). It is published as part of the computer object to which it is attached.

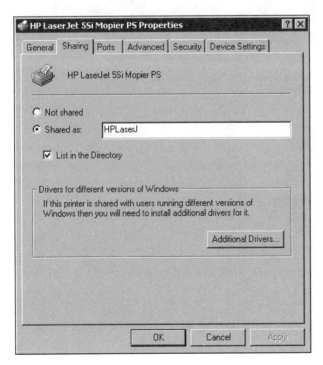

Figure 17.32
Use the Sharing tab to choose whether or not your printer should be published in Active Directory.

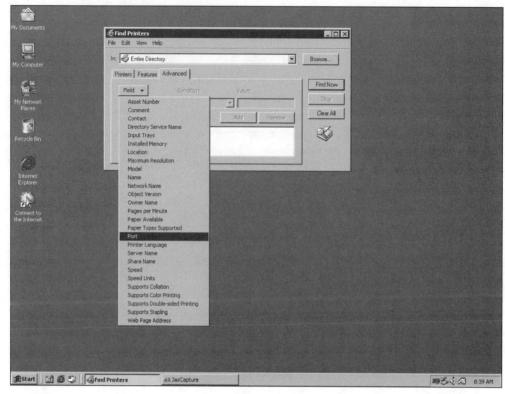

Figure 17.33
The default Active Directory schema provides a multitude of options for specifying all the relevant properties of each printer.

Moving, Renaming, and Deleting Objects

Just about any Active Directory object can be renamed or deleted, and most objects can be moved to different containers. To move an object, right-click the object, then click Move, which gives you access to a directory browser that enables you to select the destination container for the object that you are moving.

When you move objects between OUs, the permissions work like this:

♦ The object keeps the current permissions that have been directly set to the object.

♦ The OU-based permissions are changed to the ones that apply to the new OU.

The tasks of deleting and renaming an object are just as intuitive as moving an object, and thus are not set out here.

Finding Specific Objects

Active Directory offers a very powerful search functionality, called Search, which equals the Find function found in the earlier generations of Windows. Because of its power, searching for specific objects that meet a certain criteria by using this search feature often will prove much more efficient than browsing the list of objects in the results pane.

Follow these steps to initiate a search:

1. Select the OU that you want to search.

2. Open the Find dialog box, either by clicking the Find toolbar button or by right-clicking the OU and selecting Find from the Context menu.

3. Fill in the applicable information in the Find dialog box (see Figure 17.34).

So Far, So Good

By following this chapter's advice, you should be able to configure a Windows 2000 Server from the ground up, create an Active Directory, and populate the Active Directory with the most common objects. You now are prepared to start the real-life testing of the Active Directory design that you have created.

The next three chapters provide information on the more advanced (but still somewhat common) Active Directory subjects, culminating with some early advice on what to expect from your Active Directory implementation with regard to database size and replication load.

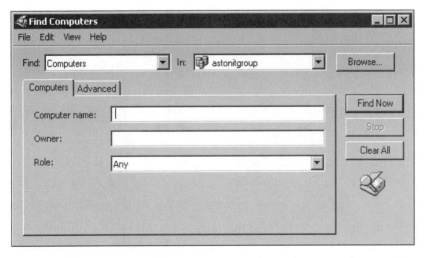

Figure 17.34
Active Directory enables you to search for specific objects and properties in a subset of the namespace. You'll discover that the Windows 2000 Server tools take advantage of that functionality in many ways.

Chapter 18

Advanced Active Directory Implementation Topics

This chapter provides an introduction to some of the more advanced implementation topics that usually are encountered in Active Directory's "proof of concept" phase—and almost certainly are encountered in the pilot phase.

These topics include the following:

♦ Setting up sites and the replication structure.

♦ Tapping into the full potential of the OUs to achieve administrative delegation and implement policies (rather than simply imposing a hierarchical structure on the directory objects).

♦ Providing for backup (and possibly the restore) of Active Directory.

♦ Understanding the decisions faced on the domain and forest levels, including how to plan the FSMO roles.

♦ Using the Support Tools utilities to achieve a better understanding of Active Directory's structures and operation and your troubleshooting options.

As this list suggests, the content of this chapter represents a variety of different subjects, some of which may not be immediately relevant to your particular situation. But, you are encouraged to take a quick tour of this chapter, because it includes some tips and tricks that may prove very valuable when you are faced with the situation covered.

Advanced Options

Before venturing into the really advanced Active Directory implementation topics, you should take a moment to appreciate some of the lower-profile features of the MMC console tools, which allow you to optimize the management of the contents of the Active Directory database. One of these features, the Filtering Options dialog box, enables you to restrict the types of objects returned to the snap-in, thus enabling you to manage Active Directory more efficiently. For example, you can choose to view only users and groups, or you may want to create a more complex filter. In addition, the Filtering Options dialog box enables you to restrict the number of objects displayed in the results pane.

The following steps describe how to use the Filtering Options dialog box to configure this limit (see Figure 18.1):

1. Invoke the Filtering Options dialog box either by selecting the Filter toolbar button or by choosing View | Filter Options.

2. Select the applicable filter condition (for example, Show Only The Following Types Of Objects) by selecting one of the radio buttons.

3. Select the types of objects that you want to show (such as Users and Groups) by placing a checkmark in the corresponding checkboxes.

Note

If you're charged with administering a very large domain, you should note that Active Directory Users and Computers will show only up to 10,000 objects inside each container. But you can increase that number by using the Filtering Options dialog box.

Note also that, by default, most of the administrative tools hide information from you. This is a very sensible design, because the hidden information includes the items you usually don't need to access.

For example, if you choose Advanced Features in the shortcut menu in the Active Directory Users and Computers MMC tool (see Figure 18.2), a handful of previously unseen

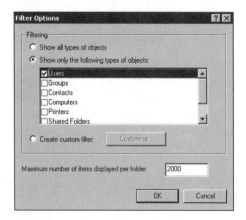

Figure 18.1
Decide which condition must be met for the object to be shown in the results pane. You can do just about any kind of customization via the Filtering Options feature.

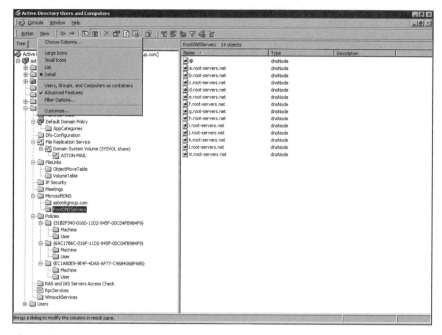

Figure 18.2
The default for most of the snap-ins hides some information from you until you check the Advanced Features choice. This shows the Active Directory Users and Computers tool with Advanced Features enabled.

containers are unveiled. One of the very interesting new folders is System, which includes information on many subjects, including a File Replication Service container that provides a way to view the progress of the FRS replication of the SYSVOL. And if you're running Active Directory-integrated DDNS, there's a MicrosoftDNS container that allows you to view (and manage) all the DNS RRs stored in the domain.

Also note the LostAndFound container, which shows objects that haven't been included in the directory due to the replication procedure being unable to determine where to place them (this could happen, for example, if you create an object at one DC while the object's container is being deleted at another DC). Examine this container occasionally to determine whether any directory objects are missing—and decide whether they should be moved or deleted.

Creating OUs for Administrative Delegation and Policies

In addition to using OUs to create a logical structure that makes navigating the company's organizational structure easier for administrators and end users, you can use OUs for these other purposes:

- To delegate administration
- To apply policies

Chapter 10 covers the base functionality (including design considerations) of OUs quite extensively, so this section shows only a few examples of the immense possibilities of using OUs to delegate administration and apply group policies.

Administrative Delegation

By default, only Administrators have the authority to join computers to a domain, because computers are security principals, just like users. However, in many cases, you may want to allow certain (or all) authenticated users to join computers to the domain without needing an administrator to preconfigure anything.

Note

Before you venture into delegating the rights to join computers to the domain, consider the security impact, because computers can be assigned permissions and rights to resources.

The following are the steps to take to enable some users or groups to join computers to a domain:

1. Within the Active Directory Users and Computers MMC tool, start the Delegation Of Control Wizard by right-clicking the Computers container and choosing Delegate Control (see Figure 18.3).

2. Skip over the Welcome page by clicking Next.

Figure 18.3
Initiating the Delegation of Control Wizard.

3. Select the security principals—typically groups—to which you want control to be delegated. Figure 18.4 shows Users being selected, to provide all members of the Users group with the option to join computers to the domain. Click Next.

4. On the Active Directory Object Type page, you can either choose the default setting (This folder, existing objects in this folder, and creation of new objects in this folder) or move the radio button to the "Only the following objects in the folder" option and choose Computer Objects (see Figure 18.5). Here, I've chosen the default settings, which will provide control on the Computers container itself. For future reference, note the many and very subtle possibilities that you are presented with here on this page. Click Next.

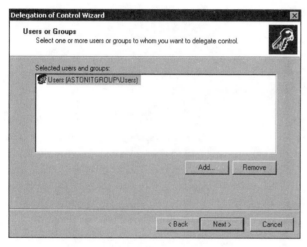

Figure 18.4
Here you specify the users and/or groups that are to be included.

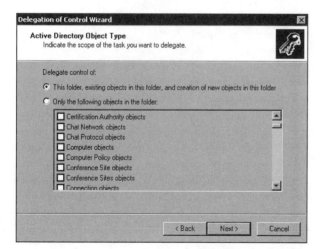

Figure 18.5
Accept the default settings for the directory objects you're delegating control to.

5. On the Permissions page, you should check the Creation/Deletion Of Specific Child Objects and check the "Create Computer Objects" and "Delete Computer Objects" options (see Figure 18.6). Click Next.

6. Click Finish to accept the choices you made (see Figure 18.7).

You should note that the "join computer" delegation of administration example actually can be done even better. Because so many people were discussing the easiest way to allow for others to join computers to the domain, Microsoft introduced a Group Policy covering this need just before the release of Windows 2000. So if you want to allow other users to join

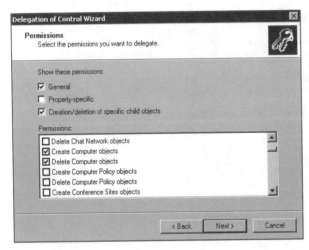

Figure 18.6
Choosing the access rights that are to be delegated to the directory objects, namely, the right to create and delete computer objects.

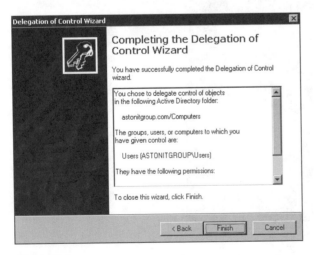

Figure 18.7
Finally, the choices are summarized, and you can click Finish to implement them.

Filter Options on the Permissions Page

Take time to appreciate the difference between the three options presented in the Delegation of Control Wizard's Permissions page when selecting access rights:

- *General*—Provides you with the general permission options used on directory objects (e.g., Full Control, Create All Child Objects, and Write All Properties).

- *Property-specific*—Provides you with all the permission options that can be assigned to the attributes of the directory objects covered by the delegation of administration rule.

- *Creation/deletion of specific child objects*—Provides you with the permission options to create or delete all the child objects that apply to the delegation of administration rule.

---

computers to the domain, you might want to follow these steps instead of the ones provided in the delegation of access scenario:

Windows 2000 Server allows users the ability to add their own computers to the domain by simply modifying the Group Policy Object for the Domain Controllers Organizational Unit. Here are the steps involved in making this change in this manner:

1. Within the Active Directory Users and Computers MMC tool, right-click the Domain Controllers OU, select Properties, select the Group Policy tab, select the Default Domain Controllers Policy object, and then click Edit.

2. Navigate to the Computer Configuration | Windows Settings | Security Settings | User Right Assignment node and double-click on the Add workstations to domain object.

3. Now you are able to add domain users and groups as you see fit to provide them the ability to create new workstations on the domain in the dialog box.

Group Policies

Group Policies enable an administrator to manage the networked computers and users by applying configuration settings inside the following areas:

- *Administrative Templates*—Allow you to configure Registry-based policies that configure the application settings, desktop appearance, and behavior of system services.

- *Security*—Decide which security rules apply inside the local computer, in the domain, and on the network.

- *Software Installation*—Allow you to perform management of software installation, updates, and removal from a central point.

- *Scripts*—Select the scripts that execute when a computer starts and shuts down and when a user logs on and logs off.

- *Folder Redirection*—Redirect some of the users' folders to a network location.

You use the Group Policy MMC snap-in and its extensions to define Group Policy requirements (which are called Group Policy Objects, GPOs) to be enforced for users and computers.

In the first example scenario, suppose that you want to remove the Run menu from the Start menu and redirect the Desktop to the Public folder on the local network share for all users who are part of the Sales OU. To achieve that, you would do the following:

1. From within the Active Directory Users and Computers MMC tool, right-click the Sales OU, select Properties, and click the Group Policy tab (see Figure 18.8) of the Sales Properties window.

2. Click New on the Sales Properties page (see Figure 18.9) and name the new GPO (in this example, it's **sales1**).

3. Click the sales1 GPO link on the Properties page and choose Edit. The Group Policy MMC snap-in will be loaded in a new window.

4. In the Group Policy MMC snap-in, double-click (expand) User Configuration, expand Administrative Templates, expand Start Menu & Taskbar; then, in the scope pane, double-click Remove Run Menu From Start Menu (see Figure 18.10), choose Enabled, and press the OK button. While you're at it, you should take a few moments to peek around at the many other options brought forward by the Group Policy MMC.

5. Still in the Group Policy MMC, expand User Configuration, expand Windows Settings, expand Folder Redirection, right-click Desktop (see Figure 18.11), and choose Properties from the shortcut menu.

6. Choose the Target tab in the Desktop Properties dialog box and specify Basic - Redirect everyone's folder to the same location in the Settings drop-down box.

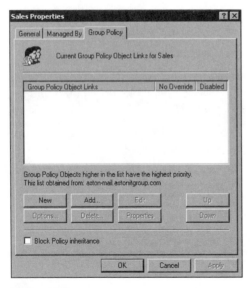

Figure 18.8
Getting access to the GPOs. The Sales Properties page shows the current GPOs defined for the site, domain, or OU (depending on your context) and provides access to attach new GPOs to the container.

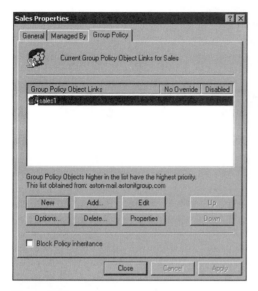

Figure 18.9
Creating a new GPO.

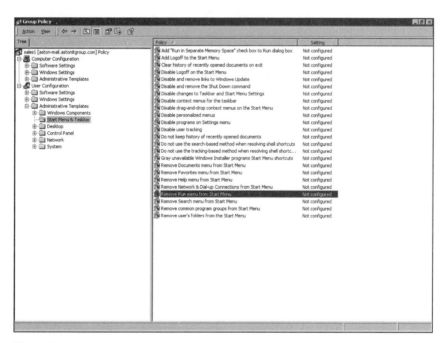

Figure 18.10
Removing the Run menu from the Start menu.

Type "\\Aston-data.astonitgroup.com\public" in the Target Folder Location box (see Figure 18.12) and click OK.

7. Close the Group Policy window, and your new GPO should be set for use.

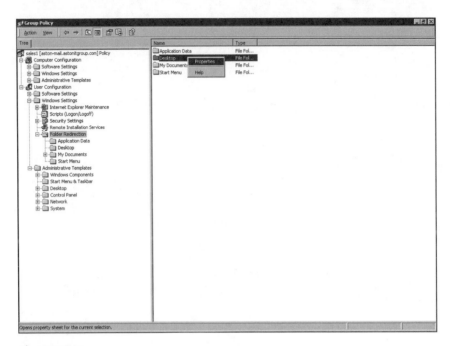

Figure 18.11
Controlling the redirection for the Desktop.

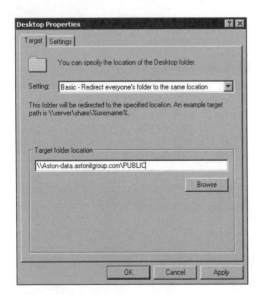

Figure 18.12
Redirect the Desktop to the Public folder on the Aston-data server.

Tip

The Group Policy possibilities are virtually infinite. But, remember to restrain yourself with regard to the number of Group Policies that a given user or computer has to process, because the average time to process a GPO should be around one to two seconds (and much more, if you're using it to distribute software and/or execute scripts).

Also, understand that GPOs can't be directly assigned to security principals (that is, groups, users, or computers). Instead, GPOs are applied to sites, domains, or OUs, and then security principals can be used to filter which objects the GPOs apply to. As you know from permissions, Deny Access always overrides Allow.

Be keenly aware that, by default, GPOs are refreshed every hour-and-a-half at the clients (and every five minutes at the servers) and that they apply only to Windows 2000-based computers and their users.

In Windows 2000 Server, all security policies are configured and managed by using the Group Policy infrastructure. If you want to configure the security policies that apply to the whole domain (for example, the minimum password length allowed), you simply follow these steps:

1. *From within the Active Directory Users and Computers MMC tool, right-click the domain (here, **astonitgroup.com**), select Properties, and click the Group Policy tab. Select Default Domain Policy and click the Edit button (see Figure 18.13).*

2. *In the Group Policy MMC snap-in, expand Computer Configuration, expand Windows Settings, expand Security Settings, expand Account Policies, and click Password Policy (see Figure 18.14).*

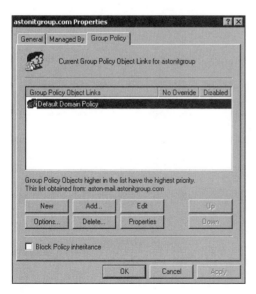

Figure 18.13
Starting the Group Policy MMC snap-in with the Default Domain Policy GPO loaded.

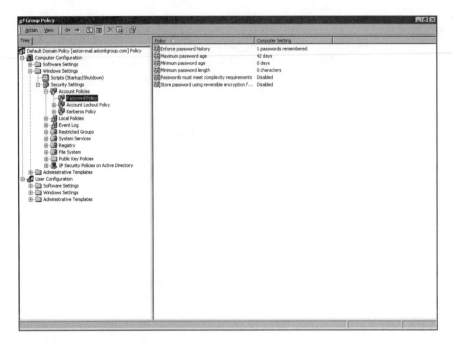

Figure 18.14
The location of the Minimum Password Length policy.

Figure 18.15
You need to input the new Minimum Password Length policy.

3. *Double-click Minimum Password Length in the scope (right) pane, implement the changes that you want (see Figure 18.15), and close the Group Policy MMC snap-in. A few moments later, your new domain-wide password policy should be implemented for all users changing their passwords.*

Creating Sites and Defining the Replication Properties

The Active Directory Sites and Services MMC tool handles everything that concerns the configuration of Active Directory for being in line with the physical properties (that is, the site and replication topology), as well as the decisions regarding which servers are to function as Global Catalogs (GCs). From this tool, you can do the following:

♦ *Manage site and replication topology*—View all sites that are part of the Active Directory forest, manage sites and subnets, manage site links, set replication schedules, set bridgehead servers, and move DCs between sites.

♦ *Manage NTDS settings*—Configure a DC as a GC and manage connection objects.

♦ *Configure other forest-wide settings*—For example, configure services information.

Note
The services registered to the forest aren't immediately visible from the default settings of the Active Directory Sites and Services MMC snap-in. The services are located in the Services container, which will only show when you select the Show Services Node on the View menu.

Except for the configuration of a DC as a GC, the management of NTDS and other forest-wide settings isn't covered in here, because you most likely won't need to change those settings in a pilot setting, if at all.

To start the Active Directory Sites and Services MMC tool, choose Start | Programs | Administrative Tools | Active Directory Sites and Services. A window similar to the one shown in Figure 18.16 should appear.

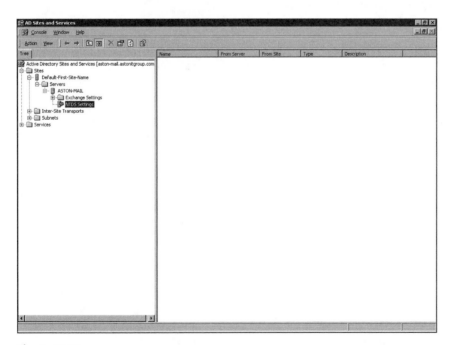

Figure 18.16
The Active Directory Sites and Services MMC tool provides you with an overview of the physical properties of your Active Directory forest.

Creating Subnets and Sites

A *site* is a collection of one or more subnets, defined by the administrator, that are assumed to be "well-connected" connections (meaning that you have at least 128Kbps available bandwidth). Sites and domains are separate objects: A *site* may contain multiple domains, whereas a *domain* may span more than one site. Also, the site topology is limited to the Active Directory forest.

When you create the first DC in a forest via the Active Directory Installation Wizard, a new site is created, called *Default-First-Site-Name* (until you change it to a more descriptive name). Each site should always be configured by following these steps:

1. *Creating the new site*—Remember to add all the applicable links to the site or do it immediately after the site has been created.

2. *Adding subnets*—The subnets found in the site are added to the Subnets container, specifying the site where the subnet is found.

3. *Adding and removing site links*—Active Directory will only accept your creating a site link that includes at least two sites, so you should postpone defining the site links until you have the sites defined. However, because of some mistake on the part of Microsoft, you are only allowed to define a new site when you point out at least one site link that applies to the site—so you might very well be tasked with having to add a site link when creating a new site and then removing that very same site link from the site, when you reach this step.

4. *Installing servers into the site*—The DC/GC servers are then installed into the site (you might also want to move some of the existing DCs/GCs into the site).

5. *Choosing the licensing computer for the site*—Active Directory will pick a licensing server for each site automatically (this is the first DC added to the site). To avoid having the first DC used as the licensing computer for the site, you need to set up yourself which server is to function as the licensing computer (the licensing computer being the server for which the License Logging service on each individual Windows 2000 Server will replicate its licensing information).

Tip

You should define all the sites and the subnets from the outset, because this will save you a lot of hassle later on. However, because of a bug in Windows 2000 Server (Microsoft has promised that the bug will be eliminated by Service Pack 2), you would be better off to install new sites immediately, before you have to create the first DC/GC for the site.

In case you choose to define all sites from the outset, you should remember, as soon as you've installed the first server to the site, to check (and delete) all DNS entries for that site that point to remote DCs and GCs. The reason for this is that Active Directory always adds links to the DCs and GCs in the nearest site to any site that is

without any local DC and GC services for more than two hours. Unfortunately,
Microsoft forgot to have these entries deleted from the DNS when local services
comes online, which means that the local users might just as well connect to DCs
and GCs that are in another site rather than the local ones.

I sure do hope that Microsoft delivers on its promise to fix this very annoying bug in Service
Pack 2, because this bug represents a major problem in distributed settings, where you might
very well have some sites being down for more than two hours from time to time. If you
need more than one site, you need to create it yourself, as follows:

1. Start the Active Directory Sites and Services MMC tool.

2. In the console tree of Sites and Services, right-click Sites and then click New Site.

3. In the Name box on the New Object - Site dialog box (see Figure 18.17), type the site
   name and click a site link that applies.

Note

To create sites and configure subnets, you must be a member of the Enterprise
Admins Group.

Each DC is represented by a server object that is distinct from the computer object that
represents the machine as a security principal (but the two can be connected, because the
server object contains a reference to the computer object). All server objects created in the
forest will be placed in the Servers folder under the Default-First-Site-Name site, unless you
have defined both IP subnets and the mappings of the individual subnets to sites. In other
words, if IP subnets and the mappings to sites are defined, your server will automatically be
placed in the Servers container in the site that provides a match to the server's IP address.

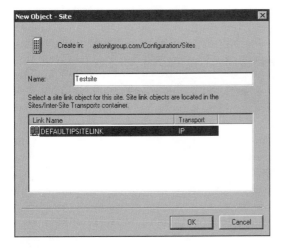

Figure 18.17
Creating a new site.

You can define the IP subnets and mappings explicitly or implicitly. To define them explicitly, follow these steps:

1. Start the Active Directory Sites and Services MMC tool.

2. In the console tree of Sites and Services, expand Sites, right-click Subnets, and then click New Subnet.

3. In the Name box of the New Object - Subnet dialog box, type the address of the IP network and its subnet mask (see Figure 18.18).

4. Choose a site with which to associate this subnet.

Note

You can associate a subnet with only one site, but you can associate several subnets to each site.

To define the IP subnets and mappings implicitly, just move the server objects to the correct sites. When doing that, Active Directory automatically assigns the subnet used in the server's IP address to belong to that given site. You move a server object by doing the following:

1. Start the Active Directory Sites and Services MMC tool.

2. In the console tree of Sites and Services, expand the site holding the server, expand Servers, right-click the server, choose the Move... option, and then select (in the Move Server dialog box) the site that the server should be moved to (see Figure 18.19).

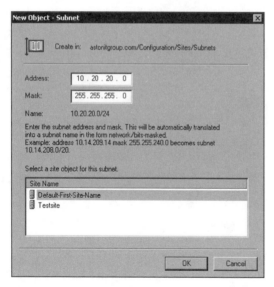

Figure 18.18
Defining a new IP subnet explicitly.

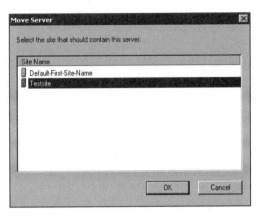

Figure 18.19
Simply moving a server often is easier than explicitly defining a subnet.

Creating the Replication Topology

As previously stated, you use *intrasite* replication inside a site and *intersite* replication between sites. If no subnets are defined and servers are all in the Default-First-Site-Name site (or any other single site), the Active Directory replication engine assumes that you need intrasite replication only—in which the replication topology is generated and kept up-to-date automatically via the Knowledge Consistency Checker (KCC)—no matter how many other sites are defined.

Although the intrasite replication topology may be suitable for small, simple, well-connected networks, it clearly isn't satisfactory in medium-size or large networks that are rife with routing concerns and varying line speeds. Wherever bandwidth consumption is a concern, *intersite* replication is appropriate, because it provides much more detailed control over the replication that is occurring.

Having a DC as a Member of Multiple Sites

A DC can be assigned as a member of only one site when using the MMC tool. But a DC actually can be a member of multiple sites, or advertise its services to additional sites. This can prove very useful if, for example, you want to configure specific DCs to be available to respond to client requests from a given site in the event that no DCs are available in the client's site.

To make a DC a member of multiple sites, you start the Registry Editor on that DC to add a new **REG_MULTI_SZ** value named **SiteCoverage** in the **HKEY_LOCAL_MACHINE\SYSTEM\ CurrentControlSet\Services\Netlogon\Parameters** Registry key. The list of additional sites for which the DC advertises services should then be listed on separate lines (the name of the second site, the third site, and so on, each on separate lines). Refer to the advanced documentation on Windows 2000 Server to check whether you need to perform any more configuration work (beyond implementing this Registry key) to be able to fulfill your precise needs.

To tap the power of intersite replication, you first need to do three things:

1. Define the necessary sites.

2. Place your server objects in the correct sites.

3. Define the replication topology that you want to implement between sites.

Warning

You might want to postpone defining each of the sites until right before the first Active Directory DC is created for the site, due to the current bug in Windows 2000 Server (which is still present at the Service Pack 1 level) discussed at the very beginning of Chapter 12's "Optimizing for Different Scenarios" section.

The preceding section describes how to perform the first two tasks. So, you simply need to know how to define the replication topology between sites. This definition can be provided by the site link or site link bridges, unless you have very specialized needs (in which case you should take a look at the options brought forward with the connection objects, as discussed in Chapter 12).

A *site link* is an object that represents how two or more sites are connected. The administrator can decide which transport to use, assign a cost to the link, and determine the schedule and frequency for replications.

Currently, you have the choice between SMTP (only applicable for GC intersite replications) and IP for the transport. The cost is an arbitrary value (the default is 100) that should reflect the bandwidth cost associated with a particular connection, thus enabling the administrator to control the replication traffic flow by defining the preferred routes throughout the network topology. Active Directory uses a "least-cost-path" evaluation (if multiple replication paths exist, Active Directory always uses the route with the lowest cost, except when it's not available) that will prove very useful if you are using a consistent cost scheme for the various site links. The schedule and frequency are decided by defining whether the site link allows replications inside each hour of the week, and how often a replication is performed (defined in minutes, with a default setting of 180 minutes).

To define a site link, do the following:

1. Start the Active Directory Sites and Services MMC tool.

2. In the console tree of Sites and Services, expand Sites and then expand Inter-Site Transports.

3. Right-click IP or SMTP (depending on your choice of transport) and click New Site Link.

4. In the New Object - Site Link dialog box, type the name for the site link in the Name box, choose the sites to be included in this site link, and then click Add (see Figure 18.20).

You configure the properties (cost, replication interval, and schedule) for the site link on the General tab of the Properties dialog box for the site link.

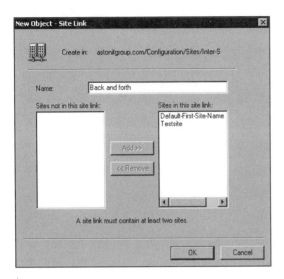

Figure 18.20
This is how you define a new site link.

Before you start defining the site links, remember to check whether Active Directory already has implemented any site links, because a site link is created automatically if a single domain applies to two sites. Also, remember that a site link isn't *transitive*, which means that traffic won't cross two site links; only traffic going to and from those sites defined in the site link is allowed.

But you can allow traffic to cross several site links, by defining *site-link transitiveness* on a given transport. Actually, this is the easiest way to set up the intersite replication topology. Enabling this little switch means that all the site links for a given transport are transitive—and, thus, that site traffic can flow through the site link(s) that Active Directory deems most appropriate, based on the least-cost-path evaluation.

To enable site-link transitiveness on a transport, following these steps:

1. Start the Active Directory Sites and Services MMC tool.

2. In the console tree of Sites and Services, expand Sites and then expand Inter-Site Transports.

3. Right-click IP or SMTP (depending on your choice of transport) and click Properties.

4. On the General tab of the IP Properties dialog box, check the Bridge all site links checkbox (see Figure 18.21).

Note

Please take note of the other available option on the transport protocol—Ignore schedules—because this might prove very handy in situations where you want the whole network to be brought up-to-date as soon as possible.

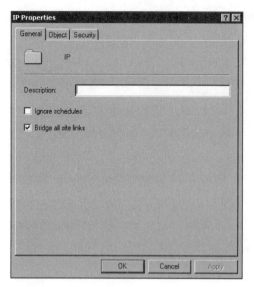

Figure 18.21
Site-link transitiveness is, by far, the easiest way to configure site link association.

If you want to minimize your manual work but retain more flexibility in controlling the traffic flow between sites, you may opt to define site link bridges instead. A *site link bridge* is a structure that builds transitive links between a limited number of sites by specifying the site links that are to be "bridged." By definition, the site link bridge always includes two or more site links.

The site link bridge uses the cost parameters specified in the site links to evaluate the least-cost path when it needs to perform a replication. Usually, a single site link bridge should prove sufficient, unless the network connecting the sites that are part of your Active Directory forest isn't fully routed.

In other words, in a medium-size or large network environment, you are able to configure site link bridges (each site link bridge can each be likened to a network router, which is able to route at will between all the sites included in the site links) to avoid explicitly defining every possible route that the replications can take. However, if you choose to declare a transport to be transitive, you won't need any site link bridges, because every site link in effect will belong to a default site link bridge.

You define a site link bridge as follows:

1. Start the Active Directory Sites and Services MMC tool.

2. In the console tree of Sites and Services, expand Sites and then expand Inter-Site Transports.

3. Right-click IP or SMTP (depending on your choice of transport) and click New Site Link Bridge.

4. In the New Object - Site Link Bridge dialog box, type the name for the site link bridge in the Name box, choose the sites to be included in this site link bridge, and then click Add (see Figure 18.22).

Note

When it comes down to it, both the site link and site link bridges are using sites as the base property. And you should note that you're allowed to designate a certain server, called the bridgehead server, to be the replication gateway to remote sites. You might actually have more than one bridgehead server per transport in each site, because servers aren't able to store and forward naming contexts that they don't host (and a DC can only be a member of a single domain). In other words, you can point out one bridgehead server per transport for each domain that is present in each site.

Active Directory also enables you to define the intersite replication topology via connection objects. *Connection objects* are truly the most precise way of controlling the replications and also, by far, the most labor-intensive proposition. The definition of connection objects isn't covered in this chapter, because connection objects usually are used only to cater to very specialized situations.

Figure 18.22
Defining a site link bridge.

Forcing the Replications

As mentioned several times earlier in this book, you sometimes need the patience of an angel to work with Active Directory, due to the rather long time that might pass before all your changes have been implemented throughout the forest.

The next-best thing to patience is knowledge on how to stress the Active Directory to clear up the replication queues as fast as possible. You have three different methods for doing that:

Using the Active Directory Sites and Services MMC tool:

1. Expand the applicable **Sites|Servers|*<server name>*** container for the server that is targeted for a new replication.

2. Click the **NTDS Settings** object, right-click the connection object representing the link to the server from which the replications are coming from and click Replicate Now.

3. Windows 2000 now initiates replication of any changes from the source server (the server represented by the connection object) to the target server for all directory partitions the target server is configured to replicate from the source server.

Using Replication Diagnostics Tool (**REPADMIN**) from Windows 2000 Support Tools:

1. Type the following command at the command prompt: **repadmin /showreps *<target server>***, where *target server* is the DNS name of the server that is targeted for replication. If the target server can be reached, **REPADMIN** will output a list of the replication partners for various naming contexts among other things.

2. Use **REPADMIN** to initiate the replication by typing: **repadmin /sync *<directory_partition expressed as a CN> <server_name> <source_server_GUID>***. Both parameters needed is shown in the output generated in the previous step (the GUID is being stated as **objectGuid**) among many other interesting data. You might want to add **/f** for overriding the normal replication schedule and **/full** for forcing a full replication of all objects from the destination server.

3. If successful, **Repadmin.exe** displays the following message: **ReplicaSync() from source: *<source server_GUID>* to dest: *<target server>* is successful**.

Using Active Directory Replication Monitor (**REPLMON**) from Windows 2000 Support Tools:

1. Click **Add Site/Server** on the **Edit** menu specifying the server targeted for replications. **REPLMON** will now identify the directory partitions and displays them as child nodes to the target server in the left pane.

2. Find and expand the directory partition that needs to be synchronized. All domain controllers listed for a given directory partition are source servers, but direct replication partners are displayed with an icon that represents two network-connected servers (they can also be identified from the Properties page).

3. Right-click the applicable direct replication partner, and then click **Synchronize Replica**. **REPLMON** will now initiate replication and report the status of the request.

You might want to note that it will take a fair deal of time using Active Directory Sites and Services for getting replications distributed from a source DC or GC that is connected to multiple DCs or GCs. Also, you won't be able to see when the replication is through or limit the replications to a certain naming context. Thus, you should generally want to perform the replications using one of the two other alternatives.

If you need to perform the same set of replications from time to time, you should want to create a Visual Basic script based on the **IADsTools COM** object (also from Windows 2000 Support Tools), which allows you to synchronize a target DC/GC with a source for a given naming context using the **ReplicaSync** function. You can find the information on the parameters needed for the **ReplicaSync IADsTools** function in the Resource Kit documentation.

Turning a DC into a GC

The last commonly occurring task in regard to the Sites and Services MMC tool is turning a DC into a GC (or removing the GC from a DC). By definition, a GC stores a partial copy of all objects in the Active Directory forest; as such, it is primarily of use for performing fast, forest-wide searches and storing forest-wide data, such as Universal Groups and UPN suffixes.

To turn a DC into a GC, follow these steps:

1. Start the Active Directory Sites and Services MMC tool.

2. In the console tree of Sites and Services, expand Sites, expand the applicable site object, expand Servers, expand the applicable server object, right-click NTDS Settings, and then click Properties.

3. On the General tab, click the Global Catalog checkbox (see Figure 18.23).

Correspondingly, you simply remove the checkmark when you need to remove the GC service from the server.

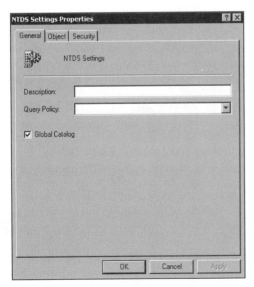

Figure 18.23
Adding the GC service to a DC is surprisingly straightforward.

Remember that you usually want at least one GC in each site, because the GC is just as vital as the DC for providing login functionality to Active Directory. And the GC will become absolutely indispensable if you plan to implement Exchange 2000 Server, because the new release of Exchange uses the GC to deliver the GAL (Global Address List) to the Outlook clients.

Disaster Prevention with Windows 2000 Server

Windows 2000 Server includes a host of features that are designed to help you prevent, and ultimately recover from, a variety of computer disasters. These features are described in Table 18.1.

The following sections provide a description of some of the more interesting aspects of the features listed in Table 18.1.

Fault-Tolerant Volumes

Even though Windows 2000 Server supports fault-tolerant volumes, I strongly advise you to implement these measures via the server hardware for *real servers* (defined as servers that support numerous users in a production environment), because this will provide you with

Table 18.1   Disaster prevention features of Windows 2000 Server.

Windows 2000 Server Feature	Description
Fault-tolerant volumes	Support RAID level 0 (disk striping), RAID level 1 (mirroring), and RAID level 5 (disk striping with parity) volumes from the OS.
Advanced Startup Options	Help you to troubleshoot startup problems, repair problems with the Active Directory database on a DC, or connect the server to a debugger. Except for Directory Services Restore Mode and the Safe Mode boot options, these features are pretty much the same as on Windows NT Server 4 (and, as before, you press the F8 key during the OS selection phase to gain access to the Advanced Startup Options).
Recovery Console	Enables you to repair the system from the command line. The commands available in the Recovery Console allow you to enable and disable services, copy system files from a diskette or CD-ROM, and repair a corrupted boot sector. You install Recovery Console by running the **winnt32** command with the **/cmdcons** switch from Windows 2000 Server. After Recovery Console is installed, you can access it from the boot menu as well as the command line. In any case, you need to access the Windows 2000 Setup disks or the Windows 2000 Server CD-ROM in order to get Recovery Console up and running.
Backup utility	Enables you to archive and restore files and folders and create an Emergency Repair Disk (ERD). You can also use the Backup utility to make a copy of a server's System State data, which is a collection of system-specific information, including the Registry, the Active Directory database, the SYSVOL directory, and the system startup files.

much better performance. But the fault-tolerant volumes do prove useful for testing purposes and for achieving a better level of fault-tolerance on low-end servers.

Note that the fault-tolerant-volume options are available only on dynamic disks (see Chapter 19 for more information on that subject), the inclusion of which in Windows 2000 Server makes creating fault-tolerant volumes much easier than before.

To create a mirrored or RAIDed volume from unallocated space, follow these steps:

1. Start the Computer Management MMC tool.

2. In the console tree of Computer Management, expand Storage and then click Disk Management.

3. Right-click an area of unallocated space and click Create Volume. The Create Volume Wizard starts.

4. Click Next, and then specify the type of volume that you want to create on the Select Volume Type page (see Figure 18.24). Click Next.

5. On the Select Disks page, select the disk(s) that is involved in the creation of the volume (see Figure 18.25). Click Next.

6. On the Assign Drive Letter or Path page, click the Assign a Drive Letter radio button and assign a drive letter to the volume (see Figure 18.26) or choose from the alternatives. Click Next.

7. On the Format Volume page, decide whether to format the volume (which usually is a good idea and sometimes will be necessary) by selecting the appropriate radio button. If you choose to format it, set the formatting options in the Formatting area (see Figure 18.27). Click Next.

8. Review your options, then click Finish to apply the settings (see Figure 18.28).

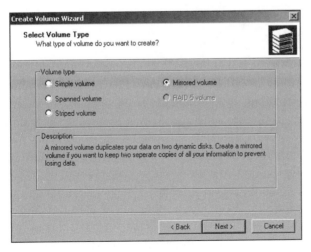

Figure 18.24
Specify which type of volume you want to create.

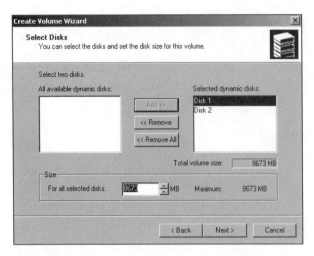

Figure 18.25
Specify which disks to include in the operation.

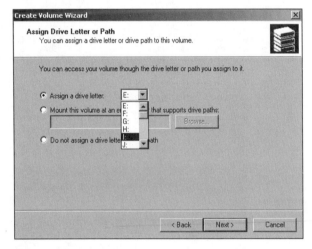

Figure 18.26
Assign a drive letter or path.

Although you have a lot of pages to go through in the Create Volume Wizard, it really makes defining fault-tolerant volumes in Windows 2000 Server so much easier than in Windows NT Server 4.

Note

In the Create Volume Wizard, you also can specify several other options not mentioned here, such as the number of disks to include in the volume and the volume size.

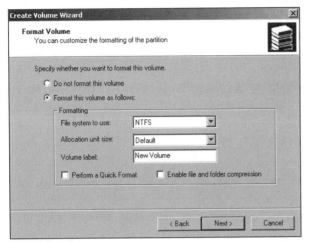

Figure 18.27
Decide whether to format the volume; if you do format it, select your formatting options.

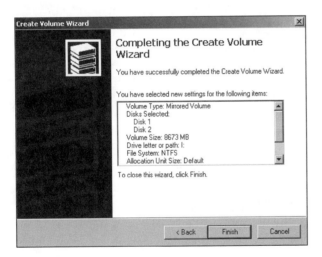

Figure 18.28
Completing the Create Volume Wizard.

To mirror an existing volume, you simply right-click the volume that you want to mirror, click Add Mirror… in the shortcut menu, and then select the second disk in the mirrored volume.

If a member of a mirrored volume fails, the other member continues to operate, so users won't even notice any changes. However, the volumes no longer are fault-tolerant. Therefore, to prevent the risk of data loss, you must recover the mirrored volume. The status of the failed volume appears in Disk Management as Failed Redundancy, and one of the disks will appear as Offline, Missing, or Online (Errors).

If the status is either Offline or Missing, fix the problem, right-click the troubled disk in Disk Management, and choose Reactivate Disk. If the problem is fixed, the status of the disk should return to Healthy, and the mirrored volume will be regenerated. If the status is Online (Errors), check whether the disk is about to fail completely (this operation typically is supported on better server hardware) or it's just a freak accident. When you are satisfied with the situation, choose Reactivate Disk and then check the status of the disk.

Backing up Active Directory

Just like its predecessor, Windows 2000 Server includes a Backup utility. This utility does represent an improvement over Windows NT Server 4 Backup utility. However, it's still limited in scope because it's a "brain-damaged" version of the well-known Veritas (formerly Seagate) Backup Exec application. For Windows 2000 Server production environments, I strongly recommend that you evaluate the full Backup Exec product and possibly some of the rival products. But Windows 2000 Server's Backup utility can and should be used if you decide not to pay for one of the commercially available backup applications.

When choosing a backup utility, you need to make absolutely sure that it is able to perform online backup (and possibly restore) of the Active Directory database. As all Exchange administrators know all too well, performing backup and restore operations on Exchange's ESE database (which Active Directory closely resembles) isn't exactly easy.

When you plan to back up the Active Directory database, realize that it consists of both the database file (*ntds.dit*), which stores all the objects in Active Directory, and log files, which store, track, maintain, and manage transactions going to and from the Active Directory database. These log files can be separated into the following categories:

♦ *Transaction log files*—Used to store, track, and maintain transactions before they are written to the Active Directory database. These include both the current transaction log file (*edb.log*) and previous transaction log files (*edb*.log*). After all the transactions in a previous log file are committed to the Active Directory database file, it will be deleted during the next garbage collection (a cleanup process that runs every 12 hours on each DC, by default).

♦ *Checkpoint files (edb.chk)*—Used to hold pointers to the transactions in the log files that have already been written to the Active Directory database. The information provided in the checkpoint files also is available directly in the transaction log files, but it's much faster to determine it via the checkpoint files.

♦ *Reserved log files (res1.log and res2.log)*—Used as a reserve to the transaction log files in case of low disk space situations. If Active Directory isn't able to create a new *edb.log* file, all outstanding transactions in memory are moved to the reserved log files, and Active Directory performs a controlled shutdown, during which an Out of Disk Space error is recorded in the Event log.

♦ *Patch files (.pat)*—Used to manage data during an online backup. During an online backup, a patch file is created for the Active Directory database, the backup operation begins, and all transactions written to a portion of the Active Directory database that has already been backed up are recorded in the database and the patch file. At the end of the backup, the patch file is written to the backup tape and then deleted.

Obviously, the Active Directory database files need to be backed up regularly. But, as is the case for Exchange, you need to make sure that you are creating a backup, which will be useful when you need to perform a restore. In other words, the database needs to be in a consistent state, which means that all the files need to be "frozen" at a certain point in time, to ensure against changes that aren't reflected in all the files.

Windows 2000 Server's built-in Backup utility provides for this need when you click the System State checkbox (which also includes a backup of the Registry, the COM+ Class Registration database, the system startup files, the Certificate Services database, the Cluster Database information, and the Sysvol folder), which is located on the Items To Back Up and What To Back Up Pages in the Backup Wizard and on the Backup tab when you expand My Computer.

If you use any other backup application for your servers, make absolutely sure that it includes support for the Active Directory database (which should be the case for all backup utilities claiming support for Windows 2000 Server, because the Active Directory backup and restore interfaces are based on the familiar ESE interfaces from Exchange Server). If the backup utility doesn't support Active directory, you'll have to perform offline backups; otherwise, a restore may leave you with an inconsistent Active Directory database.

Ultimately, when you plan your Active Directory backup, you must also understand how the Active Directory database can be recovered via the following methods:

♦ A nonauthoritative restore

♦ An authoritative restore

♦ Recovery without restore

The recovery without restore method is quite straightforward. If you can't fix the trouble by using the **NTDSUTIL** tool (described later in "The Major Active Directory Tools"), you simply demote the DC and promote it back again. Or, if you are hit by a serious disaster, you

---

Backing up All Domains

Because Active Directory is a distributed database, you don't need to perform a backup of every copy of the Active Directory database (that is, every DC) to be able to recover from a disaster situation. However, to be able to recover, you need to back up at least one Active Directory database from each domain.

Before you choose to reduce the number of DCs on which the Active Directory database is backed up, note that your backup tapes won't include the changes made at other DCs that weren't replicated to the DC at the time of the last backup. So, you might very well end up deciding to back up one or two DCs inside each domain in each site, depending upon your environment.

---

promote a replacement server instead and delete the old DC via **NTDSUTIL**. Obviously, this works as intended only if you have at least one other DC available in the given domain that is completely up-to-date, so you might find yourself in a situation in which this method won't work.

If that is the case, you have the choice between an authoritative or a nonauthoritative restore. A *nonauthoritative* restore enables you to restore a DC's entire database replica; thus, the recovery of backed-up information depends on the state of the replication and transaction logs at the time of the latest successful backup. A nonauthoritative restore is the default method used by the Backup tool for restoring the System State data to a DC. A nonauthoritative restore is performed in the following way (regardless of whether or not you're using Windows 2000 Server's Backup tool):

1. Place the DC into Directory Services Restore Mode by restarting it, pressing the F8 key during the OS selection phase, and choosing Directory Services Restore Mode.

2. Restore the Active Directory database files to the correct locations using the backup utility and restart the server after the restore is complete. After the DC is online, the replication among DCs will bring the server fully up-to-date. Please note that some services might not start correctly at the first restart; if that is the case, restart once more and things should work as before.

An *authoritative* restore enables you to select specific items (as well as all directory objects) to restore in a DC's Active Directory database, rather than just being able to restore the entire database, which may be unnecessary—or unwanted. For example, if an administrator inadvertently deletes something in the directory (which the nonauthoritative restore doesn't offer any relief for, because the DC will be brought up-to-date by the other DCs when it comes online again), you can restore the needed objects via an authoritative restore, as follows:

1. Place the DC into Directory Services Restore Mode by restarting it, pressing the F8 key during the OS selection phase, and choosing Directory Services Restore Mode.

2. Restore the needed directory objects to the directory via the backup utility.

3. Open a command prompt and type **NTDSUTIL**.

4. When in **NTDSUTIL**, type "authoritative restore" and, at the Authoritative Restore prompt, type "restore" followed by the appropriate choice ("database" for restoring the entire database; "**database verinc <version no.>**" for restoring the entire database and overriding version increase; "**subtree <full CN name>**" to restore a subtree, and "**subtree <full CN> verinc <version no.>**" to restore a subtree and override version increase). The full CN takes the shape of something along the lines of **cn=<object name>,ou=<OU name>,dc=<domain name>,dc=<top-level domain>**. Here, *object name* is the name of the object that is to be restored (if applicable), *OU name* is the name of the particular OU that needs to be restored (if you have an OU hierarchy, you need to specify multiple **ou=**parameters), *domain name* is the name of the domain the DC resides in, and *top-level domain* is the top-level domain name of the DC (such as **com** or **org**).

5. When the restore is complete, restart the server. Please note that some services might not start correctly at the first restart; if that is the case, restart once more and things should work as before.

6. After the DC is brought online again, the replication among DCs will reinstate the restored directory objects on the other DCs.

Tip

*You are able to perform an authoritative restore from Windows 2000 Server Backup as well. In order to do that, you will need to run the **NTDSUTIL** tool to mark the objects that are to be considered authoritative after you have restored the data, but before you restart the DC.*

Usually, you won't need to perform any manual work to restore a DC that has been hit with a sudden server failure (such as a power failure). When the server comes back online, Active Directory will commit any transactions that were outstanding when the server stopped. So, generally, a *real* disaster has to occur before restoring is necessary.

The Use of Vital Domain and Forest Properties

If you want an overview of the Active Directory forest, head for the Active Directory Domains and Trusts MMC tool. From this tool, you can do the following:

♦ View all domains that are part of the forest.

♦ Manage UPN suffixes.

♦ Launch the Active Directory User and Computers MMC tool for a specific domain.

♦ Modify the domain operation mode.

♦ Manage trust relationships.

♦ Manage the domain naming operations master FSMO role.

The management of trust relationships is not covered in this chapter because you won't likely need to do anything with that in a pilot. Remember that the trusts between the domains in the domain tree(s) as well as between the domain trees of the Active Directory forest are defined automatically. And so, you will only need to mess with trust relationships if you want to provide trust to domains in other forests (including Windows NT Server 4 domains), or want to improve performance between domains residing in different domains trees (by defining direct trusts).

The Active Directory Domains and Trusts MMC tool is started by choosing Start | Programs | Administrative Tools | Active Directory Domains and Trusts. Shortly thereafter, a window similar to the one shown in Figure 18.29 appears.

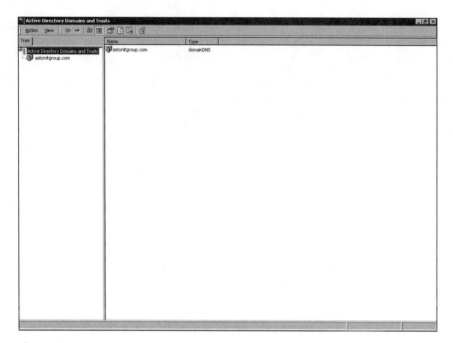

Figure 18.29
Active Directory Domains and Trusts provides you with an overview of your Active Directory forest.

What about the Clients?

Although Microsoft has developed extensions for Windows 95, Windows 98, and Windows NT 4 (still not released as of writing this; promised to be distributed with Service Pack 7), you will forego a lot of functionality by sticking with these client OSs, instead of moving to Windows 2000 Professional.

The so-called Active Directory client extensions include the following Active Directory features:

- *Site Awareness*—That is, the client will always log on to the DC in the local site and can change passwords on any Windows 2000 DC (instead of having to use the PDC Emulator, which will elsewhere be contacted by the client).

- *Active Directory Services Interface (ADSI)*—Allows you to access Active Directory using LDAP and ADSI.

- *DFS Fault Tolerance Client*—Provides access to the Distributed File System's (DFS) fault-tolerant and fail-over file shares feature, which is being made possible by the Active Directory.

- *Active Directory Windows Address Book (WAB) property pages*—Allows users who have permission to change properties on user objects (for example, phone number and address) via the user object pages, which are accessed from Start menu|Search|For People. Includes support for display specifiers that allow rendering of new schema elements stored on the user object in Active Directory.

- *NT LAN Manager (NTLM) version 2 authentication*—Allows the client to use the improved authentication features available in NT LAN Manager version 2.

In other words, you will only be able to take advantage of Group Policies, IPSEC, Kerberos authentication, mutual authentication, service principal names (the fact that you can distribute information on services through names), L2TP, a directory service entry in Network Neighborhood, searching for printers and volumes, viewing printer properties, time synchronization, and the UPN login feature when using Windows 2000 Professional.

The Windows 95- and Windows 98-based Active Directory Client is distributed with the Windows 2000 Server CD-ROM (in the Clients directory).

Changing the Domain Operation Mode

A Windows 2000 Server domain operates in either of two modes:

♦ *Mixed mode*—Allows DCs running both Windows 2000 Server and earlier versions of Windows NT Server to coexist in the domain. The domain features from previous versions of Windows NT Server are still enabled, but some Windows 2000 Server features are disabled.

♦ *Native mode*—All domain controllers must run on Windows 2000 Server, which enables you to take advantage of such new features as nested group membership and Universal Groups.

When a domain is first installed, it is operating in mixed mode. The mode of operation can be changed from mixed mode to native mode, but remember, this action isn't reversible. In native mode, down-level Windows NT Server 4 BDCs aren't supported anymore (but support does continue for member servers as well as standalone servers running Windows NT Server 4).

You change the domain to native mode by performing the following steps (see Figure 18.30), *after* you make sure all DCs in the domain are running Windows 2000 Server:

1. Start the Active Directory Domains and Trusts MMC tool.

Figure 18.30
Changing the domain from mixed mode to native mode. This is a one-way proposition, meaning it's irreversible!

2. In the console tree of Active Directory Domains and Trusts, right-click the domain for which you want to change mode, then click Properties.

3. On the General tab in the Properties dialog box, click Change Mode.

Note that it will take some time until native mode is implemented on all DCs. So, take a break (the duration depends upon your replication setup) before you start to use the feature set that is available only when running in native mode. If you are unsure whether the change has trickled down through your entire site structure, you can connect to target one or several DCs (by choosing Action | Connect to Domain Controller...) and look at the status reported on the General tab in the Properties dialog box for the domain.

Managing UPN Suffixes

The *User Principal Name (UPN)* provides an easy-to-use naming style for users to log on to Active Directory. The style of the UPN is based on the Internet standard RFC 822 and is more commonly referred to as an *Internet mail address*.

The default UPN suffix is the DNS name of the forest (the DNS name of the first domain in the first domain tree defined in the forest).

To add more UPN suffixes, perform the following steps (see Figure 18.31):

1. Start the Active Directory Domains and Trusts MMC tool.

2. Select the root node in the console tree (that is, the Active Directory Domains and Trusts container), right-click, and click Properties.

3. Add the needed UPN suffixes in the Active Directory Domains and Trusts Properties dialog box.

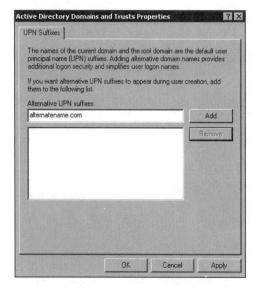

Figure 18.31
Adding or removing UPN suffixes.

The FSMO Story

As discussed in Chapter 12, Active Directory is based on a multi-master replication scheme, except for the following tasks:

♦ Schema operations

♦ Domain name assignments

♦ RID pool allocation

♦ NT 4 PDC functions (as well as a couple of related things)

♦ Interdomain consistency

For each of these operations, Microsoft has implemented the concept of an *operations master*, so that you have a single, authoritative source for information, changes, and so forth. These operations masters are usually referred to as *FSMO roles* (Floating Single-Master Operations or Flexible Single-Master Operation, depending on who you talk to at Microsoft) and are assigned automatically by Active Directory, but can be transferred between DCs by the administrator, as required.

The Schema Master and Domain Naming Master roles have to be assigned to one DC in each forest, whereas the Infrastructure Master, RID Master, and PDC Emulator roles have to be assigned to one DC in each domain. So, in a forest that consists of three domains, you have 11 FSMO roles (1 Schema Master, 1 Domain Naming Master, 3 Infrastructure Masters, 3 RID Masters, and 3 PDC Emulators). Because any DC in the forest can hold forest-level FSMO roles, and only DCs in the domain can hold that domain's FSMO roles, the example requires at least 3 DCs for the 11 roles—but the FSMO roles can be distributed among as many as 11 different DCs.

Because these FSMOs are crucial to Active Directory's well-being, and may be the reason for a lot of grief if placed less than optimally, you are well advised to decide on where to place the different FSMO roles when you do the implementation planning for Active Directory (you should refer to Chapter 12 for how to do that).

Tip

*The Windows 2000 Resource Kit contains a .cmd file called **Dumpfsmos.cmd** that you can use to quickly list FSMO role owners for your current domain and forest. The .cmd file uses **Ntdsutil.exe** to enumerate the role owners, as it's the only utility capable of showing you all the FSMO role owners at once.*

You have two options with regard to implementing changes in the current assignment of FSMO roles:

♦ *To transfer the FSMO role*—Moving it with the cooperation of the current role holder.

♦ *To seize the FSMO role*—Forcing transfer of the role without the cooperation of the current role holder.

Naturally, role transfer is always the preferred solution.

Don't Seize Any Role Unless Absolutely Necessary

Seizure of an FSMO role is a very delicate operation, so it shouldn't be done unless it is needed to get the role online again. Furthermore, the DC whose FSMO role is seized must never come back online (so, you should demote the DC if possible, or disconnect it from the network and make sure that it will not be reconnected until Windows 2000 Server has been reinstalled). If the DC were to come back online, it would wreak havoc on the Operations Masters involved as a result of having a duplication of the roles. Also, remember to move the Operations Master role(s) back when the original DC is online again.

With regard to handling the different FSMO roles, a temporary failure of the Schema Master, Domain Naming Master, or RID Master shouldn't be too significant, because it is not immediately visible to end users (and usually not even visible to administrators, except for those few situations in which these Operations Master roles are used). In other words, a temporary breakdown on a DC holding one or more of these roles usually isn't worth fixing—and should be considered only if the outage of the role holder is more or less permanent. On the other hand, you should keep an eye on the PDC Emulator at all times, especially if you've still got client accesses from computers that aren't running Windows 2000 Professional!

The FSMO role transfer can be achieved by starting up the applicable MMC snap-in (see Table 18.2). You can find an example of how to do this operation for the per-domain FSMO roles in Figure 18.32.

The seizure of an FSMO role can be done only via the **NTDSUTIL** tool. This tool also supports role transfer, but it shouldn't be used for that procedure, because using the MMC snap-ins is much easier.

The Major Active Directory Tools

The Windows 2000 Server CD-ROM actually includes plenty of very interesting utilities for the care and feeding of your Active Directory. However, for reasons unknown to me, Microsoft has hidden these tools so well that it's really not something that most people will stumble upon, unless they know where to look.

The most important new tools and utilities introduced with Windows 2000 Server are the following:

- *ADSI Edit*—An MMC snap-in used to view all Active Directory naming contexts.
- *ClonePrincipal (CLONEPR)*—Used for migrating users and groups.

Table 18.2   MMC snap-ins for transferring the FSMO roles to other DCs.

FSMO Role	MMC Snap-In
Schema Master	Active Directory Schema
Domain Naming Master	Active Directory Domains and Trusts
Infrastructure Master, RID Master, and PDC Emulator	Active Directory Users and Computers

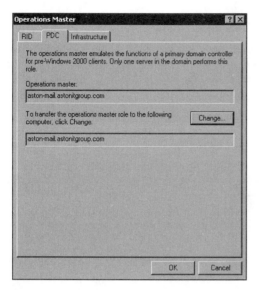

Figure 18.32
Changing the per-domain FSMO roles; access this window by clicking Operations Masters for the domain in question.

♦ *Domain Controller Diagnostic Tool (DCDIAG)*—Used to test the DC's well-being.

♦ *DSACLS*—Used to set ACLs on Active Directory objects.

♦ *DSASTAT*—Used for comparing directory trees.

♦ *Active Directory Administration Tool (LDP)*—A semi-graphical LDAP tool.

♦ *Active Directory Object Manager (MOVETREE)*—Used to move objects between domains.

♦ *Network Connectivity Tester (NETDIAG)*—Used to test end-to-end network connectivity.

♦ *Windows 2000 Domain Manager (NETDOM)*—Used to reassign computers to other domains and to manage trust relationships.

♦ *NLTEST*—Used to perform a variety of administrative tasks.

♦ *NTDSUTIL*—Used for Active Directory database management.

♦ *Replication Diagnostics Tool (REPADMIN)*—Used to check and modify replication.

♦ *Active Directory Replication Monitor (REPLMON)*—Provides graphical management of a wide range of replication related areas.

♦ *Security Administration tools (SIDWALKER)*—Used to replace one SID with another.

With the exception of **NTDSUTIL**, all the tools mentioned are part of the Windows 2000 Support Tools.

In addition, you should note that Microsoft also offers a Windows 2000 Server Resource Kit that includes a host of other tools (including some nice tools for keeping a tab on your

---

Getting Your Hands on the Windows 2000 Support Tools

You will need to install the Windows 2000 Support Tools in order to be able to tap into the various tools offered. However, this isn't a big deal, really, as the Support Tools are installed as a Windows Installer package, which means that you can remove them at any time without the risk of incurring any troubles to your server installations.

The Windows 2000 Support Tools are installed by browsing to the \Support\Tools folder on the Windows 2000 Server CD-ROM and launching the *setup.exe* file found there.

GPOs) as well as a fair number of fairly valuable scripts to ease bulk data entries and the like (you can find more information on the scripts offered in Chapter 19).

ADSI Edit

ADSI Edit is a GUI-based generic Active Directory namespace viewer (see Figure 18.33) that provides you with the following:

♦ Full access to all naming contexts.

♦ Display of all objects.

♦ Management of ACLs; you can set ACEs and take ownership for any object in the directory.

You might think of ADSI Edit as the "Registry Editor" for the directory.

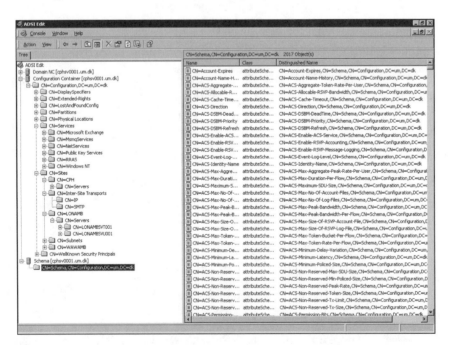

Figure 18.33
ADSI Edit allows you to inspect the objects and attributes found in all the naming contexts stored on the DC.

ClonePrincipal (**CLONEPR**)

ClonePrincipal is a nifty DLL that allows you to migrate users and groups by creating clones of the source accounts in the destination domain. This tool is primarily of interest for migrating users and groups from Windows NT Server 4 domains to Active Directory domains (see also Chapter 22). Please be aware that some scripting experience will be called for in order to make use of **ClonePrincipal**.

Domain Controller Diagnostic Tool (**DCDIAG**)

DCDIAG is a command-line tool that allows you to check that your DC works correctly. This tool is indispensable in troubleshooting situations, because it will run through all the base testing areas, including the following:

♦ Connectivity

♦ Replications

♦ Topology Integrity

♦ Netlogon rights

♦ Operations Master roles

♦ Trusts

Note

Based on my experiences, this tool works great when you just run it as is. If, however, you want to get the full story on the DC by way of the verbose option, you should not take everything that it tells you for granted. For one, I've seen the verbose mode deliver some arcane errors on DCs that are in mint condition.

Please note that **DCDIAG** is available in a newer version at **www.download.microsoft.com/ download/win2000platform/Update/5.0.2195.2103/NT5/EN-US/dcdiag_setup.exe**. The new version of **DCDIAG** adds support for verifying that it can support the Active Directory, determining if an Active Directory forest can be created, verifying that additional DCs can be added, and determining if a Windows 2000 computer can be joined to a domain.

DSACLS

DSACLS is used for command-line Active Directory ACL management. Using **DSACLS**, you are allowed to query and manipulate security attributes on Active Directory objects.

DSASTAT

With the command-line tool **DSASTAT**, you get the following:

♦ The ability to compare differences between naming contexts on DCs.

♦ Very fine-grained granularity; the entire directory, down to single objects, including the option of performing a full attribute comparison between replicated objects.

♦ Extensive statistics, such as the number of objects sorted by class and database storage information.

Active Directory Administration Tool (LDP)

LDP is a somewhat GUI-based LDAP tool (see Figure 18.34) that does the following:

♦ Supports all LDAP operations, including browse, modify, delete, and rename.

♦ Supports operational controls.

♦ Displays auxiliary data, including replication metadata and access permissions.

Because LDP is an LDAP browser, you are able to browse any domain-naming context stored on a DC, as well as a GC. In many cases, LDP will prove to be a great solution for dumping the contents or the full directory path for an object.

Active Directory Object Manager (MOVETREE)

MOVETREE provides you with the means to move directory objects from one domain to another inside the forest, within the following parameters:

♦ The objects moved can be specified as a whole domain or as a subtree in a domain (including OUs and leaf objects).

♦ Computers, Domain Local Groups, and Global Groups currently aren't covered by the move.

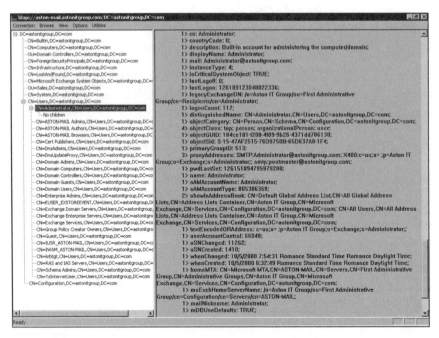

Figure 18.34
You should definitely check out LDP for dumping objects from the directory.

In other words, **MOVETREE** allows you to move most of the directory objects from one domain to another, as long as both domains are part of the same forest. Name collisions will be left in the LostAndFound container, which can be viewed in the Active Directory Users and Computers MMC tool when the Advanced Features menu option is selected. Passwords remain intact and are replicated (not copied) to the new domain, to avoid security issues. However, remember that Domain Local and Global Groups don't move (so you must find a way to deal with that situation, which is covered in detail in Chapter 22) and that machine objects must be rejoined to the new domain before they will work as intended (see **NETDOM**). You will often need to perform some sort of cleanup on ACLs, which usually is handled with the **SIDWALKER** tool.

Network Connectivity Tester (**NETDIAG**)

NETDIAG is a command-line tool for testing workstation-to-server connectivity. The tests performed include the following:

- The network layer, including IP configuration and DNS.
- The session layer, including SMB and NTLM-Secure Channel.
- The application layer, including Kerberos, NTLM, and LDAP.

The tool doesn't require the use of any parameters or switches, so it is a really good way to have end users provide the administrator with a lot of relevant network status information for isolating problems.

Please note that **NETDIAG** is available in a newer version at **www.download.microsoft.com/ download/win2000platform/Update/5.0.2195.2101/NT5/EN-US/netdiag_setup.exe**. The new release of **NETDIAG** has had the same new functionality added as mentioned for **DCDIAG**.

Windows 2000 Domain Manager (**NETDOM**)

The **NETDOM** tool gives you access to do the following:

- Move computer accounts between domains without altering any Local Groups. If the destination is a Windows 2000 domain, the sIDhistory for the workstation is updated, retaining the security permissions that the computer account had previously.
- Bulk management and monitoring of trust relationships between domains, including trusts for the Windows 2000 portion of a trust link to an MIT Kerberos realm.
- Reset machine account passwords.
- Join a computer to a domain and verify and/or reset the secure channel.
- Manage and view trust relationships between domains.
- Enumerate direct trust relationships and enumerate all (direct and indirect) trust relationships.

You might want to note that, in addition to enabling you to monitor trusts, **NETDOM** provides you with the capability of reassigning machines to another domain after the other directory objects have been moved with **MOVETREE** (see also Chapter 22). If this tool interests you, also take a look at **SIDWALKER**.

NLTEST

This command-line tool checks trust relationships, as well as the connectivity and traffic flow between a network client and a domain controller. **NLTEST** checks the secure channel to make sure that both Windows 2000-based and Windows NT 4.0-based clients can connect to domain controllers.

As such, **NLTEST** can be used to display the current list of trusted domains known by a given server. For each domain listed, you can view the following data:

♦ Trust Index (specific to each DC as the trusts are enumerated)

♦ NetBIOS Domain Name of the Trusted Domain

♦ DNS Domain Name of the Trusted Domain

♦ Trust Type (NT 4, Windows 2000, MIT, or DCE)

The tool also discovers domains and sites (and checks that your DC is in fact part of a valid site). And you can list the DCs and GCs that are available in a given domain. Additionally, **NLTEST** supports user operations to identify which DCs are capable of logging on a specific user, and browsing specific user information.

Tip

*Microsoft seems intent on reusing the **NLTEST** source code in other products (the Exchange 2000 Server being the first example) for checking that your Active Directory is okay before they start doing anything to it. So you might as well test your Active Directory yourself using **NLTEST**.*

NTDSUTIL

NTDSUTIL is a very powerful command-line tool that every Windows 2000 Server administrator should know about, because it provides a suite of Active Directory utilities. With **NTDSUTIL**, you can perform the following:

♦ Database management: Move, compact, repair, and check integrity of the Active Directory database.

♦ FSMO management: Perform either a graceful transfer of role or a seizure of role.

♦ Cleanup of directory metadata.

♦ Precreation of domain(s).

Adding Domains After NTDSUTIL

After you are introduced to **NTDSUTIL**, note that two ways are available to add a domain to a forest:

- Use Active Directory Installation Wizard.

- Use **NTDSUTIL** to connect to the Domain Naming Master FSMO role and then create the object that names the new domain. This puts a less privileged user in the position to execute the Active Directory Installation Wizard because of not having to connect to the Domain Naming Master.

You may want to note this alternative way to add a domain, because this enables a user that isn't a member of Enterprise Admins to install DCs for a new domain. This is especially handy in organizations in which the departmental administrators require the ability to install DCs, but the central IT department could find itself in a hot spot if it provided those administrators with any of the more powerful domain rights.

In short, **NTDSUTIL** is the tool that you should depend on when you need to perform advanced Active Directory management that goes beyond the scope of the functionality offered by the MMC-based administrator tools. **NTDSUTIL** really shines at performing analysis and subsequent cleanups of the core directory structures. This will come in handy if, for example, you need to recover following an error, want to reclaim disk space on the volume that holds the Active Directory database, or want to tidy up Active Directory after removing one or more DCs from the network without having demoted them via the Active Directory Installation Wizard. **NTDSUTIL** also provides some capabilities for transferring FSMO roles that can't be found in the GUI-based tools. If you're a diehard Exchange Server administrator, you will appreciate the fact that **NTDSUTIL** is a wrapper around most of the functionality found in **ESEUTIL**.

Replication Diagnostics Tool (**REPADMIN**)

REPADMIN is a command-line tool that allows you to do the following:

♦ Modify replicated naming contexts between DCs.

♦ Force replication events.

♦ Display replication metadata and the up-to-date vector.

Active Directory Replication Monitor (**REPLMON**)

REPLMON is a stellar GUI-based tool that gives you access to do the following (see Figure 18.35):

♦ View replication topology: You can display domain and site information, as well as replication partners for each naming context.

♦ View the low-level replication information for each server and domain naming context.

♦ Display replication metadata, to determine whether replication is up-to-date.

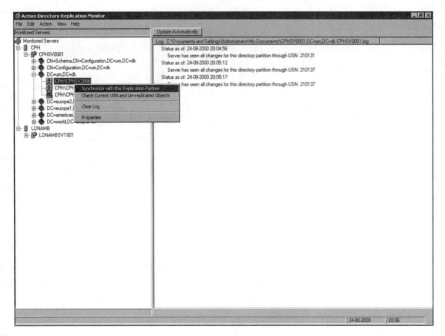

Figure 18.35
Among many other things, **REPLMON** allows you to view all the naming contexts (including partial naming context for the GC) found on each DC/GC, force replications on those, and view the state of replication with the replication partners.

♦ Force replication events.
♦ Force KCC recalculation.
♦ View status of GPOs; that is, whether the GPO and GPT versions are consistent.

You absolutely should check out Active Directory Replication Monitor. And don't let the initial confusion and frustration turn you off; this tool is the real deal—but it's just not that user friendly. The many options for forcing replication (as well as inspecting which entries are still left in the queue for replication to a certain DC or GC) will especially prove very beneficial in just about any production environment. Also, you will find the properties sheets for each server to be a true gold mine of relevant information that allows you to understand exactly what happens in the environment (see Figure 18.36). And it is quite nice that you can see which servers hold the FSMO roles and whether or not you're able to reach them.

And, well, I could go on raving a good time longer about the many features found in **REPLMON**. I just hope that I've presented my case and will see you playing around with this tool so that you can be well prepared in time for any troubleshooting.

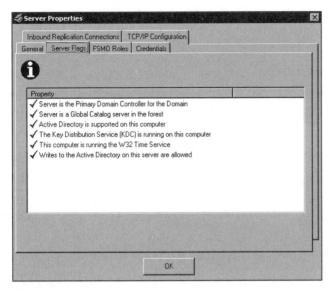

Figure 18.36
There's also a lot of valid and great information in **REPLMON** for checking out the operational
details on a particular server.

Security Administration Tools (**SIDWALKER**)

The **SIDWALKER** toolset enables you to update SIDs on ACEs and to create SID profile
files, via the following tools:

♦ *SHOWACCS*—Lists the security principals (users, computers, and groups) on all ACLs
and memberships in Local Groups.

♦ *SIDEWALKER and Security Migration Editor*—Deletes or replaces every occurrence of an
old SID with a new SID on all ACLs and Local Groups. **SIDWALKER** is a command-
line program; Security Migration Editor is an MMC snap-in.

So, although **SIDWALKER** may have a lot of interesting applications, its primary purpose
is to update ACLs on moved computers (see **NETDOM**) and Local Groups. Although the
toolset is quite fine, I sure do hope that you will be able to stay away from having to use it by
taking the advice given in Chapter 22, because this work always proves very complex (and
time-consuming).

A Mixed Bag

By now you should fully understand my assertion at the beginning that this chapter presents
a mixed bag of information. Hopefully, you also appreciate it by having found the chapter
filled with important information that proves useful to you today—or at least any day soon.

Keep Up-to-Date

I encourage you to stay up-to-date with the fixes, patches, Service Packs, additional program components, and so forth coming from Microsoft. Also, you might want to note that Microsoft finally has developed a variation of the well-known Windows Update site that is tailored for corporate use. The so-called Windows Update Corporate site (**www.corporate.windowsupdate.microsoft.com/en/ default.asp**) provides a comprehensive catalog of updates that can be distributed over a corporate network, and so it represents a one-stop location for Windows Update content and Microsoft Windows Hardware Quality Lab (WHQL) logo device drivers.

Although a lot more can be said on the subject of installing and managing Active Directory, I hope that you are able to get a pilot testing environment up and running by using the information provided in this chapter and in Chapter 17—and perhaps complemented by Windows 2000 Server's fairly fine online Help.

Chapters 19 and 20 clearly aren't everything that you need to implement a fully-fledged Active Directory environment, but they should at least present you with a host of useful information and provide you with a more practical understanding of the architecture and design of Active Directory. These next two chapters stay on course with the more hands-on-oriented approach. In Chapter 19, you learn a lot about how the Active Directory schema is constructed and how it should be handled. Chapter 20 focuses on how to size your Active Directory environment (including such things as database sizing, an in-depth discussion on the network load characteristics, and a short description on how to size the server hardware for the DCs and GCs).

Chapter 19
Schema Management

When you start tapping the real powers of Active Directory, sooner or later you'll want to extend or refine some of the properties made available in Active Directory's built-in object classes. And when you finally realize and appreciate the functionality that the directory service adds to the network infrastructure, you'll likely start wanting to add new object classes. But before you start messing with the default object classes and their properties found in the schema, you should think through the decision carefully. The schema is the heart of the directory service, and if you don't properly handle changes to it, you'll be in trouble. Also remember that trying to fix the schema while avoiding major interruptions on the whole network infrastructure (including all the directory-aware services and applications) is very difficult—if not impossible.

So read this chapter carefully before you make any such modifications, so that you know when and how to plan, prepare, and ultimately modify the directory schema. In saying that, I should also mention that this chapter is useful mainly for administrators (or programmers) who want to extend the Active Directory schema by adding new object types or attributes for their network.

Toward the end of the chapter, you'll learn how to automate the entry of bulk data in Active Directory. This should prove interesting to anyone involved with creating and managing Active Directory, because you need to input a lot of data to make Active Directory genuinely functional for both your applications and your end users.

The Schema in Brief

The kind of information that can be stored in a particular directory database depends on the schema defined for that database. A directory's *schema* defines what object classes and attribute types that directory can contain.

In Active Directory, the schema is stored in the Active Directory database. This is very different from directories that have their schema stored as a text file that is read at startup. For example, the storage of the schema in the Active Directory database means that it is dynamically available to user applications and is dynamically updateable (meaning that you can modify the schema by defining new object types and adding attributes to them and by defining new attributes for existing objects; all on the fly, without any need for rebooting the DCs).

Active Directory has only one schema for the entire Active Directory forest, which is stored in the schema naming context on every DC and maintained on a forest-wide basis to ensure that all objects created conform to the same rules. So, when changes are made to the schema, those changes will be replicated to every DC belonging to that forest.

The schema is the formal definition of all object classes and the attributes that make up those object classes that can be stored in the directory. Active Directory includes a default schema that defines many object classes, such as users, groups, computers, domains, Organizational Units (OUs), and security policies.

Every entry (container or leaf) in Active Directory belongs to some object class. That is, every user account object created is part of the object class user, every computer object created is part of the object class computer, every OU object created is part of the object class Organizational Unit, and so on.

An entry's *object class* defines what attributes (also called *properties*) that entry can contain. A sample attribute for an object of the user class might be the user's last name. Each user object has this attribute, but each user object can hold a different value that is specific to the user it represents. Each attribute can be mandatory or optional (see Figure 19.1). The type of information that is allowed in each attribute is determined by syntax rules (also known as *attribute syntax*). For example, only numeric values are permitted in the **telephoneNumber** attribute.

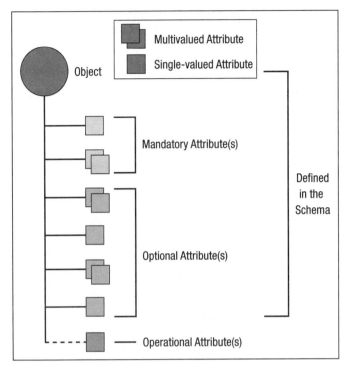

Figure 19.1
The anatomy of a directory object, which is specified by the object class.

Both containers and leaves in the Active Directory tree have attributes, so the information contained in the Active Directory tree isn't "flat," as was the case with Windows NT's directory, Security Account Manager (SAM). Instead, the information in Active Directory is spread throughout the nodes in a tree hierarchy.

Every Active Directory entry and every attribute in every entry also has an *Access Control List (ACL)*. The ACL controls which users are allowed to access each entry or attribute and, also, determines what those users are allowed to do. For example, an entry's ACL settings might allow one user to read all of its attributes, allow another user to read and write a certain subset of those attributes, and allow no access at all to other users.

Active Directory comes with a default set of classes and attributes in the schema (that's 142 object classes and 827 attributes, to be precise), but users and software vendors can add new object classes and attribute types, to add to the directory the functionality that they specifically need. Modifying a directory's schema can be very useful, but it also can have wide-ranging effects—meaning that you should make modifications only with great care. You can perform schema management either from the Active Directory Schema snap-in tool, included on the Windows 2000 Server CD-ROM, or with a programming language via Active Directory Service Interface (ADSI).

The Most Important Active Directory Object Classes

The schema consists of two types of objects:

◆ *Classes*—Each object in the directory is an instance of one class in the schema (see Figure 19.2). For example, the many directory objects include a user class, and every user account on the network is represented by an object of the user class.

◆ *Attributes*—The pieces of information that an object can hold. For example, the schema includes a **mailAddress** attribute.

So, classes actually are collections of attributes, and the attributes hold the information stored in the directory.

Plenty of Objects to Choose from

The Active Directory schema contains literally hundreds of object classes and attribute types. The following are some of the more interesting object classes:

◆ *User*—Identifies a particular user in a domain. Its attributes may include **cn** (Common Name), **userPrincipalName**, **streetAddress** (that is, the corporate address information), **telephoneNumber**, **thumbnailphoto** (that is, a picture), and many more.

◆ *PrintQueue*—Enables a client to find a printer. Its attributes include **location**, **printStatus**, and **printLanguage**.

◆ *Computer*—Identifies a machine in the domain. Among the many attributes this class includes are **operatingSystem**, **operatingSystemServicePack**, **dNSHostName**, and **machineRole** (indicating whether the computer is a DC, a member server, or a workstation).

◆ *OrganizationalUnit (OU)*—Specifies a subdivision of a particular domain. Its most important attribute is **organizationalUnitName**. As you should know by now, OUs play an important role in organizing the information within a domain.

The definitions of classes and attributes (such as the definition of the user class or the **telephoneNumber** attribute) are themselves objects stored in the directory's schema naming context. This model enables Active Directory to manage the directory schema by using

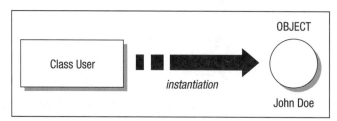

Figure 19.2
Each directory object must be an instantiation of a particular class.

the same object-management operations that are used to manage the rest of the objects in the directory.

Each *class-definition object* specifies the following:

♦ The list of attributes that can be present in an object of that class.

♦ Which of the listed attributes are mandatory.

♦ Hierarchy rules that determine the possible classes in the directory tree, if any, that are parents to the particular class.

An *attribute-definition object* specifies the syntax (the type of information, such as an integer or string) of an attribute, along with such information as whether or not the attribute can have more than one value.

The following sections list the complete information held in class-definition and attribute-definition objects. To see the default classes and attributes created by Microsoft, launch the Active Directory Schema tool in Microsoft Management Console (MMC) and click the Classes and Attributes folders, respectively, in the console tree (see Figures 19.3 and 19.4).

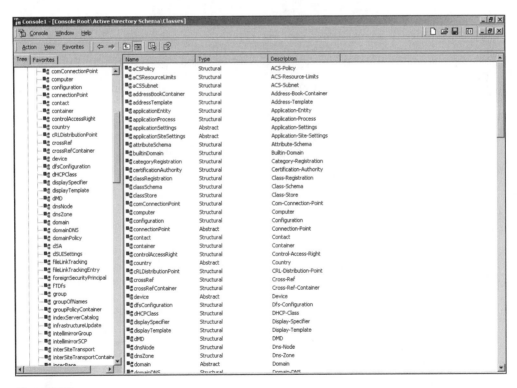

Figure 19.3
Some of the classes available in the default schema.

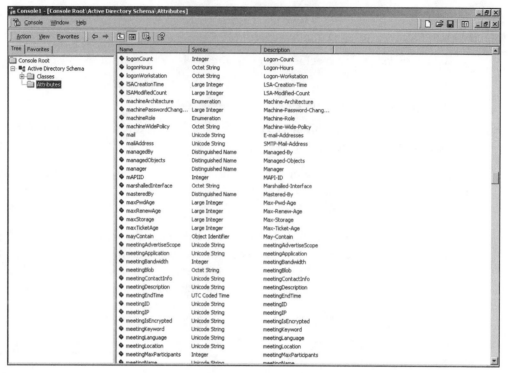

Figure 19.4
A few of the attributes available in the default schema.

The Class-Definition Object

Each class in the schema is represented by an object that defines that class. Such objects are instances of the **classSchema** class. Each class-definition object usually uses most of the attributes listed in Table 19.1. Please note, however, that many more attributes can be

Table 19.1   The most important attributes of an object for defining a class.

Property	Syntax	Mandatory	Multivalued	Description
cn	Unicode	Yes	No	Descriptive Relative distinguished name (RDN).
governsID	OID	Yes	No	Object ID (OID) that uniquely identifies objects of this class.
defaultObject-Category	DN	Yes	No	Distinguished name (DN) that defines the base object category.
objectCategory	DN	Yes	No	DN that defines the object category; this is always the **CN=Class-Schema,CN=Schema, CN=Configuration** in the forest domain context.
lDAPDisplayName	Unicode	No	No	Name by which LDAP clients identify this class.

(continued)

Table 19.1 **The most important attributes of an object for defining a class** *(continued)*.

Property	Syntax	Mandatory	Multivalued	Description
schemaIDGUID	Octet String	Yes	No	Globally Unique ID (GUID) that uniquely identifies this class.
rDNAttID	OID	No	No	RDN type of instances of this class; e.g., **OU=**, **CN=**.
subClassOf	OID	Yes	No	The class this object inherits from. To achieve inheritance from multiple parent classes, you use the **Auxiliary Class** attribute and the **System Auxiliary Class** to define the additional parents.
systemMustContain	OID	No	Yes	The mandatory attributes for instances of this class.
mustContain	OID	No	Yes	The mandatory attributes for instances of this class.
systemMayContain	OID	No	Yes	The optional attributes for instances of this class.
mayContain	OID	No	Yes	The optional attributes for instances of this class.
systemPossSuperiors	OID	No	Yes	The set of classes that can be a parent of this class in the directory hierarchy.
possSuperiors	OID	No	Yes	The set of classes that can be a parent of this class in the directory hierarchy.
systemAuxiliaryClass	OID	No	Yes	The auxiliary set of classes from which this class inherits attributes.
auxiliaryClass	OID	No	Yes	The auxiliary set of classes from which this class inherits attributes.
defaultSecurity-Descriptor	NT Security Descriptor	No	No	The default Security Descriptor (SD) is assigned to new instances of this class, if one isn't specified at creation time.
objectClassCategory	Integer	Yes	No	**Structural Class=1**, **Abstract Class=2**, **Auxiliary Class=3**.
systemOnly	BOOL	No	No	If True, only the system can create and modify instances of this class.
objectClass	OID	Yes	Yes	The class this object is an instance of.
NTSecurity-Descriptor	NT Security	Yes	No	The SD on the class-Descriptor schema object.
instance-Type	Integer	Yes	No	Instance type (internal node, NC head, etc.) of the object.

present and that only a subset of the attributes mentioned in Table 19.1 is mandatory for defining a new class.

Be Careful with the System-Attribute Setting

Some aspects of a class-definition object are contained in pairs of attributes, where the value of one of these attributes is changeable by administrators, and the other is not. These attribute pairs are the following:

♦ **mustContain/systemMustContain**

♦ **mayContain/systemMayContain**

♦ **possSuperiors/systemPossSuperiors**

♦ **auxiliaryClass/systemAuxiliaryClass**

In each of these pairs, the value of the attribute that begins with **system** can't be changed by administrators (and, conversely, the value of the other attribute in each pair can be changed by administrators). This enables Active Directory to protect certain key attributes in each class, to ensure that the schema stays consistent and usable.

Note that, as with any other system-only attribute, you can't change the value of attributes with names beginning with **system**, even for classes that you defined. So, when you define a new class and you set the initial value of the system-only attributes, you can't change those attributes ever again.

Attribute Inheritance

When you define a new class, you can have that class automatically inherit information from an existing class by making it a subclass of that class. The information inherited includes which mandatory and optional attributes the class has (the **systemMustContain**, **mustContain**, **systemMayContain**, and **mayContain** attributes) and which classes can be parents of the new class in the directory hierarchy (the **systemPossSuperiors** and **possSuperiors** attributes).

For example, you could specify an **engineeringPerson** class, which will define information about the people who belong to engineering in your company, including both their basic user information and their specialized information, such as specialty, standard rate, and authority regarding approving designs. You could specify that the **subClassOf** attribute of the **engineeringPerson** class be the **user** class. Then, the **engineeringPerson** class would instantly have all the mandatory and optional attributes (and directory-parent classes) of the user class, without your having to define these attributes specifically.

You can have a new class inherit information from more than one existing class. However, you can specify only one existing class in the **subClassOf** attribute of the new class. Any additional classes must be specified in the **auxiliaryClass** attribute. A new class inherits only mandatory and optional attributes from the classes listed in **auxiliaryClass**—it doesn't inherit the **possSuperiors** attribute from any class listed in **auxiliaryClass**.

The Schema Cache

To benefit applications and system operations that require frequent lookups of the schema, Active Directory maintains a *schema cache,* which is a representation, located in system memory, of all the class-definition and attribute-definition objects currently in the schema. The cache is loaded from the directory database when the server is booted. If you update the schema, the cache is automatically reloaded after a fixed time following the update (the default setting is five minutes).

You can also force an immediate reload of the cache after an update, if you want. However, don't do that too often, because when the schema cache is reloaded, a new cache is actually built from the schema database; the old cache remains in memory and serves existing program threads (and continues doing so until all of them are killed). So, if multiple cache reloads happen while relatively long-lasting program threads are running, many versions of the schema cache may be in memory simultaneously, causing a memory drain on the server.

Note

If you later add another attribute to a class that is specified as a subclass or an auxiliary class to other classes, the new attribute is automatically added to the other classes once the schema cache has been updated.

The Attribute-Definition Object

Each attribute in the schema is represented by an object that defines that attribute. Such objects are instances of the object class called **Attribute Schema**. Each attribute object can have the attributes listed in Table 19.2. Note that only a subset of these attributes is mandatory.

Table 19.2   Attributes of an object that define an attribute.

Property	Syntax	Mandatory	Multi-valued	Description
cn	Unicode	Yes	No	Descriptive RDN.
attributeID	OID	Yes	No	OID that uniquely identifies objects of this class.
lDAPDisplayName	Unicode	No	No	Name by which LDAP clients identify this class.
schemaIDGUID	Octet String	Yes	No	GUID to uniquely identify this attribute.
mAPIID	Integer	No	No	Integer by which MAPI clients identify this attribute.
attributeSecurityGUID	GUID	Yes	No	GUID used by security system to identify the property set of this property.
attributeSyntax	OID	Yes	No	OID of the syntax of this attribute.
oMSyntax	Integer	Yes	No	Another representation of the syntax of this attribute.

(continued)

Table 19.2   Attributes of an object that define an attribute *(continued)*.

Property	Syntax	Mandatory	Multi-valued	Description
isSingleValued	BOOL	Yes	No	Whether this attribute is single-valued or multivalued.
extendedCharsAllowed	BOOL	Yes	No	Whether extended characters are allowed in the value of this attribute.
rangeLower	Integer	No	No	Lower range of allowed values of this attribute. When range-Lower is defined for attributes that are integers, it defines the limits of the value held by the attribute; when defined for strings, it defines the number of characters that can be held in the string.
rangeUpper	Integer	No	No	Upper range of allowed values of this attribute. See the preceding description regarding **rangeLower**.
searchFlags	Integer	No	No	**0=Not Indexed, 1=Indexed**.
systemOnly	BOOL	Yes	No	If True, only the system can modify this attribute. However, the user can add this attribute while adding a new attribute-schema object.
objectClass	OID	Yes	Yes	Class the object is an instance of.
NTSecurityDescriptor	NT Security	Yes	No	The SD on the attribute-**Descriptor schema** object.
instanceType	Integer	Yes	No	**Instance type** (internal node, NC head, etc.) of the object.

Syntaxes

The *syntax* is the kind of data that can be held in a particular attribute, such as an integer, a string, or a date. Every attribute of every object is associated with exactly one syntax. The syntaxes allowed in Active Directory are predefined and preprogrammed by Microsoft, but they are not represented by actual objects in Active Directory. You can't add new syntaxes. When you define a new attribute, you must specify both the OID and the OM-Syntax numbers of the syntax that you want for the attribute. Table 19.3 lists the syntaxes understood by Active Directory.

Obtaining Valid OIDs

Active Directory uses OID strings to provide a unique identifier for all classes and attributes (that is, the **governsID** attribute of class-definition objects and the **attributeID** attribute of attribute-definition objects) stored in the schema. OID strings originated with the X.500

Table 19.3   Attribute syntaxes understood by Active Directory.

Syntax	OID	OM-Syntax	Description
Distinguished Name	2.5.5.1	127	The fully qualified name of an object in the directory.
Object Identifier (OID)	2.5.5.2	6	An OID number, which is a string containing digits and decimal points.
Case Sensitive String	2.5.5.3	20	A case-sensitive character string.
Case Insensitive String	2.5.5.4	20	A case-insensitive string containing characters from the teletex character set.
Print Case String	2.5.5.5	19	A case-sensitive string containing characters from the printable character set.
IA5-String	2.5.5.5	22	A case-sensitive string containing characters from the IA5 character set.
Numeric String	2.5.5.6	18	String containing digits.
OR Name	2.5.5.7	127	From X.400.
Boolean (BOOL)	2.5.5.8	1	True or False.
Integer	2.5.5.9	2	32-bit number.
Enumeration	2.5.5.9	10	Defined by ITU. Treated as an integer.
Octet String	2.5.5.10	4	A string of bytes.
Replica Link	2.5.5.10	127	Active Directory system-only.
UTC Coded Time	2.5.5.11	23	Time value in the UTC-Time format (see ISO 8601 and X680).
Generalized Time	2.5.5.11	24	Time value in the Generalized-Time format (see ISO 8601 and X680). This should always be your preferred choice, because the year is represented in four characters rather than the UTC Coded Time's two.
Unicode String	2.5.5.12	64	A case-insensitive Unicode string.
Address	2.5.5.13	127	A string containing OSI presentation address.
Access Point	2.5.5.14	127	From X.400.
Distinguished Name With String	2.5.5.14	127	A string that contains a string value and a Distinguished name (DN).
NT Security Descriptor	2.5.5.15	66	A string that contains a Windows NT Security Descriptor.
Large Integer	2.5.5.16	65	64-bit number.
SID	2.5.5.17	4	A SID value.
DN Binary	2.5.5.17	127	A string that contains a binary value and a DN.

directory service specifications and, thus, use the same tree structure as Active Directory, to ensure that objects defined by different entities won't conflict as various directories are brought together into a global directory. Further, OID strings are actually globally unique numeric values, because they are issued by a central issuing authority, somewhat similar to the central registration of IP addresses used in the Internet, though the mechanism is slightly different.

If you want to create a new class or attribute, you must contact an issuing authority—for example, International Standards Organization (ISO) or American National Standards Institute (ANSI). The authority will assign you an OID space, which is a branch of the universal ISO-ITU OID tree.

Note

Although it's a terribly wrong thing to do, Microsoft has included a command-line utility in the Windows 2000 Server Resource Kit (OID Generator, or simply **Oidgen.exe***) that can generate OIDs that look valid to the schema but aren't registered with the proper authorities.*

A fictional example of a space assigned to a company might be 1.2.333.4444. The company can then extend this space internally, as needed (within constraints of the structure of an OID). For example, the company can further subdivide this space by appending dotted-decimal numbers to its assigned OID root number and then assigning these subspaces to its various divisions. Each division, in turn, can further subdivide this subspace, and so on.

The example company with the OID space number 1.2.333.4444 could grant one of its divisions the number 1.2.333.4444.5. That division might then decide to use 1.2.333.4444.5.1 as the base number for classes it creates, and 1.2.333.4444.5.2 for attributes it creates. Any class this division creates would then have a **governsID** of 1.2.333.4444.5.1.*x*, where *x* is a decimal number less than 268 million (or, to be more precise: $2^{28}-1$).

For a more practical example, ISO is 1 in the OID tree, ANSI was issued 2 (that is, 1.2), ANSI issued 840 to the U.S. (1.2.840), and ANSI issued Microsoft 113556 (1.2.840.113556). Microsoft, in turn, issued 1 to Active Directory (1.2.840.113556.1), 5 to Active Directory classes (1.2.840.113556.1.5), and 4 to built-in classes (1.2.840.113556.1.5.4).

When to Modify the Schema

Before you even start planning how to modify the schema, you should spend a fair amount of time exploring all the predefined object classes and object properties in order to avoid overlooking the solutions at hand. Then, you should start your schema-modification plans only after you are totally confident that none of the predefined classes and properties will fulfill your needs (not even when the semantics of the properties are tweaked somewhat).

Exploring the predefined objects will take a while, because the default Active Directory schema has 142 classes and 827 attributes from which to choose. And these numbers will be doubled, if Exchange 2000 Server also is running inside the forest.

After you finish your review and have established that none of the predefined classes and properties meet your needs, you should evaluate the data types that you intend to fill into Active Directory. Ideally, that data should fall into the first of the following three categories:

♦ *Static*—Changes more slowly than the replication frequency of Active Directory.

- *Low-latency*—Changes faster than the replication frequency of Active Directory and thus must be replicated to other DCs every so often.
- *Transient*—Changes so much faster than the replication frequency of Active Directory that it's not sensible to replicate it at all.

The data also should meet these rules:

- It's globally relevant in the domain where it is instantiated.
- It consists of well-defined attributes: Binary Large Objects (BLOBS) are acceptable, but discrete attributes are always preferable over opaque BLOBS.
- Its useful life is at least four times the maximum replication latency.
- The size of its individual items is of "reasonable size." If the size is more than 75KB, you should consider storing the big chunks of data in the file system rather than in the directory. In this case, File Replication Service (FRS) will be able to meet your needs for replication, although no support exists for link tracking.

Finally, needless to say, clients have to be able to tolerate data being out-of-date for the maximum replication latency.

Deciding How to Modify the Schema

After you make sure that all properties of the needed directory objects meet the specifications outlined in the preceding section, you should start planning how the modifications will take place.

Here you have several very different choices (listed from the best choice to the worst choice):

- Extend an existing class by adding attributes.
- Extend an existing class by adding parent classes.
- Derive from an existing class and add additional attributes.
- Create new attributes with the needed properties.
- Create a new class with the needed (possibly new) attributes.

You should opt to extend an existing class under the following circumstances:

- The class needs additional attributes, but otherwise meets your needs.
- No requirement exists to identify the class as a separate and distinct entity.

You should opt to derive from an existing class when the following applies:

- The class needs additional attributes, but otherwise meets your needs.
- A requirement exists to identify the class as a separate and distinct entity.

You should create a new class or attribute only when:

- No existing class or attribute meets your needs, even with some tweaking.

In regard to adding new classes or attributes, remember that the scope of any new addition is the entire forest, so you should have some very serious reasons for the addition or at least be absolutely confident that no existing object class or attribute can meet your needs (see Figure 19.5).

Because the schema constitutes such a vitally important part of your corporate IT infra-structure, you should set up a rigid process regarding implementing modifications to the schema, which could include a committee that receives and debates formal requests for schema changes.

How to Handle Schema Modifications

When you add new properties and classes, take great care regarding the naming conven-tions you use. The following are the recommended naming conventions:

♦ Use a vendor-specific suffix/prefix, if applicable. For example, SAP, Baan, PeopleSoft, or any other relevant company name.

♦ Be verbose—don't use cryptic names.

♦ Understand the demographics (accessibility semantics and so forth) for the new object or property.

Also, be very persistent about securing a strong level of documentation, which should in-clude the following:

♦ A list of any new classes and attributes, with a rigorous explanation of each one.

♦ A list of any standard classes that are extended with new attributes, and a list of the attributes.

♦ A list of any new property pages, with an explanation of how to use each one.

♦ If applicable, an explanation of how the schema extensions are used by services and other applications.

Make the intended scope of the objects and properties transparent to readers. In other words, identify whether the objects and properties are going to be used in the domain partition (providing full object replicas for the domain) or the configuration partition (providing full object replicas throughout the forest). And, if you use the configuration

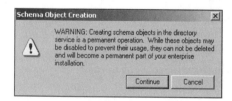

Figure 19.5
I urge you to heed this warning!

partition, decide whether the object instances should be stored in the Services child folder or the Site child folder.

You should use the configuration partition *only* when the following applies:

♦ The information is globally relevant.

♦ All attributes are highly available.

♦ The volatility of the information is very low.

♦ The volume of the information is very small.

Finally, if you expect to implement schema modifications occasionally, you should develop and publish a schema-modification policy to avoid any problems that may occur inside this vital area. Any snags might have very harsh implications for all of your Active Directory users, so play it as safe as possible. At a minimum, your schema-modification policy should include guidelines for the following:

♦ *Initiating schema modifications*—Details of what must be included in a schema-modification proposal, to whom should such proposals be submitted, and how to validate the need for the requested changes.

♦ *Planning schema modifications*—When a schema change is approved, ensure that the proposed schema modifications meet *all* the needs that initially triggered the change and implement effective offline piloting and online recovery plans.

♦ *Modifying the schema*—Make sure the right people are supervising the implementation of the actual changes and that the directory integrity is checked immediately after implementing the changes.

Modifying the Schema

To modify the schema, you can either use the Active Directory Schema tool supplied with Windows 2000 Server or extend it programmatically using ADSI. Because classes and attributes are represented in the directory as objects, to add a new class or attribute you simply need to add a new class-definition or attribute-definition object, with the necessary attributes.

On the Subject of Documenting Your Schema Changes

You should want to note that Microsoft has developed a program—SchemaDoc—for documenting extensions made to your Active Directory schema. This very nice piece of code will search your directory based on the prefix you give it and then copy the information from the classes and attributes that match the prefix into an XML file.

Although the SchemaDoc program is built for the purpose of having ISVs documenting their schema additions to Microsoft in the same way, when they apply for the coveted Windows 2000 logo, you might find the program a good fit for your own documentation needs. Currently, the SchemaDoc program is available for download at **http://msdn.microsoft.com/certification/download.asp**.

Similarly, modifying a class or attribute simply involves modifying the class-definition or attribute-definition object.

When extending the schema, you should follow this order of processing:

1. Remove the safety interlocks on the domain controller (DC), if this is the first time that you are extending the schema.

2. Add new attributes. After you do so, you may want to reload the schema cache, to avoid any trouble with the attributes not being ready when you add the classes.

3. Add new classes.

4. Add attributes to classes.

5. Trigger a schema cache reload. Although you have automatic refresh after approximately five minutes, you might want to trigger the reload so that you can immediately view the changes implemented.

Removing the Safety Interlocks to Modify the Schema

Before you can use a particular DC to modify the schema, the following conditions must exist:

♦ The DC that will modify the schema must be recognized by the other DCs as the server that can currently modify the schema (only one DC in the forest can possess this role at a given time).

♦ The DC must be enabled for schema modification.

Active Directory enables you to modify the schema at any DC in the forest. However, because simultaneous schema updates at two different DCs might conflict with each other—which can prove fatal to all directory operations—Active Directory allows schema updates at only one DC in the forest at any given time. In practice, this restriction is implemented by the Schema Master (also called the Schema Operations Master) role, which is one example of the Flexible Single-Master Operation (FSMO) functionality introduced in Chapter 12 and further explained in Chapter 18. Only the DC currently holding the Schema Master FSMO role is allowed to make updates to the schema.

The current Schema Master in the forest is always identified by the value of the **FSMO-Role-Owner** attribute on the schema container. By default, the first DC in the forest becomes the initial Schema Master and remains so until the DC either fails or is instructed by the administrator to transfer the Schema Master role to some other DC. So, to perform a schema update at a particular DC, that DC must be the current Schema Master. Otherwise, it must request the current Schema Master to transfer that power.

The process of changing the Schema Master is transparent to administrators, if you use the Active Directory Schema tool (see Figure 19.6). When you change the schema programmatically, you must explicitly check whether the DC is the current Schema Master, and if it isn't, you must explicitly request the transfer operation.

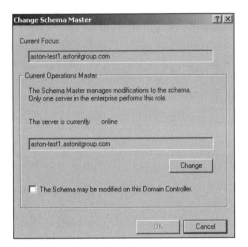

Figure 19.6
Decide whether to connect to the current Schema Master DC or transfer the role to the DC currently in use.

The current Schema Master changes the **FSMO-Role-Owner** attribute on its schema container to the name of the DC requesting to be the new Schema Master, and then sends this new attribute value back to the new master. The current Schema Master also sends any schema changes that it performed that haven't been replicated yet to the new Schema Master (this scenario is possible because of replication latencies).

The new Schema Master applies all changes that were sent by the old Schema Master and becomes the new Schema Master. This ensures that the current Schema Master always has the latest schema with all the changes. At this point, you are allowed to make schema changes at the new Schema Master. Also, by default, all DCs (including the Schema Master

---

What to Do if Disaster Strikes the DC Holding the Schema Master Role

If the old Schema Master is unavailable or has crashed, you can manually change the value of **FSMO-Role-Owner** to enable a new server to make schema changes. You do this by using the **NTDSUTIL.EXE** utility that is available on the Windows 2000 Server (you can find more information on the use of **NTDSUTIL.EXE** in Chapter 18).

However, if you opt to change the Schema Master manually, be aware that any schema changes made at the old Schema Master may not have been propagated to the new one yet, and thus may be lost. And, even worse, suppose that you switch the role manually, make schema changes at the new master, and then the old master is brought online—with the changes not previously replicated to the new master. If the two sets of changes don't conflict, they will replicate to each other and to the rest of the forest, and everything should be okay in regard to the current schema. However, if the schema changes at the old Schema Master and the new Schema Master conflict, some of the changes will be lost. And remember, you don't want two DCs holding the Schema Master role because of the risk of collisions mentioned earlier. That's why Microsoft recommends that you use the utmost caution when changing the **FSMO-Role-Owner** value manually.

Starting the Active Directory Schema MMC Snap-In

Microsoft doesn't expect schema management to be performed frequently, so at the outset, Windows 2000 Server provides neither an Active Directory Schema console nor a Start menu item to the administrator. The Active Directory Schema snap-in is actually located in the Windows 2000 Administration Tools (also known as the Admin Tools Pack), which is installed by running the *adminpak.msi* file found in the \i386 folder on the Windows 2000 Server CD-ROM. To save the console, select Console|Save and then enter a name for the saved console (for example, "schema.msc").

FSMO holder) are disabled for schema modifications. Therefore, to be able to do anything, you first need to enable write access to the schema on the Schema Master DC. You do so by placing a checkmark in The Schema may be modified on this Domain Controller checkbox, located in the Change Schema Master dialog box in the Active Directory Schema MMC snap-in.

Finally, before you try to do any schema changes, make sure that you are a member of the Schema Admins Group, because only such members are allowed to make changes to the Active Directory schema. Chances are good that you won't be a member, because Active Directory, by default, includes as members of Schema Admins only the Administrator account on the root of the first domain created in the forest.

When all the preceding items are in order, you can implement the changes that you want to make to the schema, either via the Active Directory Schema MMC snap-in tool or by using a programming language that interfaces with ADSI. The next section provides an idea of how this is done in practice.

Adding a Class

To add a new class, you add a new schema-definition object, with all the associated attributes that you want it to include. Some attributes are mandatory for every class that you define, as listed in Table 19.4. Some of these attributes are not allowed to be assigned any

Table 19.4   Mandatory attributes for new class-definition objects, including information on what happens, when defining the attribute from the Active Directory Schema snap-in.

Mandatory Information	Default
cn	No default; must be specified by administrator.
objectClass	Must be specified as **Class-Schema**.
governsID	No default; must be specified by administrator as an OID string.
subClassOf	Defaults to Top if not specified by the administrator.
instanceType	Defaults to the correct value for schema objects. Administrators never need to specify a value for this attribute.
schemaIDGUID	Defaults to new, unique value if the administrator doesn't specify a value.
NTSecurityDescriptor	Defaults if the administrator doesn't specify a value. The default value depends on the **Default-Security-Descriptor** of the **Class-Schema** class.

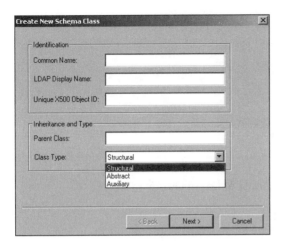

Figure 19.7
Defining the minimal entries for creating a new class.

value from the outset; in that case, they are assigned default values. A minimal definition of a new class specifies just **cn**, **objectClass**, and **governsID** (see Figure 19.7). However, to make the class useful, you probably also want to add some mandatory and optional attributes at the time of creating the class.

After the class has been defined, you might also want to add some auxiliary classes and/or possible superior attributes, as well as more optional attributes (you can't add more mandatory attributes after the class has been created). Also note that, in theory, you have three different types of classes (that is, **instanceType**) to choose from:

- *Structural*—Can be created (in other words, can be instantiated as an object).
- *Abstract*—Can't be created (can't be directly instantiated). It's a superclass that other classes can be derived from.
- *Auxiliary*—Can't be created (can't be directly instantiated). It's a superclass that other classes can include in their definition.

In almost all instances, you will want to use the Structural class.

Any attributes that you specify when adding a new class must already exist. So, if you want to add a new class with new attributes, you first must add the new attributes to the schema. Also, remember that when you add a new class, the OID specified in **governsID** must be unique not only in your forest, but throughout the world (see the earlier section "Obtaining Valid OIDs").

As a simple example of adding a class, suppose that you want to add a new class, **Friend**, to store information about friends. Any **Friend** object must contain the name of the friend and may contain their address and phone number. And, because a friend is a person, you want objects of the **Friend** class to have the same mandatory and optional attributes, as well as directory superiors, as the **Person** class. In this case, you add the following class definition:

```
cn = Friend
objectClass =  Class-Schema
subClassOf =  Person
governsID =  Your_organization's_OID_string
mustContain =  Name
mayContain =  Address, Phone-Number
```

Figures 19.8 through 19.11 show an example of how a class may look (in this instance, it's the class definition for OUs).

Modifying a Class

To modify a class, simply modify the existing class-definition object representing the class. However, some attributes of each class are designated as *system-only*, for consistency and security reasons. You can't modify system-only attributes—even for new classes that you have created. System-only attributes are designated by having their **systemOnly** attribute set to True.

The following attributes of a class-definition object are system-only and thus can't be modified:

♦ **governsID**

♦ **schemaIDGUID**

♦ **rDNAttID**

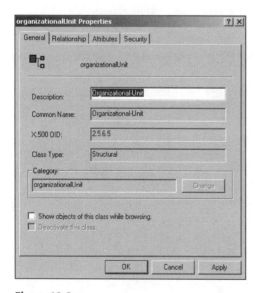

Figure 19.8
The most important definitions of the class, including the option of deactivating it.

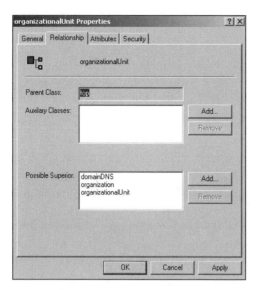

Figure 19.9
The relationship to other classes, which include possible inheritance and the classes allowed to be used as parents in the directory.

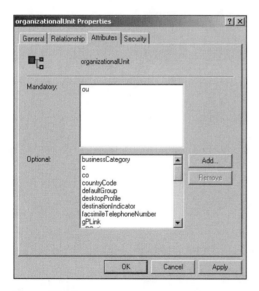

Figure 19.10
Defining the mandatory and optional attributes.

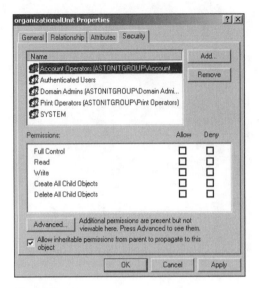

Figure 19.11
Specifies which actions (permissions) that the users and groups are allowed to perform on the class.

- ◆ **subClassOf**
- ◆ **systemMustContain**
- ◆ **systemMayContain**
- ◆ **systemPossSuperiors**
- ◆ **systemAuxiliaryClass**
- ◆ **objectClassCategory**
- ◆ **systemOnly**
- ◆ **objectClass**
- ◆ **instanceType**

Adding an Attribute

To add a new attribute, you add a new schema-definition object, with all the properties that you want to include (see Figure 19.12). Some properties are mandatory for every new attribute object that you define, as listed in Table 19.5. If you don't define values for some of these properties, they are given default values. You also need to consider whether the new attribute object should be included in the GC. For the sake of keeping the replication traffic to a minimum, always start out with the hypothesis that you do *not* need to include the attribute in the GC—and then have everybody try to convince you otherwise.

Figure 19.12
Defining a new attribute.

Table 19.5   Mandatory attributes for new attribute-definition objects, including information on what happens, when defining the attribute from the Active Directory Schemasnap-in.

Mandatory Information	Default
cn	No default; must be specified by administrator.
objectClass	Must be specified as Attribute-Schema. Thus this attribute isn't shown to the administrator.
attributeID	No default; must be specified by administrator as an OID string.
attributeSyntax	No default; administrator must specify one of the syntaxes (see Table 19.3) recognized by Active Directory.
oMSyntax	No default; administrator must specify an OM-Syntax that matches the corresponding attribute syntax.
schemaIDGUID	Defaults to new, unique value if the administrator doesn't specify a value.
instanceType	Defaults to the correct value for schema objects. Administrators never need to specify a value for this attribute.
isSingleValued	Defaults to False if the administrator doesn't check the checkbox for making it multivalued. A multivalued attribute can be assigned more than one value.
NTSecurityDescriptor	A default value that is dependent on the **Default-Security-Descriptor** of the **Class-Schema** class is inserted by default.

As an example of extending the schema with a new attribute, suppose you want to add a new attribute called **Names**. Each instance of a **Names** attribute will store exactly one Unicode string of at least 1 character and no more than 1000 characters. In this case, you add the following attribute definition:

```
cn = Names
objectClass =  Attribute-Schema
attributeId = Your_organization's_OID_string
attributeSyntax = 2.5.5.12
oMSyntax =  64
isSingleValued =  TRUE
rangeLower = 1
rangeUpper = 1000
```

Figure 19.13 is an example of how an attribute may look—in this instance, it's the attribute definition for a User Principal Name (UPN).

Modifying an Attribute

To modify an attribute, simply modify the corresponding attribute-definition object. Again, some attributes of each attribute-definition object are designated as system-only, for consistency and security reasons. You can't modify system-only attributes of an attribute-definition object. System-only attributes are designated by having their **systemOnly** attribute set to True.

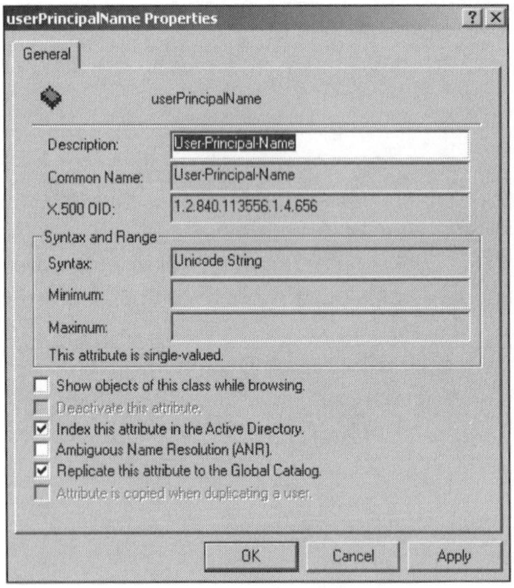

Figure 19.13
Note the options for deactivating the attribute and for replicating it to the Global Catalog.

The Attribute Options

As you can see from Figure 19.13, a couple of options are available for each attribute in the schema. The most important of those options controls which of the attributes that are used by both Active Directory and the Global Catalog (GC). These attributes have the **Index this attribute in the Active Directory** and (making an attribute indexed means that directory searches involving that attribute are going to be more efficient than if the attribute had no index—the more unique the values, the bigger the difference to the nonindexed situation; the index is built automatically by a background thread on the DC) **Replicate this attribute to the Global Catalog** options selected in their properties—and, hence, the attribute is said to be replicated to the GC.

The attributes included in the GC by default are listed in Table 19.6. The other major attribute option is the Ambiguous Name Resolution (ANR). ANR is a search algorithm implemented by Active Directory for easier searching. The whole point of ANR is that it allows objects to be bound without complex search filters when you use Lightweight Directory Access Protocol (LDAP) clients. So, rather than presenting complex filters, a search can be presented for partial matches. If a space is embedded in the search string, the search is divided at the space and an "or" search is also performed on the attributes. If there is more than one space, the search divides only at the first space.

ANR is useful when you are locating objects and attributes that may or may not be known by the client. A common use for ANR, for example, is in a situation in which a building name is known by the requesting client, but not the associated number. In this case, the **physicalDeliveryOfficeName** attribute may have a value of "Building 40" and a client might search for "Building." ANR returns a match in this instance. It also returns other matches containing the word "Building."

By default, the following attributes are set for ANR:

- **GivenName**
- **Surname**
- **displayName**
- **LegacyExchangeDN**
- **msExchMailNickname**
- **RDN**
- **physicalDeliveryOfficeName**
- **proxyAddress**
- **sAMAccountName**

Table 19.6 The attributes being replicated to the GC by default.

Name	Syntax
c	Unicode string
cA-Certificate	Unicode string
cA-Certificate-DN	Unicode string
certificate-Templates	Unicode string
description	Unicode string
distinguished-Name	Distinguished name

(continued)

Table 19.6   The attributes being replicated to the GC by default *(continued).*

Name	Syntax
dNS-Host-Name	Unicode string
domain-Component	Unicode string
driver-Name	Unicode string
dS-Core-Propagation-Data	Generalized Time
flags	Integer
frs-Computer-Reference	Distinguished name
fRS-Member-Reference	Distinguished name
gP-Link	Unicode string
home-Phone	Unicode string
meetingDescription	Unicode string
meetingName	Unicode string
meetingProtocol	Unicode string
member	Distinguished name
mSMQ-Authenticate	Boolean
mSMQ-Base-Priority	Integer
mSMQ-Dependent-Client-Services	Boolean
mSMQ-Digests-Mig	Octet String
mSMQ-Ds-Services	Boolean
mSMQ-Encrypt-Key	Octet String
mSMQ-Foreign	Boolean
mSMQ-In-Routing-Servers	Distinguished name
mSMQ-Journal	Boolean
mSMQ-OS-Type	Integer
mSMQ-Out-Routing-Servers	Distinguished name
mSMQ-Privacy-Level	Enumeration
mSMQ-Queue-Journal-Quota	Integer
mSMQ-Queue-Name-Ext	Unicode string
mSMQ-Queue-Quota	Integer
mSMQ-Routing-Services	Boolean
mSMQ-Service-Type	Integer
mSMQ-Sign-Certificates	Octet string
mSMQ-Sign-Certificates-Mig	Octet string
mSMQ-Sign-Key	Octet string
mSMQ-Sites	Octet string
mSMQ-Transactional	Boolean
mSMQ-User-Sid	Octet string
ms-RRAS-Attribute	Unicode string
netboot-Machine-File-Path	Unicode string
nT-Security-Descriptor	NT-Security-Descriptor
o	Unicode string
object-Class	Object Identifier
partial-Attribute-Deletion-List	Octet string
partial-Attribute-Set	Octet string

(continued)

Table 19.6   The attributes being replicated to the GC by default *(continued)*.

Name	Syntax
pKI-Critical-Extensions	Unicode string
pKI-Default-CSPs	Unicode string
pKI-Default-Key-Spec	Integer
pKI-Enrollment-Access	NT Security Descriptor
pKI-Expiration-Period	Octet string
pKI-Extended-Key-Usage	Unicode string
pKI-Key-Usage	Octet string
pKI-Max-Issuing-Depth	Integer
pKI-Overlap-Period	Octet string
poss-Superiors	Object Identifier
print-Color	Boolean
print-Duplex-Supported	Boolean
printer-Name	Unicode string
print-Max-Resolution-Supported	Integer
print-Media-Ready	Unicode string
print-Pages-Per-Minute	Integer
print-Share-Name	Unicode string
print-Stapling-Supported	Boolean
proxied-Object-Name	DN Binary
range-Lower	Integer
range-Upper	Integer
repl-Property-Meta-Data	Octet string
repl-UpToDate-Vector	Octet string
reps-From	Replica Link
reps-To	Replica Link
server-Name	Unicode string
service-Binding-Information	Unicode string
service-Class-ID	Octet string
service-Class-Info	Octet string
service-Instance-Version	Octet string
short-Server-Name	Unicode string
signature-Algorithms	Unicode string
st	Unicode string
street	Unicode string
sub-Refs	Distinguished name
system-Poss-Superiors	Object Identifier
telephone-Number	Unicode string
user-Certificate	Octet string
user-SMIME-Certificate	Octet string
USN-Last-Obj-Rem	Larger Integer
version-Number	Integer
well-Known-Objects	DN Binary
when-Changed	Generalized Time
when-Created	Generalized Time
winsock-Addresses	Octet string

The following attributes of an attribute-definition object are system-only and thus can't be modified:

♦ **attributeId**

♦ **schemaIDGUID**

♦ **attributeSyntax**

♦ **oMSyntax**

♦ **isSingleValued**

♦ **systemOnly**

♦ **objectClass**

♦ **objectCategory**

♦ **instanceType**

System Checks on Schema Additions and Modifications

When you complete the addition or modification of a class or attribute, Active Directory performs some checks to make sure that the changes don't cause inconsistencies or other problems in the schema.

For both class and attribute changes, the system makes sure that the values of **ldapDisplayName** and **schemaIdGUID** are indeed unique. For class changes, the system also checks to make sure that the following conditions are met:

♦ The value of **governsId** must be unique.

♦ All attributes defined in the **systemMayContain**, **mayContain**, **systemMustContain**, and **mustContain** lists must already exist.

♦ All classes defined in the **subClassOf**, **systemAuxiliaryClass**, **auxiliaryClass**, **systemPossSuperiors**, and **possSuperiors** lists must already exist.

♦ All classes in the **systemAuxiliaryClass**, **auxiliaryClass**, **systemPossSuperiors**, and **possSuperiors** lists must have Auxiliary Class specified as their **objectClassCategory**.

♦ Classes in the **subClassOf** list must follow certain X.500 specifications for the inheritance hierarchy: Abstract classes can inherit only from other Abstract classes, and Auxiliary classes cannot inherit from Structural classes.

♦ The attribute specified in the **rDNAttID** attribute must have Unicode string as its syntax.

For attribute changes, the system checks to make sure the following conditions are met:

♦ The value of **attributeID** must be unique.

♦ The value of **mAPIID**, if any, must be unique.

♦ If **rangeLower** and **rangeUpper** are present, **rangeLower** must be less than **rangeUpper**.

♦ **attributeSyntax** and **oMSyntax** must match, as previously shown in Table 19.2.

Issues Related to Modifying the Schema

This section explores several of the more advanced issues that you should be aware of before implementing changes to the schema.

Problem 1: Replication Takes Time

Because the schema is replicated across the forest, a schema update performed at one server is guaranteed to be propagated throughout the forest, guaranteeing a forest-wide, consistent schema. However, because of replication latencies, temporary inconsistencies may occur.

The fact that Active Directory uses multi-master replication means that some time elapses before the schema changes reach all the DCs in the forest, and any replication collision (however unlikely that may be due to the Schema Master FSMO methodology) can be uncovered and solved.

As an example of the possible consequences of this time window, suppose that a new class A is created at server X, and then an instance B of this class is created at the same server X. However, when the changes are replicated to another server, server Y, the object B is replicated out before the class-schema object A. When the change arrives at server Y, the replication of B fails, because Y's copy of the schema still doesn't contain the class-schema object A, and hence Y doesn't know of the existence of object A.

Active Directory solves this problem by explicitly replicating the schema container from the originating machine when such failures occur. Additionally, the replication of the schema container triggers an immediate schema cache update on the target server. Active Directory then re-replicates the object that failed. In the example, the re-replication brings in class-definition object A and puts it into Y's schema cache. Retrying the replication of B succeeds after this re-replication occurs.

Active Directory's capability to resolve the preceding scenario means that administrators and applications have to cope with only two issues: latency-induced states and multi-master-update-induced states. Latency-induced states can be further broken down into the following:

♦ *Version skew*—One replica has new values and the other has old values.

♦ *Partial update*—One replica has new values and the other has some new and some old values.

Multi-master-update-induced states deal with *intra-object inconsistency*. For example, property A is updated at DC 1, and property B is updated at DC 2, but A and B are related, and although the values were valid at update time, they are invalid together.

The possible avoidance strategies for these issues are the following:

♦ When possible, use a single object to store your information, which avoids the "partial update" case.

♦ Avoid interrelated properties, which avoids the "intra-object inconsistency" case.

When a Class or Attribute Is Ready to Retire

Classes and attributes can *never* be removed from the schema (which is why you don't want to let just anything into the schema). So, if you have some class or attribute definitions that won't be used again, your only available option is to deactivate them.

Deactivation (as well as reactivation) can be easily accomplished on the properties page for the given schema object(s). However, deactivation removes neither the definitions nor the instances of the object from the directory. Thus, you have to do your own housekeeping (remember, too, that you can delete only the instances occurring in the directory, never the schema definitions). Also, please note that you can't deactivate an attribute if it's included in any class that isn't deactivated.

However, no matter how you look at it, version skew is unavoidable in a replication system (such as Active Directory) that builds on the multi-master loose-consistency-with-convergence model.

Problem 2: Concurrency Control

Active Directory must ensure that different program threads don't perform simultaneous, conflicting schema updates (such as one thread deactivating an attribute while another adds that attribute to the **mustContain** list of a class). To ensure this, any thread that attempts to perform a schema update also writes a special attribute in the schema container as part of the same transaction (that is, Active Directory automatically causes the thread to write this attribute). Only one thread can write this attribute at any one time, which ensures that the schema updates are performed serially.

This method guarantees schema consistency, but it doesn't guarantee which of the updates will be successful. You must be aware of this fact when schema updates are made in a batch, such as in the case of the installation of directory service-aware applications. For example, consider a scenario in which two Active Directory-aware applications, A and B, are being installed simultaneously, each creating several new schema objects. Because Active Directory creates one thread per object update, it is possible that, after some of the objects in A and some of the objects in B are created (if the internal threads don't overlap), one of the installations will fail (because a thread for a schema-object creation for A overlaps with a thread for a schema-object creation for B).

Assume that A fails. Running A again from scratch won't work, because some of the objects that A creates are already created in the schema, and trying to re-create them in the second run (existing objects) will return an error. Therefore, applications that modify the schema shouldn't be run concurrently, unless the application first checks to ensure that the schema update about to be made hasn't already been made for each of the updates.

Problem 3: Handling Invalid Object Instances

A schema update can make an existing instance of an object invalid. For example, consider object X that is an instance of class Y, which in turn has an attribute Z in its **mayContain** list. Because X is an instance of class Y, X can make use of this attribute. A schema update is performed that modifies class Y by deleting Z from its **mayContain** list. This change makes the instance X invalid, because X now has an attribute Z that it isn't allowed to have, according to the class definition of Y (of which X is an instance).

In the current release of Windows 2000 Server, Active Directory allows the now-invalid objects to remain in the directory. They may be usable, but that depends on the nature of the schema changes, and thus nothing really is guaranteed. For example, if you add an attribute to the **mayContain** list of a class, no problems occur. However, if you add an attribute to the **mustContain** list, you can then read an existing object of this class, but you can't write to it until you add a value for the new mandatory attribute.

Problem 4: The Schema Cache

As mentioned earlier, Active Directory maintains a schema cache, which is a representation, in system memory, of all the class-definition and attribute-definition objects currently in the schema. Essentially, this means that two copies of the schema exist: one in the underlying directory database and one in memory. Naturally, Active Directory must keep these two copies of the schema identical when administrators make dynamic schema modifications.

When an administrator modifies the schema, the changes are made directly to the underlying database. However, for performance reasons, the schema cache in memory isn't updated on every schema update, because updating the schema cache is a costly operation in terms of performance and because schema changes tend to occur in bunches.

Instead, Active Directory waits for five minutes after the first schema update before it reloads the schema cache from the database. If multiple schema changes are being performed, this delay makes it much more likely that all (or at least several) schema changes will be finished by that time. Therefore, for at least five minutes (more, if the first cache update is made before the last of the schema changes), the schema cache contains an old copy of the schema and doesn't reflect the most recent changes. So, if someone immediately tries to add an object that is an instance of a new class that isn't in the cache yet, Active Directory returns an error, because it refers to the cache to find the class definition of an object being created.

However, you can define a new attribute and then immediately define a new class that uses that new attribute, as long as you refer to the new attribute by its OID rather than its name. (Referring to an attribute by name requires the schema cache to convert the name to its OID).

How to Do Bulk Data Entry

How to do bulk data entry is one of the issues that creep into the agenda when you create your Active Directory or when you simply want to make better use of Active Directory's many dormant attributes. Unfortunately, Microsoft hasn't been very forthcoming with information on this issue until recently (probably because of its focus on the core Active Directory functionalities and capabilities).

Although the information on bulk data entry still is rather limited, you can find quite nice support of bulk data entry (as well as bulk exporting) hidden in the depths of Windows 2000 Server. Also, Microsoft has included a fair number of tools for automating administrative tasks in the Windows 2000 Server Resource Kit.

Command-Line Utilities for Exporting and Importing Directory Information

Two command-line utilities are provided with Windows 2000 Server that support importing and exporting directory information:

♦ *LDAP Data Interchange Format Data Exchange (LDIFDE)*—Used to export and import data in Active Directory via files that conform to the LDAP Data Interchange Format defined by the Access/Synchronization of the Internet Directories (ASID) working group of the Internet Engineering Task Force (IETF).

♦ *Comma-Separated Variable Data Exchange (CSVDE)*—Used to export and import data from files that are compatible with the CSV format.

The **LDIFDE** command can be used to perform batch operations, using the LDAP Data Interchange Format (LDIF) file format, a draft Internet standard for export and import operations for directories that conform to the LDAP standard that seems set to become the standard for such things—if for no other reason than because no real competition exists in this area.

The batch operations that you can perform by using **LDIFDE** include add, delete, rename, and modify. These operations enable administrators to export Active Directory data, such as users and groups, to other applications or services. These operations also enable administrators to populate Active Directory with information obtained from other sources, such as other directory services.

You use the **LDIFDE** utility by starting a command prompt and then typing **LDIFDE**, followed by the appropriate parameters. To be more precise, the syntax is as follows:

```
LDIFDE [-i] [-f ] [-s] [-c] [-v] [-j] [-t] [-d] [-r] [-p] [-l] [-o] [-g]
[-m] [-n] [-k] [-a ] [- b][-?]
```

You can find the semantics for the utility by typing **LDIFDE -?**.

For More Information on LDIF

The current draft standard for LDIF may be downloaded from the LDAP extension group's homepage at **www.ietf.org/html.charters/ldapext-charter.html**. Currently, the latest revision, which is on the Standards Track, is available as RFC 2849 (**http://search.ietf.org/rfc/rfc2849.txt**).

The **CSVDE** command is used to import and export data from Active Directory, using files that store data in the comma-separated variable (CSV) format. Most popular spreadsheets are capable of reading and saving data in the CSV format. The CSV format consists of one or more lines of data, with each value separated by a comma. The first line of the CSV file must contain the names of each attribute in the same order as the data (for example, "**cn,first_name,surname**") and then the data is provided in any of the lines following the first line. The batch operations possible by using the **CSVDE** utility are the same as found in **LDIFDE**. Actually, the syntax is also the same—except for the **CSVDE** command and the fact that the utility expects to be fed with comma-separated files.

The Path of Least Resistance to Active Directory Bulk Data Handling

The high usability and power of the command-line utilities notwithstanding, I prefer to surround myself with a fair number of special-purpose tools—especially the ones that free me from doing a lot of hard and tedious work that has already been done. To find these kinds of tools, you should look to the Windows 2000 Server Resource Kit, which contains a plethora of useful tools, including a rather large number of scripts—which are referred to as Remote Administration Scripts. The Resource Kit features 78 scripts, so chances are quite good that one of them might be just what you're after.

The six most commonly useful tools for bulk data entry have been implemented as executables, though. These Windows 2000 Server Resource Kit tools are as follows:

♦ *Add Users (Addusers.exe)*—Allows you to create and delete user accounts (including account-creation options), Local Groups, and/or Global Groups (including adding one or multiple user accounts to groups) from a comma-delimited file. The tool also allows you to dump user accounts, Local Groups, and Global Groups to a comma-delimited file.

♦ *Find Group (Findgrp.exe)*—Allows you to find all direct and indirect group memberships for a specific domain user.

♦ *Group Copy (Grpcpy.exe)*—Allows you to copy the user accounts in a group to another group in the same or another domain.

♦ *Move Users (Moveuser.exe)*—Allows you to change the user profile from one user account to another.

♦ *Add Users to Groups (Usrtogrp.exe)*—Allows you to add user accounts to Local or Global Groups from a text file. Please note that you generally will be better served by the AddUsers tool for doing a thing like this.

♦ *Subinacl.exe*—Allows you to extract security information on files, Registry keys, and services for being able to move all security permissions from one user account to another or from one Local or Global Group to another. The tool also just allows you to inspect security information meeting certain criteria and/or change object ownership.

All of the 78 Remote Administration Scripts found in the Resource Kit are programmed in Visual Basic script and hosted by Windows Scripting Host (WSH). Each of the scripts is designed to perform specific administrative tasks using ADSI inside one of four different areas: Hardware Administration, Network Configuration, OS Configuration, and User Management. Because this section is focused on bulk data entry, it's only the User Management scripts that attract interest. Table 19.7 gives a brief description of the most interesting of those scripts.

Please stay keenly aware that you might not find the functionality offered within each of the scripts featured in Table 19.7 to be particularly exciting at first. After all, the scripts have been developed for performing only one operation each. What's exciting is the ease with which you can combine multiple scripts to deliver exactly the functionality you need. And even more exciting: How easy it is to extend these scripts with additional functionality because of the power and versatility of ADSI and Visual Basic script.

You can find more information on the scripts and utilities mentioned in this section in the Windows 2000 Server Resource Kit. But you should be forewarned: Even judged by Resource Kit tools standards, the documentation of the Visual Basic scripts is rather brief. And the documentation can be rather hard to find, too (it's found under the Remote Administration Scripts node).

Finally, if none of the previously mentioned solutions and scripts are an appropriate match for what you need to accomplish, you have one last resort: Write your own script. To do so,

Table 19.7   Some useful scripts.

Script Name	Task
ChkUsers.vbs	Checks a domain for users whose properties satisfy a specified criterion.
ClassifyMembers.vbs	Lists the members of a container object or group object in Active Directory.
CreateGroups.vbs	Creates multiple groups in a domain.
CreateUsers.vbs	Creates multiple user accounts in a domain.
DisplayOld.vbs	Lists all stale user and computer accounts based on the number of days since they were last used.
Group.vbs	Displays the groups in the specified domain.
GroupDescription.vbs	Displays the description of a given group.
ListDCs.vbs	Lists all DCs within a given domain.
ListDomains.vbs	Lists all domains within a namespace.
ListProperties.vbs	Lists properties of an Active Directory object.
ModifyUsers.vbs	Modifies attributes of one or more users.
ProgramGroups.vbs	Enumerates the program groups listed in the Start Menu for each user account on a computer.
Startup.vbs	Enumerates the startup programs on a computer.
SystemAccount.vbs	Displays system account information.
UserAccount.vbs	Displays user account information.
UserGroup.vbs	Adds or deletes one or multiple user accounts to or from a group.

Populating a Test Environment

If you need to make numerous data entries to test Active Directory, the off-the-shelf utilities and scripts don't have anything special to offer. However, some nice people inside Microsoft have built some rather advanced tools for Active Directory testing, most of which can be found in the Windows 2000 Support Tools (in the Support directory on the Windows 2000 CD-ROM) or in the Windows 2000 Server Resource Kit.

In my humble opinion, the best of these tools is the Active Directory testing utility (which is called **DSTOOL**), written by Craig Dewar and Andreas Luther. **DSTOOL** will enable you to populate your Active Directory as heavily as you want, almost instantly, with the wished-for combination of OUs, groups, computers, printers, users, and volumes.

Unfortunately, Microsoft seems to have chosen not to make **DSTOOL** publicly available. I for one haven't been able to find it anywhere. So you'd need to check with your preferred Microsoft Certified Solution Provider (MCSP), or directly with your Microsoft subsidiary, to gain access to this little gem.

When searching for this great tool, you might want to note that **DSTOOL** seems to have been superceded by **DSTOOL2**, which inlcudeds a lot more fine-grained options for population of your Active Directory. It even includes a companion tool (Ptmbx) for enabling mailboxes of objects created by **DSTOOL2**.

you should always opt for ADSI, because this is much easier to wring the necessary power out of. Also, there's actually quite a fair amount of information available on Active Directory programming using ADSI at Microsoft's Web site (you should usually start searching for your topic of interest at **http://msdn.microsoft.com**). For an example of that, you should take a look at the simple programming examples shown below. In the first example, a couple of OUs are being created at the **americas.astonitgroup.com** domain:

```
' ************************************************************************
' * Prepare the environment for this script
' ************************************************************************
' Determine the LDAP path for your domain
'Set Root = GetObject("LDAP://RootDSE")
'DomainPath = Root.Get("DC=com,DC=astonitgroup")
Set Domain = GetObject("LDAP://DC=americas,DC=astonitgroup,DC=com")

Set WshShell = Wscript.CreateObject("Wscript.Shell")
Set WshSysEnv = WshShell.Environment("Process")
upnDomain = WshSysEnv("USERDOMAIN")

'Disable error messages
'On Error Resume Next


' ************************************************************************
' * Create Top Level OUs
' ************************************************************************
```

```
Set OU1_1 = Domain.Create("organizationalUnit", "OU=Public Partition")
OU1_1.Put "Description", "Public"
ou1_1.SetInfo


' *************************************************************************
' * Create 2. level OUs
' *************************************************************************
Set ou2_1_1 = ou1_1.Create("organizationalUnit", "OU=CA")
ou2_1_1.Put "Description", "Canada"
ou2_1_1.SetInfo

Set ou2_1_2 = ou1_1.Create("organizationalUnit", "OU=US")
ou2_1_2.Put "Description", "United States"
ou2_1_2.SetInfo


' *************************************************************************
' * Create 3. level OUs
' *************************************************************************

Set ou3_1_1_1 = ou2_1_1.Create("organizationalUnit", "OU=YUL")
ou3_1_1_1.Put "Description", "Montreal"
ou3_1_1_1.SetInfo

Set ou3_2_1_1 = ou2_1_2.Create("organizationalUnit", "OU=JFK")
ou3_2_1_1.Put "Description", "New York"
ou3_2_1_1.SetInfo

Set ou3_2_2_1 = ou2_1_2.Create("organizationalUnit", "OU=LAX")
ou3_2_2_1.Put "Description", "Los Angeles"
ou3_2_2_1.SetInfo
```

And the second one creates a group in the **americas.astonitgroup.com** domain:

```
set Args  = Wscript.Arguments

'Get the domain
Set Domain = GetObject("LDAP://DC=americas,DC=astonitgroup,DC=com")

wscript.echo "Creating Groups Americas"


'
'   Create the Security Groups
'


'Get highest OU
Set ParentOU = Domain.GetObject("organizationalUnit", "OU=Public Partition")
ParentOU.SetInfo
```

```
'
' Level 3 group "New York"
'
Set SubOU = ParentOU.GetObject("organizationalUnit", "OU=US")
SubOU.SetInfo
Set SubOU1 = SubOU.GetObject("organizationalUnit", "OU=JFK")
SubOU1.SetInfo

Set NewCN = SubOU1.Create("JFK group","CN=JFK")
NewCN.Put "description", "New York group"
NewCN.Put "samAccountName", "JFK"
NewCN.SetInfo
```

With that, I hope you feel ready to jump into the world of scripting. Which scripting engine and language you prefer is much less important than the fact that you're getting started. But you might want to opt for WSH and VBScript, because you'll probably have to get used to this combo anyway, to create logon/logoff scripts and the like.

Best Practices

Before you start working with the Active Directory schema, you should carefully review the best practices for modifying it (see Table 19.8). After all, if Microsoft has its way, Active Directory will become the heart of your company—and nobody should take any unnecessary risks with an element that vital.

Keep Cool Regarding Schema Updating

The schema formally defines the universe of objects possible for a specific Active Directory. This is done by the definition of classes (the list of valid objects that can be represented in the Active Directory, such as users, computers, and printers) and attributes (the characteristics that must or may be applied to object instances, such as telephone numbers).

Remember WSH?

Windows Scripting Host is a language-independent host for ActiveX scripting engines running on 32-bit Windows platforms. It enables you to run VBScript (Visual Basic Script) and JScript natively within the Windows 98 and Windows 2000 OSs—and, provided that you install the needed code, can support the Windows 95 or Windows NT 4 line of OSs, too.

With WSH, you can run a script directly from the Windows 2000 desktop, either by clicking it in Windows Explorer or by starting from the command prompt, which eliminates the need to embed such scripts in documents. WSH is particularly useful for running noninteractive scripts that perform logon tasks, administrative tasks, and machine automation.

Table 19.8   Modifying the Active Directory schema.

Vital Points to Consider	Comments
The schema will become the lifeblood of your forest.	Make everybody involved understand that schema management is a task that mustn't be taken lightly. Even though Active Directory is dynamically extensible, it's not a playground. In other words, you should modify the schema only when absolutely necessary, and when it is, you must plan, document, and implement the modification with great care.
Don't put everything into the schema.	Model only the data that is necessary for your applications or users. When several independently developed applications or many users use the same data, you have strong motivation to instantiate that data in the schema. But, if only a single application or a select few users access the data, you might want to store it elsewhere. Also, be aware that Active Directory is best suited to storing data that is of a relatively small size or static in nature. Therefore, you should generally opt for FRS or a Relational Database Management System (RDBMS) for storing large or very dynamic data.
Opt for the simplest solution.	Reuse existing attributes and classes as much as possible when defining new classes and attributes. This will effectively make the schema much easier to manage now—and especially in the future.
Understand the properties regarding classes.	You have three different classes from which to choose: The structural class, the abstract class, and the auxiliary class. Choose any parent classes carefully, because any changes to the parent classes are inherited by the new class.
Make sure that your schema structures are unique.	All classes, attributes, and syntax types must be unique. This need for uniqueness is ensured by the Object Identifier (OID). To avoid any risk of duplication, get a registered OID and manage it rigidly.
Understand and document the structuring of your classes.	Your classes can be expressed as a tree structure, similar to OUs and domain trees. Remember to map this inheritance tree so that all other people involved with schema management will understand the implications of implementing changes to the classes used for inheritance. Also, make sure that everybody involved has a clear understanding of which classes can be leaf objects to which other classes, and vice versa.
Understand and document the content rules.	Determine the attributes that a particular class must or may contain. Remember, a new instance of a class can't be stored unless all **mustContain** (mandatory) properties are present. However, be careful not to use the schema to enforce a detailed object structure. Must-Contain is a blunt tool, at best, and shouldn't be overused. Ultimately, applications are much better suited to enforce meaning ful constraints on attributes.
Be sure to follow the correct order for schema changes.	Define all the needed attributes before defining the class. Also, when you want to define objects based on the newly founded schema definitions, consider the time lag involved with replication and caching of the schema throughout the forest.
Make the schema entries easy to understand.	Prefix a new class or attribute with a name that is meaningful to everybody involved with schema management, and prepare the documentation before you implement the schema changes.

(continued)

Table 19.8 Modifying the Active Directory schema *(continued)*.

Vital Points to Consider	Comments
Don't overuse the GC unnecessarily.	Be very selective about the attributes that you allow to be included in the GC, to keep the replication load in check. And remember that any change to the attributes that are replicated to the GC will have all GCs in the forest being reloaded—thus quite a lot of replication traffic will ensue!
Study information on Active Directory Display Specifiers for schema changes that are relevant to end users.	If you are creating new classes and attributes that are meant primarily for use by end users, refer to Microsoft's documentation on Active Directory Display Specifiers, which are Active Directory objects that store user interface (UI) information used to form different user interfaces for administrators and users. To be precise, the Active Directory Administrative Tools (such as the Active Directory Users and Computers snap-in) and the Windows shell extensions use Display Specifiers to dynamically create context menu items and property pages. Thus, Display Specifiers permit localization of class and attribute names, context menus, and property pages and also support new classes and attributes— such as those created by you or third-party applications. Display Specifiers are objects of class **Display Specifier** and are stored in a container in Active Directory that corresponds to the local ID. This container is stored in the Display Specifiers container in the Configuration partition.
Take great care to avoid hitches on the schema.	Don't mess with the Schema Master FSMO unless you want to take the current role holder offline or it crashes (and thus has been taken offline with no intention to put it online again within the current Active Directory forest). Also, keep The Schema May Be Modified On This Domain Controller checkbox unchecked on your Schema Master, except when you impose changes to the schema. Like- wise, closely guard the memberships of the Schema Admins Group.

The schema is a separate partition whose replication scope is the entire forest. The Active Directory Schema MMC snap-in allows administrators to manage the Active Directory schema by creating and modifying classes and attributes, and specifying which attributes are indexed in the Active Directory and which will be replicated to the Global Catalog.

Management of the schema isn't supposed to be a frequently performed task, and you must take care when modifying the schema. For this reason, you must meet the following safety procedures before you are allowed to modify the schema:

◆ The schema object is protected by the Windows 2000 Security model; therefore, to ef- fect schema changes, you must either be given explicit permissions or be a member of the Schema Admins Group.

◆ Only one DC at a time is allowed to write to the schema—the DC that has the Schema Master FSMO role. You must be connected to the Schema Master to manage the schema.

◆ By default, all DCs permit only read access to the schema. A checkbox must be checked for the Schema Master DC via the Active Directory Schema MMC snap-in to permit write access to the schema.

Microsoft has placed many constraints on schema updates, to make it less likely that one application's updates cause problems for another application. The most notable constraint is that the set of **mustContain** attributes on a class can't be changed after a class is defined.

You are well advised to remove any potential trouble spots in regard to the schema management, because the schema represents the "crown jewels" of your corporate infrastructure. Remember, too, that your schema management is only as good as the weakest link (which usually turns out to be the manner in which the administrators handle schema management). Removing potential trouble spots requires understanding both schema management and schema modification and the implications of each. A carefully designed strategy for managing the schema is essential. This strategy should at the very least provide operative control on when and how schema modifications are implemented. Also, keeping everything in order regarding schema updates won't help much if you ignore the schema updates that stem from the applications. Active Directory-aware applications will be ubiquitous in the future, so you should prepare for an avalanche of applications that need to extend Active Directory. The prospect of having schema extensions executed in conjunction with installing new applications requires that all administrators receive a good refresher on old-fashioned administrative virtues—and you must maintain some rigid guidelines regarding who can be trusted to be made a member of the very powerful Schema Admins Group.

Finally, although Microsoft has tried to protect the schema by denying overwriting of the key classes and attributes, you still should look out for "rogue" applications and, ultimately, implement a procedure for piloting new Active Directory-aware applications in a separate test environment. Also, be keenly aware that the next generation of viruses and Trojan Horses might target Active Directory as an instrument to wreaking havoc on the entire network.

Chapter 20

Mastering the Art of Active Directory Sizing

Depending on the size and complexity of your corporate surroundings and the number of narrow WAN alleyways, you might fear the overhead that Active Directory will put on your current server and networking infrastructure. Well, the best way to overcome fear is through knowledge, which is what you can gain in this chapter. This chapter gives you the inside track on what to expect of Active Directory regarding the size of the database and the DC/GC load, as well as the load added to the network by replication traffic. By reading this chapter, you'll learn to do an approximation of your situation with respect to these two all-important areas. And even more importantly: You'll be able to use your knowledge for troubleshooting and performance optimizations inside these vital areas.

And for those of you who are implementing Active Directory in a WAN setting, you will be in for a treat later on in this chapter, where I've jotted down my quite extensive WAN experiences. Believe me, you'll find several hard-learned lessons to be found there, which to my knowledge aren't available anywhere else.

At the very end of the chapter, you will also be treated to a short description on how to size your server hardware for DC and GC use. So, after you successfully complete this chapter, you should be able to provide answers to the following questions:

♦ How do I size my domain controllers (DCs)?

♦ How do I size my Global Catalog servers (GCs)?

♦ How does replication traffic affect my namespace planning?

♦ How well does my physical network support my directory namespace?

This chapter doesn't discuss how to automate the directory population. For that information, refer to Chapter 19, which includes a section devoted to how to do bulk data entry into Active Directory. This chapter doesn't cover the pilot testing of your Active Directory setup, either. The planning stage of pilot testing is covered in some detail in Appendix A, whereas a lot of advice regarding the implementation stage is presented in Chapters 17 and 18. However, for a comprehensive treatment of pilot testing, you need to refer to a more hands-on-oriented book.

Active Directory Internals

For a refresher on how Active Directory works, review the section "How Active Directory Fits within the Windows 2000 Server Architecture" in Chapter 4, which explains (among other things) that Active Directory is an improved version of the database engine that is used in Microsoft Exchange Server—called *Extensible Storage Engine (or simply ESE)*—and that the database engine reserves storage only for the properties that are in use in each object. However, to understand the more precise properties of Active Directory with regard to database (and, ultimately, hard disk) sizing, you must know exactly how the ESE database engine works. This section should provide you with that knowledge.

Because the ESE database is flat (and thus can't explicitly express a hierarchical namespace, such as Active Directory), the DataBase Layer (DB) provides an abstract object hierarchy. What connects the distinguished name (DN) and relative distinguished name (RDN) used by Active Directory's Lightweight Directory Access Protocol (LDAP) interface with the underlying entries in the ESE database is the Globally Unique Identifier (GUID), which is assigned to each database object and can't be changed after the object is created.

So, even though the LDAP interface exposes objects through their DNs and RDNs, internally the value is converted to the GUID of the object they want to refer to. This, in turn, also ensures that a reference always points to the same object, even if that object is renamed or moved. Again, the LDAP interface automatically converts these GUID references back to the DN, so that when an LDAP client reads these attributes, it gets back a distinguished name, not a GUID.

> **Note**
>
> *If the system always had to store and compare bulky GUIDs, identifying an object within a table in the ESE database would take too long; therefore, every object is also identified by a Distinguished Name Tag (DNT). The DNT is a 4-byte DWORD value that is incremented when a new object is created in the store. Thus, it represents the database row number for a given object. Each object's parent relationship is stored as a Parent Distinguished Name Tag (PDNT), and so the resolution of parent-child relationships is optimized because the DNT and PDNT are indexed fields in the database.*

The ESE database has two main tables:

♦ *Data table*—Sometimes referred to as the *object table*, this table holds common objects and attributes, such as users, printers, application-specific data, and just about any other information stored in Active Directory since it was installed. In this table, the rows represent objects, and the columns represent attributes. You can choose between fixed columns and tagged columns.

♦ *Link table*—The table in which object relationships are expressed. The table contains data representing linked attributes, which contain values referring to other objects in Active Directory (for example, the **MemberOf** attribute on a user object, which contains values that reference groups to which the user belongs).

Apart from these primary tables, you also can find a *schema table*, which is Active Directory's schema, with its object and attribute definitions and the relationships between them. However, neither the schema table nor the link table is really very important in regard to database sizing, because these tables should prove to be much smaller than the data table (which represents most of the actual information stored in Active Directory). Because the data table is far larger than the link and schema tables in all "real-life" installations, it is the focus in much of the rest of this section.

Getting Acquainted with the Data Table

Although the data table is actually a flat file, it can be thought of as having rows (each representing an instance of an object, such as a user) and columns (each representing an attribute in the schema, such as **userPrincipalName**). The data table contains a column (or field) for each attribute in the schema. Each column can be either of the following types:

♦ *Fixed column*—Storage is allocated for the column on every row, which means that it consumes the maximum space allowed for the given attribute, regardless of whether it's being used by the objects.

♦ *Tagged column*—Storage is allocated only if a value is present, which means that it consumes exactly the space that is needed to store values in the objects.

By default, the data table contains only a relatively small number of fixed columns and a large number of tagged columns. Generally, fixed columns are exclusively used for maintaining the structure of the directory and thus are invisible to clients, whereas tagged columns contain the attributes that clients see and need. So, if you feel that Active Directory is hungry for disk space, you can at least console yourself with the fact that things could have been much worse.

Further, each of these columns can be either of two size types:

♦ *Fixed size*—Contains an integer or long integer as its data type.

♦ *Variable size*—Typically contains string types (for example, Unicode strings and multi-valued attributes). The database allocates only as much space as a variable-size column

Table 20.1 Data table with four tagged columns and one fixed column.

Column Header	DNT	CN	objectclass	OS	userPassword
Row x	3512	JDavies	Top# person# organizational Person# user		******
Row y	4092	KJensen	Top# person# organizational Person# user	Windows 2000	********

needs; for example, 16 bits for a 1-character Unicode string, 160 bits for a 10-character Unicode string, and so on.

Table 20.1 shows a subset of the fields in the actual data table with one fixed column (the DNT) and four tagged columns, in order to give you an idea of what the data table looks like. Remember that *all* attributes defined in the schema (the default Active Directory schema comprises approximately 800 attributes) are inserted into every row, regardless of whether or not they are utilized or apply to the object in a given row. The data table doesn't indicate structural rules; this is done by the Directory Service Agent (DSA) in conjunction with the schema table. Thus, the example in Table 20.1 shows only a tiny subset of the columns available in the real data table.

Due to the preference given to tagged columns, the precise space used to store an object in the database depends on both the number of attributes for which values are set and the size of those values. For example, if you have two user objects with attributes of the same size and length and then later add a 20-character description to one of the attributes (of the Unicode string type) available to the first user, the space used for the first user will consume 40 bytes more than the second user.

Note

The current ESE database engine doesn't allow records to span database pages, so each object is limited to 8KB. However, some attribute values of an object don't count fully against this limit. Long, variable-length values can be stored on a different page than the object record, leaving behind only a 9-byte reference. In this way, an object and all of its attribute values is allowed to grow beyond the 8KB limit.

Understanding How the Database Works

As noted earlier, Active Directory is implemented on top of an ESE database engine. ESE is an *indexed sequential access method (ISAM)* table manager. Earlier versions of ESE were called *Jet* and have been put to use in WINS, Certificate Services, FRS, Security Configuration Editor (SCE), and various other Windows 2000 Server components.

The file that holds the ESE database (and thus the Active Directory database), is called *ntds.dit*, which is located in the folder that you specified to the Active Directory Installation Wizard (the default setting is the WinNT\NTDS folder). ESE is a *transacted database system,* which uses log files to support rollback semantics, to ensure that transactions are committed to the database. In other words, every change to the database happens as a single operation, so that every time anything is changed in the database, the following four actions happen as a group (that is, if one fails, they all fail):

♦ Write to log

♦ Write to memory

♦ Confirm transaction

♦ Write to *ntds.dit*

Note

When the current log fills up—that is, when the log reaches a specified number of files—you must decide whether the system should create a new log file (noncircular logging) or overwrite the oldest log file (circular logging). The default setting is noncircular logging. If you want circular logging instead, simply change the Registry key HKEYLocalMachine\CurrentControlSetServices\NTDS\Parameters\ CircularLogging from 0 to 1. If you decide to stick to noncircular logging, be aware that it saves all database changes and won't be deleted by the garbage collection before all entries have been implemented in the database.

Log files should always be 5MB in size. Log files that are not of this size are most likely damaged. All log files used by ESE are quite easy to spot, because they end with the extension .log.

This is also why, ideally, the system database (*ntds.dit*) and log files (**.log*) should be located on separate drives. If you do separate these different types of files, you will notice an improvement in performance and have much better support of recovery in case of a major disk crash. The performance gain will be proportional to how many writes are occurring in your Active Directory domain—as you might be familiar with from Exchange Server 4/5, which comes with the same design recommendations. Also, be aware that you should opt for RAIDed drives for the disk partitions that store the system, database, and log files, to prevent data loss from a hard disk crash.

As far as database internals go, you also should be acquainted with a bit of *garbage collection* ("house cleaning") basics. Garbage collection is the rather prosaic term referring to the fact that Active Directory needs to perform a clean up on itself now and then. This garbage collection process runs independently on every DC (by default, after every continuous 12 hours of operation), deleting objects and files no longer needed by Active Directory. To be more precise, the garbage collection process accomplishes the following tasks:

♦ *Deletes unneeded log files*—A log file is unneeded once all changes (and all previous log files) have been written to the database file.

♦ *Deletes tombstones*—Rather than physically delete objects from the database, Active Directory removes most attributes and then tags the object as being in the "tombstone"

Practicalities of the ntds.dit File

All use of the *ntds.dit* database file is handled by **lsass.exe**. So, when Active Directory needs to access data, **lsass.exe** loads pages from the *ntds.dit* file into memory. It reserves a pool of memory for these operations and moves the pages between the database and the pool on a *least recently used* (LRU) basis.

Some pages in memory and in the database file get out of synch whenever the DSA performs a write operation on an object. To correct this condition, all pages in memory are flushed to the database file every time the database shuts down. The DC also swaps pages from memory back to the hard disk (in the background) whenever it is in an idle or low-load state.

All changes are made to in-memory copies of the directory objects. When a transaction is performed, it will be written to the log file first. Writing the changes to the log file is much faster than writing them to the database file, because log files are written to sequentially (eliminating seek time). Also, the log boosts recoverability, because log files can be used to recover the changes if a hardware failure corrupts the database file, provided that the logs are backed up and intact. Log files are typically kept on a separate physical disk drive from the information store and directory database files, to ensure that a failure affecting the database files won't affect the log files. Any data that has not been backed up, but that has been written to the transaction logs, can be "played back" to restore the database file. As part of its background work, the database engine continually updates the database file with recently committed changes, getting them from memory directly (not from the log files).

When you perform bulk load operations to Active Directory, you might have noticed that the **lsass.exe** process keeps growing bigger and bigger. This is by design and is caused by the database system's memory buffer allocation: The database continues to allocate memory until its requests for still more buffers are denied by the OS. In its quest to squeeze the optimum performance out of the server, the database tries to grab hold of as much memory as it can. When the database is updated later, the memory buffers are released again, and **lsass.exe** shrinks.

If the DC can't shut down in an orderly fashion or Active Directory comes to an abrupt halt, chances are that the database will be left without some of the recent changes, because the most recent in-memory pages have not been written to the disk. This is where your log files come into play, because they can be used to recover the changes that have been written to memory, but not yet sent to the disk. This recovery is performed automatically on the next restart of the DC.

---

state, to alert replication partners that the object was deleted. The database removes tombstones after a configurable interval (the default tombstone lifetime is 60 days; in all but very special circumstances, you should not change this default, because tombstones are used to replicate object deletions).

♦ *Online database defragmentation*—To update the database file, the database system uses the quickest way, which isn't always the most efficient way: It simply fills up database pages. Defragmentation rearranges how data is written in the database, to fill the database pages more efficiently. The online defragmentation used by the garbage collection process doesn't reduce database file size (for that, you need to perform offline defragmentation), but it makes more space available for new objects and optimizes the database layout.

Warning

If you restore a directory server from a backup tape older than the tombstone lifetime, the server won't know about some deletions, which will lead to having the deleted objects brought back into the Active Directory database unless the backup application accounts for any such discrepancies by flagging to the Active Directory DC that this is a non-authoritative restore (see Chapter 18 for more information on this). Also, to accommodate occasional disruption of replication caused by communication failures (as well as time spent for transport, if you're staging the Active Directory DCs at a central location after which the DC is taken offline in order to be moved to its final destination), you should keep the tombstone lifetime substantially longer than the expected worst-case replication latency.

Tip

*You can change the tombstone lifetime (60 days per default; 1 day minimum) and the garbage collection interval (12 hours per default; 1 hour minimum) used throughout your forest by changing the **tombstoneLifeTime** attribute and the **garbageCollPeriod** attribute, respectively, on the Directory Services container (which is stored in the Configuration container in **cn=WindowsNT, cn=Services**), which is replicated to every Active Directory DC.*

How to Perform Offline Defragmentation

To perform offline defragmentation of the *ntds.dit* file, you need to do the following:

1. Take offline the DC to be defragmented.

2. Boot the DC into Directory Services Repair mode. On Intel machines, select F8 during the boot options phase and then select Directory Services Restore Mode. The reason for needing to do this is that Active Directory will open its database files in Exclusive mode by default, which means that the files can't be managed while the system is booted as a DC.

3. When the system is through booting in Safe Mode, you should defragment the *ntds.dit* file by using the ntdsutil.exe tool. This is done by writing "files" (followed by Enter) and then specifying **Compact to *target_directory***. This command will instruct the server to defragment the existing database file and write the compacted database file to the specified directory.

4. Move the current *ntds.dit* file somewhere else and move the newly defragmented version of *ntds.dit* into the current *ntds.dit* file's place (by using the **Move DB to *target_directory*** command, also found on the Files submenu). You can delete the old *ntds.dit* file when you are absolutely certain that the defragmented version runs fine.

Booting in Directory Services Restore Mode temporarily converts your DC into a standalone server, so expect some services to fail to start (and, thus, a fair deal of additional time spent on booting), especially those that are integrated with the directory service. Also, when booted in Directory Services Restore Mode, the system is running off a minimal set of user and group definitions stored in the Registry, so you aren't able to make use of all the users and groups found in Active Directory. If your DC isn't physically secured, you should password-protect access to the Directory Services Restore boot to avoid any back doors to the system from this angle.

Provided that you keep your DCs up for more than 12 hours continuously, garbage collection should take care of all the housekeeping needed. Thus, offline defragmentation should prove needed only on one seldom seen occasion: when your database contents have shrunk considerably (for example, when a GC in a large forest is reduced to just serving as a DC) and you need that space for other uses.

Although chances are good that you'll never need to perform offline defragmentation in a production environment, you will need to do offline defragmentation to test the database size, because these kinds of tests mostly require a method to determine the "fair" size of the *ntds.dit* file. However, in a production situation, the best that you can expect to establish is the size of the fragmented *ntds.dit* file, making it impossible to tell how much space the objects really consume in the database file.

If you do want to know the size of the fragmented *ntds.dit* file, be careful about how you ascertain it, because Active Directory opens the database file when the DC boots and does not close it again until the computer shuts down. Unfortunately, NTFS records the size of a file only when the file is opened and does not refresh before the file is closed again. Therefore, you can't just use the size of the *ntds.dit* file reported by Windows Explorer or a command prompt to find out how big the file actually is.

Always use one of the following methods to determine the fragmented *ntds.dit* file's exact size:

♦ Use the Windows Explorer Properties dialog box on the partition containing the *ntds.dit* file. This dialog box always reports the correct available space.

♦ Reboot the DC, which closes the file and reopens it when the directory service restarts, allowing NTFS to report the correct file size until the first write is performed to the database file.

Active Directory Database Sizing and Optimization

Always select online defragmentation in a production environment (except for very extreme cases), because it leads to the same results in the database as the offline process but won't require taking the DC offline. For database growth testing, however, you should utilize offline defragmentation of the database file after a bulk load of objects, because only the offline defragmented version of the directory database allows you to assess how much space really is consumed by the objects (by way of comparing the size of the defragmented database file before and after the object load).

Performing Your Own Tests to Determine Database Size

Because only a defragmented database shows actual space consumption, you should rely on the size of the database given only immediately *after* you defragment the database. If you want to run some incremental test scenarios, perform the test runs as follows:

1. Load the set of objects.
2. Run **ntdsutil.exe** and run an offline defragmentation of the database.
3. Get the size of the database.

Follow these steps for each of the scenarios you want to test. However, note that this test method provides you with the fair benchmark in regard to the *minimum size* of the database (hence, the space needed for the objects added to Active Directory), not the *real size* of the database in use, because you won't do offline defragmentation in a production environment. Consequently, you might want to ascertain the database's size before you run the defragmentation, too, so that you can analyze how effective (or ineffective) Active Directory is at adding new objects and attributes under different conditions.

Getting a Feel for Database Size

Whereas large and complex Active Directory setups may require detailed studies of database sizes, you likely won't need to do much testing to set up an average environment. "Average" in this context refers to a setup that uses standard Active Directory features (that is, no additional objects and attributes added to the schema) in an environment with up to a few thousand users/computers spread out pretty evenly over a few locations, with links that are fairly stable and have plenty of bandwidth available.

Generally, you should be able to optimize the size requirements in an average environment simply by following the information provided in this section. For larger or more complex settings, you also should study the information provided here, to acclimate yourself to Active Directory, but you likely will want to perform some pilot testing that includes database sizing.

The figures and tables provided in this section and the next section actually are provided by Microsoft. Initially, they were copied from the whitepaper "Active Directory Database Sizing: Optimizing Size Requirements for Growth in Directory Service," which Microsoft made available for download at its Web site for a while (and then, after only a few weeks, it disappeared mysteriously). According to the information provided in the whitepaper, it represents an excerpt from a book called *Optimizing Network Traffic*, which is part of Microsoft Press's "Notes from the Field" series. Maybe that's the reason why the whitepaper went missing very soon afterwards.

To my big surprise, the whitepaper has now resurfaced on the Web in the TechNet forum (it can currently be downloaded from **www.microsoft.com/TechNet/win2000/win2ksrv/ technote/adsize.asp**), which is very curious, because the information provided in the whitepaper, as well as in the book, now is incorrect. The many minor changes implemented from Windows 2000 Server Beta 2 to the release of Windows 2000 Server actually did add some additional overhead to most directory objects.

Tip

Some of the tests being discussed in the whitepaper can also be found in Chapter 3 of the Distributed System Guide of the Windows 2000 Server Resource Kit. So, although the tests performed are exactly the same as originally performed, I've updated the material in this chapter to reflect what will be experienced in the real life nowadays.

In general, two different kinds of tests were performed by Microsoft: The first series (the single objects loads) loaded the database with a large number of identical objects, to show both how the database grows when objects are loaded and how much space is consumed for these object types. To apply more of a real-situation approach, the second series (the corporate scenarios loads) created a sample company with user objects, group objects, and file shares. It was designed to show how big the database grows for small, medium, and large companies. All test numbers quoted are for the defragmented versions of the database file.

Tip

Because the database engine consumes space only for attributes that are assigned values, the number of attributes that have values for an object will change that object's size dramatically. So, be very observant of what was done in each test quoted, and remember to compare it to your situation.

Single Objects Loads

Table 20.2 shows the growth for an Active Directory database with up to 500,000 users, in increments of 100,000 users. In this test, only mandatory attributes were set. Note that the database file growth pattern is linear. The growth between two load operations is always almost identical: Each user object is some 4,370 bytes. The test shown in Table 20.2 has also been performed by Compaq with 16 million user objects, showing the same results. So you can be sure to find a linear growth pattern for user objects, no matter what size your company is.

Tip

*For a cool demonstration of Active Directory's immense scalability, you should have a go at **www.demo.esc.compaq.com/phonebook/**. Here, you'll find an Active Directory DC with approximately 100 million objects and 1.3 billion attributes, which results in a 268 GB ntds.dit file. Actually, this isn't just a nice demonstration, you might also be able to do something good with it, because it was built on the U.S. White Pages.*

Similar tests performed on contacts show that each contact object amounts to some 1,700 bytes. Table 20.3 shows the growth for an Active Directory database that is loaded with up to 16,000 OUs, in increments of 2,000 OUs. In this test, only mandatory attributes were set. Again, the database file growth pattern is fairly linear, except for the second rounds of loads, in which the OUs seem somewhat smaller; this probably is because the defragmentation

Table 20.2   Single object load with user objects.

Number of Users	Size of *ntds.dit* (in KB)	Growth (in KB)	Bytes per User
0	10,256		
100,000	436,240	425,984	4,362
200,000	864,272	428,032	4,373
300,000	1,290,256	425,984	4,369
400,000	1,716,240	425,984	4,367
500,000	2,142,224	425,984	4,366

Table 20.3   Single object load with OUs.

Number of OUs	Size of *ntds.dit* (in KB)	Growth (in KB)	Bytes per OU
0	10,256		
2,000	14,352	2,048	2,097
4,000	16,400	2,048	1,573
6,000	22,544	4,096	2,097
8,000	26,640	2,048	2,097
10,000	28,688	2,048	1,887
12,000	32,784	2,048	1,922
14,000	36,880	2,048	1,947
16,000	40,976	2,048	1,966

is unable to optimize the database entirely when it's rather small. Besides these first loads, the growth between two load operations is approximately identical: each OU object is some 2,000 bytes.

Table 20.4 shows the next series of tests in which user objects have between 1 and 11 attributes added. These attributes are defined in the schema as string value attributes, and each of them was filled with 10 characters. The test began with a store containing 100,000

Table 20.4   Addition of one attribute at a time to the directory's user objects.

Number of Additional Attributes	Size of *ntds.dit* (in KB)	Bytes per User	Bytes per Attribute
0	436,240	4,362	
1	430,080	4,404	42
2	434,176	4,446	40
3	434,176	4,446	27
4	438,272	4,488	30
5	442,368	4,530	33
6	442,368	4,530	27
7	448,512	4,593	32
8	448,512	4,593	28
9	454,656	4,656	32
10	540,672	5,536	117
11	540,672	5,536	106

user objects, with only the mandatory attributes set. The DC was demoted, promoted back, and loaded with 100,000 user objects again, this time with one additional attribute, continuing until a level of 11 attributes was reached.

This test paints a much less predictable picture with regard to the database file growth pattern. However, as a general rule, you can conclude that each 10-character string will add, at most, approximately 100 bytes to the size of the user object. The growth of the defragmented database is not linear; it seems to jump at certain steps (which may be caused by the nature of the ESE database, in which space is allocated in pages) and then stay at that plateau for some time.

Because of space limitations, the very important question of how much space each group object will take up in the Active Directory database isn't covered in detail here. However, you shouldn't be cheated on the results:

♦ A Security Group will amount to some 2,100 bytes.

♦ A Distribution Group (that is, a non-Security Group) will also amount to some 2,100 bytes.

And then, there's the question of how much overhead each member will add to a group:

♦ Each group member will add some additional 200 bytes to the size of the group.

♦ When you hit the 100-member mark, you should expect each member to take up only 100 bytes.

♦ And if you're working with really huge groups (more than 500 members), you should cut the estimate by another 30 percent, to 70 bytes per member.

The above-mentioned numbers will be the same no matter whether you're talking Security Groups or non-Security Groups.

Table 20.5 shows the growth in user objects when public key certificates (X.509 v3 certificates issued by Windows 2000 Server's Certificate Service) are deployed in a 100,000-user Active Directory database. The size of an X.509 certificate stored as a file is 1,294 bytes.

Table 20.5   Addition of public key certificates to a directory with 100,000 users.

Number of Certificates	0	1	2	3
Defragmented store before certificate deployment	434,192	577,552	790,544	1,003,536
Growth of defragmented store after certificate deployment	0	143,360	212,992	212,992
User account size in defragmented store after certificate deployment (bytes per user)	4,341	5,809	7,990	10,171
Growth of user account per additional certificate (bytes per user)	0	1,468	2,181	2,181

As the test results demonstrate, the user object grows with some 2,100 bytes, which is a fair amount more than what should be expected when comparing to the theoretical value of 1,294 bytes.

This test is quite interesting for two reasons:

♦ Many companies will most likely start adopting public key certificates in the coming years as a result of the technology now being fully integrated into the OS (remember this when summing up the database size needed).

♦ Public keys are larger than most other attributes in the directory, so the test provides an insight to how well the database handles attributes of a larger size.

According to the early experiences, you should expect each printer and volume to amount to some 2,400 and 1,600 bytes, respectively.

Corporate Scenarios Loads

Modeling different corporate scenarios might provide a more realistic look at the database size. In this case, the maximum sample corporate scenario is set to 100,000 computers, 100,000 users, 10,000 groups, 10,000 printers, and 10,000 volumes. The number of members of each group is 25.

Each test cycle loads one-tenth of the full corporate scenario—that is, at each round, 10,000 computers, 10,000 users, and so on, are being added to the database. Table 20.6 shows the corporate scenario when the minimum number of attributes is used (only the mandatory attributes are assigned values). The growth pattern in Table 20.6 is essentially linear, with a growth of some 88MB in each stage (that is, for every 10 percent of the full scenario loaded).

Table 20.7 shows how the database responds to the addition of attributes. In the test, 30 commonly occurring attributes (first name, last name, office number, phone number, and so

Table 20.6   The corporate scenario with only mandatory attributes.

Load Cycle No.	Size of *ntds.dit* (in KB)	Growth (in KB)
Initial state	10,256	
1	98,320	88,064
2	184,336	86,016
3	272,400	88,064
4	360,464	88,064
5	448,528	88,064
6	534,544	86,016
7	622,608	88,064
8	708,624	86,016
9	798,736	90,112
10	884,752	86,016

Table 20.7   The corporate scenario with additional attributes.

Load Cycle No.	Size 0f *ntds.dit* (in KB)	Growth (in KB)
Initial state	10,256	
1	139,280	129,024
2	268,304	129,024
3	397,328	129,024
4	526,352	129,024
5	655,376	129,024
6	784,400	129,024
7	913,424	129,024
8	1,042,448	129,024
9	1,171,472	129,024
10	1,300,496	129,024

on) were added to the user objects, 8 attributes were added for workstations, 4 attributes were added for groups, and 4 attributes were added for volumes. All attributes were filled with strings of 10 characters.

Again, the growth is close to being linear, with a growth of approximately 130MB in each stage. Note that the scenario defined actually is pretty fitting for most real-life cases, so using these results will provide you with a good yardstick for the size of the "base" Active Directory database in your corporate setting.

Table 20.8 shows the results of testing on another very important subject: the impact that delegation of access rights has on the database size. This impact is bound to be significant, because Active Directory is built upon *static inheritance* for ACEs. This means that any Access Control List (ACL) changes caused by the delegation of access rights on Active Directory containers are pushed down to all objects covered by the change (either explicitly or by inheritance, defined via the hierarchical structure inside the domain). Thus, affected objects will have this ACE added to their ACL. For this reason, you should delegate access rights on directory objects only to groups rather than to a specific security principal.

Table 20.8 also shows the results of adding ACEs granted to a group on all objects in a whole domain on a DC that is loaded with 10 OUs and 100,000 users. Each step shows an ACE being added to all user objects in the domain. The test results show that each user object grows between 29 and 105 bytes—the large differences being because *ntds.dit* only jumps in size for every five ACEs that are added to the domain—so you should be safe in assuming that each ACE added will take up, on average, about 75 bytes on each object that is inside the scope of the administrative delegation.

Active Directory Replication Load

Active Directory is a forest-level directory service in which updating of the DCs and GCs is done through replication. For network administrators, this replication raises the question of how much and how often the network (LAN as well as WAN) will be subjected to

Table 20.8   A subset of the results when adding ACEs to the full domain.

Number of ACEs	Size of *ntds.dit* (in KB)	Bytes per User	Bytes per ACE
0	436,240	4,362	
1	436,240	4,467	105
2	440,336	4,509	74
3	440,336	4,509	49
4	440,336	4,509	37
5	440,336	4,509	29
6	481,296	4,928	94
7	481,296	4,928	81
8	481,296	4,928	71
9	481,296	4,928	63
10	481,296	4,928	57
15	483,344	4,949	39
17	552,976	5,662	76
20	552,976	5,662	65

replication traffic. This question can't be answered easily, because Active Directory provides several options for controlling when replication traffic occurs. However, you can determine how much replication traffic needs to be sent between the DCs and GCs.

With regard to replication, you should remember that the following two different replication types exist, and the type that you use depends on your site infrastructure:

♦ *Intrasite replication*—All replication that takes place inside the same site. By default, the replication topology used inside the site is constructed by the Knowledge Consistency Checker (KCC).

The Exchange 2000 Server Object Size Experiences

Exchange 2000 Server is the first application that replaces its own directory with that of the Active Directory. As such, Exchange 2000 Server introduces a very high number of new objects and attributes, almost doubling both the number of objects and attributes to be found in the Active Directory schema and adding 4MB to the size of *ntds.dit* in the process.

Because Exchange 2000 Server most probably will be implemented in a lot of Active Directory environments, I don't feel that you should be cheated from the early object sizing experiences with it:

• *Mailbox-enabled users*—Using the mandatory attributes, you should expect a size of approximately 8,000 bytes per mailbox-enabled user.

• *Mailbox-enabled contacts*—Using the mandatory attributes, you should expect a size of approximately 4,900 bytes per mailbox-enabled contact.

• *Mailbox-enabled groups*—Using the mandatory attributes, you should expect a size of approximately 3,400 bytes per mailbox-enabled group—whether it be a Security or non-Security Group.

All other database sizing guidelines will prove the same, regardless of whether or not you've implemented Exchange 2000 Server.

◆ *Intersite replication*—All replication that takes place between sites. You create the Intersite replication topology by defining sites and connecting them using different types of site links. However, it's the KCC that will be charged with managing all the minor topological details.

In addition to controlling replication, the site infrastructure also provides client affinity, which means the control of how clients locate a DC and a GC (it always opts for a DC and a GC belonging to the same site as the client) and allow applications to become site-aware. This is actually a big step forward compared to earlier releases, in which you had no control over the DC location. The client just logged on to the DC that responded first (except in Windows NT Workstation 4 SP4 and later, which allow you to specify a preferred Windows NT 4 DC).

Although the jury is still undecided regarding many of the finer points of replication (largely because very little documentation exists in this area), all the information that you need to gain a broad understanding is readily available and is provided in the following sections.

Intrasite DC Replications

Intrasite DC replications are always performed by using DS-RPC (RPC over IP), which assumes that all the DCs are connected by good, relatively stable network connections. Also, no compression is used, because Microsoft assumes that you prefer to spend the CPU horsepower available in the DC for end user operations rather than for compressing the data flowing between the DCs inside the site.

The DCs notify their replication partners periodically (the default interval between notifications is five minutes) as to whether any changes have happened since the last replication. Because of this rather high frequency of notifications, not using compression makes very good sense. Usually, you won't find that many changes inside each five-minute cycle, so compression would actually work to increase the replication load compared to the non-compression scenario (you need a fair amount of data before you will start seeing some payoff from using compression).

The available data on Intrasite DC replication paints the following picture:

◆ The minimum replication size (including handshaking) for directory objects is approximately 4KB, with the size growing in 16-byte increments from there on.

◆ Each user object is approximately 4KB.

◆ Each Global and Universal Group object with no members is approximately 2.1KB.

◆ Each volume object is approximately 1.8KB.

The quoted size of the directory objects is valid only when you replicate more than 100 objects at a time. Thus, for example, if you replicate only one of the aforementioned directory objects, approximately 12KB will be consumed.

A Primer on Replication Load Testing

You can view replication traffic using any of the following tools delivered on the Windows 2000 Server CD-ROM:

- *Network Monitor*—Enables you to measure Remote Procedure Call (RPC) and Simple Mail Transfer Protocol (SMTP) replication traffic flowing between DCs.

- *Performance Monitor*—Enables you to measure replication data coming in to and going out of a specific DC.

- *Active Directory Replication Monitor (**REPLMON**)*—Enables you to view your replication topology.

Network Monitor measures all incoming and outgoing packets from a particular DC. This includes *all* packets, including those from other services. One way around this problem is to identify the IP port being used by replication. This is easy for replications using SMTP as the transport, because SMTP always uses port 25, so you can find all replication-related traffic by filtering on that port with Network Monitor (provided that you don't transfer any SMTP mail during the test period).

However, isolating the RPC over IP replications isn't as easy, because these replications use dynamic RPC port mapping, for heightened security. But you can configure each Active Directory DC to use a certain port (which also proves very useful, when dealing with VPNs and firewalls), by adding this value to the Registry: **HKEY_LOCAL_MACHINE\CurrentControlSet\Services\NTDS\ Parameters\TCP/IP Port**. For example, if you choose to set this value to 1349 (in decimal), you can view all replications by filtering on that port. Be aware, however, that you need to perform this operation on all the DCs on which you want to measure the replication load.

Alternatively, you can use Performance Monitor's replication counters, which provide you with the sum of incoming and outgoing bytes for replication (showing bytes before and after compression, if using intersite replication). Although this won't supply you with the individual replication packets for analysis, it does provide you with the figures for the bandwidth consumed by each DC.

Finally, if you're only curious as to what the replication topology looks like in your site, you can try out Active Directory Replication Monitor (**REPLMON**), located in the Windows 2000 Support Tools. **REPLMON** allows you to view a limited graphic display of the replication topology between DCs in the same site or forest (however, my experience suggests that there are bugs in the graphical view feature, so you shouldn't put too much trust in the graphic that is displayed), but most importantly enables you to gain information on the low-level status and performance of the replications going on and, optionally, the status of GPOs, FSMOs, and the other details that make up the vitally important support Active Directory structures.

You might also want to check out the Replication Diagnostics tool (**REPADMIN**), also located in the Windows 2000 Support Tools. Among several other things, **REPADMIN** enables you to force replications, and thus should prove a boon to speeding up the replication testing. Using **REPADMIN** for that purpose does have one drawback: Notification calls between the replication partners for that specific replication are skipped, for obvious reasons (as such, the replication load is a bit smaller than one would experience in real life, and so this tool doesn't apply to performance testing).

The overhead per member of a group is always around 180 bytes. Unfortunately, the replication size of the most commonly occurring changes in the Active Directory database—password changes—seems to vary a lot. Each password change seems to take up between 400 and 600 bytes, depending on the number of password changes that have occurred since the last replication (except for the case in which you change only one password; then it's approximately 1.8KB).

Intrasite GC Replications

The GC consists of a partial copy (defined by the schema) of all the domains in the forest, with some additional objects (namely, Universal Groups). Intrasite GC replications are done in the same way as for DCs, using DS-RPC with no compression and notifications every five minutes.

The available data on Intrasite GC replication paints the following picture:

♦ Each user object is approximately 3.0KB.

♦ Each Global and Universal Group object with no members is approximately 2.1KB.

♦ Each volume object is approximately 1.8KB.

Again, these figures are valid only when you replicate more than 100 objects at a time. For example, if you replicate only one of these directory objects, approximately 12KB will be consumed.

The overhead per member of a Universal Group seems to be approximately 200 bytes. No additional overhead is expended on members of Global Groups, because they aren't published in the GC. As you can see, most of the GC replication that occurs is smaller than the comparable DC replication. This is exactly as it should be, because the GC carries only a subset of the attributes stored in the DCs. Further, this margin is bound to grow wider as you start to use still more attributes stored in the DCs that won't be replicated to the GC. Conversely, be aware that the GC will hold more objects than each of the DCs in a multiple domain environment.

Intersite DC Replications

Intersite DC replication is done in much the same way as Intrasite DC replication, except that Intersite DC replication uses compression, which nearly always reduces the replication traffic on the wire (the more data, the better the compression rate), but carries a penalty in use of CPU cycles.

Also, you have full control regarding how often and when the replication partners will be communicating. But, in a departure from Intrasite DC replication, the DCs set up the communications channel every time (adding some overhead, but reducing the chances of having something go haywire because of unstable connections). Also, because of this marked difference, no notification takes place between the two partners. Instead, changes are requested for each naming context.

The available data on Intersite DC replication paints the picture shown in Table 20.9, when replicating 10, 100, and 1,000 of the listed directory objects. By comparing these figures to the Intrasite DC replications, you can see that compression really works wonders—and the payoffs

Table 20.9   Intersite DC replication.

Object Type	10 Objects (size per object)	100 Objects (size per object)	1,000 Objects (size per object)
User	4,560 bytes	400 bytes	290 bytes
Global and Universal Group, no members	2,675 bytes	295 bytes	200 bytes
Volume	2,170 bytes	230 bytes	155 bytes

increase with the number of objects replicated. Generally, if you have 100 objects or more to replicate, you will find that the replication load is reduced to some 10 to 15 percent of what is needed for the Intrasite DC case (if you have less objects, you will find the data load to be approximately the same as for the Intrasite DC replications). So you don't want to replicate more often than is needed in the Intersite case, because infrequent replications, all things being equal, yield a larger data payload and thus the optimum compression rate.

Intersite GC Replications

Intersite GC replication can be done in exactly the same way as Intersite DC replication—using DS-RPC (RPC over IP) with compression. However, for Intersite GC replications, you also have another option: use SMTP as the replication transport. Choosing SMTP makes sense if you are faced with unstable line conditions (because SMTP is an asynchronous protocol) or you encounter situations in which you can't use TCP/IP and/or RPC.

Note

The SMTP transport is built upon the SMTP component that comes as part of Internet Information Server 5, which is included on the Windows 2000 Server CD-ROM.

The available data on Intersite GC replication with DS-RPC provides the picture shown in Table 20.10, when replicating 10, 100 and 1,000 of the listed directory objects. The available data on Intersite GC replication with SMTP provides the picture shown in Table 20.11, when replicating 10, 100, and 1,000 of the listed directory objects.

Again, most of the GC replications are smaller than the comparable DC replications—exactly as should be. Also, the replications using RPC as the transport cause less network traffic than those using the SMTP transport. Thus, you should always opt for RPC, unless a strong reason exists for not doing so.

Table 20.10   Intersite GC replication with DS-RPC.

Object Type	10 Objects (size per object)	100 Objects (size per object)	1,000 Objects (size per object)
User	3,600 bytes	325 bytes	235 bytes
Global and Universal Group, no members	2,680 bytes	290 bytes	195 bytes
Volume	2,320 bytes	245 bytes	170 bytes

Table 20.11   Intersite GC replication with SMTP.

Object Type	10 Objects (size per object)	100 Objects (size per object)	1,000 Objects (size per object)
User	5,290 bytes	600 bytes	440 bytes
Global and Universal Group, no members	4,040 bytes	555 bytes	395 bytes
Volume	3,540 bytes	415 bytes	350 bytes

Understanding and Optimizing Network Behavior

Unless, you have plenty of available bandwidth throughout your enterprise at all times, you should take the time to understand the network behavior that can be attributed to the Active Directory. Just learning a few important issues might put you in a position to lessen the Active Directory's impact on your WAN.

The first and foremost lesson lies in the area of creating an Active Directory design that maps properly to your network infrastructure. This was the subject of Chapter 12, so I won't dwell further on that here.

But you can still learn a few important lessons from the details. If you are to understand the network behavior attributed to Active Directory, you should focus on these two very different things:

◆ *Server traffic*—Replication traffic between the DCs and GCs and the user accesses to the servers. Although you generally won't be able to forecast the user component of server load, the replication traffic can be predicted fairly accurately because it relies on the namespace design and the number of object changes inside each time slot.

◆ *Client traffic*—Client logon and the actual usage of the computer. It's generally not possible to forecast the user load, but the client logon traffic is pretty well documented.

It can prove quite interesting to understand client logon dynamics, because that will allow you to predict the load on the network in a business where most users are logging on at the same time. And the replication traffic between servers isn't entirely without interest, because it should be considered a baseline of the minimum additional load that will be imposed on the existing WAN lines, when Active Directory is put into production.

The Client Logon Situation

Generally, you should expect each client logon to generate network traffic in the 95 to 170KB range (which is a stark contrast to the approximately 50KB generated when logging on from a Windows 9x-based computer). The first number quoted is for a "bare-bones" client logon that doesn't include anything but the default feature set (that is, a plain-vanilla user account that doesn't include any use of the advanced Active Directory features); the second number quoted pretty much should be viewed as the case for a client that is making use of a fair number of the GPO options.

And the more group memberships, Group Policy settings, security settings, and software distribution that you employ—the larger the size will get.

The client logon consist of two parts:

♦ *The computer startup*—A "bare-bones" computer startup hovers around the 57KB mark.

♦ *The user login*—A "bare-bones" computer startup hovers around the 36KB mark.

The steps involved in the computer startup are outlined below. It will usually result in some 60 to 90KB of data being carried over the network, depending on the number of Group Policy options and group memberships:

1. The computer issues a DHCP request and receives an acknowledgement from the DHCP server, at which point the DHCP server registers the reverse lookup pointer address supplied with the DDNS server. Three ARP broadcasts are done to check for a duplicate IP address on the one received from the DHCP server. Approximately 700 bytes.

2. The computer multicasts to 224.0.0.2 (ICMP Router Solicitation) to query for the nearest routers and then goes on to query the DNS server for any DCs that are members of the computer's domain to be found in the local site. Approximately 1,500 bytes.

3. The DC is queried for a variety of records in order to establish the name and context of the logon server. Approximately 2,000 bytes.

4. DDNS is queried for the IP address of the preferred DC and sets up a TCP session for a MS RPC conversation that is used for accessing the **NETLOGON** service. Approximately 3,000 bytes.

5. TimeSync is established with the preferred DC using NTP (Network Time Protocol) over UDP (port 123). Approximately 150 bytes.

6. Steps 2 and 3 are performed again, the server is **PING**ed, and a new session is set up for catering to the needs of an SMB session. Approximately 1,150 bytes.

7. The Kerberos authentication of the machine account takes place and will hopefully wind up with the computer now being in possession of a Ticket Granting Ticket (TGT). Approximately 12,000 bytes (it can grow a bit, depending upon the number of groups that the machine is a member of).

8. The computer connects to the **IPC$** Share on the DC and gets all DFS referrals on the domain back from the server in the process. Approximately 6,000 bytes.

9. The DC is queried once more, much along the lines of Step 3. Approximately 550 bytes.

10. The RPC port mapper function is set up, the computer requests a Ticket Granting Service ticket for the **DC$** (the domain controller account) service, three calls to the Active Directory are carried out, and the DC is **PING**ed. Approximately 10,000 bytes.

11. The computer requests a Ticket Granting Service ticket for the **LDAP.DC.domain.com** (the domain controller account) service and queries the Active Directory for a range of base data, including the LDAP attributes supported. The computer requests a Ticket Granting

Service ticket for the **WS$** (workstation) service and ask for the GPOs for the site, domain, and workstation. Approximately 16,000 bytes (depending upon the number of GPOs).

12. The GPOs of relevance to the computer are downloaded. Approximately 12,000 bytes or more (depending on whether you've added additional GPOs that are of relevance to the machine).

13. The DDNS SOA (Source of Authority) is requested, CNAME and A records of the computer are added to the DDNS database, and the DDNS server is then queried for that very record in order to check that everything works on the DDNS side of things. Approximately 1,000 bytes.

14. Everything is torn down, and the computer is ready to accept a user login. Approximately 1,500 bytes.

The steps involved in the user login are outlined below. It will result in some 40 to 100KB of data being carried over the network, depending on the number of Group Policy options and group memberships:

1. Kerberos tickets are exchanged between the computer and the DC (that is, the computer requests a Ticket Granting Ticket, receives it, and then sends the ticket back to receive a Ticket Granting Service ticket. Approximately 8,000 bytes (depending upon the number of groups that the user is a member of).

2. An LDAP search query (which include the computer's domain GUID and domain SID) is launched against the DC. The DC returns the name and context for the **LOGON** server. Approximately 500 bytes.

3. RPC port mapper function is set up, three calls to the Active Directory are carried out, and Kerberos tickets are exchanged again. Approximately 12,000 bytes (depending upon the number of groups that the user is a member of).

4. The existing RPC session executes three more calls to the Active Directory and the session is torn down. Approximately 7,000 bytes.

5. An LDAP authentication is established and is used for executing an LDAP search for GPOs for the site and then the domain. Approximately 12,000 bytes (depending upon the number of GPOs).

6. Kerberos tickets are exchanged. Approximately 9,000 bytes (depending upon the number of groups that the user is a member of).

7. An SMB session is set up to download the applicable GPOs. Approximately 6,000 bytes.

8. Kerberos tickets are exchanged once more. Approximately 11,000 bytes (depending upon the number of groups that the user is a member of).

9. The applicable GPOs are downloaded. Approximately 20,000 bytes or more (depending on whether you've added additional GPOs that are of relevance to the machine).

10. The computer **PINGS** the DC, all outstanding TCP and SMB connections are torn down, and the user is logged on. Approximately 500 bytes.

Because so many Kerberos ticket exchanges occur in the user login, the membership of groups have a lot bigger impact on the user login than is the case with the computer startup. You should expect the growth in network traffic to be more linear between the computer startup and the client login, if you have the same number (and size) of GPOs being loaded here. You can check out the size of each GPO in the **SYSVOL***Sysvol* folder (see Chapter 10 for more information on that).

And you should remember that software distribution using GPOs and roaming user profiles in particular would work to move the network traffic to a whole other dimension than what's quoted and discussed here.

In addition to these things, you should always stay alert to the following features that may work to add a fair amount of load to your network (but usually far from being in the class of software GPOs and roaming user profiles):

♦ Offline files and folders

♦ Folder redirection

The Server Replications

As mentioned earlier in this chapter, the Active Directory replications are quite predictable, generally exhibiting a near-linear growth.

The Active Directory replications adhere quite closely to these rules of thumb:

♦ Set-up traffic for Intrasite replications: None

♦ Set-up traffic for Intersite replications: About 13KB per naming context

♦ Intrasite replications (uncompressed data): 110 to 120 percent of actual size

♦ Intersite replications (compressed traffic): 10 to 15 percent of actual size, when more than 100KB of data

But you should acquaint yourself with a couple of other important details before venturing further.

Watch Those Roaming User Profiles

Roaming user profiles store user preferences for hyperlinks, Start menu items, and system and application settings, as well as all user documents located in the My Documents folder and its subfolders. Temporary and local computer information will not roam with the user. That is, the roaming user profile doesn't include the following items:

- The user's personal Temp directory.
- All temporary files created by Internet Explorer (Temporary Internet Files during a browsing session).
- Locally stored application data (Application Data).
- The list of recently accessed Web pages (History).

When a user logs on, the server-stored profile is merged with the local cached copy of the user profile (provided that one already exists). If the user logs on to the computer for the first time, all the profile information, including any Start menu customizations and the My Documents folder, are copied to the local hard drive.

As you might suspect, the addition of roaming user profiles adds more data to the user login. A "bare-bones" user profile will usually add some 270KB of network traffic and more, when the user begins adding to his profile. However, there's even worse things ahead: Although a logoff amounts to less than 1KB of network traffic when not using a roaming user profile, you will find the size of the logoff growing to a whopping 521KB and more, after the user starts adding data to his profile.

The profile size increases significantly as more applications and user data are added. You should note that the merging algorithm used by Windows 2000 would work to reduce the data traversing the wire, because only changed data is copied to the workstation at logon and to the network server at logoff. However, field experiences point to the quite scary conclusion that it does very little to change the data transferred at logoff; at the very best, it should reduce the logon traffic by some 50 percent. In other words, you should perform some real-life field tests and carefully weigh the benefits of enabling this option against the network traffic it will generate based on those test results.

Depending upon your network infrastructure, you might find yourself in a very tight spot on the roaming user profiles. If that's the case, take some joy from the fact that you can set quotas for user profile size and can manage user settings centrally. A most elegant method for making sure that the remaining user profiles won't grow out of bounds is to redirect the My Documents folder and make it available offline.

First of all, chances are that you will have several other kinds of replications going on in your environment, including the following:

♦ *File Replication Service (FRS) replications*—Exists between all DCs in each domain running off the replication topology defined by you and the KCC. FRS is running in uncompressed RPC, so it might add a fair amount of load to your WAN.

♦ *Active Directory Connector (ADC)*—Chances are high that you will sooner or later need to implement this feature, if you have Exchange Server 5.5. ADC connects to Exchange Server 5.5 and DCs/GCs using LDAP over RPC.

♦ *DNS replications*—Unless you've chosen to make use of the Active Directory-integrated DDNS feature, you need to get a separate DNS replication topology up and running.

You should note that you can't get around RPC replications inside each roam (due to FRS), so you'll be hard-pressed to partition the various subnets inside a roam into separate security boundaries by using a firewall. Or, to be more precise, although you can always implement a firewall, you won't be able to make it very secure because of all the RPC traffic that has to pass through it.

Secondly, you should take care to establish a fairly high stability of your lines, because RPC is notorious for being less than forgiving to unstable connections. However, field experience shows that the improvements in the Windows 2000 TCP/IP stack do indeed make Active Directory much more forgiving of these things than has been the case before.

And third, you should be aware that Active Directory DCs/GCs are quite chatty. By default, you'll have some chatting (that is, a couple of network packets of very small sizes) going on every 3 to 10 minutes, in effect making the servers unsuitable for dial-up lines. Although this no doubt won't present a large company with a problem, it does present small and geographically disparate companies with some major headaches.

As mentioned in the later-coming "Reducing Your WAN Load" section, several tweaks are available to help you improve on the situation. However, although these things do go a long way to reduce the bandwidth spent (and Active Directory's inherent chattiness), you really shouldn't expect to get much above 30 minutes between each chat "session." And when you start adding third-party applications, you will most probably find them to add a fair bit of chat as well. So, in my experience, you might as well get used to the fact that Active Directory isn't built for dial-up lines.

Watch Those All-Encompassing Replications

A full replication to a DC or GC is certainly the worst-case scenario one can face. And that's why you should understand that that will happen in these cases:

- *Installation of a DC or GC*—Each time you promote a server to the status of Active Directory DC or GC, you will have a lot of replication going on. And that's why you should be careful to check when the replication traffic will be passing over the WAN and when it won't be. You should obviously be facing replications, when you're installing the first DC or GC in a site. But you might also encounter it under several other situations.

- *DC being off more than the tombstone period*—Any DCs that aren't connected to any other Active Directory DCs for more than tombstone period (60 days default) will get a full replication from the nearest DC (and GC), when they get back online.

- *Changes in attribute set being replicated to the GC*—Any change in a GC's available attributes will cause a full synchronization of any and all GCs found in the forest.

Usually, it will make good sense to change all applicable attributes as soon as the first two DCs and GCs have been installed. Also, in order to avoid overstretching the WAN, you might consider installing the DCs and GCs at a hub site rather than on-site.

Reducing Your WAN Load

Microsoft is right when they claim that the DCs and GCs are optimized to reduce network usage from the outset. So when you've carefully decided how often and at which times of the days of the week replications are allowed for the various Intersite replication connections, there's really not any more optimization left to do. After all, the replications are a consequence of the day-to-day management of the environment—that is, creation and deletion of users, creation and deletion of group memberships, creation of new non-security principals such as printers, volumes, computers, and so forth—and thus can't be postponed indefinitely.

Note

Please remember that although SMTP is a bit more forgiving to unstable lines, it uses up more bandwidth (also, it's much harder to configure). So never choose SMTP if you can avoid it.

However, there are, in fact, a couple of very powerful things left for you to do outside the scope of replications.

NetBIOS: Still Alive and Kicking

It's easy to spot anyone who has been tasked with optimizing the bandwidth usage on Windows NT Server 4 domains. You just have to mention something about NetBIOS and network communications in the same sentence, then sit back and wait for their reaction. And yes, the NetBIOS legacy still haunts Active Directory despite Microsoft's initial promise that Active Directory would represent a radical break with the past with regard to network communications.

When you get up close to the network traffic, you will find that there's a lot of NetBIOS hiding underneath the covers. As such, you will be subjected to lots of NetBIOS packets, if you just perform a trace of the network communications going back and forth between your Active Directory DCs.

Note

It's quite easy to get a feeling for the NetBIOS communications added to the equation even if you're not that much of a networking type of person. You can simply install Network Monitor, ask it to look for all packets departing from the local DC/ GC when there's nobody accessing the server, jot down the number of bytes transmitted after a couple of hours, disable NetBIOS support on the network card, and ask Network Monitor to do the same once more.

There's one recurring set of NetBIOS network packets that stands out from the others. And that's the master browser and backup browser traffic, which also gained notoriety in Windows NT Server.

What's Browsing?

Browsing is what happens when a user takes a peek at Network Neighborhood. Although this is a great feature for peer-to-peer LANs, it's really not something that is very interesting in a client/server setting. In order to effectively locate network resources, Microsoft Windows 2000 Server implements browsing—just as was the case with its predecessor.

The browsing is done by having the client connect to a master browser or a backup browser for getting the current list of hosts known to the master browser. Browsing is limited to the client's own domain or work group. All computers with server components—that is, the ability to share network resources—announce themselves to the master browser in their local domain. Additionally, servers that operate in any capacity as a potential browser, backup browser, or master browser become involved in several other communications as well:

- Browser elections occur whenever the master browser cannot be located on the local subnet and whenever a domain controller initializes.
- Master browsers in different domains communicate with each other so that servers and resources can be accessed throughout the network.
- Backup browsers receive updated browse lists from the local master browser.

The basics of the server browsing process are:

- Upon startup, the primary domain controller of a domain assumes the role of domain master browser.
- Upon startup, each backup domain controller of the domain becomes either a backup browser or a local master browser, depending on whether there is already a master browser for that domain on that subnet.
- Every 15 minutes, each master browser (on each subnet) announces itself to the master browsers of other domains on the local subnet.
- Every 12 minutes, each domain master browser contacts WINS for a listing of all domains (<1B> names).
- Every 12 minutes, each master browser contacts the domain master browser to update the browse lists.
- Every 12 minutes, each backup browser contacts its local master browser to retrieve an updated browse list.

All hosts that have a server component—such as computers running Windows for Workgroups, Windows 95, Windows NT Workstation, and Windows 2000 Professional—announce themselves every 12 minutes to the local master browser. This allows the host to be included in the browse list for the domain.

Having a single domain that is separated by routers (as is a common scenario nowadays) makes browsing more difficult, because browsing relies on broadcast messages. But, thanks to the master browser and backup browsers, it's possible to browse an entire domain on a WAN, even though subnets are separated by IP routers through WINS (which registers the domain master browser).

The browser traffic adds at least 17KB of communications (on top of that come the entries in the master browser as well as the domain browser list; each entry in the browse list is 27 bytes plus space for the server comment, if any) for every time that a master browser is elected. By default this happens every 12 minutes, which means that you'll have approximately 85KB traversing your WAN lines in an hour, just for the sake of keeping NetBIOS happy.

Admittedly, this figure doesn't look that bad initially—after all, it's a measly 24 bits per second going to waste. But as a master browser is elected on each TCP/IP subnet (and for each domain represented on the subnet, as well as for each installed and bound protocol), you will find NetBIOS adding some 2MB load per domain per WAN location each day of the year. So if you have 100 locations/subnets, which on average are having DCs from two domains each with two protocols, you will find 800MB of bandwidth going to waste every day of the year—and, perhaps worst of all, each 200MB piece of this traffic is heading to the DC holding the PDC Emulator role for the applicable domain.

Fortunately, it's quite easy to get rid of those master browser elections, as well as the backup browser, which you might as well change now that you're at it, because both are controlled by changing the following two Registry settings:

◆ *MasterPeriodicity*—Specifies how frequently a master browser contacts the domain master browser. The default is 720 seconds (12 minutes) with a minimum of 300 seconds (five minutes) and a maximum value of 0×418937 (4,294,967 seconds). The parameter is added as a **REG_DWORD** and can be changed dynamically without restarting the computer.

◆ *BackupPeriodicity*—Specifies how frequently a backup browser contacts the master browser. The default value for BackupPeriodicity is 720 seconds, with a minimum of 300 seconds (five minutes) and a maximum value of 0×418937 (4,294,967 seconds). The parameter is added as a **REG_DWORD** and requires you to restart the computer to be changed. This parameter shouldn't affect the WAN (that is, provided that no computers that are part of each subnet are connecting over WAN lines), because backup browsers always communicate with a local master browser, never with a remote one. But you'd better change this setting, too, just to be on the safe side.

Warning

The master browser needs WINS to be present to locate the domain master browser. For this reason, each master browser generates a host of errors on each subnet. So you will need to address this feature, whether or not you have WINS running on your network.

Both Registry keys are found in **HKEY_LOCAL_MACHINE\SYSTEM\CurrentControlSet\Services\Browser\Parameters.** You need to change the setting on all Windows computers (including the clients) if you are to be absolutely certain to avoid wasting any bandwidth for this.

You should note that the only viable alternative to changing the Registry keys is to disable the server component or the NetBIOS protocol on all computers running in the whole enterprise. Neither will prove feasible in most environments, and the latter will also make the computers unable to work with other NetBIOS applications, which can't be recommended because of the tens of thousands of old NetBIOS applications still out there.

Knowing Your Passwords

Another thing that you should look into is the handling of password changes in your domains. Although changes to account passwords can be made at any DC, the change will immediately be pushed to the PDC Emulator role holder in the domain by that DC. In other words, depending upon the number of password changes occurring inside each location, you might have a fair number of connections to the PDC Emulator role holder DC caused by password changes.

The reason for this is quite simple: There must be a point of reference with regard to passwords to ensure that a user that has just changed password at DC1 and then attempts to log in using DC2, for which the password hasn't yet replicated, won't experience that his new password is seen as being invalid (and his user account being subjected to an account lockout), just because he tries to log on to another DC for one or another reason.

In Windows NT Server 4, if authentication fails at a BDC, the authentication is remoted to the PDC. Active Directory exhibits a similar behavior: The authentication is retried at the PDC role holder, when an authentication fails at a DC other than the PDC role holder. If you're able to make do without the PDC Emulator being employed as a kind a tie-breaker (and would rather save the bandwidth spent for the push of new passwords), you can disable that functionality by way of setting the Registry key **HKLM\ CurrentControlSet\Services\Netlogon\Parameters\AvoidPdcOnWan** to 1 on all DCs in the domain. **AvoidPdcOnWan** is of the type **REG_DWORD** and is disabled by deleting the Registry key or setting it to 0.

Please note that there are two kinds of password changes to take into account—user passwords and computer passwords—when calculating the WAN bandwidth spent on this chore.

Additionally, you will also be able to save some bandwidth by moving from Windows 9x or Windows NT Workstation to Windows 2000 Professional with regard to password changes, because all non-Windows 2000 Professional clients will attempt to contact the PDC role holder directly to make a password change (this is because of the Windows NT Server 4 legacy).

Along the same lines, you might want to note that Active Directory includes four events that prompt an immediate replication:

♦ Replicating a newly locked out account

♦ Changing an LSA secret

♦ State changes in RID Manager role

♦ Changes in Inter-domain trust passwords (trusts between domain A and B) to any Windows NT Server 4 BDCs, which only applies to Active Directory mixed mode domains

Unfortunately, you can't do anything to optimize on these four events. Your only consolation to that is that all other Active Directory replication takes place only at the intervals defined by you.

Staying Clear of the Forest Root

Another optimization well worth doing centers on the DNS records. First of all, you should make absolutely sure that all applicable DNS records are stored in one or multiple DNS databases that are found in the site rather than across the WAN. You might also want to enable the Active Directory-Integrated DNS feature (see Chapter 7) to save yourself a bit of bandwidth by not having to keep a separate DNS replication topology in place beside the Active Directory replication topology.

However, more interestingly, you should also delegate the zone _msdcs.<Name_of_forest> and make one or multiple DNS servers in every location secondary for this zone. The reason this will save you some precious bandwidth is that the mentioned DNS zone contains RRs for GC location and DC location by GUID, both of which will be looked up quite frequently by the DCs and GCs.

Note

This will only work to save you bandwidth if you have more than one domain in the Active Directory forest or if you're not running Active Directory-Integrated DNS.

The WINS Options

As mentioned in Chapter 7, you should also implement WINS in your environment to avoid any trouble with regard to performing NetBIOS name lookups. And just as was the case in Windows NT Server, you should put a fair amount of effort into the design to avoid having the WINS database changes replicated too often (or too seldom). You should also only want the servers to be registered in WINS, unless some very good reasons exist for also allowing clients to do this.

Taking Care of Slow WANs

My own experiences show Active Directory to be very stable, indeed, when it comes to slow links. The replications work fine (albeit take a fair amount of time to complete) on line speeds all the way down to 19,200 bits per second (bps).

Time outs will begin to occur at 9,600 and 2,400 bps line speeds, but these generally also will prove suitable, provided that you optimize the settings used by the TCP/IP protocol stack. However, depending on your setting (that is, the number of objects changed per day, the inherent risk of having to re-replicate the full GC context, the amount of FRS traffic, etc.), you might still find the time spent on performing each replication so painstakingly long that it simply doesn't apply to your scenario.

In addition to the things mentioned in the last section, you should also do the following to optimize your Active Directory solution for slow WANs:

♦ *Adapt the TCP/IP stack to the exact properties of the slow link*—Windows 2000 allows you to configure a lot of interesting features that has been introduced to the Windows 2000's TCP/IP stack. For doing so, I urge you to study the "Microsoft Windows 2000 TCP/IP Implementation Details" whitepaper (currently found at **www.microsoft.com/WIN-DOWS2000/library/howitworks/communications/networkbasics/tcpip_implement.asp**) with a keen eye toward TCP-scalable windows size, Delayed Acknowledgements, and TCP Selective Acknowledgements.

♦ *Optimize the Time Service*—Each DC will try to synchronize its clock periodically. You are allowed to specify how many minutes the DC initially waits until next try in the case of time-sync failure (using the Registry key **HKLM/CurrentControlSet/Services/W32Time/Parameters/GetDcBackoffMinutes**), where the initial value will be doubled for each retry. Also, you can specify the maximum number of minutes that the Time Service can wait (using the Registry key **HKLM/CurrentControlSet/Services/W32Time/Parameters/GetDcBackoffMaxTimes**).

♦ *Optimize the time-out on each login using Netlogon*—The time-out interval, which is specified in seconds, can be configured at **HKLM/CurrentControlSet/Services/Netlogon/Parameters/ExpectedDialupDelay**.

♦ *Optimize Netlogon's password handling*—Netlogon performs a set of "scavenging" operations in which it checks to see if a password on a secure channel has to be changed or if a secure channel has been idle for a long time, sends a mail slot message to each trusted domain for a DC that hasn't been discovered (if NetBIOS enabled), and attempts to add <Domain>[1B] **name** to WINS (if NetBIOS is enabled). These chores are performed every 15 minutes by default, but can be changed at **HKLM/CurrentControlSet/Services/Netlogon/Parameters/ScavengeInterval** (specified in minutes).

♦ *Optimize dynamic registration of the SRV records added by the DC and GC service*—You are allowed to specify how often Netlogon will try to re-register DNS entries at **HKLM/CurrentControlSet/Services/Netlogon/Parameters/DnsRefreshInterval**. By default, the DNS re-registration entry will happen with the same interval as the scavenging. Additionally, you also are allowed to control the Time-to-Live (TTL) value attributed to the DNS entries registered by Netlogon, which specifies for how long the client is allowed to use the DNS entries by tweaking the Registry key **HKLM/CurrentControlSet/Services/Netlogon/Parameters/DnsTtl**.

♦ *Optimize the RPC session expiry*—By default, the OS will kill all RPC sessions after they've been idle for five minutes. Because a fair level of bandwidth is spent on setting up (as well as tearing down) each RPC session, you should advance the current expiration time of five minutes quite a lot, which is done by using the Registry key **HKLM/ CurrentControlSet/Services/NTDS/Parameters/Replicator RPC handle expiry check interval**. You should remember to also change the **HKLM/CurrentControlSet/Services/NTDS/Parameters/Replicator inter site RPC handle lifetime**, which specifies the same value for Intersite RPC sessions. Both Registry keys are specified in seconds.

Finally, you should also disable the browser service (or NetBIOS, if possible). You can disable NetBIOS from the TCP/IP properties sheet, whereas you can only disable the browser service by inserting the Registry key **"MaintainServerList"=No** in **HKLM/ CurrentControlSet/Services/Netlogon/Parameters**.

Improving DC/GC Performance: Adding More Load to the Network

As mentioned in the last section, Microsoft has done a good job of optimizing the DCs and GCs for keeping the network load to a minimum. And although that's good news for all of you who are trying to get by with the least possible bandwidth, it actually also goes to prove that there's a lot to be done, if you need to have the DCs/GCs performing at their optimum (including working with the least delay with regard to distributing changes) and have plenty of bandwidth to spare.

You should look into the following options for improving on the DC/GC performance compared with what you'll experience when using the default settings:

♦ Size of network packets

♦ Number of packets allowed between each ACK from the receiver

♦ Adding more priority to replication chores (possibly by adding additional processors)

♦ The latency set up with regard to:

♦ When Active Directory anticipates that it won't receive more changes

♦ When the next replication partner is notified of new changes

Best Practices

The behavior of the Active Directory database seems very predictable (linear growth with more or less approximation), which is very nice. However, the future demands on Active Directory don't look to be nearly as predictable, because you likely will be implementing a lot more schema extensions (explicitly as well as implicitly coming from Active Directory-aware applications).

So I urge you to be very careful regarding how much space you have available for the *ntds.dit* file. In general, always size the disk space to handle at least double the size of your estimated Active Directory database, to handle tombstones (all deleted objects stay in the database for 60 days, by default), database defragmentation, and future expansions with regard to objects and attributes. Also, consider providing even more expansion potential, because no one is able to foresee just how large the Active Directory database may become in the future, because it in large part will be dependent upon how many third-party applications become Active Directory-integrated in the future and your incentives for letting them into the Active Directory in the first place.

Note

The tombstone lifetime of 60 days means that in a DC's first 60 days, the database will grow, even if a large number of objects are deleted. After 60 days, the database either stays the same size or grows slightly. The fact that the file doesn't shrink after objects are deleted doesn't mean that new space hasn't been made available—it simply means that the space hasn't been reclaimed for other uses, which requires that you run offline defragmentation.

When you estimate the size of your Active Directory database, you should use the following guidelines (which admittedly are rough and conservative, but you'd better be on the safe side):

♦ Start with an Active Directory size of 10.5MB.

♦ Treat any security principal like a user object; each user has a size of 4.4KB.

♦ Treat nonsecurity principals like OU objects; each OU has a size of approximately 2.0KB.

♦ For delegation of access rights, add 75 bytes per directory object that is covered by each new ACE.

To estimate the size of your own attribute extensions, current available information provides the following guidelines:

♦ Every extra string attribute will add approximately 100 bytes to each object that it is attached to (and more if the string exceeds 10 characters).

♦ Binary data seems to take up 25 to 40 percent more space in the database than its actual size.

To assess the Active Directory database size in your organization, try following these steps:

1. Find the size that best approximates your company in Table 20.7 and note the corresponding database size.

2. Compare the objects that you expect to use with the number of objects used in the example. If you have additional objects that are security principals, add 4,400 bytes per instance; if they are not security principals, add 2,000 bytes per instance.

3. Compare the number of attributes that you intend to make use of on each type of object with the number of objects used in the example. For additional attributes, add 100 bytes per attribute. For binary data, such as pictures, add the file size, plus a buffer of 35 percent of the file size.

4. Make an estimate of the number of ACEs that will be added to some of the objects in the domain. Add 75 bytes per ACE per object.

5. To be properly prepared for the future, you should at least double (or triple) this base estimate.

Finally, remember to factor in the additional room needed for DCs that also act as GCs. Accounting for the GC sizing is a bit too complicated, given the many parameters that need to be considered. However, look at these factors when trying to determine the additional load added by the GC:

♦ How many objects are in place in all the domains that are part of the forest?

♦ Which groups are the most commonly used? Universal Groups or Global Groups? Universal Groups are stored in the GCs (that is, you need to account for the number of members of each group), whereas only the Global Group name is registered in the GC. Universal Groups are comparable to Global Groups with regard to the size claimed in the database.

♦ How many attributes are being replicated to the GC and approximately how many of each of those is actually in use (and thus claiming precious database space)?

♦ Is the schema changed to include attributes in the GC that aren't replicated by default?

As a very rough "guesstimate" for GCs, you should expect to have approximately 50 percent of each domain copied to the GC. The number will grow beyond that if you are using Universal Groups, because this kind of group and its members are stored in the GC instead of the DC. But because of the very complicated nature of making a correct estimate of the size of the GC, be sure to tread very carefully here. Also, remember that a GC will require much more room than a DC when you have several large domains that are part of the same forest.

Windows 2000 Server features two kinds of DC and GC replication: Intrasite (inside a site) and Intersite (between sites). Always strive to use *Intersite* replication across physical boundaries connected via WAN links, because Intersite replication will compress the traffic traversing the link and will provide you with a much easier and more detailed control of the traffic flowing on the link. You want to use this detailed traffic control to ensure that it uses the least trafficked times of day and happens as seldom as possible—doing so will get the most out of the compression.

For Intersite GC replication, you have the choice between RPC and SMTP. Always opt for RPC transport, because it causes less network traffic. Use SMTP transport only if you have no IP connectivity or the link is very unreliable.

When you try to estimate the replication load for your environment, remember that, except for having a new domain going online and such matters, the size of your replications depends on how many objects are changed in Active Directory within each cycle. In large environments, password changes (each password taking up some 400 to 600 bytes; and a single password change amounting to approximately 1.8KB) are one of the most important recurring sources of change.

Warning

You are advised to be very careful with regard to administrators and applications making changes to the attributes that are being replicated to the GC (that is, the **Replicate This Attribute To The Global Catalog** *option).*

Any change in the attribute set being replicated to the GC will trigger a full re-replication of all data stored in the GC. And as you can see, this could amount to so much data that you might find your WAN clogged for a while!

Table 20.12 provides a summary of how much bandwidth the replication of different numbers of the most commonly occurring directory object—the user object—will take up. However, please note that in reality the bandwidth for replicating the stated number of users should be less, because it's not common that one would change all the attributes on a lot of user objects and thus provoke a replication of the full object.

Warning

There's one very important exception to the rule that Active Directory should only replicate the data that has been changed. This exception incorporates all groups. Because the members of each group are stored in a multivalued attribute, you will find the whole list of members being replicated with every membership change— and so, if you add a single user account to a group with 5,000 members, you will have all 5,001 members being replicated throughout the group's scope (which translates into replication traffic of more than 2MB on the wire).

For this reason, Microsoft recommends that you keep your groups as small as possible, and especially refrain from building large Universal Groups. You might want to note that the group nesting functionality (Native Mode domains only) will allow you to split one large group into multiple smaller ones.

Table 20.12   The possible replication situations with varying numbers of user objects.

No. of Users	Intra-Site DC	Inter-Site DC	Intra-Site GC	Inter-Site GC with RPC	Inter-Site GC with SMTP
1	13KB	14KB	12KB	13KB	22KB
10	47KB	46KB	36KB	36KB	53KB
100	386KB	40KB	273KB	32KB	60KB
1,000	3,818KB	291KB	2,641KB	234KB	440KB

A Little-Known Detail Regarding Password Changes

Don't be fooled into believing that user passwords are the only ones that need to be considered. Each Windows 2000 (and Windows NT) computer also has a machine account that includes a password that frequently needs to be renewed.

For each Windows 2000 computer that is a member of a domain, a discrete communication channel (the secure channel) to the DC is created when the machine boots. The secure channel's password is stored along with the computer account on all the DCs and, thus, is replicated throughout the domain.

By default, the computer sends a secure channel-password change every 30 days, and the computer account password is updated. In other words, all things being equal, in a 1,000-computer domain, a computer account password change occurs on average every 43.2 minutes.

This isn't unique to Windows 2000—it's the same on Windows NT. However, in NT, the default update frequency is every seven days, thus worsening the number of replications that happen.

Summing It All Up

The storage requirements of the Active Directory database are pretty dependable, growth-wise; it approximates linear growth, which should come as a consolation for everybody involved with Active Directory design. Nothing yet seems to indicate that Active Directory has any major shortcomings in this area.

Computing a good approximation for the database sizing of DCs is relatively easy, whereas the sizing of GCs currently is a bit harder to predict. Remember that users won't be able to log in if no GC is available anywhere on the WAN, so hitting the disk space limitations on the GCs will be just as bad as for the DCs. Additionally, Exchange 2000 Server adds a lot of attributes to the GC, because it depends on the GC to present the Outlook clients with the Global Address List (GAL) and to answer queries, which increases the load experienced on GCs quite a bit compared with the "clean" Active Directory case.

Because most companies will not achieve a 100,000-user directory any time soon, it is appropriate to note that (from the perspective of disk space usage) DC hardware requirements are not overwhelming—in most cases, the directory database remains significantly below 1GB. However, to lower total cost of ownership of these systems, you should strive for dimensioning the disk space for three to four times the expected initial size of the database. Additionally, for large or heavily used DCs and GCs, you should hold the database and the log files on separate hard drives, for better performance and stability.

The replication load of Active Directory will prove fairly predictable provided you are familiar with the size of the objects and attributes being stored in the directory and their rate of change. It goes with the territory that you should remember to avoid adding redundant information or many large objects to your Active Directory, because this will lead to unnecessary increases in the replication load.

Sizing Your DCs and GCs

If you're charged with sizing the server boxes that are responsible for bringing Active Directory into life (and keeping it alive and kicking), you should check out Microsoft's Active Directory Sizer Tool (**ADSIZER**). The Active Directory Sizer Tool allows you to estimate the hardware required for deploying Active Directory in your organization based on a number of fairly tough questions probing your organization's profile, domain structure, and site topology. The tool will ask you to specify the total number of concurrent users; the number of dial-in connections per day; average number of groups a user belongs to; average logon rate per second during peak hours; number of Windows 2000-based computers in the domain; number of other computers in this domain; if Exchange 2000 Server will be deployed; and a great deal of other such things.

Based on the information provided by you, **ADSIZER** will provide you with estimates of the following:

- DCs per site
- GCs per site
- CPUs per machine as well as type of CPU
- Amount of memory required
- Disk storage needed for Active Directory

In addition, **ADSIZER** will deliver estimates on the following items:

- DC data size
- GC data size
- Network bandwidth utilization
- Intersite replication bandwidth required

Although **ADSIZER** definitely is a nifty tool that will allow you to cut a few corners, you should avoid putting all your faith into this one tool. For one, its scope is limited to just one domain; secondly, there's really no substitute for getting some real-life experience with Active Directory in your own setting. **ADSIZER** is a free download that is available at **www.microsoft.com/windows2000/downloads/deployment/sizer/default.asp**.

Part V

Fitting into a Current Infrastructure

Chapter 21

Implementing NT Server 4 with Active Directory in Mind

You may indeed have some very good reasons for choosing to implement Windows NT Server 4 rather than Windows 2000 Server in your infrastructure design—for the present. Some of the more significant reasons include the following:

- *A Service Level Agreement exists*—You may want to outsource all or part of the NT Server 4 installation on a Service Level Agreement (SLA) that guarantees a very high level of uptime or percentage availability. Until recently, major service and support organizations have been reluctant to offer such guarantees to their NT Server-based customers. However, several organizations lately are getting very aggressive in offering agreements that go up to 99.9 percent availability. The same guarantees for a Windows 2000 Server/Active Directory setting probably won't be available for a while.

- *Implementation plan for Windows 2000 Server would need to be extremely aggressive*—I, for one, would never try to convince any medium-size company to design an implementation plan in which the planning, proof-of-concept, and pilot phases are to be executed in less than a year. Correspondingly, a major company would need at least a year and a half, probably two years, to do the same. This timetable may be deemed unacceptable in some circumstances. If that holds true to your situation, you have to stick to NT Server 4 this time around.

- *Fear of the unknown*—Because Windows NT Server 4 essentially is a souped-up version of NT Server 3.51, many Value-Added Resellers (VARs), independent consultants, and corporate IT organizations have now accrued substantial experience with NT Server 4 design and implementation. Windows 2000 Server design and implementation is a much different story. Thus, judging from history and the complexity of the product, you'll have to wait for quite some time before you will be able to find a substantial talent pool that is very familiar with Windows 2000 Server and Active Directory. If this talent shortage poses a problem in your company, a bit of conservatism might be in order.

If you do choose to continue using NT Server 4 for one or more of the previously listed reasons (or for some other reason), you really should factor Windows 2000 Server into your short-term plans, because sooner or later—and probably sooner than you might think—you'll need to upgrade to Windows 2000 Server.

Given Microsoft's massive push for Windows 2000 Server—and the product's strong support from the Independent Software Vendor (ISV) community—chances are pretty high that you will need to upgrade to Windows 2000 Server in 2002 or at the latest in 2003. And, the 2002/2003 timeframe is close enough that you currently need to consider this upgrade with regard to hardware and software write-offs, staffing of the IT department, and presentation of your long-term plan to the corporate entities.

In short, when planning your NT Server 4 design, you should factor in the Windows 2000 Server upgrade, because doing so could potentially save you a lot of hassle when you migrate to Windows 2000 Server. The focus of this chapter is to help you form your NT Server 4 plan today with a keen eye toward the future—which is Windows 2000 Server.

If you don't have much NT Server 4 experience, don't despair! If you are unfamiliar with some of the concepts presented in this chapter, consult some other NT Server 4 design references (for example, *MCSE NT Server 4 in the Enterprise Exam Prep* and *MCSE NT Server 4 Exam Prep* both published by Coriolis), because this chapter assumes that readers know all the NT Server 4 core concepts. Consulting an NT Server 4 primer should help you understand all the finer points presented here.

Vital Advice about Designing Your NT Server 4 Solution

When you begin your NT Server 4 design (or redesign), keep this advice handy:

♦ Use TCP/IP only.

♦ Keep your TCP/IP address structure neat and tidy.

♦ Implement DHCP for allocation of TCP/IP addresses to clients.

♦ Reduce the reliance on NetBIOS as much as possible (especially on the third-party applications being deployed).

♦ Strive to implement applications that have been proven fully compatible with Windows 2000 at present time or—almost as good—an application for which an upgrade that is Windows 2000 Certified already is in existence.

- Implement solutions that use DNS for name resolution, wherever you can.

- Go with as few domains as possible, and stay clear of the complete trust model, when possible. If you need more than one domain, you should set your goal for using the single master domain or multiple master domain models.

- Keep your group structure as simple as possible.

- Use groups for assignment of all permissions; avoid doing any permission assignments directly to users and computers and try to stay clear of the built-in domain local groups (Administrators, Users, Account Operators, etc.).

- Think carefully before implementing non-English versions of Windows NT 4 on servers and clients.

- Always implement NT Server 4 with the latest Service Pack (or at least SP5).

- If in doubt about the OS for clients, choose Windows NT Workstation 4.

- Dimension your new hardware (clients and servers) in anticipation of the Windows 2000 upgrade.

For users of Exchange Server, add the following to your list:

- Strive to minimize the number of Windows NT domains that are used by Exchange Server.

- Limit the number of containers created to the absolute minimum.

- Use only Exchange 5.5 Service Pack 3, when possible.

- Try to keep the number of Exchange sites down.

If you follow these simple guidelines, you should be much better off when you perform the actual Windows 2000 Server migration. You'll find that most of the above-mentioned advice is examined in more detail in the rest of this chapter.

One more thing: Try to do at least some of the planning and architecture of Active Directory that is outlined in this book before you wrap up your NT Server 4 design. You might find one or two important lessons in store for you, regarding how you should or shouldn't structure the NT Server 4 design.

The Boring TCP/IP Details

You should strive to make your NT Server 4 implementation a TCP/IP-only proposition. This will work to ease your Windows 2000 Server migration substantially, because Active Directory works on TCP/IP networks only. Also, TCP/IP is NT Server 4's default selection, so virtually all NT Server 4 implementations done in recent years have been built on TCP/IP.

To use TCP/IP, your network infrastructure must be able to handle TCP/IP. Luckily, because of the runaway success of the Internet, this demand already is met by most existing LANs and WANs. Consequently, the demand for TCP/IP usually affects legacy devices the most. Many big iron (DEC VAXs and different kinds of IBM-compatible mainframes and AS/400s) systems that are still in use aren't TCP/IP-compatible. In such situations, you are usually faced with the following possible solutions:

♦ Bite the bullet and add TCP/IP support to the computers in question.

♦ Isolate the non-TCP/IP resources on a separate part of the LAN and put up a TCP/IP gateway to the rest of the network environment or put up such gateways directly "in front" of each computer.

♦ Learn to cope with the aspects of a multi-protocol LAN: higher complexity (more administration and a higher risk of trouble), higher overhead on bandwidth usage, less interoperability, and more demands on each client.

Often, the easiest and fastest solution to the problem is to employ a few gateways that bridge the gap between the legacy protocols and the rest of the network environment (a few Microsoft SNA Servers/Host Integration Server 2000s often prove to be a good solution, except in very specialized situations). However, you still might encounter some problems, caused by old terminals and printers and by mission-critical connections between legacy devices in different sites. But that's beyond the scope of this discussion.

Regardless of whether or not you are faced with implementing a whole new TCP/IP network infrastructure, always be cognizant of the TCP/IP address plan. If you want to avoid troubles later, don't be too inventive with your TCP/IP address plan. The simpler, the better, so the ideal situation is to have one subnet (be it class A, B, or C) at each location. Oppositely, you should definitely go to great lengths to avoid subnetting schemes in which you use subnet masks that are out of the ordinary (the ordinary being 255.0.0.0, 255.255.0.0, or 255.255.255.0) in an effort to save IP addresses.

A Brief Look at DHCP, WINS, and DNS

Properly configuring TCP/IP on each computer on the network can involve significant administrative overhead and a lot of opportunities for misconfigurations. The point of the Dynamic Host Configuration Protocol (DHCP) is to centralize and manage TCP/IP configuration information by automatically assigning to IP hosts IP addresses and other IP configuration information.

DHCP is one of the cornerstones of Active Directory, so you might as well get used to it now—and reap the ample rewards that it brings. In regard to Windows 2000 Server readiness, you really don't need to use anything but common sense (and current best practices for NT Server 4 environments) when implementing DHCP.

NetBIOS Is the Name of the BackOffice Game

If you are intent on implementing some Microsoft BackOffice applications in your Windows NT Server environment (such as Exchange Server 5.5, SQL Server 7.0, SMS 2.0, and so on), you should know that they're also essentially NetBIOS-bound.

For example, although you can avoid using NetBIOS in the core Exchange Server setup, you need NetBIOS support to use all the utilities for administering Exchange Server 5.5. Also, Exchange Server "talks" NetBIOS to the domain controllers. So, you really don't have to look any further than Microsoft's own applications to find a looming NetBIOS hassle.

Windows Internet Name Service (WINS) is a whole other story, however. WINS provides a name resolution service for NetBIOS over TCP/IP-based hosts, which eliminates the NetBIOS broadcasts. You need WINS for all the Microsoft OSs preceding Windows 2000 Server (because of the need for NetBIOS for name resolution); and, although WINS strictly speaking isn't a requirement for Windows 2000 Server/Active Directory, chances are you'll need to keep it running after the upgrade. Thus, regardless of your feelings toward WINS (for those unfamiliar with it, WINS is a pain to administer in a large setting; it has a lack of good tools and a lackluster replication engine), you'll need it to make your NT Server 4 network buzz and most probably will need it to some extent (that is, you might be able to avoid it being used by the clients) after having upgraded.

However, except for the compulsory NetBIOS-to-TCP/IP name resolution for Windows NT Servers and Windows clients, you should attempt to reduce the use of NetBIOS on the network as much as possible. NetBIOS should be considered a legacy solution in regard to Windows 2000 Server, which is why you want to avoid introducing more NetBIOS dependencies from other applications. If presented with the choice, opt to use DNS instead, because DNS is the name resolution standard used in Windows 2000 Server. And, for homegrown applications, you should start pondering a conversion from the NetBIOS APIs to the Winsock APIs.

In anticipation of Windows 2000 Server, you should make sure that you use only DNS-compatible NetBIOS names for all of your network Windows clients and servers. The standard DNS characters are A through Z, 0 through 9, and the dash (-). Also consider the length of the domain name, because migrated NT Server 4 domains most easily will maintain their domain name. Remember that names in Active Directory consist of several parts (for example, **exchserv.finance.bigwig.com**), so if you aren't careful, the resulting full name of the domain could be very cumbersome and difficult to read. Shorter names are easier to remember and use for both users and administrators.

With respect to DNS, you should at least incorporate a DNS domain structure into your NT Server 4 environment. Chapter 7 thoroughly presents the steps to implement a DNS domain structure, so they won't be repeated here. However, you should understand that implementing DNS-to-WINS name resolution might be helpful for migrating your legacy

NetBIOS solutions. This means that all of your NetBIOS names could just as well be re-solved via DNS as WINS because the DNS Server will query WINS on behalf of the client if it doesn't include an RR that matches the query—and considering the bleak future out-look for WINS, you really should get everybody used to using DNS right from the outset.

Everything has its price, however, and it may be steep in some cases. For example, DNS-to-WINS name resolution is a Microsoft proprietary DNS extension, and thus requires use of Windows NT Server 4's built-in DNS Server. Therefore, if you have an existing DNS do-main structure, you have the choice of migrating it to Microsoft's DNS Server or delegating a zone to the NT Server 4 DNS infrastructure, that is, if you want to use DNS-to-WINS name resolution.

If you don't have a DNS domain structure in place today, you should opt for Microsoft DNS Server: it's included with Windows NT Server 4, it has DNS-to-WINS name resolution, and it's obviously the perfect match for the souped-up DNS version included in Windows 2000 Server.

Clients and Servers

As you head toward Windows 2000 Server, you should *always* opt for Windows NT Server 4 instead of NT Server 3.51. Although upgrading directly from NT Server 3.51 to Windows 2000 Server is possible, some small backward-compatibility problems exist (see Chapter 22 for more information) with this upgrade that you would do well to avoid.

Also, you should use at least Service Pack 5 (and preferably SP6a or later) for all NT Server 4 servers, because this provides the best insurance against all sorts of inconveniences that may arise during the migration. Although it is still too soon to provide a rundown of any of those inconveniences, I'm confident that they'll occur—if for no other reason than that Microsoft invests fewer resources to ensure that the upgrade from NT Server 4 SP5 or SP6 is a breeze than it invests to ensure the same holds true for earlier Service Packs. And so, if you're experiencing difficulties, chances are that Microsoft will advise you to do the maxi-mum amount of patching, and to start over again.

Items to Remember When Designing Your DNS Solution

The following are some general rules for designing a good DNS solution that is optimized for migra-tion to Windows 2000 Server:

- Create a DNS domain for each NT Server 4 domain. Remember that Windows 2000 Server as-sumes that Active Directory domains map to DNS domains.

- If a site has servers, then it should also have a DNS server. The DNS server should be either primary or secondary for the DNS domain used for that site and secondary for the parent DNS domain. Placing the Windows-based clients in a separate DNS domain in the zone, based on site, often will prove useful.

- Servers running Windows NT Server should be registered in a master DNS domain. This will ensure that the presence of each NT Server is being made known to any DNS-only hosts.

To maximize the many TCO-related features of Windows 2000 Server, you need to implement Windows 2000 Professional on your desktops. The best way to prepare for Windows 2000 Professional is to deploy Windows NT Workstation 4 on any new client PCs that you install, because this will provide the fastest and smoothest upgrade (mainly because of its better software, hardware, and file system compatibility with Windows 2000 Professional). Obviously, you might also want to ponder going straight to Windows 2000 Professional, if your PC client hardware and client applications are up to it.

Choosing NT Workstation 4 also enables your support organization to develop advanced NT skills on the desktop, which later will prove valuable for ensuring an easy and rapid deployment of Windows 2000 Professional. Additionally, Microsoft claims that a lot of benefits can be derived from using NT Workstation 4 rather than Windows 98/Me.

Sure, the distinction of Windows NT Workstation 4 versus Windows 98/Me isn't a crucial one if you expect to do a total reinstallation on desktops when you migrate to Windows 2000 Professional. But there are still some very substantial reasons (and hundreds of subtle ones) for choosing NT Workstation 4 over Windows 98/Me in a corporate setting, and only a few reasons for doing the opposite.

Choose the Right Hardware from the Outset

Choice of hardware is an issue that probably is just as important as the OS considerations. Here, you should try to stay clear of any skimping on the dimensioning of the hardware components used for clients and servers. Windows 2000 Professional and Windows 2000 Server put even higher demands on the boxes than before. So, factor in this extra burden for all hardware that you buy today, because it likely will still be in use when you implement Windows 2000, regardless of the depreciation schedule used.

Reasons to Avoid Windows 95/98

The reason why you don't want to implement Windows 95/98 (as well as Windows Millennium Edition) on your clients, if presented with the choice, is quite simple: A Windows 95 or Windows 98 upgrade may require a lot of special handling.

Windows 95/98 is actually a very different kind of technology from Windows NT Workstation 4. If you delve further into the subject, you'll find many subtle differences (the worst difference, migration-wise, probably is the different Registry structures) in the architectures that, combined, have a negative impact on application migration.

When migrating Windows 95/98 platforms, you'll need help from the application vendor for the transition. To accomplish this, Microsoft is touting a technique that implements *migration DLLs,* which enable applications to recognize which OS they are running on and to update themselves accordingly. Migration DLLs (Dynamic Link Libraries) are called by the application to verify that all the appropriate application components are installed for the OS running. If not, the application setup program is called and the appropriate application components are loaded.

So, even though Microsoft will support the upgrade process from Windows 95/98 to Windows 2000 Professional and is working with application vendors to encourage their work on the migration DLLs, you will likely face more difficulties doing an in-place upgrade from Windows 95/98 than from NT Workstation 4.

If you want to avoid spending a lot of time and money on hardware upgrades (and the support time involved in executing them) later, you should dimension your hardware with plenty of RAM and CPU horsepower today (review the guidelines presented in Chapter 2, remembering to factor in your applications' needs and some room for growth in their hardware demands).

When purchasing hardware, remember that Windows 2000 has full support for Plug and Play, Advanced Configuration and Power Interface (ACPI), and many other new technologies. On the server side, note especially the support of hot-pluggable PCI devices, hot-pluggable array controllers and hard drives, and the much-improved support for clustering.

Consider the Language Version

Take a long, hard look at the options available when you choose the language version of NT 4 (especially for Windows NT Server 4), because the choice of language potentially could pose a problem regarding the Windows 2000 upgrade. The reason for this potential problem is quite simple: Generally, you won't be able to do an in-place upgrade to any Windows 2000 version other than the version that is of the same language as used by NT 4.

Tip

An undocumented and unsupported exception exists for upgrading from a local language version of Windows NT Workstation to the English version of Windows 2000 Professional. This exception is documented in Windows 2000 Professional: Advanced Configuration and Implementation, *also from The Coriolis Group.*

Although you might be very satisfied with your current language version for NT 4, you eventually could find that version to be a second-rate solution in a multinational Windows 2000 setting. Microsoft has introduced a new, multilingual user interface (MUI) edition of Windows 2000 (called Windows 2000 MultiLanguage Version), which is a version addressing global deployment scenarios. Thus, this version enables users to access information in their preferred language. In the MUI edition, you are able to localize everything except the following (which stay in English):

♦ All 16-bit pieces of the OS

♦ Bitmaps

♦ All Registry keys and values

♦ Folder and file names (including folder and link names found on the Start menu)

The localization is done by implementing one or more of the 24 language packs available. If you need to implement many of those language options, note that each will claim quite a bit of additional space on the hard disk: Each language adds up approximately 25MB for the UI and between 1MB and 20MB for data support to the hard-disk space used by the OS. Thus, you may discover ample need for the large hard disks being offered on the new PC clients.

The MUI version is a good choice for all situations except those in which the users don't understand any English. Furthermore, the MUI version is a very attractive proposition for the IT department, because it promises to eliminate many of the complexities of deploying multiple "flavors" of the same OS, resulting in easier deployment, feature parity across all languages, less technical support burden, and easier Service Pack and update deployment.

However, upgrading to the MUI version is possible only from a U.S./English-language edition of Windows NT Workstation 4, which is why you should avoid implementing anything but the U.S./English-language version of Windows NT Workstation in a corporation. And yes, I do know that this might prove to be a hard task, considering the variance of English skills among end users around the globe.

Thus, for the preceding reasons, if you opt to use non-U.S./-English-language versions of Windows NT Workstation 4, your only way of implementing the MUI edition when transitioning to Windows 2000 Professional is an all-out reinstallation of all clients. Planning upfront to do that doesn't seem too likely in the more decentralized types of organizations, unless you obtain this permission from users and management alike well before the NT 4 rollout starts.

However, before you insist on choosing the U.S./-English-language version of Windows NT Workstation 4—which could prove very unpopular among non-U.S./-English-language users—to secure the option of moving to the MUI version later, consider the fact that every Windows 2000 Professional local language version is much better than Windows NT Workstation 4 versions at handling the many different languages and preferences that exist in the world. Because Windows 2000 uses a single worldwide binary for core executable files (based on Unicode 2.0), you will be able to create scenarios such as multilingual user environments, mixed-language networks, and multilingual documents regardless of the language version chosen.

However, you still will be subjected to current problems associated with data sharing, support of roaming users, and basic connectivity when you mix different language versions of Windows 2000 (not to mention the support headaches). Thus, if you are stuck with non-U.S./-English-language versions of Windows NT Workstation 4, you may find that your company is ill-prepared to take full advantage of the options presented for global deployment.

Tip

When choosing the OS, and when choosing applications you must consider any language restrictions imposed. That's why you should strive to use applications that are prepared for the new Multilingual API (MLAPI), which will enable applications to handle keyboard input and fonts from different language versions and, thus, enable users to run applications in their preferred language. For example, a Japanese user will be able to sit down at any Windows 2000 Professional-based PC and switch the MLAPI-compliant text processor to Japanese characters regardless of which local language version is implemented on the PC, assuming that the appropriate language support has been installed in advance.

Choosing a Domain Model

The following are the four Windows NT Server 4 domain models defined by Microsoft:

♦ *Single domain*—Best model for many small and medium-size companies.

♦ *Single-master domain*—Best choice for companies that don't have too many users relative to the hardware, has a centralized IT department, and must have shared resources split into groups for management purposes.

♦ *Multi-master domain*—Often proves to be the only sensible choice for large companies with many users and fairly centralized IT operations (that is, companies which are operated from one or a few operations centers).

♦ *Complete trust*—Usually considered only by companies with no central IT department. Should be implemented only where none of the three other models fit, because the potential security risk posed by users from other domains that have access to resources requires that you have a high degree of confidence in all the other administrators.

Each of these domain models has various advantages and disadvantages that must be understood, which is why almost all major books on Windows NT Server 4 discuss these models in depth. Such in-depth analyses are beyond the scope of this book, and thus the pros and cons of each model are summarized in Table 21.1.

Basically, the following are the good, well-understood reasons for adding domains:

♦ For organizational reasons

♦ To improve network performance

However, the advent of Windows 2000 Server/Active Directory adds a new variable to the equation—the ease of transition to Windows 2000 Server. The net effect of this variable is really quite simple: Use as few domains as possible.

Therefore, although migrating to Windows 2000 Server is possible regardless of the domain model chosen, you should first look closely at your company's needs to determine whether you can use the single-domain model. If the single-domain model doesn't meet your company's needs, always opt for the single-master domain model, because this is the next-best choice of the three remaining options with regard to Windows 2000 Server migration.

Vital Group and User Lessons Learned

The migration from Windows NT Server 4 to Windows 2000 Server will be greatly simplified if you can do a straightforward upgrade that includes all the security principals (groups and users). If you are able to do that, you won't need to implement any changes to the users' basic setup and security permissions when migrating SID changes. However, such a migration also includes inheriting every inappropriate security permission setting, and thus does not allow you to clean up any security inexpediences during the migration. Consequently, you might want to be even more attentive than usual regarding how permissions are set up

Table 21.1   Each of the four domain model choices has its pros and cons.

Domain Model	Major Advantages	Major Disadvantages
Single domain	Centralized management of users and resources.	Potential for PDC overload.
	No trust relationships are required.	No grouping of users and resources into departments.
	Group definitions are simpler.	Ceiling on maximum number of users.
		Potential for slow browsing with numerous servers.
Single-master domain	Centralized security management.	All logon activity occurs in a single domain, thus posing a potential for performance problems.
	Resources are grouped logically in resource domains.	Local Groups must be defined in each resource domain.
	Browsing activity is distributed through the department domains.	Local administrators rely on master-domain administration for grouping of users.
	Global Groups in the master domain enable departments to establish local permissions easily.	
	Departments can manage the resources in their own domains.	
Multi-master domain	Scalable to any organizational size.	The number of Local and Global Groups and trust relationships multiplies rapidly as the number of domains increases.
	Centralized security.	User accounts and groups are not located in a single domain.
	Departments can manage the resources in their own domains.	
	Related users, groups, and resources can be grouped logically.	
Complete trust	Scales to any organizational size.	Central security control is lacking, and all participants effectively surrender their control by trusting everybody.
	No central MIS department is required.	Numerous trust relationships required.
	Departments retain control of their users and resources.	Departments are dependent on the management practices of other departments.
	Users and resources are grouped logically by departments.	

in the NT Server 4 design. If you want to do things right in the NT Server 4 design, then heed these five messages:

♦ *Keep your group structure as simple as possible*. Don't overload each group with several semantics.

♦ *Stay clear of the built-in domain local groups*. Although they work fine on Windows NT, these groups can't be migrated easily to Active Directory.

♦ *Use groups for assignment of all permissions*. Never implement any permission assignments directly to user accounts.

♦ *Strive to invest more time than usual on setting up the file system(s) permissions*.

♦ *Prepare for Active Directory's requirement of global uniqueness in user naming*. In Windows NT Server 4, user naming has to be unique only inside each NT Server 4 domain. So, to ease the transition to Active Directory, implement a naming scheme in NT Server 4 that ensures uniqueness across all domains implemented. For groups, use the same names for Local Groups that have the same semantics inside each domain. And, depending on what applies for each Global Group's Active Directory future, try to anticipate either convening the identical Global Groups in a Universal Group on a forest-wide scale (by choosing a descriptive name for that upfront) or turning the Global Group into a Universal Group (by securing forest-wide uniqueness of the Global Group naming).

The Exchange Server Angle

While preparing your design, don't neglect the server and client applications, because they may pose the harshest design challenges of all. For example, you must consider the following:

♦ Whether legacy client applications will be incompatible with Windows 2000 Professional.

♦ Whether newer Windows client applications will be incompatible with Windows 2000 Server user roaming, the improved security features, and the more rigid DLL handling.

♦ Whether you need to develop new custom scripting files for application assignment and publishing via Group Policies (if the applications are not Windows Installer-compliant).

Additionally, in a worst-case scenario, you could have server applications that include some level of looming incompatibility with Windows 2000 Server. Also, try to find out how each server application's vendor foresees integrating to Active Directory, because you may be able to avoid some harsh migration hazards by massaging the application setup before you implement it on Windows NT Server 4.

This section presents a less theoretical example, using Exchange Server 5.5, of some of the perils of server application integration with Active Directory. It also provides some words of advice on how to handle that integration. Exchange Server 5.5 is used as the example because many organizations adopt it to handle their messaging needs when they implement Windows NT Server 4. This example sets forth the reasoning that should be used for an Exchange Server 5.5 installation (you can't make use of the newer Exchange

2000 Server version because it relies on Active Directory) that will be migrated to Windows 2000 Server at a later time.

Thus, your likely migration scenario for Exchange Server is the following:

1. Implement Windows 2000 Server.

2. Set up integration between Active Directory and the Exchange directory via the Active Directory Connector (ADC), which is delivered in the Windows 2000 Server package and in an improved version in the Exchange 2000 Server package. ADC implements a bi-directional LDAP-based replication between Active Directory and Exchange Server 5.5 Service Pack 3 (it must be version 5.5, because that is the only version of Exchange that supports writes and paged results).

3. Migrate from the current Exchange Server environment to Exchange 2000 Server.

Your first goal is to try to implement as few Exchange sites as possible, because of the challenges of implementing ADC. Each Exchange site must be mapped to Active Directory by defining an ADC connection. Thus, if you implement a relatively low number of sites, your administrative work spent setting up and maintaining the ADC connection will be reduced, and the load on the servers will be minimized (each ADC connection adds some load).

The second piece of advice is that you should try to limit the number of containers created—and, at best, use only the predefined containers in Exchange—because you might need to create one ADC connection for each container that is to be replicated depending upon your precise replication needs. Additionally, you will face trouble if you try to replicate two containers to the same Active Directory OU and need to replicate any changes made in Active Directory to the applicable Exchange container; this quite simply is impossible, because Active Directory doesn't have any way to determine whether a newly created object should be placed in one or the other Exchange container. Further, strive to implement only Exchange Server 5.5 with Service Pack 3, because Windows 2000 Server's ADC demands that.

If you do, for some reason, have difficulty implementing a "pure" Exchange Server 5.5 installation, try to make sure that you have at least one Exchange 5.5 Server in each site, to be able to implement ADC and ease the migration to Exchange 2000 Server.

Note

Don't worry if you can't implement an Exchange Server 5.5 in each site. You are allowed to have the ADC replicate between Active Directory and Exchange Server 5.5 from another site. However, please keep in mind that not having an Exchange Server 5.5 in each site will work to limit your migration flexibility, and it should be avoided, whenever possible.

Finally, you may want to contemplate how to map the objects between Active Directory and the Exchange directory, because you certainly want to make sure that objects with similar semantics are merged. However, this merger is possible only if you have some unique identifier shared by the objects in each directory. Usually, this unique identifier is the SID (Windows 2000 Server contains user accounts with SIDs, and Exchange mailboxes usually are associated with user accounts). But, if you choose to move some of the user accounts to new domains or create new user accounts for every user, you could find it difficult to provide the correct mappings.

Best Practices

One more word of advice—plan your Active Directory namespace as soon as possible. Remember this advice, because it may be the best advice of all! Designing your Windows NT Server 4 implementation with an Active Directory namespace in mind provides the best insurance possible that you won't implement something that you'll regret later, when you begin the actual Windows 2000 Server/Active Directory migration exercise.

At best, you will be able to gather and plan most of the items outlined in Chapters 6 through 12 when you design for Windows NT Server 4. Realistically, although you probably realize the obvious advantages of striving for that goal, you should be doing reasonably well, if you are able to address the topics listed in Table 21.2 as these things usually will turn out to be of the greatest consequence to the future Active Directory design. That is, these things usually will be among the most important influencers on the structures laid down for the Active Directory domain, site and OUs (which should be compared to the DNS domain structure and domain structure used in the Windows NT Server 4 design), and the groups.

A Last Word of Advice

Microsoft undoubtedly will support you in your migration from a Windows NT Server-based design to a Windows 2000 Server-based design, because this is in its own interest, and Microsoft recognizes that it is facing the legacy questions that have haunted almost all of its

Table 21.2   Essential issues in NT Server 4 design.

Tasks	Points to Consider
Do your TCP/IP housekeeping.	TCP/IP rules! But avoid the potential potholes by doing a "best practices" TCP/IP implementation.
Reduce the use of NetBIOS.	NetBIOS is a legacy protocol. Thus, you should always use DNS-compatible NetBIOS names and strive to minimize use of NetBIOS among applications and users.
Deploy DNS now.	In the best of worlds, you will be able to implement your DNS structure on the NT Server 4 platform, because this will ease the migration to Windows 2000 Server DDNS. And, for applications that need name resolution, always prefer DNS over NetBIOS.
Limit the number of NT Server 4 domains.	The fewer domains, the easier the migration.

(continued)

Table 21.2   Essential issues in NT Server 4 design *(continued)*.

Tasks	Points to Consider
Keep it simple in regard to groups.	Use groups for assignment of all security permissions, and avoid overloading the coverage of each group. Don't use the domain local groups, if you can help it.
Go with the newest OS versions and Service Packs.	Choose Windows NT Server 4 and Windows NT Workstation 4 over any alternatives. Patch the OSs to the highest possible level (currently, Service Pack 6a). Avoid non-U.S./English-language versions of Windows NT Workstation 4, if possible, because using other language versions limits your options when doing an in-place upgrade to Windows 2000 Professional.
Watch the dimensioning of the hardware.	Be aware that Windows 2000 includes support for a lot of new hardware and puts even higher demands on the hardware than the earlier Microsoft OS versions.
Watch the future prospects of your applications.	Always try to keep things as simple as possible, to ease the migration pains. Do a detailed analysis of the upgrade options possible for each application, to avoid dead ends (such as software that isn't compatible with Windows 2000 and that can't be upgraded when Windows 2000 is released). If you currently use Exchange Server 4 or 5, read the more detailed advice presented earlier in this chapter; also, you might want to go back to Chapter 15 for the full story on how to design for Exchange 2000 Server.
Start designing your future Windows 2000 Server infrastructure now.	It makes good sense to have a point of reference (that is, the base Windows 2000 Server/Active Directory design) at the time of doing the Windows NT Server 4 design.

competitors for years. But be careful not to direct all of your attention to the Microsoft products. As part of the Windows NT Server 4 planning process, your organization should identify applications that will need to be supported in the coming Windows 2000 Server environment. As soon as these applications are identified, the organization should begin to communicate with the application vendors, to understand the vendors' plans for Windows 2000/Active Directory development and to help your organization avoid any surprises. The same is true for any existing specialized hardware that you expect to keep in operations when Windows 2000 is deployed in your organization.

Finally, acknowledge that some designs migrate to Windows 2000 Server more easily and quickly than others. This chapter attempts to point out the important traits of a Windows NT Server 4 solution, which generally will prove fairly straightforward to migrate. Most of these recommendations are based on the experiences shared by Microsoft's Rapid Deployment Program (now re-christened the Joint Development Program) customers, and a few of the recommendations stem from my own experiences.

In the next chapter, you'll learn the most important lessons of handling the actual migration to Windows 2000 Server/Active Directory—whether or not you are coming from the ideal Windows NT Server 4 design.

Chapter 22

Migrating to Active Directory

If your organization is happily toiling away on a Windows NT Server-based infrastructure, you probably should start pondering how you are going to migrate that infrastructure to Windows 2000 Server. If you still aren't sure whether this migration will ultimately prove worthwhile (or even necessary), consider the history of the software industry: Being a successful software company requires being able to move existing customers to a new product periodically. And, undeniably, Microsoft has been the most successful at doing this. (Windows 95 may be Microsoft's greatest example of moving its customer base to a new product.) Based on its history, Microsoft very likely will be able to pull off the same trick with regard to moving its customer base to Windows 2000 Server and Windows 2000 Professional. This is reinforced by the early, heavy backing from independent software vendors (ISVs), as well as Windows 2000's very radical feature set, which will cater to virtually everyone's wishes.

Thus, the nearly unavoidable conclusion is that migrating to Windows 2000 Server not only will prove worthwhile, but also may ultimately prove a competitive necessity. So, you might as well begin looking at Windows 2000 Server now, because you most likely will have to do so soon anyway—and if you wait, you may face the worst-case scenario of having to learn all about Windows 2000 Server and Active Directory while a tough deadline dangles over your head. This chapter outlines some of the things that you should and should not do when migrating from Windows NT Server to Windows 2000 Server, as well as when consolidating or migrating from one Active Directory environment to another, which might prove necessary not that many years from now.

> **Note**
>
> *You should note that Chapter 15 includes a rather detailed discussion on some of the most vital points regarding Exchange Server migration. And you definitely should check that out before getting to work on the migration, because Exchange will need to be catered to, when migrating from Windows NT Server to Windows 2000 Server. In many cases, you should perform the migration from Exchange Server 4/5 to Exchange 2000 Server hand-in-hand with the Windows 2000 migration, because the Exchange 2000 Server product often will give you the first taste of the many possibilities and capabilities offered by Active Directory-integrated applications, as well as a couple of fairly serious challenges.*

If you currently have less than a complete Windows NT installation and still are rolling out NT Servers, take a look at Chapter 21, which discusses what you should and shouldn't do when designing NT projects with an eye toward migrating to Windows 2000 Server in the near future. You might learn something valuable in that chapter with regard to "tuning" the NT Server rollouts for a later Windows 2000 Server migration project.

The Broad View on Upgrading

Ultimately, when you upgrade from Windows NT Server, you have to choose from among the following three very different scenarios:

♦ Keep the existing domain structure as is.

♦ Collapse and rearrange the existing domain structure.

♦ Create a completely new Active Directory domain structure and move the existing Windows NT-based user credentials and resources to the new domain structure (or, in the best of worlds, reduce the migration coverage to only the existing data and possibly the applications currently implemented).

To migrate from a Windows NT Server environment to a Windows 2000 Server/Active Directory setting, you have to complete the following planning tasks:

♦ Examine the existing NT Server structures (domains, groups, users, and machines) and all applicable restraints (that are posed primarily by applications that utilize the current NT Server infrastructure).

♦ Determine a strategy for migrating the existing NT Server domains to your future Active Directory domain architecture (including the order of upgrade of domains).

♦ Determine a strategy for upgrading the PDC and BDCs in each domain to Windows 2000 DCs (if applicable).

♦ Develop a recovery plan.

♦ Determine when to move to native mode.

♦ Determine how to handle the application migration (for example, Exchange Server, as discussed in Chapter 15).

♦ Determine exactly how you restructure the domain (if you plan to restructure or consolidate the current domains) with respect to the domain objects (for example, servers, groups, users, machines, and permissions).

After you complete these planning tasks, you should be ready to execute the actual migration to Windows 2000 Server. The rest of the chapter addresses each of the planning tasks in detail.

Preplanning: Examining Current NT Server Structures

Before you begin your detailed plan of the NT Server-to-Windows 2000 Server migration, you need to understand thoroughly the current Windows NT Server environment, including the following:

♦ The type of domain model being used.

♦ Existing trust relationships and which domains you may not want to include in the coming Active Directory forest.

♦ Mapping of PDC/BDC servers, member servers, and standalone servers within each domain (as well as their placement on the network).

♦ OS versions and Service Pack levels.

♦ The current WINS, DHCP, and DNS architectures.

♦ The current setup of users, groups, and machines, as well as rights and permissions. This work will usually entail some rather heavy tasks, such as:

  ♦ Documenting registry, share, and NTFS file system permissions on source domain controllers.

  ♦ Documenting the membership of each source group to be migrated.

  ♦ Identifying Global Groups in source account domains that might be combined in the target domain.

  ♦ Identifying obsolete and disabled user accounts.

  ♦ Documenting special user rights assignments and Built-in Group membership.

  ♦ Identifying empty or obsolete groups.

♦ The various client OSs and configurations (including system policies) currently connecting to the NT environment.

You also should understand which (if any) restraints on the migration are posed by the applications that use the current Windows NT Server infrastructure.

Regarding the OS versions, remember that you can do an in-place upgrade only on Windows NT Server 3.51 and 4 machines. Thus, you must upgrade any NT Server 3.1 and 3.5 systems to NT Server 3.51 or 4 before you are able to subject them to an in-place upgrade to

Windows 2000 Server. So, if you still have any Windows NT Server 3.1 or 3.5 systems, the simplest approach usually consists of redoing the base OS configuration on new Windows 2000 Server machines, moving the data on the old servers to the new servers, and retiring the old servers.

Also, consider streamlining and updating the current NT Server infrastructure, to ease the transition to Windows 2000 Server. The following are some of the streamlining exercises that could prove highly advantageous:

♦ Clean up old directories, user accounts, and groups.

♦ Consolidate user accounts into one or more master account domains (try to establish the fewest possible master account domains needed).

♦ Establish TCP/IP as the primary (preferably the only) network protocol used.

Before updating from Windows NT to Windows 2000, consider implementing the latest Service Packs on the OSs and deploying key services, such as DNS, DHCP, and WINS.

But don't get carried away in updating your infrastructure. For example, the solution available on Windows NT for dynamically updating DNS tables—that is, integrating DNS and WINS—will prove a fairly short-lived solution with regard to upgrading to Windows 2000 Server. Windows 2000 Server is based on Dynamic DNS (DDNS), which eliminates the need for WINS altogether—with a few notable exceptions, which are discussed in Chapter 7—because it allows clients with dynamically assigned addresses to

---

Watch Out for SID Trouble

If you plan to do an in-place upgrade of Windows NT Servers or Windows NT Workstations, be keenly aware of a problem that is haunting many early NT deployers: SID duplication. The Security Identifier (SID) is the component that is supposed to provide a unique ID for every Windows NT Workstation and Server inside each domain. The domain-unique SID is created when the machine joins the domain.

If you manually installed all of your machines either by using the Windows NT installation CDs or via an **UNATTEND.TXT** script, you will be in the clear regarding the SIDs. However, if you employed some sort of cloning (streaming a reference machine's copy of the setup to many other similar machines) without using a tool to generate a unique SID, you are headed for trouble, because all the cloned machines will in fact have the same SID. You should remedy this problem before you continue the in-place upgrade—for example, by using the NewSID tools available for free download at **www.sysinternals.com**, or by simply opting to do a fresh installation of Windows 2000 on all machines involved. Please be aware that you are on soft ground when doing that kind of SID regeneration—doing anything like this isn't supported by Microsoft and might leave some problems in regard to pre-existing rights and permissions—and so you have to be very careful in executing this process.

If you choose to change the SID before you upgrade to Windows 2000 using some sort of SID regeneration tool, check to make sure this change won't have any impact on the functionality and security settings in the domain—to avoid having this cause a problem with the Windows 2000 upgrade later.

---

register directly with the DNS server and update the DNS table on-the-fly. So, although implementing DNS with WINS integration is a fine solution for the challenges faced in a Windows NT setting, it won't do much if you intend to fully migrate your environment to Windows 2000 Server very soon. In other words, the time spent at the pre-planning stage for making absolutely sure that you've chosen your pre-migration tasks wisely will prove a boon later on, because it will work to avoid your doing anything that might prove superfluous later on.

Deciding How to Migrate Your NT Domains

As mentioned a bit earlier in this chapter, you have two very different choices when it comes to migrating your existing Windows NT domains:

♦ *The clean-sheet approach*—Here, you are building a new Active Directory forest in parallel with the existing Windows NT environment, after which you start migrating. When you are through migrating all users and resources to your new Windows 2000 infrastructure, all the existing Windows NT servers are shut down forever.

♦ *The in-place approach*—Here, you will be upgrading your existing Windows NT domains to Active Directory by way of in-place upgrading of each PDC and BDC to Windows 2000 Server until all servers have been upgraded.

Microsoft was preoccupied with the in-place approach all the way during the beta testing of Windows 2000 Server and after the release of the product. Thus, the world was left with no other option but to endorse the in-place migration approach (which was reflected in the first edition of this book).

And that's really a pity, because the in-place migration approach also proves to be the hardest of the two to perform; you will have to perform a "live" upgrade on top of a more or less well-designed (and stable) OS configuration that might include one or multiple third-party applications, as well as small bits and pieces of applications that have been installed earlier on. And you might even need to upgrade the hardware at the same time, adding further to the complexity.

Additionally, you will often be limited in your migration choices (especially in regard to the structure of the resulting Active Directory forest), as well as being faced with the less gratifying task of having to upgrade on top of the current operations environment. This works to add a fair number of new risks for downtime (as well as work to limit the options for backtracking) in conjunction with the upgrade.

The in-place upgrade will surely be preferred in some scenarios. However, this typically will only be the case in small companies and in companies that operate some very well-defined server configurations (in terms of software and hardware, as well as the usage of the domain) and have the resources for testing the upgrade thoroughly before deployment. And, although you will be able to find a lot of small businesses running off a couple of NT Servers, you really won't be able to find many companies that meet the very rigid demands put up for the in-place approach.

Needless to say, Microsoft got a lot of heat as still more companies were inching closer to the actual deployment. And Microsoft did the only sensible thing: They acknowledged that in-place upgrades didn't meet the needs faced by most companies and subsequently went out and purchased one of the best third-party tools available. This tool was eventually re-packaged as Active Directory Migration Tool (ADMT) and released to the public as a free supplement to Windows 2000 Server in March 2000. And based on my experiences with the real world and the application of Active Directory Migration Tool to it, I strongly suggest that you choose the clean-sheet approach for your migration unless there's a strong reason not to do so.

Tip

Active Directory Migration Tool not only proves a great solution for making the clean-sheet approach come through, when faced with migrating from Windows NT Server to Active Directory. It will also prove highly useful for the Active Directory-to-Active Directory consolidations and migrations that no doubt will become an inevitable ingredient of the not-so-distant future.

Understanding the Clean-Sheet Approach

The base premise of the clean-sheet approach is quite simple: You are allowed to start from a clean sheet in building your new Active Directory environment, rather than being stuck with the current more or less well-designed and well-managed Windows NT infrastructure.

When you use the clean-sheet approach, all decisions are left to you on what you migrate over to the Active Directory environment from the current Windows NT-based environment and when you migrate the various parts of the current infrastructure. And you're able to build a brand new domain structure that is better in sync with the features and capabilities put forward by Active Directory, rather than having to migrate the current domain model to Active Directory and then going on to change it, which usually will prove a fairly tough task, as you will see from the discussions later in this chapter. In other words, the clean-sheet approach allow you the optimum level of flexibility without any major limitations with regard to interim interoperability between the old and the new environment.

Note

You should note the fact that most of the tools used for the clean-sheet approach also are applicable to consolidating new NT or Active Directory domains (which, for example, might arise out of a merger of new companies) into the new environment at a later time.

And what will maybe prove even more important in many situations: You are allowed to migrate to Active Directory without messing with the production environment. And if you get in trouble on the new Active Directory environment, you will be able to perform an immediate fallback to the existing Windows NT Server-based production environment, so long as you haven't started moving your clients and servers into Active Directory.

There's only one real disadvantage to the clean-sheet approach: It demands a fair number of additional servers in the interim, because you need to build your new Active Directory environment in parallel with the existing environment. It's only when you're coming to an end with the migration (that is, when you're able to close down some NT domains) that you will be able to cut down on the number of servers again.

At first, you might also suspect that the clean-sheet approach demands more planning than is the case for in-place migrations. However, that usually isn't the case (that is, unless you've assigned permissions using the Local Domain Groups rather than your own groups or the Global Groups, as is called for by best practices), because in-place migrations are complicated by the fact that you need to plan more in order to avoid the inherent limitations of the migration method and to make sure that you're able to backtrack, if the upgrade should go wrong for some reason.

Apart from this, the clean-sheet approach might prove to be a bit more bandwidth-hungry, depending upon your current LAN/WAN setup. But the bottom line is the same almost regardless of the scenario faced: Not only is the clean-sheet approach less taxing from an administrator's perspective, it is also ripe with possibilities of doing the right thing from the outset.

Understanding the in-Place Approach

Although the in-place approach usually won't provide the same level of migration flexibility, as is the case with the clean-sheet approach, you might be in a situation where it proves the best—or maybe just the safest—choice. You should note that the in-place approach does allow you to perform an incremental upgrade, enabling you to migrate at your own pace, based on your business needs. This option is available because Windows 2000 Server supports a mixed environment (a mix of Active Directory DCs and Windows NT BDCs inside the same domain). The mixed environment tricks down-level clients into believing they are accessing NT 4 DCs regardless of whether that is actually the case.

Choosing an incremental, in-place upgrade means that you don't have to upgrade all systems in your network simultaneously—if at all—and means that you can start either with PDCs/BDCs or with clients, or use a mixed form.

Tip

Even though Active Directory allows you to proceed at your own pace with regard to the upgrade to Windows 2000 Server, you should understand the drawbacks of retaining some of the existing Windows NT Server BDCs. Most important of all, if a Windows 2000 client can't find an Active Directory DC (this is done via DNS lookups), it will use the old NTLM protocol to log on to an NT Server BDC. But when logging on to the BDC, the Windows 2000-based Group Policies—that is, software, policies, logon scripts, and so forth—aren't available, and thus won't be processed at the client.

Avoid Using Windows NT 3.51 Server (and Earlier Versions) in Active Directory Domains

No matter whether you're using the in-place or clean-sheet approach for migrating to Active Directory, you should stay clear of servers running Windows NT 3.51 Server (and earlier versions) being members of Windows 2000 Server domains. Two serious deficiencies exist in NT Server 3.51 regarding authentication that involves groups and users in domains other than the logon domain, when used in a Windows 2000 Server environment.

The first problem involves having Windows NT Server 3.51 in a resource domain. If a user from an account domain logs on to the server, only the groups from the account domain of that user are used to construct the token. With Windows NT Server 4 and Windows 2000 Server, the access token can contain groups from the account domain, any resource Domain Local Groups, and Global/Universal Groups. This in turn means that, with NT Server 3.51, ACLs and Local Groups containing groups from domains other than the account domain of the user logging on are ignored when evaluated for access control.

The second problem involves the user identities of moved users. When a user account is moved to another domain, it is given a new SID and the SID that it had from the previous domain should be added to the **sIDhistory** attribute (see the sidebar "Understanding sIDhistory" later in this chapter). Placing the Windows NT Server account SID in the Windows 2000 account's **sIDhistory** preserves access to network resources for the user logging on to his new Windows 2000 account. And so, the **sIDhistory** attribute is a great facilitator for many Windows 2000 deployment scenarios. In particular, it supports scenarios in which accounts in a new Windows 2000 forest are created for users and groups that already exist in a Windows NT Server production environment.

However, when a Windows NT Server 3.51 system performs a logon for a user, it can use only SIDs relative to the domain in which the logon is being performed. Because the sIDhistory SIDs aren't from the domain in which the account currently resides, those SIDs are not added to the user's access token. Note that the **sIDhistory** deficiency also applies to Windows NT Server 3.1x and 3.5, whereas it's handled in the proper way by Windows 95 and Windows 98.

*Additionally, the well-known LAN Manager Replication (**LMRepl**) service, which is used to replicate policy and logon script files among the Windows NT Server DCs, isn't applicable to Windows 2000 Server. In Windows 2000, **LMRepl** has been replaced with the File Replication Service (FRS), and FRS doesn't include any support for **LMRepl**. So you must find a suitable way of handling the two different file replication architectures in a mixed domain.*

Currently, the only viable (but lousy) solution is to create a batch script that copies the script directory from Windows NT Server to Windows 2000 Server and schedules it to run at intervals to keep the scripts and policies up-to-date.

*The Resource Kit includes a utility (**Lbridge.cmd**) that does just that. **Lbridge.cmd** is a script that pushes files from the system volume (Sysvol) on a Windows 2000-based server to the Export folder on a Windows NT server. By default, this script uses **Xcopy** to copy the files, or you can configure it to use **Robocopy**. Microsoft recommends that you schedule the script to run every two hours at the Windows 2000-based DC.*

An incremental, in-place upgrade does the following:

♦ Maintains access to Windows NT Server 4 domains through existing NT-style trust relationships (that is, one-way non-transitive trusts).

♦ Maintains transparent access to Windows NT 4 Servers from the user's point of view.

In-place migration enables you to keep the existing Windows NT Server domain relationships within the Windows 2000 Server domain structure. In fact, you will keep the existing domain structure in place when migrating to Active Directory. You can then choose to restructure the Windows 2000 Server domains at a later time (see the section "Domain Restructuring and Consolidation," later in this chapter).

What is important in this design is that you never have to experience a state in the migration process where a special OS version on a server or client is required. Furthermore, you will never face the need to take a complete domain offline to migrate PDCs/BDCs or clients. The individual PDC/BDC is unavailable only during the OS update, which guarantees that companies can migrate to Active Directory without imposing big interruptions in business.

In a typical incremental-upgrade scenario, you map the existing Windows NT Server domain structure to the future Active Directory structure, domain by domain. As a result, you create an Active Directory domain tree or forest that incorporates the same domains that are present in the current NT domain structure—the only change being that you will need to impose some level of hierarchy in the domain structure (for example, the first domain that is migrated will become the root of the domain tree).

You can migrate any of the four Windows NT Server domain models (single domain, single-master domain, multiple-master domain, and complete trust) to an Active Directory tree or forest. The following sections include some migration suggestions pertaining to each of the four domain models. These suggestions may help you decide how to handle your domain structure during and after your upgrade to Windows 2000 Server/Active Directory. You should also study the section "Domain Restructuring and Consolidation," later in this chapter, for more information about how to achieve the domain restructuring goals outlined in the rest of this section.

Single Domain Model

When you upgrade from Windows NT Server to Windows 2000 Server, a single domain model usually ends up with a single domain in Active Directory (see Figure 22.1). You can add new twists to the Active Directory domain in the process, such as adding an OU hierarchy and delegation of administrative rights.

Single-Master Domain Model

The upgrade from a particular single-master domain model to Windows 2000 Server typically takes place from the top down: The master domain is the first domain to be migrated, followed by the resource domains.

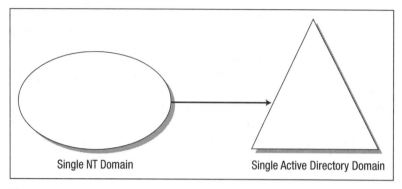

Figure 22.1
A single NT Server domain usually winds up being a single domain in an Active Directory setting.

If your company has centralized IT administration, you may want to consolidate the whole domain structure into a single Active Directory domain, to lessen the administrative work of maintaining multiple domains (see Figure 22.2). You should remember that Active Directory allows you to retain the organizational structure of multiple domains by way of OUs (again, remember that this domain consolidation can't be performed until the source and destination domains have been migrated to Windows 2000 Server).

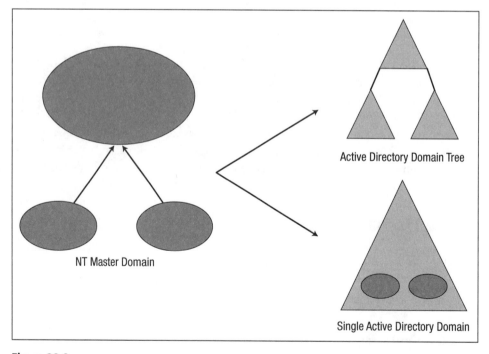

Figure 22.2
A single-master domain can be converted into a domain tree or consolidated to fewer domains in an Active Directory setting.

A very decentralized company (or a centralized company that wants to keep the highest possible leverage for buying and selling business units) usually opts to keep the current resource domains as Active Directory domains. At a later time, you might even choose to make them into full-fledged domains that contain users and resources, enabling you to move user accounts to the domains in which the people actually work, rather than storing the user accounts in the central master domain.

Multiple-Master Domain Model

If your company has a multiple-master domain model, it probably has chosen this model for one of the following reasons:

♦ Your network is so large that all users and groups don't fit into one domain database.

♦ Your network has several main geographical sites, each with its own sets of users and resources. The sites are linked by slow links, so you want to minimize replication traffic traveling across the links.

♦ The domain model mimics your business structure, in which different business units must have complete control over their own users and resources.

Active Directory addresses the first two points directly. So, if your company chose a multiple-master domain model for the first reason listed, you should consider doing some sort of radical domain consolidation (see Figure 22.3). This also is the probable outcome if your company chose the multiple-master domain model for the second reason (however, you may need to retain separate domains in the different sites in case your business structure mirrors your geographical boundaries).

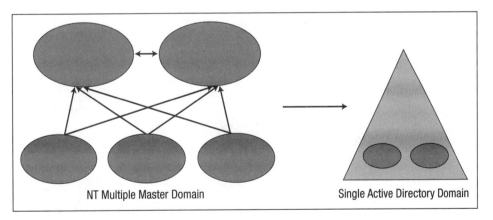

Figure 22.3
Your multiple-master domain may or may not be a candidate for a radical consolidation to a single Active Directory domain. It depends on the circumstances.

If your company chose the multiple-master domain model for the third reason listed, you will still be able to benefit from a consolidation of domains after migrating to Active Directory. In this scenario, you are left with two possible options (see Figure 22.4):

♦ Get rid of all the resource domains by merging the resource domains associated with each master domain into the master domains.

♦ Retain the domains that you have now, organize each current master domain as the root domain of a Windows 2000 Server domain tree, and make all the domain trees part of the same forest. This especially makes sense either if your company's DNS namespace is split along the same lines as your current master domain structure or if your company often buys and sells individual business units.

Complete Trust Model

If your company makes use of the complete trust model, it probably does so for one of two reasons:

♦ The current Windows NT Server structure is the result of a "grass roots" implementation throughout the organization. In other words, your network wasn't planned and established in an organized fashion, but rather it's the result of various islands that started deploying Windows NT Server and grew together as the company moved completely to NT.

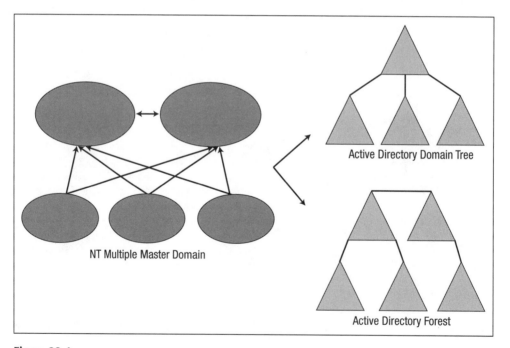

Figure 22.4
A multiple-master domain may turn out in one of quite a few different ways, depending on your organizational needs. The most probable scenario is turning it into a single domain tree or a forest.

♦ You are part of a very decentralized company that doesn't have a common IT department to manage common resources or to establish a set of common "rules" for the sake of securing interoperability.

If the complete trust model was implemented for the first reason cited, you will be happy to know that Active Directory provides a suitable base for executing the needed consolidation of your network (again, you need to migrate the domains in question to Windows 2000 Server before you can start consolidating).

If the complete trust model was chosen for the second reason, you can retain most of this independence (you still will have to learn to cope with the Enterprise Admins and Schema Admins Groups, and their vast power over the whole enterprise, so you might want to implement a placeholder domain as discussed in Chapter 11) within the Active Directory structure by setting up each of the current domains inside a single domain tree or multiple domain tree. If you choose this method (see Figure 22.5), the administrative burden of trust relationships is reduced dramatically, because each domain needs only one transitive trust relationship, which provides access to all other domains that are connected in the forest—and this trust relationship is defined automatically by Active Directory.

Be aware, however, that you may need to establish separate forests (see Figure 22.6), if some parts of the enterprise can't accept being part of the same forest. Although there might be some very profound reasons for this choice, it can't be recommended unless

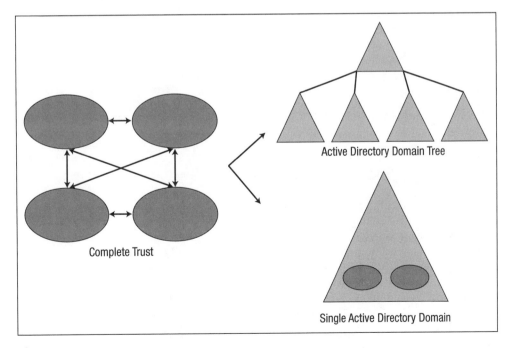

Figure 22.5
How the complete trust model ought to look in an Active Directory setting: as a single domain or a domain tree.

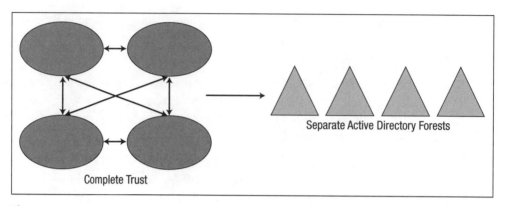

Figure 22.6
How a complete trust model shouldn't turn out in an Active Directory setting (separate forests), if any trusts between domains are needed. Try to reserve one-way trust relationships for business partners.

absolutely necessary, because you are faced with defining one-way trust relationships—similar to those known from Windows NT Server—between the domains that need to allow users from other domains some sort of access.

Know Your Tools

As you might already have guessed, Microsoft offers several different tools for the two kinds of migration. And there's a fair number of very powerful tools available from various third parties (including Aelita Software Corporations, FastLane Technologies, and Mission Critical Software) for easing your migrations.

Although Microsoft's tools usually won't prove to be the best tools available, they have two things going for them:

♦ They're free of charge (or, to be correct, they're included with the Windows 2000 Server license).

♦ They're usually well known in the community, so chances are that any quirks are already well documented in the Knowledgebase (or ironed out in more recent releases).

But you might note that it's fairly easy to find people acquainted with the Microsoft tool set, and you also might want to note that the tools are in fact not officially supported by Microsoft, because they're part of the Support Tools or Resource Kit tools. But you will most probably find that the "unofficial" support is very close to what you are used to from the official channels.

Personally, I've only found the third-party tools to apply to migrating very large or compli-cated Windows NT environments to Active Directory as well as improving on the interoperability between those two environment during the migration period. But before you venture further into any of those tools, you should be aware that these tools do cost a fair amount of money (they're usually built upon a per-user licensing scheme). So, unless these tools also fill some other needs, you will probably find them too costly, indeed.

For these reasons, I won't be covering the third-party tools here. Instead, I'll keep focusing on the following tools supplied by Microsoft:

♦ Active Directory Migration Tool

♦ **ClonePrincipal**

♦ **MoveTree**

♦ **NetDom**

♦ **SIDWalker**

Understanding sIDhistory

It's imperative that you understand that it's really not possible to move security principals between domains, because the Security Identifier (SID) used for ensuring uniqueness in all security principals is domain-relative (as opposed to the globally unique GUIDs that are also assigned to all Active Directory objects, but can't be used for assigning permissions and rights). Thus, although you can move nonsecurity principals inside as well as outside of the Active Directory forest without much ado, you've got some work on your hands with regard to moving security principals across domain boundaries.

Luckily, Microsoft did recognize this issue when designing Windows 2000 Server. Although Microsoft might have avoided these problems altogether by allowing GUIDs to be used instead of SIDs when assigning permissions and rights, they did at least do something to relieve the headache. This "something" is called *sIDhistory*.

sIDhistory is an optional attribute available for all security principals that allows you to store more than one SID for every security principal. And so, you are able to move a security principal across the domain boundary (that is, creating a new SID) without losing track of the permissions and rights assigned to the security principals in the source domain (by adding the object's source domain SID to the **sIDhistory** before writing the new SID to the object). The **sIDhistory** attribute can actually hold multiple values. And so, you are allowed to move security principals more than once without losing the old SID—and the permissions and rights assigned to that SID.

The reason for maintaining a SIDhistory is obvious: Even though you might want to move a security principal—for example, a user—it doesn't necessarily mean that you want the user's rights and permissions to change. For example, this will usually prove to be the case in a migration scenario.

By using the **sIDhistory** attribute, you can avoid having to change the ACLs on any resource because of moving the security. The reason for this is that the ACL still has the user's old SID (not the new one) and the old SID still is found in the user's access token (thanks to **sIDhistory**), which means that the user will be granted or denied access based on the old SID.

To be precise, when a user logs on and is successfully authenticated, the domain authentication service will query Active Directory for all of the SIDs associated with the user—the user's current SID, the user's old SIDs stored in **sIDhistory**, and the SIDs for the user's groups. All of these SIDs are returned to the authentication client and are included in the user's access token. When the user tries to gain access to a resource, any one of the SIDs in the access token, including one of the SIDs in **sIDhistory**, could allow or deny the user access.

Develop a Recovery Plan

When you do the actual upgrade from a Windows NT Server infrastructure to a Windows 2000 Server infrastructure, you should be very concerned about the following:

♦ Maintaining uninterrupted service to clients

♦ Preventing data loss

♦ Being able to recover from any problems encountered because of the upgrade

To ensure against loss of data or prolonged downtime during the upgrade process, you must develop a recovery plan that provides answers to the following questions for each step involved in performing the migration:

♦ How do you roll back the system to the previous state?

♦ What administrative tools do you need to recover to the previous state?

♦ How long will recovery to the previous state take?

And before you execute the upgrade on each domain, you are recommended to do the following:

♦ Add a BDC, if the domain contains no BDCs. This ensures that the domain doesn't become orphaned in case an upgrade to the PDC fails miserably (applicable only to in-place migrations).

♦ Determine whether any services are running on the PDC and BDCs in the domain in question. Back up the data needed for those services to tape, and test the backup tapes.

♦ Fully synchronize all BDCs with the PDC.

♦ Take one BDC from each domain offline before doing anything to the domain. Before beginning the migration, subject the offline BDC to the following tests:

   1. Promote the offline BDC to a PDC in an isolated network environment.

   2. Check the integrity of the SAM data and try to log on with a client from the domain. Do a backup of the BDC.

   3. Demote the PDC to a BDC and verify that the SAM data didn't become lost or corrupted in the process.

Native Mode Doesn't Change Relationship to Down-Level Machines

A lot of confusion exists about what native mode is—and especially about what it isn't. Basically, the issue of native mode versus mixed mode is related only to which DCs are used within the domain. In short, even though the domain is running in native mode, down-level client systems, member servers, and standalone servers continue to see and interoperate with the domain within the limits imposed by NT Server 4 domain functionality. So, as far as down-level member servers and clients are concerned, whether they are part of a mixed mode domain or a native mode domain doesn't really matter.

---

4. Shut down the server and leave the BDC offline and untouched for at least a week after the migration so that you can do a disaster recovery via this BDC.

If you run into heavy problems during the migration process, you can remedy the situation by following these three simple steps:

1. Remove the Windows 2000 machines from the production environment.

2. Reinstate the offline BDC(s) in the production environment.

3. Promote the offline BDC(s) to PDC(s). Each new PDC then replicates its data to all applicable BDCs, and the domain is returned to its previous state.

Tip

When using the clean-sheet approach, you often won't need to adhere to the fallback method discussed above. Fallback will usually prove as simple as removing the trusts between the new and the old domains and making sure that all clients and servers are still logging on to the old domain. On the other hand, things will prove more complicated if you've gone on to move the machine accounts to the new domain.

However, remember to track all changes to the domain(s), while the spare BDC is kept offline. If you don't track all domain changes made while the BDC is offline, the changes are lost forever if you later need to turn the BDC back into production as a PDC. If you are daring, you can minimize this loss of SAM changes by periodically turning on the offline BDC (and turning it off again) during the migration process when the domain is in a stable state, to update its copy of the SAM database.

Actually, you have another (less practical) alternative to "saving" a BDC before executing the domain upgrade: Remove the PDC from the network (you must have at least one BDC installed to provide authentication in the interim) and do the migration on that PDC in an isolated lab setting. After you've successfully migrated one or more PDCs in isolation, you can gradually start adding clients and additional DCs to the domain. If everything goes smoothly, you can return the upgraded PDC(s) to the network and turn them on.

The advantages of using this quite offbeat upgrade method are that the network environment remains untouched until the migrated environment has proven stable, and you're allowed to do a complete Active Directory migration without affecting production. A disadvantage is that you can't make changes to your network until the PDC(s) are put online. Thus, considering the number of password changes and the amount of administrative work occurring each day in most Windows NT Server environments, this option should prove very theoretical.

If you adhere to the basic rules outlined in this section when you perform the migration, you should be able to recover from almost any kind of disaster possible—at least any disaster that can be linked to the migration. (Microsoft is quite influential, but you can hardly attribute to it such calamities as flooding, lightning, and hurricanes that could occur during your upgrade of Windows NT Server to Windows 2000 Server.)

Decide When to Move to Native Mode

When a new Active Directory domain is created or when an existing Windows NT Server domain is being upgraded, the domain is in the intermediate operational state known as mixed mode. You can leave the domain operating in mixed mode indefinitely, or you can move it to the final operational state, known as native mode, after you get rid of all Windows NT Server-based PDC and BDCs in that particular domain.

Native mode means that the domain is considered an Active Directory-only domain, and thus can take advantage of the full range of Active Directory features. The switch from mixed mode to native mode isn't performed automatically by Active Directory. Instead, it must be initiated by the administrator, because of the effects imposed on the Active Directory DCs. Make this switch only after you are fully committed to an Active Directory infrastructure, meaning that you'll never want to add another Windows NT Server BDC to the domain in question.

After you switch to native mode, seven major things happen:

♦ The domain uses only the new Active Directory replication protocol, even for security principals.

♦ The FSMO PDC ends the support of NTLM replication.

♦ Windows NT-based BDCs can't join the domain; only Active Directory DCs are allowed.

♦ The domain is still capable of hosting various down-level client computers, member servers, and standalone servers that are running Windows NT.

♦ The server that served as FSMO PDC when the domain was running in mixed mode no longer acts as the master of the domain. All DCs now perform as peers.

♦ Down-level clients will begin to benefit from Active Directory's transitive trusts and can access resources anywhere in the domain tree(s). Although down-level clients aren't Kerberos-enabled, the pass-through authentication provided by the DCs allows the clients to be authenticated in any domain in the forest, which enables the user to access resources from all over the forest. Other than enhanced domain tree access, down-level clients won't be aware that any changes have occurred to the domain.

♦ You have access to the Universal Group functionality, group nesting, and several other minor functionality enhancements.

You should switch to native mode at the earliest possible time, because doing so removes the most dominant single-point-of-failure risk of a Windows NT Server domain—the PDC functionality. The side effects of going to native mode really aren't scary, because legacy clients, member servers, and standalone member servers still regard the Active Directory domain as a Windows NT Server domain. Actually, going to native mode will seem like an improvement, because legacy clients and servers will be able to take advantage of the transitive trust relationships—and thus be able to access resources from all over the forest.

Additionally, you might want to move to native mode in the destination domain(s) for reasons of migration ease. That is, the sIDhistory attribute and the Universal Groups (which are great for migrating Global Groups between domains that are part of the same forest, because the Universal Groups can contain members from the source domain that haven't been migrated yet, whereas Global Groups can only contain members from their own domains) are only applicable to domains running in native mode.

Tip

If a domain is operating in mixed mode, the old domain restrictions still apply, according to Microsoft: The number of objects (including users, groups, and computers) in that domain shouldn't total more than 40,000.

However, as far as I've understood, this isn't because of a restriction in Windows 2000 Server. The limitation is imposed by the NT BDCs. And so if you're certain that no NT-based BDCs are present (nor will be added in the future), you should in fact be able to move beyond the 40,000-object limit with less fear than before. But, well, if you're absolutely certain of that, you might as well switch to native mode anyway!

Migration and Domain Consolidation Fundamentals

As mentioned earlier, the tools and processes vary quite a lot, depending upon what you want to achieve. And you will find that things are working markedly different (see Figure 22.7) when performing:

♦ *Inter-forest migration*—If your source and destination domains cross forest boundaries (which will usually be the case for clean-sheet migrations from NT to Windows 2000). Active Directory Migration Tool and **ClonePrincipal** are used for performing clean-sheet and in-place upgrades, respectively.

♦ *Intra-forest migration (and domain consolidation)*—If your source and destination domains are located in the same forest (which will usually be the case for in-place upgrades from NT to Windows 2000). Active Directory Migration Tool and **MoveTree** apply to clean-sheet and in-place upgrades, respectively.

Tip

Windows NT Server domains are by definition not in a forest; thus, you will always be facing the inter-forest migration scenario if you are migrating from Windows NT to Active Directory.

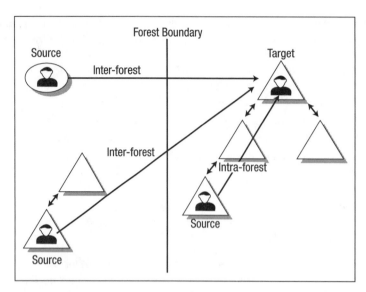

Figure 22.7
It will make a world of difference, between using inter-forest or intra-forest migrations.

As mentioned earlier, you should always preserve the SID of the source object(s) by using a tool that supports the **sIDhistory** attribute—which is the case for all the Microsoft tools mentioned here. However, you might want to be aware of the fact that you need the following to be true in order to make use of the **sIDhistory**:

◆ *The SID(s) in question should be unique*—This will always prove to be the case with objects defined manually using Windows NT Server's own tools, but you should note that it might not be the case for SIDs that have been generated by various early cloning and copying tools. And the Built-in Groups (which include the Account operators, Administrators, Backup operators, Guests, Print operators, Replicator, Server operators, and Users Local Groups; despite much information saying otherwise, the user accounts Administrator and Guest are in fact not built-in accounts) are identical in every domain—therefore, you would be violating the SID uniqueness requirement by adding them to the **sIDhistory**. Also, the Domain Local Groups are shared among the PDC and all the BDCs of each domain, which might give you trouble with regard to duplicating the same groups several times.

◆ *Administrator privileges in both domains*—You simply won't be able to perform all the needed operations unless you have Administrator privileges in the source and destination domains.

◆ *Auditing is enabled in both domains*—Because of the risks inherent in copying and moving directory objects, Microsoft demands that you have auditing enabled in both the source and destination domains. And you really shouldn't be too unhappy about this, because it will allow you to be able to see what has happened later on in case any issues should surface with regard to security or consistency.

> ### Note
>
> *You should also note that any domain includes a number of so-called "well-known accounts." A well-known account is an account that has a well-known relative identifier (RID) and a domain-specific prefix. The well-known accounts include Administrator, Guest, Domain admins, Domain guests, and Domain users.*

And you obviously also need to make sure that the source domain trusts the destination domain so that you can move or copy objects at all (Active Directory Migration Tool requires trusts in both directions).

On Inter-Forest Migrations

The three main reasons for doing inter-forest migrations are as follows:

♦ Migrating a Windows NT Server domain to Active Directory without impacting the current production environment.

♦ Incorporating a Windows 2000 Server/Active Directory "grassroots" domain into the forest.

♦ Consolidating two separate Windows 2000 Server/Active Directory forests into one (which, for example, might very well happen because of a merger).

In an inter-forest migration, you basically just need to clone the objects in question—you won't get in trouble over uniqueness, because the cloned objects exist in separate forests.

And There's More...

You should be keenly aware that you will most probably encounter a least a couple of issues that aren't touched upon here (because this book focuses on Active Directory) in your migration project. For example, it's quite common that you will be faced with some issues—it might be on DNS, DHCP, WINS/NetBIOS, RAS, migrating system policies to Group Policies, or other such things—depending upon the pre-existing and future environments.

And then, you also need to face the more mundane challenges, including settling a fairly high proportion of details that you will need to cater to in order to be able to initiate the migration or consolidation tasks. For example, you should decide in advance how to handle any naming clashes between pre-existing objects in the destination domain and the objects from the source domain, how to generate new passwords for the moved user accounts, and whether the objects should continue to be active in both domains or not.

And you will need to determine whether accounts should be disabled during the migration process, how to distribute passwords to users, when clients will be allowed to log on using target cloned accounts, whether service accounts should be handled differently, whether the services being serviced by the individual service accounts allow a migration of the particular service account, and so on.

As always, a couple of details need some attention, when cloning objects:

◆ Inter-forest migration of user objects:

  ◆ How do you want to handle the user's profile? That is, do you want to issue a new profile, copy the existing profile, or share the same profile between the source and the destination domain? Active Directory Migration Tool copies profiles, whereas **ClonePrincipal** doesn't maintain profiles.

  ◆ How do you want to handle Active Directory profiles (only applies if the source domain is an Active Directory domain)? Currently, Microsoft doesn't provide any support for migrating Group Policies and, thus, you'll have to untangle the policy side of things yourself.

  ◆ How do you want to handle any rights being assigned to the user? Active Directory Migration Tool allows you to update user rights in the destination domain, whereas you have to handle this manually with **ClonePrincipal**.

  ◆ You might encounter several other things that are bound to the user (and might be vitally important to the user), for which the tools don't include any support as of now. Such things include the Protected Storage (PStore), Encrypted File System (EFS), and Smart Cards.

◆ Inter-forest migration of group objects:

  ◆ *Moving Domain Local, Global, and Universal Groups*—You can move Domain Local, Global, and Universal Groups between two domains without any problems whatsoever. You might note that you're able to move native mode Active Directory Domain Local Groups more easily than their NT counterparts, because they have slightly different properties (the NT groups and mixed mode Active Directory Domain Local Groups only apply to DCs, whereas the native mode groups apply to everything inside the domain).

  ◆ *Moving Built-in Domain Local Groups*—It's simply not possible to move Built-in Domain Local Groups. Consequently, they have to be handled manually (and it goes with the territory that you're in serious trouble, if you've assigned permissions and rights using the Built-in Domain Local Groups). Usually, you should create some parallel groups in the destination domain.

◆ Inter-forest migration of resources:

  ◆ *Clients and member servers using Windows NT or Windows 2000*—Moving these types of computers should prove no big deal, because the member servers and clients take their local SAM database with them. In other words, users can access machine resources after the move as they did before. The move of machines can be accomplished using Active Directory Migration Tool or **NetDom**.

  ◆ *Domain Controllers using Windows NT or Windows 2000 (that is, PDC/BDCs as well as DCs)*—You will have to perform an in-place upgrade of the Windows NT servers to Windows 2000 Server, as discussed later on in this chapter. After that, it's a question of manually taking care of any rights and permissions assigned to the Domain Local Groups (including the built-in ones), demoting the server to a member server, and performing the move as discussed above.

On Intra-Forest Migrations and Domain Consolidation

Contrary to what one might think, intra-forest migration is a more complicated matter than the inter-forest case. You have to be very careful as to how you handle an intra-forest migration because of the potential for creating several instances of the same object (which obviously is a very bad thing, because several things need to stay unique inside a forest, including object naming and the handling of Global, as well as Universal Groups). For this reason, you will generally need to move objects rather than clone them.

Warning

*You must always avoid duplicate SIDs—whether appearing as primary SIDs or **sIDhistory** values—created inside the same forest.*

But that's really not sufficient. In order to be able to avoid any problems with regard to uniqueness, you also need to make sure that the objects you're moving constitute a closed set:

♦ *Intra-forest migration of users and/or groups*—A closed set is the set of users and groups for which no other users are members of the groups, and no users are members of other groups. You should note that this only applies to Global and Universal Groups. You will have to handle any issues with Built-in Domain Local Groups manually, exactly as in the inter-forest case.

♦ *Intra-forest migration of resources*—A closed set is the set of computers and Local Groups for which no other computers are members of the groups, and no computers are members of other groups.

Tip

*You have several alternatives to creating closed sets with regard to moving Global Groups. First of all, you can convert the Global Group to a Universal Group and move it to the destination domain. Although a Global Group can only include members from its own domain, the Universal Group is capable of having members from multiple domains inside the same forest (and, thus, include all the previous members in the source domain). Second, you can just create parallel groups; that is, you can copy the Global Group without **sIDhistory** (rather than moving it) to the destination domain, add it to the ACLs using the original group, and then restore the group memberships as the group's members are moved to the destination domain.*

Active Directory Migration Tool will help you to check whether you have a closed set or not. If that's the case, you are allowed to move objects with the old SID intact. If it isn't, you have no other option except to create new objects and set up the same permissions and rights for them, as is the case in the source domain.

MoveTree doesn't include any features that help you determine whether the set of objects constitutes a closed set or not. And so, you are faced with having to do a lot of manual pre-planning work or simply consolidating an entire domain.

If you are doing intra-forest migration, you should remember to check that all the accounts in the source domain have been disabled or—better yet—deleted, because this will ensure that you won't run into trouble later on. Also, if you have computers that are members of other groups than Domain Computers, you should always migrate those computers prior to migrating the groups they belong to; this is the only way to prevent these computers from losing their group membership.

Getting a Handle on the Tools

As mentioned earlier, Microsoft does put a fair number of different tools at your disposal:

- *Active Directory Migration Tool*—Applies to clean-sheet migrations, domain consolidation, and moving directory objects. Available as a free download at **www.microsoft.com/ windows2000/downloads/deployment/admt/default.asp**. As a nice departure from most other Microsoft tools, Active Directory Migration Tool is available in all the languages for which a localized version of Windows 2000 Server exists.

- *ClonePrincipal*—Used for cloning (copying) directory objects between domains in different forests. Applies to inter-forest migrations and other types of object copying tasks. Available in Windows 2000 Support Tools.

- *MoveTree*—Used for moving directory objects between domains that are part of the same forest. Applies to domain consolidation and other kinds of intra-forest moves. Available in Windows 2000 Support Tools.

- *NetDom*—Used for moving machine objects. Applies to inter-forest as well as intra-forest migrations. Available in Windows 2000 Support Tools.

- *SIDWalker*—Used for cleaning up and monitoring ACLs. Applies to domain consolidation and moving directory objects. Available in Windows 2000 Support Tools.

*Active Directory Migration Tool, **ClonePrincipal**, **MoveTree**, and **NetDom** all use the sIDhistory attribute. Therefore, the information on the limitations on the usage of sIDhistory provided in the sidebar "Avoid Using Windows NT 3.51 Server (and Earlier Versions) in Active Directory Domains" applies equally well to all these tools. Likewise, you should note the fact that sIDhistory is available only in Active Directory native mode domains—thus, you will need to switch your destination domain into native mode for gaining access to that prized functionality!*

The Active Directory Migration Tool

The Active Directory Migration Tool promises to be an easy, secure, and fast way to migrate from Windows NT Server to the Windows 2000 Server Active Directory service. And believe me, I've tried it and it works—most probably because this fine tool actually has been programmed outside of Microsoft (it's been licensed from Mission Critical Software).

Note
There are a few handfuls of quirks left in the tool at present time. However, the majority of them are thoroughly documented in the README file delivered with the application.

To be more precise, Active Directory Migration Tool provides you with a set of wizards that make it fairly easy to migrate users, computers, and groups:

♦ *From Windows NT Server domains to Windows 2000 domains*—That is, doing an inter-forest migration.

♦ *Between Windows 2000 domains in different forests*—That is, doing an inter-forest migration.

♦ *Between Windows 2000 domains in the same forest*—That is, doing an intra-forest migration or domain consolidation.

Note
*Active Directory Migration Tool can operate on source domains running Windows NT Server 4 (the PDC must be running Service Pack 4 or later), as well as Windows 2000 Server. The destination domain must be running in Active Directory native mode (because of the need for **sIDhistory**).*

Active Directory Migration Tool includes tools for getting an overview of the current state of the source and destination domains, setting correct file permissions, and migrating Microsoft Exchange Server mailboxes. Further, the reporting feature allows you to assess the impact of the migration, both before and after executing the operations, and includes limited support for rollback of the previous migration.

Maybe most important of all, the Active Directory Migration Tool is for doing clean-sheet migrations. And so, at most of the steps in the migration process, your users will still be allowed to access the services in the old domain as well as the new domain (and services in all domains that trust these two domains). Or to put it another way: You're allowed to migrate to Active Directory without messing with the production environment, and you have all the time that you need for cleaning up and moving services and permissions from the old domain (and any other domains that trust the old domain), because the permissions and rights assigned to the users, computers, and groups in the old domain will "survive" the move to the new domain. And if you get in trouble on the new Active Directory environment, you will be able to perform an immediate fallback to the existing Windows NT

Server-based production environment as long as you haven't started moving computers and servers into the new Active Directory.

Active Directory Migration Tool is a fairly nonintruding tool. That is, Active Directory Migration Tool installs services, called agents, on the source computers only when migrating computers or translating security on resources. The agents are dispatched automatically (that is, you don't have to perform any manual installations on the source computers) from the computer on which Active Directory Migration Tool is running and are installed on other computers using the security credentials of the user account used to run Active Directory Migration Tool (the agents run as a service using the local system security credentials). After the agent's task is completed, it uninstalls itself.

Active Directory Migration Tool is built around a set of wizards for performing the commonly occurring migration and domain consolidation chores:

♦ *User Migration Wizard*—For user accounts.

♦ *Group Migration Wizard*—For group accounts.

♦ *Computer Migration Wizard*—For computer accounts.

♦ *Security Translation Wizard*—For migrating local profiles and user rights and replacing the usage of a source account SID on resource ACLs with the new target account SID (this usually won't be needed unless you decommission a source account domain before its resource domains).

♦ *Reporting Wizard*—For creating reports that contain the status information you need in order to plan the migration of your Windows NT or Windows 2000 domains.

♦ *Service Account Migration Wizard*—For service accounts (that is, accounts used by services beside the local system authority).

♦ *Exchange Directory Migration Wizard*—For updating the SIDs used by Exchange Server mailboxes from the ones used in the source domain to the new ones used in the target domain.

♦ *Undo Wizard*—Allows you to undo the last user, group, or computer migration operation performed.

♦ *Retry Tasks Wizard*—For retrying an operation that is performed by agents on a local computer and that failed the first time around.

♦ *Trust Migration Wizard*—For maintaining resource access during migration—that is, to establish the same trust relationships in the target domain as exist in the source domain. The Trust Migration Wizard is fairly smart; it compares the needed trusts to the existing ones and thus often simplifies the old trust relationships defined in the Windows NT domains (remember that Active Directory uses a more powerful type of trust relationship that usually will allow you to cut down on the number of trusts).

♦ *Group Mapping and Merging Wizard*—For preparing groups for migration. That is, you are allowed to map the source group to a different target group (and, thus, move the membership of a group in the source domain into a new or different group in the target domain).

Tip

Active Directory Migration Tool includes an option to remigrate previously migrated users. This is a very neat feature, because a remigration will ensure that the group memberships of the destination user account are upgraded with the changes that have happened to the user account in the source domain since the previous migration. In case the remigration behavior isn't desired and you want to completely reset the destination account to only be a member of the source user's groups, you should just delete the target domain user and migrate the source user again.

All the wizards for migrating objects allow you to do a dry run (that is, running through the migration process without doing any actual changes to the domains in question) as well as a real migration. You should always perform a dry run before the actual migration, because it will allow you review the log files and reports to identify and troubleshoot any potential problems before performing the actual migration.

A lot more could be said on the many options—for example, you can choose to copy users rights assigned in the source domain to the target domain; you can copy groups along with their members to the target domain to ascertain a closed set; you can leave user accounts active in both the source and target domains; you can copy roaming profiles to the target domain for selected user accounts; and you can migrate to OUs—available in Active Directory Migration Tool and how they suit the many different possible migration and domain consolidation scenarios, but you will have to refer to Active Directory Migration Tool's built-in help files and other documentation for that.

A Few Important Notes from the Field

If you have more than 10,000 user accounts, groups, or computers, you need to increase the Maximum size of Active Directory Searches group policy in the target domain. By default, this value is set to 10,000.

If you want to translate Exchange security for Exchange mailboxes, distribution lists, custom recipients, organizations, sites, and containers, the account credential that you specify during the translation process must be a Permissions Admin in the Exchange site of the applicable Exchange server. And if you want to translate Exchange security, you must install Microsoft Exchange Administrator on the computer where you run the Active Directory Migration Tool.

Also, the computer running the Active Directory Migration Tool must be able to connect to all domains related to the information in the sIDhistory property of each migrated account. In addition, the user account that you log on with when you run the tool must have administrator rights in each domain from which SID information is used. For example, if you migrate accounts from Domain A to Domain B, then migrate accounts from Domain B to Domain C, your account must have administrator rights in Domain A to copy the sIDhistory information related to that domain. If Domain A is no longer available, the tool cannot copy the sIDhistory information related to Domain A.

ClonePrincipal

ClonePrincipal is a scriptable COM object (in the shape of a .DLL) for doing inter-forest clean-sheet migrations. That is, **ClonePrincipal** allows you to copy users and groups from Windows NT Server or Active Directory domains to an Active Directory native mode domain without impacting your existing production environment.

ClonePrincipal is delivered with a series of sample Visual Basic scripts designed to serve as building blocks for the supported migration scenarios. The scripts included are the following:

♦ *sidhist.vbs*—Updates the sIDhistory attribute. That is, it copies the SID of a source principal to the sIDhistory of an existing destination principal.

♦ *clonepr.vbs*—Copies a single user or group. That is, it copies the properties of a source principal and copies the source SID to the sIDhistory of the destination object. The destination principal need not exist, but if it does, both destination SAM name and distinguished name must refer to the same object.

♦ *clonegg.vbs*—Copies all Global Groups. That is, all Global Groups in a domain are cloned, including well-known accounts (such as Domain Guests), but excluding Built-in Domain Local accounts (such as Backup Operators).

♦ *cloneggu.vbs*—Copies all Global Groups and users. That is, all Global Groups and users in a domain are cloned, including well-known accounts, but excluding the Built-in Domain Local accounts.

♦ *clonelg.vbs*—Copies all Domain Local Groups. That is, all the Local Groups in a domain are cloned, including well-known accounts, but excluding Built-in Domain Local accounts.

> **Note**
> *It's fairly unlikely that the sample scripts will prove an exact match to the migration requirements of your enterprise, and so you should factor in some Visual Basic scripting for the migration work.*

MoveTree

MoveTree is able to move part of an OU tree from one domain to another inside a single forest. So **MoveTree** applies to intra-forest migration and domain consolidation, where you need to be able to move Active Directory objects, such as organizational units, users, or groups, between domains.

Just as **ClonePrincipal**, **MoveTree** makes use of the sIDhistory attribute to preserve access to resources after a group, user, or computer is moved from one Windows 2000 domain to another. **MoveTree** is a command-line tool, so it should prove easily scriptable. And it includes a switch for performing a "dry run" that tests whether or not the options specified are valid.

But you will most probably find **MoveTree** inadequate for all your intra-forest migration needs, because it's restricted to only moving Global Groups as a closed set of groups in the source domain. Also, **MoveTree** doesn't deal with the changes needed on associated data, such as policies, roaming profiles or logon scripts, and user's personal data.

NetDom

NetDom is a tool that has many purposes—including making queries for trust relationships; creating new trust relationships; adding, removing, and querying client computer accounts; joining a computer to a domain; verifying and resetting the computer's secure channel; and a few more things. But **NetDom** only has one purpose with regard to domain migration: Moving a computer account from one domain to another without losing the old SID. **Netdom** is a command-line utility, so it should prove easily scriptable.

SIDWalker

SIDWalker is designed for ACL management. **SIDWalker** allows you to monitor ACLs, to clean up ACLs for now-defunct ACLs, to delete and replace SIDs, and to convert the SIDs residing in the ACLs. As such, **SIDWalker** should prove highly beneficial, if you need to clean up the existing ACLs as well as for "tuning the ACLs" and the sIDhistory attribute after the migration and domain consolidation chores are completed. **SIDWalker** applies to all possible migration and consolidation scenarios, depending upon your needs for tidiness. **SIDWalker** is an MMC-based tool that is somewhat hard to understand at first. But relax, you'll get used to it after a couple of hours.

Clean-Sheet Migrations

Although it does take some effort with regard to pre-planning as well as fine-tuning the migration options, it's fairly straightforward to perform a clean-sheet migration—no matter whether we're talking intra-forest or inter-forest scenarios.

As a rule of thumb, you should follow this recipe for doing a full inter-forest migration of a single-master domain setup. In the account domain:

1. Create the destination Active Directory domain, if not already present.

2. Establish trusts between the source and target domain.

3. Migrate Global Groups.

4. Migrate user accounts.

In the resource domain(s):

1. Establish trusts between the source and target domains.

2. Migrate workstations and member servers.

3. Migrate local profiles.

4. Migrate Domain Local Groups.

5. Migrate the service accounts not running under the local system (if needed).

6. Update user rights.

7. Migrate a single DC from the resource domain.

Decommission account and resource domains.

Warning

How to perform each of these steps is left to you, because there are several different options for doing that. Which options you choose depend upon the tool set and the specialties of the task at hand.

The recipe for doing an intra-forest migration of a single-master domain setup is a bit more complicated, but it should still prove a manageable task. In the resource domain(s):

1. Migrate workstations and member servers.

2. Migrate the service accounts not running under local system (if needed).

3. Update user rights and group memberships.

4. Migrate Domain Local Groups.

5. Migrate member server or one DC from the resource domain.

Decommission the resource domain(s).

In the account domain:

1. Migrate Global Groups.

2. Migrate user accounts.

3. Migrate service accounts not running under local system authority.

4. Migrate roaming profiles.

5. Update user rights and group memberships on any applicable member servers.

6. Migrate local profiles on workstations.

7. Migrate one DC from the account domain.

Decommission the account domain.

The above-mentioned schemes for inter-forest and intra-forest migration and domain consolidation also apply to the three other domain models—you just need to take their peculiarities into account.

Also, please stay alert to the fact that you should defer migrating your clients and servers to the Active Directory target domain until the latest possible time. This is because, until you move the machine accounts, you are able to fall back to the old environment more or less immediately (although you might face some trouble over such mundane things as passwords and group changes that have only been implemented in Active Directory).

With regard to the actual migration, you should be in good shape if you remember to perform the migration and merging of security principals on the LAN—*never* across a WAN, if you can help it. Although it is possible to perform the migration over a WAN link, you should try to avoid it because of the inherent risks of losing the link during the migration (an error that doesn't sit very well with most migration and domain consolidation tools).

In-Place Upgrades

As mentioned earlier, in-place upgrading is a bit more complicated than clean-sheet migrations. However, as this section hopefully will prove to you, you're by no means faced with an impossible situation.

Decide How to Form the Active Directory Domain

After you examine the current Windows NT Server infrastructure thoroughly and consider the different upgrade scenarios for the domain model used, you should be ready to make the first major decision: how to form the Active Directory domain tree.

To form an Active Directory domain tree, you must perform the following:

♦ Choose the domain that will become the root of the domain tree. This domain has to be the first to be migrated.

♦ For each nonroot domain, decide which domain will be its parent. This determines the order in which the domains are migrated, because you have to have a parent domain in place before you add the child domains.

The first domain migrated to Active Directory becomes the root of the Active Directory domain tree (see Figure 22.8). In the current version of Windows 2000 Server, you aren't allowed to change the root of the domain tree (because it holds the configuration and

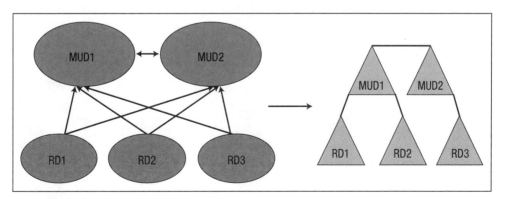

Figure 22.8
Example of an initial Active Directory domain tree design based on a multiple-master domain.

schema information for the entire forest), so you had better invest some time in making an informed decision here.

When you form the domain tree, you should know how to implement the desired DNS domain infrastructure, and you should have your DNS namespace and Active Directory domain name ready (in other words, decide whether you want to reuse the current NT Server domain name for the Active Directory domain name). Regarding the domain naming, note that Windows 2000 Server gives you the option of implementing a down-level domain name (the NetBIOS name), which can be different from the Active Directory domain name (the DNS name). This can work to sidestep any problems with the NetBIOS resources, which are still using the old NT Server domain name.

However, in some circumstances you might not want to use one of your current Windows NT Server domains as the domain tree root of the forest. You might instead want to use a construct known as a placeholder domain (or a structural domain), a dummy domain that doesn't contain user, group, or computer accounts.

You can use a placeholder domain to provide the following:

◆ An anchor for its child domains in the namespace, allowing for future domain restructuring.

◆ A common link for accessing data that has to be replicated, to avoid tying up resources in the child domains.

Figure 22.9 shows the same Windows NT Server multiple-master domain structure being upgraded to a single Active Directory domain tree using a placeholder domain.

The choice of whether to consolidate domains when you actually perform the domain upgrade or to postpone the domain consolidation until later depends on your preferences. You should take a look at the section "Domain Restructuring and Consolidation," later in this chapter, for guidance on how to achieve the domain consolidation that you desire.

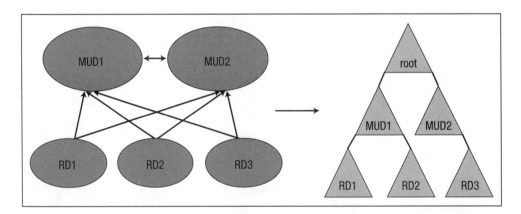

Figure 22.9
The same multiple-master domain migrated to Active Directory through help of a placeholder domain to avoid creating two domain trees.

Decide How to Upgrade the DCs

The migration process for the Windows NT Server environment actually is a simple, iterative process of separately upgrading each domain. The upgrading of each domain is always performed in the same way, regardless of the domain model (and variations on it) used.

The migration process is divided into two parts (see Figure 22.10):

1. Upgrade the PDC.
2. Upgrade each of the BDCs.

These steps are performed the same way regardless of the domain model(s) in use. The only difference is the number of times each step needs to be performed.

After you migrate all PDCs and BDCs to Active Directory, consider going to native mode to exploit Active Directory's many advanced features (see the section "Decide When to Move to Native Mode," earlier in this chapter, for more information). To reap Active Directory's full benefits, also consider upgrading all member servers, standalone servers, and workstations used in your domains.

Step 1: Upgrade the PDC

The PDC is the first server in the domain that you must upgrade. This upgrade converts the existing Registry-based Security Account Manager (SAM) database to an Active Directory store. The existing objects in the SAM are copied from the Registry to the new Active Directory database.

The following are the advantages of upgrading the PDC first:

♦ The domain can immediately join the Active Directory domain tree, even though it still includes Windows NT Server-based BDCs.

♦ Administrators can immediately start using the new administration tools and create Active Directory objects, such as OUs. However, Active Directory structures such as OUs are visible only to Active Directory-aware computers.

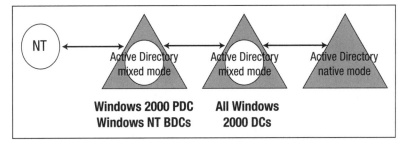

Figure 22.10
This is how your upgrade of any domain always will be executed.

Watch Out for File Replication

Windows NT Server can be configured to synchronize the contents of the Netlogon shares on each of the domain controllers (DCs) in a domain. This functionality is called LanMan Directory Replication (**LMRepl**).

Windows 2000 Server includes the same functionality, which now is being dubbed File Replication Service (FRS). Unfortunately, FRS isn't backward-compatible with **LMRepl**. This incompatibility between the replication engines used in Windows NT Server (**LMRepl**) and Windows 2000 Server (FRS) will often prove to be a major problem when doing in-place migration, because you would need to keep data synchronized between the two environments.

But there's help to be found in the Windows 2000 Resource Kit in the shape of the L-Bridge (**Lbridge.cmd**) tool. **Lbridge.cmd** is a script that pushes files from the system volume (Sysvol) on a Windows 2000-based server to the export directory used by **LMRepl** on a Windows NT-based server. Microsoft recommends that you schedule this script to run every two hours on a Windows 2000-based DC.

It is strongly suggested by Microsoft that you plan to upgrade the server working as the **LMRepl** export last. Therefore, you will usually need to move the Export server functionality from the PDC to another BDC (because the PDC usually is employed as the Export server). You should move the Export server functionality to the BDC that you project will be the last one to be upgraded to Windows 2000 Server in order to avoid having to move it several times during the upgrade. Also, before each upgrade (whether it's a PDC/BDC or a member server), you should remember to manually disable the Directory Replicator service so as to avoid any hiccups on this account.

After the upgrade, the PDC has been transformed into an Active Directory DC that uses the Active Directory store to save objects (see Figures 22.11 and 22.12). However, the former PDC is still fully backward-compatible, because it exposes the directory objects as a flat store and hides all the new Active Directory objects to down-level computers, making the domain appear unchanged. Thus, the domain really has one foot in each camp, which is why it is said to be operating in mixed mode.

The PDC now appears as an Active Directory DC to other Active Directory-aware computers, and as a Windows NT Server 4 PDC to computers that aren't yet upgraded (as the PDC will be awarded with the PDC Emulator FSMO role). This, in turn, means that down-level workstations (as well as member servers and standalone servers) can use the PDC as a possible logon server, without noticing any changes.

And, you can still use the former PDC to create new security principals and then replicate those changes to the Windows NT Server BDCs, because the former PDC behaves like the domain master to the BDCs—through the PDC Emulator FSMO role (refer to Chapters 12 and 18 for more information). If the Windows 2000 Server DC that has the PDC Emulator FSMO role goes offline (or otherwise becomes unavailable) and no other Windows 2000 Server DCs exist in the domain, then a BDC running Windows NT Server can be promoted to PDC.

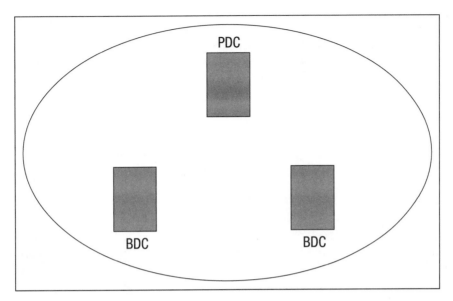

Figure 22.11
The initial configuration of the domain, poised for migration to Windows 2000 Server: a simple Windows NT Server domain with a PDC and two BDCs.

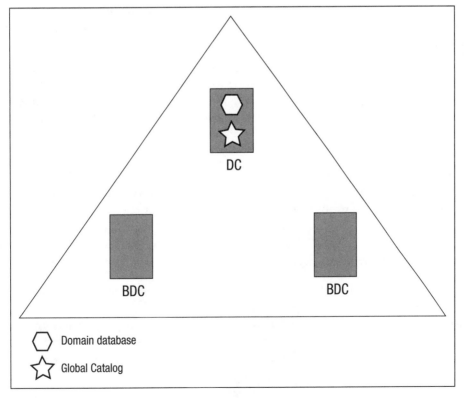

Figure 22.12
The domain after migrating the PDC to an Active Directory DC.

> **Note**
>
> *The PDC is often configured to be the Export server for **LMRepl**. Before you upgrade the PDC to a Windows 2000-based DC, you should configure the **LMRepl export** function on a backup domain controller (BDC) and remove it from the PDC.*

After the PDC is running Active Directory, you can proceed in either of two ways:

♦ Upgrade all other BDCs to Windows 2000 Server and Active Directory.

♦ Install Windows 2000 Server and Active Directory on only one more server for redundancy, leaving all other BDCs configured with Windows NT Server.

Either method is appropriate, but you won't be able to tap the full functionality of Active Directory until you have migrated all BDCs and turned the domain into native mode. However, experience shows that compromise often proves to be the best strategy—so staying in mixed mode and upgrading the BDCs over time will probably prove the best solution for most environments. Regardless, you will need to install at least two DC servers, to provide fault tolerance for the Active Directory database.

> **Tip**
>
> *If you're upgrading a multiple domain environment, you might find yourself between a rock and a hard place. If you choose to in-place upgrade each Windows NT Server domain and thus retain your previous domain structure, you will need to make sure that the explicit trusts used today are upheld until the PDCs in all domains are upgraded to Windows 2000 Server.*
>
> *Alternatively, you can start performing domain restructuring or consolidation. But you should note that this will add a lot of work to your plate (see the later section, "Domain Restructuring and Consolidation") and you will often wind up needing to uphold all explicit trust relationships to the down-level domains during the migration process anyway.*

Step 2: Upgrade the BDC(s)

After you upgrade the PDC to Active Directory, you can move to the second stage of the upgrade process, which involves upgrading the BDCs. As mentioned before, you can perform this upgrade at your own pace. As each BDC is converted to an Active Directory DC, it becomes a peer of the former PDC; thus, the existing Windows NT Server 3 and 4 replication is being replaced by Windows 2000 Server's multi-master replication (see Figure 22.13).

Just like the migrated PDC, the former BDCs represent themselves as Active Directory DCs to other Active Directory-aware servers and clients, and as NT Server 4 BDCs to servers and clients that aren't Active Directory-aware. After the domain is completely upgraded to Active Directory-only DCs, it is ripe for transformation into native mode operations (this is a manual task, accomplished by checking a checkbox). When your domain is operating in

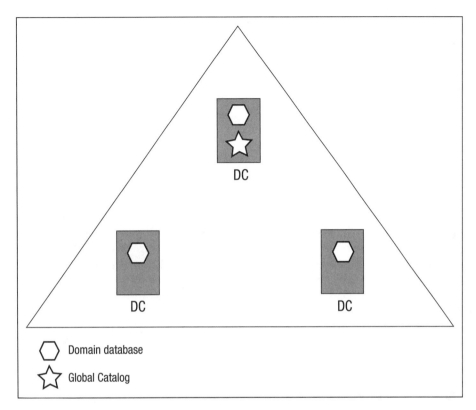

Figure 22.13
The domain after migrating all the BDCs to Active Directory DCs. If you throw a switch (shifting the domain to native mode) in this setting, you obtain access to Active Directory's full functionality set.

native mode, you have access to the full set of Active Directory features. The only downside to moving to native mode is that no Windows NT Server BDCs can ever again be added to the domain.

Domain Restructuring and Consolidation

In some cases, when you are performing the incremental, in-place upgrade, you may antici-pate a need to impose some changes on the structure of the Active Directory forest that you are creating at this point. Implementing changes in the Active Directory structure generally is known as either *domain restructuring*, which implies making changes inside and between the domains, or *domain consolidation*, which implies collapsing some of the domains into others.

Before you venture further into the subject of domain restructuring and domain consolida-tion, be aware that it is a fairly intensive operation—both mentally and time-wise; you might want to postpone these operations until later, because, strictly speaking, they aren't required for deploying Windows 2000 Server or Active Directory.

Domain Restructuring

Domain restructuring enables you to organize the objects in the Active Directory domains to suit the needs of your organization. The tool set delivered with Windows 2000 Server (and the Resource Kit) enables you to perform such restructuring activities as the following:

◆ Moving users across domains

◆ Moving groups across domains

◆ Updating access rights to reflect changes in organization or philosophy

◆ Moving computers to different domains

Of course, you might also want to restructure objects inside the domain, implement new Group Policies (especially inside the security area), move a DC to another domain, and other such things. However, these tasks are quite straightforward to achieve with the common Active Directory tools, so they won't be covered in any more detail here.

Executing the actual domain restructuring isn't too difficult with the assistance of the Microsoft tools mentioned earlier in this chapter. However, planning the domain restructuring is another story, because you have to figure out exactly what effect the changes will have on the permissions (that is, ACLs and groups) and take the steps necessary to avoid any adverse effects—usually by using one or several of the tools.

Domain Consolidation

With Windows NT Server, delegation of administration is achieved by introducing resource domains. This method for providing administration is somewhat expensive, because it requires administrative personnel to manage trusts and requires the purchase of additional hardware for DCs.

If your current domain model is anything but a single domain, Active Directory potentially can reduce the number of domains by collapsing second-tier domains into the master domain. Doing so gives you two major benefits:

◆ There are fewer domains to manage. Now, it's true that a group of Windows 2000 Server domains is easier to manage than the same number of domains in earlier versions of Windows NT Server, because using Kerberos transitive trusts lessens the number of trust relationships needed. However, having fewer domains still works to lessen the administrative burden in many other ways.

◆ By merging resource domains and a master domain into a single domain, with a structure of OUs to retain the current container structure, you cause all resources—users, groups, file shares, and printers—to be grouped together in one domain, where they logically belong. This is different (and quite a bit more logical) than the previous model, in which the resources would be in a department resource domain, but the users in that department would have their accounts in a master domain.

Considering Active Directory's fine-grained delegation of authority, retaining resource domains in the longer term has little advantage. You can reduce the administrative and hardware costs by merging your existing resource domains into your master domain. If necessary, you can create an OU structure in the master domain that mirrors the previous resource domain structure. However, collapsing resource domains into OUs isn't an entirely free proposition. It requires reworking many of the Domain Local Groups after they've been folded into a single domain. So you should carefully weigh the costs required to collapse the resource domains against the costs of leaving them in place.

If you find that the advantages of getting rid of one or more resource domains outweighs the costs of collapsing the resource domains, you should follow this seven-step recipe for getting the work done:

Step 1: Upgrade the Master Domain
Migrate the master domain to Windows 2000 Server by installing Active Directory on the PDC and BDCs and then turning the domain into native mode.

Step 2: Add OUs
If you are dissolving resource domains into OUs in the master domain, you will usually want to first create an OU structure that corresponds to the resource domains. During migration, only Active Directory-aware clients and servers can see the new OU containers. Down-level machines can still access resources that are in OUs, but they can't see the OU structure.

Step 3: Upgrade Resource Domain PDC and BDCs to Windows 2000 Server
You also need to migrate the resource domain PDC and BDCs to Windows 2000 Server, install Active Directory, and switch the domain to native mode. This is because you need to use the Microsoft tools to move security principals between domains. However, don't try to move the resource domain server into the master domain yet. At this step of the process, keep the resource servers in their current domain.

Step 4: Move Security Principals and Member Servers to the Master Domain
Move all security principals (users and groups) and servers to the master domain by using **MoveTree** or Active Directory Migration Tool. Be forewarned that this is a very delicate process that varies quite a bit depending on the exact circumstances, so you will have to do a bit more studying on this subject. However, if you don't need to uphold the current group types, you might get by with these steps:

1. Make the group a Universal Group.

2. Consider renaming the group (for example, [*current domain*]_[*current group name*]), to avoid experiencing a clash of names if you have a group with the same name on other resource domains to be migrated.

3. Move the group from Step 2 ([*current domain*]_[*current group name*]) to the master domain.

If you need to assemble several similar groups from different resource domains, you would implement an "Umbrella" Group the first time around, as follows:

1. Make the group a Universal Group.

2. Rename the group (for example, [*current domain*]_[*current group name*]).

3. Create a new Universal Group (for example, [*current group name*]) in the master domain.

4. Move the group from Step 2 ([*current domain*]_[*current group name*]) to the master domain.

5. Add the group from Step 4 ([*current domain*]_[*current group name*]) to the group from Step 3 ([*current group name*]).

When you move member servers from the resource domains to OUs in the master domain, the computer account for each server is moved along with it. Any Local Groups created on the member server are also moved with the server, and thus will continue functioning exactly as before the move.

Note that the users preserve their access rights during the move. However, the procedure doesn't deal with moving roaming profiles, logon/logoff scripts and other such things. These components need to be handled separately.

Step 5: Move the Resource Domain Local Groups to the Master Domain
Then, move any Domain Local Groups that you want to preserve from the resource domain to the master domain. You should move these groups by using the three-step procedure outlined in the preceding section ("Step 4: Move Security Principals and Member Servers to the Master Domain").

The moved groups will appear as Universal Groups in the master domain and can be converted to other group scopes as soon as the domain is running in native mode. You will have to change the resource ACLs using the old Domain Local Groups to point to the SID in the master domain for getting things to work correctly, when the PDC and BDCs of the resource domain are moved (you don't have to make these changes to permissions, if you don't need to move any PDC or BDCs to the master domain).

Step 6: Move All Workstations to the Master Domain
You need to move workstations and standalone servers from the resource domain to the master domain. For Windows 95 and 98 computers, this only requires changing the computers' Work Group name. For computers running Windows NT Workstation or Windows NT Server, you need to move them from the old domain to the master domain (this can be achieved using the **NetDom** tool or Active Directory Migration Tool, as mentioned earlier). You may ease the transition costs if you choose to implement these changes while upgrading the clients to Windows 2000 Professional.

Step 7: Eliminate the Resource Domains
You now can eliminate the resource domains, either by turning off all DCs in the resource domain or by moving the DCs to the master domain (by demoting them and then having them join the master domain). If you are running applications on any of your BDCs, you

Why Access Rights Are Preserved in this Way

Companies that use the master domain model usually create only Local Groups in the resource domains, not Global Groups or user accounts. These companies then assign permissions for resources in second-tier domains in one or more of the following ways:

- To Global Groups coming from the master domain
- To Local Groups created on member servers in the resource domain
- To Domain Local Groups created on the PDC and BDCs in the resource domain

When a resource domain is dissolved into an OU in the former master domain, the SIDs of the users and groups created in the resource domain are no longer valid. This is a concern if you have assigned access rights to Domain Local Groups in the resource domain itself—but not if you assigned the permissions to Local Groups on member servers in the resource domain, because these Local Groups are moved along with the servers (see "Step 4: Move Security Principals and Member Servers to the Master Domain"), and thus the SIDs remain valid.

So, when a resource domain is merged into a master domain, permissions assigned in the manner of the first two bullets are automatically preserved. Permissions assigned to the resource domain's Domain Local Groups aren't automatically preserved, but you can preserve them by following the simple seven-step recipe provided in this section.

When the resource Domain's Local Groups have permissions assigned, you can use Active Directory to copy security principals—such as resource Domain Local Groups—from one domain to another (Step 5). A security principal that is moved to another domain then carries two SIDs: one from the old domain (stored in **sIDhistory**) and one from the new domain.

---

should demote each specific BDC to a member server (this can't be done until you have upgraded to Windows 2000 Server, if you want to avoid reinstalling the server from the ground up). This will work to get rid of the Domain Local Groups available in that domain before moving the server to the master domain, which might prove a problem, if they're used for assigning permissions (as mentioned in "Step 5 Move the Resource Domain Local Groups to the Master Domain").

You should do some "housekeeping" on the ACLs (usually done by using the **SIDWalker** tool) with regard to the SIDs pointing to the resource domain after you've removed the resource domain.

Heed the Advice

You should collapse kinds of child domains other than the ones encountered when using a master domain model into the parent domain in much the same way as outlined in the preceding seven-step procedure. You also should heed the implicit advice given in the seven steps described in this section. If you want to consolidate or restructure the current domains, you need to determine exactly how you want to handle the domain restructuring with respect to the domain objects (for example, servers, groups, users, and permissions). And to make that determination, you need to understand the finer points of handling security principals when moving servers between Active Directory domains, as well as the power (and shortcomings) of the individual Microsoft migration tools.

Why Local Groups on DCs Require Special Handling

You need to be very careful moving any DCs that include Local Groups, because of the marked difference in the semantics of Local Groups defined on member servers and those defined on BDCs or PDCs:

- *Local Groups on member servers*—Remain local; exist only in the SAM on the member server, and aren't migrated into Active Directory.

- *Domain Local Groups on PDCs and BDCs*—When you create a Domain Local Group on a BDC, the create operation is remoted to the PDC and replicated back to all BDCs (because the BDCs have only a read-only SAM). So, although these Domain Local Groups look identical to the Local Groups on a member server, they actually exist on the PDC and all BDCs (and thus more correctly should be referred to as Domain Local Groups rather than Local Groups).

If you move each former BDC or PDC to Active Directory in the same way as you move member servers, the migration process will create a new Domain Local Group object in the Active Directory for each of the Domain Local Groups used in that domain. That's the reason you should always demote each BDC that you want to move to another domain.

Tip

Remember that Microsoft doesn't support the Support tools (as well as any Resource Kit tools), so you should make it a habit to check whether new versions of the tools have been released.

Best Practices

Review the questions in Table 22.1; you should be able to provide detailed answers to them when you are planning a migration from Windows NT Server to Windows 2000 Server.

Performing the Actual Upgrade

After you complete all the planning tasks outlined in this chapter, you should be ready to test and execute the actual migration to Windows 2000 Server. And, as you have probably recognized by now, planning the move from Windows NT Server domains to Active Directory isn't simple. However, after you have acquired broad knowledge of the Active Directory terms and the important phases of performing a successful migration plan, the exercise should prove fairly straightforward.

But don't you go forgetting the mantra for making the actual migration a breeze: Planning, planning, and more planning. And take one step at a time. You should migrate fully to Windows 2000 Server (in the in-place migration case) and clean up the permission assignments (in the clean-sheet migration case) before you try to perform any kind of domain consolidation, server application integration, or the more advanced tasks. If you take one step at a time, the work will be much more manageable for everybody involved, and isolating any faults will be much easier (and, in the worst-case scenario, recovering the previous environment will be possible).

Table 22.1   Issues to resolve in Windows 2000 migration.

Task	Questions to Consider
Migration Pre-planning	Have you examined the existing domain structure?
	Have you developed a recovery plan?
	Have you designed the initial Active Directory domain tree or forest?
	Have you designed the site topology?
	Have you determined the domain upgrade order?
	Have you determined when to switch to native mode?
	Have you determined (and tested) how to handle server applications in regard to the Active Directory upgrade?
Migration Planning	Have you determined whether you will need to perform inter-forest and/or intra-forest migration?
	Have you determined whether you want to use in-place or clean-sheet migration?
	Have you settled on which tools to use to perform the migration?
In-place Migration	Are all NT computers (servers and clients) used in the domains running Windows NT 4 already?
	Have you determined the upgrade strategy imposed on PDCs and BDCs?
Domain Restructuring	Have you determined how to structure Active Directory groups?
	Have you determined whether any restructuring of the domain namespace is needed?
	If any domain restructuring is needed, have you determined how to do it?

Chapter 23

Migration from and Coexistence with Non-Microsoft Environments

D espite Microsoft's hopes to the contrary, many popular server platforms are available other than Windows. And, because the Windows platform is becoming ubiquitous in larger IT shops that usually have several operating system (OS) platforms running, customers increasingly are demanding integration between Windows and their other OS platforms.

Although Microsoft is aware of its customers' demands that it ease the migration from other server platforms to the Windows platform, its performance in the coexistence field has been a mixed bag—to put it mildly. Until now, Microsoft seemingly has ignored the need for coexistence with other server platforms and has focused entirely on providing a strong set of migration tools for migrating from its closest rival on the server market—Novell NetWare. However, based on Windows 2000 Server's feature set, Microsoft apparently has heeded some of the demands of its customers regarding the need to facilitate migration and coexistence.

This chapter outlines Microsoft's current support (and future plans) for migration from, and coexistence with, each of the prevalent server OSs, including Novell NetWare 3.x/4.x/5.x, Unix (for practical reasons, all versions are discussed as one group, although quite a few differences exist among the prevalent Unix versions), Apple Macintosh, IBM OS/2, Banyan VINES, and the host systems. And, as you will see, the outlook for migration and coexistence isn't really as bad for Windows 2000 Server as one might be led to expect, when judging from past experiences with Windows NT Server.

Understanding Microsoft's Integration Strategy

Before heading into the detailed discussions of Microsoft's integration support for each of the prevalent non-Microsoft server OSs, this section examines Microsoft's general view on integrating Windows 2000 Server and Active Directory with competing server OSs and third-party applications. This information will help you understand the functionality—and the shortcomings—presented by Windows 2000 Server's interoperability capabilities and what is to be expected of the future. The much sought-after Single Sign-On (SSO) feature is one of the first things that Microsoft is betting on bringing about by way of Active Directory. SSO enables enterprise network users to access all authorized network resources seamlessly, based on a single authentication that is performed when they initially access the network. By saving users from today's hassle (that is, having to log in multiple times in various applications), SSO has the potential of improving productivity of network users, reducing the cost of network operations, and enhancing network security.

For a truly ubiquitous SSO functionality, the network resources accessible through SSO should range from printers and other hardware to applications, files, and other data, all of which may be spread throughout an enterprise on servers of various types running different operating systems. However, this "computing nirvana" won't happen any time soon, as the more experienced of you might already suspect.

This is in large part because, until recently, Microsoft's integration strategy has been centered exclusively on two concepts:

♦ *Providing strong migration tools*—The rule seemed to be, the bigger the competitor, the better the migration tool set offered by Microsoft.

♦ *Providing integration from Active Directory to the primary non-Microsoft OS competitors*— For obvious reasons, Microsoft has been quite narrow in their focus on the main OS competitors. And because of that, you would generally be able to attain a fair level of integration with other OSs only by providing information stored in Active Directory's database *to* those other OSs—never in the opposite direction. Microsoft would usually reserve the possibility of providing two-way replication to a select few products (usually their own server application products).

So, if you were planning on keeping and updating your core network information at close proximity to the clients (that is, on the NOS servicing each client subset), you were at odds with Microsoft's strategy. Windows 2000 Server and Active Directory simply weren't cut out to help you achieve this sort of peer-to-peer integration. And so, your only option for achieving any level of peer-to-peer integration was to locate a third-party tool that could provide the required functionality between each of your platforms (which usually prove very difficult and quite expensive, if possible at all). However, there's been a lot of softening on Microsoft's position in the year 2000. As part of its decision to start encouraging integration of third-party applications, Microsoft is slowly starting to cozy up to the option of doing two-way integration with Active Directory.

The detailed discussion on application integration with Active Directory is the subject of Chapter 16.

However, you should stay observant of the fact that Microsoft still has a fair level of warming up to do before reaching a level of true openness toward all the other major OSs. So you would be wise to study the comments made on the various technologies and solutions in the rest of this chapter.

The Three Founding Elements of Microsoft's Strategy

Microsoft is intent on eliminating the remaining competition coming from Novell in the PC server market space. Thus, historically Microsoft has been concentrating its efforts on making migration from Novell's NetWare/NDS platform to their platform a very attractive proposition. And it seems that this strategy will pay off quite handsomely, because Novell hasn't been making much progress in the directory services space in recent years. Historically, low growth rates have proved a very good indicator of a product in trouble inside the software segment, so it is fair to expect that Microsoft will see an increasing number of migrations from Novell's DNS directory service to Active Directory in the years to come.

But Novell isn't the only game in town. Realizing this, Microsoft has begun adding integration capabilities for other popular NOSs. And Microsoft is increasingly viewing integration as more than a defensive effort—that is, it's an effort to deter people from choosing NetWare on this account (even though Novell also has its work cut out on the coexistence issue). However, Novell is a much less feared opponent these days due to being on the verge of being overtaken by Linux as the primary competitor to Windows 2000 Server inside the PC segment. Additionally, Microsoft now also targets Windows 2000 Server at the high-end market segment, which means that the Unix migration and interoperability features are becoming still more important.

Another very important founding element of Microsoft's integration strategy is their desire to position Active Directory as the heart of the network—as a *metadirectory*. That is, Microsoft wants to persuade companies to place Active Directory at the hub of the enterprise (for holding user accounts and any other relevant information regarding integration to third-party applications, networking hardware, and, potentially, other OSs).

In order to do that, the company needs to develop Active Directory into a central resource that provides the core services to everybody on the network (see Figure 23.1). Microsoft is currently hard at work delivering just that with a product known as Microsoft Metadirectory Services (MMS), which allows you to solve just about any need you may have for providing integration to other directories.

Chapter 16 includes a more detailed discussion on MMS.

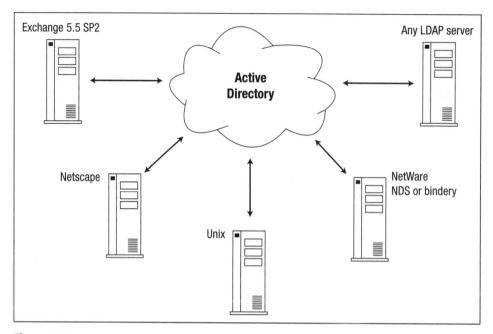

Figure 23.1
Microsoft's strategy for Windows 2000 Server/Active Directory is very simple: Make it the hub of the enterprise.

And MMS isn't just another new product from Microsoft. MMS is a repackaging of one of the best metadirectories (Zoomit VIA) on the market, which has been purchased by Microsoft. Also, MMS is targeted to become an integral part of Active Directory a bit further down the road (which is one of the chief reasons Microsoft is vending it free of charge with authorized partners). However, just like any other metadirectory product, MMS demands some fairly specialized skills for successful deployment. For that reason, MMS currently only is available to customers from a select number of authorized partners as part of the purchase of consulting time.

Active Directory: The Hub of the Enterprise

Microsoft's strategy for Active Directory not only is very logical; it's also been Microsoft's official position for quite a while. In the now-defunct white paper, "Planning for a Global Directory Service," the following key passage appears regarding Microsoft's official position:

"In addition to providing comprehensive directory services to Windows applications, Active Directory is designed to be a consolidation point for isolating, migrating, centrally managing, and reducing the number of directories that companies have. This makes Active Directory the ideal long-term foundation for corporate information sharing and common management of network resources including applications, network operating systems, and directory-enabled devices."

Goal No. 1: Providing Single Sign-On

As previously mentioned, SSO is the ability of users to authenticate themselves (prove their identity) to all services available on the network one time only.

Every computing enterprise can benefit from having SSO capability:

♦ Users are more productive when barriers are removed between them and the resources that they are authorized to use.

♦ Networks can be managed with fewer administrators, because of the consolidation of management information.

♦ Network security is improved via secure authentication protocols and the elimination of the most common threat to network security: users writing down their passwords.

However, although SSO potentially is very advantageous to all parties involved, it has never been fully realized, except in a few enterprises that have consolidated around some kind of mainframe-class SSO product, such as IBM's Resource Access Control Facility (RACF) or Computer Associates CA-Top Secret.

Full SSO capability already is supported in a homogeneous Microsoft environment (see Figure 23.2), consisting entirely of Windows 2000 Server and Windows 2000 Professional and most Microsoft BackOffice applications, a.k.a., the .NET Enterprise Servers. However, this should come as no surprise, based on the tight integration already found in Microsoft's earlier server applications and its Windows NT Server 4 OS.

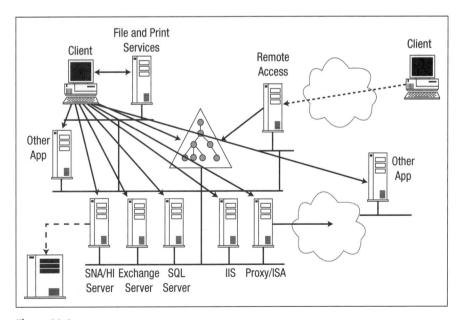

Figure 23.2
You will, of course, only need one logon to access all services made available via Microsoft's own server applications product set.

What should prove far more important is Microsoft's intention to provide the flexibility to support SSO within a network that consists of a variety of vendors' platforms via its support for standards-based authentication protocols, and Microsoft gateway products that address the specific options and challenges of the most popular non-Microsoft OS platforms.

To be more precise, Windows 2000 Server/Active Directory provides standards-based SSO within mixed networks through its native implementation of the Kerberos and Secure Sockets Layer (SSL) protocols. But again, this is only part of the story: As mentioned in the last section, Microsoft's ultimate goal is to make Active Directory the best choice to serve as an interchange point within large, mixed-platform environments. So, Microsoft targets a near-future scenario where all of Microsoft's product line not only will enable enterprise customers to extend the benefits of SSO to their entire network, but also will serve to establish Active Directory as one of the best platforms to act as a mediator between disparate systems using MMS. Again, when discussing its support for SSO capability on heterogeneous networks, Microsoft assumes that Active Directory is present and used as the hub of the network (see Figure 23.3).

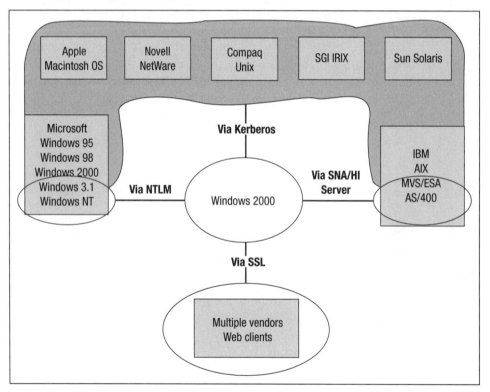

Figure 23.3
Microsoft envisions providing SSO interoperability to other OS platforms in this manner.

SSO with Kerberos

The Kerberos protocol is based on the idea of *tickets*, encrypted data packets issued by a trusted authority called a *Key Distribution Center (KDC)*. A ticket vouches for a user's identity and carries other information (such as security data). A KDC provides tickets for all the users in its area of authority, or *realm* (the correct Kerberos term). In Windows 2000 Server, every Active Directory DC is a KDC, and you have one realm for each domain.

The operation of the Kerberos protocol is simple, as shown in Figure 23.4. At logon time, the user authenticates to a KDC, which provides it with an initial ticket, called a *Ticket Granting Ticket (TGT)*. When the user needs to get in touch with a network resource, the user's user session presents the TGT to the DC and requests a ticket for the particular resource, called a *Service Ticket (ST)*. The user presents the ST to the resource, which then grants access to the user.

Microsoft's implementation of the Kerberos protocol in Windows 2000 is fully compliant with the Internet Engineering Task Force (IETF) Kerberos v5 specification (RFC 1510). This, in turn, enables Active Directory domains to interoperate seamlessly with standards-compliant, third-party Kerberos implementations (such as CyberSafe's TrustBroker), thereby allowing SSO between Windows 2000 Server and mixed-vendor networks running MacOS, AIX, Digital Unix, HP-UX, IRIX, NetWare, Solaris, SunOS, Tandem, and MVS/ESA (Multiple Virtual Storage/Enterprise Systems Architecture) OSs, provided that they also implement support for Kerberos v5.

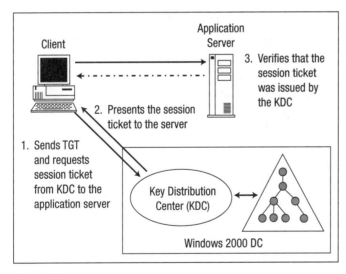

Figure 23.4
The basic operation of the Kerberos protocol—providing user authentication.

> **Tip**
> Please note that only DES-CBC-MD5 and DES-CBC-CRC encryption types are available for Kerberos interoperability and that the most common error for Kerberos interoperability is clock skew (Kerberos cross-realm authentication will fail unless the system clocks are closely synchronized; that is, within two minutes of each other). You can find more information on how Kerberos works in Chapter 14.

Establishing a trust relationship between Windows 2000 Server and other platforms via Kerberos is really quite simple. The administrator establishes a trust relationship between the KDCs in the different realms, and tickets are provided via cross-realm referrals. The administrator of Windows 2000 Server sets up a user account to which the incoming user(s) from the other system will be mapped. After this has been done, the rights and privileges of incoming users are managed via their Active Directory-based user accounts, using the same administrative tools that are used for native Active Directory users.

Cross-realm referrals in a heterogeneous environment are similar to those for homogeneous Windows 2000 Server networks (also known as *trusts*). When a user on the other system needs to access a network resource in the Windows 2000 Server domain, the user's user session requests a ticket for the resource. The KDC, seeing that the resource lies in the Active Directory domain, refers the user to the Active Directory DC and vouches for the user's identity. The Active Directory DC then maps the user's identity to the corresponding user account and issues the ticket to the user, who then presents the ticket to the resource. For a Windows 2000 Server user who needs to use a resource in the other system, the process happens in reverse, although the administrative procedures that are used on the other system will vary.

Note that working in a heterogeneous environment does introduce an unavoidable loss of administrative simplicity, because some administrative actions that happen transparently under Windows 2000 Server must be performed manually when joining heterogeneous networks. For example, in contrast to Windows 2000 Server, when trust is established in a heterogeneous environment, the administrator must manually synchronize keys between the Active Directory DC and the other system's KDC. Likewise, the administrator loses the advantage of having a single set of administrative tools and a single repository of SSO-related information. Instead, at best, a single set of tools and a single repository of SSO-related information exist for each platform. However, the ability to provide seamless sharing of resources is clearly a boon to enterprise customers and frequently is worth the additional administrative burden.

SSO with Public Keys

Today, not all enterprise computer users will enter the network via internal connections. Modern enterprise computing must increasingly also support users who access their corporate network via public networks (most often the Internet). Microsoft's SSO answer to that need is the Secure Sockets Layer (SSL) security protocol.

SSL is able to use digital certificates as a basis for authentication. And you are well advised to use the digital certificate option, because this is the only fairly secure and standards-based token of authenticity available at present. A *digital certificate* is a tamper-proof packet of data issued by a *Certificate Authority (CA)*; a CA provides a public key and a name and vouches for the fact that the person or server named is the owner of the public key. In the mode used for SSO, the Web client and server exchange certificates and then use the public keys embedded in them to exchange information, such as session encryption keys. This serves to authenticate both users, because if either is not the actual entity named in the certificate that they present, they will be unable to decrypt what the other party sends.

All the components needed to provide SSO via SSL are natively included within Windows 2000 Server, and all are fully integrated into the Windows 2000 Server security architecture. Management of digital certificates is provided by the Windows 2000 Server *Public Key Infrastructure (PKI)*, which has two components:

◆ *Certificate Services*—Enables administrators to issue and revoke certificates.

◆ *Active Directory*—Provides CA location and policy information and enables revocation information to be published.

Microsoft's SSL-based SSO is fully standards-based and, thus, should interoperate with other standards-compliant products. It supports SSL v3, the most widely used version of the SSL protocol, which has been submitted to the IETF under the name *Transport Level Security (TLS)* protocol. Microsoft Internet Explorer, Netscape Communicator, and most other Web browsers support this standard and actively support the adoption of TLS by the IETF.

The Windows 2000 Server PKI supports digital certificates using ISO's X.509 v3 standard, which is a nearly universal standard for digital certificates. For example, it allows Windows 2000 Server to use digital certificates issued by VeriSign, Thawte, BelSign, and most well known CAs.

Many Other Uses for Public Keys

SSL only represents one possible usage scenario for digital certificates. For example, Windows 2000 now allows login using Smart Cards holding an X.509 v3 digital certificate, and digital certificates can be used for establishing tunnels between secure networks on unsecured lines using Layer 2 Tunneling Protocol/Point-to-Point Tunneling Protocol (L2TP/PPTP) protocols and/or IP Security (IPSEC).

PPTP is a proprietary Microsoft solution, whereas L2TP and IPSEC are through IETF. L2TP represents the combination of Microsoft's proprietary Point-to-Point Tunneling Protocol and Cisco's proprietary Layer 2 Forwarding (L2F) technology. As you might expect, L2TP is heavily supported by Microsoft and Cisco, whereas the rest of the market has been somewhat more reluctant to jump onto the L2TP bandwagon—but it seems that most companies are in the process of adding L2TP support these days.

Administrators have considerable flexibility in configuring the network's use of PKI security information to suit their corporate needs. For example, the following are but a few of the decisions that they are able to make:

♦ Specify, via Internet Information Server (IIS), what a given certificate can be used for. For example, certificates can be used only to authenticate to a Web server, or they can serve as the basis of a full network logon.

♦ Associate individual certificates with individual user accounts or state that all certificates from a particular CA map to a single Active Directory user account.

♦ Enable the use of certificates issued by an external CA within the enterprise or a Windows 2000-based CA in the enterprise.

Access control can be easily and effectively managed because, although digital certificates are used for the initial authentication of the user, the control point for access to network resources remains the user account. After authenticating the user, Active Directory maps the certificate to the appropriate user account and uses the user's normal security credentials to determine whether the user has access rights to specific network resources. This eliminates the need to keep multiple copies of the user's privileges synchronized.

Session security is quite fair because encryption is provided as part of the SSL protocol implementation. This allows an enterprise to determine the preferred level of encryption for Web-based network access and to establish that level when the session begins. Windows 2000 Server's SSL implementation exists in two versions because of the U.S. export laws: the North American version (the 128-bit version) and the international version (the 56-bit version) for use outside of North America. The North American version provides 40-bit and 128-bit versions of the RC2 and RC4 cryptoalgorithms; 512-, 768-, and 1024-bit versions of RSA; and 56-bit Data Encryption Standard (DES) encryption. The International version provides 40-bit RC2 and RC4 and 512-bit RSA encryption. Because of softening of the U.S. export laws that basically allow everyone except a few embargoed states access to commercial-grade encryption products, most enterprises are now allowed to upgrade to the North American versions by obtaining (or downloading) the Windows 2000 High Encryption Pack from Microsoft.

SSO with Host Integration Server

If you have no way of reaching the intended audience via SSL or Kerberos, your last resort likely is Microsoft Host Integration Server 2000 (previously known as SNA Server). Just like its predecessor, Host Integration Server 2000 works in conjunction with some of the prevalent host security protocols implemented by RACF, ACF2, and CA-Top Secret, to provide SSO between Windows NT Server- and Windows 2000 Server-based networks and MVS/ESA host environments.

In SNA Server's case, SSO to an MVS security system was executed by installing the proprietary Proginet SecurPass solution on the relevant hosts, because SNA Server came packaged with Proginet SecurPass, and the two products work in tandem. For AS/400 password synchronization, you had to turn to Open Universal Software, which sells the security provider necessary for support of OS/400 V2R3 and earlier.

SecurPass provides password-synchronization services that ensure that a user's security credentials are always identical on both systems (that is, two-way password synchronization). SecurPass also performs *password harmonization,* meaning that when the user's password is changed on one system, it is subjected to the password rules on both systems before it is accepted. This effectively secures that the corporate password policy is the stronger of the Windows NT/IBM policies and prevents weak password policies on one system from threatening the security of the other.

This password synchronization enables SNA Server to perform its *password stuffing;* that is, when the mainframe's security provider requires authentication, SNA Server supplies the user's Windows NT password (which is identical to the user's mainframe password, because of password synchronization) via an automated 3270 or 5250 logon.

In Host Integration Server 2000, Microsoft has opted to implement native SSO (making SecurPass superfluous) to the RACF, ACF/2, and Top Secret host security systems. However, you should note that Host Integration Server 2000 only allows for the simple one-way password synchronization going from Active Directory to the host environment. You will have to turn to third-party solutions for getting two-way password synchronization—unfortunately, to my knowledge no such products are available at present time.

Goal No. 2: Providing Tighter Integration

Although it does add some significant improvements to the table, SSO represents only a small (and relatively simple) fragment of turning Active Directory into a fully-fledged metadirectory (a directory that functions as the integration point for all the corporate directories).

The really hard part about transforming Active Directory into a metadirectory is providing some form of mapping of the main objects—besides user accounts handled by SSO—between Active Directory and the many different directories available (whether they are OSs or applications). Such directory-synchronization capabilities are important to Microsoft, because they will enable companies to focus on using Active Directory as their command center for information storage and management, and then propagate subsets of information out to other directories automatically.

Active Directory's much-vaunted synchronization capabilities will come in several forms. From a standards-based perspective, Microsoft is working with other vendors to ensure that upcoming versions of the LDAP specification will include support for synchronization features—and Microsoft has pledged to move quickly to support LDAP synchronization, when available. However, you might want to note that Microsoft's name is conspicuously missing on the most important draft documents from IETF in the area of improving LDAP interoperability. So I'm no longer certain that Microsoft will make good on this promise—or they have changed their focus so much in the direction of MMS that they only look to LDAP as just being one among many different directories. As mentioned earlier, Microsoft is all set to move the MMS product into the mainstream in 2001 and 2002 by moving it into the box—probably with the next major release of Windows 2000 Server, which is known as Blackcomb. But you probably won't be subjected to much marketing surrounding MMS until then, unless Microsoft feels pressured on this account, because a fair bit of work is needed before MMS can be said to work as an integral part of Active Directory—that is, unless you happen to be in the Fortune 1000 league and have a pressing need for tight integration with several different applications.

But LDAP isn't going away anytime soon. Rather the opposite: MMS is heavily LDAP-based and Microsoft seems to have gotten a taste for the fact that they can claim to be complying with industry standards. And so, you should be safe in implementing any kind of LDAP-based interoperability solutions and directory services in any Active Directory infrastructure.

MS DirSync

In the short term, Microsoft is delivering a synchronization service called MS DirSync with Active Directory in the form of "synchronization connectors." MS DirSync is a general-purpose version of the replication functionality presented by Active Directory Connector (ADC); ADC provides integration between Exchange Server 4.x/5.x directory services and Active Directory (you can find a very thorough treatment of the ADC in Chapter 15).

The initial goal of MS DirSync was to provide the following:

♦ Directory synchronization from Active Directory to the target directory (usually one-way synchronization, caused by competitive considerations).

♦ A single point of administration (implemented as an MMC snap-in) for daily, user-related tasks.

♦ Less dependence on secondary tools to complete commonly performed administration of the other directory.

The first (and current) version of MS DirSync (see Figure 23.5) includes functionality to provide session-based synchronization that supports multiple targets (for example, trees), the definition of schedules, and any necessary class and attribute mappings. Or, more precisely, you will find the functionality to perform namespace mappings, class and attribute mappings, and rights and permissions mappings. Also, change events occur any time an object is added, deleted, or modified in the directory service. More broadly speaking, Microsoft's design of the DirSync control represented an advance in synchronization technologies for directories inside the following areas:

♦ Support for capturing changes at the attribute level, enabling developers to build high-performance low-bandwidth connections between directories.

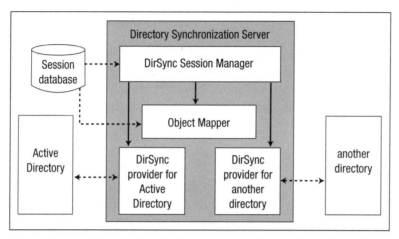

Figure 23.5
The MS DirSync architecture.

♦ Instant compatibility with the design of most replicated directory services.

♦ Efficient resynchronization after server failures.

♦ Optimal use of existing investments in LDAP.

In March 1999, Microsoft went so far as to publish the specification for MS DirSync as a nonstandards-track IETF Internet draft submission in a move designed to garner some interest among third parties for this LDAP-based control. However, Microsoft's move didn't impress the LDAP community much, and Microsoft's purchase of Zoomit Corporation a few months later made even avid Microsoft followers reluctant to build anything on top of MS DirSync.

And that seems quite wise, because Microsoft hasn't delivered anything but the ADC and an MS DirSync-based connector for synchronizing with NDS to date, despite the fact that Microsoft was very keen on stating that MS DirSync being one of the technologies that wasn't fully exploited at the time of Windows 2000 Server's release, because of time restraints—raising the expectation that we should expect to see many further developments from Microsoft regarding MS DirSync shortly after the release of Windows 2000 Server, in terms of both platform coverage and the depth of coverage. Likewise, Microsoft's expectation that several third parties would deliver DirSync-based synchronization connectors and support of non-LDAP directories using interfaces such as ADSI in the year 2000 has been proven wrong.

The Current State of Affairs

Although MMS appears very much to be Microsoft's choice for the future, you really shouldn't waste too much time on it now, if you're in need of a basic level of directory integration with one or two OSs. MMS is just getting started in the Active Directory bracket; the skills available on this product are very scarce (and thus expensive), and the probability is high that you'll see some rather hefty changes in the product as it gets further integrated with Active Directory. Additionally, MMS is generally much better fit to provide directory integration with application directories than between different OSs. And so, MMS really only will make sense if you're facing some very complex or advanced directory integration needs in a very large enterprise setting immediately. On the other hand, you should also stay attentive to the fact that you're well advised to forget about MS DirSync for anything but short-term solutions.

Thus, unless you're in the lucky position of being able to make good on an existing Kerberos implementation or something along the lines of that, you're left to choose between the future and the past. Which way you should go will depend on a fair number of different parameters—but some thinking definitely is required. For most of the time, focusing on the other integration and migration tools that Microsoft provides for the various popular OSs should prove a much more practical and interesting exercise. Therefore, the following sections include a review of Microsoft's various tools for integration and migration.

Although some information is included on tools and services delivered from third parties (mostly third parties who have strategic partnerships with Microsoft), this is in no way a complete presentation of the options available on the market. Therefore, you are encouraged to research the many third-party offerings, especially if your needs are beyond what's detailed here—the chances of finding what you need should get better every day.

Novell NetWare Interoperability and Migration

Windows 2000 Server's core feature set includes the same interoperability components as Windows NT Server 4 out of the box. These components include the following:

- *NWLink*—An IPX/SPX-compatible network protocol that is fully compliant with Novell's own IPX/SPX protocol, which in turn enables you to add a Windows 2000 Server to a NetWare 2.x/3.x and NDS-based network without requiring modifications to other servers or clients, and enables you to have Windows 2000 Professional clients communicating with NetWare servers.

- *Client Services for NetWare (CSNW)*—A Novell-compatible client that enables Windows 2000 Professional-based clients to access files and print resources on Novell NetWare 3.x and NDS servers with a single login and password for Windows 2000 Server and NetWare. However, if you have this need, I strongly suggest that you get a better client directly from Novell. CSNW includes only a fraction of the functionality found in NetWare's own client for Windows 2000.

- *Gateway Services for NetWare (GSNW)*—A Novell gateway that enables clients to access IPX/SPX-based NetWare resources (bindery as well as NDS) from the Windows 2000 Server that is serving as a gateway. By doing that, you remove the technical requirement of installing NetWare client software and the IPX/SPX protocol stack on the clients. However, the gateway functionality also represents a compromise with regard to security, because all clients coming from the Microsoft environment are governed only by the Microsoft security setup, and so you are only able to set up share-level security—not user-level security—on the files and printers that originate from NetWare resources.

♦ *Active Directory Service Interface (ADSI)*—Provides easy interfacing to Novell NDS and bindery (NetWare 2.x, 3.x, and NDS bindery emulation) with regard to automation of commonly performed tasks by way of scripts and other programming.

Additionally, Microsoft offers another set of tools—known as Services for NetWare (SFN) version 5—targeted at easing NetWare-to-Active Directory interoperability and migration. The SFN product enables companies to migrate their NetWare bindery (NetWare 2.x, 3.x, and possibly 4.x and 5.x) and/or NDS (NetWare 4.x and 5.x) servers to Active Directory in a semi-automated fashion, as well as optimizing the coexistence.

Tip

Services for NetWare version 5.0 aren't free—but it's a very cheap product that comes with a per-customer client and server license.

Services for NetWare includes three major tools:

♦ *Microsoft Directory Synchronization Services (MSDSS)*—Two-way synchronization information stored in the Active Directory service with information stored in NDS or Netware 3.x binderies.

♦ *File Migration Utility (FMU)*—Migrates NetWare files to Windows 2000 while preserving their access control permissions.

♦ *File and Print Services for NetWare (FPNW)*—Allows a Windows 2000-based server to emulate a NetWare file and print server to users, clients, and administrators alike.

You might want to note that Services for NetWare also includes the following tools that were available in the previous version of the product:

♦ *File and Print Services for NetWare version 4 (FPNW4)*—FPNW4 performs the exact same functions as the FPNW. It's just built for Windows NT Server 4 rather than Windows 2000 Server.

♦ *Directory Service Manager for NetWare (DSMNW)*—Allows you to manage NetWare 2.x and 3.x binderies from Windows NT Server 4. That is, DSMNW copies the NetWare user accounts to the SAM and then propagates any changes back to the NetWare server's bindery. This, for example, allows you to consolidate the management of the NetWare servers to a single location.

The File and Print Services for NetWare helps your company make good on its NetWare skill set by providing a NetWare 3.12 user interface to a Windows 2000-based server. That is, even though they might be using a Windows 2000 server for file and print services, the administrators and users will be able to access it with the well-known NetWare user interface. Additionally, the same single logon for clients is maintained without a need for any client configuration changes.

To make a long story short, File and Print Services for NetWare allows a Windows 2000 Server to emulate a NetWare 3.12 compatible file and print server. This can be quite useful, because you are able to replace a NetWare file and print server with a Windows 2000-based file and print server without inflicting any changes on users and administrators—they will still believe they're using NetWare if they don't know otherwise.

The File Migration Utility works along the same lines. Using the File Migration Utility, you are able to reduce the challenges involved (and, thus, the time spent) with migrating files from NetWare to the Windows 2000 Server platform. Not only does the File Migration Utility allow you to point out a grouping of NetWare files that has to be copied to one or many "destination" Windows 2000-based servers—it will also keep track of the files, allowing you to migrate at your own pace—and it will ensure that the rights and permissions unique to each file are preserved during the migration process.

Tip

In order to migrate file-system permissions, you must have already migrated the users before you migrate the file system. That is, in order to be able to migrate files with their access rights, you must first use Microsoft Directory Synchronization Services to migrate NDS directory or bindery objects to Active Directory, selecting the optional Migrate Files checkbox, because this creates a migration log that is used by the File Migration Utility. You then use the File Migration Utility to migrate the files and their access rights to a Windows 2000 NTFS share (you need NTFS to avoid losing the file rights and permissions).

The File Migration Utility supports both TCP/IP and IPX/SPX protocols to allow seamless migration of NetWare files and their permissions from the most popular versions of NetWare.

The Microsoft Directory Synchronization Services product provides the following functionality:

♦ *One-way synchronization from Active Directory to Novell NDS or bindery via periodic push/pulls*—This functionality allows you to manage objects in the Novell directories from Active Directory. The synchronization is incremental and works at the attribute level (that is, changed objects are read from Active Directory and only the modified attributes are written to NDS or bindery). One-way synchronization doesn't require any schema change to NDS.

♦ *Two-way synchronization between Active Directory and NDS via periodic push/pulls*—This functionality lets you manage shared data, such as user account information, from either directory. While the synchronization from Active Directory to NDS works at the attribute level, the synchronization going in the opposite direction happen with object-level granularity (that is, all objects are read from NDS, the objects that are unchanged are filtered out, and only the modified objects are written to Active Directory). The two-way synchronization feature requires extending the NDS schema to stamp a globally unique identifier (GUID) on all objects of interest—that is, user accounts, group accounts, and OUs.

♦ *Synchronization to NDS can be restricted to certain Active Directory domain(s) or OUs*—You might want to note that synchronization to bindery can only cover a single Active Directory OU level.

♦ *Cover synchronization of user accounts, group accounts, distribution lists, and OUs with support for all objects that have been added, deleted, renamed, moved, and modified*—So, although you do have support for the most important directory objects, you will miss a fair number of object types—including machine accounts, printer objects, and application objects—that might prove important to ascertain a fair level of coexistence. Also, it's only the most common attributes (not including the security permissions attributes) that are carried over between the two platforms.

♦ *Single sign-on*—Allows you to implement single sign-on between Novell NetWare and Active Directory. However, it does come at a cost. Because passwords are stored in separate formats (and encrypted methods) in the Windows and Novell operating system directories, it isn't possible for MSDSS to retrieve the encrypted passwords that are stored in an NDS or bindery directory at the time of implementation. And so, MSDSS needs to create new passwords (which can be set up to adhere to several different password generation schemes) for each user that is migrated to Active Directory or whose account will be synchronized between Active Directory and NetWare. After the initial password change, MSDSS can be instructed to keep the user passwords synchronized between the two platforms, providing you with the vaunted single sign-on functionality. However, the single sign-on is available only when users are changing their passwords from a client that connects to the Active Directory (that is, the passwords can only be pushed to Novell, not the opposite).

♦ *Allows scheduled as well as manual synchronizations*—Thus, MSDSS applies equally well to migration as well as coexistence scenarios.

MSDSS supports all versions of Novell's NDS (to be exact, that is NDS for Novell NetWare 4.0, 4.1, 4.11, 4.2, 5.0, 5.1, and 5.0 with NDS 8) and the NetWare 3.x bindery (bindery for Novell NetWare 3.1x and 3.2). MSDSS doesn't introduce any components that need to be installed on the NetWare servers, and it is able to cover multiple NDS trees and binderies.

Tip

MSDSS is based on the MS DirSync technology discussed earlier in this chapter. The product uses Novell's own client—that is, Novell Client Access, a.k.a., Novell Client or Client32—and supports all protocols that it supports, including IPX/SPX and TCP/IP.

So, although the migration covers user accounts, group accounts, files, and permissions from just about any NetWare server to Active Directory, you are left on your own with regard to the following:

♦ Logon scripts and NDS templates (although you are able to migrate bindery logon scripts by using Microsoft's File and Print Services for NetWare)

♦ ZENworks policies

How Does It Work?

The synchronizations going on between Novell NetWare and Active Directory are set up by defining synchronization sessions. A synchronization session is required for each association between an Active Directory OU and a NetWare container/subtree. Up to 50 sessions are supported on each server running Microsoft Directory Synchronization Services.

MSDSS migration creates a structure of Active Directory objects that mirrors the bindery or NDS structure. Here, NetWare user, group, and distribution list objects are mapped to Active Directory users, groups, and group objects, respectively, and Novell containers are mapped to Active Directory OUs.

However, because Active Directory doesn't support a container comparable to the NDS organization and because Active Directory doesn't allow using the OUs as security principals (that is, assigning rights and permissions using OUs), MSDSS creates a corresponding Domain Local Security Group in Active Directory for each NDS OU and organization, when being run in migration mode. MSDSS then goes on to map the content of each Novell OU or organization to the corresponding Active Directory domain local security group.

◆ Applications (server NLMs and client NAL)

◆ Schema extensions

◆ Macintosh namespace

◆ Computer accounts, printers, and other hardware devices

◆ Inheritance of object permissions in NDS—that is, when OUs are used as security principals or security equivalence is used—in a coexistence scenario

I hope that this section has given you good insight into the interoperability and migration options available with Microsoft's products, and you can also find a summary of the migration services available, in Table 23.1. Obviously, all elements not listed in this table will have to be migrated manually or by using tools from other vendors.

Table 23.1   Summary of the migration services made available by Microsoft's product set.

NetWare Element	NetWare Versions Supported	Tool Used
Files	NetWare 3.x, 4.x and 5.x	File and Print Services for NetWare.
Directory information	NetWare 3.x, 4.x, 5.x and NDS 8	Microsoft Directory Synchronization Services.
File and print servers	NetWare 3.12, 4.2 and 5.x	File and Print Services for NetWare. Please note that you've got full support of NetWare 3.12, whereas NetWare 4.2 and 5.x are only partially supported (that is, only bindery).
NLMs/Applications	No versions supported	No product available.

In summary, you might want to note that a quick, complete, one-time migration often will prove a better choice than anything else for a small or medium-sized organization that has yet to deploy any NDS-dependent applications because of the limitations in the NDS interoperability. If you have a complex or large NDS environment, you will most probably have to make some sort of sliding migration, which can prove fairly painful.

You will have much greater freedom of choice in how to handle an organization running off Novell NetWare 3.1x (or using the newer versions of NetWare running in bindery mode only); this type of interoperability and migration setting should prove relatively simple.

Unix Interoperability and Migration

Until recently, Microsoft's support for interoperability on Unix has largely been nonexistent. However, the release of the Windows Services for Unix add-on product has improved this situation vastly.

The core interoperability capabilities included in Windows Services for Unix v2 are the following:

♦ *NFS client and server*—Support for Network File System (NFS) v2 and 3, the standard file-sharing protocol for Unix environments. The NFS server supports PCNFSD (a PC-compliant version of the NFS daemon) as well as native NFS authentication. And so, the NFS client and servers support authentication by connection and PCNFSD or Network Information Service (NIS) authentication.

♦ *NFS gateway*—Shares Unix-based NFS exports as Windows-based file shares allowing seamless client access from any Windows client to the NFS exports.

♦ *Telnet client and server*—Support for several new Telnet terminal types compared to the terminal emulator built into Windows NT/Windows 2000: VT100, ANSI, and the Microsoft-developed VTNT. VTNT is to be published as a Request for Comments (RFC) supported by Microsoft and, incidentally, also provides support for NTLM authorization.

♦ *ActiveState ActivePerl 5.6*—Allows you to automate administrative tasks by running new or existing Perl scripts natively on the Windows NT and Windows 2000 platforms.

♦ *Unix scripting commands*—A KORN Shell and 60 other Unix bins, such as **cat**, **grep**, **ls**, **touch**, and **tee**.

♦ *User Name Mapping*—You might want to refer to this feature as SSO for NFS and NIS, because it allows you to associate users and groups from a Windows domain to a Unix NIS domain or a PCNFS server. The user name-mapping feature is usually needed to implement a proper level of security for cross-platform NFS file sharing. Otherwise, the users will have to enter separate credentials when accessing shares on the other platform or you will have to lessen the security.

♦ *Integrating NIS domains with Active Directory*—The **Server for NIS** feature enables a Windows 2000 DC to act as the primary NIS server, thus allowing administrators to manage an NIS domain from within Active Directory. Using this feature, you create a common namespace and thus allow Unix users and groups to be administered the same way (and with the same tool set) as Windows users and groups. Additionally, you'll get one-way password synchronization in the process (from Windows to Unix). Server for NIS implements the NIS 2.0 protocol and supports both Unix-based NIS subordinate (slave) servers as well as Unix-based NIS clients. When moving NIS domains to Active Directory, you might very well want to make use of the **NIS to Active Directory Migration Wizard;** this wizard allows you to move Unix source files (such as password and host files) from pre-existing NIS domains into Active Directory.

♦ *Two-way Password Synchronization*—The Password Synchronization feature provides the ability to synchronize password changes in both directions (as well as one-way password synchronization from Windows to Unix). The Password Synchronization feature supports synchronization of Windows NT and Active Directory domains and standalone Unix-based computers, such as those that use /etc/passwd, as well as Unix-based computers using NIS or NIS+. For domain passwords, Password Synchronization must be installed on Windows NT or Windows 2000-based DCs. Please note that password synchronization only applies to users with the same user name on both Unix and Windows and that the supported Unix platforms are Solaris 2.6 and above, HP-UX 10.3 and above, IBM AIX 4.2 and above (only one-way synchronization from Windows to AIX), Digital Tru64, and Red Hat Linux 5.2 and above.

Basically, Windows Services for Unix provides a fair level of SSO functionality, a fully fledged NFS client that enables Windows NT /Windows 2000 to mount and access files on Unix and other systems acting as NFS servers, and a fully fledged implementation of NFS Server that enables Unix or other NFS clients to mount and access files located on Windows NT Server/Windows 2000 Server file shares.

Apart from the preceding Unix integration features, you should note that Windows 2000 Server is quite Unix'ed by nature, because it is based on TCP/IP, DNS, DHCP (BOOTP), and Kerberos, among other things. Of these features, Kerberos probably will represent the most important change in regard to a lot of Unix environments.

Tip

Chapter 14 provides an in-depth introduction to Kerberos.

Today, the Kerberos v5 protocol is already implemented for a variety of systems (including almost all Unix variants). Thus, as previously mentioned in the section on SSO, Microsoft's choice of using Kerberos (which is based on the Kerberos v5 protocol using the RFC 1510 and RFC 1964 token format) will certainly provide you with the much-demanded cross-platform interoperability in regard to authentication, message integrity (sign/verify), and confidentiality (seal/unseal) to a fair number of Unix platforms.

Kerberos interoperability provides a common protocol that, at least in theory, enables you to implement a single (possibly replicated) account database to authenticate users on different OS platforms, and provide them SSO access to all services in a heterogeneous environment. Kerberos interoperability is based on the following characteristics:

♦ A common authentication protocol is used in a network connection to identify end users or services by their principal name.

♦ The ability to define trust relationships between Kerberos realms and to generate ticket referral requests between realms.

♦ Implementations that support the "Interoperability Requirements" defined in RFC 1510 regarding encryption and checksum algorithms, mutual authentication, and other ticket options.

♦ Support for Kerberos v5 security token formats for context establishment and per-message exchange, as defined by the IETF Common Authentication Technology working group in RFC 1964.

Tip

Despite the flack that Microsoft has gotten in the press and among purists for using RFC 1964 to add SID information to Kerberos, Active Directory has been proven to interoperate with a fair number of the most prevalent third-party Kerberos implementations. The most important of those probably is CyberSafe's TrustBroker, which will provide you with SSO between Windows 2000 and networks running the Mac, AIX, Digital Unix, HP-UX, IRIX, NetWare, Solaris, SunOS, Tandem, and MVS/ESA OSs.

A lot of rumors have been circulating that allege the Windows 2000 Server implementation of Kerberos incorporates a lot of incompatibilities to "plain-vanilla" Kerberos. However, these rumors grossly exaggerate the facts. True, the implementation isn't DCE-compatible—that is, it isn't compatible with DCE Privilege Attribute Certificates (PACs)—nor SESAME-compatible. However, Windows 2000 Server's Kerberos implementation does conform to RFC 1964, the Generic Security Services (GSS) Kerb5 Mechanism token formats.

The interoperability issue is centered on Windows 2000's use of the extensibility features of the Kerberos protocol (as defined in RFC 1964) to handle authentication data (which, in Active Directory's case, primarily means user and group SIDs). The interoperability issues arise out of the fact that the extensibility feature already is being used by other security architectures, including Distributed Computing Environment and SESAME.

This issue (which should be blamed on the standards rather than on Microsoft) has led to a lot of confusion and Microsoft-bashing. However, you will probably be relieved to hear that the actual interoperability issues seem to be quite limited, because the Active Directory authentication data that is carried in the Kerberos session tickets is ignored by most of the Unix implementations of Kerberos.

Tip

*In order to improve the interoperability between Windows 2000 Server's implementation of Kerberos and other Kerberos implementation, Microsoft has made its usage of the authorization data field in the Kerberos session ticket publicly available (currently it can be found at **www.microsoft.com/technet/security/kerberos/default.asp**).*

A much more important issue is the fact that, because of the implementation choices made by Microsoft (some of them probably are more strategic than technology-based), not every type of interaction between Kerberos realms is supported. Not surprisingly, the choice that presents you with the most interoperability possibilities is when you have Windows 2000 Server host the KDC (see Figure 23.6), which provides the following interoperability:

♦ Unix clients to Unix servers

♦ Unix clients to Active Directory-aware servers

♦ Active Directory-aware clients to Unix servers

If you are in search of interoperability with existing Unix-based Kerberos servers (which, by the way, has to be based on MIT Kerberos to work at all), the outlook is less promising. If you want to base your infrastructure exclusively on MIT Kerberos-based KDCs, your configuration of Windows 2000 Professional is limited to interoperating with the KDC (that is, ruling out the usual tight integration to Active Directory DCs in the process). Also, only those

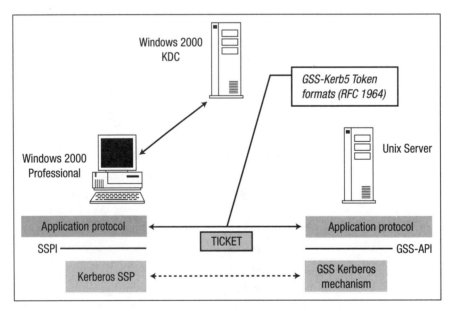

Figure 23.6
Having Windows 2000 Server host the KDC is the preferred option.

Windows 2000 applications that accept using name-based authentication (as opposed to Windows 2000 Server-style access control) will be able to use an MIT Kerberos-based solution.

Because name-based authentication usually isn't sufficient, your best (and Microsoft-endorsed) option is to create a multiplatform Kerberos environment in which Windows 2000 Server interoperates with MIT Kerberos via a cross-realm trust (see Figure 23.7). In this case, the Unix KDC can act as an account domain, and Windows 2000-based services are located in the Windows 2000 resource domain (and thus the Windows 2000 KDC is the authorization server for Windows 2000-based services). In other words, clients that obtain initial Kerberos TGT tickets from KDCs on non-Windows 2000 Server-based systems will be able to use the Kerberos referral mechanism to request a session ticket from the KDC in the Active Directory domain. The referral ticket is created by cross-realm trust relationships between the KDCs.

So, in the cross-realm situation, you actually are presented with the same set of options as when using the Windows 2000 Server-exclusive design. However, you should take note of the fact that this introduces an additional management burden, because you need to implement name mappings between security principals in the Unix realm and shadow or proxy user accounts and their group membership in Active Directory—worst case you will be charged with the task of mapping every account in the Unix realm to the corresponding Active Directory account, which kind of offsets a lot of the reasons for implementing Kerberos in the first place.

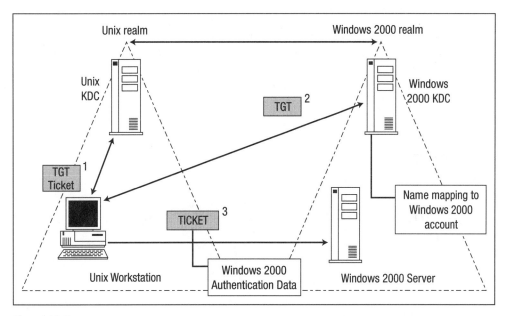

Figure 23.7
If you need to include in your Kerberos setup one or more KDCs that aren't hosted on Windows 2000 Server, always opt to keep the Windows 2000 Servers in a Windows 2000 realm.

Unifying File Access Using DFS

Before you venture into a painful migration of your current file systems to NT File System (NTFS), you ought to do yourself the favor of reviewing a much simpler solution, the Distributed File System (DFS), provided as part of the Windows 2000 Server product.

DFS makes finding and managing data on a network easier by uniting files on different machines into a single namespace. That way, IT managers can build a single, hierarchical view of multiple file servers and file server shares on a network.

In effect, this means that NTFS (Windows 2000 Server), NetWare file system (Novell NetWare), NFS (Unix), and other file systems all can be unified under a common naming structure. Both internal and external file systems, including files on the Internet, can be mapped into a DFS structure as long as a Windows 2000 redirector (in the form of either a client redirector or some server-based gateway technology, such as Services for Unix) exists for the given file system.

The DFS functionality provides significant benefits to users working on a heterogeneous network: Rather than seeing a physical network consisting of many file servers with a different directory structure, users see the few key logical directories that they need to use. And, at its best, using DFS could postpone your migration pains.

The reason you can't use a "plain-vanilla" MIT Kerberos-based KDC as the authorization server for Windows 2000 Server services is actually quite simple: The Windows 2000 security model depends on more than a list of SIDs for authorization data in Kerberos tickets. For example, to manage security on NTFS files, the ACL editor requires a domain service that uses RPC over the Netlogon secure channel to the DC for performing SID-to-name lookups.

Actually, because Windows 2000 reuses the security subsystem from NT, you need to enhance the MIT Kerberos implementation with the following functionality (besides the support of SIDs in session tickets) before you will be able to replace the Windows 2000 Server KDCs:

♦ Netlogon secure channel

♦ Authenticated RPC

♦ NetBIOS naming

♦ Lightweight Directory Access Protocol (LDAP)

The Interoperability and Migration Story on the Other Prevalent OSs

As you will see in this section, Microsoft's commitment to the less prevalent—and, in some cases, legacy—OSs leaves something to be desired.

Apple Macintosh

When it comes to interoperability with Apple Macintosh from a Windows 2000 environment, it's pretty much business as usual. By natively supporting the core Macintosh standards,

Windows 2000 Server allows a Macintosh client to use a Windows 2000 Server as if it were a Macintosh server. As with Windows NT Server 4, this feature is provided via the following built-in components of Windows 2000 Server:

♦ *File Services for Macintosh*—Enables Apple Macintosh clients to use Windows 2000 Server as their file share.

♦ *Print Services for Macintosh*—Enables Macintosh users to access Windows 2000 Server shared printers.

Both of these AppleShare-compatible services presuppose that Microsoft's AppleTalk-compatible network protocol already is installed and in operation at the Windows 2000 Servers in question. Besides that, not much is left to say regarding Macintosh interoperability and migration.

IBM OS/2 Warp

The interoperability and migration description for the legacy OS/2 Warp Server (formerly OS/2 LAN Server) and OS/2 Warp Client (formerly OS/2) environments is even shorter than the description for Macintosh: Interoperability and migration are simply nonexistent.

Even though IBM basically halted development of its OS/2 operating system overnight (and denied having abandoned its customers, claiming that OS/2 is in the process of being reincarnated as a network computing platform), Microsoft doesn't provide any relief for the migration pains of porting a current OS/2 installation to Windows 2000. The IBM-developed OS/2 Warp Server clients for Windows NT 4 (IBM Networks Coordinated Logon Client for Windows NT and IBM Networks Primary Logon Client for Windows NT) and Windows 95 (IBM Networks Client for Windows 95) are the only products available to help migrate OS/2 to Windows. In other words, your options are quite limited.

You Can Still Connect

OS/2 diehards might want to note that it is possible to connect to Windows 2000 Server from an OS/2 client (and an OS/2 server) using NetBEUI and NetBIOS over TCP/IP, just as has been the case in Windows NT Server 4 environments. This is because OS/2 and Windows NT platforms both were based on the same network code initially.

However, because of the diverging paths of the two OSs, you are basically limited to the same level of interoperability as from a plain-vanilla Windows NT Workstation 4—and so, you really don't have much more than the basic connectivity available when hooking up OS/2 computers to a Windows 2000 Server. Therefore, while it might prove a viable interim solution to hook up a couple of OS/2 clients to your Active Directory domain, you won't get much out of hooking up an OS/2 server. If you desperately need to hook up OS/2 to your Windows 2000 environment, you should check out **www.haynes97.freeserve.co.uk**, which provides some sound information on how to perform this trick with Windows NT.

Banyan Systems VINES

Banyan VINES was the first major player in the PC-based directory services market with their StreetTalk directory service. However, their first-mover advantage didn't help them make good on the healthy growth rates inside the directory services field in the latter half of the 1990s. Realizing this, Banyan Systems (now ePresence) had to give in to the free-market forces late in 1999. All support for StreetTalk and VINES ended May 1, 2000, and so StreetTalk and VINES are currently being phased out at most customer sites.

ePresence recommends migrating to Active Directory and actively encourages this through a services offer going by the name of BridgeNET 2000. BridgeNET 2000 includes migration consulting advice, account management, and support services. To my knowledge, no interoperability and migration tools for Windows 2000 Server/Active Directory are in existence, except for a Windows 2000 network client (Enterprise Client for Windows 2000) for VINES. So chances are that you'll be in for a rather rough ride in the transition to Active Directory. Banyan customers might also want to note that ePresence also offers coexistence and migration of BeyondMail and Intelligent Messaging with Microsoft Exchange Server and the Outlook client.

Host System Interoperability

As mentioned in the earlier section on SSO, the Host Integration Server (formerly SNA Server) product is Microsoft's primary vehicle for providing interoperability between Windows 2000 environments and the host systems that it believes are important. Host Integration Server 2000 primarily focuses on the IBM hosts (that is, MVS/ESA-type machines as well as AS/400 and AS/36) and nothing indicates that this is likely to change any time soon. So, if you need a solution for integration to Windows 2000 from other host environments, you may just as well start looking at the third-party options offered.

SNA Server 4 offers two-way synchronization and password harmonization as an option (which means that password changes aren't permitted to take place until a new password has been confirmed to comply with the password rules on both platforms) between Windows 2000 Server/Windows NT Server and SNA hosts, when run in concert with SecurPass's tool set. The supported security products on the mainframe hosts are ACF/2, RACF, and CA-Top Secret. For AS/400 password synchronization, Open Universal Software sells the security provider necessary for support of OS/400 V2R3 and earlier.

On Host Integration Server 2000, one-way password synchronization from Active Directory (as well as SAM) to mainframes with RACF, ACF/2, and Top Secret is offered by default. So you no longer need a third-party host component to initiate a password change from Microsoft Windows NT or Microsoft Windows 2000.

Host Integration Server 2000 uses the standard Password Expiration Management (PEM) component on the host to make changes on the host and thus allows Windows 2000 to act as the central/master security database. The PEM component is part of the Advanced

Program-to-Program Communication/Customer Information Control System (APPC/CICS) on the host, so you don't have to impose any changes in the current host security environment to enable the one-way password synchronization feature.

You might also want to note that the maintenance of the user ID and password for the single sign-on feature isn't done using a proprietary flat-file database (as was the case in SNA Server). Rather, Host Integration Server 2000 uses the Microsoft Data Engine (MSDE).

Apart from the SSO functionality, you will also find the following interoperability features in a Host Integration Server 2000 environment that are related to the core NOS services:

♦ *Shared Folders Gateway*—Enables users to access AS/400 shared folders-based files as if they were located on a local drive of a Windows NT Server/Windows 2000 Server. The same security permissions and access rights that can be applied to any other NTFS file can be applied to shared folders. Additionally, you've got AS/400 file system access using OLE DB.

♦ *Host Print Service*—Enables mainframe and AS/400 print jobs to be printed on LAN-attached printers. Mainframe printing support includes LU1 and LU3 data streams, with pass-through support for Intelligent Printer Data Stream (IPDS). IPDS pass-through support enables organizations to send mainframe print jobs to LAN printers without changing their host applications. Full Advanced Function Presentation (AFP) support can be obtained through third-party add-on products for Host Print Service. AS/400 printing support includes standard SNA Character String (SCS) line printing as well as pass-through support for host-based 3812 graphics printer emulation by using AS/400's native Host Print Transform function.

♦ *FTP-AFTP Gateway Service and AFTP Service*—Enables any FTP client to access host files on any mainframe or AS/400 system running APPC File Transfer Protocol (AFTP).

♦ *VSAM File Transfer Service*—Enables users to transfer VSAM files to Windows NT/Windows 2000 with a simple command-line interface.

♦ *TN5250 Service*—Enables a customer to offload the AS/400 from providing this functionality.

♦ *TN3270 Service*—Allows host access from any TN3270, TN3270E, or TN3287 client.

♦ *Native 3270 and 5250 access*—Allows you to access the host with native 3270 and 5250 functionality (thus you don't necessarily have to make do with the TN3270 and TN5250 subsets).

♦ *Multiple sessions per client desktop*—Allows users to have up to 16 instances of the 3270 client running on the desktop. In theory, a user should be able to have as many sessions as there are local computer resources, but 16 is the number that has been tested and verified.

♦ *Many security-enhancing features*—Allows you to shut out users that have not been authenticated in a domain, control assignment of Logical Units (LUs) to users and groups, assign LUs to particular desktops (by IP address or workstation name), provide automatic logon to host applications using the SSO feature, and perform encryption of all host-bound or host-originated data between the desktop and Host Integration Server 2000.

Additionally, Microsoft has added a fair number of new integration capabilities (for example, you've got transparent access to relational DB2 data and flat-file data on mainframes, AS/400, and Unix, as well as integration between Microsoft Transaction Server and COM+ with IBM's CICS or IMS transaction environments, including support for two-phased commit between platforms) that allows Microsoft's .NET services to be integrated much more tightly to hosts than was previously the case. It seems that the host folks at Microsoft are working from the rather ambitious target of turning Host Integration Server into a middleware component that allows Windows 2000 Server and the core .NET services to act as some kind of virtual host for a select number of applications (typically, for message queuing, transaction services, and DBMS applications) that will be indistinguishable from the "real thing".

The Migration and Coexistence Story Thus Far

Where is that all-inclusive enterprise directory service that vendors have been promising for several years? Don't look too hard, because you won't find it. Today's enterprise looks more like an archipelago—a group of islands occupied by many different OSs and application directories—than a unified network.

That probably is one of the main reasons that Microsoft is more focused than ever on providing interoperability and migration tools for the key non-Microsoft OS platforms and cooperating with the major application vendors on making their applications able to tap the power of Active Directory. However, up until now, the majority of Microsoft's tools have been reflecting its current dominant standing in the server OS market. For example, historically Microsoft's array of interoperability and migration tools have included far better support for Novell's OS platform than any other platform. But now Microsoft seems quite focused on creating the same set of migration and integration tools for Unix—their second-largest competitor nowadays in the server OS space.

However, the newly found focus on SSO means that Microsoft probably will finally broaden the scope of its interoperability offerings, going from its historically narrow, competitive focus on OSs to a situation in which Active Directory will be increasingly well positioned inside the metadirectory fray. However, Microsoft still has much to accomplish before it will be able to convince customers that Active Directory is a metadirectory, because a real metadirectory should provide support for tying together a large number of third-party directories (such as the directories associated with databases and email applications) into a single, logical directory. And that's really the plain, but true, answer to why they went out and purchased Zoomit Corporation in mid-1999, and are very keen on getting the MMS' metadirectory product tightly integrated with Active Directory. The fact that MMS will eventually be using Active Directory as its main delivery vehicle (as opposed to being just another support directory) improves the chances that Active Directory will actually wind up being viewed as a true metadirectory.

However, you might also want to note that, although Microsoft undoubtedly has heeded the demands for a metadirectory, it also is very intent on partnering with key independent software vendors (ISVs). Microsoft has garnered a lot of support from many different sources, ranging from Cisco to Enterprise Resource Planning (ERP) providers (including SAP and Navision), on the topic of directory service integration. But the customers are still waiting for the smooth marketing messages to be turned into real solutions.

So, if you still have doubts regarding whether Active Directory will indeed wind up as the much-vaunted enterprise metadirectory that is able to integrate with most third-party OSs and applications, you might want to stay alert to the development of real Active Directory-integration offerings from the ISV community. If you do see a fair share of the popular applications on the verge of becoming Active Directory-aware or having a clearly defined goal of doing so within a few years, then Microsoft will indeed be on the way to successfully transforming Active Directory into a metadirectory.

But until these trends become apparent, you are well advised to concentrate on the short-to medium-term benefits of moving to Active Directory. Given its tight integration with Microsoft's own .NET Enterprise Servers applications line (formerly known as BackOffice applications), the breadth of interoperability that is planned for Windows 2000 Server, and the steady improvement in the level of ISV commitment, you surely can find some real advantages in moving to Active Directory. Just getting SSO in place should prove to present a big advantage in many organizations.

Finally, before you convince yourself that a metadirectory is the solution to all the ills of the enterprise, remember that a metadirectory usually brings no improvements with regard to niche OSs (be they legacy or not), legacy applications, and custom-built applications, unless you have a lot of money to spend on doing it yourself. So, I strongly suggest that you play it safe and make sure that you've realized all real (and measurable) advantages before you try your luck at such a time-intensive and money-demanding venture as directory integration.

Appendix A

A Guide to Handling a Windows 2000 Server Implementation Project

The implementation project, like most other projects, consists of a series of phases and associated steps, set forth in Table A.1.

Table A.1   Implementing Windows 2000 Server.

Phase	Steps
Conceptual	Determine needs
	Examine alternatives
	Identify necessary resources
	Determine initial feasibility
	Establish a project organization
Definition	Identify the preferred solution
	Define performance requirements
	Develop risk management plan
	Develop system support plans
Configuration	Validate specifications
	Update plans
	Produce and verify solution
Operational	Use the solution
	Integrate the solution into organization
	Perform the final evaluation and feedback
Divestment	Perform transfer of responsibility
	Give out "lessons learned"
	Accept divestment of resources

Getting Started

This appendix stops short of providing in-depth coverage of each of the items just listed. Instead, its aim is to provide you with a hands-on introduction to navigating safely through the implementation of Windows 2000 Server in your corporate setting. Also, this appendix skips the preplanning activities, which will prove vital to any large-scale Windows 2000 Server implementation project. However, Chapter 6 provides extensive advice on the necessary preplanning activities for Windows 2000 Server. At the preplanning stage, you should perform the following activities:

♦ *Gather information*—The end of Chapter 6 provides a lengthy table that contains the essential information that you need to gather.

♦ *Create the project team/working group*—Seek team members with proven skills in the fields of leadership, communication, business knowledge, and technical prowess—however impossible that may sound. For the technology project teams, you will need people with skills in the fields of directory services, DNS, base OS, security, workstations, networking and migration, and coexistence (which, at its best, includes a solid knowledge of the legacy systems that you want to migrate or coexist with).

♦ *Define goals and obtain executive sponsorship*—Research previous successful infrastructure projects accomplished inside the particular organization. Also, always address the following topics in the goal document:

   ♦ Up-time (stability) goals

   ♦ Mobile user support goals

   ♦ Cost-reduction goals

   ♦ Functionality goals

   ♦ Productivity goals

   ♦ Growth and expansion goals

   ♦ Risk assessment (typical risks include change of business drivers or user requirements, slipped schedules, and larger-than-anticipated costs)

Please be aware that it really isn't possible to provide precise advice on how to handle these activities, because they will usually differ in each corporate setting.

After you execute the preplanning activities, you should be left with the following main project areas:

1. Creating a design

2. Proof of concept (lab)

3. Pilot (production)

4. Deployment

Choosing the very best people to handle the first two project areas listed is key to your success; after that, you can start slowly adding the less skilled people to the project.

Tip

To make your project a sound success, as well as to make possible the future assignment of less-skilled people to the project, you need to have available very detailed documentation of the work done. This task alone often proves to be very tough, because most technically inclined IT personnel are loath to document anything.

Microsoft Solution Framework (MSF)

If the organization in question doesn't already have a project model in place, you might want to take a look at the Microsoft Solution Framework (MSF), which is an incremental, milestone-driven, team-oriented project framework developed by Microsoft. If nothing else, it should help you impose some structure to the project and deliver a checklist of the documentation needed.

Note

Understand that MSF is a framework, not a methodology; consequently, it is not nearly as hands-on focused as you might be hoping for.

The MSF project model allegedly is based on the best practices at Microsoft and its partners inside application development. Not that long ago, Microsoft mapped the project model to the infrastructure deployment field, which still is reflected in some of the naming conventions for the definitions:

♦ *Incremental*—MSF encourages you to complete your project plan on time/budget, almost regardless of which new requirements are identified as part of the process. All new requirements should be pushed aside, instead of wasting time and money redefining the existing project. So, the basic premise is that after you finish the goal definition of the current project (which happens in the first and second milestone, depending on what level of details you're referring to), you should focus only on putting the existing project to life on budget/time, and should include all new requirements in the next version.

♦ *Milestone-driven*—Any MSF project is based on reaching four milestones: Vision/Scope Approved, Project Plan Approved, Release, and Deployment Complete (see Figure A.1). These four milestones are based on Microsoft's belief that the life-cycle definition of any IT project can be summed up as these phases: Envisioning, Planning, Developing, and Deploying.

♦ *Team-oriented*—The MSF project is staffed from six team roles: Product Management, Program Management, Development, Testing, User Education, and Logistics Management. One or more individuals can be assigned each of these six roles or have several of these roles. So, the only factor that actually remains constant is the team roles.

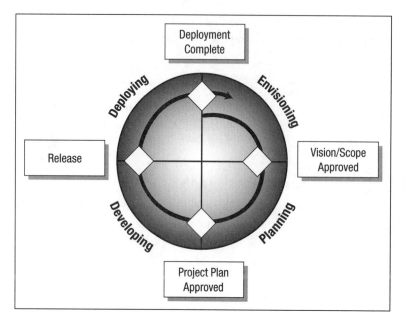

Figure A.1
The MSF project model comprises four milestones.

The MSF Process Model

The MSF process model for infrastructure deployment consists of four phases, each culminating in an externally visible milestone. These four phases (again see Figure A.1) are as follows:

♦ *Envisioning*—The period during which the team and the customer define the business requirements and the overall goals of the project. This phase culminates in the Vision/Scope Approved milestone, indicating team and customer agreement on project direction.

♦ *Planning*—The period during which the team and the customer define what will be built and deployed, as well as how and when. This phase culminates in the Project Plan Approved milestone, indicating the project team, customer, and key project stakeholders agree on what will be delivered and when.

♦ *Developing*—The period during which the team builds and tests the solution. After testing, the team pilots the technology and stabilizes it in preparation for release. This phase culminates in the Release milestone, indicating that the solution is ready to be deployed.

♦ *Deploying*—The period during which the team deploys the solution to all sites and ensures that it is stable and usable. This phase culminates in the Deployment Complete milestone, at which point responsibility for the solution shifts to the operations and support teams.

For the Envisioning phase (that is, reaching the Vision/Scope Approved milestone), you have to complete the following documentation:

♦ *Vision Statement document*—Outlines the settings of the project in a very abstract fashion, which is created by Product Management (which could be either one person or a team) with input from other team members.

♦ *Design Goals document*—Provides an idea of the project scope. It may be created by Program Management or Product Management. This document should identify issues that need resolution and solicit input before the specification process begins.

♦ *Risk Assessment document*—Identifies the upcoming technologies and organizational issues that might impact the progress of the project. It is a dynamic document that is updated as the project proceeds.

♦ *Project Structure document*—Defines the administrative structure for the project team. It outlines the structure for moving into the Project Plan Approved milestone.

♦ *Functional Specification document*—Describes what capabilities the resulting "product" will have. Most of Microsoft's MSF documentation implies that a draft of this document should be completed in this phase.

For the Planning phase (that is, reaching the Project Plan Approved milestone), you need the following deliverables:

♦ *Functional Specification document*—Describes what capabilities the resulting "product" will have, and is a prime deliverable of this milestone. In other words, the only things that might be missing in this document are the detailed technical solutions to the needs at hand.

♦ *Risk Assessment document*—Reviewed and updated by team leaders based on known issues.

♦ *Draft Master Project Plan document*—A collection of the plans from each of the roles. The tasks outlined are based on the functional specification and are grouped into major interim milestones. The content of the project plan includes approach, dependencies, assumptions, and budget and cost information. Remember to address the following topics: Pilot Plan, Purchasing and Facilities Plan, Test Plan, Training Plan, Communications Plan, Capacity Plan, Security Plan, and Budget Plan.

♦ *Draft Master Project Schedule document*—Incorporates all schedules from each team role. All roles base their schedules on what is stated in this document.

When doing the Developing phase (that is, reaching the Release milestone), you should have the following documentation available:

♦ *Risk Assessment document*—Reviewed and updated by team leaders based on known issues.

- *Performance Solutions Draft document*—Includes the design of all performance assistance solutions created by the User Education team.

- *Test Specification document*—Covers all aspects of the infrastructure solution that are of relevance to testing it, and then defines the testing requirements for each area.

- *Test Case documents*—Describe how to test each individual area of the infrastructure solution, meeting the requirements of the test specification.

- *Versioned Functional Specification document*—At the Project Plan Approved milestone, this document is "frozen". That is, subsequent changes should be reflected in new releases of the functional specification.

- *Updated Schedule document*—Reviewed and updated based on risks and known variance.

The primary deliverable of this milestone is a fully functional result that is stable enough for a first pilot test, which is executed as part of the Developing phase.

The Deploying phase (that is, reaching the Deployment Complete milestone) is an active phase in which the rollout of the full infrastructure solution takes place. In other words, the project goes through the following transitions:

- *Deployment of the core technology*—The rollout of the enabling components of the solution, which usually is placed in one or more central locations.

- *Completion of the site-specific technology*—The rollout of the components in the different locations, which enables the end users to tap the power of the new infrastructure solution.

- *Completion of the stabilization phase*—Completes the transition into the operations phase, which is usually handled by staff other than the one that built the infrastructure solution.

Unlike the previous milestones, the Deployment Complete milestone doesn't culminate with a major deliverable, other than the deployed solution. Nonetheless, this milestone requires several key deliverables:

- Release notes
- Training manuals, documentation, and performance assistance tools
- Issues and bug database
- Release of all the documentation generated during the other phases of the infrastructure project

The Team Roles

The overall idea of the team roles is to encourage a small team of peers to work in interdependent, multidisciplinary roles. Additionally, the team roles model provides a quite flexible approach, depending on project scope, team size, and team member skills.

The six team roles identified in the MSF Team Model (see Figure A.2) are:

♦ *Product Management*—Identify and set priorities for the product or service being deployed. Establish and sustain the business case for the project. Simply stated, the goal for this role is a satisfied customer.

♦ *Program Management*—Drive the critical decisions necessary to release the right product at the right time. Create the functional specification as a tool for making decisions about how the product or service will be implemented. Facilitate the day-to-day coordination required to deliver the product or service in a manner consistent with organizational standards and interoperability goals. Simply stated, the goal for this role is delivery within project constraints.

♦ *Development*—Build or implement a product or service that meets the specification and customer expectations. Evaluate technical solutions to be acquired or utilized. Simply stated, the goal for this role is delivery to project specifications.

♦ *Testing*—Ensure all issues are known before the release of the product or service. Simply stated, the goal for this role is that the project isn't released until all issues are addressed.

♦ *User Education*—Design, develop, and publish user performance solutions, online help, and training systems, including instructional materials that enable users to get the most out of the product or service. Package the system so that it can be supported and used effectively. Simply stated, the goal for this role is enhanced end-user experience.

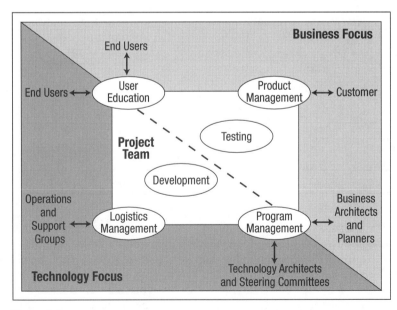

Figure A.2
Illustrating the differences in the team roles.

♦ *Logistics Management*—Ensure smooth rollout, installation, and migration to the operations and support groups. Simply stated, the goal for this role is a smooth deployment of the infrastructure project.

IT organizations may have additional requirements that call for supplementing the team with supporting roles, such as Systems Management, Help Desk, and Communications.

Because having one individual handle more than one team role often is desirable (when the project size doesn't warrant having six individuals assigned), Table A.2 provides a matrix that identifies the compatible and incompatible combinations of team roles. You should take care to note that MSF was designed for large projects because of its great scaling feature: Introducing feature teams that take care of one or more specific features of the project. Each of such feature teams is staffed in accordance with the specific role needs for executing the task at hand (see Figure A.3 for an example).

Additionally, you're allowed to split the responsibility for each role onto more than one individual. However, Microsoft advises that the size of each team should never exceed eight individuals. So, if you need more than eight individuals, you should specify that some of the tasks be handled by a feature team.

Table A.2   Team roles that are compatible (C), unlikely (U), and incompatible (I).

Role	Product Management	Program Management	Development	Testing	User Education	Logistics Management
Product Management	N/A	I	I	C	C	U
Program Management	I	N/A	I	U	U	C
Development	I	I	N/A	I	I	I
Testing	C	U	I	N/A	C	C
User Education	C	U	I	C	N/A	U
Logistics Management	U	C	I	C	U	N/A

Additional Project Material

You should note that the Deployment Planning Guide included in the Windows 2000 Server Resource Kit and as a help file in the Support Tools contains a lot of information on deployment that supplements the discussions in this appendix. And you definitely don't want to miss the Windows 2000 Enterprise Planning Workbook featured at **www.microsoft.com/Office/Project/ w2kMigration.htm**. Although the workbook text is quite disappointing considering the rather high-flying title of this meager document, the accompanying deployment template (note that the template only can be viewed using *Microsoft Project 2000*) is great. This template includes a rundown on a lot of the tasks that are required to accomplish each phase of the project and thus will prove invaluable when you need to build a Windows 2000 implementation project from scratch.

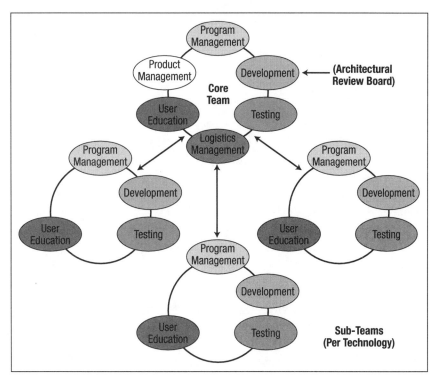

Figure A.3
An example of feature teams in a large infrastructure project.

The Implementation Project

The rest of this appendix will provide you with a little bit more detail on each of the implementation project's four phases and some checklists for the work that needs to be accomplished inside each phase.

The tables in the following sections list the activities that are involved for each of the usual project areas when pushing through each of the phases in your Windows 2000 Server/Active Directory implementation project. Each table lists (in the far-right column) the teams that should be involved for each activity. The abbreviated forms of the team names shown in Table A.3 are used in later tables in this chapter.

Creating a Design

To ensure a successful project, *never* underestimate this phase, because all the major decisions should be made here. Remember that the validity of these decisions will have a huge impact on the execution of the remainder of the implementation project—as well as the network situation for years to come for administrators, users, and business managers.

Table A.3 Team name abbreviations.

Abbreviation	Team Name
DS	Directory Services Team
DNS	DNS Team
OS	Base OS Team
Sec	Security Team
Cli	Client Team
Net	Networking Team
M&C	Migration and Coexistence Team

In a medium-sized company (1,000 to 5,000 desktops), expect this phase to last *at least* two months—assuming the availability of heavyweight skills on Windows 2000 Server and Active Directory and a lot of time to spare for the implementation project. If your IT department and Microsoft Solution Provider are like most (overworked, ripe with clashes of personalities, and generally hard to control), you realistically should expect this phase to take three to nine months.

Table A.4 lists only the major activities that go into creating the design (that is, you are likely to find several other major activities not listed that need to be addressed). You should

Table A.4 Major steps of design creation.

Major Steps	Detailed Steps	Team(s)
DNS and root namespace selection	Review existing DNS tree	DS/DNS
	Identify and resolve issues	DS/DNS
	Identify external naming requirements	DS/DNS
	Identify internal naming requirements	DS/DNS
	Select proposed root namespace	DS/DNS
	Review proposed root namespace design	DS/DNS
	Document proposed root namespace design	DS/DNS
	Review proposed root namespace design with relevant parties	DS/DNS
	Finalize the root namespace design	DS/DNS
	Publish finalized first draft version	DS/DNS
Namespace design	Review existing NT architecture	DS/M&C
	Gather information on number of NT resource domains	DS/M&C
	Gather information on number of NT master account domains	DS/M&C
	Gather details on largest resource domain (number of groups, printers, file shares, etc.)	DS/M&C
	Gather details on largest master account domains (number of groups and users)	DS/M&C
	Collect server hardware inventory listing	DS/M&C
	Collect server software OS version and Service Pack inventory listing	DS/M&C

(continued)

Table A.4   Major steps of design creation *(continued).*

Major Steps	Detailed Steps	Team(s)
	Collect server roles listing (PDC, BDC, File, and Print, BackOffice applications, etc.)	DS
Develop domain tree/forest architecture	Assess new capabilities of Windows 2000 Server and its impact on existing architecture	DS/M&C
	Identify political considerations	DS
	Define Active Directory domain-creation criteria	DS
	Develop proposed domain tree architecture	DS
	Document proposed domain tree architecture	DS/M&C
	Review proposed domain tree architecture with relevant parties	DS
	Finalize domain tree architecture	DS
	Publish finalized first draft version	DS
Active Directory domain	Review existing NT DNS naming conventions	DS
	Review existing non-NT DNS naming conventions	DS/M&C
	Propose server naming conventions	DS/M&C
	Propose machine naming conventions	DS
	Review proposed domain naming conventions	DS
	Document proposed domain naming conventions	DS/M&C
	Review domain naming conventions with relevant parties	DS
	Finalize Active Directory domain naming conventions	DS
	Publish finalized first draft version	DS
DNS design	Review existing DNS namespace design	DNS
	Review DNS administration model	DNS/M&C
	Review Active Directory service namespace architecture	DNS/M&C
	Propose DNS design	DNS
	Draft DNS design architecture	DNS
	Review proposed DNS design	DNS
	Review DNS namespace design with relevant parties	DNS/M&C
	Publish DNS namespace design	DNS
DNS interoperability requirements list	Gather requirements for DNS interoperability for all DNS-dependent systems	DNS
	Develop and review interoperability dependencies on Active Directory and DNS	DNS/M&C
	Publish interoperability requirements	DNS
Number of DNS zones and the administration model	Review current DNS administration model	DNS
	Review what's new in DNS administration	DNS/M&C
	Review group ownership of DNS administration	DNS
	Develop and review DNS administration model	DNS
	Publish DNS zones and administration model	DNS/M&C

(continued)

Table A.4   Major steps of design creation *(continued)*.

Major Steps	Detailed Steps	Team(s)
Develop OU architecture	Assess OU capabilities of Active Directory and its impact on existing architecture	DS
	Identify political considerations	DS/OS
	Define Active Directory OU creation criteria	DS/OS
	Develop proposed OU architecture	DS/OS
	Document proposed OU architecture	DS/OS
	Review proposed OU architecture with relevant parties	DS/OS
	Finalize OU architecture	DS/OS
	Publish finalized first draft version	DS/OS
User and group design	Review current user and group design	OS/Sec
	Assess capabilities of Windows 2000 Server and its impact on existing design	OS/Sec
	Develop user and group guidelines	OS/Sec
	Develop naming conventions for users (user account full name/UPN names/down-level names)	OS/Sec
	Develop naming conventions for groups	OS/Sec
	Document proposed user and group design	OS/Sec
	Review proposed user and group design with relevant parties	OS/Sec
	Finalize user and group design	OS/Sec
	Publish finalized first draft version	OS/Sec
Security design	Review current security design	Sec
	Assess capabilities of Active Directory and its impact on existing design	Sec
	Develop password requirements guidelines	Sec/M&C
	Develop default domain policies guidelines	Sec
	Document proposed security design	Sec
	Review proposed security design with relevant parties	Sec
	Finalize security design	Sec
	Publish finalized first draft version	Sec
Delegation of administration design	Assess capabilities of Active Directory and its impact on existing administrative routines	OS/Sec
	Develop delegation of administration guidelines	OS/Sec
	Document proposed delegation of administration design	OS/Sec
	Review proposed delegation of administration design with relevant parties	OS/Sec
	Finalize delegation of administration design	OS/Sec
	Publish finalized first draft version	OS/Sec
Capacity and deployment planning	Choose a deployment approach	All
	Create the preliminary implementation schedule	All
	Develop test procedures	All

(continued)

Table A.4   Major steps of design creation *(continued)*.

Major Steps	Detailed Steps	Team(s)
	Develop testing strategies and set up the test lab	All
	Determine typical space and hardware requirements	All
	Develop quality assurance methods	All
	Develop training and Help Desk plan	All
	Document proposed deployment plan	All
	Review proposed deployment plan	All
	Finalize proposed deployment plan	All
	Obtain executive support for deployment plan	All
Group policies design routines	Assess capabilities of Active Directory and its impact on existing routines	OS/Cli
	Develop group policies guidelines	OS/Cli
	Document proposed group policies design	OS/Cli
	Review proposed group policies design with relevant parties	OS/Cli
	Finalize group policies design	OS/Cli
	Publish finalized first draft version	OS/Cli

note that, because of the tight integration introduced by Active Directory, you will generally be able to do concurrent designing in regard to each of the project activities only if you employ some highly professional project leaders and have closely knit teams with strong communication skills.

Again, note that the preceding table stops short of detailing *all* the activities involved with a typical implementation project. For example, the Client Team did not take part until the group policies design activity, the last of the main activities listed, and the Networking Team and the Migration and Coexistence Team don't even have any activities listed.

And you also have an issue that shouldn't be taken too lightly: the compatibility with existing applications inside the server and client space. This will probably prove to be one of the most likely hotspots with regard to a well-executed Windows 2000 Server project—and in the worst-case scenario (serious teething troubles with a vital business application) could prove to be a showstopper for the whole project!

Proof of Concept

After you complete the numerous design decisions that Windows 2000 Server and Active Directory present, proofing the concept is of paramount importance. In a medium-sized company, expect to spend at **least** one month—and hopefully much longer—on the concept-proofing phase.

Table A.5 provides a list of the most common concept-proofing activities. Please remember that the primary purpose of this table is to provide you with *examples* of the activities that need to be performed; it does *not* present a complete list of the activities that your company needs to perform.

Table A.5   Some of the steps in proof-of-concept.

Major Steps	Detailed Steps	Teams Responsible
Server functionality testing	Implement HSM, including backup and restore	OS
	Do disk quotas	OS
	Test DFS	OS
	Test administrative roles—filtered view—delegate an administrative view in MMC	OS
	Delegate administration	OS
	Demote a DC to a member server	OS/DS
	Confirm that users maintain access to resources on demoted server	OS/DS
	Confirm that machine account remains in original domain	OS/DS
	Create member server	OS/DS
	Promote member server to DC	OS/DS
	Confirm that DC receives a full replica of DS	OS/DS
	Update attributes on DS objects and confirm their propagation	OS/DS
	Confirm that client validates against DC/GC within the same site	OS/Cli
	Confirm that workstation validates against DC/GC within the same site	OS/Cli
	Confirm that workstation validates against DC/GC in a separate site	OS/Cli
	Implement schema extensions	DS
	Test for server limits	OS
DNS/DHCP/WINS functionality testing	Ensure that DHCP is configured to provide both WINS and DDNS data	DNS/OS
	Test DC and DDNS registrations	DNS/OS
	Test DNS replication (primary/secondary configuration)	DNS/OS
	Implement Active Directory-integrated DDNS	DNS/OS
Server coexistence testing	Install and test Certificate Server	M&C/OS
	Implement X.509 certificate-based logon	M&C/OS
	Ensure X.509 certificate interoperability	M&C/OS
	Do X.509 certificate mapping	M&C/OS
	Check Kerberos interoperation with other OSs	M&C/Sec
	Integration with Exchange administration	M&C
	Check RADIUS compatibility	M&C/Net
Server migration testing	Try out DS migration tool(s)	M&C
	Windows NT Server 3.51 upgrade	M&C
	Windows NT Server 4 upgrade	M&C
	Windows NT Server 4, Enterprise Edition upgrade	M&C
	Perform System recovery	OS/M&C
	Backup and restore	OS/M&C

(continued)

Table A.5 Some of the steps in proof-of-concept *(continued)*.

Major Steps	Detailed Steps	Teams Responsible
Client OS installation testing	Unattended install	OS/Cli
	Windows 95/98 upgrade	OS/Cli
	Windows NT Workstation 3.51 upgrade	OS/Cli
	Windows NT Workstation 4 upgrade	OS/Cli
Desktop applications testing	Test standard applications	Cli
	Test mission-critical applications	Cli
	Test custom-built applications	Cli
	Test other applications in use	Cli
	Test migration DLL specs	Cli/M&C
Network testing	Test WINS interoperability	Net
	Test DHCP interoperability	Net
	Test Security policy for access (Internet, intranet, RAS, VPN)	Net/Sec
	Test IIS compatibility	Net
	Test RRAS	Net
	Test PPTP and L2TP	Net
	Test IPSec	Net/Sec
	Test QoS/ACS	Net
	Test Mac services	Net/M&C
Hardware testing	Test device enumeration	Cli
	Test FAT32 upgrade	Cli
	Test hot docking	Cli
	Test remote boot	Cli
	Test PnP, APM, ACPI, OnNow	Cli

Pilot

After you complete the design and proof-of-concept phases, you should be ready to put a select few pilot users into life. This pilot production phase should span a period of at least six weeks to give you a real chance of getting some valuable feedback from end users. This, in turn, will work to make the pilot phase last for some two-and-a-half months at the least, because you also have to allocate time for execution of the activities before and after the parts of the pilot in which end users are involved. Ultimately, the pilot might take three to five months because you likely will find and fix a fair number of problems inside the pilot period, and you might need to prolong the phase so as to allow everything to be left untouched for approximately four weeks before ending the pilot.

Generally, your pilot should encompass 20 to 60 people (depending upon the size and variety of the IT usage in the organization). If you have less than 20, some serious problems likely won't be uncovered during the pilot; if you have more than 60 people, too much time will be spent on end user installation, migration, and support, which doesn't really provide much value to the implementation project, per se. So, unless you're in a pinch, you should strive to do a pilot with between 30 and 50 people who are genuinely interested in being used as "guinea pigs" in the implementation project. For the sake of your own corporate survival, I recommend that you let the pilot users keep their old computers for use in case of "emergencies."

When choosing pilot users, strive to include many different types of personnel. And do yourself and the project a favor by including a few high-profile users (that is, managers and other persons who have a certain clout inside the organization). But don't include too many, because this could cause teething troubles (minor but nonetheless annoying problems) more likely to backfire on the project.

Apart from the staging and subsequent rollout of PCs (which should be done according to the plans for the real deployment phase), most of your time will most likely be spent solving problems with your concept, the OS, and the applications used. Table A.6 lists the important pilot activities.

Table A.6   Important pilot steps.

Major Steps	Detailed Steps	Teams Responsible
Initiate the pilot	Define the scope and objectives for pilot rollouts	All
	Create structure for operational support (e.g., Help Desk)	All
	Locate appropriate end users	All
	Deliver communications plan to pilot end users	Cli
	Create the pilot plan (including schedule)	All
	Do a risk management plan for the pilot	All
	Obtain pilot plan approval and sign-offs	All
Pilot planning	Gather and compile server hardware configurations	OS
	Implement server infrastructure	OS
	Gather and compile standard applications used	Cli
	Brief the end users	Cli
	Roll out PCs to the end users	Cli
Pilot experiences	Obtain top ten support issues from IT group	OS/Cli
	Perform TCO and ROI analysis	OS/Cli
	Gather end-user feedback	Cli
	Gather pilot group feedback	Cli
	Gather deployment staff feedback	Cli
	Gather project team feedback	All
	Review pilot experiences with relevant parties	All
	Implement changes necessary to the implementation project	All
	Finalize the pilot report	All
	Review the pilot report with relevant parties	All
	Publish finalized report	All

Deployment

If your pilot turns out to be a success, then you're destined for even more hard work: the deployment phase. In this phase, logistics rule (providing you have done your homework in the previous three phases). However, don't dismantle the project team until two or three large-scale deployments have been successfully completed, because a lot of opportunity to uncover new problems still exists at the beginning of the deployment phase.

For this reason, you should consider using this well-known, conservative stance toward the deployment phase:

♦ *Go slowly with your deployment*—Instead of simultaneously installing every server, install just a few at first. Populate those few servers with the immediately necessary information and then provide a well-defined group of users with access to the directory service. See how your users actually make use of the directory service (what their access habits are like) and how well your network infrastructure responds to the increased network load. Be prepared to add or eliminate servers as a usage pattern becomes clear.

♦ *Continue to deploy in stages, after experiencing how your directory service is performing for the initial rollout*—Don't try to roll out your entire directory all at once, especially if you are deploying into a large, complex environment. Instead, continue extending the directory service in stages to other central locations around your enterprise.

♦ *Deploy in parallel with existing directories*—Give Active Directory some time in your operations environment before dismantling your legacy directories and databases (if that is your goal). You may want to start with Active Directory running as a secondary or backup service to your existing infrastructure. After Active Directory has proven itself, you can start to use it in the primary role and downgrade your legacy systems to the secondary or backup role. After a sufficient amount of time has passed without any significant problems, you can eliminate your legacy directories altogether, if you so desire.

♦ *Determine when to rely entirely on Active Directory*—The amount of time that should pass before you rely entirely on Active Directory depends on the state of your computing environment, including the reliability of your networks, the complexity of your data management tasks, and the availability of LDAP- or ADSI-enabled software that allows you to manage information directly in Active Directory. You will probably find that the biggest hurdle to moving to an Windows 2000/Active Directory-only environment is getting all of your mission-critical applications moved to the Windows 2000 OS.

By following this cautious deployment strategy, you can achieve several desirable effects:

♦ This staged approach provides you with the opportunity to locate unexpected problems in your design *before* they become mission-critical problems.

♦ A phased rollout helps you keep your problem-set to a containable size, which in turn helps reduce the total amount of work needed to deploy the new Windows infrastructure solution—thus reducing TCO.

♦ A slow, deliberate rollout serves to increase your users' confidence in the implementation project by avoiding unexpected and embarrassing outages.

Appendix B
Active Directory Design Cases

What could be more fitting than ending this book with a small handful of design references? And so, it will indeed be done. This appendix outlines some of the cornerstones in solutions designed by me, and my closest colleagues, for the following kinds of companies:

♦ Small company with sales offices

♦ Mid-size company with many offices

♦ Mid-size company with many offices and high-latency, low-bandwidth links

While it isn't possible to get into every detail of those designs, and the underlying reasoning, the designs will hopefully prove for some stimulating reading.

Note
Please note that the discussions on the three designs might look a bit odd, due to the fact that they've been made anonymous to simply refer to each of the companies as company.

Small Company with Sales Offices

The small company includes around 500 PCs, where approximately 300 are found at the headquarters, and the rest are spread out rather unevenly among some 10 offices. The reason why the small company chose to take a gamble on Windows 2000, at a relatively early time, was that it provided a much better match to their overriding goals than the alternatives. Due to this fact, they did acknowledge that they would have to migrate to Windows 2000 not that long after its release anyway, and thus would stand to save a lot of money by heading straight for Windows 2000.

The Vision

The vision for the company reads something along the following lines:

Global efficiency and local proximity (presence).

A combination of global efficiency and local proximity will enable the company, partly to design, partly to establish a number of business systems so flexible, that they reflect and support changes in the market—including fluctuations in the demand.

The global efficiency is established by production departments, the Logistics Department, and resources in the head office. Local proximity is established by the sales function.

It is the corporate vision through global efficiency to create local proximity, represented by our salesmen, representatives, and importers. In this context, IT must contribute to a strengthening of the sales role. The success criteria are correct products, consultancy, visibility, distribution, installation, service and prices. In brief, increased demand.

The sales function must have access to training, information, response to questions, support, drawings, quotation material, and order registration 24 hours a day. This should be provided by sales companies, central knowledge centers, and on-site by a sales backup service.

A combination of global efficiency, local proximity, and a homogenous business system in relation to each individual role will provide the following:

♦ The possibility to increase or reduce the company's capacity, in general, or in response to the demand of each individual market. Adaptation of sales capacity and focus can be done through internal, as well as external collaboration partners. This enables growth through the establishment of alternative sales channels at low costs.

♦ Design and change of the company's business system and services, in accordance with the needs of the market and interested parties.

♦ The local partner provides customer contacts in the local market—providing proximity, flexibility, and readiness—while the company provides knowledge of equipment and solutions, as well as experience with design, production, distribution, installation, and service. Further, IT services will be made available for the new partner.

Thus, the core business driver for the Windows 2000 project was to provide an IT platform, which makes it possible to carry out the "global efficiency and local proximity" vision.

Other business objectives are as follows:

- To provide a robust, standardized, and flexible platform that allows for future growth and demands.

- To allow new applications to be developed and deployed more quickly.

- To consolidate the current IT usage for being able to achieve the optimum The Cost of Ownership (TCO) situation.

- To establish a platform that is of lasting value to the company.

Note

The only dedicated IT department is found at the company HQ. The offices had been used to having a fair deal of freedom for implementing their own IT solutions, but it was decided by management at an early stage, that the company would focus on in sourcing more of the IT work to the central IT department, due to this being the only available option for meeting the goals set up in the Vision and Scope. Also, it was believed that an "in sourcing" of the IT responsibilities to the central IT department would add improvements to the overall stability of the solution and optimized IT spending, among other things.

The Design

As the company was running off a very diverse (and totally undocumented) Windows NT Server/MS Mail solution, featuring all kinds of hardware brands in both servers and clients, as well as all kinds of Windows client versions from Windows 3.1 to Windows NT Server 4, it was decided to forfeit any work on migration (with the exception of the mail system), and focus entirely on moving the company to Windows 2000 as fast as possible. Thus, there were no strings attached to the design worth mentioning—so it was simply a question of matching Windows 2000 to the needs at hand.

The Windows 2000 project was initiated by performing a validation, where the only purpose was to get the high-level Vision and Scope in place (see Appendix A for more explanation on this), as well as making sure that Windows 2000 was indeed the best match to the needs at hand. The ultimate validation of Windows 2000 in the company proved to be the assemblage of all the business-critical applications, and performing a rough testing on their compatibility with the new OS. After that, the validation phase was declared a success, and the actual design of the Windows 2000 could begin. The most important design decisions (and the reasoning behind them) are listed in the following sections.

A Single Domain

This will be a single domain solution, because a multiple domain solution (be that a forest or a tree), will only add overhead to hardware and administration. The company is one, and so no one part should have reason to act as a totally separate entity.

The company is using COMPANY.NET for the internal domain (which also goes as the internal DNS domain name). The external DNS domain name is COMPANY.COM. The company uses the Active Directory domain download name of COMPANY, for seamless backward-compatibility with the current EDI solution, and other solutions, that will prevail during the worldwide rollout of the Windows 2000 infrastructure.

Integrated DNS is used (that is, all DNS records are integrated in the Active Directory, to avoid designing a separate replication infrastructure for DNS). The Active Directory domain operates in native mode right from the outset as no integration was needed to NT 4-based PDCs or BDCs.

Note
It was validated that neither Windows NT Workstation 4, nor Windows 9x based PCs, have any trouble in logging on to the Active Directory domain in the interim.

The OU and Group Structures
The OU and group structures have to be determined. As part of the determination of the OU and group structures, the exact organizational diagram was outlined by the company. After a detailed study of the possible OU structures, the following OU structure was chosen:

♦ First level: Country

♦ Second level: Organizational grouping

♦ Third level: Section/department

The group structure has to be viewed in close connection to the OU structure, as the group structure should provide a complement to the OU structure, so that it can be used for filtering the relevant Group Policies, if needed.

The group structure wound up being a combination of job description (for instance, secretary, production, R&D, or manager), geography, and reflecting the OU structure.

Note
When settling on the OU and group structures, one should take care to note that the OU structure merely is of use to the administrators (that is, for applying policies and doing administrative delegation), whereas the group structure will be the primary tool for assigning privileges to resources, as well as providing email distribution lists and filtering capabilities as to GPOs.

The groups were set up as Universal Groups, or with a combination of Universal Groups and Global Groups (that is, Universal Groups at the top level and Global Groups as "feeders" to these groups).

GPOs

After careful consideration, it was decided that all software will be distributed using GPOs, as SMS or another separate application distribution tool wouldn't add enough value compared to the additional expenses and time needed for implementing it.

The company manages three very different kinds of applications:

- Computer-specific applications
- Role-specific applications
- *Ad hoc* applications

At an early time, it was decided that the two overriding goals for the software distribution solution were the following:

- Its ability to support central administration in an efficient way.
- The option to delegate parts of the application management to the individual offices and administrators.

Consensus was created between two possibilities being up for consideration:

1. To have the GPOs follow the OU hierarchy, letting the inheritance take care of who should, and who shouldn't, be subjected to a given application policy.
2. To use the NT 4-style method, where group membership is the deciding factor on who should, and who shouldn't, be subjected to a given application policy.

While the first solution clearly is the preferred one from an Active Directory point of view, due to taking advantage of the OU hierarchy, the customer did find this solution to be unnecessarily complicated, as it would prove hard to keep an overview of the consequences of implementing each of the application policies (especially if "corrections" to the base policies would be needed in the lower level OU containers), and it would prove somewhat more complicated to delegate the management of the individual policies to other administrators, as most policies would be scoped to the top-level OUs.

Instead, the customer opted for using the group-based application management due to the following reasons:

- It is closer to what the administrators were used to from Windows NT, and thus, didn't bring a need for understanding the Active Directory structures in every detail.
- It's immediately possible to see exactly which users are covered by each policy.
- All policies (including applications policies) will be administered from one level only.
- One would be able to make use of the groups created for assigning rights and permissions to other resources.

One Site for Each Geographic Location

One site is defined at each geographic location. The naming of the individual sites are in line with the naming of the second level OU structure.

> **Note**
>
> *The IP address structure has to consist of one or multiple full subnets at each location for fulfilling the assumption of having separate sites.*

It's expected that each site will host one DC and GC (except for the HQ, which hosts multiple DCs and GCs). This is due to not wanting to be held hostage to any Internet outages, which, without a DC, will lead to the users not being able to login after the password cache on the local PC has expired.

If the DC or GC at a site is down, this will lead to an increased bandwidth demand as all logins, directory accesses, directory searches, and other directory related activities will be carried out over the WAN at the server, which provides the fastest reply. There's no optimum way of handling this potential bandwidth drain.

> **Warning**
>
> *During the lab testing of the solution, it was determined that the customer's wish to employ dial-up links (ISDN) between the offices and HQ wasn't feasible, primarily due to Active Directory being fairly chatty (see Figure B.1). As a consequence to that, the customer chose to implement a frame relay solution between the HQ and the offices.*

The replication structure is set-up with the RPC transport. The site replication topology is set up using site links and site link bridges due to the WAN design being inherently hub and spoke.

> **Note**
>
> *Due to the company having a fair number of mobile workers, a scheme based on Microsoft IPSEC (and Kerberos) was outlined. However, the solution has later been proven wrong due to these users' PCs not being part of the domains. After that, an IPSEC solution based on Certificate Services and Cisco networking components was chosen, which was severely hampered by various technical issues at first. The final solution has proven somewhat less ideal from the user's viewpoint, due to them having to manually apply for the needed certificates among other things.*

User Structures

The company's own personnel settled the exact naming conventions for the following user properties themselves:

◆ User Account Full Name

◆ UPN Name

◆ Downlevel Name

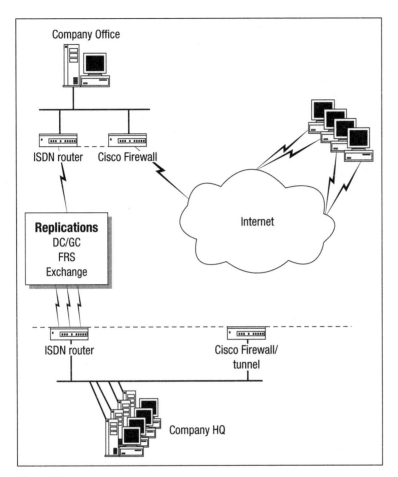

Figure B.1
The initial design based on ISDN links was proven unsuitable during lab testing. And so, the ISDN was eventually replaced with frame relay.

Additionally, the IT personnel had to spend a fair amount of time, deciding on more subtle manners, such as the set up of the individual account properties (password, password change policy, stricter rules on passwords, and so on), and which additional user account options to use (for instance), address fields, telephone fields, organization fields, and more), as well as the precise semantics for their use.

Mid-Size Enterprise with Many Offices

The company covers some 3,500 PCs and 100+ locations around the world that connected in a private WAN design, based on a combination of frame relay and fixed lines. The company is very decentralized as the HQ includes fairly few people, the total number of PCs amounting to a couple of hundred.

The company has been running off Windows for clients, as well as servers, for several years. Currently, most servers are running Windows NT Server version 4, and the clients are running Windows 95, Windows 98, or Windows NT Workstation 4. The company is a conglomerate, that includes three large divisions, and a handful of smaller entities, that operate highly autonomous, due to them operating in very different markets. It also has a central IT department, which is charged with designing and operating the common infrastructure components. Each of the three large divisions has an IT department of their own.

The reason that the central IT department picked up on Windows 2000 at a relatively early stage, was due to wanting to consolidate their current OS platforms further (the target being a Windows 2000-only solution), and for being in a position to lay down the groundwork for the enterprise-wide design in advance of any one of the entities having implemented Windows 2000. The company's central IT people had a relatively good understanding of the fact that it would take much longer to get from the drawing board to the real world on Windows 2000.

The Operational Vision

The value of ownership proposition for upgrading to Windows 2000 is as follows:

♦ *A consolidated IT infrastructure will allow for knitting the different divisions closer together*—A Windows 2000-based infrastructure will by itself bring improved standardization across the divisions and allow for new types of cross-divisionary cooperation.

♦ *Improved handling of changes in the business conditions*—Windows 2000's overall properties will provide the organization with improved responsiveness in regard to meeting new demands and needs.

♦ *Improved potential for introducing new solutions and services*—A Windows 2000-based infrastructure will improve the possibility of implementing new solutions that support the higher-level IT vision (which might be focused on furthering the integration at the company or allowing for a "connected everywhere" vision). Also, the responsibility and control of the solutions now can be delegated to the proper parties, without imposing security risks to the organization, as was previously the case.

♦ *Improved integration with the Internet*—The company will be allowed to move further in its Internet integration (for example, commerce, stronger partnerships, etc.) whenever that may be wished for, due to the Windows 2000 feature set (security-, as well as functionality-wise).

♦ *A consolidated IT infrastructure will allow for faster integration of new mergers and acquisitions*—The standardization of the OS usage across the different divisions will make it easier to handle new mergers and acquisitions, as well as generic growth.

The cost of ownership reasons for upgrading to Windows 2000 are as follows:

♦ *Improved administration flexibility*—Windows 2000 includes much-improved features for delegation of administration on all levels, and will make it possible to let the control follow the responsibility throughout the organization.

- *Improved security properties*—Windows 2000 includes a host of security functionality that will allow for improving the overall security of the corporate environment, at the same time as implementing further flexibility.

- *Improved reliability and scalability*—Windows 2000 provides a much more scalable and reliable infrastructure than its predecessor, leading to less downtime.

- *Connected everywhere*—The features and security delivered with Windows 2000 allow for implementing ubiquitous corporate access. This will allow people traveling to log on to their work space, as well as allow any small office to be included in the company's IT infrastructure.

The Design

The scope of the first phase of the company's Windows 2000 project was to develop a range of specifications for Windows 2000 for all parts of the company to adhere to in order to avoid any mishaps in regard to implementation as well as operations. Due to the company's highly decentralized structure, the specifications brought forward by the central IT department represent the very minimum of regulation that can be imposed in a Windows 2000 solution. And so, for instance, the first phase of the design didn't do anything to settle OU and group structures.

The second phase of the company's Windows 2000 project was charged with developing a set of guidelines, though, for helping the divisions steer the path to "Active Directory nirvana."

Note

Due to the sheer size of the company, it was recognized that much emphasis had to be put on how to migrate without disruptions to the current Windows NT Server single master domain infrastructure (with approximately 30 grass-roots/stand-alone domains) to Active Directory.

A Domain Tree

The emphasis was put on the following items, when designing the domain structure:

- *Bandwidth usage*—Keeping the bandwidth usage to a minimum has been of paramount importance to the design, due to the rather harsh consequences (economical as well as practical) that will result in the Active Directory replications gobbling up a lot of bandwidth.

- *Flexibility*—As to the different needs and wants of the divisions. The IT usage patterns are different between the divisions inside the company. It's important that the design is able to accommodate for that.

- *Administrative model*—One of the major goals for the implementation of Windows 2000 at the company is to improve the administrative model in such a way that the handling of users, rights, printers, etc., is eased compared to today, and that it becomes more straightforward to implement new solutions. Also, the design is intended to consolidate the number of domains and different administrative approaches that are currently in existence.

♦ *Security considerations*—It's considered important that the company uses this historic opportunity for improving and consolidating its overall security in its IT systems.

After a lot of discussions, it was decided to go with a two-layer domain tree structure in which the root domain would be acting as a placeholder domain. The reason for choosing the domain tree is outlined in Table B.1. The high level of autonomy in the divisions (which would demand Domain Admins privileges in many cases and thus full control with the other divisions in the company), was the reason why a single domain wasn't deemed feasible.

The domains are structured and named, based on the divisions/business units, as this is the only structuring that makes any sense to this particular company.

Note
Each location constitutes a separate site.

The DNS Structure

The company currently operates a flat DNS structure, with registrations of servers and other services in the COMPANY.COM domain. The COMPANY.COM domain resides on two Unix servers (one of which is the primary name server for COMPANY.COM), and a Windows NT-based DNS. The Windows NT-based DNS replicates to all servers, which are found at the major locations throughout the company.

Due to Active Directory's use of Dynamic DNS (DDNS), some changes are called for in the current DNS infrastructure. In order to reduce the changes brought forward to the existing DNS infrastructure, the following solutions have been developed:

Table B.1   The pros and cons of implementing a two-layer domain tree structure with a placeholder domain.

Pros	Cons
Less troublesome administration than for the alternative domain tree designs.	Higher bandwidth usage than the alternative domain tree designs (expected to be in the 20% range).
Is able to cater to even very large organizations, as they can be represented as OUs rather than domains.	If GPOs are used for software distribution, this could impose some additional bandwidth usage across the WAN.
Medium bandwidth usage.	Fewer DCs and GCs than for the alternative domain tree designs.
Security flexibility.	Each domain can sport its own security properties, and all the powerful forest-wide administrator roles are separated into the placeholder domain.
Administrative flexibility.	The different needs and wants of the divisions can be accommodated immediately, as each domain usually will be under the division's full control.

- The authority of the COMPANY.COM domain is transferred to an Active Directory DC, being a member of the top-level domain. The Active Directory DNS servers will be using Microsoft's proprietary Active Directory-integrated DNS functionality, which avoids having to implement a separate DNS replication topology, and secures against the risk that any dynamic DNS registrations overwrite existing entries. All the existing server and services entries in COMPANY.COM are secured from being overwritten from the outset.

- All existing DNS servers stay unchanged, except for the fact that the Unix servers are upgraded to BIND 8.1.2 in order to be able to support DDNS, and the other new DNS standards used by Windows 2000/Active Directory. This is strictly speaking not necessary, but it will provide a good security against any teething problems in the Windows 2000/ Active Directory DDNS functionality.

Note

It has to be ensured that all Windows NT-based DNS servers are running Windows NT Server 4 at the Service Pack 4 level or later.

The new DNS infrastructure is outlined in Figure B.2.

In other words, the following rule set applies to the company's DNS infrastructure:

- All authoritative servers are upgraded for handling DDNS, SRV records, and the other DNS improvements brought forward with Windows 2000/Active Directory. This in turn, means that no existing DNS servers will need to be changed, except for the central ones.

- The DNS naming follows the names of the Active Directory domains, and each of these domains are set up using the Active Directory-integrated DNS feature (meaning that all Windows 2000/Active Directory DCs will be acting as "virtual primary name servers").

- All mission-critical legacy DNS records (that is, records that are used for referring to servers and services) should be protected from erroneous writings from DDNS-compliant servers and clients.

Migration Fundamentals

It was found that the easiest and most convenient way to implement Windows 2000 Server/ Active Directory at the company entailed performing the following:

- The new Active Directory top-level domain (COMPANY.COM) is implemented running in native mode. The top-level domain is running separately to the present Windows NT Server 4 domains.

- At least one second-level domain is implemented running in native mode.

- All existing users and groups are copied from the Windows NT Server 4 master domain database to the applicable second-level Active Directory domain. In order to ensure full backward-compatibility, the SIDs used in the Windows NT 4 master domain database are transferred to the Active Directory domain using Active Directory Migration Tool (ADMT).

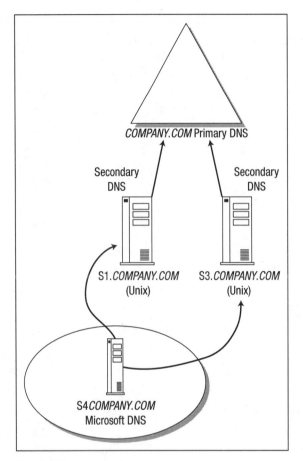

Figure B.2
The new proposed DNS infrastructure.

♦ The current master domain BDCs running in the divisions and remote offices are re-placed incrementally with Active Directory DCs from the applicable second-level domains. This DC will also replace all of the present BDCs responsibility (that is, DNS lookups, email services and logon validation) in regard to the clients and servers found in the site—in other words, the old trust relationships are deleted, and new trusts to the Active Directory DC are implemented.

♦ The division/remote office's existing Windows NT 4 PDC/BDCs can be migrated at will to Active Directory DCs from the corresponding second-level domain. When all clients have been moved to logging in at the second-level domain DC, the local replica of the top-level domain is removed.

Using this methodology, it will be possible to continue satisfying the needs of the downlevel clients (and servers), until the division/remote office have performed a full migration to Windows 2000, without imposing any changes to the current client and server configura-tions, except for the trust relationships.

Thus, the divisions continue retaining full administrative control and operational responsibility over their own servers during the migration to Active Directory, as well as after the migration has been completed. Also, it's crucial to understand that the implementation of Windows 2000/Active Directory won't change the physical location of DCs.

Other Corporate Rules

There are a fairly limited number of actions (which should be occurring quite seldom), for which a common rule set needs to be established in an Active Directory environment.

The actions that call for a common set of rules are the following:

♦ Implementing Universal Group modifications

♦ Implementing domain modifications

♦ Implementing schema modifications

♦ User naming conventions

All of the company should adhere to the same user naming conventions in order to allow everyone to use the same login and email name, and ensure every person an identical corporate identity (which for instance will enable a global Yellow pages directory and similar services), regardless of which part of the company they come from.

Implementing Universal Groups

While the Universal Group can prove very valuable, due to the fact that it sports the same properties as Global Groups, and adds the possibility of including members from multiple domains, it's also highly dangerous to Active Directory's well being.

The Universal Groups are stored in the Global Catalog (GC), which has a global scope—in other words, all Universal Groups will be replicated throughout the Active Directory domains. And so, thoughtlessly implementing Universal Groups could potentially wind up clogging up parts of the WAN (especially at small offices carrying very little bandwidth). Due to these rather harsh global consequences of doing local configuration, a strict set of rules governing the usage of Universal Groups will be called for.

Note

It's important to note that Active Directory doesn't provide any solution for controlling which persons hold Domain Administrator privileges, and who are allowed to create Universal Groups. Presently, all members of Domain Administrators are able to create new Universal Groups.

Adding and Deleting Domains

The creation and deletion of domains represents a rather delicate operation in regard to the Active Directory consistency, as well as the bandwidth usage. Due to these facts, any changes imposed to the domain structure should be authorized in order to avoid any mishaps on this account (including any deviation from the DNS naming scheme, which is outlined for the first and second level domains in the "Domain Implementation" Microsoft whitepaper).

> **Note**
>
> *It's important to note that Active Directory will presently allow Domain Admins to create and delete child domains relative to the domain administered. Also, Enterprise Admins is allowed to add and delete all domains.*

Implementing Schema Modifications

The schema lays the foundation for the objects available in the Active Directory, and so it really constitutes the crown jewels of your corporate infrastructure. And so, the company will be well advised to take good care of removing any potential trouble spots with regard to the schema management.

The company will also be in need of a carefully designed strategy for managing the schema that includes controlling when and how schema modifications are tested and implemented. It will make sense to discern between schema modifications imposed by users or administrators and schema modifications stemming from applications (as well as upgrades to the Active Directory).

> **Note**
>
> *It's important to note that Active Directory allows you to define which persons are allowed to edit the schema. Presently, only members of the Schema Admins Group are able to edit the schema.*

User Naming

It's important that the user naming make sense to the end user, as well as allowing for easy identification of a given user. Also, the user-naming scheme should prove to work in all situations (including when logging on from a localized version of Windows 2000 Professional). And not in the least: The user naming should prove to be unique throughout the company, as this is demanded by Windows 2000/Active Directory, due to the fact that it allows UPN (User Principal Name) logins.

After careful consideration, it was found that the current user-naming scheme used at the company's email systems meet all the above-mentioned requirements. And using the email name brings the added benefit of the user being able to log in using his email address.

It is advisable that the company defines what constitutes the proper usage of the most important other user attributes (such as the UPN suffix(es) used, the User Account Full Name, and any of the optional attributes that are decided to be put to use).

In other words, all user accounts created in the Windows 2000/Active Directory domain should have an email address so as to avoid any naming clashes. And so, an email address complying with the corporate guidelines for email names must always be present before creating the corresponding user account in the applicable Windows 2000/Active Directory domain.

No User Database Integration

The company also wished to move to Exchange Server at the time of migrating into Windows 2000. This was because Microsoft Mail was causing a lot of grief to users and administrators alike, and the customer wanted to be able to create and manage mail users from Active Directory right from the outset.

However, the company eventually decided to give up on consolidating the user databases found in Active Directory and the Exchange Server 5.5 directory, due to Windows 2000 ADC being less than well-understood at the time of implementation, and the fact that it proved quite problematic to set up and operate.

Note

It's important to note that Active Directory allows you to define which persons are allowed to create new user accounts at any given domain or OU hierarchy level. Presently, all Administrators are able to create new user accounts by default.

Mid-Size Company with Many Offices and High-Latency, Low-Bandwidth Links

The company has some 3,000 PCs. Approximately 1,200 of those PCs are found at the headquarters, whereas the rest are scattered fairly evenly around the globe in some 110 locations. While the company does operate a fairly sizable central installation that is being handled by the central IT department (which also is in charge of all IT use in the whole organization), the administrative responsibilities are fairly decentralized. That is, the customer only wants to administer the things centrally that are absolutely necessary, leaving the rest to administrators (and consultants) at the locations. Most of the company is running Windows NT Server 4 and Windows NT Workstation 4. But you can still find Windows 3.1 or Windows 9x, as well as other NOSs at some locations.

The Vision

The overriding vision for the customer was to establish a common and standardized IT infrastructure, covering all kinds of data (information), for all employees across the world. The underlying reasoning is that it would make it possible to better exploit the sizable investments being done continually in IT, and thus improve the quality being delivered by the organization, as well as providing for improved efficiency for each of the individual activities.

Most of these improvements will be due to the company being able to work off the same set of data at any given time, and thus allowing for much-improved knowledge transfer to the management as well as the individuals. In addition, it is expected that a common and standardized IT infrastructure will ease the operations environment, which will lead to improved uptime, without additional operations expenses.

The Design

As a consequence of the vision, the customer decided that they wanted to standardize on Windows 2000 across the board. That is, the customer wants to have all servers and clients migrated to Windows 2000 Server and Windows 2000 Professional, respectively, as soon as possible.

> **Note**
>
> *The customer also wanted to migrate their current email systems to Exchange 2000 Server at the same time. The majority of the existing email infrastructure is based on Exchange Server 5.5, but there are other email systems present in some of the WAN "pockets".*

In addition to the usual data migration, the solution entails a fair level of migration with regard to the domains (the customer currently operates one domain at the HQ, and one separate domain for each location running Windows NT Server), as well as the messaging infrastructure (the customer currently operates one Exchange Organization covering most of the company).

The security characteristics of the system, as well as the option for decentralized operations and management, were deemed highly important by the customer. Due to the sheer size of the IT infrastructure, and a wish to get started implementing the new Windows 2000-based environment, it was decided to separate the project into four constituents:

♦ Implementation of Windows 2000 from scratch at the individual locations

♦ Migration to Windows 2000 from Windows NT at the individual locations

♦ Migration to Windows 2000 from other OSs at the individual locations

♦ Migration to Windows 2000 at the HQ

A Domain Tree

All the possible domain designs—including the very improbable ones—were under heavy scrutiny by the customer in advance of opting for a domain tree solution with the root domain operating as a placeholder domain. The single domain design was turned down on the grounds of being a very bandwidth-hungry proposition, in addition to being very hard to secure to the level wished for, as well as constituting a single point of failure.

On the other hand, the customer was keenly aware of the need to keep the number of second-level domains to a minimum, due to the wish for administrative ease. However, the total number of domains wound up to be eight, despite the relatively small number of users found in the company (see Figure B.3).

> **Note**
>
> *Four domains were due to the need for keeping the bandwidth to a minimum, and easing the administration by implementing DFS replication (which you can only*

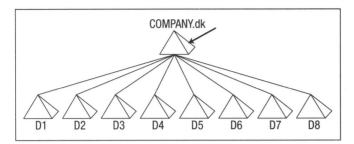

Figure B.3
The customer went for a domain tree design.

have 32 of), whereas the rest represent the fact that the customer's security needs prompted a need for doubling the number of domains, due to the domain constituting Active Directory's only true security boundary.

The DNS design follows the domains and is based on the proprietary Active Directory-integrated DDNS feature found in Windows 2000 Server.

OU Design

The OU design is similar for all domains. It comprises four hierarchies:

♦ Country

♦ Location name

♦ Sections at the location

♦ Special organizational groupings inside each section

The two first OU levels are defined in advance and the administrators at the individual locations aren't allowed to make any changes here, whereas the rest of the OU levels can be changed to match the local needs. All applications are distributed from the central IT department, by using GPOs and DFS replicas. Any instance of the DFS replica found in each location allow for LAN-based application installation.

Network Design

Each location is provided with two DCs/GCs to allow for local logons (as two domains applies to each location). Each location constitutes an Active Directory site. In order to minimize the bandwidth used up by the Active Directory, the WAN optimizations outlined in Chapter 20 were employed (actually most of the optimizations outlined in this chapter stem from the experiences in the lab test of the customer's setup). Because of the less than perfect solution delivered by Active Directory's Intersite KCC, with regard to handling WAN links or Active Directory DCs that are unavailable for just a few hours, the Intersite KCC was disabled. In addition, changes were implemented in the TCP/IP stack for allowing Windows 2000 to make the most of the high-latency links used.

The Exchange Dimension

Due to the customer's wish to keep its current SMTP mail domain, and the gradual migration from Exchange Server 5.5 to Exchange 2000 Server, the Exchange 2000 Server ADC was implemented to keep the Active Directory and the Exchange Server 5.5 directory in sync. See Chapter 15 for more information on the hows and whys for integrating Exchange with Active Directory, and vice versa.

A Job Well Done?

As you can see, the needs and demands vary quite a lot in these three cases. And that obviously also amounts to some very large changes on the scope and goal of the project, and thus the resulting design. And that's the reason why you should be very careful about getting the Vision and Scope established from the outset. Otherwise, you might find yourself venturing down the wrong path, and having to face a full or partial redesign, or an upset customer.

With regard to the actual designs, I admit that I could find a thing or two that I would change in hindsight, but the three solutions constitute a very good match to the needs, if I may say so. If nothing else, you won't be able to find any major errors along the lines of this one stemming from another real-life Windows 2000 installation that was coined by a very large consultancy house: This 1,500+ PC environment, comprising a dozen locations, are being stored inside one Active Directory domain and *one site*. Additionally, all DCs have been placed in two data centers, adding a need for implementing some needlessly big (and maybe even more important, very expensive) WAN links, to even the smallest of their offices.

I do hope that the company or the consultants that did this design will wise up and reconsider before any major disasters occur, such as the following:

♦ *The WAN links going down for an extended period of time*—This will effectively leave the clients unable to log on after the grace period of three logins, using the same user credentials locally as were used the last time the WAN links were up.

♦ *Being faced with rolling out a large application to every desktop using GPOs*—This would bring their WAN, as well as their servers, to their knees, if a fair percentage of the users were logging on during the same timeframe.

♦ *Allowing roaming profiles to grow larger in the user population*—If a fair percentage of the users are logging on or off during the same timeframe, this will leave the links oversubscribed, and might even prove to bring the servers to their knees.

With this scary solution in mind, I want to express a hope that you and I will be able to treat many more companies to the experience of a job well done in the coming years.

Appendix C
Whistler: What's in Store for the Next Version?

Microsoft is busy specifying and programming the next version of Windows 2000, which currently is known by the codename of *Whistler* (and probably will end up being named Windows.NET, or something akin to that).

Whistler is scheduled for release in the second half of 2001. But judging from Microsoft's history, it might very well slip into early 2002. But no matter the precise release date of Whistler, you will want to keep abreast of the changes being implemented in this product, due to the long-planning horizon of Active Directory.

While you shouldn't expect any revolutionary changes in the product, compared to Windows 2000 (due to Whistler being a minor release), the current rumors and speculations surrounding the product indicate that Microsoft will be improving on a fair number of Active Directory's weak spots.

Warning

Please understand that this appendix is based entirely upon rumors and speculations from a variety of sources at a very early point in the development of Whistler. So things might very possibly end up being very different from what's detailed here. So don't take things too literally, and keep an eye out for your Microsoft representatives, as well as any third parties close to the information loop.

The Major Active Directory Improvements

The most notable improvements are expected to take place in the following three areas:

♦ Scalability

♦ Management

♦ Monitoring

Microsoft seems poised to add the following major improvements to Whistler, compared to Windows 2000 Server:

♦ *It will become possible to logon without contacting a GC every time, allowing you more flexibility in placing the GCs in your environment.* This will be implemented by having the Universal Groups memberships cached by the nearest DC at the first logon to a given site, and by having all DCs inside the site, refresh the cache entries periodically from the nearest GC.

♦ *An Active Directory DC will be populated from an offline media, and thus allow you to avoid performing large replications after a server is promoted to a Domain Controller.* That is, you can now copy a DC to tape or CD-ROM, and use it to create new, unique Active Directory DCs. As such, the feature will eliminate the need to build a DC from scratch over the network. At the next scheduled replication, the DC will be "patched up" with any missing or changed directory attributes. This functionality might also be applied to GCs.

♦ *Active Directory will become much smarter in its handling of group memberships.* Only the individual memberships that have changed will be updated at next replication. So, the current need for staying away from creating groups with a large number of objects (discussed in Chapter 9) won't apply to Whistler. You will also most definitely be saving a fair deal of bandwidth to the replication of groups. This functionality will probably only apply to the "pure" Whistler environment—that is, when all DCs are running off the Whistler release.

♦ *Adding attributes to the GC won't prompt a full re-replication of all data to all GCs.* Full replication throughout the Active Directory infrastructure is a very scary event in most installations, and this has worked to put a damper on the interest of adding new Active Directory-aware applications (especially Exchange 2000 Server) to the existing infrastructures. This functionality will probably only apply to the "pure" Whistler environment—that is, when all DCs are running off the Whistler release.

♦ *The Intersite KCC will be changed to become smarter and less CPU-intensive.* You can find more information on the Inter-Site KCC in Chapter 14 and 20. This functionality will probably only apply to the "pure" Whistler environment—that is, when all DCs are running off the Whistler release.

♦ *It will become possible to rename the DC/GC server with a flick of a switch.*

♦ *There will be an improved tool set for documenting, managing, and troubleshooting Group Policies.* This will most probably include improvements with regard to viewing the resulting set of Group Policies for a given user or OU, as well as getting a low-down on the possible Group Policy conflicts.

♦ *The MMC snap-ins will become more powerful and flexible, and will add some new features, making things easier on the administrator.* Also, Microsoft seems poised to add more bells and whistles to the Active Directory Migration Tool (see Chapter 22).

Finally, Microsoft will work on making Active Directory more ubiquitous than before. This means that Microsoft will probably expand the scope of data that can be stored in the Active Directory to also cover binary large objects (BLOBs), as well as fairly volatile data. Also, query functionality, programming features, and other such things seem destined for some marked improvements.

The Major Windows 2000 Improvements

Whistler is scheduled to become Microsoft's first OS with support for 64-bit processors, which should prove beneficial to Intel's new family of high-end processors (IA-64, codenamed Merced). At the same time, it's planning to eliminate the old 16-bit Windows client family (Windows 9x/Windows Me) at the low-end. So, it's going to be interesting to watch how Microsoft will make ends meet for both the high-end and low-end client needs, as well as the server needs.

Note
The needs in an enterprise setting, are quite different from that of a home user. For instance, a high level of backward-compatibility with games, as well as older hardware, is a priority for most home users, whereas it doesn't matter that much in a corporate setting.

As part of the standardization on one platform, Microsoft is expected to change the user interface (UI) so that it becomes more easily customizable, allowing the user and/or administrator to fit the UI to the user at hand. Microsoft also seems confident that they'll finally be able to put the DLL hell to rest.

Some of the improvements that are likely to be found in the Whistler Server line of OSs include the following:

♦ You will be able to administer remote servers fully from a distance. This ability will include support for all kinds of disasters and hardware changes.

♦ Microsoft DNS Server will add support for DNSSEC, and several other nice-to-haves.

♦ Encrypted File System (EFS) will add support for file sharing, and offer improved performance.

♦ Services will be met with several different standard privilege account levels. This should mean a great improvement compared to the limited choice faced with Windows 2000 Server (you can either use LocalSystem, or an ordinary user account).

Index

A

Access methods
   Active Directory and wire protocols, 77
   MMS (Microsoft Metadirectory Services), 555–556
Access rights
   domain restructuring and consolidation, 789
   OUs (Organizational Units) and, 214
Access tokens, user accounts and SIDs
  (Security Identifiers), 248–249
Account Operators Group, Built-in Groups, 269
Account Policies
   Security Settings, 310
   security templates, 500
ACEs (Access Control Entries), 110, 246–247. *See also*
User account and group management.
   ACLs (Access Control Lists) and, 245–246
   Active Directory security, 110
   static inheritance, 706
   SystemAudit, 246
ACLs (Access Control Lists), 110. *See also* User account
and group management.
   ACEs (Access Control Entries) and, 245–246
   Active Directory security, 110
   Group Policies, 306
   OUs (Organizational Units) and, 210
   schema and, 655
   structure of, 246
   user accounts and, 245–246
   Windows 2000 security elements, 443
Active Directory, 28–30, 57–58, 61–114, 438–448, 693–729.
  See also Directory services; Planning; Results assessment.
   accessing, 77
   administering, 593–605
   Administration Tool (**LDP**), 646
   ADSI (Active Directory Service Interface), 30, 436, 437
   advanced implementation topics, 607–652
   attributes, 63, 64
   Backup utility, 634–637
   BDCs (Backup Domain Controllers), 30
   bulk data entry, 683–689

client extensions, 638–639
components interaction, 90–94
Connector. *See* ADC.
container objects, 63, 64
core concepts, 439–448
database architecture, 694–700
databases and **DCPROMO** (Active Directory Installation
  Wizard), 579
DCs (domain controllers), 73–74, 360–361, 381–383, 446
DDNS (Dynamic DNS), 67, 94–95, 165–166, 439–441
delegation of administration, 294–298
delegation of authority, 442
design elements, 449
design scenarios, 841–858
DNs (distinguished names), 106
DNS (Domain Name System) integration, 76
DNS zones and. *See* Active Directory-integrated
  DNS zones.
DNS-SRV (service records), 76, 168–169
domain naming, 576–579
domain structures, 203–239
domain trees, 64, 87–88, 333–358, 444
domain trees and in-place upgrades, 779–780
domains, 68–72, 86, 441
domains and Exchange 2000 Server, 532
ESE (Extensible Storage Engine), 109, 694–697
Exchange 2000 Server and, 505–506, 527–530
Exchange 2000 Server design interdependence, 532–533
features of, 75–79
forests, 70–72, 88–90, 335–336, 337–338, 532, 533
forests and Exchange 2000 Server, 532, 533
GCs (Global Catalogs), 72–73, 98–99,
  361–362, 383–386, 448
Group Policies, 298–331
groups and, 91, 257–289, 444–446
GUIDs (Globally Unique Identifiers) and objects,
  106, 443
hierarchies of domains, 90–94
HTTP URL Names, 107
implementing, 561–605
implementing on legacy DNS servers, 182

B

S

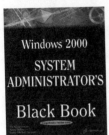

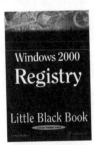